The Cambridge Companion to
the First Amendment and Religious Liberty

This book is an interdisciplinary guide to the religion clauses of the First Amendment with a focus on its philosophical foundations, historical developments, and legal and political implications. The volume begins with fundamental questions about God, the nature of belief and worship, conscience, freedom, and their intersections with law. It then traces the history of religious liberty and church–state relations in America through a diverse set of religious and nonreligious voices from the seventeenth century to the most recent Supreme Court decisions. The *Companion* concludes by addressing legal and political questions concerning the First Amendment and the court cases and controversies surrounding religious liberty today, including the separation of church and state, corporate religious liberty, and constitutional interpretation. This scholarly yet accessible book will introduce students and scholars alike to the main issues concerning the First Amendment and religious liberty, offering incisive new insights into one of the most important topics in American culture.

Michael D. Breidenbach is Assistant Professor of History at Ave Maria University, Florida, and Visiting Scholar at Corpus Christi College, Oxford. His work has been published in the *William and Mary Quarterly*, and his book on American religious liberty and church–state relations is under contract with Harvard University Press. He has held research positions at the Universities of Oxford, Cambridge, and Princeton.

Owen Anderson is Professor of Philosophy and Religious Studies at Arizona State University. He has published seven books, including *The Natural Moral Law* (Cambridge University Press, 2012) and *The Declaration of Independence and God* (Cambridge University Press, 2015). He studies rational presuppositionalism and how it approaches basic questions about God and the good.

Cambridge Companions to Law

Cambridge Companions to Law offers thought-provoking introductions to different legal disciplines, invaluable to both the student and the scholar. Edited by world-leading academics, each offers a collection of essays which both map out the subject and allow the reader to delve deeper. Critical and enlightening, the *Companions* library represents legal scholarship at its best.

The Cambridge Companion to European Private Law
Edited by Christian Twigg-Flesner

The Cambridge Companion to International Law
Edited by James Crawford and Martti Koskenniemi

The Cambridge Companion to Comparative Law
Edited by Mauro Bussani and Ugo Mattei

The Cambridge Companion to Human Rights Law
Edited by Conor Gearty and Costas Douzinas

The Cambridge Companion to Public Law
Edited by Mark Elliott and David Feldman

The Cambridge Companion to International Criminal Law
Edited by William A. Schabas

The Cambridge Companion to Natural Law Jurisprudence
Edited by George Duke and Robert P. George

The Cambridge Companion to Comparative Family Law
Edited by Shazia Choudhry and Jonathan Herring

The Cambridge Companion to Comparative Constitutional Law
Edited by Roger Masterman and Robert Schütze

The Cambridge Companion to the First Amendment and Religious Liberty
Edited by Michael D. Breidenbach and Owen Anderson

The Cambridge Companion to

the First Amendment and Religious Liberty

Edited by

Michael D. Breidenbach
Ave Maria University

Owen Anderson
Arizona State University

CAMBRIDGE
UNIVERSITY PRESS

CAMBRIDGE
UNIVERSITY PRESS

University Printing House, Cambridge CB2 8BS, United Kingdom

One Liberty Plaza, 20th Floor, New York, NY 10006, USA

477 Williamstown Road, Port Melbourne, VIC 3207, Australia

314–321, 3rd Floor, Plot 3, Splendor Forum, Jasola District Centre, New Delhi – 110025, India

79 Anson Road, #06–04/06, Singapore 079906

Cambridge University Press is part of the University of Cambridge.

It furthers the University's mission by disseminating knowledge in the pursuit of education, learning, and research at the highest international levels of excellence.

www.cambridge.org
Information on this title: www.cambridge.org/9781108417471
DOI: 10.1017/9781108277716

First published 2020

A catalogue record for this publication is available from the British Library.

ISBN 978-1-108-41747-1 Hardback
ISBN 978-1-108-40529-4 Paperback

For Paul Thomas, with love

– M.D.B.

For Alyssa, with many thanks

– O.A.

Contents

Notes on Contributors

Owen Anderson is Professor of Philosophy and Religious Studies at Arizona State University. He is the author of several books, including *The Declaration of Independence and God* (Cambridge University Press, 2015) and *The Natural Moral Law* (Cambridge University Press, 2012). He has been a research fellow at Princeton University and a visiting scholar at Princeton Seminary. He teaches philosophical theology at Phoenix Seminary and is currently interested in the role of reason and general revelation in social and individual life.

Chris Beneke is Professor of History and Director of Academic Integrity at Bentley University. He is the author of *Beyond Toleration: The Religious Origins of American Pluralism* (Oxford University Press, 2006) and co-editor of *The First Prejudice: Religious Tolerance and Religious Intolerance in Early America* (University of Pennsylvania Press, 2001), *Profane: Sacrilegious Expression in a Multicultural Age* (University of California Press, 2014), and *The Lively Experiment: Religious Toleration in America from Roger Williams to the Present* (Rowman & Littlefield, 2015).

Gerard V. Bradley is Professor of Law at the University of Notre Dame, where he is the co-director of the Natural Law Institute. He is also an editor-in-chief of *The American Journal of Jurisprudence*. His most recent book is *Catholic Social Teaching: A Volume of Scholarly Essays*, edited with Christian Brugger (Cambridge University Press, 2019).

Michael D. Breidenbach is Assistant Professor of History at Ave Maria University and Visiting Research Scholar at Corpus Christi College, Oxford. His research interests concern the history of political, legal, and religious thought in the Atlantic World. His work has been published in the *William and Mary Quarterly*, and his current book, a history of American religious liberty and church–state relations, is under contract with Harvard University Press. He received his PhD from King's College, Cambridge, and has held research positions at Princeton University; the Rothermere American Institute, Oxford; St John's College, Oxford; and Wolfson College, Cambridge.

Janice Tzuling Chik is Assistant Professor of Philosophy at Ave Maria University; Associate Member of the Aquinas Institute at Blackfriars Hall, University of Oxford; and a research fellow at the University of Pennsylvania. Her research spans the philosophy of action, metaphysics and philosophy of science, and human rights. She holds degrees in philosophy, public policy, and music performance from Princeton University, the University of Texas at Austin, and the University of St Andrews.

Marc O. DeGirolami is the Carey Fields Professor of Law at St. John's University School of Law, where he is the Associate Director of the Center for Law and Religion. His book *The Tragedy of Religious Freedom* was published in 2013 by Harvard University Press. His writing concerns the First Amendment, constitutional interpretation, and constitutional history. He is now working on an account of American church–state relations, focusing on the thought of George Washington, Patrick Henry, and John Marshall.

Jonathan Den Hartog is Professor of History at Samford University in Birmingham, Alabama. He is the author of *Patriotism and Piety: Federalist Politics and Religious Struggle in the New American Nation* (University of Virginia Press, 2015). He is also the co-editor, with Carl Esbeck, of *Disestablishment and Religious Dissent: Church-State Relations in the New American States, 1776–1833* (University of Missouri Press, 2019).

Donald L. Drakeman is Distinguished Research Professor in the Program on Constitutional Studies at the University of Notre Dame and a fellow in Health Management at the University of Cambridge. He is the author of numerous works on religion and law, including, most recently, *Church, State, and Original Intent* (Cambridge University Press, 2010) and, with John F. Wilson, *Church and State in American History*, fourth edition (Routledge, 2020). His church–state writings have been cited by the Supreme Courts of the United States and the Philippines. He received his AB from Dartmouth, JD from Columbia, and PhD from Princeton.

John Finnis is Professor Emeritus of Law and Legal Philosophy at the University of Oxford and Biolchini Family Professor of Law at the University of Notre Dame, Indiana. His books include *Natural Law and Natural Rights* (Oxford University Press, 1980, 2011); *Fundamentals of Ethics* (Clarendon Press, 1983); *Moral Absolutes: Tradition, Revision, and Truth* (Catholic University of America Press, 1991); and *Aquinas: Moral, Political and Legal Theory* (Oxford University Press, 1998). To accompany the second edition of his first book, Oxford University Press in 2011 published *Collected Essays of John Finnis* in five volumes: vol. V is *Religion and Public Reasons*. He is a Fellow of the British Academy (in the Philosophy as well as the Law section) and an honorary Queen's Counsel.

Anthony Gill is Professor of Political Science at the University of Washington and Distinguished Senior Fellow at Baylor University's Institute for Studies of Religion. He hosted the podcast series Research on Religion from 2010 to 2018 and is author of *Rendering unto Caesar: The Catholic Church and the State in Latin America* (University of Chicago Press, 1998) and *The Political Origins of Religious Liberty* (Cambridge University Press, 2007). He is currently interested in the topic of how informal norms act as a substitute for formal regulation and law, and is a spirited writer on the topic of gratuities.

Paul E. Kerry is Associate Professor of History at Brigham Young University and a visiting fellow at the University of Oxford in the Programme for the Foundations of Law and Constitutional Government as well as the Centre for Theology and Modern European Thought. He researches in intellectual history, historiography, and the transatlantic transmission of ideas in the eighteenth and nineteenth centuries. He is a fellow of the Royal Historical Society and honorary secretary to the All-Party Parliamentary Group for the Prevention of Sexual Violence in Conflict. He has held fellowships at Princeton, Cambridge, Edinburgh, and the London School of Economics and Political Science.

Glenn A. Moots is Professor of Political Science and Philosophy at Northwood University in Midland, Michigan, and has served as William E. Simon Visiting Fellow in the James Madison Program at Princeton University in 2013–14. He is co-editor of *Justifying Revolution: Law, Virtue, and Violence in the American War of Independence* (University of Oklahoma Press, 2018) and author of *Politics Reformed: The Anglo-American Legacy of Covenant Theology* (University of Missouri Press, 2010) and of essays in *American Political Thought*, *Locke Studies*, and *Hebraic Political Studies*. He earned his undergraduate degree at the University of Michigan and graduate degrees in political science and philosophy from Louisiana State University.

Vincent Phillip Muñoz is the Tocqueville Associate Professor of Political Science and Concurrent Associate Professor of Law at the University of Notre Dame. He is the founding director of Notre Dame's Program in Constitutional Studies and author of *God and the Founders: Madison, Washington, and Jefferson* (Cambridge University Press, 2009).

Zoë Robinson is Professor of Political Science at the School of Politics and International Relations, Australian National University. She also holds positions as Professor of Law at DePaul University College of Law and Professorial Research Fellow at Deakin University.

Steven D. Smith (JD, Yale; BA, Brigham Young) is the Warren Distinguished Professor of Law at the University of San Diego and co-director of the Institute for Law and Religion. His works on law and religion include *Foreordained Failure: The Quest for a Constitutional Principle of Religious Freedom* (Oxford University Press, 1995), *The Rise and Decline of American Religious Freedom* (Harvard University Press, 2014), and *Pagans and Christians in the City: Culture Wars from the Tiber to the Potomac* (Eerdmans, 2018).

Acknowledgments

The idea of this volume began while we were fellows at the James Madison Program at Princeton University. We would like to thank the Madison Program, particularly Robert P. George and Bradford P. Wilson, for offering us the fellowship that inspired this collaboration. We would also like to thank John Berger and our editorial team at Cambridge University Press.

M.D.B. and O.A.

Introduction

Assessing the First Amendment and Religious Liberty in America

Michael D. Breidenbach and Owen Anderson

In 1789, when the First Federal Congress discussed James Madison's proposed constitutional amendments on religious liberty and nonestablishment, the lawmakers did not debate many of the concerns related to the First Amendment today. They did not argue over whether religious imagery should be excluded from civic spaces, or whether government should refrain from funding activities that include a religious purpose, or whether religion should be separated from politics generally. To these issues, many of the American founders had already replied with a resounding "no." Instead, the question during that sweltering summer in 1789 was more narrowly conceived: What juridical prohibitions should be placed on the federal legislature with respect to a national church and religious conscience, liberty, or exercise? After a month of deliberations, Congress agreed on the following text: "Congress shall make no law respecting an establishment of religion, or prohibiting the free exercise thereof."

Around this text, now aged 230 years, turn today's church–state jurisprudence as well as much political, cultural, and religious discourse in America. The religion clauses remain one of the most contested constitutional texts: Free exercise and establishment clause cases are common in state and federal courts, and those that rise to the Supreme Court are often the centerpieces for contentious debates among scholars, practitioners, and the public at large. Their decisions fundamentally shape how individuals live and organizations operate. Just in the first two decades of the new millennium, the Supreme Court has decided whether students can initiate and lead prayer in public schools, whether the government can fund secular programs at religious schools and organizations, whether religious organizations can access public school facilities, whether religious imagery

Thanks to Janice Chik for her helpful comments.

can be displayed on public property, whether an illegal substance can be used for religious purposes, whether religious organizations can exclude certain people from membership based on religious beliefs, whether corporations can obtain religious exceptions from laws, and whether businesses can deny certain services based on religious convictions. Similar questions have appeared in previous Supreme Court cases and will no doubt reappear on future dockets. The contemporary importance of the religion clauses of the First Amendment cannot be underestimated, even though their initial purpose was less ambitious than their expansive reach today.

The First Amendment is such contested territory because it relates to fundamental questions about the nature of humanity, morality, religion, government, and God. When these questions are renewed, or when novel answers are offered, changes in societal views on the content and parameters of religious liberty often follow. First Amendment cases often appear at times when fundamental values seem to be in tension. For instance, the first landmark Supreme Court decision on the free exercise clause, *Reynolds* v. *United States* (1879), concerned whether a federal law criminalizing plural marriage violated the religious liberty of a Mormon who considered polygamy his religious duty. Divergent views on sexual morality continue to ignite conflicts concerning religious liberty. Recent cases across the United States, including *Masterpiece Cakeshop* v. *Colorado Civil Rights Commission* (2018), have considered whether those who provide services for weddings can lawfully deny, on religious liberty grounds, those services for ceremonies celebrating same-sex unions.

Resolving these disputes requires comprehension beyond knowledge of constitutional law and legal precedents. However, Supreme Court justices rarely wrestle with fundamental questions about human nature and the transcendent and often decline to address what religion is and what it is not. This judicial modesty is in fact fatal to their jurisprudence: By punting the question of what religion is, the Court cannot reasonably judge what religious liberty, exercise, organizations, or establishments are. Part I of this interdisciplinary volume, therefore, grounds the discussion of First Amendment jurisprudence with philosophical foundations.

Owen Anderson considers areas of natural religion, reason, and presuppositional thinking with respect to the First Amendment. He argues that the right to religious liberty is grounded not on the belief that all religious knowledge is impossible, but that there are truths about God, human nature, and individual rights knowable by natural reason, as the Declaration of Independence avers. Anderson argues that the religious liberty protected by the First Amendment applies to all persons inasmuch as all persons participate in the characteristic human search for meaning, which is the defining feature of religious beliefs and activities. This is a pursuit that requires freedom from external coercion if it is to have any coherence. Anderson's metaphysical view shows how some knowledge is possible in the realm of natural religion, how humans can access these truths through reason alone, and how greater agreement can therefore be achieved concerning religion. The value of the First Amendment lies precisely in the fact that disagreement exists, even as it was founded on the belief that some agreement is possible.

In a complementary but unique approach, Janice Tzuling Chik defines what religion is, and is not, by the human activities essential to it. By centering the question of religion's nature within action theory, she challenges the catchall account of religion – that it is simply a set of beliefs concerning the cosmos and ethics – and thus denies that religion can be reduced to a philosophy, a mere matter of conscience, or "religious atheism." The paradigm case of religion, Chik maintains, is an activity that is ordered to a concept of superior nature, what has traditionally been called "God." While worship is the exemplar of religious activity, all moral action can be religious, even if only in a secondary sense, as long as it is ordered to the transcendent. Religious exercise also includes voluntary act omissions – the choice not to perform an action – when the agent sincerely believes that such an action would violate his or her religious convictions. This account offers philosophical grounding to the claim, often found in free exercise clause cases, that in principle one has the religious liberty to act, or (more commonly) refrain from acting, on account of religion, even when such activities are seemingly secular, such as refraining from attending public schools, denying mandates that require certain health care, and objecting to serving in armed conflicts. The reasoning and implications of this metaphysical view of action, Chik concludes, are available to all rational beings, regardless of one's religious or nonreligious commitments.

Yet even if one agrees with Anderson that there are certain knowable truths about God, human nature, and individual rights, and with Chik that religion is defined as activities ordered to the divine, one might still object that the Constitution need not protect the liberty to hold these beliefs and perform these distinctive activities any more than it protects conscience rights or other human activities. John Finnis argues against contemporary legal scholars who have insisted that religion does not require special protections, privileges, exemptions, or immunities under generally applicable laws. He maintains that religious liberty is a special right because of religion's ultimate interest in and search for "the truth about truth." Religion thus transcends, incorporates, and illuminates, rather than floats at the same level as, all other truths, such as those pertaining to science and morality. This distinctive relevance demands special status in law – a status enshrined in as diverse a canon as the US Constitution, Indian Constitution, Second Vatican Council, and the European Convention on Human Rights.

The foregoing chapters point to the distinctive good of religion and the special legal protection required for its free exercise. But what are the practical applications of these philosophical views? Should there be limits to the legal protection of religious exercise? Should religion generally or some religions in particular receive special treatment or even be established as the state religion? What would governmental favor of religion entail? Throughout American history, lawmakers, religious leaders, and the general public have registered divergent, incompatible responses to these and similar questions. Part II of this volume traces these historical developments of religious liberty and church–state relations in America.

The arc of church–state relations in America did not inexorably bend toward the First Amendment. Colonies with church establishments in early America outnumbered those without establishments, and many colonial and state laws restricted religious exercise or full participation in public life to anyone who fell outside a colony's or state's defined orthodoxy. There were, of course, notable exceptions: Maryland, Rhode Island, and Pennsylvania all offered varying degrees of religious toleration during at least part of their colonial histories, but even then their religious tests and other laws restricted religious minorities from public office and other privileges. As Glenn A. Moots demonstrates, establishments and penal laws were justified, as in Europe, on the grounds that religion was vital to good government, that civil rulers had a duty to protect and promote the true faith, and that religious dissent presented not only spiritual problems but also the political problems of disunity and even treason. If religious liberty existed for religious minorities, it was at best a liberty to be left alone. Yet Moots notes that because not all Americans agreed on what true faith should be established, protected, or promoted – a fact only more pressing as America grew from small settlements to fully functioning colonies – there were religious minorities who agitated for toleration and against their colonies' establishments. This struggle for greater liberty, Moots shows, was local, uneven, and argued mostly with Christian sources and British law, favoring Protestant dissenters more than Catholics and Jews.

The complicated picture of church–state relations and religious liberty that Moots depicts in the seventeenth century remained in the immediate context of framing the First Amendment. Chris Beneke maintains that the congressional record and available historical evidence present a messy, mysterious picture of what "free exercise" and "respecting an establishment of religion" meant. But there are some clear conclusions that may be drawn from the historical record. Free exercise at least meant the right to worship according to one's religion, which was a more expansive liberty than simply the "right of conscience," and which was often couched in terms of natural rights rather than a concessionary toleration. Despite its ambiguity, Beneke argues, the free exercise clause did signal greater religious liberty by not restricting it to any religion in particular and by not protecting conscience only. Moreover, the establishment clause did not, as Thomas Jefferson famously glossed, build "a wall of separation between Church & State." While the First Amendment prohibited the federal government's establishment of one particular religion to the detriment of others, it also allowed religious accommodations, including federally funded Christian missions in the territories as well as congressional chaplains and prayer. Beneke stresses that none of these conclusions challenges the generally secular foundation of the federal government, even as individual states maintained confessional establishments or laws.

The First Amendment was, of course, an amendment to the Constitution, and as the Anti-Federalists were at pains to point out, the original document did not explicitly protect religious liberty or prohibit the establishment of a national church. Yet Michael D. Breidenbach argues that a nonestablishment clause did exist in the Constitution before the First Amendment: the no religious test clause in Article VI. Since religious tests were the clearest manifestation of state sovereignty over religion, their prohibition in Article VI prevented an establishment of a "Church of the United States" (to use Donald L. Drakeman's phrase), even before the First Amendment. Unlike previous oaths in Britain and the colonies, the federal oath for officeholders – codified in the first act of Congress – did not require a denial of specifically Catholic beliefs, yet undivided civil loyalty remained a prerequisite to securing religious liberty. When Congress later debated the First Amendment, Breidenbach shows how the establishment clause was based on what Congress had already stated in 1783: that powers in "purely spiritual" matters were "reserved to the several States, individually." Congress had declared this principle in response to the Holy See's request for it to approve a Catholic bishop, one of the few instances in which Congress made a policy decision concerning church–state relations before the First Amendment. In doing so, Congress had renounced one of the rights of patronage that governments traditionally held over ecclesiastical affairs. Although "an establishment of religion" could mean many things, the one element of a church establishment that Congress had already explicitly and definitively denied was the right of a government to present or approve bishops. Breidenbach explains how this context adds to the original meaning of the establishment clause, for prohibiting a "Church of the United States" did not necessarily forbid this particular right of patronage.

Even after the ratification of the First Amendment, some state establishments remained – a reminder that the nonestablishment clause was originally intended to be a federal prohibition only. Religious persecution or discrimination, too, did not abate after the First Amendment. Most religious liberty laws and enforcement were still handled on state and local levels, and the free exercise clause again pertained to the federal government only until the Bill of Rights was incorporated into state constitutions in the twentieth century. The nineteenth century, therefore, witnessed a patchwork of contradictory principles and practices concerning religious liberty among the states and federal territories. Like Beneke, Jonathan Den Hartog sheds light on the shadow that Jefferson's wall metaphor cast onto church–state relations in America. He finds that many Protestants across political parties, ideologies, and even Union–Confederate divisions continued to believe that federal and state governments could and should promote Christianity, at least Protestant Christianity. In 1892, Supreme Court Justice Josiah Brewer declared what many Americans had believed all along: "[T]his is a Christian nation." Freethinkers, like secularists today, bristled at such a bald statement and argued that governmental promotion of Christianity was detrimental to the United States. Even those who were sympathetic to Brewer's assessment could not all agree about what it meant; still others worried whether they were included in it. Despite the religious liberty that Catholics gained in the American founding, as Breidenbach shows, many Americans continued to single them out for their uncivil, potentially dangerous allegiance to the pope. Den Hartog demonstrates that Catholics still needed to prove their loyalty and protect their religious liberty, often appealing to the First Amendment. Mormons, too, presented a singular challenge to the Protestant moral establishment, particularly with the practice of plural marriage, which the Supreme Court decided had exceeded the bounds of religious liberty. If there was a metaphorical wall between church and state, Den Hartog concludes, it was one-sided: to protect general Christian faith and morality from government obstruction while permitting explicit and powerful religious influence on politics and society.

Part II of this volume closes with a critical review of landmark Supreme Court cases on the First Amendment religion clauses from the late nineteenth century to the present. Zoë Robinson notes that the religion clauses have been idealized as a vanguard against religious majoritarianism, but argues that Supreme Court decisions have often reinforced this majoritarianism. Except for a handful of significant cases during the Warren Court (1953–1969), she contends, First Amendment jurisprudence has generally reinforced the majority's political, social, economic, and religious views. If the framers of the First Amendment sought to prevent a "tyranny of the majority" concerning religion, Robinson suggests, modern jurisprudence has not on balance lived up to that ideal. Her findings in modern Supreme Court cases complement what the previous chapters detected: that America's moral establishment, if not de jure establishment, has privileged America's majority religions in law, politics, and the broader culture while often looking askance at those who challenge it.

Church–state issues are not the exclusive purview of the courts, however. Debates about religious liberty and church–state relations are also the concern of scholars, whose work has influenced not only the political and religious landscape but also Supreme Court decisions. To begin Part III on law, politics, and economics, Paul E. Kerry canvasses recent historical, political, legal, and philosophical interpretations on the subject and examines how certain presuppositions have informed scholars' accounts of the meaning, scope, and implications of the First Amendment. Kerry agrees with Steven D. Smith's typology of dividing First Amendment scholarship between providentialist and secularist understandings. Providentialists view America as founded on certain religious or religiously inspired principles and seek to favor that heritage in law, politics, and culture. Secularists, on the other hand, view America as founded on more classical sources and seek to dislodge religion from politics in order to better approximate equal rights for all. Yet Kerry also identifies a pragmatic strand that sees religious liberty as a useful, if not essential, policy in a religiously pluralistic society – a view that Anthony Gill will later characterize in economic terms. Ultimately, Kerry cautions that, in the ideologically charged battles over the First Amendment, the meaning of the text and its influences defy tidy explanations and further warns against constructing a narrative with a predetermined end for which evidence is pressed into service. Analyzing scholarly presuppositions, he concludes, can lead to a better understanding of the dynamics of religion, politics, and jurisprudence in America.

Vincent Phillip Muñoz's account of natural rights theory occupies a middle ground between these providentialist and secularist camps. He argues that the American founders advanced a natural rights view of religious liberty. They believed that this right, like all other God-given rights, is inalienable – no reasonable person would surrender it in order to enter into government – yet citizens may forfeit it if they violate the moral or civil law. Therefore, while the government does not have direct cognizance or jurisdiction over religious belief or practices, it may inflict indirect burdens on religious practices as a side effect when pursuing legitimate, limited, constitutional interests. Muñoz contrasts this natural rights theory with what he calls "modern moral autonomy exemptionism." This second view seeks to guard against not only direct burdens on religious practices but also indirect burdens – and not only religious practices but also "conscience." While this modern autonomy view in principle expands the protection of religious liberty, it also broadens the scope of government: As long as the government has a "compelling" interest, its acts are lawful. Under this second regime, Muñoz maintains, the best that religious dissenters can do is to appeal for an exemption, which places them again at the mercy of the government.

Scholars will continue to debate which jurisprudence guides the American constitutional order, but the very fact that religious liberty exists at all, Anthony Gill marvels, is a rare instance in human history. Employing the methods of political economy, he demonstrates that both civil and ecclesiastical leaders have compelling reasons to monopolize the religious market. Why, then, would they sunder the symbiosis of church and state?

Rather than retracing the ideological origins of religious liberty, Gill contends that civil officials in fact possess economic incentives to codify religious liberty – or, in economic language, to deregulate the religious marketplace. This was especially true in America, he argues, in which colonial leaders such as William Penn recognized that greater religious liberty could increase revenue collection, trade, immigration, and overall economic growth. Gill concludes that this pragmatic virtue was at the core of the First Amendment.

The pursuit of profit might have accounted for the rise of religious liberty for individuals, but do corporations that seek profit possess the right to religious liberty as well? Steven D. Smith argues that they do by virtue of the Religious Freedom Restoration Act of 1993 and the long-standing precedent that corporations are legal persons that can possess rights. Incorporated religious organizations also possess religious liberty, he affirms, by virtue of the ancient freedom of the church. Recent Supreme Court cases such as *Burwell* v. *Hobby Lobby* (2014) and *Hosanna-Tabor Evangelical Lutheran Church and School* v. *Equal Employment Opportunity Commission* (2012) have upheld these views, yet opposition to them betrays more fundamental normative questions about whether the government should demand that business owners forfeit their religious liberty if they choose to operate their business as a corporation and whether the government should grant special constitutional protections to religious organizations. He argues that hostility to corporate religious liberty, whether for a business or a religious organization, is part of a broader culture war that views religious liberty as an outdated, discriminatory privilege. Smith shows how yet again the Supreme Court has become a battleground where culture wars are fought – but perhaps never definitively won.

From political, economic, and legal considerations of religious liberty, the volume then turns to the establishment clause. Like Muñoz, Donald L. Drakeman employs originalism – a theory of legal interpretation based on the original meaning of the Constitution – in contrast to living constitutionalism, the view that constitutional meaning should evolve in order to adapt to the changing needs and values of the times. As Drakeman notes, interpreting the establishment clause usually divides into three groups: strict separationism, non-preferentialism, and federalism. Strict separationists, often employing Jefferson's "wall" metaphor, argue that the establishment clause prohibits not only governmental interference directly in the realm of religion (such as establishing a church) but also religious interference in government (such as religious images in civic buildings). Non-preferentialists, also called accommodationists, agree with the strict separationists that the establishment clause forbids a national church, but argue that the clause still allows for governmental support of religion (even over non-religion) so long as such aid does not unduly prefer one religion to the detriment of others. Finally, federalists view the prohibition of a national church as the consequence of a prior principle: that all matters pertaining to religion are within the jurisdiction of the states, not the federal government. The corollary of the federalism view is that the clause recognizes states' right to establish churches, adopt strict separationist policies, or non-preferentially support religion. The common denominator among these three dominant interpretations is that the clause prohibits the establishment of a "Church of the United States," which, Drakeman argues, is exactly how the framers and the public understood the clause – no more, no less. Because the Supreme Court has since incorporated the First Amendment at the state and local levels, he argues that the federalist interpretation, in conjunction with the no-national-religion prohibition, best articulates the original meaning of the clause.

As Drakeman and the other historians show, discussions of the establishment clause often concern whether it codified a "separation" of church and state. Marc O. DeGirolami rescues the idea of "separation" from the assumption that it is simply strict separationism. He identifies another type of separation – the ancient Christian idea of juridical separation of church and state – intended to benefit the Christian church and civil society. These two versions of separation – one that sees Christianity as a positive force in America, another that characterizes Christianity as irrelevant, obnoxious, or even dangerous – have coincided, albeit unevenly and uneasily, for much of American history. The jurisprudential shift to doctrines of equality and nondiscrimination with respect to religion is, he argues, simply a derivation of the secularist version of separation. DeGirolami insists that these modern doctrines are not neutral with respect to religion and to Christianity in particular; instead, they have sought to suppress Christian influences that have been foundational to American law and politics.

Gerard V. Bradley claims that the moral and cultural transformations diagnosed by Smith and DeGirolami, especially over sexual identity and marriage, are fundamentally altering how Americans perceive and ascribe importance to religious liberty. Many Americans now understand religious commitments as a mere matter of self-expression, one of many possible subjective identities. In this culture war, what once was a conflict over rights is now a contest over identities, not all of which are treated equally. Bradley argues that the relegation of religion to personal identity and the further demotion of religious identity with respect to other identities threaten a core of American constitutional liberties. His conclusion to the volume is in some ways a return to its beginning: a call to restore religion as a unique public good, grounded in reason, whose exercise deserves special protection under law.

Taken together, these chapters at once show the great divisions concerning religious liberty and church–state relations, as well as the promise of a way forward. Today's public controversies are symptomatic of deeper problems witnessed before and beyond the First Amendment. Are there truths about God knowable by reason? What is religion, and what is it not? Is religion a special good deserving of legal protection? Should governments promote, to the extent possible, religion generally or a particular religion, even to the exclusion of other religions or non-religion? What is legitimate religious dissent, and what kind of loyalty should be required to ensure religious liberty? What laws and practices might secure civil peace in light of the intractable fact of religious pluralism? Should governments grant religious toleration – a concession dispensed by political authorities who otherwise seek to promote "the one truth faith" – or should governments recognize and protect the inalienable natural right to religious liberty?

Questions concerning the taboo topics of religion and politics do not admit of easy answers. Yet the brilliance of the First Amendment is that it recognizes and protects the freedom not only to practice or refrain from practicing religion but also to discuss and debate our differences – including the meaning and significance of the First Amendment itself.

Part I

Philosophical Foundations

The First Amendment and Natural Religion 1

Owen Anderson

Introduction

The United States was founded on natural religion. The grievances justifying independence rest on the claim that there are some things self-evident about God and human nature and from these come human rights and the structure of human government. Specifically, the Declaration of Independence claims it is self-evident that there is a Creator and that humans are created. Human equality and rights rest on this claim about creation. The eventual Constitution and Bill of Rights are further examples of the development of general revelation into the political and social realms as opposed to appeals to divine origination or special revelation. The exact quote is so well known it hardly needs repeating, but we can benefit from thinking about its structure: "We hold these truths to be self-evident: that all men are created equal and endowed by their Creator with unalienable rights." We can discern three parts here: epistemology, metaphysics, and ethics. There is the epistemological claim, or a claim about knowledge, that some things are self-evident. There is the metaphysical claim about what is real: God the Creator and human nature. And there is the ethical claim about equality and rights.

The present chapter will look at religious liberty and natural religion. This will involve questions about reason, knowledge, meaning, and critical thinking. We will discover three overlooked areas where this critical thinking needs to take place and then use a paradigmatic religious freedom trial to illustrate the form such trials take and identify a solution that has been available to us for some time but left neglected. These three areas are natural religion, reason, and presuppositional thinking. For a paradigmatic religious freedom trial, we will examine the trial of Socrates. The argument is, first, that religion has to do with meaning, and the beliefs that provide meaning cannot be compelled. We will see this explained by Thomas Jefferson and exemplified in Socrates. Second, the First Amendment is not aimed at promoting unending religious pluralism, but instead it provides the context for seeking to understand how lasting meaning can be attained.

The First Amendment has a practical application simply because people disagree about religion. And, indeed, disagreement about religious opinions is sometimes taken as a trademark of *religion*. But religious knowledge is like knowledge in any field. It has as its goal not merely true belief (opinion) but a true justified belief. And when we have this we can have agreement among all. Universal agreement is not a guarantee of truth, but nor is it an indication of error. J.S. Mill said it this way:

> But what! (it must be asked). Is the absence of unanimity an indispensable condition of true knowledge? Is it necessary that some part of mankind should persist in error to enable any to realize the truth? Does a belief cease to be real and vital as soon as it is generally received – and is a proposition never thoroughly understood and felt unless some doubt of it remains? As soon as mankind have unanimously accepted the truth, does the truth perish within them? The highest aim and best result of improved intelligence, it has hitherto been thought, is to unite mankind more and more in the acknowledgement of all important truths; and does the intelligence only last as long as it has not achieved its object?[1]

Disagreements about revealed religions (which constitute most if not all of the First Amendment cases) are grounded in disagreements about natural religion, especially about God and the good.

Are the First Amendment religion clauses universal, or do they apply only to some persons? The answer to this is the same as the answer to why we are starting with natural religion. The First Amendment applies to everyone. And this is not just because everyone might potentially join an institutional or traditional religion. It is because there is an important way in which all persons are religious. Religion cannot be defined primarily in terms of an organization, or rituals, or the supernatural, or scriptures, or belief in God. Not all religions have these. Nor can religion be primarily defined in terms of dualities like sacred/secular, or holy/profane, or natural/supernatural, or immanent/transcendent. To claim that such dualities are real already begs the question; many of the world's religions deny the reality of such dualities and instead make their core teaching that *all is one*.

[1] John Stuart Mill, "Liberty of Discussion," in *A Great Books Primer: Essays on Liberal Education and the Uses of Discussion and Rules for Reading*, ed. Robert Hemenway (Chicago: The Great Books Foundation, 1955), 55.

Instead, the universality of religion is in its connection to meaning. Religion is uniquely connected to how a person attempts to find meaning, and it is not strange to say that how a person finds meaning is through their religion. The beliefs we use to find meaning and interpret our experiences are the basic beliefs that are foundational to the rest of our belief system. An objection to this is that it makes religion too common. Indeed, this could mean that activities like sports or hobbies are religions. In such cases we use the adverb *religiously* (as in, he pursues baseball religiously). This makes sense precisely because of how religion relates to meaning, while also noting that such cases are instances of pursuing a hobby *like* a religion without it actually being a religion. As such, it is not a sufficient objection but instead helps illustrate the role of religion in the search for meaning.[2]

This also explains why we are looking at natural religion. Not all religions involve scripture (revealed religion), and revealed religion presupposes natural religion. All religions make claims about natural religion. Religious liberty begins in our freedom to form beliefs about authority, reality, and value that are parts of natural religion. This will also help us understand how religion and reason are related. The liberties protected by the First Amendment are for all persons. An example of an application of this is that religious beliefs cannot be separated from the public square because religion (at least in this universal form as natural religion) permeates the public square and all discussions.

What do we do when disagreements in the public square would appear to compel a person to abandon their religious convictions? Or, can the government compel us to be religious? This can be done by first narrowly defining religious activity and then regulating it and giving out freedoms limited to this narrow definition. On this basis, people are forced to participate in religious ceremonies they do not agree with. Must we accept a narrow definition of religion given by the government, or is that merely another attempt at control? The solution is to understand the universality of religion, its connection to the search for meaning, and that pragmatism and pluralism will never be final solutions for religious belief. Instead, in the area of religion, like any other, we must pursue knowledge to come to unity and agreement. We must be able to show what is clear at the basic level in the pursuit of meaning instead of falling into antinomies about

[2] Victor Frankl, *Man's Search for Meaning* (Boston: Beacon Press, 2006).

government control or individual licentiousness. Let us look at the aforementioned three elements more closely.

What Is Natural Religion?

We will start by looking at natural religion. When we speak about the First Amendment our attention almost always, perhaps always, goes to revealed religion. This is true in part because the history of our First Amendment comes out of the conflicts among those who appealed to revealed religion. It is also true in part because many of the religious sects that have been a part of the important religious liberty Supreme Court cases made an appeal to revealed religion or personal religious experience.

Nevertheless, revealed religion presupposes natural religion. Revealed religion (scripture, redemptive revelation) presupposes that there is a God and that there is sin that requires redemption. Keeping our primary focus on natural religion will serve to illustrate what it means to think presuppositionally before we look at it directly. If by revealed religion we mean the Christian scriptures, then these affirm the clarity of natural religion so that unbelief is without excuse; it is this failure to know what ought to be known from natural religion about God that leads to the need for revealed religion and its redemptive content. Revealed religion presupposes humans can understand and then offers them some new message in addition to what they can already know.

Natural religion, also known as natural theology, is the study of general revelation. General revelation is what all persons at all times can know about God and the good. Philosophical skepticism says that no knowledge is possible about God or the good. The fideist agrees with this but insists that it is impossible to live without believing something, and therefore we must choose what we will believe in the absence of knowledge. In contrast to these, we can see that knowledge is possible through reason and argument by learning to think presuppositionally. To think presuppositionally means to think of what is less basic in light of what is more basic. It is to begin with first things.[3] It

[3] I am using this term purposely to identify the structured order to thought and not as a reference to the apologetic system of Cornelius VanTil. I have written about that specific kind of presuppositional argument in Owen Anderson, *Reason and Worldviews: Warfield,*

is to trace our disagreements to their most basic starting point. This is first done in natural religion.

Thomas Jefferson

In order to illustrate the above point about natural religion, we can refer to the Virginia Statute for Religious Freedom. Commenting on this document will help us define terms like *religion* and *liberty* and will also illustrate presuppositional and critical thinking. Specifically, it will require asking what is meant by the crux terms (critical thinking) and what the conclusions presuppose (presuppositional thinking) about *religion*. In defending the *Virginia Statute for Religious Freedom*, Thomas Jefferson stated:

> Well aware that the opinions and belief of men depend not on their own will, but follow involuntarily the evidence proposed to their minds; that [Whereas] Almighty God hath created the mind free, and manifested his supreme will that free it shall remain by making it altogether insusceptible of restraint; that all attempts to influence it by temporal punishments, or burthens, or by civil incapacitations, tend only to beget habits of hypocrisy and meanness, and are a departure from the plan of the holy author of our religion, who being Lord both of body and mind, yet chose not to propagate it by coercions on either, as was in his Almighty power to do, but to extend it by its influence on reason alone.[4]

Notice the theological, or what I will here call the "metaphysical," assertions that Jefferson makes to justify his view of human nature and religion. Metaphysics is the study of what is real. Since what changes is not permanent, when we ask what is real, we are asking what is impermanent and unchanging: what is eternal – without beginning. And so we will see that when we find someone giving a theory of human nature, they will also give us, explicitly or as a presupposition, a theory of what is eternal. In the Declaration of Independence, this is the distinction between the Creator and humans who have been endowed with rights. Here, in the Virginia Statute, Jefferson affirms this distinction between God the Creator and

Kuyper, Van Til and Plantinga on the Clarity of General Revelation and Function of Apologetics (Lanham, MD: University Press of America, 2008).

[4] Thomas Jefferson, "Virginia Statute for Religious Freedom," The Jefferson Foundation, accessed online, www.monticello.org/site/research-and-collections/virginia-statute-religious-freedom.

humans as the creation. God is eternal, without beginning, and created all else. In this act of creation, God determines human nature.

The critical aspect of human nature considered here is that it is free. Freedom is not here defined as uncaused but instead as unrestrained. Those who define freedom as "the ability to do otherwise" must emphasize that a free will is one that has no cause and is not predetermined. In the century after this Statute, both Immanuel Kant and William James rejected any theory of a free will that makes freedom compatible with causation. Yet, the emphasis here is on the will as free from restraint or coercion, not necessarily causation.

Taking the time to define freedom is important because it helps set the distinction between God and the creation. This is an important distinction because it is a basic distinction. Natural religion begins in the general revelation distinction between God and the creation. As created beings, humans are always contingent and caused. It is impossible for a creation to be uncaused. To desire an uncaused will is to desire to be the uncreated Creator: to be God. It is impossible for a human to be God, and so the human will must be caused. And yet, in contrast to bare material objects, Jefferson affirms that the will is created free. A free will is a will that is not restrained; it is free to will or to do what it wants. This is consistent with it having causes: We can name many different causes of the will, including background, personality, mood, and beliefs. Causes are unavoidable and are compatible with a free will.

Jefferson names the effects of attempting to restrain or coerce the will in matters of religion. These are the habits of hypocrisy and meanness. Here we have a hint at the role religion plays in human life. Not all coercion leads to hypocrisy. On less weighty matters one might go along or even change one's opinion. But in the case of religion, coercion creates hypocrisy because religion involves our most basic beliefs (those underlying the rest of our belief system) about what is meaningful. Attempts at coercion in religion are attempts to force a person to act against the very way they find meaning in life. Even if a person goes along with this, it will only be a kind of outward conformity that is inconsistent with the person's actual beliefs; the outward conformity will revert to authentic action as soon as the pressure is removed.

By contrast with coercion, Jefferson asserts that God Himself propagates religion through its influence on reason. Reason here is connected to beliefs and so references that by which we come to understand and believe.

A person's religion is addressed through their understanding. Or, the way a person finds meaning in life has to do with what they believe about reality and value. Religion and reason are therefore related here in the same way truth and meaning are related: For a person to believe something as true, it must first have meaning (meaningless noises cannot be true and cannot be believed).

Finally, we can note here that God is said to propagate religion. The spread of religion is through the influence of reason on the mind. The implication is that religion and reason grow together, and irrationality or failure to understand goes hand in hand with the decline of religion. We can wonder if this opens the subject of redemption. Reason can be used to understand anything, not only matters of religion. But humans in the condition of failing to use reason to know basic things are in the condition of failing to find meaning: Religion is the subject of how redemption from this condition is possible. It introduces the subjects of general revelation and redemptive revelation.

And so we have here these important definitions that can be inferred from the Statute and discernable in later documents like the Declaration of Independence: God the Creator, humans as dependent on God, the liberty of will to do what one wants, and the role of reason to shape beliefs that inform a person's religion in the pursuit of meaning. Finally, the role of general revelation and redemptive revelation will be central to the First Amendment and its history in American thought and life.

In the next passage, Jefferson introduces the role of civil rights, government, and the need for limitations and restrictions on power. This helps us think about the First Amendment and religion because it defines the limits of governmental authority. Jefferson writes:

> That our civil rights have no dependence on our religious opinions, any more than *on* our opinions in physics or geometry ... *that the opinions of men are not the object of civil government, nor under its jurisdiction;* that to suffer the civil magistrate to intrude his powers into the field of opinion and to restrain the profession or propagation of principles on supposition of their ill tendency is a dangerous fallacy, which at once destroys all religious liberty, because he being of course judge of that tendency will make his opinions the rule of judgment, and approve or condemn the sentiments of others only as they shall square with or differ from his own.[5]

[5] Ibid.

In this passage, Jefferson affirms different spheres of authority. The civil government has authority in some matters of life, but it does not extend to our religious opinions. He likens religious opinions to those in other fields of inquiry like physics or geometry. Now, these fields are two of the most certain where we believe knowledge is possible. This hints to us that his use of "opinion" is not here meant to be contrasted with "knowledge." One story that we will consider in more detail is that religious liberty is needed because religion is a private matter where knowledge is not possible; it is more like a matter of taste. That does not seem to follow from what Jefferson says.

Instead, this reminds us of different spheres of authority in human life which may share the same goal but contribute different means to that goal. There is a strain that will be introduced into a given society or civilization when multiple authorities compete within the same sphere. This could be true when the civil magistrate interferes into the realm of the church. Religions are protected from this interference by religious liberty laws. But, it can also occur when multiple religions conflict with each other within one civil realm. Religious liberty protections do nothing to address this problem of pluralism, and it can increase until civil laws are not sufficient to hold back the tide of division. This should help us realize that unity in religious matters is an important goal necessary for unity in society and the achievement of final ends. The need for religious liberty need not imply the need for unending religious pluralism but instead the need for liberty to pursue the truth, just like in subjects such as geometry and physics.

The special reason that Jefferson gives here is that the civil magistrate will be tempted to make his own opinions the rule of judgment and approve or condemn others on this standard. This tells us that Jefferson recognizes something about the post-lapsarian human. Far from being a benevolent ruler, those with power will be inclined to abuse that power for their own selfish ends, and there need to be checks of law in place to prevent this. This inner conflict is not limited to the magistrate, but each person will themselves be inclined toward this tendency. This corruption is not due to civilization but is checked by the laws of civilization. In itself, it speaks about the need for redemption. We will see various solutions offered for this redemption either from historic Christianity, those who break away from it and offer variations of redemption in Christian terminology, or even secular versions that propose self-help cures (what Christian Smith calls “moralistic therapeutic deism”). Interestingly, the need for laws about religious liberty is itself an indicator of our need for religion as redemptive.

For Jefferson, law is above any civil ruler or form of government. We might be tempted to think this is due to Enlightenment influence. Indeed, it may be true that books like Samuel Rutherford’s *Lex Rex* as well as events like the English Civil War and Bloodless Revolution were indicative of law above all, including the monarchy. Yet the Magna Carta is pre-Enlightenment, and it binds the king to law. And we can find this emphasis even further back: The Decalogue serves as the law for Israel, and no king is above this law. The preface to the Decalogue begins by affirming not only God the Creator but also God the Redeemer, and then its first law corresponds to affirming the role of God. In the same way, Jefferson is appealing to a natural law and civil rights and that these are given by God. And so, whether it is the law in revealed religion or the law in natural religion, we see the same starting point in God the Creator and the same authority over all things.

The liberty of religious opinion is not absolute. It can infringe on the civil realm, and Jefferson identifies this as overt acts against peace and good order. This summarizes for us the purpose of the civil realm: the protection of peace and good order. So just as the civil magistrate cannot interfere into matters of religious belief, so too religion cannot break its bounds by causing disorder or outward harm to others. Laws for religious liberty create obligations on both sides. There is the obligation to protect peace and good order but also the obligation to pursue and promote truth. He says:

> That it is time enough for the rightful purposes of civil government for its officers to interfere when principles break out into overt acts against peace and good order; and finally, that truth is great and will prevail if left to herself; that she is the proper and sufficient antagonist to error, and has nothing to fear from the conflict unless by human interposition disarmed of her natural weapons, free argument and debate; errors ceasing to be dangerous when it is permitted freely to contradict them.[6]

This describes a battle between truth and error. And the only way to ensure that truth has victory is to promote free argument and debate between these. This could be called a spiritual battle to contrast it with a physical

[6] Ibid.

battle. And a spiritual battle is fought not with weapons of the world but with truth.

It is correct to wonder if there has been any progress since the time of Jefferson. Was he too optimistic about the outlook for reason? Pessimism might be in order but for the fact that free and open debate about presuppositions has not been the practice. There may indeed have been debates. However, these often occurred between persons who otherwise share presuppositions that remain unconsciously held and not critically examined. Jefferson himself may have fallen into this, and so we can hold him to the standard of this text. His deism and modification of the New Testament may not live up to the very standard of reason and general revelation to which he appeals.

Knowledge and Fideism

Much attention has been given to the obligation or duty of the civil magistrate in the history, law, and literature since Jefferson's time, but what about the obligations of religion? What if those holding to religious opinions increase division, disunity, and discord? This occurs when personal opinions are held as if they were actual knowledge when they are not. Knowledge carries with it obligation. Knowledge is not mere assertion. We will call mere assertion "fideism." Any group can assert itself in a fideist fashion. The strong impression that I am correct does not always, and perhaps very rarely, correspond to actually being correct. To call this strong impression the work of God does not change it from fideism into knowledge. What separates knowledge from true opinion is being able to give an account of why one's belief is true.[7] Those who speak highly of the value of reason have not themselves been able to show what is clear to reason about religion.

By comparing it to geometry and physics, Jefferson has given us an indication of how religious knowledge is attained. Like any discipline of knowledge, but especially exemplified by these two, knowledge begins with basic things and grows from there. These use the laws of thought (noncontradiction) to rule out what is impossible. This is not

[7] This is true for any definition of "knowledge" because it is inescapable. It is the case even if one is *giving an account* of alternative definitions of knowledge.

Enlightenment foundationalism, since both geometry and physics were doing this before the Enlightenment. But we can use the term "foundation" since this is used in the scriptures (also pre-Enlightenment). We must get the first principles or foundation in place and take care on which foundation we are building.

So when religion is in disarray and causing division that threatens the peace and good order of civilization, we can safely assume that there is division about basic things. Here I will call this "presuppositional thinking" and spend more time on it in a later section. However, the idea is that if we disagree about a less basic issue, this is because we also disagree about a more basic issue. Often, it is the less basic issues that get attention and are the source of heated argument. However, they will not be resolved as long as they are the product of more basic but unnoticed disagreement. This requires a greater level of consciousness about our own belief system and critical analysis of how disagreements work.

A religious believer's fideism shares the same presupposition as the non-believing skeptic: knowledge is not possible. The skeptic presupposes that knowledge is not possible and argues that we should not believe. The fideist also presupposes that knowledge is not possible but argues that we must believe something. The alternative to both is to critically analyze the presupposition that knowledge is not possible. As we have seen in the history of American religious life, fideism begets fideism: the multiplication of fideistic groups, each claiming to have a revelation or the correct understanding of revelation but without knowledge.

Fideism places a stumbling block in the path of others and hinders the fideist from entering as well. It strengthens the position of the skeptic, the naturalist (material monist), and the deist in their confidence that either there is no God or God does not act in human and natural history. This view is strengthened by the confusion among religions about God's activities. This stumbling block can also affect the civil realm by increasing tension and disturbing good order. The alternative is to prepare the way, remove stumbling blocks in the form of objections, by showing that basic things are clear to reason. Perhaps without knowing it, this is what Jefferson is calling for when he appeals to the role of reason in religious belief. This requires identifying the basic things and then showing what can be known about them. Basic things include concepts about God and creation, good and evil.

Jefferson has confidence in truth. He believes that when humans are free to debate and argue, they will come to know the truth. This might be called an optimistic view of humans. Truth will prevail over ignorance. Given what Jefferson said about those in power misusing their power, one might wonder why he thinks truth will prevail. To borrow a theological term, if humans are *fallen*, then why would we think they will ever seek the truth over their own selfishness? There is a tension here that needs to be resolved. On the one hand, Jefferson affirms that humans are easily corruptible, and this especially is evident when they have power. On the other hand, humans are also oriented toward the truth and truth will prevail. Perhaps, this indicates something other than the natural course of things. Under the natural course, selfishness will stay selfishness. It indicates that God's redemptive work will renew the person so that they begin to seek the truth. It seems doubtful that Jefferson would want to go there in light of his deism and his reworking of the New Testament. And it is also true that this is the only way that we can combine the corruption of human nature with the idea that truth will prevail. For our purposes here, this raises the reality of the need for redemption. Jefferson connects freedom of religion and worship with freedom of belief and opinion:

> That no man shall be compelled to frequent or support any religious worship, place, or ministry whatsoever, nor shall be enforced, restrained, molested, or burthened in his body or goods, nor shall otherwise suffer, on account of his religious opinions or belief; but that all men shall be free to profess, and by argument to maintain, their opinions in matters of religion, and that the same shall in no wise diminish, enlarge, or affect their civil capacities.[8]

Liberty is set in contrast to coercion. It is in contrast to Augustine asserting, "Compel them to enter," in his misapplication of the parable (Luke 14:23).[9] This mistake reverberated throughout church history. In this passage, Jefferson specifically mentions religious worship. This includes attempts by the state to use taxes to support religious worship that might seem foreign to us now but were well known at the time. Worship is related by Jefferson to religious beliefs because it is a fundamentally cognitive, rather than a merely noncognitive, activity. While there may be noncognitive aspects, the foundational and fundamental activity is the affirmation of

[8] Ibid.

[9] Owen Anderson, "Augustine's Ethics of Belief and Avoiding Violence in Religious Disputes," *New Blackfriars* 91, no. 1031 (2010): 81–101.

basic truths: the praise of God (consider how the Psalms praise God through remembering his qualities, promises, and acts in history), the hearing of the Word of God, and discipline in applying this Word to life. None of these can be coerced so that, even if one tried, one would only produce the hypocrites Jefferson already mentioned: persons who do not believe but act as if they do believe. This is the opposite of disciplining the nations and teaching them to obey whatsoever has been commanded. What would the consequences of lack of discipline and this form of hypocrisy be on the church? What might the influence be on the life of true believers and on the health of correct doctrine?

Next, we need to pay special attention to how Jefferson expects us to maintain our religious beliefs. Humans are free to profess their religious opinions and to maintain them by argument. This is a further development of his affirmation of the relationship between religion and reason. Among its various uses, reason is used to construct arguments to support conclusions. Truth will prevail because reason leads to truth, not error. And, reason will prevail because it is the distinguishing feature of human nature. To disconnect religious belief from reason and argument is to disconnect religion from meaning.

This is the tension mentioned already between affirming that humans seek the truth and their fallenness. This kind of Enlightenment optimism is set in contrast to the claim that power corrupts and the fact that humans do not seem to seek the truth. If humans are not in the condition of seeking, then what could make them begin to do so? Or, if humans have the potential to use reason but have failed to do so (about basic things, only doing so about less basic and superficial things), what could make them begin to do so? In other words, the ability to use reason could be a defining feature of what it means to be human despite the possibility that humans do not use that ability or do not use it in a manner that leads to knowledge of what is clear at the basic level. Humans want the freedom to profess whatever belief, but not the responsibility to know what is clear about God.

This presses us to notice another purpose of reason. Although reason does aim at truth, it first and foremost aims at meaning. We cannot know if an opinion is true if we don't know what it means. Reason gives meaning by distinguishing between things (A and non-A) and then forming beliefs from these distinctions in a coherent way. Our need for meaning is our most basic need, and humans regularly give up the other needs commonly listed (food, water, shelter, friends, life) in the pursuit of meaning. It is on the concept of meaning that reason and religion overlap; each of these is undeniably concerned with meaning.

Will the desire for meaning prevail and motivate a specific human to pursue truth? Perhaps. Perhaps not. The lack of need for meaning will always be compelling, but it could compel in one of two directions. It could compel a person to abandon what is meaningless and grow in meaning. But, it could also compel a person to move from what is meaningless into even less meaning. It moves to either greater understanding (light) or greater misunderstanding (darkness). How could we know which way it would work in a given person? This again raises the problem of redemption. Jefferson himself seems to have believed that self-improvement, including moral self-improvement, was possible through learning and good advice. Yet, the text of what someone has written takes on a life of its own, and we are not bound by the author's understanding. The problems that arise in this text make us doubt that self-improvement is sufficient in this area. If I am not seeking, then I won't listen to good advice, and I won't correctly learn or apply my learning. This problem will remain with us throughout the chapter, and we will need to return to the central role of redemption in religion.

It is hard not to see the comparison with what Jefferson here says about establishing our religious opinions through argument and what Martin Luther said at the Diet of Worms. There, when his religious beliefs were on trial, and he was accused of error and folly, he famously replied:

> Unless I am convinced by Scripture and plain reason – I do not accept the authority of the popes and councils, for they have contradicted each other – my conscience is captive to the Word of God. I cannot, and I will not recant anything for to go against conscience is neither right nor safe. God help me. Amen.[10]

Although he says it is not safe or right to go against conscience, he is also affirming that belief and conscience are insufficient grounds for religious freedom since both belief and conscience may be in error. Instead, a belief must be supported by scripture and plain reason. Appeals to scripture require the further step of demonstrating that scripture has been correctly understood. We understand by the use of reason. So whether we are

[10] Martin Luther, "Luther at the Imperial Diet of Worms," accessed online, www.luther.de/en/ws.html.

attempting to understand scripture or nature, we ultimately make our appeal to reason.

What Jefferson is most concerned to protect then is the liberty to hold religious opinions and support them by rational argument. This creates a social value that affirms and encourages the use of reason in the self and others and turns away in disgust from those who fail to use reason and instead rely on mere assertion and fideism. The bald assertion of religious experience or enthusiasm is not sufficient since experiences can be misunderstood and misinterpreted even by the one who has had them. Liberty is, therefore, a means to an end. It is a means for the thriving of rational discourse about religious opinions, which are the most basic and most important of opinions because they address the very questions needed for meaning. If liberty is given but not used for this end, then it is of questionable value. Nonthinking animals don't need this kind of liberty because even if they had it, they couldn't benefit from it.

Socrates: The Paradigm of a Religious Trial

We can use Socrates as a paradigmatic example of a religious trial to illustrate what was just considered in Jefferson. This trial involves both revealed and natural religion. Socrates is responding to the claim by the oracle that he is the wisest. He has a hard time believing this and sees it as a kind of religious duty to discover if it is true. After examining those persons considered wise by society and finding that they think they know, but they do not know, he concludes that the oracle spoke about Socrates as a type, "[H]e is wisest who, like Socrates, knows when he does not know." When he is asked by the court to stop his questioning, he points out that this would involve breaking his religious duties. His questioning also involves a kind of natural religion in that he is asking those who are considered wise to explain what it is to know and what is good. Their inability to do this is a matter of natural religion.

Socrates summarizes the charges against him as follows: "What do they say? Something of this sort: – That Socrates is a doer of evil, and corrupter of the youth, and he does not believe in the gods of the state and has other new divinities of his own."[11] Socrates responds to these accusations

[11] Plato, *The Apology*, MIT: The Internet Classics Archive, accessed online, http://classics.mit.edu/Plato/apology.html.

showing that he is the last who could be accused of corrupting the youth and that he cannot be called an atheist since he is in this difficulty from his commitment to the words of the oracle.

By questioning those who are considered wise by society, Socrates finds that, while people consider themselves wise, they are not actually wise and cannot give an account of their lives. This is a kind of self-deception. When Socrates questions them, and their lack of wisdom is discovered, they engage in self-justification. This self-justification carries itself to the point of a trial and eventual death penalty for Socrates. Although Socrates uses arguments to support his beliefs, he does not persuade his opponent. This once again raises a problem we have already encountered: How can it be that humans have the capacity for reason and yet do not use it? A sound argument will not persuade those who are not making use of reason, nor will it change them from not using reason to using reason.

Was Socrates engaged in a fool's errand? We need not conclude so. We noted above that reason and argument are not always persuasive, but they are compelling. They will move a person either to greater understanding or greater misunderstanding. And so it is with the trial of Socrates. His arguments moved the hearers into greater misunderstanding, and this in itself is a revelation of something worth knowing. This process reveals the fool and the simpleton. The fool is the one who thinks he knows when he does not know. The simpleton is the one who does not care to know. Neither appreciates the Socratic method of questioning.

Nevertheless, he is found guilty. His liberty will be taken away either by his agreeing to remain silent or by his death. The opposition asks for the death penalty. Socrates initially proposes that he should be rewarded for his endeavors since he tirelessly sought the betterment of others. But he admits this is unlikely and considers what other possible penalties are available:

> Someone will say: Yes, Socrates, but cannot you hold your tongue, and then you may go into a foreign city, and no one will interfere with you? Now I have great difficulty in making you understand my answer to this. For if I tell you that this would be a disobedience to a divine command, and therefore that I cannot hold my tongue, you will not believe that I am serious; and if I say again that the greatest good of man is daily to converse about virtue, and all that concerning which you hear me examining myself and others, and that the life which is

unexamined is not worth living – that you are still less likely to believe. And yet what I say is true, although a thing of which it is hard for me to persuade you.[12]

The unexamined life is not worth living. The liberty to dialogue in the pursuit of wisdom is necessary for the greatest good. To ask Socrates to stop doing this is to ask him to live as less than a human. He is responding to the divine command of the oracle, but he is also doing what falls under the heading of natural religion. Without the Oracle at Delphi we could know from general revelation that the unexamined life is not worth living; we could know that wisdom is the highest good.

Socratic skepticism should not be confounded with the skepticism mentioned earlier. Socrates comes to realize that he is wise in that he knows that he does not know, whereas those he questioned believed they were wise but were not wise. His condition is superior because he knows the truth about himself. But he does not intend to stay in the condition of not knowing, nor does he conclude that knowledge is not possible. Instead, he is an example of the life of inquiry and rational dialogue to clarify definitions and give arguments.

There are inherent consequences for any human who does live the examined life. The failure to seek wisdom, the failure to know the good, results in the accuser uncovering the meaninglessness in one's life. Socrates phrases it this way:

> And I prophesy to you who are my murderers, that immediately after my death punishment far heavier than you have inflicted on me will surely await you. Me you have killed because you wanted to escape the accuser, and not to give an account of your lives. But that will not be as you suppose: far otherwise. For I say that there will be more accusers of you than there are now; accusers whom hitherto I have restrained: and as they are younger, they will be more severe with you, and you will be more offended at them. For if you think that by killing men you can avoid the accuser censuring your lives, you are mistaken.[13]

In his analysis of what sentence or consequence he should face for having been found guilty, Socrates considers two options: death as nonexistence or as a continuation of his present consciousness. If it is the former, then it is not to be feared since it is nothing. And if it is the latter, then it will be a continuation of his present search. He says:

[12] Ibid. [13] Ibid.

> Now if death is like this, I say that to die is gain; for eternity is then only a single night. But if death is the journey to another place, and there, as men say, all the dead are, what good, O my friends and judges, can be greater than this? If indeed when the pilgrim arrives in the world below, he is delivered from the professors of justice in this world, and finds the true judges who are said to give judgment there, Minos and Rhadamanthus and Aeacus and Triptolemus, and other sons of God who were righteous in their own life, that pilgrimage will be worth making. What would not a man give if he might converse with Orpheus and Musaeus and Hesiod and Homer? Nay, if this be true, let me die again and again. I, too, shall have a wonderful interest in a place where I can converse with Palamedes, and Ajax the son of Telamon, and other heroes of old, who have suffered death through an unjust judgment; and there will be no small pleasure, as I think, in comparing my own sufferings with theirs. Above all, I shall be able to continue my search into true and false knowledge; as in this world, so also in that; I shall find out who is wise, and who pretends to be wise, and is not.[14]

We are using the trial of Socrates as an exemplar of a religious trial. Socrates represents the iconic philosopher. But his trial is also a religious trial. Athens does not permit religious liberty. Although it is a polytheistic center and, as such, could exemplify the kind of pagan pluralism that some hold in regard, what in fact happens is that only some gods or worship are permitted. When Socrates is perceived to teach other gods than those the city recognizes, he runs afoul of the authority. Or, more importantly, when Socrates raises questions about whether those in authority know or if they only think they know, he is then targeted as a problem. Religious liberty is about what is real (which gods), and it is about authority (who is wise, who has knowledge).

Although there can be a kind of pluralism, in theory, even the pluralism of polytheism has its limits. Those limits aren't merely against the addition of new gods. They are about maintaining the same epistemology that supports the authority necessary for the cultural order. So, presumably, gods that affirm this order can be added indefinitely. However, when Socrates begins to question if those in authority are actually wise, this order is threatened.

Reason and Religion, or, Epistemology and Authority

Religion and government both make claims about what is real and rest these claims on authority. Ultimately, reason is the highest authority

[14] Ibid.

because it is self-attesting. Religious and political sources, at least implicitly, appeal to reason and argument to justify their claims. This is true of an Enlightenment figure like Jefferson, of a Reformation figure like Martin Luther, and of an ancient Greek philosopher like Socrates. We are bringing these many threads together to help us more clearly identify religious liberty and its goal. We need to get *reason* into greater focus to help us in this. Reason and faith are not in tension but are necessarily related.

In defining "reason," we are looking to define reason in itself. This is not exactly the same as defining reason as we use it, or defining reason in us (the sense in which we are rational). Understanding reason in its use or reason in us will follow from having defined reason in itself. When we do not define reason in itself, we tend to focus on some one aspect of rationality, reasoning, or rationalizing. This then leads us into confusion about the relationship between religion and subjects like religion or scripture.

Reason is sometimes thought to be nice but not necessary for faith and life.[15] It is thought to be for some personalities and not others. Or, it is contrasted with the simple who are authentic and do not need reason. The simple have a simple faith, and reason is said to be for the worldly-wise. Here we will see that reason and faith are inseparable and are united in their common emphasis on the need for meaning. Meaning is not just for some personalities, and the simple need meaning as much as anyone else. Reason is for all and is fundamental to our humanity.

Reason in itself is the laws of thought.[16] These laws have been defined as the law of identity (A is A), the law of excluded middle (either A or non-A), and the law of noncontradiction (not both A and non-A). These are interrelated so that affirming one of them affirms all of them and denying one denies all of them. These also operate at a meta-level over logic (classical, modern, or postmodern – if there is such a thing) in that a law of inference is what it is (law of identity). God is God. Humans are humans. A right is a right. Scripture is scripture. Whatever the subject, we study what *is* and distinguish it from what *is not*.

[15] Anderson, *Reason and Worldviews*.

[16] For further discussion of reason and general revelation, see Surrendra Gangadean, *Philosophical Foundation: A Critical Analysis of Basic Beliefs* (Lanham, MD: University Press of America, 2008).

The laws of thought can become more concrete for us as we think about their use. Defining *reason in its use* will also help define what reason is not. These are the laws of thought in that they are the basis for understanding anything. In understanding, we distinguish between *A* and *non-A*. We distinguish pencil, desk, computer, book, under, red, fast, being, God, the good. This first use of reason is to form concepts, judgments, and arguments, which are the forms of all thought. Consider a person who objects to reason: In objecting an argument (however unsound) is being formed, and reason is being used in the objection to reason. Thought about the mundane and secular, as well as about the eternal and transcendent, is both dependent on reason for the formation of concepts, judgments, and arguments. There are other things that are sometimes confused with *thought*, such as impressions, the senses, intuitions, feelings; but reason is the laws of thought. And even with these, we distinguish senses from nonsenses, intuition from non-intuition. We use reason to understand.

In seeking to understand we use reason critically as a test for meaning. *Teaching critical thinking* has become a standard phrase in the academy. It would be hard to find any school that does not affirm this value. And yet, what this means is often lost when we see it is performed in so many conflicting ways. We are doing critical thinking by asking "what does it mean to think critically?" Asking about the meaning of a phrase is more basic than (prior to) asking about whether it is true or false. If we do not know what something means, then it cannot be assigned a truth-value. Many disagreements occur at this level because the participants are arguing about true/false but actually have different meanings in mind. Reason is a test for meaning in that if a law of thought has been violated, then there can be no meaning. *It is A and non-A at the same time and in the same respect* "means" that nothing has been distinguished, nothing has been understood, and no concept has been formed.

This presses us to consider our interpretation and is the third use of reason. We use reason to interpret our experiences. Experiences are not self-verifying. We have an experience, and then we have a meaning and explanation we assign to the experience. Sometimes, this happens so quickly that we do not notice our interpretive lens and need to take time to disconnect the experience itself (an event) from how we interpret it and explain it (it was the most important event of my life and means God exists). This builds on the formative and critical uses of reason. When we interpret, we are "giving meaning" to an experience or text. This is a necessary part of understanding.

The fourth use of reason is constructive. We use reason to build a coherent world and life view. This is the systematic application of reason into all areas of human life. We see it illustrated in the use of "philosophy" before the various features of human society: philosophy of law, philosophy of medicine, philosophy of religion, philosophy of business, philosophy of politics, etc. We seek to understand how these relate to each other and their own internal structure as it relates to our basic understanding of what is real and the purpose of human life. In all of these, we are using reason to understand.

Different philosophers and individuals might emphasize one or another of these uses, and this gives a stamp on their approach to thought and understanding. Descartes might emphasize the critical use of reason; G.W.F. Hegel might emphasize the constructive use of reason; Foucault might emphasize the interpretive use of reason. It is appropriate for a person to emphasize a particular part of reality for greater study, but when we isolate any one of these from the rest or when we confuse their order, then we will end up with a misunderstanding of reason and perhaps even deny reason. Consider how Michel Foucault (as the exemplar of postmodern philosophy) built his career on the role of interpretation but ends with arguing that there is only interpretation and takes this one use of reason out of the context of the reason to understand what is real and permanent. We use reason to understand being. Religion is about being. And so we use reason to understand religion.

If these are the uses of reason, in what sense are we rational? What is reason in us? This is a natural question to ask because reason is natural in us. This is in contrast to saying that reason is cultural or conventional. It is natural for a human to form concepts, judgments, and arguments; it is natural to ask what something means; it is natural to interpret experience; and it is natural to form belief systems. These are formal similarities that run throughout human history and around the globe. Reason is universal – the same in all. The ancients used the law of identity to make distinctions; the moderns used the law of identity to make distinctions; and the postmoderns use this same law to make distinctions. On this basis, we can learn foreign languages in the present, and we can translate ancient texts. If anything comes natural to humans, it is thinking and the use of reason.

Second, reason in us is ontological. This is to say that reason applies to being as well as thought. Thought is an activity of being, so these are not absolutely distinct categories. Reason is not merely a mental game that rules over what we can and cannot think about; reason is also about the nature of being. What is a contradiction cannot be thought and cannot be. It is the most basic law or starting principle that something cannot both be and not be in the same respect and at the same time. The standard example of this is the square-circle. A circle has no corners, and a square does have corners, and so a square-circle is an object that both has and does not have corners at the same time and in the same respect. This means that there aren't square-circles in our thought, and there aren't any on the dark side of the moon or within black holes. This also serves as an example of the critical use of reason. Although both *square* and *circle* have meaning by themselves, when we combine them in this manner the result is the loss of meaning.

Third, reason is transcendental. Reason is the highest authority. It cannot be questioned because it makes questioning possible. If we were to question reason, we would be using reason to form concepts, judgments, and arguments. Reason is inescapable. Insofar as we are thinking, we are using reason, and where we fail to use reason we are also failing to think. As rational beings, we cannot finally abandon reason without silencing all thought. To call reason the highest authority will inevitably raise questions about the relationship between reason and faith, or reason and scripture? Although there is a perceived tension (especially when we slip from *reason* as the laws of thought into *reason* as naturalism), the tension is not real; we use reason to understand, and we want to understand our faith and understand scripture. These are not competing authorities but categorical distinctions; reason is that by which we understand anything from the natural world to special revelation.

Fourth and finally, reason is fundamental. It is fundamental to the other aspects of the human personality, and it is fundamental in the order of understanding anything else about what is real. Great attention is often paid to either desire or the will; reason and the formation of beliefs shape how these are understood. This is true both in the sense that we use reason to understand our desires and choices and in the sense that the extent to which we use reason to understand will shape our desires and choices. This lays bare to us the order of the human personality and the order between human talents. Reason is fundamental in that its use is the source of meaning and its denial is the source of our greatest misery.

Discussion of reason and religion usually brings to mind the dichotomy of naturalism and religion, or atheism and religion, or secularism and religion. This need not be so and is due to a failure to think presuppositionally in our definitions. Indeed, we will be working on defining presuppositional thinking and use this as one example. Naturalism, atheism, and secularism are beliefs about what is real. When adherents of these systems say that we can only appeal to *reason* and not faith or scripture, *reason* means empirical data, the senses, because this is the only source of information available if all is matter. Their presupposition about what is real has limited how they interpret their experiences. However, if there is more to reality than matter, then we need to be able to use reason to understand this as well. *Reason* has been used ambiguously by the naturalists. It refers to the laws of thought but is used by naturalism to refer to sense data about matter. This misuse of the term is a source of skepticism because empiricism by itself can never lead to knowledge, and thus by identifying it with reason this also is implicated in the skepticism.

Naturalism is one example of what reason is not, or of an ambiguous use of the term *reason*, or of a misuse of *reason* that leads to skepticism. There are other examples worth considering. Sometimes *reason* is used to mean *reasoning*. This is the human thought process. It could mean the uses of reason mentioned above. But more often it means the way a person thinks so that it can be said: "your reasoning is flawed." *Reason* as the laws of thought cannot be flawed, but a person's thought process could be unsound. For instance, a person might be using the various informal fallacies and drawing fallacious conclusions. These pseudo-arguments might pass as sound arguments to many in the audience because of their own failure at reasoning. In other words, fallacies can be persuasive, but they can never be sound. When *reason* is used to mean this kind of pseudo-argument, then it becomes a source of skepticism.

Reason is sometimes also used to mean *common sense*. What counts as common sense takes the condition of the perceiver for granted. What one person takes to be common sense, another person does not. Thomas Paine praised common sense but did not think critically about his own assumptions that led to deism and the denial of special revelation. Paine spoke highly of reason but in identifying it with common sense implicated both as skepticism. Common sense differs from society to society, and so dependence on common sense easily leads to relativism, the denial of absolutes, and the inability to come to agreement with those that have differing systems. Intuition, although different than common sense, shares this same problem. Sometimes *be reasonable* means *share my intuitions* when there is not actually common agreement about basic understanding.

This use of intuition, or common sense, in place of reason as critical thinking, leads all three into skepticism.

Reason is also sometimes contrasted with the individual. Reason as the system that has come down to us through the collected wisdom of the ages or the great teachers can be set over and above individual expression. This then creates dichotomies, including tradition and individual or reason and art or reason and creativity. Tradition is not the same as reason in itself; tradition can depart from reason or have failed to use reason critically. The individual who does critically examine the presuppositions of an age is expressing reason. Art as aesthetics or impression is not in contrast or conflict with reason but is a category that needs interpretation so that we perfectly well know what it means to speak of the philosophy of art or the art critique/commentary.

Sometimes *reason* is spoken of boldly in its systematic function and given great expression as in the works of Hegel. Here consistency as a criterion for truth is affirmed with great vigor. Castles of beliefs can be built brick by brick through systematization and the affirmation of noncontradiction. Yet these will be castles on sand if they do not get built presuppositionally (identifying what is most basic first through critical thinking) and if they first pursue truth over first using reason as a test for meaning. Modern logic puts its students through the rigors of truth tables and gives the rules for inferring true conclusions from true premises; sometimes it even attempts to build systems of inference that deny one or the other of the laws of thought (noncontradiction and excluded middle have come under special attack). These are misusing *reason*, which is not first a test for truth or a rule of inference but is first and fundamentally a test for meaning. A rule of inference is what it is (obeys the law of identity), and where it violates a law of thought it loses meaning. This misuse of reason leads to skepticism and many that are otherwise very proud of their logical prowess have fallen into as a slough of despair that reverberates throughout the rest of their life and choices.

Reason is not naturalism. It is not reasoning, it is not common sense or intuition, it is not tradition, and it is not merely systemization. Reason as the laws of thought is the source of meaning. And meaning is intimately connected to religion. And yet *faith* is often synonymous with *fideism*. Here we are distinguishing these two. *Faith* is the evidence of things not seen; faith is contrasted with sight, not with reason. Faith is understanding of what is not seen so that it can be said both that Abraham had faith and that he reasoned God would raise Isaac from the dead.

The privatization of faith is an attempt in modernity to distance religious opinion from the public and from law. It is part of the Westphalian solution to religious wars. Most of the notable religious liberty cases are about times when this private bumps into the public and a decision must be made about which will have greater weight. However, the privatization of religious does not and cannot distance them from reason. The goal of religious beliefs remains the same: to provide meaning. And reason is the test for meaning. So whether they are left in the private realm (which turns out to be impossible in the end) or they are in the public realm, when they are void of meaning this will become evident through the critical use of reason.

The privatization of religious belief tends to focus on the conflicts surrounding revealed religion. The Peace of Westphalia settled conflicts between Protestants and Roman Catholics. Since that time there have been many new religious movements introduced into the field and greater contact between the previously existing world religions. What all of these share in common is that humans think, that thinking involves the use of reason, that thinking is presuppositional, and that our basic beliefs are about natural religion.

The First Amendment does not strike us as being about natural religion because we don't see great divisions about natural religion. Indeed, perhaps all persons are united about natural religion in their general neglect of its study. The Declaration of Independence makes a bold claim about natural religion when it affirms that there are self-evident truths about God the Creator and God's role in endowing humanity with rights. Although it might be readily knowable that God the Creator exists, it is not self-evident, and in a way this might be an indication of the neglect of natural religion: Rather than do the work of giving the arguments necessary to show this is the case, it is assigned *self-evidence* and has been attacked ever since by atheists and naturalists. It is now largely replaced by a naturalist account of right or at least sufficiently challenged to undermine any claims to *self-evidence.*

Presuppositional Thinking: Applying Reason in Our Thinking about Religion

It is self-evident that we think. To deny this one must engage in thinking. We cannot deny our natures as thinking beings; we can only forfeit our integrity. Compare this to other assertions about what is self-evident, including that all men are created equal. This might be commonly agreed upon and readily knowable, but it is not self-evident.

The simple form of a thought is to affirm or deny something of a subject. The pencil is yellow. The chapter is engaging. The dog is not loud. Here we see the work of reason in forming concepts to distinguish things (pencil and non-pencil, etc.) and forming these concepts into judgments.

Our judgments have presuppositions. A presupposition is what is assumed, or must be true, for the judgment at hand to be true: for instance, the existence and nature of the being in question. When we are told that a pencil is yellow, we operate within a framework of what it means for there to be pencils. Our framework includes that pencils exist and have properties like colors. This presupposes the concept of being.

When we think about our presupposition *being*, we naturally begin to ask *where did this come from*, or *has this always been*? This is a natural question for young children to ask just as they begin to learn to think, and if it now seems unnatural to the adult, it is only because the adult has abandoned that original curiosity in favor of skepticism. For the pencil, we conclude it has not always been. It came from something else: wood. For wood, we conclude that it has not always been; it came from something else: a tree. And a seed, and back to the first tree, and this makes us ask about the origin of life, and ultimately since we cannot press this back to infinity, it forces us to ask *what has existed from eternity?*

Our most basic belief, or our most basic presupposition, has to do with what has existed from eternity (without beginning). If we transport the judgment, *the pencil is yellow*, into one or another framework about what is eternal, we will see how the meaning is altered once we ask questions outside of the immediate practical. Is the pencil part of the creation of God, is it an illusion in the mind of Brahman, is it a merely material object composed of eternal atoms? This is called philosophical ambiguity.

We can map the possible presuppositions about what is eternal and in doing this learn to locate ourselves and others on the map about basic beliefs. At first, there appears to be three possibilities: all is eternal; only some is eternal; none is eternal. *At first*, because we can use critical analysis to find that one of these is not possible. This will be a useful illustration of what it means to think critically as well as to help narrow the spectrum of possible beliefs about what is eternal.

None is eternal is not one of the basic beliefs because it involves an impossibility. Remember that reason is ontological, meaning that it applies to being as well as to thought. If we find a contradiction, it is not possible in thought nor being (thinking is an activity of being, and so these are not absolute distinctions). *None is eternal* is not the same as saying all is change. The latter (in Heraclitus, Buddha, and others) affirms that while no individual thing has existed from eternity, the flow of these extends into eternity; it is a form of *all is eternal.* Rather, *none is eternal* asserts that all is temporal, all had a beginning, all came into being, and finally all came into being from nonbeing. The claim of *none is eternal* is that *being came from nonbeing.* There was once nothing, and then something came into existence.

The distinction between *being* and *nonbeing* is the most basic and fundamental distinction we can make in thinking. It is the absolute distinction. No one confuses these two. We might disagree about what exists, but we don't confuse existing with non-existing. And no worldview confuses these. *From nothing nothing comes.* Nonbeing cannot give rise to being, and cannot be such that it existed, and then something came from it, nor can being come out of nonbeing. To say that the laws of thought did not yet exist if there was only nonbeing and therefore do not apply is to still affirm that at some point nonbeing existed. Each time we see this kind of assertion and inquire further (a universe from nothing; a universe that creates itself) we find that *nothing* is really something (quantum foam; gravity). If *none is eternal* cannot be true, then it follows that something must be eternal.

It is clear to reason that something must be eternal. We find the world's belief system lumped into these two presuppositions: All is eternal (material monism; spiritual monism; dualism); only some is eternal (theism; deism). We can use the same method seen above of critical analysis to find that there is indeed both eternal and temporal being, God and the creation, so that only some is eternal and the contrary assertion confuses temporal being (or denies its existence) with external being (confuses the creation with God; non-God with God). This illustrates both what it means to think presuppositionally and what it means to think critically. True critical thinking must identify our presuppositions and test them for meaning.

We can also identify what it means to think presuppositionally in subject matter. Our beliefs, or suppositions, have assumptions, or presuppositions. These follow a pattern from ethics, to metaphysics, to epistemology. Ethics is the study of what we ought to do. Our choices presuppose beliefs about what is good. These, in turn, presuppose beliefs about human nature and what is real. This is the study of metaphysics. The good for a being is based on the nature of that being (good for a human; good for a horse; good for a car). And so to know what is good requires knowing about the nature of the being. Consequently, people make different and competing choices precisely because they have different and competing beliefs about what is good. To think presuppositionally is to analyze how these beliefs about what is good are grounded in beliefs about human nature and what is real.

Presupposed in these beliefs about what is real, about human nature and what is eternal, are beliefs about how knowledge is possible. Sometimes these are articulated and conscious, but many times a person's epistemological framework operates at an unobserved level. People are often not aware of their epistemology in forming beliefs and conclusions. We can say they are unconscious and inconsistent. The Socratic process was one of growth in consciousness and consistency through defining meaning.

Presuppositional thinking relates to religious liberty because we can identify the assumptions on which such liberty rests. The liberty of Athens could only extend so far. Its extension was to the borders of presumed knowledge. When this was called into question, those in authority had to act.

Liberty in the modern age cannot simply rest on skepticism. This is often how such liberty is presented: Since each person has an opinion, and since knowledge of religious matters is not possible, the government or society cannot take a position on religious matters and must instead take no position and allow each person to worship as seen fit. This skepticism only lasts as long as it is not consistently applied. The resulting pluralism extends until it is too much for the civil order.

The alternative formulation is that some things about God and the good are clear to reason and make up the foundation of religious belief. It is true that religious worship or belief cannot be compelled. Belief or assent cannot be compelled. And so while the government can indeed affirm what counts as religious beliefs (we hold these truths to be self-evident, etc.), it does not follow from this that it must compel individuals or groups in religious matters. So, it can be true that religious liberty and constitutional government rest on known presuppositions about the nature of reality and the good and also true that it is not possible to compel persons to believe what they do not think is true. The responsibility is on each person to pursue meaning by knowing what is clear.

Conclusion

We need not accept a narrow definition of religion. Religion is a human activity aimed at finding meaning. Nor must we accept pragmatic and pluralist solutions as final solutions. These are at best a means to an end. And that end is the same in religion as in any other human discipline: to come to have knowledge that provides unity and agreement. This knowledge begins with the kinds of questions asked in the field of natural religion. There are ways in which pluralism might be enforced that are essentially attempts at coercion of religious beliefs.

The general neglect of natural religion is not surprising. And this neglect is behind many of the false antinomies that arise, including private–public. We can continue to smooth out our approach to First Amendment cases by weighing where burdens fall to the individual and society in cases of conflict. An increasingly pluralistic society makes this increasingly difficult. Our conflicts reflect competing values that are grounded in contradictory beliefs about what is real. To continue to operate together requires common ground about what is real, about what is good, about reason, and about thinking.

As we saw in our consideration of Jefferson, it is not possible to coerce agreement. This, combined with philosophical skepticism about basic beliefs (we cannot know), leads to a kind of pluralism that is understood to be inevitable. This view says that knowledge is not possible and we will never agree. It says that nothing is clear to reason. This is not the only way to interpret pluralism. The current reality of pluralism can be agreed upon (and explained) without the specious conclusion of philosophical skepticism. Knowledge of basic things is possible through the diligent use of reason in seeking to know. The current reality of pluralism could be explained either as the result of people seeking to know while knowledge is impossible or as people not seeking to know while knowledge in reality is available (clear to reason). We have considered examples above to argue for the latter: It is clear to reason that something is eternal, that only God the Creator is eternal. As thinking beings, our highest good is to know this.

The reality that it is clear that God exists can be true, and it is also true that political and legal coercion in this matter is not useful, profitable, or even possible. It need not be enforced by law, although the law can affirm important truths that it takes to be the groundwork for all else (again, consider the Declaration of Independence). This is what it means to say that religion is propagated by reason.

However, there is a kind of coercion that naturally occurs and is unavoidable. This is the coercion that arises from the need for meaning. The loss of meaning, and the attending boredom and guilt that accompany it, is unbearable. It pushes us either to the use of reason to find meaning or into excess to cover-up our loss of meaning and distract us from its consequences. The latter is self-destructive and a kind of death. By way of contrast, it highlights all the more the life of reason as the light of humanity (John 1:4). The reality of this death raises for us the question of redemption and highlights the need for the diligent study of natural religion.

We need not be restricted to the actual and continuing cases about religious liberty. We can raise questions about whether pluralism must presuppose philosophical skepticism and what the law must presuppose about pluralism. Westphalia was a kind of stopgap measure that allowed for the liberty and time to come to knowledge and agreement. It need not be understood as the final end. If it has been our common state to neglect what is clear about God from natural religion, then we can and should acknowledge this and turn from it.

The Philosophical Meaning of Religious Exercise 2

Janice Tzuling Chik

Defining "Religion"

In Herman Melville's *Moby-Dick*, the narrator Ishmael, a Presbyterian, befriends the cannibal pagan Queequeg, who invites Ishmael to join him in worship of a wooden idol. Caught in a dilemma between the embrace of his new friend and loyalty to his religious commitments, Ishmael reflects dialectically:

> I was a good Christian, born and bred in the bosom of the infallible Presbyterian Church. How then could I unite with this wild idolator in worshipping his piece of wood? But what is worship? thought I. Do you suppose now, Ishmael, that the magnanimous God of heaven and earth – pagans and all included – can possibly be jealous of an insignificant bit of black wood? Impossible! But what is worship? – to do the will of God – *that* is worship. And what is the will of God? – to do to my fellow man what I would have my fellow man to do me – *that* is the will of God. Now, Queequeg is my fellow man. And what do I wish that this Queequeg would do to me? Why, unite with me in my particular Presbyterian form of worship. Consequently, I must then unite with him in his; ergo, I must turn idolator.[1]

Whatever humorous absurdities Melville intended to illustrate about the apparent contradictions of religious commitments, Ishmael's internal dialogue emphasizes the importance of distinguishing properly between an act of worship as religious activity par excellence and our sundry moral obligations to others and ourselves. Failure to do so, I argue in this chapter, results in a serious misconception of the meaning of religious activity in its most paradigmatic form. Without recognition of the centrality of this paradigm, it is impossible to affirm religion as a distinctive form of human activity with multiform instantiations. Indeed, it would be impossible to affirm it as a special class of human activity and worthy *as such* of specific legal protections under the US Constitution. The central contention

[1] Herman Melville, *Moby-Dick; or, the Whale* (New York: Norton, 1851), 52–53.

of this chapter is that it is possible to give such an account. Moreover, the concept of religion as a distinctive, special form of human activity is one that anyone can comprehend, whatever one's religious beliefs or indeed whether one is religious or not at all.

The free exercise clause of the US Constitution states: "Congress shall make no law … prohibiting the free exercise [of religion]." What is religion, and what constitutes its "free exercise"? These are historically vexed questions, and the legal literature purporting to answer them is vast. In contrast, this chapter engages with recent attempts to redefine "religion" from a philosophical perspective.[2] My intention is to show that, among the most prominent recent innovations on the concept, none in fact improves on the traditional understanding of religion and religious exercise, nor do these revised accounts plausibly hold coherent application under the free exercise clause. Insofar as I defend a variation of a traditional account of religion, the arguments advanced are not in themselves new. However, there seems to be rare acknowledgment that the success of these arguments, as well as an understanding of their conceptual implications, depends substantially on a thorough analysis of the question "What is religion?" as a subject properly belonging to the philosophy of action. That is, the concept of religious exercise is preeminently an action-theoretic concept, since religion is a special form of human action and activity. The original contribution of this chapter, therefore, is to provide such an analysis.

The first contention of this chapter is that the concept of religion cannot be coherently developed if it is assumed that "religion" is only a species of propositional belief. Instead, the concept depends on the comprehension of social practices as foundational to human life in general, where such practices are integral to religion as offering a distinctive set of practical commitments for its followers. This claim, which accords with an ancient, pre-Christian concept of *religio*, rejects modern arguments that religion is simply a cosmological view conjoined with a moral system, or as Ronald Dworkin puts it, "a science part and a value part."[3] The toleration of religious belief, on the modern view, is no more unusual or distinctive

[2] For comparison of a representative legal perspective defending the conclusions of this chapter, see, for instance, John Finnis, "Does Free Exercise of Religion Deserve Constitutional Mention?" *American Journal of Jurisprudence* 54 (2009): 41–66.

[3] Ronald Dworkin, *Religion Without God* (Cambridge, MA: Harvard University Press, 2013), 23.

than the toleration of a moral worldview in general.[4] Religious freedom is therefore "a central case of a more general right to ethical independence."[5] Yet to any member of a religious tradition, or indeed to any careful observer of religious sociology, such assertions about the essential character of religion appear patently false. Nobody who diligently shadows a devout Jew or Muslim for even a day could possibly claim that his or her religion consists merely in a set of propositional beliefs pertaining to metaphysics and morality. In *The Meaning of Belief: Religion from an Atheist's Point of View*, Tim Crane frames my objection in the following way:

> What the cosmology-plus-morality picture leaves out ... is something that seems absolutely central to the religions I am considering here: *religious practice*. Being a believer essentially involves doing certain things, performing certain activities, either once in one's life (baptism, confirmation, the hajj) or on a regular, repeated basis (ritual prayers, giving alms, the Sabbath). These activities are absolutely fundamental to anything that we recognize as a religion, but they are neither matters of morality nor simply the straightforward expression of some cosmological belief. This is why the cosmology-plus-morality picture of religion is so inadequate. It does not account for religious practice.[6]

[4] Besides Dworkin, other scholars who have advanced the claim that religion is not a special class of belief have gone further in questioning whether it therefore merits protection under the First Amendment at all. See, for instance, Micah Schwartzman, "What If Religion Is Not Special?" *The University of Chicago Law Review* 79 (2002): 1351–1427; Brian Leiter, *Why Tolerate Religion* (Princeton, NJ: Princeton University Press, 2013). My account challenges their central claim on the basis that their arguments rely on a fundamentally flawed premise, that religion simply is a species of belief.

[5] Dworkin, *Religion*, 146. Leiter goes further in insisting that the nature of such ethical norms captured by *all* religions is that of a moral system issuing in *categorical* demands: "for all religions there are at least some beliefs central to the religion that ... issue in *categorical* demands on action – that is, demands that must be satisfied no matter what an individual's antecedent desires and no matter what incentives or disincentives the world offers up." Leiter, *Why Tolerate Religion*, 33–34. There is, however, no good reason why one must accept the assertion that the ethical norms related to religion in general must universally be of this sort of categorical character and, by implication of the assertion, why such moral beliefs must be insulated from "ordinary standards of evidence and rational justification, the ones we employ in both common sense and in science." Ibid. Even a cursory survey of the major world religions reveals that its scholars engage philosophically with reasons offered on nonreligious grounds, suggesting that this particular claim about religion as being intrinsically nonreasonable lacks serious merit or is simply based on ignorance about specific religious traditions themselves.

[6] Tim Crane, *The Meaning of Belief: Religion from an Atheist's Point of View* (Cambridge, MA: Harvard University Press, 2017), 87–88. In this passage, Crane identifies "religious practice" as actions pertaining to worship or otherwise having a religious character clearly

My account does not assume that propositional beliefs (for instance, about the cosmos and transcendence, or God) are irrelevant to religion. However, I prefer an alternative to the view that religion is *fundamentally or primarily* a system of propositional beliefs, which are potentially expressed in certain kinds of action and activity in the life of a religious believer. This standard view is typically given a causalist gloss, in which beliefs are the causal determinants of action. Aside from the metaphysical inadequacies of such an action theory, the standard view is unable to accommodate the complex, variegated ways in which religious commitments are intermeshed with pre-religious, natural practices, including moral commitments.[7]

Action and activity are central to the meaning of religion, just as they are central to human life in general. The question "What is religion?" therefore has a reply whose content, if compelling, necessarily refers to a more specific, meaningful question: "What is religious activity?" The latter question assumes a unique species of human action demarcated by the US Constitution as indeed worthy of moral and legal protections. Indeed, if religion is not a distinctive form of human activity, then the free exercise clause is either of trivial significance or bombastically based on deceit. That is, were one to presume that religious activity is merely one exemplification of "meaningful human activity in accordance with sincerely held beliefs" among many instantiations of the latter, then there could in fact be no curtailing of the variety of activities that could be cited as constituting an exercise of religion. What is to prevent the prima facie absurd yet apparently inevitable conclusion that, for some Americans, baseball sincerely *is* a religion? On the other hand, if there is no account that can show why religion is a special or unique case of human social practice, then the

demarcated from the class of activities pertaining straightforwardly to morality. One of the major arguments of my chapter is to show that, for the religious practitioner, even those matters normally pertaining to morality may come to acquire a religious character, such that "religious practice" in fact is inclusive not only of activities of worship, prayer, and sacrifice but also of those pertaining to normal human excellences and the pursuit of happiness in a virtuous life. Elsewhere, Crane does acknowledge that "morality is part of the practical element of religion, but is not the whole of it." Crane, *Meaning*, 7. My aim is to show precisely *how* we ought to recognize the place of morality within religion, and its relationship with a tradition's distinctively paradigmatic religious duties of worship, sacrifice, and prayer.

7 For recent arguments against a causalist view of action, see Helen Steward, *A Metaphysics for Freedom* (New York: Oxford University Press, 2012).

widespread assumption that the free exercise clause ought to be upheld appears to stand on questionable philosophical foundations.

The Challenge of "Religious Atheism"

Given the centrality of human activity to the concept of religion, a successful defense of the philosophical integrity of the free exercise clause relies on an inquiry into the following question: What constitutes "religious activity" as a unique and distinctive sphere of human activity?

The traditional reply is that religious activity as such has an end (*telos*) in, or directedness toward, a divine being, or God. This reply is no longer fashionable, however, and is generally regarded as naïve. In its place are a number of recent arguments for the claim that the concept of religion should be expanded to include even atheistic forms. Dworkin introduces the issue in the following way, in his endorsement of "religious atheism":

> Would it not be better, for the sake of clarity, to reserve "religion" for theism and then to say that Einstein, Shelley, and the others are "sensitive" or "spiritual" atheists? But on a second look, expanding the territory of religion improves clarity by making plain the importance of what is shared across that territory. Richard Dawkins says that Einstein's language is "destructively misleading" because clarity demands a sharp distinction between a belief that the universe is governed by fundamental physical laws, which Dawkins thought Einstein meant, and a belief that it is governed by something "supernatural," which Dawkins thinks the word "religion" suggests. But Einstein meant much more than that the universe is organized around fundamental physical laws; indeed, his view ... endorse[s] ... the supernatural. The beauty and sublimity he said we could reach only as a feeble reflection are not part of nature; they are something beyond nature that cannot be grasped even by finally understanding the most fundamental of physical laws. It was Einstein's faith that some transcendental and objective value permeates the universe, value that is neither a natural phenomenon nor a subjective reaction to natural phenomena. That is what led him to insist on his own religiosity. No other description, he thought, could better capture the character of his faith.[8]

[8] Dworkin, *Religion*, 5–6. Although it is not my concern here to evaluate Einstein's statement – he is cited merely to support "religious atheism," which is my principal interest – it is worth offering the quotation attributed to him by Dworkin: "To know that what is impenetrable to us really exists, manifesting itself as the highest wisdom and the most radiant beauty which our dull faculties can comprehend only in their most primitive forms – this knowledge, this feeling, is at the center of true religiousness. In this sense, and in this sense

In this passage, Dawkins's argument assumes the requirements of traditional atheism, which (1) distinguishes sharply between "the natural" and "the supernatural," and (2) argues that the supernatural does not exist – therefore "religion," which is essentially committed to the latter, is an incoherent concept. Dworkin appears unwilling to dispense with the idea of the supernatural, or what Rudolf Otto calls "the numinous," as necessary for "religion."[9] From a traditional atheist perspective, the combination of these ideas appears prima facie to involve a contradiction: How is it possible to affirm the supernatural, a realm of things that exists beyond the physical, natural world, while simultaneously denying the existence of a superior being (or beings) traditionally assumed to inhabit that realm most of all? Furthermore, how could such an account ever be recognized as "religious"?

Dworkin argues that the standard atheistic account (supported by Dawkins and other so-called new atheists) maintains a problematic view of nature, via its sharp distinction between belief in the natural and belief in the supernatural. He names this problem "naturalism," defined as "the very popular metaphysical theory that nothing is real except what can be studied by the natural sciences, including psychology. That is, nothing exists that is neither matter nor mind; there is really, fundamentally, no such thing as a good life or justice or cruelty or beauty."[10] In place of such "naturalism," he argues that atheists should embrace a "religious attitude": one that recognizes that (1) human life has objective meaning and importance, and (2) the physical universe is something containing intrinsic value

only, I belong in the ranks of devoutly religious men." Albert Einstein, in *Living Philosophies: The Reflections of Some Eminent Men and Women of Our Time*, ed. Clifton Fadiman (New York: Doubleday, 1990), 6, quoted in Dworkin, *Religion*, 3.

[9] Dworkin, *Religion*, 19–20. Dworkin comments: "I mean to suggest that convictions of value are also complex, sui generis, emotional experiences … [W]hen scientists confront the unimaginable vastness of space and the astounding complexity of atomic particles, they have an emotional reaction that matches Otto's description surprisingly well. Indeed, many of them use the very term 'numinous' to describe what they feel. They find the universe awe-inspiring and deserving of a kind of emotional response that at least borders on trembling." It is unclear, however, to what extent Dworkin embraces Otto's concept of the numinous. In *The Idea of the Holy* (1917), Otto introduces the numinous as something set apart from "the rational … and which remains inexpressible … in the sense that it completely eludes apprehension in terms of concepts." Rudolf Otto, *The Idea of the Holy*, trans. John W. Harvey (Oxford: Oxford University Press, 1917), 5. Dworkin, however, argues that there must be a final, comprehensive explanation of the numinous, for instance in beauty. Dworkin, *Religion*, 82, 104.

[10] Dworkin, *Religion*, 12.

and wonder.[11] One need not think that theism is true if one embraces these two proposals. One can have a metaphysics of value without God, and therefore a religion without God, all without contradiction.

Dworkin's account of "religious atheism" has been echoed by a number of recent legal scholars and philosophers.[12] The concept of religion without God is possible because "religion," as Dworkin argues, is really reducible to an attitude that is shared by theists and nontheists alike. This "religious attitude" encompasses two major themes concerning one's beliefs: The first asserts that moral responsibility is an objective feature of human nature, while the second asserts that one's cosmological or metaphysical views of the natural world should exclude "naturalism," as already defined.

However, the plausibility of the argument for "religious atheism" depends on a number of tenuous premises. The first is that religion is constituted by what Dworkin identifies as an "attitude." The second concerns the content of this attitude: namely, that religion is reducible to the fact that human beings are moral beings, as well as our sense that there is more to the natural world than what is studied by the natural sciences. The third assumes that any entity or event that metaphysically supervenes on the physical world – such as consciousness, goodness, or beauty – simply *is* the supernatural or something religiously transcendent. All three of these presuppositions are problematic, and if shown to be false, the idea of religious atheism cannot stand.

I have already argued against the first premise in the first section. Here, I first consider Dworkin's claim that metaphysical transcendence implies a rejection of naturalism, and that such transcendence is conceptually interchangeable with the supernatural. Problematically, however, Dworkin's examples of what he considers "the supernatural" seem to be instantiations of thoroughly *natural* phenomena: beauty and our sense of sublimity about the universe, values concerning goodness, such as justice or human acts of cruelty. There is no reason why a naturalist must deny that such phenomena is real in a world of causal sufficiency, in which all phenomena can be explained by natural causes.[13] What Dworkin envisions to be his target, therefore, is not

[11] Ibid., 10.

[12] See, for example, Alain de Botton, *Religion for Atheists* (London: Penguin, 2012). For an account from the Continental philosophical tradition, see Bradley B. Onishi, *The Sacrality of the Secular: Postmodern Philosophy of Religion* (New York: Columbia University Press, 2018).

[13] Even most traditional theists would be hard-pressed to defend the view that phenomena such as beauty or goodness are explained *exclusively* by recourse to divine power. Morality

"naturalism" per se but rather a form of reductive materialism that regards concepts like beauty and goodness as epiphenomenal or causally inefficacious in a strictly physical world without nonphysical values. One who rejects reductive materialism finds a range of alternatives: supernaturalism and transcendence, but also non-reductive materialism, which affirms the very phenomena and values that Dworkin seeks to affirm. But supernaturalism or transcendence is not identical with non-reductive materialism, and although many non-reductive materialists would deny the supernatural, very few would assume that their account is an affirmation of the supernatural or transcendent.[14] Since the concept of religion, even for Dworkin, necessarily implies transcendence, it cannot be the case that what Dworkin proposes is "religion" without God. Rather, it appears that his thesis is simply *non-reductive materialism without God* – but that is hardly an innovative account.

The second major premise of "religious atheism" may now be understood as follows: The concept of religion is reducible to or may be generalized as a commitment to non-reductive materialism, with its admittance of certain nonphysical phenomena such as beauty and morality. But is it plausible to think that non-reductive materialism on its own is a religion? The affirmative case implies that there is a general category or genus of phenomena that we identify as "religion," under which falls Christianity, Judaism, Islam, Hinduism, and other traditionally recognized world religions, *alongside* a broad conception of non-reductive materialism. But why stop there? Why not admit of other theories of mind, human nature, ethics, and aesthetics as found in philosophy and elsewhere? That which unifies the genus of "religion," under which the traditional world religions are gathered, must be something more specific in order to avoid trivializing the concept of religion: It would be absurd to identify anyone as "religious"

has a natural explanation as well as a supernatural one, and likewise the presence of beauty in the natural world. For instance, the Third Earl of Shaftesbury defended the presence of beauty in the universe within a naturalistic account. See Anthony Ashley Cooper, 3rd Earl of Shaftesbury, *Characteristics of Men, Manners, Opinions, Times*, ed. Laurence Klein (Cambridge: Cambridge University Press, 1999).

[14] As Crane argues, "Religion without transcendence is no religion … What these 'religious atheists' tend to lack are … two essential elements of religious belief … what I call the religious impulse, and the element of identification. The religious impulse, roughly speaking, is the belief in the transcendent: 'something beyond all this.' The element of identification consists in the fact that religion involves institutions to which believers belong and practices in which they participate. Dworkin's *Religion without God* includes none of this. De Botton's *Religion for Atheists* does attempt to introduce a kind of identification, but it has no place for the religious impulse." Crane, *Meaning*, 23.

who merely affirms the existence of beauty and morality in the universe. Additionally, the aesthetic stance and the ethical attitude are human phenomena worthy of independent inquiry in themselves: Why should one bias these disciplines by identifying them also as "religious attitudes"?

If defenders of the traditional concept of religion were unable to offer an explanation for what grounds the unity of world religions as diverse as Judaism, Islam, Christianity, and Hinduism, then one might accept Dworkin's assertion that "religion is an interpretive concept," entirely open to whatever one thinks it *should* mean.[15] But there has always been a perfectly coherent and sound definition of the concept, which adherents to the various religious traditions intuitively understand and affirm (even if most are unable to articulate it in precise philosophical terms), and which modern critics have not given sufficient attention. As I have suggested in the first section, the essential concept depends on treating religious *activity* as central to the account. To this topic I now turn.

What Constitutes "Religious Activity"?

In response to the challenge of "religious atheism," one may unproblematically grant that religion generally requires certain forms of ethical commitments, as well as support for the metaphysical claim that reductive materialism must be false. However, these requirements are merely incidental to the central contention of religion, which I defend as a distinctive form of human activity that is paradigmatically ordered toward some form of transcendence – a being or beings, possessing a nature superior to ours. The form of this definition most familiar to Western minds is that such superior being is "God," understood as Creator of the universe; however, the term "God" need not universally have such an implication. On my account, use of the term "God" may be broad enough to include certain faith traditions that do not explicitly assume the existence of a metaphysical Creator but sufficiently narrow that it excludes systems of pure philosophical thought.[16] Any argumentative use of the term

[15] Dworkin, *Religion*, 7.

[16] Religion can be characterized as a search for life's meaning: "But not every search for meaning is religious." Crane, *Meaning*, 7. Since my account excludes systems of pure philosophical thought that deny a sense of the transcendent, there may be borderline cases about which there is doubt: whether we should, for instance, classify certain varieties of

"religion" as applicable to secular humanism or any philosophical commitment to non-reductive materialism is merely analogous and not univocal to the concept of religion properly understood.

Crane delineates two central requirements as distinguishing the category of the religious among similar forms in which there exists a search for life's meaning. Religion includes what he calls "the religious impulse," a "need to live one's life in harmony with the transcendent (for example, the will of God)" and "identification," or "the fact that religions are social institutions; the fact that, as Durkheim says, one does not just believe in a religion, one belongs to it."[17] My account in this section aims to articulate precisely *how* religious practice actualizes the desire to practically engage with one's respective concept of the transcendent. I argue it is necessary to affirm a paradigmatic form of religious practice, understood broadly as activity directed to the transcendent (such as worship and devotion), from which other forms of religious practice are derived and informed with similar meaning.

One might object that ethical commitment *does* require a distinctive form of human activity, with responsibilities toward another outside of oneself. Thus Dworkin observes: "Godly religions impose serious duties and responsibilities, including not just duties of worship and diet but also social responsibilities."[18] There indeed exists a variety of duties and responsibilities that have significance for religious practitioners, but the social responsibilities typically required by religious traditions are not precisely on par with duties of religious worship. Such responsibilities, in the context of their respective traditions, would not contain their proper significance without recognition of the activity of worship as central and foundational to the concept of religion. Indeed, worship *is* religious activity par excellence, from which all other subsidiary forms of activity relating to one's religion are derived. Viewed in this light, it cannot be the case that such social and ethical

Buddhism and monistic thought as religion. Certainly, the latter has religious aspects: for instance, the practice of monastic community, the use of shrines with images and statues of the Buddha (certainly recognized by devotees as a superior model for emulation), liturgical rituals, devotion to the dead, social prayer such as chanting, and meditation. Buddhists themselves frequently seem ambivalent about whether theirs is a religion, a philosophy, or merely a set of teachings. For some, the lack of determinacy about religions that explicitly deny transcendence (even while appearing to affirm it in practice) is a cost associated with my account, but if it is, it is surely one that Buddhists themselves appear to regard as unimportant, as is consistent with monistic thought.

[17] Ibid., 11. [18] Dworkin, *Religion*, 113.

activity is identical across contexts as radically diverse as, for instance, atheism or Judaism.[19] An indication of their differentiation is provided by the fact that "religious atheism" or secular humanism requires only the belief that human beings have certain ethical obligations: For the most part, it leaves open precisely what those obligations are, resolving them in only the most general terms.[20] In contrast, theistic traditions characteristically articulate very specific moral obligations and prohibitions, with duties to others understood as deriving from – and simultaneously essentially ordered to – one's more primary commitments to a transcendent or divine being (or beings).

The distinction between primary and secondary activities pertaining to religion is not new. Aquinas, for instance, argues in the *Summa Theologiae*:

> Religion has two kinds of acts. Some are its proper and immediate acts, which it elicits, and by which man is directed to God alone, for instance, sacrifice, adoration and the like. But it has other acts, which it produces through the medium of the virtues which it commands, directing them to the honor of God, because the virtue which is concerned with the end, commands the virtues which are concerned with the means. Accordingly "to visit the fatherless and widows in their tribulation" is an act of religion as commanding, and an act of mercy as eliciting; and "to keep oneself unspotted from this world" is an act of religion as commanding, but of temperance or of some similar virtue as eliciting.[21]

The "proper and immediate acts" of religion, such as sacrifice and adoration, are those "directed to God alone": These constitute what I have called the "primary activity pertaining to religion." What I have called the "secondary type of activity" is differentiated from the latter by *not* being directed to God[22] alone: Such activities can be directed to oneself, as in

[19] Indeed, it seems utterly implausible to claim that even across diverse theistic religions there is a shared univocal concept concerning one's social and ethical responsibilities, and how they should be derived.

[20] For instance, Dworkin writes, "[The religious attitude] includes a responsibility of each person to decide for himself ethical questions about which kinds of lives are appropriate and which would be degrading for him." Dworkin, *Religion*, 114.

[21] Thomas Aquinas, *Summa Theologiae*, trans. the Fathers of the English Dominican Province, 2nd edition (London: Burns, Oates & Washbourne, 1920), 2a 2ae, 81, 1, ad. 1.

[22] Henceforth, I use the term "God" simply to mean a transcendent nature or being(s) of a superior nature – a definition that is intended to have broad application, covering more than merely Western conceptions of divinity. Indeed, in this context of q. 81 of 2a 2ae, it does not appear to be the case even for Aquinas that "God" necessarily designates a divine Creator Being; his citation of Cicero suggests an application to what may be universally understood as *being in some form*, of a superior nature to human nature.

the case of sexual purity ("to keep oneself unspotted from this world"), or directed to others, as in the case of visiting orphans, widows, and the poor. Activities of this secondary type can be "elicited" or "commanded," according to Aquinas, because it is possible for them to be performed simply as acts of virtue or morality, and not as *religious* acts per se.

Visiting orphans and widows, giving alms to the poor, and keeping oneself chaste (among many other possible examples) acquire the character of "religious activities" only when they are "commanded." What this means, for Aquinas, is that "the virtue which is concerned with the end, commands the virtues which are concerned with the means." Religion is a *virtue*,[23] in accordance with the Aristotelian conception of *areté*, and like the other virtues, it consists of a habit or disposition for *doing* certain things at the appropriate moments and under the right circumstances: courage for doing courageous things, temperance for doing temperate things, and so on, when these are called for. Religion, in turn, is the habit or disposition for doing things "directed to God alone": This is commonly called "worship" or "religious devotion" and comprises activities ranging from individual prayer ("adoration") to communal sacrifice and liturgy. On Aquinas's view, worship and devotion[24] are clearly prior and more fundamental to the social and moral responsibilities associated with it, and they stand in relation to these latter responsibilities as an end stands in relation to its means. His account entails that the demands of the regular virtues – those *not* "directed to God alone" – must be understood by the agent as standing in relation to religious worship in the primary sense, as a means to an end. Otherwise, the fulfillment of such commitments may not be identified as "religious" but simply constitute regular acts of excellence that would be good for *any* agent, religious or not, to do. Hence, the usual ethical obligations required of any human being, *qua human*, must be "commanded" or directed by the agent's ultimate intention of honoring God in order to acquire the character of being a religious act. Where no such ultimate intention exists, these ethical obligations are merely "elicited" by the demands of the virtue itself. Thus, Aquinas observes that the

[23] Aquinas argues that religion is a species of the virtue of justice, in that worship is due to God. Aquinas, *ST*, 2a 2ae, 81, 4.

[24] Aquinas in fact gives priority to devotion and prayer, the principal and interior acts of religious worship. Acts of bodily reverence follow from these as secondary, external acts. Only then does he discuss the offering of material things to God: sacrifices, oblations and first-fruits, tithes, and vows. Aquinas, *ST*, 2a 2ae, 82–88.

same action – visiting orphans and widows – *can* be an act of religion, but also may be simply an act of mercy.

Acts "directed to God alone" cannot possibly admit of this dual analysis, such that an act of worship *could* be a religious act but need not be. Such acts – assuming they are voluntary and not coerced – necessarily *are* religious acts. Someone may object, however, that it is possible to engage in acts of worship without *intending* that such acts be directed to God alone. For instance, Tom Sawyer attends church at the bidding of his aunt only in order to attract the attention of the charming female creature in a nearby pew. He *could* direct his further intention with which he attends church toward the end of honoring of God, but he does not; therefore, the primary activity of religion appears to be not necessarily religious in character at all. In Tom's case, it is simply the pursuit of girls where they happen to be congregated. Alternatively, consider the case of an atheist priest who performs the ritual movements required by a religious liturgy. Since he does not believe in God, he cannot intend that his performance be directed to an object assumed by him to be nonexistent. It appears implausible that his activity of worship should count as an act of religion.

My reply to this style of objection is that religious activity, like many other distinctive forms of human activity, has a certain characteristic form that exists regardless of one's personal and private intentions. Religion is not unique in this regard. Many social activities or practices are of this form: for instance, attending a baseball game or the opera. One may not be paying any attention to the proceedings, or may be entirely ignorant about the rules of the game or the basic libretto and story line. Or hypothetically someone may try to *will*, with all his might, to be anywhere but there. In such cases, however, one's intention or comprehensive knowledge is not necessary for it to be the case that one *is* attending a baseball game or the opera. Minimally, one must understand certain basic concepts constituting these forms of social practice – that baseball is a game involving bats, balls, and bases and that the libretto being sung is part of a musical-theatrical performance.[25] Furthermore, the movements constituting one's attendance must be minimally voluntary and conscious. But one need not believe that

[25] No special knowledge is required, but simply some minimal comprehension of the general form of activity: one must recognize that *such-and-such* is a baseball game and not, say, a form of public torture. In the very rare case that someone (a rational Martian, for instance) does *not* recognize that this game involving bats, balls, and bases is indeed baseball, then admittedly it could be claimed that the Martian is "not attending a baseball

either baseball or opera has any point whatsoever, nor understand any of the means undertaken (or indeed the detailed rules of the game) to achieve their ends. Hence, there exists what I call a kind of "material sufficiency" for these forms of activity, such that any reasonable observer would instantly recognize, without question or doubt, that what you are engaged in *is* attending a baseball game or the opera.

The claim that certain activities possess an intrinsically characteristic form of this kind may be supported by arguments made by G.E.M. Anscombe in her monograph *Intention.*[26] Anscombe argues that there is a class of action descriptions that *must* imply an occurrence that is voluntary or intentional, such as "marrying," "contracting," "sending for," "hiring," "dismissing," "paying," "selling," "buying," or "greeting." By contrast, action descriptions that lack this characteristic form *might* be simply occurrences that are entirely unintentional or events unrelated to one's agency. Some of her examples of this latter class are "intruding," "offending," "coming to possess," "kicking," and "abandoning." She further comments on the example of "kicking": Such a description is simply one of many "descriptions connoting characteristically animal movement," which suggests that one of the criteria for distinguishing between these two classes of action descriptions may be a form of activity that could only be attributed to human beings or to some rational being with powers of agency. Only a rational kind of creature could have a social practice such as "marrying" or "contracting." Furthermore, in carrying out such activities, it must be the case that a rational agent does them voluntarily or intentionally, even under conditions in which one does not fully comprehend the specific terms of one's marriage or contract, or in which one wishes hopelessly (at the very moment of being married) that such a union, to such a person, were otherwise.

Religious activity in the primary sense possesses the kind of characteristic form described by Anscombe: It is a form of rational activity that is essentially directed to God, and it retains this form even if one's personal and private intentions should diverge from the end of honoring God. For someone to be engaged in religious activity, all that is required is the sort of material sufficiency I have outlined. That is, one's presence must be voluntary and

game." But such cases are so rare, if not nonexistent, with regard to the forms of social activity with which human beings are familiar, that the possibility of nonrecognition of them does not impinge on my overall argument.

[26] G.E.M. Anscombe, *Intention* (Cambridge, MA: Harvard University Press, 1957), 85.

one must have a basic concept of religious activity as essentially directed to God. Religion is a virtue, and one's attempt to perform any virtue, in order to become virtuous, can be flawed or incomplete – as are Tom Sawyer's attempts, whether he is attending church or school, since he wishes to engage in neither. The performance of any virtue can also be incomplete where one does not fully understand the meaning of what one does. For this reason, Aristotle identifies such performances as arising from "natural virtue," which lacks the perfection and maturation of authentic virtue. But engagement in religious activity does not require that one must fully comprehend the rationale and significance of one's activity: The vast majority of religious practitioners would not be able to give such explanations of the rituals, liturgies, and requirements of their respective traditions. Yet their voluntary practice and participation in the requirements of worship and devotion undeniably constitute religious activity.

This account has the consequence that the atheist priest, who performs the ritual movements required by a liturgy, is in fact engaged in religious activity. This conclusion seems to me correct. One need not actually believe in God so long as one performs an action *understood* to be an act of worship directed toward God: Such an act is a religious act, regardless of one's personal beliefs, because it is the kind of action that possesses the characteristic form of religion. Religious activity in my secondary sense, in contrast, does not have this sort of characteristic form. It is entirely possible to observe someone giving alms to the poor without ever knowing whether such an action is religious in character or simply an act of mercy. It is impossible to know, merely from the basic action description, "abstaining from eating meat," whether the agent does so because she is a Stoic, a vegetarian, or a Catholic on Good Friday.[27] However, religious activity in the primary sense is prima facie recognizable by an onlooker as such. By this, I do not mean that such an onlooker necessarily comprehends the religious significance of what one observes, but that such activity is immediately obvious as falling outside the ends that govern human social practices. The latter forms seek either the material support of life and existence (such as food and textile production) or various ideals of human leisure (such as art, sport, music, philosophy, and mountaineering).

[27] My claim is not that such actions lack a characteristic form altogether: "giving alms to the poor" has the characteristic form of mercy or pity, but not in itself the characteristic form of *religion*.

A primary act of religion, in contrast, cannot possibly be reduced to one of these natural social practices, even if it may *very* occasionally be mistaken as such.[28] The act of reserving and burning on an altar the very best edible portion of one's healthiest lamb (as Judaic law prescribes[29]) cannot possibly be construed as a regular human activity for either material support or human leisure, for sacrifice has an intrinsically religious, supernatural character (being above what is natural).

I have argued that religious activity in the primary sense retains a characteristic form of religion regardless of the agent's own beliefs and intentions. This argument has the consequence that an atheist priest may conduct a liturgical ritual and yet even unwillingly be a participant in that religious act.[30] One may object that this amounts to a severe account. If a state were to coerce its citizens to participate in religious activities of a particular kind, as Nebuchadnezzar required all of his subjects to bow before and worship a golden idol,[31] my account entails that a reluctant subject could not resort to an internal act of willing against the very activity that one's body performs: Any bodily participation in state-enforced religion *must* be a religious act for even an unwilling subject.

[28] One who mistakes sacrifice as a form of material support for human life we would call incoherent; arguably, one who mistakes sacrifice as a form of natural human leisure holds an account of leisure that is not only incomprehensible but also perverse. It may be possible for an observer ignorant of Islamic prayer requirements to mistake a Muslim engaged in *salat* prayer for someone who is merely resting, but it can only be from an extreme perspective of ignorance to be so mistaken.

[29] At the very least, the animal to be offered for sacrifice must be absolutely perfect in form and health, and to offer a blemished animal was considered sacrilegious. Deut. 15:21, 17:1; Lev. 22:18–25.

[30] There are other aspects of this characteristic form of religious practice that I have not discussed, such as Crane's suggestion that we "need to reflect on two obvious and often overlooked features of such practices: the fact that believers generally don't invent religious practices themselves; and the fact that they participate in practices together with other people. Of course, there is private prayer and private worship, and there is inspiration and spontaneous invention. But the paradigm of religious practice is repetition – doing something that has been done before many times – and doing it socially, along with other people. These are not incidental or accidental features of religion but things that lie at its very heart." Crane, *Meaning*, 88. However, it seems possible to give an account of a social practice that includes both of these aspects, but is not itself a religion. Certain practices deriving from complex social traditions, for instance, or even a superstitious practice that comes to be handed down through generations, might exhibit both of these aspects by manifesting as a communal repetition of a practice not invented by the practitioners themselves.

[31] Dan. 3:1–7.

Again, it seems to me that this is the correct conclusion: It is precisely for this reason that we identify religious coercion to be an intolerable assault on human rights and dignity.

The case of blasphemy or sacrilege bears a similar analysis. Activity that directly repudiates or slanders God has a characteristic form that exists *qua* blasphemy, merely by a criterion of material sufficiency. For instance, someone who is ordered to blaspheme by trampling on a holy image may attempt to internally deny that the meaning of such an action *is* that it is blasphemous, perhaps by willing that one's action is only the saving of one's own life. But such an attempt cannot be made coherent, any more than an act of embezzlement may be conveniently redescribed by the embezzler as "saving for retirement." Certain action descriptions are necessarily associated with certain forms of activity, regardless of one's personal and private further intentions.

The account I defend clearly excludes a conception of "religious atheism" from the first exercise clause. However, this should not be construed as a discriminatory move, for atheism and other forms of philosophical expression are protected by the free speech clause of the First Amendment.[32] Still, my account appears to privilege traditional monotheism as the only real candidate for comprehension of the concept of "religious activity," particularly since the Thomistic explanation speaks only of "God" as its end. Contrary to these appearances, my account is expansive enough to include possible ideas of "God" beyond merely the Judeo-Christian conception. Notably, Aquinas quotes Marcus Tullius Cicero, of pre-Christian era, to support his essential definition of "religion": "Tully says (Rhet. ii, 53) that 'religion consists in offering service and ceremonial rites to a superior nature that men call divine.'"[33] It matters not to this account precisely *how* someone conceives of this "superior nature," or whether there is one or many beings identified as divine.[34] Should someone regard an evil being as divine and worthy of worship,[35] according to

32 It should be obvious that my account disagrees sharply with a view that assumes religion is simply a form of free speech.

33 Aquinas, *ST*, 2a 2ae, 81, 1, *Sed contra.*

34 However, I assume that a polytheist must have a plausible metaphysical account of how multiple gods of co-equal power can exist simultaneously.

35 Likewise, I assume that an adherent of such a religion would need to defend the logical and ethical coherence of worshipping an evil being, if the existence of a good and *superior* being is also assumed.

my account, such an object would constitute an end for one's religious activity, so long as one's belief in such an object, *qua* "superior" in nature (or "supernatural"), is sincerely held.[36] In this respect, my account accords with a *pre-Christian* concept of religion, on which religion is essentially a form of activity or human action, rather than something primarily epistemological – in strictly the propositional sense that is commonly assumed by modern and post-Christian era thinkers.[37]

It is possible, of course, for one to agree with my account of religious activity and yet contend that such activity is in itself not worthy of special legal and moral protections. This is precisely the conclusion tendered by so-called new atheists, who argue that since there is in reality no God, human activity ordered to a nonexistent being is incoherent, and constitutional protections of such activity should be jettisoned accordingly. However, my argument does not depend on the success of any prior case to be made for theism. In order to affirm the free exercise clause, one need not assume that the object of one's sincerely held belief be necessarily veridical or in correspondence with metaphysical reality. This suggests that the success or failure of proofs for God's existence is irrelevant to the legal protection extended by the free exercise clause: Such protection instead aims to guarantee one's sincere conscience and commitment to the practical implications thereof, whatever the divine object of belief, and whether it is real or illusory. Hence, my account is neutral as to whether or not "God" exists in actuality.

[36] So-called Pastafarians, those who jokingly profess belief in the existence of "the Flying Spaghetti Monster," and other satirical movements, are therefore excluded from this account of what constitutes "religion."

[37] Teresa Morgan offers a rich account of the historical context for this distinction between action and epistemology in ancient *religio*: "Varro, one of the few ancient systematists of religion, categorizes Roman religious matters under priesthoods, holy places, festivals, rituals, and gods, but not beliefs. In Cicero's *On the Nature of the Gods*, the Academic Cotta divides them even more simply into rituals, auspices, and warnings. In his own voice at the start of that work, Cicero offers a longer list of elements of *religio*, religious observance, which depend on human understanding of the nature of the gods: reverence, piety, holiness, ritual, *fides*, the swearing of oaths, temples, shrines, solemn sacrifices, and auspices. Even this taxonomy, though, is not usually seen as encompassing statements of belief. Belief, it seems, does not constitute a category in Greeks' and Romans' thinking about their own traditions." Teresa Morgan, *Roman Faith and Christian Faith: Pistis and Fides in the Early Roman Empire and Early Churches* (New York: Oxford University Press, 2015), 125–126.

Can Act Omissions Constitute Religious Exercise?

The Problem of Act Omissions

My account of religion so far has been presented in terms of human action and activity. Does this account plausibly include *not* doing something, in which an agent refrains or refuses to engage in an activity whose performance is sincerely believed to be contrary to one's religious beliefs? Strictly speaking, act omissions are not actions or any kind of activity at all, so how can the absence of activity be understood as religious activity? Furthermore, the account I have defended defines religion as constituting a kind of voluntary activity, directed toward honoring a divine or transcendent being, or some superior nature; whereas in a secondary sense, religious activity is directed toward the good of others or oneself. How can an act omission fulfill either of these ends?

The threat of religious coercion highlights the problem of act omissions in a peculiar way: If religious exercise includes only act commissions, then what precisely is the problem with coercion that simultaneously encourages the private exercise of one's personal religion? This is the scenario raised by Charles Carroll of Carrollton's poem, "A Letter from the Tyrant Almachius to St Cecilia," composed in 1753. One of the American founders, and the only Roman Catholic to sign the Declaration of Independence, Carroll presents Almachius's solution in these lines:

> *Worship the Gods with your lips, Christ's Godhead in your mind.*
> *Pretend to be pious: this pretense will give you life.*[38]

Almachius does not prevent Cecilia from worshiping her own God, so long as she merely pretends to worship his; thus, he dismisses her claim that such pretense of piety contradicts her own free religious exercise. Why refrain from doing what Almachius asks, when he is all too willing to grant her the right to free religious exercise, having fulfilled her secular obligation in merely "pretending to be pious" in the state's mandated religion? Since religious activity is the actual doing of something, and such exercise

[38] Charles Carroll of Carrollton, "Almachius, Tyrant, to Saint Cecilia: A Letter," 1753, in *A Letter from the Tyrant Almachius to St Cecilia*, trans. Anastassi Callinicos (Clitheroe, UK: St Omers Press, 2013). Thanks to Michael Breidenbach for a helpful discussion of this work, and to Stonyhurst College curator Jan Graffius for discovering this manuscript and bringing it to our attention.

is not prevented by the state's injunction, the tyrant understands his request as being perfectly compatible with the sort of freedom extended by the free exercise clause.

It is possible for the analysis of the above case to prescind altogether from the issue of act omissions. One might argue that coercion in this case is a violation of Cecilia's right to free religious exercise simply because Almachius enjoins her to perform an act that contradicts a central commitment of her personal conscience, that she not worship other gods. Certainly, this claim is undeniable: that religious coercion contradicts personal conscience and that for this reason such coercion is morally wrong. However, this simple explanation does not sufficiently account for the fact that, in such cases, one is applying for an exemption from law based on one's religious beliefs, with the assumption that an act omission – *not* doing what the law requires – constitutes a form of religious exercise. And although the threat of religious coercion by a tyrant such as Almachius is nowadays relatively rare, the fundamental question about act omissions raised within Carroll's poem remains relevant to a number of prominent legal challenges examined in free exercise clause discourse. It has been questioned, for instance, whether a Jew or Seventh Day Adventist's refusal to work on Saturdays[39] should be protected as legitimate religious exercise, and whether a Catholic employer might legitimately refuse to provide insurance coverage that includes contraceptives for its employees, citing the free exercise clause.[40] Whether or not legal protections should be (or have been) granted in such cases, the philosophical path to resolving the legal challenges represented by them must include a coherent account of how such refusals, *qua* act omissions, might be counted as instances of religious exercise.[41]

The Solution of "Two-Way Powers"

Some act omissions are involuntary, in that the agent is unaware of his failure to act at the moment that he could and should act. Other act omissions are voluntary, in that the agent is both aware of his failure to act when he is bidden by circumstances (or explicitly by an authority such as the state) and

[39] *Sherbert* v. *Verner*, 374 U.S. 398 (1963). [40] *Zubik* v. *Burwell*, 578 U.S. ___ (2016).

[41] It is possible to defend either case as instances of religious exercise without granting that the right to refuse in these cases is absolute. However, as I have expressed above, the scope and limitations of religious exercise in legal history are beyond my present concern.

may actively choose upon deliberation not to act.[42] It is clear that the act omissions under current scrutiny are of a kind freely *chosen* by an agent: In refusing to comply with a higher-order directive, one deliberately chooses not to do something that one might otherwise do, in the absence of practical religious commitments.

However, on this basis one may try to argue that voluntary act omissions *are* actions, since they are deliberately chosen and clearly intentional: that is, the agent can cite a reason (or reasons) for not doing something that he otherwise might have done. Bruce Vermazen, for instance, has argued that such act omissions should be conceived as "negative actions."[43] In her reply to his account, Maria Alvarez rightly notes that if "action" is understood to be anything that is voluntary and intentional, however, then we must include passive occurrences in this definition of "action," such as allowing oneself to be anesthetized or having one's hair styled.[44] But this results in a radical, overly broad definition of action. Unless we are willing to concede that the patient being anesthetized performs an action in the very same sense that the anesthesiologist performs an action in anesthetizing him, the definition of "action" and "activity" must be limited to instances of actually *doing* something, where the agent is understood as the primary cause[45] of some change or as producing some novel state of affairs.

[42] I include the qualification that the agent *might* choose not to do the action upon deliberation, but some act omissions may be voluntary but not chosen. For example, a beachgoer refrains from moving away from the water's edge, finding the sensation of the waves unexpectedly pleasant. Harry Frankfurt offers the example of "a driver whose automobile is coasting downhill in virtue of gravitational forces alone [who] may be entirely satisfied with its speed and direction, and so he may never intervene to adjust its movement in any way. This would not show that the movement of the automobile did not happen under his guidance. What counts is that he was prepared to intervene as necessary, and that he was in a position to do so more or less effectively." Harry Frankfurt, "The Problem of Action," in *The Philosophy of Action*, ed. Alfred Mele (Oxford: Oxford University Press, 1988), 48. The driver refrains from doing anything, but his act omission is voluntary since he is aware of and consents to the speed and direction of the car. The speed and direction are not therefore *chosen* in the sense of Aristotle's concept of *prohairesis* as the product of deliberation, but choice nevertheless remains a possibility on this account, of course, with the possibility of the driver's intervention as necessary at any moment.

[43] Bruce Vermazen, "Negative Acts," in *Essays on Davidson: Actions and Events*, ed. Bruce Vermazen and Merrill B. Hintikka (Oxford: Oxford University Press, 1985).

[44] Maria Alvarez, "Agency and Two-Way Powers," *Proceedings of the Aristotelian Society* 113, no. 1 (2013): 105.

[45] Still, one might insist that the patient being anesthetized is also a cause of the change at hand: his becoming anesthetized. Although true that without his voluntary and intentional

So voluntary act omissions, or not doing something, are *not* actions or activities. Even Vermazen admits that "negative events do not, strictly speaking, exist."[46] Nonetheless, since voluntary act omissions can be freely chosen, and although the result of such choice is neither an action nor an activity, it is possible to claim that what happens nevertheless constitutes an exercise of *agency*. The latter claim, I will argue, is sufficient for affirming that voluntary act omissions may be counted as legitimate instances of religious activity. On this solution, it is possible for an agent to exercise her agency without performing an action.

The distinction between actions and exercises of agency may arguably be attributed to Aristotle. In *Nicomachean Ethics*, he gives his account of choice (*prohairesis*) as a special class of the voluntary, that which is willed and proceeds from deliberation. Choosing *not* to do something clearly falls within this subclass of the voluntary, as a matter of something proceeding from agential powers: "For when acting depends on us, not acting does so too, and when saying no does so, saying yes does too."[47] Alvarez interprets this claim as implying the existence of "a two-way power": agency is constituted by a single power, such that "when the conditions for the exercise of the power obtain, the power need not be manifested . . . [for] whether the power is manifested depends on the thing whose power it is."[48] Citing Anthony Kenny's distinction between "ability" as something internal to the agent and "opportunity" as something external, Alvarez specifies that the possession of a two-way power requires that I have both the ability and opportunity to φ, where φ-ing is an action, *and* it must be "up to me" whether I exercise my ability to φ at that time or not.[49]

cooperation, *his* agency is not the primary mover of the change, for that is the physician's work, and it is *prima facie* clear that there is a distinction between and certain order in these respective exercises of agency. The distinction and order corresponds precisely with Aristotle's account of active versus passive potentialities, in *Physics*, Book II.

46 Vermazen, "Negative Acts," in *Essays on Davidson*, ed. Vermazen and Hintikka, 100.

47 Aristotle, *Nicomachean Ethics*, trans. Christopher Rowe (New York: Oxford University Press, 2002), 1113 b7–8. The context of Aristotle's comment here, in Book III of *Nicomachean Ethics*, concerns excellence in acting "when it is a fine thing to act" and for which one's act omission is blameworthy and shameful.

48 Alvarez, "Agency," 102. While identifying her thesis as Aristotelian, Alvarez notes its medieval development in Aquinas, citing *ST* 1a 2ae, 49, 4: "Some capacities can be realized in more than one way (*ad multa*)," while others "can be realized in only one way (*ad unum*)."

49 Alvarez, "Agency," 109.

If Alvarez's account is correct, then it is possible to construe religious exercise as simply a special instantiation of a two-way power belonging to human agents. Religious exercise is not only the active pursuit of religious activity in the primary and secondary senses defined earlier, for it includes the election of certain voluntary act omissions, being passive in certain other actions and activities over which human agents have agential control, such that it is "up to us" whether or not we pursue them. Thus, deliberately opting to refrain from performing an action, or choosing not to φ when φ-ing is required by the state, *can* be construed as legitimate religious exercise where φ-ing is reasonably understood as gravely contradicting a citizen's practical religious commitments.[50] That is, an account of "religious exercise" should be broad enough to include not only actions but also exercises of one's agency that do not in themselves constitute actions. This is precisely what voluntary act omissions are, when they are chosen by the agent in order to avoid what can be reasonably construed as a grave contradiction of one's religious commitments.

The account I have outlined may be challenged on a number of points, each of which I will canvass and address in turn. First, it may be thought that the concept of a two-way power is vulnerable to the objection that the existence of such powers, where it is up to the agent to do and also *not* to do, does not entail that the exercise of an agent's ability to φ bears the same relation to the agent as the exercise of her ability to *not* φ. That is, even if someone concedes that such two-way powers exist, there is no reason to think that agential exercise of this power has the same metaphysical structure in both directions, nor that the same analysis could be given for both φ-ing and not φ-ing. Alvarez's account appears to leave this question open. It seems plausible to think, however, that in φ-ing I am exercising a power to φ in a way that actualizes or fulfills the power itself: It exists in an agent to be fulfilled in such a way that the agent moves his body and causes a change in material state of affairs. On the other hand, *not* φ-ing is simply a failure to realize this power: Although it may be a *deliberate* failure to actualize a particular ability, the relation of this exercise of agency to the agent herself is metaphysically distinct. For when one

[50] Again, this does not entail, on my account, that all religious activity is absolutely protected. But the fact that there is at various times and circumstances the need to curtail one's religious exercise does not amount to a denial that such activity *is* religious in character, and counts as religious activity.

refrains from φ-ing when one could φ (or "it is up to the agent to φ"), the power to φ still exists, unactualized: One's body does not move, and no state of affairs is altered. It would be extremely odd, on this description of agential power, to assert that such a power has *two* ends that define the power itself: both to φ and not to φ. Yet this appears to be the result of claiming that a single power has bi-directionality. Rather, we should say that there is a single power with a single end and one normative direction, which the agent may choose *not* to actualize.

Alvarez avoids this conclusion because she does not wish to characterize agential powers as merely the conjunction of two one-way powers. She justifies this on the basis that

> one-way powers are characterized by the fact that when the conditions for their manifestation obtain, the power will be necessarily manifested. But if an agent had the ability and opportunity to φ and also the ability and opportunity not to φ at *t*, and this were the conjunction of two one-way powers, then the agent would both φ and not φ at *t* – but that is impossible. Thus, if an ability I have is genuinely two-way, and if the opportunity to exercise that ability is present, then it will be up to me whether I exercise the ability.[51]

Alvarez's examples of one-way powers are abilities like perception, where certain conditions need only obtain in order for the power to be actualized: So long as the eye is not blind or covered, the perceiver is conscious and functioning, and there is a veridical object of sight in proximity, then necessarily one *is* perceiving. However, I fail to see why this must be the only characterization of what is called "one-way powers": Why cannot there be "one-way powers" that I am free to refrain from actualizing? To attribute bi-directionality to a power implies that there are two ends, both of equal metaphysical standing. And yet Alvarez does not wish to conclude that act omissions are actions: precisely because they are not actualizations of the power that exists in order to be actualized in a certain way.

Perhaps this worry about the concept of two-way powers is justified: What then are the implications for my account of religious exercise? Even if one were to reject the concept of two-way powers, Alvarez's account highlights the Aristotelian distinction between actions and exercises of agency, which underpins my analysis. So long as one agrees that some act omissions may be voluntary and intentional – that an agent can give

[51] Alvarez, "Agency," 109–110.

reasons for choosing to refrain from doing – then it is possible to recognize such act omissions as exercises of one's agency without thinking that they constitute actions per se. Alvarez's account of two-way powers usefully illustrates how an exercise of agency not constituting actions or activity per se might be understood, but there may be variations on this view, as I have suggested.

What Constitutes "Grave Contradiction"?

I have argued in this section that deliberately opting to refrain from performing an action, or choosing not to φ when φ-ing is required by the state, *can* be construed as legitimate religious exercise where φ-ing is reasonably understood as gravely contradicting a citizen's practical religious commitments. Someone may challenge certain terms in this thesis. For instance, what counts as "grave contradictions" of one's religious commitments, and how far does this concept extend? In addition, to whom should "reasonable understanding" of this contradiction be attributed? Is it sufficient for the agent herself to claim that such contradiction exists, or must the appearance of contradiction be accessible to any reasonable observer, including someone who stands outside of the agent's religious tradition?

Specifically, there may be a concern that a fundamental problem with my account thus far is that it offers no objective basis for demarcating religious activity from other forms of human life. In some cases there may remain ambiguity as to whether any natural human activity whatsoever might be "commanded" by the end of worshipping God, to use Aquinas's language.[52] Could a religious citizen not abuse such ambiguity for the purposes of securing an overly broad application of the free exercise clause? A few examples may help in illustrating this particular objection.

In the case of Almachius and Cecilia, the contradiction between the commitments of one's religion and what is required by the state is obvious and appears sufficiently grave for the justification of Cecilia's refusal to obey civic orders. A paramount requirement within Cecilia's duty to worship precludes the worship of other gods, or indeed any idolatrous expression, in accordance with the way her religious tradition defines idolatry. Avoiding this sort of grave contradiction is a paradigm exemplification of

[52] Aquinas, *ST*, 2a 2ae, 81, 1, ad. 1.

legitimate act omission as religious exercise, since her obedience to civic obligations would otherwise amount to blasphemy, a violation of her basic religious commitments. In this case, *not* refraining from action constitutes a grave contradiction of one's religion in the primary sense, and one's chosen act omission is an exercise of one's agency in the paradigmatic way, for it fulfills one's obligation to direct honor to God. Distinguishing the primary sense of religion as a duty of worship, unique among other human activities, is relatively simple and straightforward. Furthermore, it is easy for any reasonable observer, someone who is in Almachius's position, to understand the grave contradiction that his edict poses for Cecilia: For this very reason, Almachius proposes that she need only obey his edict with insincerity.

More problematic cases arise upon consideration of religion understood in the secondary sense: naturally moral human activity, which comes to acquire a religious significance for a member belonging to a religious tradition. The trouble with this particular class of religious actions is that it may be possible to give a philosophical account of "moral activity" that encompasses every aspect of human life. If this is the case, then any distinction between religious activity and other forms of human life appears incoherent. Consequently, it appears to be impossible to set conceptual limits on what constitutes religious exercise in this secondary sense, as well as when a citizen is justified in disobeying the state to avoid contradicting her religious commitments. Worst of all, if *anything* at all can come to acquire a religious meaning, then the free exercise clause extends protection that is either trivial in its attempt to distinguish religious activity as a special kind among human forms or abusively overexpansive.

Concrete consideration of specific religious traditions seems to deepen, rather than alleviate, the basis of this critique. The major world religions have a shared comprehension of social and moral obligations as specific obligations to be fulfilled on every practical level and every detailed sphere of human life. Moral activity within such religious traditions is therefore not restricted only to overt acts of charity, such as visiting widows and orphans, giving alms to the poor, or visiting the sick and imprisoned. Rather, it is inclusive of all aspects of a religious believer's life, being instantiated, to name a few general examples, in one's honest work for pay, in the fulfillment of the domestic needs of a home and child-rearing, and in educating and being educated.[53] As Aquinas argues, every human action has a moral aspect: All action is *moral* action.[54]

It appears undeniable that a moral aspect is ubiquitous within the scope of human action and activity, and it follows that a religious significance may be attributed to this extensive range whenever it is sincerely and deliberately an agent's intention to honor a transcendent or divine being through the medium of her moral actions. For some, this conclusion may be difficult to accept. Yet for many people of faith, sincere in the practice of their religion, there can only be this very conclusion. For religion is not merely a system of beliefs, ethical theories and judgments, and metaphysical opinions. As I have already argued, its distinctiveness and internal coherence relies on its ability to provide concrete proposals for a certain comprehensive way of living one's life, complete with specific practical obligations and often mundane or quotidian commitments, with the duty of worship and devotion as a central, organizing principle, without which the concept of religion would lack coherence. The all-encompassing character of religion, inclusive of both its primary and secondary forms of activity, is perhaps something to be simultaneously admired and feared. In any case, it is clear that its free exercise must, at the very least, be respected.

This account does not imply the impossibility of conceptually demarcating "religion" from other forms of human activity; nor does it entail a gross over-extension of the rights to religious liberty. That the concept of religion *may* have such extensive reach in one's life will normally entail no contradiction whatsoever between one's civic commitments and religious duties. This is because, on my account, religious activity in the secondary sense assumes that one's activity is in itself already an exemplification of human excellence, or that it is

[53] Aquinas says, "*Every virtuous deed* is said to be a sacrifice, insofar as it is done out of reverence of God. Hence this does not prove that religion is a general virtue, but that it commands all other virtues ... *Every deed insofar as it is done in God's honor, belongs to religion*, not as eliciting but as commanding: those belong to religion as eliciting which pertain to the reverence of God by reason of their specific character." Aquinas, *ST*, 1a 2ae, 81, 4, ad. 1–2 (emphases mine).

[54] See in particular Aquinas, *ST*, 1a 2ae, 18. Aquinas also argues that "religion" in some sense just is "sanctity," *qua* "the works of the other virtues [and not pertaining specifically to divine worship]," citing sexual temperance as an example. Aquinas, *ST*, 2a 2ae, 81, 8, ad. 1. Temperance in general has many other applications, for instance to the more paradigm case of eating food. See John Haldane, "Is Every Action Morally Significant?", *Philosophy* 86, no. 3 (2011): 375–404.

a morally good activity prior to that activity coming to acquire a religious character. So any genuinely grave contradictions that do arise, such that a religious citizen would feel the necessity of refusing to obey a civil order, must arise from either one of the following two reasons: the state may be mistaken about the moral propriety of its directive, or else the religious believer may be mistaken about her religious commitment being well-ordered to what is good. Aquinas's theoretical framework potentially resolves this difficulty by presupposing that the state should have the same comprehensive account of moral virtue as any religious citizen: but unanimity in this matter, of course, cannot be assumed in practice.

The difficulties that inevitably arise from disparate accounts about natural moral excellence may be significant and deeply vexing, and the legal resolutions attempted will no doubt prove unsatisfactory to settling certain fundamental questions concerning our social and ethical responsibilities. Importantly, however, such disputes have little to do with the concept of religion per se. On my account, religion is paradigmatically concerned with worship and devotion to the transcendent, rather than with the natural moral excellences over which near-universal consensus is typically sought. Certainly, true moral excellences can come to acquire the character of religion, in a secondary way. But human reasoning can also lead to irreconcilable conflicts in its attempts to ascertain what constitutes a true moral excellence. Such conflict is unfortunately pervasive, and there are few signs that it will ever disappear entirely from human society. In any case, any progress to be made about the latter problem will be located beyond an account of religion and religious exercise. For those hoping to reconcile potential and existing conflicts between religious citizens and the rule of law, perhaps there is some basis for optimism: namely, to promote deeper reflection about the fact that grave contradictions, and the act omissions consequently chosen to avoid them, may arise from mistakes in moral reasoning committed by *either* side in these matters. In the meantime, religious exercise as a distinctive form of human activity continues to enjoy protection by law, which – like those subject to it – should exercise its own forms of epistemic restraint concerning judgments about human goodness.

Conclusion

I have argued that religion should be understood primarily as a characteristic form of human activity directed toward a being (or beings) whose nature transcends that of human nature. The paradigm of religious exercise therefore is worship, defined as human activity directed toward the transcendent. Rejection of this paradigm, I have argued, debases the concept of religion and trivializes its distinctive status among other forms of human activity. Worship, as a paradigmatic religious exercise, is further distinguished from basic moral actions – such as Ishmael's commitment, voiced in Melville's *Moby-Dick*, "to do to my fellow man what I would have my fellow man to do me" – although such moral obligations *can* acquire the character of religion. I have likewise defended the inclusion of voluntary act omissions under the concept of religious exercise and argued that grave contradictions between civic obligations and religious commitments are fundamentally conflicts about moral values rather than over religious obligations per se.

This account ultimately affirms and defends the ancient and nearly universal intuition that religion refers to a special category of human activity. Religious liberty is a unique human right: It is not reducible to or identifiable with other rights, which may share similar aspects but in fact refer to fundamentally distinct human powers, such as the right to free speech or the right to espouse certain metaphysical or ethical views. Religion therefore *is* special, and it deserves respect and protection as such.

3 Freedom of Religion
Special, Valuable, and Qualified

John Finnis

Freedom from, Not a Freedom to

What is religious liberty? As with all "What is?" questions about human matters, an adequate answer must depend (as Aristotle advises) on first answering the question "Why?" – *Why value religious liberty?*[1] Of course, the latter question presupposes some beliefs, indeed shared beliefs, about what the words "religion" and "liberty" mean. For this and other reasons, it is reasonable to follow some other advice and practice of Aristotle: begin with common sayings. The relevant common sayings are the main public declarations and constitutional provisions that articulate a right to religious liberty or, in the US Constitution's First Amendment phrase – reiterated (one may fairly say) in the Second Vatican Council's Declaration on Religious Freedom (*Dignitatis Humanae*) – "the free exercise of religion."

A representative example of these public declarations and constitutional provisions is Article 25 of the Constitution of the Republic of India, brought into effect in January 1950 after more than two years of lucid and intelligent public debate in a constitutional convention:

Right to Freedom of Religion

(1) Subject to public order, morality and health and to the other provisions of this Part, all persons are equally entitled to freedom of conscience and the right freely to profess, practise and propagate religion.

The first four sections and elements of the fifth section originally appeared as "Why Religious Liberty is a Special, Important and Limited Right," Notre Dame Law School Legal Studies Research Paper No. 09–11, an address to a conference in October 2006 at Princeton University on religious liberty in the contemporary situation. We thank the organizer of that research paper series for permission to present here a version adapted by incorporating in the fifth section the main elements of my nearly contemporaneous paper "Discrimination Between Religions: Some Thoughts on Reading Greenawalt's *Religion and the Constitution: Establishment and Fairness*," *Constitutional Commentary* 25 (2008): 265–271.

[1] John M. Finnis, "Law and What I Truly Should Decide," *The American Journal of Jurisprudence* 48 (2003): 107–129 at 107–108, republished in *Philosophy of Law*, vol. 4 of *Collected Essays of John Finnis* (Oxford: Oxford University Press, 2011), 23–45 at 23–25.

(2) Nothing in this article shall affect the operation of any existing law or prevent the State from making any law –
   (a) regulating or restricting any economic, financial, political or other secular activity which may be associated with religious practice;
   (b) providing for social welfare and reform or the throwing open of [Hindu, Sikh, Jaina, or Buddhist] religious institutions of a public character to all classes and sections of [persons professing the Hindu, Sikh, Jaina, or Buddhist religion].

Later in the same year, the European Convention on Fundamental Rights and Freedoms articulated:

Article 9 – Freedom of thought, conscience and religion

(1) Everyone has the right to freedom of thought, conscience and religion; this right includes freedom to change his religion or belief and freedom, either alone or in community with others and in public or private, to manifest his religion or belief, in worship, teaching, practice and observance.
(2) Freedom to manifest one's religion or beliefs shall be subject only to such limitations as are prescribed by law and are necessary in a democratic society in the interests of public safety, for the protection of public order, health or morals, or for the protection of the rights and freedoms of others.

Common to all these formulations, including the American First Amendment, is the term "free[dom]." And these declarations of constitutional rights imply that what they declare and establish as legal and constitutional was already, and foundationally, a moral right of essentially the same extent. So the question arises whether these declarations teach that there is a moral, that is a natural, right to profess *whatever religion or religions one chooses.* Or again, is the liberty or freedom that is being asserted a moral *freedom from all obligations* (for instance, all vows) in matters of religion, as the French revolutionary tradition proclaimed (and insisted upon by dissolving all religious orders)? It was this kind of understanding of religious liberty that led the mid-nineteenth-century popes to denounce claims to religious liberty as "madness." And the answer to that question that was eventually given by the Second Vatican Council, in its 1965 Declaration on Religious Liberty, *Dignitatis Humanae,* is this: The right to religious freedom is a right to be *free from coercion* when one is exercising one's conscience in – within due limits – forming, holding, or giving effect in action to one's beliefs "in matters religious" (*in re religiosa*). This freedom from coercion was often described by the Council's drafting committee as an immunity. And though it is not an immunity in the sense stipulated by Wesley Hohfeld in his analysis of jural relations, there is no objection to using "immunity" as a synonym for a claim-right not to be interfered with or coerced. The "religious liberty" is nothing more, nor less, than a *claim-right not to be coerced in performing religious acts, individual or corporate, within due limits.*

It follows that the fundamental topic of *Dignitatis Humanae* is in substance not a liberty-right (*stricto sensu*), not a freedom to act, but a duty – the duty of state government and law, and of other groups and individuals in civil society, not to coerce anyone's religious acts unless they threaten the rights of others, public peace, or public morality. The right of religious liberty – freedom from coercion – which is the subject-matter of *Dignitatis Humanae*, is nothing other than the correlative of that duty, that is, *nothing other than that duty considered from the point of view of the beneficiary* of (the performance of or compliance with) that duty.

If we now ask *why* there is this duty to respect (or more precisely, to leave uncoerced) the conscientious religious beliefs and acts of anyone and everyone, even beliefs that are false and acts that are accordingly ill-justified, the Second Vatican Council gives more than one answer, but most prominently and fundamentally points to another duty. This is one's serious duty, the duty of each and every person, to seek truth, particularly truth *in re religiosa* – obviously we will need to try to find content for this vague phrase "religious matter(s)" – and then to shape one's life in line with what one judges one's search has discovered about such matters. And that duty is only fulfilled if pursued with an authenticity that would be prejudiced, corrupted, and even nullified by coercion and "psychological pressure."

Why Specifically Protect *Religious* Choices?

To understand all this a bit better, and to move a little closer to understanding what it is about religion – about the *res religiosa* – that calls for respect, we can look at the arguments of contemporary American legal and constitutional theorists who hold that there is nothing about religion or religious liberty that calls for particular respect or for mention in constitutional bills of rights. Religion, these theorists say, has no such dignity, though some of them wryly grant that religions or religious believers may have a historical vulnerability (especially to other religions and believers) that explains and in a weak sense justifies the mention of religion in the first limb of the First Amendment. A principal proponent of such a theory was Ronald Dworkin.[2] Likewise, Christopher Eisgruber and Lawrence Sager, in work culminating in their book *Religious Freedom and the Constitution*, argue for a principle they call "Equal Liberty," a principle that "denies that religion is a … category of human experience that demands special benefits and/or necessitates special restrictions" or any "special immunity for religiously motivated conduct."[3]

Their principle of "Equal Liberty" as a demand of fairness in a religiously diverse society has much about it that may seem welcome. They argue strenuously against the metaphor of "separation of Church and State," and their theory equally discredits not only the slogan but also the once prevailing Supreme Court interpretation of "no establishment of religion" that forbad any state aid to religious or religiously affiliated enterprises. They offer to defend not a secularism that would reject, exclude, or disparage religion but the healthy secularity of nonreligious institutions that decline to be – and are prohibited from being – "overtly or specifically religious."[4] They have no time for Rawlsian proposals to expel from the public domain all religious arguments or grounds for decision-making.[5] As to free exercise of religion, Eisgruber and Sager support the approach in *Employment Division* v. *Smith*, upholding "neutral and generally applicable" laws even when they happen to restrict some religious practices that no "compelling state interest" required be legally restricted.[6] That approach is much less welcome to many who recognize the particular good of religion and religious liberty, but I shall not be arguing against it here. Instead, I shall say why I think the theory of Equal Liberty proposed by Eisgruber and Sager is radically unsound, at the very least insofar as it denies to religion and religious liberty any moral or constitutional status distinct from other "deep commitments."

[2] The final, posthumously published presentation of his thesis was in Ronald Dworkin, *Religion without God* (Cambridge, MA: Harvard University Press, 2013), 105–147 at 132–133.

[3] Christopher L. Eisgruber and Lawrence G. Sager, *Religious Freedom and the Constitution* (Cambridge, MA: Harvard University Press, 2007), 6, 13.

[4] Ibid., 313. [5] See ibid., 48–50 (not explicitly mentioning Rawls's "political liberalism").

[6] *Employment Division* v. *Smith*, 494 US 872, 890 (1990).

Eisgruber and Sager's first exposition of their theory was entitled "The Vulnerability of Consciences: The Constitutional Basis for Protecting Religious Conduct."[7] But the title can give a mistaken impression of their central thesis. For they *deny* that conscience as the rational faculty of practical judgment has any more claim than religion to constitutional privilege or even protection.[8] Rather, the proper object of constitutional protection is any "deep concern," any and all "deeply" motivated and self-shaping attitudes and behavior. Whether or not these are religious *or even conscientious*, all alike are entitled to "equal regard." There is, they say, a "grand diversity of relationships, affiliations, activities, and passions that share a constitutional presumption of legitimacy" because in them members of "a modern, pluralistic society ... find their identities, shape their values, and live the most valuable moments of their lives."[9] Religious acts do, they concede, have the same dignity and constitutional status as the "relationships, affiliations, activities and passions" under discussion. Their article did not say how far this wider category extends, and their book, too, is not much concerned to clarify the matter. But it does make clear that, in their view, the freedom of a religious association such as the Catholic Church to maintain a male priesthood is defensible only as an instance of the constitutional principle that "there are a variety of personal relationships in which members of our political community are free to choose their partners [as in *Lawrence* v. *Texas*], associates or colleagues without interference from the state."[10] And their 1994 article had several times explicated the phrase "deep concern(s)" (which in the book is usually rendered "deep commitment(s)") as including "passionate" acts and relationships.[11]

Eisgruber and Sager are right to think that if religion is just one among the deep passions and commitments that move people, it does not deserve constitutional mention on account of any special dignity or value, and that if its mention in constitutions is defensible at all, the defense must be the

[7] Christopher L. Eisgruber and Lawrence G. Sager, "The Vulnerability of Consciences: The Constitutional Basis for Protecting Religious Conduct," *University of Chicago Law Review* 61, no. 4 (1994): 1245–1315.

[8] Ibid., 1263, 1268–1270. [9] Ibid., 1266.

[10] Eisgruber and Sager, *Religious Freedom*, 65; *Lawrence* v. *Texas* (2003) 539 U.S. 558, involving partnership in casual homosexual sodomy, is cited on the preceding page.

[11] Eisgruber and Sager, "Vulnerability of Consciences," 1263, 1266, 1269, 1292, 1302. At the very outset, the authors say that "an important theme of this essay is that religion does not exhaust the commitments and passions that move human beings in deep and valuable ways." Ibid., 1245n.

backhanded argument according to which religious people have been so beastly to each other that historical constitution-makers have not necessarily been unreasonable in treating the religious as specially vulnerable to discrimination. But the hypothesis – that religion is just one deep and passionate commitment among others – is, of course, lethal to religion. It adopts an unqualifiedly external view, which treats religious propositions as if they were inherently incapable of conveying any understanding of or rational response to any feature of objective reality.[12] They treat religion in the way that Ronald Dworkin regularly treated those views of legislators or "majorities" with which he was unsympathetic, that is, not as propositions *about* rights, or common good, or as any other proposition or premise justifying a normative conclusion, but instead as mere expressions of distaste or disapproval, accompanied by an (implied) appeal to the power of those who hold these views – their power as a majority to give effect to their attitude, *their* passionate political commitment.[13]

Eisgruber and Sager fall into that Dworkinian sort of sophism on the last pages of their book, when they twice reduce the concerns of religiously minded people – particularly their concern that America acknowledge its dependence on God – to a mere concern for "their [own] wellbeing," a mere complaint that "*they* are being deprived of an environment" that they value.[14] The externality of Eisgruber and Sager's view of religion – that is, their refusal to enter into the line of rational inquiry, reflection, and judgment that leads people to affirm the existence of a transcendent intelligent and provident creator – is manifested by their repeated remarks about "intelligent design." Going beyond the rational (albeit not wholly compelling) objection that gaps in experimental science call for more experimental science, they claim that the "suggestion" that there exists an intelligent designer is merely "a vague kind of religious view," "a hypothesis grounded in religion," and that identifying the transcendent

[12] In their book, they explicitly speak from, or on behalf of, "an external, secular perspective." Eisgruber and Sager, *Religious Freedom*, 103.

[13] I first pointed to this sophistic technique of Dworkin's in J. M. Finnis, "A Bill of Rights for Britain? The Moral of Contemporary Jurisprudence," *Proceedings of the British Academy* 71 (1986): 309–311 (republished as "Human Rights and Their Enforcement" in *Human Rights and Common Good* vol. 3 of *Collected Essays*, 19–45 at 24–26), and again, with reference to its pernicious echoes in then recent Supreme Court doctrine, in "Universality, Personal and Social Identity, and Law," in *Intention and Identity*, vol. 2 of *Collected Essays*, 100–121 at 110–112.

[14] Eisgruber and Sager, *Religious Freedom*, 284–285.

Creator God as designer, rather than gods, wizards, fairies, or "transcendental pasta," is a mere profession of religious faith.[15] The truth, of course, is that, whatever should be said about particular theories of evolution, the general hypothesis of intelligent design of the whole cosmos, including all the scientifically verifiable mechanisms of evolution, is one of the rational *grounds*, not a mere subrational consequence, of religious faith.

Now suppose that Eisgruber and Sager had followed the drafts (but not the final version) of the First Amendment, the Indian Constitution, and the European Convention on Human Rights (ECHR) in associating religious liberty with freedom of conscience. Would that have provided them, or us, with a ground for according religion, or conscience and religion together, a particular constitutional status, as worthy of special mention in enumerating fundamental rights?

You might think so. After all, *Dignitatis Humanae* defines religious liberty in close conjunction with conscience, a conjunction eliminated by the lamentable English mistranslation of section 2 on the Vatican website. An accurate translation of the Latin would read:

> This Vatican Council declares that human persons have the right to religious freedom. This kind of freedom consists in this: that all human beings ought to be immune from coercion whether by individuals or social groups and by every kind of human power, so that in religious matters no-one be compelled to act against his or her conscience or be impeded from acting according to his or her conscience, whether acting publicly or privately, alone or in association with others, within due limits.[16]

But it would have been no improvement if Eisgruber and Sager had treated conscience, or if the reader of the Council treats conscience, in the way that Robert Bolt, to almost universal applause, treats conscience in his 1960

15 Ibid., 190, 281, 310n56.

16 "Haec Vaticana Synodus declarat personam humanam ius habere ad libertatem religiosam. Huiusmodi libertas in eo consistit, quod omnes homines debent immunes esse a coercitione ex parte sive singulorum sive coetuum socialium et cuiusvis potestatis humanae, et ita quidem ut in re religiosa neque aliquis cogatur ad agendum contra suam conscientiam neque impediatur, quominus iuxta suam conscientiam agat privatim et publice, vel solus vel aliis consociatus, intra debitos limites." The English translation on the website of the Holy See, in 2019 as in 2008, astonishingly reads: "This Vatican Council declares that the human person has a right to religious freedom. This freedom means that no one is to be forced to act in a manner contrary to his own beliefs, whether privately or publicly, whether alone or in association with others, within due limits." Second Vatican Council, *Dignitatis Humanae*, December 7, 1965, accessed online, www.vatican.va/archive/hist_councils/ii_vatican_council/documents/vat-ii_decl_19651207_dignitatis-humanae_en.html.

play about Thomas More, *A Man for All Seasons*. For there he makes More say: "But what matters to me is not whether it's true or not but that I believe it to be true, or rather, not that I *believe* it, but that *I* believe it."[17] In Bolt's conception, what matters about fidelity to conscience is that it is fidelity to oneself, to one's inmost core, one's authenticity. But in the real world, and in the actual thought of Aquinas, More, and the authors of *Dignitatis Humanae*, what matters about one's judgments of conscience is that one considers them to be *true*, so that failure to act in line with those judgments, while one holds them, is infidelity to *truth*.[18] An observer then and there, or I myself later, may be able to see that my judgments are not true but mistaken. But that is scarcely relevant at all. For in making a judgment that *p* – that is, in asserting my belief that *p* – I am doing nothing other than asserting that *p* is true. So if *p* bears on my actions – on what I ought or ought not to do – and I fail to act accordingly, I act against the *truth* and against morality. That it is only the truth as I see it, and morality as I see it, and that I may have been mistaken in judging it true and morally required, are neither here nor there in relation to the question whether I was loyal or disloyal to truth and morality. Those who think that what is at stake in acting conscientiously and refusing to act against conscience is loyalty to oneself, or to one's self, are unable, so far as I can see, to make sense of repentance. Bolt is one of them: he has everything exactly backwards, and his misunderstanding, being a denial or sophistical mishandling of the *transparency*[19] of judgments for truth, is practically identical to Dworkin's, Eisgruber's, and Sager's sophistical premise mentioned above: that a group whose views they disfavor is concerned not with truth or true human welfare but with enforcing, maintaining, or disseminating the views it happens to have – with the result that they need not engage with that group's reasons for holding those views, nor with reasons that might in any case support those views. Bolt's misunderstanding of conscience is forerunner or progeny of the worldview that makes autonomous *commitment* what

[17] Robert Bolt, *A Man for All Seasons* (1960), Act 2 (New York: Vintage Books, 1990), 91.

[18] See John Finnis, *Aquinas: Moral, Political and Legal Theory* (Oxford: Oxford University Press, 1998), 123. See also John Paul II: "In any event, it is always from the truth that the dignity of conscience derives. In the case of the correct conscience, it is a question of the *objective truth* received by man; in the case of the erroneous conscience, it is a question of what man, mistakenly, *subjectively* considers to be true." John Paul II, *Veritatis Splendor*, August 6, 1993, §63.

[19] See "Human Rights and Their Enforcement," n. 13 above, at 25.

matters, even if the commitment be passionate in the sense of "passions" in which they may well be *over and against* reason and in need of subjection to reason's properly constitutional mastery and rule.[20]

One's concern for one's conscience, then, is worthy of respect only because, even when one's conscience happens to be mistaken, it is concern for *truth* (and one *cannot* know that one is here and now in error). Concern for religious conscience is warranted only because, or on the assumption that, there can be religious judgments that are true, *true* judgments about religious matters. And one of the most important truths about religious matters is that divine creativity and intelligence are at the source of every truth there is, and above all of our ability to make judgments that at least sometimes are true and thus at least sometimes link us, in ways otherwise simply unavailable, with realities past and present, and with real opportunities of our truly flourishing, individually and all together. Religion's supreme relevance – or at least an integral element in religion's relevance – to human life and well-being is that it articulates, more or less adequately, a main truth about truth (and thus about conscience and everything else). The truth about truth that it articulates is the truth that everything we experience and envisage is utterly dependent upon the originating and sustaining intelligence and will of a Creator whose existence, intelligence, and freedom provide the explanation that our inquiring reason imperiously (because by force of reasons) demands, but provide it only if understood to be utterly free from the contingency – the falling short of pure actuality unmixed with mere potentiality – that marks the nature of everything known to experience and natural science, and marks too the imagined natures of polytheistic gods, or wizards, or fairies, or transcendental pasta.[21]

[20] On this constitutional or civil rule of reason over passions, see Finnis, *Aquinas*, 72–78.

[21] Ibid., 306: "Polytheisms, idolatries, and gnosticisms propose a multiplicity of more or less creative and providential divinities, all falling short of God's simplicity of actuality, and reflecting rather the profusion of natures in the universe of experience. Pantheism proposes that the universe itself, precisely as informed by intelligibility and thus by mind, is divine. Though not as foolish, in principle, as atheism, polytheism and pantheism alike are philosophically arbitrary and misguided. They presuppose a semi-materialist underestimation of intellect's capacity to grasp (and project) multiple and changing realities (actual or possible) in a single act of mind. They veer towards the pernicious in the character they ascribe to a divinity or divinities falling short of the perfection of a pure and limitless act(uality), and imaging moral weaknesses of the people who project them. They are utterly inconsistent with a logically necessary implication of the arguments which justify affirming divine existence: that existence (pure act) is what divine being is. For, that being so, whatever we understand of something which can be or not be cannot

Inquiring reason outruns the methods of natural science, but not its own capacities and integrity, when we affirm – not merely as a product or consequence of faith, but in the first instance as a reasonable preamble to faith – that the success of everything we attempt is dependent upon the cooperation, the co-working, of God. Natural reason, apart from any faith in any divine revelation, endorses the full reasonableness and the importance of the prayer (the Regents' prayer) that was expelled from the public schools of New York by the Supreme Court in *Engel* v. *Vitale* (1962): "Almighty God we acknowledge our dependence upon Thee, and we beg Thy blessings upon us, our parents, our teachers and our Country."[22]

Such is the core of natural religion, and of any paradigmatic *res religiosa*, even one as richly elaborated by revealed doctrine and worship as, say, Orthodox or Catholic Christianity.[23] There can be non-paradigmatic, more or less watered-down instances of religion, some of them historically highly significant such as Buddhism. The human good of religion is centrally the good of being aligned in one's intelligence, will, and freedom with the intelligence, will, and freedom of the Creator. Wrongdoing, temptation, repentance, forgiveness, and redemption are all within the ambit of that generic *alignment*, that *assimilatio* and *adhaesio*, as Aquinas puts it. One does not get the measure of religion's dignity and value if one remains with the conception of religion's value that Andrew Koppelman has proposed on the basis, not least, of the "place-holder" sketch of a good of religion that I have previously offered.[24] Koppelman's intentions in this enterprise are

be true of God, and the supposed divine principles posited by polytheism or pantheism, being intelligible to us, cannot be God. Pantheism and polytheism are rationally ineligible because they stray from the only way in which anything can be rationally affirmed of the divine: the way which Aquinas calls *remotio* – connoting both the utter separateness or transcendence (removed-ness) of God and the fact that affirmations about God can be made *only* by negating (removing) creaturely imperfections."

22 *Engel* v. *Vitale*, 370 U.S. 421 (1962) at 422.

23 On the importance of natural religion, and the idea of natural religion, in the thought of the founders of the American republic, see Gerard V. Bradley, *Religious Liberty in the American Republic* (Washington, DC: Heritage Foundation, 2008), 8–9, 29, 40–41, 46. The report of the US Senate Committee on the Judiciary on petitions to abolish the office of chaplain, January 21, 1853, lucidly affirms that "our fathers ... did not intend to send our armies and navies forth to do battle for the country without any national recognition of that God on whom success or failure depends."

24 See Andrew Koppelman, "Secular Purpose," *Virginia Law Review* 88 (2002): 130–131; Andrew Koppelman, "Is It Fair to Give Religion Special Treatment?" *University of Illinois Law Review* 2006, no. 3 (2006): 593–594; and John Finnis, *Natural Law and Natural Rights*, 2nd edition (Oxford: Oxford University Press, 2011 [1980]), 83–84, 89–90.

good – he is a critic of the unadmitted secularism of Eisgruber and Sager – but the content and dignity of the good of religion cannot be identified (as he attempts to identify them) without regard to the arguments that point to the existence of God and to something of the divine nature and activity.

Nor should we neglect the importance of natural religion's underpinning of the idea, the truth, of human equality, the equality of human beings as animals who, unlike (as far as we can tell) all other animals, have, each and all, the *radical* capacities of persons. Those capacities are to participate in the immaterial life of the spirit, the life of meanings, logic, truths, and errors (known by their consistency with evidence, not by their correlation with any brain-state), about the past and the possible. As Article 25(2)(b) of the Indian Constitution reminds us, it is possible for a developed religion to distort natural religion's awareness of human equality under, and in relation to, the supreme, creative spiritual reality.[25] But the greater threat to human equality is materialist, scientistic denials of spirit, denials which strip away that one aspect of human reality which makes us equal in dignity despite the manifold inequalities between us. It is very significant that those who expend the patrimony of a religious, anti-materialist civilization, the patrimony we call *rights*, by extending rights to sub-personal animals, are characteristically to be found denying the equal rights of young or disabled human persons. Prayers like the New York Regents' prayer, acknowledging to God our dependence and addressing to the unseen God a petition, both presuppose and reinforce the anti-materialist truth so essential to human rights and their acknowledgment.

Disparagement or Denial of Equal Membership?

Eisgruber and Sager admit that the rule in *Engel* v. *Vitale*, expelling all such prayer from public schools even when opting out of prayer sessions is fully permitted and protected, cannot be adequately justified by simple appeal to the risk of coercion by social pressure. Certainly, they concede, *Engel*'s progeny, such as *Santa Fe Independent School District* (2000), could not be

[25] "[The state may make law] providing for social welfare and reform or the throwing open of Hindu religious institutions of a public character to all classes and sections of Hindus." Constitution of India, art. 25 is quoted above (text after n. 1) as affected by the second of the two "Explanations" with which that Article concludes.

so justified. After all, anyone can stay away from a football game at which there will be school-sponsored prayer. But they vigorously defend the absoluteness of the rule in these cases by deploying a wide-ranging principle of *disparagement*:

> Government-sponsored prayer rituals involve a public embrace of the faithful ... more precisely, of those whose faiths are consistent with mainstream public prayer. As a result, their social meaning includes this blunt message: *The real members of this community (the school community and by extension the larger community serviced by the school or school district) are practicing Christians of a certain sort; others dwell among us but lack the status of full membership.* The public rituals create a class of outsiders and thereby disparage those relegated to that status. ... Proponents ... will no doubt object that neither they nor school authorities have any intention to disparage anybody; their goal is simply to make prayer rituals available to those who will appreciate them ... [But] the relevant question is not about the intentions of particular speakers, nor about the perceptions of particular audiences, but rather about the social meanings of rituals, practices, and religions.[26]

You are entitled to be puzzled by a "meaning" that floats free both of the intentions of the speaker or acting person and of the perceptions of the audience. Yet this argument from unintended but supposedly real disparagement is now a mighty force in constitutional and political arguments against not only our religion or religions but also against the institution of marriage, the primacy of our language within our own country, and every other aspect of our culture that is not universally shared and about which some are discontented. To require immigrants to speak our language, argues Joseph Raz, is to disrespect them, to express a judgment that their culture is inferior, and to be eliminated.[27] Here Raz, for so many years a stern critic of Ronald Dworkin, implicitly throws in his lot with Dworkin's long-running sequence of arguments, each one springing up when its predecessor twin or cousin was refuted, all revolving around the claim that some state action manifests disrespect, or

[26] Eisgruber and Sager, *Religious Freedom*, 163–164 (emphasis added). See also Justice Stevens' opinion for the Court in *Santa Fe Independent School District* v. *Doe*: "School sponsorship of a religious message is impermissible because it sends the ancillary message to members of the audience who are nonadherents 'that they are outsiders, not full members of the political community.'" 530 U.S. 290 (2000) at 309–310.

[27] Joseph Raz, "Multiculturalism," *Ratio Juris* 11, no. 3 (1998): 200, referring also to Raz, *Ethics in the Public Domain*, 2nd edition (Oxford: Oxford University Press, 1995), 178. On all this, see "Universality, Personal and Social Identity, and Law," n. 13 above, at 112–119.

lack of equal respect, for those persons whose conduct it restricts or otherwise affects – restricts or affects perhaps, in truth, out of lively concern to protect them from their own folly or weakness.

To all these attributions of disrespect, insult, disparagement, unhinged from any intent, we should reply that they are gratuitous and groundless, essentially sophistic fictions. The meaning of the resolve to pray together is simply *not* that those who abstain or absent themselves are not full members of the community. They are full members of the community with every single right that everyone else in it enjoys, and every single right enjoyed by those who engage in the corporate activity from which they are entitled to dissent, and with whom they have, *pace* Eisgruber and Sager, equal constitutional stature.[28] Similarly, those countries or legislatures or citizens who insist that immigrants learn the country's language, lest the country be Balkanized with seriously bad consequences for all its residents alike, need neither have nor convey any view that the immigrant culture is inferior, nor any intent to eliminate it. And in those cases where they do judge some such particular culture to be significantly and damagingly inferior, and hope or even plan for that culture's gradual elimination in their country by robust assimilation, their judgment, if sincerely and thoughtfully and carefully made, need not be unfairly disrespectful of persons, any more than, say, the comparable judgment that sexual relations between grown men and nine-year-old girls are immoral, harmful, and are to be eliminated from our community.

Bad Side Effects and the Need for Limits to the Duty of Non-restriction

I have just touched on one of the morally necessary limits to the right of religious freedom. That the right is limited was stated upfront in the Indian Constitution's articulation of the right and was made plain in the provisos or riders or qualifying clauses of the ECHR and in *Dignitatis Humanae*. The terms of these last two documents are very close to each other. The

[28] See Eisgruber and Sager, *Religious Freedom*, 130, where the authors gratuitously postulate that a (hypothetical?) "mainstream Christian" majority consciously treat dissenters as "less than full members of our community," as members who lack "equal constitutional stature." See *Santa Fe Independent School District* v. *Doe* as quoted in n. 26 above for the same eisegesis and fallacy in the Supreme Court.

European Convention states that limits are "necessary in a democratic society in the interests of public safety, for the protection of public order, health or morals, or for the protection of the rights and freedoms of others."[29] Likewise, *Dignitatis Humanae* affirms limits justified by "the need for an effective safeguard of the rights of all citizens and for the peaceful settlement of conflicts of rights, also out of the need for an adequate care of genuine public peace, which comes about when people live together in good order and in true justice, and finally out of the need for a proper guardianship of public morality."[30]

There can be problems about the boundaries of these exceptions; many of them are explored in the American cases on free exercise of religion. There can also be problems that are not really about boundaries but about abuses, moral errors by legislators or judges, errors that can scarcely be protected against by sound constitutional provisions. The application of general and (in intent) religiously neutral laws against discrimination can be unjust and a grave imposition on religious or religiously organized and inspired enterprises. Such is the case with laws prohibiting discrimination against persons who make no secret of their engaging in same-sex sex acts but wish to be employed as teachers in Muslim, Catholic, or Evangelical schools or to make use of Catholic or Evangelical facilities such as adoption agencies or church halls, or who demand from believers that they use their commercially available skill and labor to make products specifically for use in celebrations of same-sex sex acts. The consequent unjust impositions on right-thinking religious or religiously motivated activities and associations are probably best – most truthfully – resisted by protesting not so much that they are impositions on religious liberty but, rather, that they are impositions on associational freedom and perhaps the rights of parents, and that in their rationale they are, in many ways, profoundly wrong-headed about both sex and marriage, are abuses of children's innocence, and are reckless about the future of the country's common good. To make and persist in such strong, substantive claims will not be easy. But unless religious believers are willing to go on proposing and defending – in season and out of season – the rationality and soundness of moral judgments rejected by newly prevalent secular (or liberal-religious) proponents of sex acts (e.g. same-sex) outside genuine ("traditional") marriage, they will

[29] European Convention on Human Rights, art. 9.

[30] Second Vatican Council, *Dignitatis Humanae*, §7.

succumb to the hostile (and false) designation of their beliefs and judgments as bigotry, no better than the prejudices of slave-owners or the Ku Klux Klan.

To this I should add a pair of different but complementary lines of thought. One concerns the necessary and appropriate limits on the right to religious freedom. The other concerns just and lawful accommodations[31] of religious beliefs and practices in the interests of the great human good – truth about, and orientation toward, the framework and source of reality – that religion (unlike irreligion) more or less appropriately cultivates, participates in, and makes available to others. Suppose a religion rejects on principle the right to religious freedom as defined, for example, in the ECHR's reference to freedom to change one's religion, and rejects also other fundamental elements of our constitutional order. This is no idle hypothesis. In 2003, eighteen judges of the European Court of Human Rights (ECtHR) held unanimously, in *Refah Partisi (No.2)* v. *Turkey*, that

> the Court considers that sharia, *which faithfully reflects the dogmas and divine rules laid down by religion, is stable and invariable.* Principles such as pluralism in the political sphere or the constant evolution of public freedoms have no place in it . . . [A] regime based on sharia . . . clearly diverges from Convention values, particularly with regard to its criminal law and criminal procedure, its rules on the legal status of women and the way it intervenes in all spheres of private and public life in accordance with religious precepts. . . . [A] political party whose actions seem to be aimed at introducing sharia . . . can hardly be regarded as an association complying with the democratic ideal that underlies the whole of the Convention.[32]

On that basis, the ECtHR upheld the Turkish Supreme Court's dissolution of Turkey's elected government and of the country's main party on the grounds that the government in which that party was dominant was preparing – or might well be preparing, and there is no obligation to wait until the last moment to be sure of such intentions – to introduce sharia, the religious law of

[31] On accommodation, see now Finnis, "Equality and Religious Liberty: Oppressing Conscientious Diversity in England," in *Religious Freedom and Gay Rights: Emerging Conflicts in the United States and Europe*, ed. Timothy Shah, Thomas Farr, and Jack Friedmann (New York: Oxford University Press, 2016), 21–40 at 26–40.

[32] *Refah Partisi (No. 2)* v. *Turkey* 37, European Human Rights Reports 1 (2003), §123 (emphasis added), Grand Chamber, upholding and adopting the language of the Third Section of the ECtHR in *Refah Partisi (No. 1)* v. *Turkey* 35, European Human Rights Reports 3 (2002).

Islam, either as law applicable to all or as part of a scheme in which all citizens would be subjected to the law of their respective religion.

If it is hard for *contemporary* American constitutionalists to take this sort of "militant democracy" – preemptive defense of democracy – at all seriously, it is even harder to get them to do so when it involves steadily focusing on the possibility that a particular religion might be different from all other religions in its core beliefs about the Constitution, and about the legitimacy of long-term deception and intimidation in the cause of overthrowing it or, much more immediately, in the cause of rendering certain constitutional guarantees inapplicable within the religion's zone of dominance. For I should not conceal the fact that it was part of Turkey's case before the ECtHR that "[i]n order to attain its ultimate goal of replacing the existing legal order with sharia, political Islam use[s] the method known as '*takiyye*,' which consist[s] in hiding its beliefs until it ha[s] attained that goal." The Court did not make any explicit finding about Islamic *takiyye* (a practice which had not, it seems, been denied by the applicant members of the dissolved government and party), but it did observe more broadly that political parties and movements may conceal their aims and profess their adherence to democracy and the rule of law until it is too late to prevent them from overthrowing both.[33] Still, for present purposes, we do not really need to speculate about the possible secret intentions of particular members of the Islamic religion. We can study the open public documents and declarations of states holding themselves out as Islamic, such as the Cairo Declaration on Human Rights in Islam, adopted by the governments of forty-five states in August 1990. Purporting to track the Universal Declaration of Human Rights, this 1990 Declaration's article on religious freedom reads as follows: "(10) Islam is the religion of true unspoiled nature. It is prohibited to exercise any form of pressure on man or to exploit his poverty or ignorance in order to force him to change his religion to another religion or to atheism." But Articles 24 and 25 add, for good measure: "(24) All the rights and freedoms stipulated in this Declaration are subject to the Islamic Shari'ah. (25) The Islamic Shari'ah is the only source of reference for the explanation or clarification of any of the articles of this Declaration."[34]

These realities put a question mark over more than one part of the orthodoxy of American freedom of religion doctrine. They raise a doubt about the

[33] *Refah (No. 1)*, §48, 80; *Refah (No.2)*, §101.

[34] U.N. GAOR, World Conference on Human Rights, 4th Sess., Agenda Item 5, U.N. Doc. A/CONF.157/PC/62/Add.18 (1993).

part that says the law and the Court must make no investigation of a religion's doctrines and over the part, treated as axiomatic by justices of every shade of opinion, that forbids any discrimination between religions. What if the "theological propositions of a religion" *include political* teachings "wholly at odds with premises of our liberal democracy," or, to speak like the ECtHR, "with the democratic ideal that underlies the whole of the [Constitution]," or, to speak I think more suitably, with the Constitution and other principles that we have taken as foundational for our law? Is it unconstitutional to discriminate between religions at our border? Does doing so wrongly *disparage* adherents of the religion who are citizens already resident? Does it coerce *their* liberty *in re religiosa*? Or coerce the human right to religious liberty of those who would be kept out of our community in the interests of our community's public order?

In relation to the last question, it is essential to make a distinction which recalls the second fundamental ground for religious liberty identified in *Dignitatis Humanae*, the argument from the division of jurisdiction implicit in "Render to Caesar the things that are Caesar's, and to God the things that are God's" – the argument, that is, from the fundamental difference between church and state, religious and secular community. *Dignitatis Humanae* states:

> The religious acts whereby men, in private and in public and out of a sense of personal conviction, direct their lives to God transcend by their very nature the order of terrestrial and temporal affairs. Government therefore ought indeed to take account of the religious life of the citizenry and show it favor, since the function of government is to make provision for the common welfare. However, it would clearly transgress the limits set to its power, were it to presume to command or inhibit acts that are religious [*actus religiosos dirigere vel impedire*].[35]

The difference between church and state reappears, implicitly, in one of Pope Benedict XVI's first statements:

> Single believers are called to open their arms and their hearts to every person, from whatever nation they come, allowing the Authorities responsible for public life to enforce the relevant laws held to be appropriate for a healthy co-existence.[36]

[35] Second Vatican Council, *Dignitatis Humanae*, §3.

[36] Benedict XVI, Address to the Pontifical Council for Pastoral Care of Migrants and Itinerant People, May 15, 2006 (*Acta Apostolicae Sedis* 98 (2006) 453 at 454).

One might add this about the difference between church and state. Within a universal *religious community* (say, church) there need be no distinction between male and female, slave and free, citizen and foreigner. It does not follow, however, that all such distinctions are irrelevant to the common good and indeed the public order of *political communities*. The question comes plainly into view: Can political communities – states and their governments and laws – rationally and responsibly be neutral between religions (or between religions and irreligion) and indifferent to the distinctions between religions?

Neutrality between Religions (and Irreligion): Irrational Unless Qualified

The orthodoxy – neutrality between religions – is expounded in the second volume of Kent Greenawalt's *Religion and the Constitution*, entitled *Establishment and Fairness*. The First Amendment's two religion clauses each, he argues, "forbid discrimination *among* religions." He explains, "[O]ne of the most powerful principles of the religion clauses is that the government may not favor some religions at the expense of others."[37] Into the American context so meticulously explored by Greenawalt, how might one transpose a contemporary problematic that elsewhere – in many of the countries party to the ECHR – is very real, transcends bigotry, and calls on responsible people to set aside their feelings of embarrassment? And is the intuition enshrined in Greenawalt's title, that nonestablishment and fairness go hand in hand (the former required by the latter), really sound?

[37] Kent Greenawalt, *Religion and the Constitution*, vol. 2, *Establishment and Fairness* (Princeton, NJ: Princeton University Press, 2008), 13, 212. The former statement is supported with *Larson* v. *Valente*, where Justice Brennan for the Court puts forward a characteristically maximalist articulation and application of that principle (though there were two dissenters, Justices White and Rehnquist, not "only one," and two others dissented on standing grounds). Brennan assembles a good deal of Supreme Court rhetoric in support. See 456 U.S. 228 (1982). The effect, of course, is not, *pace* some of this rhetoric, an "absolute," but instead is "strict scrutiny": the discrimination, as Greenawalt puts it, must "be needed to satisfy a compelling state interest." Greenawalt, *Religion and the Constitution*, 2:13. This orthodoxy has support from the unorthodox, too: Greenawalt quotes Justice Thomas's opinion for the plurality in *Mitchell* v. *Helms* that courts should not be "trolling through a person's or institution's religious beliefs." 530 US 793 (2000) at 828, quoted in Greenawalt, *Religion and the Constitution*, 2: 410–411.

If, as I said above, it is hard for *contemporary* American constitutionalists to take seriously the sort of "militant democracy" – preemptive defense of democracy – that the ECtHR unanimously upheld in *Refah*, will it not be even harder for them when doing so involves them steadily focusing on the possibility that a particular religion – the private faith of fellow citizens or of hard-up immigrants – might be different from all other religions in its core beliefs about the Constitution and about the legitimacy of long-term deception and intimidation in the cause of overthrowing it or, much more immediately, in the cause of rendering certain constitutional guarantees inapplicable within the religion's zone of dominance? The challenge to American legal imagination is apparent in Justice Stephen Breyer's *Active Liberty: Interpreting a Democratic Constitution.*[38] To the US-oriented first edition, subtitled *Interpreting Our Democratic Constitution,*[39] Breyer added a ten-page discussion of the *Refah* decision's immediate successor, *Sahin* v. *Turkey*, in which the ECtHR Grand Chamber, in a 17 to 1 decision, upheld the Turkish Supreme Court's ruling that universities *must* prohibit the wearing of religious headscarves even when the effect was to deny a university education to women who held themselves bound to wear such a scarf. Justice Breyer's discussion never alludes to the *Refah* decision (presupposed in *Sahin*) or to its essential holding about the nature of the religion in question. In his exposition of the *Sahin* decision, Breyer quotes the passage in which the ECtHR explained that permission to wear such scarves opens women to pressure from extremists, especially from extremists outside the university (including, implicitly, their own families) and in Turkish society at large, including from extremist political parties seeking to "impose on society as a whole their religious symbols *and conception of a society founded on religious precepts.*" But in his "reconsideration of these factors," Breyer narrowed and reduced this "factor" dramatically, adverting only to pressures that might be imposed "on ordinary non-religious students . . . *by religious students.*"[40]

[38] Stephen Breyer, *Active Liberty: Interpreting a Democratic Constitution* (Oxford: Oxford University Press, 2008).

[39] Stephen Breyer, *Active Liberty: Interpreting Our Democratic Constitution* (New York: Knopf, 2005).

[40] Ibid., 137 (emphasis added), where Breyer imagines a second kind of pressure: discouragement of "less religious Turkish women" from attending classes where scarves were widespread among "more religious Turkish women," "thereby helping to bring about a more religiously-oriented university atmosphere." Breyer's thoroughly inadequate attention to realities seems, however, a model of attentiveness compared with the unrealism of

On these matters, Greenawalt's 2008 commentary is rather oblique. He persuasively defends the pre-*Smith* balancing test for religious claims to exemption from generally applicable prohibitions, against Eisgruber and Sager's thesis that claims of religious exercise should enjoy constitutional protection if and only if non-exemption (failure to accommodate) would manifest a discriminatory legislative "failure of equal regard." In doing so, Greenawalt takes a critical look at Eisgruber's and Sager's suggestion (as he paraphrases it) that "[i]f legislators or administrators fairly considered the imposition on members of minority religions of a uniform dress code, they would have made exceptions."[41] He comments that this overlooks a significant complexity:

> It might be that the reason *not* to make a particular exception – say for girls in school wearing head scarves – is that usage reflects and conveys (for some people) a prescribed role for women that does not correspond to liberal democratic values.[42]

Greenawalt's point is a fair one. But his dialectic with Eisgruber and Sager does not require or even allow him to reach some key issues: (1) What if the prohibition were aimed precisely at a practice demanded or encouraged by a particular religion, *because* it is demanded or encouraged by that religion *as part of a unitary package*

"Fearing Strangers Again: The Alleged Muslim Threat," the relevant pages of the contemporaneous book on religious liberty and equality: Martha Nussbaum, *Liberty of Conscience: In Defense of America's Tradition of Religious Equality* (New York: Basic Books, 2008), 346–353. Dealing mainly with Europe, Nussbaum here gives attention to the House of Lords judicial decision in *R (Begum)* v. *Denbigh High School Governors* [2006] UKHL 15, [2007] 1 AC 100. But she relies on a brief newspaper report of it, thoroughly misstates the reasoning, and is unaware that the Law Lords' judgments rest on the line of thought relied on in *Sahin* and so, ultimately, on the line of thought in *Refah*, a line of thought which in its full (*Refah*) version is to the effect that Islam involves (risk of) intimidation of its own milder or lukewarm adherents and of any political community in which its robust adherents are inclined, and feel strong enough, to seek dominance (which is not at all the same as thinking that all Muslims favor such intimidation – it was the Muslim headmistress of Begum's school who forbad her religious attire, and many professing Muslims in Turkey still support the principle of a secular state defended in *Refah* and *Sahin*). See John Finnis, "Discrimination between Faiths: A Case of Extreme Speech?" in *Extreme Speech and Democracy*, ed. Ivan Hare and James Weinstein (Oxford: Oxford University Press, 2009), 430–441.

[41] Greenawalt, *Religion and the Constitution*, 2: 475. Eisgruber and Sager might protest that this absolutizes their claim, quoted by Greenawalt in the preceding sentence, that equal liberty "will call for exemptions in *most* dress code cases."

[42] Ibid.

of tenets of that religion which as a package is opposed to the constitution? Or again: (2) What if the prohibition were aimed precisely at a practice demanded or encouraged by a particular religion, *because* it is often imposed on members of that religion by (a) unlawful intimidation, or (b) unjustified pressure, otherwise impossible to combat effectively?

Or again, to get a little bit closer to matters of immigration: (3) What if the prohibition were in the context of state aid, e.g. vouchers available for schools, including religious schools, provided that they undertake neither to advocate nor to teach the desirability of introducing sharia law into the United States? Greenawalt's discussions of the conditions that states may impose on the ideas that schools receiving aid may teach are, doubtless necessarily, somewhat inconclusive. "[C]ertain [legislative] judgments about good and bad values would be constitutionally foreclosed as criteria for a state providing aid," but "courts will permit states to set some conditions . . . as Ohio required that schools receiving voucher money in Cleveland not teach hatred of groups classified by race, religion, or ethnic background."[43] On the other hand, "Justice Souter amply demonstrates that the rule against teaching hatred of groups is fuzzy enough at the edges, so that it might be understood to cover teaching of various ideas that are embraced by many religious groups."[44] But Souter's point falls short of ample demonstration; it is in fact no more than the simple observation that Ohio's rule "could be understood (or subsequently broadened) to prohibit religions from teaching traditionally legitimate articles of faith as to the error, sinfulness, or ignorance of others, if they want government money for their schools." To illustrate such teachings, Souter cites texts in the Book of Mormon, the Pentateuch, and the Koran announcing the damnation, in the next life, of unbelievers and adds a reference to 2 Corinthians 6:14,[45] which in the interpretation that is more genuinely "traditionally legitimate"[46] means no more than that believers should not associate

[43] Ibid., 459. The reference is to *Zelman* v. *Simmons-Harris*, 536 U.S. 639 (2002).

[44] Greenawalt, *Religion and the Constitution*, 2:418, citing 536 U.S. 639 at 713–714. See also Ibid., 416, where Greenawalt suggests a list of other religious (Catholic and Protestant – conspicuously not Islamic) beliefs that might be regarded as hatred of others.

[45] Souter quotes the King James Version: "Be ye not unequally yoked together with unbelievers, for what fellowship hath righteousness with unrighteousness? And what communion hath light with darkness?"

[46] For example, Thomas Aquinas, *Super 2 ad Corinthios*, cap. 6, lect. 3, para. 234.

themselves with nonbelievers *in works (actions) that are specifically of unbelief*, for example in worshipping idols.

Souter concluded that any state aid to religious schools threatens religious liberty and equality among religions (or entangles the state in discrimination between religions), and Greenawalt seems unwilling to go so far. His book's treatment, at this point, lacks the absolutism foreshadowed by its initial acceptance of the sponsorship of Brennan in *Larson* v. *Valente* for a near-absolutist rule of nondiscrimination among religions. Greenawalt does not accept Noah Feldman's argument that a decisive reason for avoiding or outlawing state aid is that the constitutional rule of neutrality, applied to such aid, would entail permitting the beneficiaries to both take the money and teach, for example, "anti-Americanism, or sexism." Greenawalt's objection is:

> Although a state cannot discriminate on the basis of theological propositions of a religion, it may be able to require that a school's ethical and political teachings be not wholly at odds with premises of our liberal democracy.[47]

And thus a central underlying issue comes again into view. What if the "theological propositions of a religion" rather clearly include *political* teachings "wholly at odds with premises of our liberal democracy"? Or, to put the question in the language of the ECtHR, what if a religion's doctrine demonstrably conflicts "with the democratic ideal that underlies the whole of the [Constitution]" or, to speak more suitably, with the Constitution and other principles that we have taken as foundational for our law?

The matter is not settled by cases declaring, "The Bill of Rights is a futile authority for the alien seeking admission for the first time to these shores."[48] Such sweeping declarations are qualified even by those who,

[47] Greenawalt, *Religion and the Constitution*, 2:470; see also 2:459, 2:469. Greenawalt adds, to me somewhat obscurely: "If the only concern is about discrimination, the inquiry should be whether state restrictions on forms of teaching constitute some kind of discrimination. Presumably more would need to be shown than that some religious groups actually do want to engage in the kind of teaching that is disallowed." Ibid., 2:470. Then he further adds, to me more intelligibly: "[H]owever, the concern here goes beyond discrimination to whether the government impedes religious liberty by setting up standards for instruction about morals and politics with which religious groups wanting state assistance for their schools must comply." Ibid.

[48] *Bridges* v. *Wilson*, 326 U.S. 135 (1944) at 161 (Justice Murphy concurring), quoted in *U.S.* v. *Verdugo-Urquidez*, 494 U.S. 259 (1990) at 271 (Chief Justice Rehnquist for the majority).

like the majority in *U.S.* v. *Verdugo-Urquidez* (1990), recite them in the context of a rights-articulating provision such as the Fourth Amendment. The declarations, like the result in *Verdugo-Urquidez*, were rejected by the same Justice Brennan who authored *Larson* v. *Valente*. It is easy to envisage judges of Brennan's (and is it also Greenawalt's?) persuasion jumping off from the absoluteness of the prohibition: "shall make no law respecting an establishment of religion." No need (the argument might run) to predicate a correlative right in aliens abroad; many citizen members of the "dis-established" religion might be deemed to have standing to challenge its discriminatory, "other-religions-establishing" restriction on their opportunity to be joined by co-religionists (family members, imams, etc.) from abroad.[49]

Other absolutist pronouncements of the Court would be called in aid, e.g. from the other case cited by Greenawalt along with *Larson* v. *Valente*: "a law targeting religious beliefs as such is never permissible, if the object of a law is to infringe upon or restrict practices because of their religious motivation, the law is not neutral; and it is invalid unless it is justified by a compelling interest and is narrowly tailored to advance that interest."[50] Would ending immigration by Muslims, or by Muslims who will not publicly renounce sharia for America,[51] be "*targeting* their *beliefs as such*"? Would it be "to infringe upon or restrict their practices *because of*

49 What was easy to envisage in 2008 was amply illustrated in June 2018 in the dissent by Justices Sotomayor and Ginsburg in *Trump* v. *Hawaii*, 585 U.S. ___ (2018), in relation precisely to a supposed presidential rationale for restricting immigration from countries considered predominantly Muslim. And the Opinion of the Court recites, "Our cases recognize that '[t]he clearest command of the Establishment Clause is that one religious denomination cannot be officially preferred over another.' Larson v. Valente, 456 U.S. 228, 244 (1982)."

50 *Church of the Lukumi Babalu Aye* v. *City of Hialeah*, 508 U.S. 520 (1993) at 533 (Justice Kennedy for the Court); Greenawalt, *Establishment and Fairness*, 2:13.

51 Consider s.2 of the bill for a Jihad Prevention Act, introduced on September 18, 2008, by Representative Tom Tancredo as H.R. 6975:

2. Section 212(a)(3) of the Immigration and Nationality Act (8 U.S.C. 1182(a)(3)) is amended by adding at the end the following:

(G) SHARIA LAW SYSTEM- Any alien who fails to attest, in accordance with procedures specified by the Secretary of Homeland Security, that the alien will not advocate installing a Sharia law system in the United States is inadmissible.

This is a low-key version of the option, because "advocate" is given a stringently narrow meaning in *Yates* v. *U.S.*, 354 US 297 (1957).

their *religious motivation*"? The categories I have italicized are strained, artificial, and rhetorical. But one can readily foresee the first part of Justice Kennedy's loosely constructed sentence being pressed into service.

To be sure, Greenawalt nowhere opts for absoluteness, but instead for a no-discrimination demand that is defeasible in principle. But any defeater is subject to strict scrutiny – scrutiny seeking a compelling state interest – and while strict scrutiny in religious *liberty* cases has proved "feeble," in religious *discrimination* ("no establishment") cases it has hitherto been strict enough to be uniformly fatal,[52] absent historic practices such as legislative prayers (anomalies bitterly repudiated by the Brennan absolutists).

Because numbers – critical masses – matter, times change. About polities such as ours, it seems reasonable to think that a forward-looking legislature might responsibly decide that the only likely medium-term constructive alternative to forbidding immigration by persons unwilling to renounce their religion's core theologico-political and numbers-dependent drive to impose political and legal domination will foreseeably prove to be the *state-promoted* introduction – as is beginning to be ventured in France, Germany, and the United Kingdom – of an emasculated version of that religion, supervised by state instrumentalities responsible for selecting the teachers and preachers of that highly distinctive religion in the hope of watering down its inbuilt focus on domination, violence, and submission, its division of the world into the world of submission and the world of war, its public and private subjection of women, and other features that (so the legislature might judge) make it at best inassimilable and at worst a clear and mounting danger to the public good. If the latter alternative (a state-sponsored form of that religion) is to be judged permanently unavailable here, because of a plain "establishment of religion," still the resort to it by centrist European governments may go some way toward showing a compelling state interest in not leaving this religion and its followers to their own devices, and thus surmounting the bar raised by the beguiling but curious doctrine of the Supreme Court that discrimination against one religion is (as Greenawalt seems implicitly to contend) not only unfair but also an establishment of all the others (and of irreligion?).

[52] Adam Winkler, "Fatal in Theory and Strict in Fact: An Empirical Analysis of Strict Scrutiny in the Federal Courts," *Vanderbilt Law Review* 59 (2006), 793 at 860–862.

Part II

Historical Interpretations

4 Religious Exercise and Establishment in Early America

Glenn A. Moots

The free exercise of religion protected by the First Amendment, together with its prohibition of national establishment, reflected a long debate in the century and a half preceding the amendment's ratification. The debate over religious liberty and church–state authority in America was first waged at the colonial and provincial levels. This chapter chronicles the diverse approaches to religious liberty and church–state authority in the colonies prior to ratification of the Bill of Rights.

Fundamental Political Questions

While every polity has confronted the question of religion's role in the formation of the good ruler and the good citizen, polities made up of Christians confront additional challenges. In the Bible, Jesus and the Apostles assert that the scope and authority of the church stand apart from, and may even contend against, civil authority (e.g., Matthew 22:21, John 19:11, Acts 5:29, Hebrews 11:23). This idea of dual ecclesiastical/civil authority has been contested throughout church history, particularly during the Investiture Controversy of the eleventh century and the Protestant Reformation that began in the sixteenth century.[1] Applied at the level of an individual soul, the idea of dual authority encouraged the seminal idea of "conscience" motivating many early modern advances in religious toleration or liberty.[2]

[1] For a discussion of these events as reformulations of dual authority, see Harold J. Berman, *Law and Revolution: The Formation of the Western Legal Tradition* (Cambridge, MA: Harvard University Press, 1985) and Eugen Rossenstock-Huessy, *Out of Revolution: Autobiography of Western Man* (West Haven, VT: The Eugen Rossenstock-Huessy Fund, 1969).

[2] For a good example of how the Protestant idea of conscience, for example, separates civil and spiritual authority, see John Calvin, *Institutes of the Christian Religion*, trans. Henry Beveridge (Grand Rapids, MI: Wm. B. Eerdmans, 1989 [1559]), 3.19.15, 16 and 4.10.3 and 4.

Colonists not only shared concerns about protecting an individual's conscience, however; they also believed that Christian faith was conducive to, if not coterminous with, being a good citizen and a good ruler. Both the citizen and the magistrate were therefore expected to support religion. Religious toleration and liberty in America often reflected a desire to accommodate both goals: increase piety and faithfulness *while still respecting the believer's conscience*. Religious toleration and liberty therefore reflected not a *declining* interest in religion among Americans but instead an *intense but more diverse interest* in religion. Though there was indeed a rising temper of skepticism and heterodoxy in the Anglo-American eighteenth century, such ideas remained very much in the minority. Toleration and liberty owed very little to skepticism and much more to increased religiosity.

But while colonists desired to protect the private and public benefit of piety, they increasingly disagreed about what true piety meant. Greater diversity of religious interests and ideas, introduced both by immigration and by proliferating Protestant theologies, forced Americans to accept the idea of a civil sphere operating *despite* disagreement on religious questions. In states with an established religious tradition, such as Massachusetts or Virginia, toleration enabled worship by dissenters (albeit with varying degrees of restrictions) while still providing financial support for the established denomination. Over time, dissenters and nonconformists increasingly enjoyed *religious liberty*, meaning that there were no impositions on worship or ordination and that their taxes did not support a denomination to which they did not belong.

In true Anglo-American style, debates about toleration or liberty usually turned more on particular rights and liberties in law and the British constitution rather than to philosophical or theological arguments.[3] Though the most influential defenses of toleration or liberty published on both sides of the Atlantic were published by 1670, toleration officially flowered for Protestant nonconformists or dissenters beginning only in the 1690s. In other words, the force of tolerationist arguments does not appear to have compelled much immediate progress. By the 1690s, no new arguments for

[3] Thomas J. Curry, *The First Freedoms: Church and State in America to the Passage of the First Amendment* (New York: Oxford University Press, 1986), 93. I, like others, am deeply indebted to Curry's rich and careful chronicle. I am also indebted to James Hutson, *Church and State in America: The First Two Centuries* (New York: Cambridge University Press, 2008) for its broad sketch of religious liberty in colonial America.

toleration were being published; however, changing political dynamics (especially passage of the English Bill of Rights and Toleration Act in 1689), combined with demographic realities to force real change (at least for Protestant minorities).[4]

Precedent: Church and State in the Old World

The dominant legal paradigm for British colonies in North America was existing church–state relations in Britain. European civil authorities in the sixteenth and seventeenth centuries enjoyed a remarkable degree of authority over religious matters. Regardless of whether rulers wielded their power for the sake of piety, avarice, or expediency, the wide scope of their power over religious exercise was a precedent emigrating to America with the earliest English settlers. Furthermore, America was overwhelmingly Protestant, and Protestant rejection of papal authority in the sixteenth century actually necessitated *increased* civil authority over religion.[5] The notion of an autonomous church – in other words, a civil society silent or neutral on religious matters, and a magistrate without some responsibility for ecclesiastical matters – would have been either unknown or else held in contempt by most colonial Americans, especially those in the magisterial Protestant traditions (e.g., Congregational, Anglican, Presbyterian, and Lutheran). As one New England minister expressed it in the Stuart era of expanded toleration, unbounded toleration was "the first born of all abominations."[6]

Martin Luther is often cited as the earliest and most influential Protestant reformer, but Luther's influence on tolerationist arguments is speculative at best. Though Luther's early "two kingdoms" theology separated church and state in important ways, Luther himself did not become a champion of religious freedom. Like other early magisterial reformers, Luther did not want to be associated with what were then considered

[4] Andrew R. Murphy, *Conscience and Community: Revisiting Toleration and Religious Dissent in Early Modern England and America* (University Park, PA: The Pennsylvania State University Press, 2001), 124–128, 146–161.

[5] This was Luther's argument in *An den christlichen Adel deutscher Nation* (1520), his letter to the German nobility.

[6] Rev. Urian Oakes, *New England Pleaded With* (Cambridge, MA: Samuel Green, 1673), 54.

radical or revolutionary ideas.[7] Furthermore, Lutherans did not play a significant role in colonial American politics. Lutheranism was confined to German settlements; congregations also formed slowly, disconnected from one another, and were hampered by the absence of a seminary.[8]

Reformed Protestantism, not Lutheranism, influenced the earliest colonial approaches to religious toleration. Most Britons and Americans confessed some variant of a Reformed tradition. Reformed Protestant leaders from the continent (e.g., John Calvin, Theodore Beza, Henry Bullinger, Peter Martyr Vermigli, and Martin Bucer) influenced British Protestants by their own example (in Protestant polities such as Geneva, Zurich, or Strasburg) and through personal correspondence, popular publications, and at teaching posts in England.[9] English bishops (including Thomas Cranmer) looked to continental reformers for direction in reforming the Church of England, and so did nonconformists and dissenters resisting religious uniformity. Britons brought these diverse opinions with them to North America.[10]

Unlike later sects within Protestantism (e.g., Baptists or Quakers), most early Protestant reformers on the continent and Britain desired to partner with civil magistrates in advancing piety: hence the appellation "magisterial Protestants." Drawing from Isaiah 49:23, almost all Anglo-American Protestants in the magisterial tradition – even after the American Revolution – asserted that magistrates were to serve as "nursing fathers" to the church. That is, churches looked for legal and financial support from the civil magistrate, including prosecution of religious dissenters. Even after toleration and liberty advanced, and financial support waned, the

[7] Nicholas P. Miller, *The Religious Roots of the First Amendment: Dissenting Protestants and the Separation of Church and State* (New York: Oxford University Press, 2012), 15–48. Miller argues that while Luther himself did not champion toleration or religious liberty in principle, his ideas did inspire later advocates of toleration. For Luther's own intolerance of radical Protestants, see his *Wider die Mordischen und Reubischen Rotten der Bawren* (1525).

[8] American Lutherans were not effectively networked or organized until the 1740s. Even by 1790, Lutheran congregations claimed only 25,000 formal members. See Mark A. Granquis, "Lutherans in America," in *Oxford Research Encyclopedia of American History*, accessed June 3, 2017, http://americanhistory.oxfordre.com/view/10.1093/acrefore/9780199329175.001.0001/acrefore-9780199329175-e-381.

[9] Martyr and Bucer had appointments at Oxford and Cambridge respectively – both of them approved by Archbishop Cranmer.

[10] Diarmaid MacCulloch, "The Church of England and International Protestantism, 1530–1570," in *The Oxford History of Anglicanism, Volume I: Reformation and Identity, c. 1520–1662*, ed. Anthony Milton (New York: Oxford University Press, 2017), 326–332.

"nursing father" might still be expected to punish public blasphemy or working on the Sabbath, for example.[11]

Magisterial Protestants distanced themselves as much as possible from those they viewed as "radical reformers," especially those Anabaptists who had threatened to pull down existing civil authority. Protestant radicalism inspired the German Peasants' War (1524–1525) and the Münster Rebellion (1535–1536), and both were crushed with savage violence by civil authorities. The idea of the "nursing father" considered such rebellions equivalent to patricide. Though most Anabaptists were pious, peaceful believers who denied the possibility of a Christian political order and desired to separate from what they considered a secular world, a minority of radicals lingered in Protestant memory for centuries. "Anabaptist," like "Papist," became an epithet for Protestants to use against one's opponents, and religious toleration was associated with Anabaptism because they opposed the idea of Christendom and a church–state partnership.[12]

Protestant confessional statements written after 1527 implicitly referenced and rebutted Anabaptist rejection of any church–state partnership. The Second Helvetic Confession, written by Henry Bullinger of Zurich, assigned to the magistrate not only the duty of preserving public peace but also "the preaching of the truth and sincere faith" and "root[ing] out lies and all superstition, together with all impiety and idolatry." The magistrate was to "defend" the church. Bullinger's scope of public peace was not confined to the narrow range of life and property – as Thomas Jefferson would have defined it, for example.[13] The magistrate was to guard against threats to *spiritual* peace as well: false doctrine, impiety, heresy, or blasphemy. Chapter 30 of Bullinger's Second Helvetic Confession commands the magistrate, "Let him draw this sword of God against all malefactors, seditious persons, thieves, murderers, oppressors, blasphemers, perjured persons, and all those whom God has commanded him to punish and even to execute." Such appointing of *civil* authority over church affairs, also

[11] See, for example, Rev. John Hancock, *Rulers Should Be Benefactors* (Boston: B. Green, 1722).

[12] See the Schleitheim Confession (1527) for a statement of Anabaptist beliefs.

[13] Jefferson argued, "The legitimate powers of government extend to such acts only as are injurious to others. But it does me no injury for my neighbor to say there are twenty gods, or no god. It neither picks my pocket nor breaks my leg." Thomas Jefferson, *Notes on the State of Virginia*, ed. William Peden (Chapel Hill: University of North Carolina Press, 1955), 159.

found in Erastianism or Marsilianism, was a response to *papal* claims of authority over civil affairs.

The Erastian position is evident in the Thirty-Nine Articles (1571) of the Church of England. Article 37 assigns considerable authority to the "Queen's Majesty," specifically "chief power ... ecclesiastical or civil." The monarch's power is not "subject to any foreign jurisdiction," an obvious reference to the pope.[14] The magistrate did not have clerical power to "minister by word or sacrament," but did possess a prerogative similar to that enjoyed by rulers in the Old Testament.[15] Prescriptions of both Bullinger and the Thirty-Nine Articles, therefore, evince a stubborn fear of ecclesiastical authority asserting itself against civil authority as well as a clear charge to the magistrate to govern religious affairs. One Church of England bishop summarized the standing opinion thus: "In a word, all mankind must be under one obedience and one authority."[16] Religious supremacy was reflected in the Clarendon Code (1661–1665) passed by Parliament after the Restoration (1660), asserting Anglican supremacy over dissenting faiths. Aided further by the Act of Toleration (1689) and the Act of Union (1707), the Church of England therefore enjoyed significant legal advantages in America thanks to its partnership with the monarch, bishops, and Parliament. Where the Church of England did not enjoy advantages in America (such as in New England or the Carolinas), circumstances (e.g., lack of clergy or low popular adherence) overwhelmed legal prerogative.

An alternative to this robust civil supremacy in England and Zurich was prescribed by John Calvin and Theodore Beza in Geneva. While Genevan magistrates did suppress "stubborn heretics" by execution (most prominently, Michael Servetus) or exile (Jerome Bolsec), and its consistory

[14] Civil affairs were also addressed in Articles 36, 38, and 39. Under Edward VI, the first great Protestant monarch, this assertion of supremacy was much shorter: "The king of England is supreme head in earth, next under Christ, of the church of England and Ireland." Pope Pius V's excommunication of Elizabeth in 1570 was a *de facto* call for revolution in England because it released English Catholics from their civil oaths and made them liable to excommunication if they obeyed an excommunicated ruler. Bullinger's subsequent defense of Elizabeth raised his stock even further in the Church of England.

[15] Thomas Rogers, *The Catholic Doctrine of the Church of England, An Exposition of the Thirty-Nine Articles:* ed. J.J.S. Perowne. Publications of the Parker Society (Cambridge: Cambridge University Press, 1854 [1586]), 40:338–339.

[16] Gilbert Burnet, *An Exposition of the Thirty Nine Articles of the Church of England by Gilbert, Bishop of Sarum*, ed. James R. Page (New York: D. Appleton & Company, 1842), 498–505, 505–506.

concerned itself with questions of public morality, Calvin asserted the autonomous right of *churches* to discipline members for scandal or heterodoxy. Bullinger, by contrast, did not assert such a right. According to Calvin, not only were magistrates *not exempt* from such discipline, but they should even *desire* to submit themselves to ecclesiastical authority should they engage in scandalous conduct.[17] While Calvin's ideal church–state relationship is not entirely clear (many of his desired reforms were blocked by Geneva's civil authorities), he did encourage distinguishing civil from ecclesiastical authority.[18] Calvin's and Beza's Genevan model influenced many Puritans in England and America. As far as many English bishops and rulers were concerned, however, there was no difference between Puritans and "Papists" because each made civil authority "very precarious and feeble" by not also giving it ecclesiastical supremacy.[19] Puritans in New England feared extremes of ecclesiastical tyranny or anarchy. Given a laboratory in North America, they wrestled with the proper relationship of church and state.

Not only did these two visions of church–state authority (civil supremacy versus limited ecclesiastical autonomy) contend with one another in America, denominations and sects arose that rejected the "magisterial" tradition altogether. Most prominent among these groups were the Quakers and Baptists who, together with other minority sects, catalyzed legal steps toward transatlantic toleration. Charles II's Declaration of Indulgence (1672) and James II's in 1687 and 1688, though short-lived in giving Protestant nonconformists and dissenters (and Catholics) toleration, were no doubt seen as prudent reactions to the proliferation of Protestant sects.

As for Catholics in the English North America, English fear and loathing of "popery" frustrated almost every attempt at toleration for them, except for a brief time in Maryland, then in Pennsylvania and Rhode Island. Catholics would have enjoyed great toleration if Protestants had not forced retraction in Charles's case and deposition in James's case. Stuart attempts at enlarged toleration for Catholics failed thanks to Protestant insistence on oaths of supremacy and allegiance that limited the political and religious rights of Catholics. As part of these oaths, officeholders were obliged to reject transubstantiation, affirm the Trinity (a move directed not at

[17] Calvin, *Institutes of the Christian Religion*, 4.3.6, 4.12.1–7. [18] Ibid., 4.10.9, 4.11.3.
[19] Rogers, *The Catholic Doctrine*, 338–339.

Catholics but Quakers), and receive communion according to the *Book of Common Prayer.*

While the Act of Toleration (1689), passed in the wake of the Glorious Revolution, eased the crueler persecution of Protestant dissenters and nonconformists on both sides of the Atlantic, it was advanced largely for economic and political motives and opposed by the Church of England. Indeed, Catholics saw their religious rights and liberties limited further, along with their right to vote or hold office. Dissenting or nonconforming Protestants enjoyed a greater foundation for their religious rights and liberties, but their political rights were still precarious.[20]

New England

The Puritan Challenge in New England

The most famous, and perhaps most misunderstood, tale of religious liberty in America begins in New England. New England consisted of five colonies (Massachusetts Bay, Plymouth, Connecticut, New Haven, and New Hampshire) settled mostly by Puritans.[21] They disagreed about the appropriate degree of separation from the Church of England, but they all desired to effect significant reform in it. Before coming to America, they opposed civil or royal supremacy when it blocked their desired reforms.[22] Indeed, King James I famously summarized the civil implications of Puritan ecclesiology in 1604 when he said, "No bishop, no King." Nevertheless, Puritans readily summoned the authority of the magistrate, especially in the New World, when it was to their advantage.[23] In New England, Puritans could

[20] Compared to the toleration ordered by Charles and James, the Revolution of 1688 was a considerable step backward. See Murphy, *Conscience and Community*, 157–161.

[21] Plymouth was eventually merged with Massachusetts Bay. New Haven was eventually merged with Connecticut. New Hampshire was formally established after the Restoration.

[22] For example, Congregational founders Robert Browne and Henry Barrow advanced reforms without civil approval and threatened magistrates with discipline for their religious opinions.

[23] Congregationalists William Bradshaw and Henry Jacob, for instance, argued for self-government by congregations, and against episcopacy, by arguing that bishops had usurped the rights of the king. Michael P. Winship, *Godly Republicanism: Puritans, Pilgrims, and a City on a Hill* (Cambridge, MA: Harvard University Press, 2012), 76–80, 83–84. English dissenters also defended civil supremacy against episcopal authority when the latter was used against them, as in the case of Archbishop Parker's *Advertisements.*

no longer protest the establishment as they had in England. They *were* the establishment. Against the Puritan religious establishment stood dissenting individuals (e.g., Roger Williams or Anne Hutchinson) and sects (most notably Baptists and Quakers).

John Cotton and the Puritan Way

Debates over religious toleration in New England prompted some of the seventeenth century's most articulate and lengthy statements regarding establishment and dissent. These debates were often motivated by New England colonies instituting a form of ecclesiastical establishment funded by compulsory tithing paid to Congregational ministers. Each colony also obliged church attendance by law, though membership and access to sacraments required evidence of conversion.[24]

Motives for religious establishment in New England are reflected in a document that was part legal code and part constitution, John Cotton's *Abstract of the Laws of New England.* Cotton was one of the most important Puritan leaders in New England. A minister educated by Puritans at Emmanuel College, Cambridge, Cotton had served as vicar of St. Botolph's in Lincolnshire for twenty years and became a popular and influential voice for nonconformity in England. Cotton was not a "separatist" as such: He did not insist on full separation from the Church of England, but his opinions did eventually elicit a summons to appear before the High Commission Court for his nonconformity. Though Cotton had previously declined an invitation to join the colonists across the Atlantic, he faced an English church and state increasingly averse to leniency for nonconforming Puritans such as himself. He and his wife soon fled to Massachusetts Bay Colony.

Though proposed by Cotton for Massachusetts Bay, the *Abstract* was adopted by New Haven instead. However, Cotton's provisions are reflected in two founding legal documents of Massachusetts Bay: *The Body of Liberties* (1641) and the *Laws and Liberties of Massachusetts* that succeeded it in 1648. Cotton's *Abstract* came to be published in 1641 as *Moses His Judicials*, a title evincing that these colonies were not simply new Englands; they were also to be new Israels. As in Old Testament Israel, there could be no religious liberty because Puritans believed that divine blessing was conditional on punishing blasphemy and heresy. Because

[24] One exception to this was Portsmouth, New Hampshire.

Cotton drew from the books of Deuteronomy, Exodus, and Leviticus, he believed his code to be superior to "all the municipal laws and statutes of any of the Gentile nations and corporations under the cope of Heaven." He cited Exodus 32:25 and 32:27 in support of giving the general court, the governor, and his counselors the power to "preserve religion." Cotton's criminal code likewise drew from Old Testament civil and moral law to prescribe capital punishment for blasphemy (particularly atheism), perjury, slavery, idolatry, witchcraft, rebellion by children, rape, treason, prostitution, and "profaning of the Lord's Day." Lesser penalties included corporal punishment or fines.[25]

In principle, Cotton and the Puritans adopted a model more like Calvin's and less like England's brand of Erastianism; they supported greater separation of ecclesiastical and civil authority than existed in England. Ecclesiastical leaders did not hold civil office: Cotton argued that such power would make a "beast" of the church. The franchise and office-holding were limited to church members, but such limitations, Cotton argued, *did not* invite ecclesiastical subversion of civil authority.[26] In Massachusetts Bay, even though magistrates could be subject to church discipline, such discipline did not necessarily disqualify them from holding office. In contrast with England, Puritans also did not create standing ecclesiastical courts with authority over civil matters such as marriage or estates. However, Puritans went *further* than Calvin in separating church and state; no civil-ecclesiastical consistories regulated morality as they did in Geneva or Scotland. It is also important to note that Puritans did not aggressively pursue heretics so long as they kept their opinions to themselves. Relatively speaking then, New England was generally progressive.

These were baby steps away from British or continental precedent, but they in no way meant religious toleration, let alone liberty. Puritans understood liberty not as a positive liberty to do what one wanted, nor was it a negative liberty to be "left alone." To do whatever one desired tempted what John Winthrop had criticized as "natural liberty" – an equal freedom to do evil or good. Such natural liberty, Winthrop argued, resisted authority and made men worse than beasts. What Winthrop approved

[25] Even tolerant colonies such as Pennsylvania, for example, did not consider Sabbath-breaking, atheism, or blasphemy to be protected by liberty of conscience. Instead, each was considered a threat to good civil and personal conduct.

[26] John Cotton, *An Exposition upon the Thirteenth Chapter of the Revelation* (London: 1655), 17–18.

instead was what he called "civil" or "federal" liberty.[27] Law governed federal liberty and protected freedom to do only what is good and honest. Such liberty, Winthrop asserted, is the only appropriate Christian liberty.[28] Similarly, Cotton argued that freedom is the right to assert the liberty of conscience not in *any way* that one pleased, but only insofar as liberty was *rightly informed* by scripture. According to this Puritan concept of liberty, to assert an opinion contrary to scripture was to exercise a right that did not exist; it was to sin against one's own conscience, and there was no right to sin against one's own conscience.[29] Persecution by authorities was therefore not the punishment of *any* dissenting, unpopular, or minority opinion. Unlawful libertine opinions, morally and legally speaking, should not be held in the first place. Therefore, punishing such opinions did not constitute "persecution."

In the Puritan mind, therefore, there was a limit to the extent of liberty. "There is never peace," Cotton wrote, "where full liberty is not given, nor never stable peace where *more* than full liberty is granted."[30] Too much liberty, *especially* the liberty inviting the "infection" of impiety, idolatry, or blasphemy, was poison; and no society was at liberty to poison itself. Cotton explicitly proscribed this "soul-stealing danger of blasphemy, a liberty that men never had in the first place."[31] New England magistrates were further encouraged by their idea that while church and state were no longer one (as they were in the Old Testament), the Old Testament legal and moral codes were no less relevant for informing civil law.[32] Finally, Puritans feared that disorder in the church would become disorder in the state. Cotton concluded, "Purity, preserved in the church, will

[27] Federal was a word derived from the Latin for "covenant," so this was essentially "covenantal" liberty.

[28] John Winthrop's address at this trial, known as his "Little Speech on Liberty," delivered on July 5, 1645.

[29] John Cotton, *The Answer of Mr. John Cotton of Boston in New-England Against the Aforesaid Arguments Against Persecution for the Cause of Conscience,* in Roger Williams, *The Bloudy Tenent of Persecution, for Cause of Conscience, discussed, in a Conference Between Truth and Peace* (London, 1644), 41–54.

[30] Cotton, *An Exposition,* 73.

[31] Ibid., 71–72; John Cotton, *The Bloudy Tenent, Washed and Made White in the Bloud of the Lambe* (London: Printed by M. Symmons for H. Allen, 1647), 34–35, https://catalog.hathitrust.org/Record/100872567.

[32] Cotton, *The Bloudy Tenent, Washed,* 126.

preserve well-ordered liberty in the people, and both of them establish well-balanced authority in the magistrate."[33]

Though the church had only spiritual weapons (including synods, the Bible, or church censure) against blasphemy or heresy, magistrates must ensure that such weapons were deployed, and that religious differences did not undermine the civil order. Magistrates did not control the churches, but they must act when religious differences threatened public order. While the *primary* responsibility of the civil magistrate encompassed secular matters such as "disposing of men's goods or lands, lives, or liberties, tributes, customs, worldly honors, and inheritances," that did not preclude civil authorities addressing religious matters of a "second sort" affecting the civil peace, however: "the establishment of pure religion, in doctrine, worship, and government, according to the word of God."[34] Cotton's reasoning was clear enough: If laws are to protect the public good, and religion is essential to the public good, why would the magistrate and the laws not concern themselves with religion?[35]

The Challenge of Roger Williams

Roger Williams, who immigrated to Massachusetts Bay from England in 1631, was unconvinced that political well-being necessitated spiritual conformity. His extended argument with Cotton over religious liberty has made him, among modern scholars at least, the most celebrated religious dissenter of colonial America. Whereas Cotton has gone from great fame among his contemporaries to relative infamy today, Williams progressed from infamy among his contemporaries to obscurity and finally to great fame beginning in the nineteenth century.[36] Williams' fame has even

[33] John Cotton, "Cotton to William Fiennes, Lord Saye and Sele," in *The Correspondence of John Cotton*, ed. Sargent Bush, Jr. (Chapel Hill: University of North Carolina Press, 2001), 246–247. Cotton and Winthrop, or Puritan leadership in general, did not always agree. Their disagreement was certainly evident in the trial of Anne Hutchinson, for example. See Michael P. Winship, *Making Heretics: Militant Protestantism and Free Grace in Massachusetts, 1636–1641* (Princeton, NJ: Princeton University Press, 2002).

[34] John Cotton, *The Keyes of the Kingdom of Heaven, and Power Thereof, according to the Word of God* (Boston: S.K. Whipple & Co., 1852 [1644]), 95.

[35] Cotton, *The Bloudy Tenent, Washed*, 67–68, 151. Magistrates would govern ecclesiastical questions with clerical guidance, however. Ibid., 95–97.

[36] Dozens of biographies and celebrations of Williams have been published, most recently by John M. Barry, Martha Nussbaum, and Teresa Bejan.

eclipsed William Penn's, even though Thomas Jefferson (a great American champion of religious liberty) knew nothing of Williams but called Penn "the greatest lawgiver in the world."[37] It is especially ironic that Jefferson knew nothing of Williams, however, because it was Williams who first proposed a "wall of separation." In 1644, Williams wrote, "When they [the Church] have opened a gap in the hedge or wall of separation between the garden of the church and the wilderness of the world, God hath ever broke down the wall itself, removed the Candlestick, etc., and made His Garden a wilderness as it is this day."[38]

Though Williams has been lionized as a proto-liberal or a man ahead of his time, he was neither.[39] Williams' prescription for the strict separation of church and state (or, as he cast it, the church and the world) was rooted in his conviction that the world was , from a religious or spiritual perspective, a lost cause. God separates the church to save it from the corruptions of the world.[40] Cotton placed more spiritual value and hope in the world than Williams did. Whereas Cotton hoped to protect the world in part by protecting the integrity of the church, Williams hoped to protect the integrity of the church by essentially *abandoning* the world to its corruption. Against Cotton's fear of religious or spiritual infection of those outside and inside the church (because of lax civil enforcement of blasphemy or heresy) Williams simply replied of those outside, "Dead men cannot be infected."[41] Those inside were best protected by the church keeping to its own business and leaving the civil sphere to its own business.

[37] Thomas Jefferson to Peter Stephen Duponceau, November 16, 1825, accessed June 28, 2017, http://rotunda.upress.virginia.edu/founders/default.xqy?keys=FOEA-print-04-02-02-5663.

[38] Roger Williams, "Mr. Cotton's Letter Lately Printed, Examined and Answered," in *The Complete Writings of Roger Williams* (New York: Russell & Russell Inc., 1963), 1:108.

[39] For examples of this hagiography, see Vernon Parrington, *Liberalism, Puritanism and the Colonial Mind: Main Currents in American Thought* (New Brunswick, NJ: Transaction Publishers, 2011 [1927]), 62; Samuel Hugh Brockunier, *Irrepressible Democrat: Roger Williams* (New York: The Ronald Press Company, 1940).

[40] Roger Williams, "Mr. Cotton's Letter," in *The Complete Writings of Roger Williams*, 1:108.

[41] Williams, *Bloudy Tenent*, 125, 111–113. In contrast to my argument, Teresa M. Bejan calls Williams' scheme "evangelical toleration wherein 'civil life' would prepare nonbelievers for conversion." Bejan, "'When the Word of the Lord Runs Freely,' Roger Williams and Evangelical Toleration" in *The Lively Experiment: Religious Toleration in America from Roger Williams to the Present*, ed. Chris Beneke and Christopher S. Grenda (New York: Rowman & Littlefield, 2015), 65–81.

While modern Americans might therefore presume they have found a kindred soul in Williams, a separatist Puritan, they would be wrong. Williams would have certainly opposed public school prayer, but not because he feared imposition on tender young consciences. Rather, he considered prayers by unconverted persons to be "forced worship" that is "hypocritical stench" in God's nostrils.[42] So while Supreme Court Justice Hugo Black conveniently cited Williams to oppose to school prayer in *Engel* v. *Vitale* (1962), Black surely did not share Williams' conviction that a national church was the "Whore of Babylon" depicted in Revelation 17.[43]

Williams was certainly progressive in his reasoning about separating church and state, but the actual influence of his ideas is speculative at best. The Cotton–Williams debate, which lasted seven years and stretched across three long polemics, was published in London and read on both sides of the Atlantic. Williams may have had some influence on British advocates for toleration, but he was inconsequential for the progression of religious toleration in early America.[44] If Americans remembered Williams at all in the decades after his death, it was scornfully.[45] If not for Baptist minister Isaac Backus, a champion for toleration who pressed Williams' ideas into service beginning in 1773, Williams might have been forgotten.[46] William G. McLoughlin, an eminent historian of Baptist attempts to gain toleration, spoke to Williams' dubious legacy when he wrote, "Those who fought hardest for religious freedom in Massachusetts, Connecticut, Vermont, and New Hampshire considered Rhode Island an embarrassment rather than an asset to their cause."[47] It is therefore absurd to assert, as Supreme Court Justice Thomas Clark did in the majority opinion in *Abington School District* v. *Schempp* (1963), that Williams, along with

[42] Roger Williams to Major John Wilson and [Connecticut] Governor Thomas Prence, Providence, June 22, 1670, in *The Correspondence of Roger Williams*, ed. Glenn W. LaFantasie (Providence and London: Brown University Press/University Press of New England, 1988), 2: 617–618.

[43] *Engel* v. *Vitale*, 370 US 421 (1962), 434 n. 20.

[44] Williams arguably had some legacy among English tolerationists, however, including Sir Henry Vane the younger (1613–1662) who helped Williams secure the Rhode Island patent.

[45] Miller, *The Religious Roots of the First Amendment*, 61.

[46] LeRoy Moore, Jr., "Religious Liberty: Roger Williams and the Revolutionary Era," *Church History* 34, no. 1 (1965): 57–75.

[47] William G. McLoughlin, *Soul Liberty: The Baptists' Struggle in New England, 1630–1833* (Hanover, NH: University Press of New England, 1991), 20.

James Madison and Thomas Jefferson, was influential not only on the Federal Constitution but also on constitutions of the states.[48] Despite only the most speculative traces of Williams' influence, however, it is important to understand his groundbreaking and powerful arguments – even if only to appreciate how they have become popular in hindsight or paralleled similar tolerationist arguments.

When Williams arrived in America, his radical separatist ideas became evident when he refused a call to become pastor of the First Church of Boston – a post that Cotton later accepted. The church at Boston, Williams believed, had not sufficiently repented of (separated from) fellowship with the Church of England. When Williams eventually secured an appointment in 1634 to the pulpit in Salem in Plymouth, he publicly advanced a variety of political complaints that got him banished from Massachusetts Bay: Williams denied that the king (whom Williams considered unconverted and a "horn of the Whore of Babylon's beast") had authority to grant charters to Native American lands.[49] Williams also resisted what he considered polluted and hypocritical worship: the prayers of "unconverted" children, hearing of sermons by unconverted persons, and (most significantly) the administering of civil oaths. Williams was directly attacking the colonies' political order because unconverted persons did not yet have equal political rights (including the right to vote) and stood outside the authority of ministers because they had not entered church covenants. Their loyalty was bound only by civil oaths. If administration of these civil oaths to unconverted persons was forbidden because it constituted a form of hypocritical worship, how could their civil loyalty be secured? Williams also refused to acknowledge the civil magistrate's authority in all matters related to the "First Table" of the law – those commandments dealing with God rather than man. Expressing these and other complaints, and exploiting whatever avenue of authority or protest he thought expedient, Williams was soon counseled by ministers and magistrates to cease. Williams refused and was banished in 1635 not for his religious opinions as such, but for the way in which they disturbed (as Cotton called it) the "civil and holy peace."[50]

48 *Abington School District* v. *Schempp*, 374 US 203 (1963), 214.

49 Williams established good relations with Native Americans and respected their culture and government. His first published book was a study of Indian language and society titled *A Key into the Language of America* (1643).

50 John Cotton, "A Letter of Mr. Cottons, Teacher of the Church in Boston, in New-England, to Mr. Williams, a Preacher There," 1643, in *The Complete Writings of Roger Williams*, ed.

The Bloudy Tenent *Controversy*

Williams did not disseminate his full argument for religious liberty until almost ten years after his banishment when he hoped to deter the progress of the Presbyterian-leaning Westminster Assembly in London and also rebut a Congregational manifesto written by Cotton and Massachusetts Bay ministers titled "A Model of Church and Civil Power" (1644). Both groups opposed religious toleration. The Westminster Confession, for example, charged the civil magistrate in Chapter 23 to "suppress all blasphemies and heresies" as well as "all corruptions and abuses in worship and discipline." Williams' attack on what he called the "bloudy tenent of persecution" elicited Cotton's attempt in 1647 to "wash it white in the bloud of the lambe" (as Cotton's title asserted). Williams followed in 1652 with a lengthy polemic that Cotton's attempt to wash the "bloudy tenent" in fact made it "yet more bloudy" – particularly with the blood of Christians.

Williams argued that civil prosecution of dissenters, no matter how well-intentioned, committed two errors. The first error was a typological or interpretive error: Persecution confused the sword of the magistrate in Israel (used before Christ) with the sword of the Word (used after Christ).[51] The second error was that persecution potentially invested *all* civil rulers (even pagan or heathen nations) with control over religion.[52] Such power would not only disturb the civil peace (regardless of who was persecuted) but also (in the case of persecuted Christians) invite the judgment of God.[53] Unlike Cotton, Williams did not believe the example of ancient Israel to be relevant for polities after the coming of Christ; therefore, while blasphemy and idolatry did not invite divine judgment, murder of true Christians did. Williams' alternative to the idea of the New Israel was a polity rooted only in "civil and moral duties."[54] Pagans were capable of constructing a perfectly adequate civil order, Williams argued, wherein bodies and goods (rather than souls) are protected.[55] After Christ's first

Rueben A. Guild (New York: James H. Trumbull, 1963) 1:298. A timely warning from Winthrop enabled Williams to flee to Narragansett Bay rather than be forced to return to England. In fact, Winthrop and Cotton were relatively moderate in their judgment of dissenters compared with New England Puritans Thomas Dudley or Thomas Shepard, for example.

[51] Williams, *Bloudy Tenent*, 251–252. [52] Ibid., 249–250.

[53] Ibid., 6, 43, 60–62, 247. Roger Williams, *Bloody Tenent Yet More Bloody* (London: Giles Calvert, 1652), 71–72, 170, 179, 180, 189.

[54] Ibid., 413–415. [55] Ibid., 5.

coming, the church *alone* had spiritual responsibility; polities were merely civil.[56] To enforce the First Table of the Ten Commandments was to disobey Christ's command in Mark 12:17 to "Render unto Caesar the things that are Caesar's."[57]

Rhode Island

Williams' solution was established in a sixth New England colony, Rhode Island. The Providence Agreement (1637), an early founding document, was akin to the Mayflower Compact, but it included neither an oath nor explicit theological language. Its adherents promised only "active and passive obedience to all such orders or agreements as shall be made for the public good . . . in civil things." Likewise, the revised patent for Rhode Island (1643) made no mention of religion. When a royal charter was secured for Rhode Island (incorporating settlements in Providence Plantation, Newport, Portsmouth, and Warwick) in 1663, it referred to the colony as a "lively experiment" granting "full liberty in religious concernments." This legal arrangement would enable "true piety rightly grounded upon gospel principles" and secure "the free exercise and enjoyment of all civil and religious rights." The charter stated that no one was to be "molested, punished, disquieted, or called in question, for any differences in opinion in matters of religion." All would be free to enjoy "their own judgments and consciences, in matters of religious concernments" provided that they did not disturb civil peace or promote "licentiousness and profaneness."[58]

Toleration did not result in political concord, however. The colony not only became a refuge for dissenters from Massachusetts Bay (Samuel Gorton and Anne Hutchinson were two of the most prominent), and eventually Quakers and Baptists, it also attracted malcontents and subversives. Other colonies either paid it no mind or else held it in contempt. This meant that Rhode Island was either misunderstood (some presumed the colony to have an established church) or considered scandalous. Dutch

[56] Ibid., 160, 281, 317–321. [57] Ibid., 45; Williams, *Bloody Tenent Yet More Bloody*, 414.

[58] Both documents are available in Francis Newton Thorpe, *Federal and State Constitutions Colonial Charters, and Other Organic Laws of the States, Territories, and Colonies Now or Heretofore Forming the United States of America Compiled and Edited Under the Act of Congress of June 30, 1906* (Washington, DC: Government Printing Office, 1909), 3209, 3211.

minister Johannes Megapolensis summed up the opinions of many when he referred to Rhode Island as the "latrine" of New England.

Nevertheless, Williams' "lively experiment" was a relative haven of toleration for Protestants, and even for Jews. Though Jews could not vote, hold office, or perform wedding ceremonies, the first American synagogue was established in Newport and is notable for receiving a letter from George Washington in 1790 praising religious liberty.[59] Quakers enjoyed Williams' (and the Rhode Island government's) toleration but not Williams's personal approval. Catholics also enjoyed toleration, though they could not worship publicly nor vote in the colony after 1716. They were later excluded from holding public office and then subject to oaths of allegiance during the French and Indian War. Restrictions on Catholic rights and liberties were not unique to Rhode Island, however. Intolerance of Catholics was characteristic of almost all colonies after the 1689 Act of Toleration.

Tolerance and Intolerance Elsewhere in New England

Beginning in the 1640s and 1650s, the original four New England colonies began to contend with groups that advanced toleration far more than Williams did: Quakers and Baptists. Founded by George Fox (1624–1691) in England around 1647, the Society of Friends (or Quaker) movement urged believers to look to an "inner light" for direction. Quakers eschewed the authority of trained ministers, creeds, and confessions. Even scripture was not considered a final authority. They flouted not only orthodox Trinitarian theology but also many customs of both church (including the sacraments) and society; some were wont to disrupt the worship of non-Quakers. Some early Quakers even paraded naked in public to symbolize their spiritual nakedness before God. Edward Bond argues that given their reputation for disruption in England, there was good reason in the early years of their migration to America to worry about a "Quaker menace."[60] The English people hated Quakers at first, and Oliver

[59] George Washington to the Hebrew Congregation in Newport, Rhode Island, August 18, 1790, in *The Papers of George Washington, Presidential Series*, ed. Mark A. Mastromarino (Charlottesville: University Press of Virginia, 1996), 6: 284–286.

[60] John Norton argued against "destructiveness of the doctrine and practice of the Quakers unto religion, the churches of Christ, and Christian states" in *The Heart of N- England Rent at the Blasphemies of the Present Generation* (1659), 31.

Cromwell's relative indulgence of them may have even undermined his regime.

That loathsome reputation followed them to America, though their reputation gradually improved after the movement renounced violence.[61] When they began making evangelistic inroads in New England and elsewhere against traditional denominations, authorities pressed them hard.[62] Quakers were whipped and imprisoned, and their writings were burned. Beginning in 1656, Massachusetts Bay fined shipmasters who brought them. New Haven did likewise in 1657 (though they allowed Quakers to trade if they did not preach). New Haven fell in line with Massachusetts by 1658, and persecution of Quakers was politically popular in Plymouth. Connecticut was a bit gentler under the leadership of John Winthrop's son, however. Quakers were pragmatically drawn to the tolerant shores of Rhode Island, of course, though Massachusetts Bay threatened their neighbor with economic sanctions for providing refuge. When banished Quakers returned to Massachusetts Bay, leaders drew on the example of Solomon executing Shimei and threatened Quakers with the death penalty; four recalcitrant returning Quakers were hanged in 1660.[63] Besieged by Quaker appeals for intervention, Charles II ordered an end to the executions in 1661. The Massachusetts General Court repealed its death penalty but handed off whipping of Quakers to local officials.[64] New England Puritans, even Roger Williams, continued to contend against Quaker doctrine in print, but Quakers eventually won the right to establish their "meeting houses" by the 1680s.[65]

Baptists fought similar prejudice. Doctrinally and socially speaking, Baptists were not remotely like Quakers. Baptists at this time were essentially (Reformed) Congregationalists in doctrine who came to reject infant baptism. Also, with only a few exceptions, Baptists were not given to social disruption. Unlike Quakers, whose early petitions and protests aggravated civil authorities, Baptist protests and petitions were more winsome and

[61] Edward L. Bond, *Damned Souls in a Tobacco Colony: Religion in Seventeenth-Century Virginia* (Macon, GA: Mercer University Press, 2000), 172.

[62] Notable among them was William Coddington, who came over on the Arabella with Winthrop but later became a Quaker and appealed for Quaker liberty.

[63] 1 Kings 2:41–43.

[64] For a history of the Quakers, see Rufus Matthew Jones, *The Quakers in the American Colonies* (London: Macmillan and Company, 1911), 3–271.

[65] Roger Williams attacked Quaker beliefs in *George Fox digg'd out of his burrowes* (1672).

respectful.[66] However, the Baptists' refusal to baptize infants enabled critics to compare them to the aforementioned Anabaptists of the sixteenth century. Indeed, many in North America referred to Baptists as "Anabaptists," a confusion born of both malice and ignorance. The moniker was correct insofar as Baptists would "re-baptize" (the linguistic root of the term "Anabaptist") those previously baptized as infants. However, this re-baptism was not considered a *second* baptism; Baptists simply did not recognize infant baptism in the first place. Most importantly, Baptists did not subscribe to the Anabaptist Schleitheim Confession, but subscribed to Reformed confessions modified in areas concerning infant baptism or ecclesiastical polity. The label therefore served to slander by association.[67]

Because Baptists had shed blood fighting alongside Cromwell, they enjoyed increasing freedom in England; New England was a different story, however. At first, Baptists were able to find refuge only in Rhode Island. John Clarke, a Baptist physician, was responsible for securing and penning part of the Rhode Island charter, for example. When New England began to reconsider its intolerance of Baptists, Massachusetts Bay took advantage of the formation of the United Colonies (a mutual defense pact) to push for more stringent intolerance against Baptists. The General Court of Massachusetts voted in November 1644 to banish Baptists, and Puritan clergy pressed the court to hold firm against petitions to repeal the act. By 1645, deputies to the Plymouth General Court flirted with an idea to "allow and maintain full and free tolerance of religion to all men that would preserve the civil peace." The list excluded the usual heterodox suspects, "Turk [Muslim], Jew, Papist, Arian, Socinian, Nicolaytan, Familist, or any other," but did not exclude Baptists. This would have given Baptists toleration, but Governor William Bradford blocked a vote on the motion. However, through migration and evangelism and the sympathy of their

[66] For an excellent study of both groups and the struggle for toleration, see Carla Gardina Pestana, *Quakers and Baptists in Colonial Massachusetts* (New York: Cambridge University Press, 1991).

[67] Baptists rejected the comparison. The London Baptist Confession of Faith (1644) identifies itself as a doctrinal statement of "seven congregations or churches of Christ in London, which are commonly, but unjustly called Anabaptists." For similarities, compare the London Baptist Confession with Congregationalist confessional statements including the Cambridge Platform (1648) or the Savoy Declaration (1658).

neighbors, Baptists eventually settled into New England and achieved toleration.[68]

The last group to gain toleration in New England was the Anglicans, the tradition most advantaged elsewhere in North America. Puritan ministers in New England were technically Anglicans already as ordained ministers in the Church of England, but they did not worship according to the *Book of Common Prayer* and considered it, and episcopacy, odious. Charles sent commissioners to New England in 1664 to, among other things, secure toleration for worship according to the prayer book, to encourage public support for Anglican ministers, and to enable the franchise for Anglicans in Massachusetts. The commissioners were reasonably successful elsewhere, but not in Massachusetts Bay. Freedom from "prayer book worship" was, after all, arguably the first "freedom" that the Puritans had sought in braving the wilds of settlement, and they resisted every imposition on that freedom. When New England and New York were put under the rule of Sir Edmund Andros and the Dominion of New England (1686–1689), for example, the Old South Congregational Church chafed under the obligation to share its facilities with a Church of England minister. Hating such encroachments by their ecclesiastical archenemy, Massachusetts Bay ministers dug in for a long fight against Anglicanism throughout the eighteenth century, including resistance to missionaries from the Society for the Propagation of the Gospel in Foreign Parts, formed in 1701 to promote the Church of England in America.[69] Congregational clergy in New England, notably both Jonathan Mayhew and Charles Chauncy, fought hard against the establishment of an Anglican bishop in America, particularly in the decades before the American Revolution.

The greatest blow against religious intolerance and the Congregational establishment in New England fell, ironically enough, after the Revolution of 1688 that New England ministers hailed as a new dawn of Protestant freedom from "popery." With the Glorious Revolution came the Act of Toleration and new government charters for New England. When Connecticut's provincial government attempted to forbid Quakers or any other "notorious heretic," it found itself in violation of both the Act and its

[68] Michael P. Winship, *Hot Protestants: A History of Puritanism in England and America* (New Haven, CT: Yale University Press, 2018), 122, 239–240.

[69] John Frederick Woolverton, *Colonial Anglicanism in North America* (Detroit, MI: Wayne State University Press, 1984); Frederick V. Mills, Sr., *Bishops by Ballot: An Eighteenth-Century Ecclesiastical Revolution* (New York: Oxford University Press, 1978).

charter. Cruel or violent intolerance of Protestant dissenters in New England was forbidden. Nor could the franchise be confined to church members; it was extended to any Protestant who subscribed to the loyalty oath. Catholics, of course, remained stripped of many political and religious rights.

Unable to stop this wave of toleration forced from across the Atlantic, New England clergy not only fell in line but also changed their own narrative about religious freedom.[70] Sermons of New England ministers celebrated English rights and liberties (including a more robust liberty of conscience) while insisting that their old vision of a shining city on a hill had *not* been lost. Ministers increasingly retreated from doctrinal orthodoxy and toward virtue as proof of their faithfulness to their founders. Cotton Mather, one of the most influential and important intellectual leaders among Boston's clergy, considered Quakerism a damnable heresy but nevertheless extolled Quakers' "liberty of conscience" in a 1691 sermon and again at a Baptist ordination ceremony in 1717.[71] Connecticut passed its own toleration act in 1708. Within fifty years of the Act of Toleration, everything had changed. By 1747, it was remarked that Boston – once the great stronghold of Puritan Congregationalism – had, in addition to its eleven Congregational congregations (ten likely in fellowship with one another, one not), three "pretty large" Anglican congregations: two Baptist congregations, one Huguenot congregation, and one Quaker congregation. The observer of this new landscape remarked that even Papists "may be many," but they were "too conceal'd" for an "accurate accounting."[72]

All of that said, Congregationalist leaders in New England did not submit quietly to advancing religious toleration. Those who published criticism of Congregationalism and its treatment of dissenters (e.g., Thomas Maule and John Checkley) were arrested or fined. The provincial government of Massachusetts still mandated that each town select and pay a minister at public expense. In theory, a non-Congregationalist minister *could* receive that support, though it was evident to all that only Congregationalists

[70] See, for example, Rev. Peter Clark, *The Ruler's Highest Dignity, and the People's Truest Glory* (Boston: Printed by S. Kneeland, printer to the Honourable House of Representatives, 1739).

[71] Cotton Mather, *Little Flocks Guarded against Grievous Wolves* (Boston, MA: Benjamin Harris and John Allen, 1691).

[72] Frank Lambert, *The Founding Fathers and the Place of Religion in America*, (Princeton, NJ: Princeton University Press, 2003), 153–154.

would receive that support. Connecticut not only mandated tax support for Congregational churches but also adopted the Saybrook Platform (1708) that strengthened the authority of their Congregational churches. The province of New Hampshire featured a looser establishment, however. It obliged, but did not enforce, local taxation to support ministers. The province also exempted Quaker constables who, in good conscience, refused to collect support for other churches.

Competing denominations chafed at the remaining Congregational establishment. Anglicans did not object to religious establishment *in principle*; they enjoyed establishment in most of the colonies, after all. But they asserted that they, rather than Congregationalists, were entitled to such support in New England. When concessions were given to non-Congregationalist believers, it was often with petulant and scornful expressions about "alleged" or "professed" conflicts with conscience.[73] When Baptists were exempted from taxation to support Congregational worship, they had to procure certificates. This left them at the mercy of local administrators who were usually inclined to deploy any obstacle they could to delay approval. Only beginning in the 1730s could members of denominations dissenting from established Congregationalism (with conditions) be exempt from ministerial taxes used to support Congregational churches. Even Anglicans would eventually be able to support their own ministers with tax monies.

The Southern Colonies

Virginia

Though Virginia is sometimes contrasted with New England as having commercial rather than pious motives for colonization, the Anglicans who settled there felt no less called to establish their own version of Christendom – and Christendom meant establishment.[74] John Rolfe sounded like a New England Calvinist and compared himself to Caleb and Joshua when he wrote of the settlement in 1616: "God's hand hath

[73] Recall the previous discussion of Cotton or Winthrop on conscience.

[74] Studies of Protestant dissenters in Virginia include Henry Read McIlwaine, *The Struggle of Protestant Dissenters for Religious Toleration in Virginia* (Baltimore, MD: The Johns Hopkins University Press, 1894).

been mighty in the preservation thereof hitherto; what need we then to fear, but to go up at once as a peculiar people, marked and chosen by the finger of God, to possess it."[75] Charters issued to the Virginia Company of London in 1606, 1609, and 1612 express similar missionary zeal. Instructions given to civil leaders in 1578, 1584, and 1607 likewise instruct them to promote and provide for the Christian faith and the Church of England. *Articles, Laws, and Orders, Divine, Politic, and Martial* (1610), a document drawn up by military officers and imposed by the governor empowered by the Virginia Company of London, was a body of laws (though neither legislated nor enforced by a court) used to administer the colony of Jamestown. It was a law code as severe and Hebraic as anything established in New England, deploying Old Testament juridical ideas, mandating attendance at worship, and prescribing the death penalty for various violations of Old Testament civil or moral law. But unlike Cotton's *Abstract*, for example, *Articles, Laws, and Orders* did not make comparable provision for English rights or liberties.

The governing authorities of this royal colony decreed uniformity and made provision for Anglican ministers' salaries. Unlike the New England Puritans who followed Calvin in establishing some small distance between church and state, Virginia's Church of England was even more unified with civil authority. In declaring their support for the Church of England (and royalism) in 1643, the governor and assembly pledged their support to the "purity of the doctrine and unity of the church." Those who did not conform to the practices of the Church of England (including Puritans, Baptists, and Quakers) were expelled.[76] When Anglican uniformity was reestablished in England in 1662, and then again in 1693, Virginia law pressed nonconformists and dissenters even further. Attendance at Anglican worship became compulsory. Office-holding and voting privileged Anglicans above others. Ministers were forbidden to preach without episcopal ordination in England.[77] A December 1662 statute levied

[75] John Rolfe, "Virginia in 1616," in *Virginia: Four Personal Narratives*, Reprint Edition (New York: Arno Press, 1972), 113.

[76] Intolerance was viewed by its victims on all sides as inviting the judgment of God. John Easton in *A Relation of the Indian War, by Mr. Easton, of Rhode Island* (1675) asserted that mistreatment of Quakers provoked God to bring King Philip's War to New England. Winthrop thought God's displeasure with Virginia's persecution of Puritans brought Indian massacres there in 1644.

[77] The absence of a bishop in North America posed real challenges for ordination, but many vestries also appreciated the freedom it afforded them in making decisions. Hence, while

a penalty of 2,000 pounds of tobacco for anyone who refused infant baptism. Marriages and funerals could not be performed except according to the *Book of Common Prayer*, imposing yet another limitation on dissenters.[78] When concessions were available in the form of special building permits or preaching licenses, as in New England, these concessions existed more in statute than in practice. Local administration proved quite capricious in handling appeals for these concessions.

Quakers first arrived in Virginia in 1656 and were vigorously persecuted until 1663. Quaker meetings were banned, shipmasters were penalized for bringing Quakers to the colony, and Quakers were arrested or jailed on any number of pretenses. As in New England, authorities banished Quakers and threatened them with death if they insisted on returning a third time. Over time, however, Quakers proved themselves harmless and even salutary; it helped that their evangelistic efforts did not draw heavily from the lower classes (as they had in England) but from the more elite ranks of society. They were eventually accepted – provided that they paid their parish levies to support the Church of England.[79]

Exemptions for other dissenting groups were eventually given, but exemptions were few and far between. French Huguenots were exempted from ministerial taxes in 1700, and German Lutherans were granted the same exemption in 1730. No one else was technically exempted until 1776. Virginia's regime was so hard on dissenters that it discouraged their migration to the colony. Presbyterians and especially Baptists struggled hard against the regime of licensing. Disestablishment came only because of negotiation forced by the American Revolution.[80]

What motivated Virginia's treatment of non-Anglicans? Unlike the loquacious New England Puritans, Virginian authorities did not write extensive treatises to explain their views concerning church and state. Also, Virginian authorities were not forced to defend themselves in print against a verbose Roger Williams, for example. Like good Anglicans, they

New England Congregationalists opposed the move to establish a bishop in North America for fear of "popery," many Virginia Anglicans provided only ambivalent support in hopes of preserving their autonomy.

[78] Charles Fenton James, *Documentary History of the Struggle for Religious Liberty in Virginia* (Lynchburg, VA: J.P. Bell Company, 1900), 17–20.

[79] Bond, *Damned Souls*, 162–174.

[80] John A. Ragosta, *Wellspring of Liberty: How Virginia's Religious Dissenters Helped Win the American Revolution and Secured Religious Liberty* (New York: Oxford University Press, 2010).

took their cues from their superiors such as the Bishop of London (who had some ecclesiastical jurisdiction over the colonies). Anglicans stood alone as the established Church of England and considered themselves privileged on both sides of the Atlantic. Ironically, however, establishment did not do much to increase the number of Anglican ministers (and, by implication, Anglicans) in the colony or elsewhere. In 1671, there were only 30 Anglican ministers in both Virginia and Maryland, the other colony with Anglican establishment at the time. By 1700, the Church of England had managed only to double that number, with just twenty clerics operating outside of Maryland or Virginia.[81]

Nevertheless, Virginia enjoyed a degree of religious uniformity in the 1730s comparable perhaps only to Protestant polities two centuries prior.[82] Given this fact, it is remarkable that New England's persecution of dissenters is so much more widely known than Virginia's. Ironically, Virginia's legacy became not its vigorous persecution of dissenters. Instead, Virginia's legacy became the landmark work of James Madison and Thomas Jefferson for religious liberty.[83] The reason that Madison and Jefferson pushed so vigorously for religious freedom in their home state was *because* Virginia was so *intolerant* of those dissenting from the Church of England. Indeed, Jefferson himself considered Virginia equal to New England in its poor treatment of dissenters. He wrote that if Virginia's leaders did not execute dissenters, it was only due to "historical circumstances which have not been handed down to us."[84]

Maryland

Virginia's neighbor Maryland, like Rhode Island, became an experiment in religious liberty. Unlike Virginia and the colonies of New England, Maryland was a proprietorship. This meant that the crown could enjoy the benefits of colonization without incurring its cost, and that the

[81] Arthur Lyon Cross, *The Anglican Episcopate and the American Colonies* (New York: Longmans, Green, and Co., 1902), 33.

[82] Hutson, *Church and State in America*, 75.

[83] Though Jefferson and Madison are often cited as key inspirations for the First Amendment, a persuasive alternative view is presented by Mark David Hall, "Madison's Memorial and Remonstrance, Jefferson's Statute for Religious Liberty, and the Creation of the First Amendment," *American Political Thought* 3, no. 1 (Spring 2014): 32–63.

[84] Jefferson, *Notes on the State of Virginia*, 168.

proprietor himself became a kind of king. Its visionary founder and proprietor was George Calvert (1st Lord Baltimore), a Roman Catholic convert who secured his charter in 1632. Administration passed to his descendants. Maryland was the first polity in the Anglo-American Protestant world, on either side of the Atlantic, to give explicit freedom to Catholics to worship publicly. Maryland was unique in the Anglo-American world at that time because Catholics and Protestants coexisted peacefully (relatively speaking). This was especially remarkable insofar as British identity came to be increasingly defined by hatred of the Church of Rome.[85] Even more astonishing was that the Calverts attempted such coexistence *before* the more Catholic-tolerant regimes of Charles II or James II. No religious or political tests (beyond allegiance to authorities and the law) were required in the early days of the colony. Protestants and Catholics often shared places of worship. Incidents of early religious "intolerance" were minor.[86]

What motivated Calvert? Again, one can only speculate about such things outside of prolix New England. It is very likely that Calvert desired to provide a haven for persecuted English Catholics, though Calvert had instructed his governor (and brother) to restrain overt Catholic worship, ritual, or discussion of religious questions so as not to antagonize Protestants. Calvert, no doubt, also understood what others would realize only in time: support of toleration and liberty attracted settlers, especially settlers willing to engage in productive commerce.[87]

Despite these noble and practical motives, religious freedom for Catholics remained a hard sell in an increasingly Protestant Anglo-American world.[88] "Papists" were no more welcome near Virginia than in New England, and Virginians resented having them as neighbors. The king himself had to restate emphatically his protection of the Maryland charter in 1637. What's more, Calvert made the mistake of bringing Jesuits to the colony – those Roman Catholics most feared by Protestants. Even Calvert in 1642 privately expressed his reservations about the zeal of the Jesuits

[85] Linda Colley, *Britons: Forging the Nation 1707–1837* (New Haven, CT: Yale University Press, 2009), 11–54.

[86] William Hand Browne, *Maryland: The History of a Palatinate* (Boston, MA: Houghton, Mifflin, 1890), 48–71.

[87] John D. Krugler, *English and Catholic: The Lords Baltimore in the Seventeenth Century* (Baltimore, MD: Johns Hopkins University Press, 2004).

[88] Antoinette Sutto, *Loyal Protestants & Dangerous Papists: Maryland and the Politics of Religion in the English Atlantic 1630–1690* (Charlottesville: University of Virginia Press, 2015).

and considered them a potential threat to this colony.[89] In an effort to refute the charge that Maryland had become a haven for threatening Papists, and to mollify Cromwellian England, the assembly passed the "Act Concerning Religion" in 1649. This was arguably a step backward for toleration in Maryland. It limited the free exercise of religion to Trinitarian Christians only (threatening non-Trinitarian Christians such as Quakers with hanging), but it did protect Roman Catholics from insult.

Such measures did not mollify Protestants at home, however. Protestant rabble-rousers took advantage of parliamentarian sentiments and Cromwellian prejudices. In 1645, Protestants Richard Ingle and William Claiborne took control of the colony by force. Priests like Father Andrew White were sent to England in irons to stand trial for treason. (White was acquitted.) The Calverts fled to Virginia. Returning with a hired band of soldiers, they secured the colony again but soon lost it to Puritans striking from Annapolis in 1654. The Puritans expelled the Jesuits, repealed the Act Concerning Toleration, and outlawed "prelacy and popery." When the Calverts again regained control, they reinstated the Act Concerning Religion. By this time, Quakers were thriving in Maryland and eventually gained full religious freedom by 1660. George Fox himself came to Maryland to preach in 1672. By the late 1670s, over 15 Quaker meeting houses were established in Maryland.

While Protestant hopes for toleration in Maryland were brightening, however, Catholic fortunes were fading. Beginning around the time of the Exclusion Crisis, Protestants in Virginia, Maryland, and elsewhere became obsessed with Catholic conspiracies. The epithet of "papist" or "Jesuit" became applied to anyone suspected of either tyranny or lawlessness. Allegations arose of alliances between Maryland's Catholic governors and either the French (alleged in 1676) or the Indians (alleged in 1681). Anglican minister John Coode capitalized on the hysteria and seized the government of Maryland in the name of a so-called "Protestant Association" – though Protestant support for Coode was not exactly widespread. Lord Baltimore eventually lost control of his own colony (though he retained proprietorship).

The Church of England was eventually established in Maryland, consistent with a trend after the Act of Toleration and Clarendon Code.

[89] Owen Stanwood, *The Empire Reformed: English America in the Age of the Glorious Revolution* (Philadelphia: University of Pennsylvania Press, 2011), 57.

Marylanders would have to pay a tax for its support, though toleration was eventually extended to "dissenters." Consistent with the oaths and tests obliged by the 1689 Act of Toleration, Quakers and Catholics were denied office, though Quakers eventually recovered that right. Catholics continued to live in Maryland, but they could worship only in their homes. In 1756, Catholic property owners were subject to a double tax. In a colony where Catholics once chided Protestants for reading Protestant books, the situation was now reversed; it would not be until 1774 that the first openly Catholic book would be published in Maryland.

Carolina and Georgia

Virginia's other neighbor, Carolina, was a proprietary colony founded in 1663 when Charles II granted a charter to eight men who were advisors on foreign trade, colonization, and investment. Notable in this project was Anthony Ashley Cooper, the first Earl of Shaftsbury. As a Presbyterian who had supported toleration, Shaftsbury was a pioneer in his own right. Even more notable than Shaftsbury was his physician and secretary, the political philosopher John Locke who had a hand in the 1669 constitution. The 1669 constitution (which also divided the colony into two provinces) took cues from the 1665 royal charter, which in turn borrowed language from the Rhode Island charter of 1663. This 1669 charter granted a broad liberty of conscience to Jews, non-Trinitarian Christians, and any group of seven people who formed a church to worship God. Assemblies were not to be disturbed and persons were not to be molested or persecuted for their opinions or way of worship. Early settlers were recruited with the promise of "full and free Liberty of Conscience."[90] In the wake of the Restoration, the constitution was amended in 1670 to establish the Church of England. This establishment continued into the eighteenth century. This establishment was fairly passive, however; unlike Virginia's establishment, it did not deter immigration. In 1696, a law was passed guaranteeing all Protestants full liberty of conscience.

[90] Gloria Beth Baker, "Dissenters in Colonial North Carolina" (PhD Dissertation, University of North Carolina at Chapel Hill, 1970), 37–38. The quotation is taken from Robert Horne, *A Brief Description of the Province of Carolina* (1666), a document intended to entice migration to the colony.

The religious population of the northern province (which became North Carolina in 1712) reflected the "unwanted" of Virginia: primarily Quakers who took advantage of their ability to flourish without expense or infrastructure. Proliferating Quaker settlements gave them leverage to influence laws and thereby avoid oaths, military service, or fines for refusing military service. Hard pressed by both shrewd Quakers and an inhospitable wilderness, the Church of England struggled in North Carolina. Indeed, the governor told the Bishop of London in 1703 that there was "neither priest nor altar" in the colony.[91] Even the Society for the Propagation of the Gospel could make little headway there. One historian for the Society said of the colony, "In none of the States did the Missionaries undergo greater hardships from the dearness of provisions, the great extent of their cures, and the indifference or hostility of the people."[92]

The population of the southern province of Carolina (which became South Carolina) reflected an inflow of English immigrants from Barbados, English Presbyterians and Baptists, and French Huguenots. The need for economic development there discouraged religious uniformity despite a formal Anglican establishment in the law. The colony's assembly appropriated only a small maintenance for the minister of St. Philip's Episcopal Church in Charleston. After a vigorous but failed effort toward a more aggressive establishment, the Assembly settled in 1706 on providing for only ten parishes with elected (Anglican) ministers supported by public monies. More notable is that a 1710 act made South Carolina the only colony with provision for a tax-supported clergy funded from the public treasury rather than from direct taxes – a measure that had aggravated dissenters in other colonial establishments. Therefore, not only did dissenters enjoy protection for their own worship, but they also did not have to chafe at paying money directly to a church they did not attend. German, French, and Irish came to the colony in subsequent decades, their immigration further blunting the ambitions of the Church of England. Jews were permitted to worship, but barred from holding office, and after 1721 they were denied the vote. Catholics were first barred from holding office. After 1759 they were denied the vote.[93]

91 Curry, *The First Freedoms*, 56.

92 Earnest Hawkins, *Historical Notices of the Missions of the Church of England in the North American Colonies, Previous to the Independence of the United States* (London: B. Fellowes, 1845), 67.

93 A survey of the relatively extensive freedom available to dissenters in South Carolina is in William Lewis Burke and James L. Underwood, eds., *The Dawn of Religious Freedom in South Carolina* (Columbia: The University of South Carolina Press, 2009).

South Carolina's neighbor, Georgia, was established by royal charter in 1732 as the last of the thirteen original colonies. Though populated by Scottish Presbyterians, French Huguenots, German Moravians, and a host of other Protestant groups, Georgia established the Church of England in 1758. However, this weak establishment still tolerated Protestant dissenters. Georgia also hosted the colonies' largest group of Jews, a group that came to Savannah in 1733. (Jews had previously settled in New York and Newport and would later settle in Philadelphia and Charleston.) This Jewish settlement would have founded the first synagogue *except* for two difficulties: ethnic division among the settlers and the threat of persecution by Spanish troops during the War of Jenkins' Ear.[94] In many ways, Georgia was a case study of how religious toleration and liberty played out in southern colonies besides Virginia. The government still saw itself as a guardian of public morality and religion and thus did not embrace a robust separation of church and state. However, the magistrate's responsibility to public morality and piety was moderated by a desire for immigration and commercial development.[95]

The Middle Colonies

New York and New Jersey

Between the southern colonies and New England lay middle colonies who exemplified both the virtues and vices of their northern and southern neighbors. New York, originally New Amsterdam, was captured from the Dutch by a British fleet in 1664. Under the proprietorship of the Duke of York (later King James II), it first reflected his tolerant (and more mercantile) attitude toward religion. Under the duke's direction, New York's governor advanced an establishment under which two-thirds of voters in each town decided which church would be tax-supported. Minority believers could still worship without interference, however. This tolerant policy was more sensitive than Dutch precedent to the diversity of settlers

[94] Congregation Mickve Israel, accessed July 5, 2017, www.mickveisrael.org/museum-and-tours/the-story-of-mickve-israel.

[95] Joel A. Nichols, "Religious Liberty in the Thirteenth Colony: Church-State Relations in Colonial and Early National Georgia," *New York University Law Review* 80, no.6 (2005): 1693.

there.[96] Nevertheless, many still refused to pay the obligatory taxes. New York, like other colonies, was also stirred up both by Quakers who refused to conform and by fears of Catholic conspiracies. As in Boston and Maryland, a self-appointed Protestant savior (Jacob Leisler) rose up to throw off a "Popish" threat in 1689.

After Leisler's demise in 1691, the new royal governor attempted to force the colony to fall in line with expectations in England, including some form of Anglican establishment and exclusion of Catholics from civil protections and office-holding. When financial maintenance for Anglican worship met opposition from dissenters, Anglicans insisted that the Ministry Act of 1693 provided maintenance for Anglican ministers. Other denominations disagreed, noting that the act referred only to support for "good sufficient Protestant" ministers. The Anglican establishment technically won, but Trinity Church in Manhattan was really its only success. Protestant dissenters (notably Presbyterians, Quakers, and the Dutch Reformed) held their own but struggled to attain full toleration, let alone release from financial maintenance of the Church of England. New York authorities even doubled down on Anglican establishment to the point of insisting that the 1689 Act of Toleration did not apply in the colonies. (Virginia likewise made this argument until 1776.) Jews living in New York benefitted from being outside the sectarian battles and enjoyed some degree of toleration. Catholics were, of course, not tolerated. Priests were banned from entering the colony.

New Jersey, as an English colony, was created when James II gave friends some of his land south of Manhattan. These proprietors were, like James, more interested in practical matters of trade than with perpetuating Christendom. Proprietors made vague provision for a weak establishment at the discretion of the citizens. Some towns decided to adopt voluntary maintenance, but the actual result was no establishment at all. Baptists and Quakers took advantage of the circumstance, as did Congregationalists, Dutch Reformed, and Presbyterians. For reasons administrative and financial, Jersey split into West and East and remained two distinct provinces between 1674 and 1702. West Jersey became an English Quaker refuge controlled by Quaker proprietors. East Jersey received an inflow of New

[96] For a new consideration of the Dutch precedent, see Evan Haefeli, *New Netherlands and the Dutch Origins of American Religious Liberty* (Philadelphia: University of Pennsylvania Press, 2012).

England Congregationalists and Scottish Presbyterians. In 1702, the two proprietary colonies of East and West Jersey became one royal colony. As elsewhere, the governor was under orders to ferret out "Popish Recusants" by oaths of allegiance. Provision was made for Quakers who would hold office only by affirmation rather than by oath – an allowance Quakers managed to make official in 1718.

Pennsylvania and Delaware

Pennsylvania was also a proprietary colony, founded in 1681 by a royal charter granted to William Penn, a Quaker.[97] Penn's persuasive thoughts on toleration are articulated in *The Great Case of Liberty of Conscience* (1670), a work comparable to (but more systematic than) Williams' *Bloudy Tenent.* Penn may even have taken cues from Shaftsbury and Locke, insofar as Article 35 of his 1682 Frame of Government resembles The Fundamental Constitutions of Carolina (1669). The Carolina Constitution obliged only that one "confess and acknowledge the one Almighty and eternal God, to be the Creator, Upholder and Ruler of the world." This technically meant toleration for Catholics, Jews, Muslims, or non-Trinitarian Christians – though religious tests excluded all three groups from holding office.[98]

Delaware was originally leased by Penn and joined to the Pennsylvania administration in 1682, but it was then chartered as a separate colony in 1707. Neither Pennsylvania nor Delaware established support for ministers and both admitted all Protestants who desired to settle there. There were rumblings against Catholic churches in the 1730s, but no legal action was pursued. As in most colonies, laws remained against actions judged to be impious or contrary to good civil order. In Pennsylvania, this not only included fornication or drunkenness but also "stage-plays, cards, dice." Such activities did not constitute what the First Amendment would later call "free exercise," nor were they protected matters of conscience. Pennsylvania was briefly rent by a theological schism within its Quaker ranks threatening the colony's ambitious tolerationist goals. As with

[97] See, for example, J. William Frost, *A Perfect Freedom: Religious Liberty in Pennsylvania* (Cambridge: Cambridge University Press, 1990).

[98] For more details on Muslim toleration, see Denise Spellberg, "Muslims, Toleration, and Civil Rights from Roger Williams to Thomas Jefferson" in *The Lively Experiment*, ed. Beneke and Grenda, 85–100.

Massachusetts Bay's banishment of Williams, the resulting justification for prosecuting rival religious leaders was civil and not religious.[99]

Quakers and others heard Penn's summons for toleration, and by 1685 as many as eight thousand Quakers had settled in Pennsylvania. Not surprisingly, Pennsylvania became a haven for other religious pariahs from Europe, including Mennonites and other sects previously unknown in North America (e.g., Dunkers, Schwenkfelders, Rosicrucians, German Baptists). Pennsylvania's leaders did retreat from some of Penn's ideals over time by, for example, barring Catholics and Jews from holding office. Nevertheless, Pennsylvania's stable government, growing cities, and economic success made it a model for religious liberty in North America. In being both successful and influential, Pennsylvania (and Delaware) became what Roger Williams' "latrine" of Rhode Island could not become – a venerable model of religious freedom in colonial America.[100]

The Great Awakening

The First Great Awakening (c. 1730–1750) provided the last great occasion for ecclesiastical or church–state conflict before the Revolution and the Founding.[101] Religious revivals opened schisms among Protestant groups and undermined what was left of religious establishment before the Revolution. Skirmishes during this time mainly pitted "New Lights" or "New Side" ministers (those who supported the revivals and the rights of itinerant preachers) against the "Old Lights" or "Old Side" ministers who deployed ecclesiastical, theological, and civil arguments against both revivalism and the disruptions of itinerant preachers. In states with any form of tax-funded maintenance, churches split by the Awakening had to confront the question of which faction was entitled to that maintenance. Groups without financial maintenance fought over the status of their

[99] Andrew R. Murphy, "Persecuting Quakers? Liberty and Toleration in Early Pennsylvania," in *The First Prejudice: Religious Tolerance and Intolerance in Early America*, ed. Chris Beneke and Christopher S. Genada (Philadelphia: University of Pennsylvania Press, 2011), 143–165.

[100] Andrew R. Murphy, "'Livelie Experiment' and 'Holy Experiment': Two Trajectories of Religious Liberty," in *The Lively Experiment*, ed. Beneke and Grenda, 37–52.

[101] Chris Beneke casts the Great Awakening in the struggle for religious toleration more broadly in *Beyond Toleration: The Religious Origins of American Pluralism* (New York: Oxford University Press, 2006), 49–77.

exemptions. In Connecticut and Massachusetts, Baptists who struggled through persecution to obtain tax exemptions from Congregational establishment resented exemptions now demanded by new sects of "Separate" or "Separatist" Baptists. Old Light Baptists viewed New Light Baptists with suspicion and resentment. Separate Baptists arriving in Virginia in the 1750s clashed with establishment Anglicans and now-tolerated Presbyterians.

Old Lights sometimes gained the ear of legislators. The Connecticut Assembly banned itinerant preachers in 1742 and stripped local courts of jurisdiction over New Lights. New York passed similar legislation in 1744. In Virginia, both Presbyterians and Baptists already had to submit to licensing and a prescribed area for preaching, a requirement that impeded itinerancy. In April of 1745, Governor Gooch of Virginia pressed his opposition further. He lamented to the grand jury of the general court that "false teachers" under the "pretended influence of new light" were disrupting the colony's remarkable "uniformity in worship." Gooch claimed that any who challenged Anglican establishment elsewhere in the "British dominions" would be "very severely handled" and asked why Virginia should not do the same.[102] Some Anglicans in Virginia were not content to wait on the law and instead deployed mob violence against groups they considered a threat to the Church of England's establishment.

Of course, one solution to such dilemmas was to abolish establishment altogether. The Great Awakening emboldened Presbyterians and Baptists against establishment in Virginia and stirred Baptists against establishment in Connecticut and Massachusetts. Presbyterian revivalist Samuel Davies pressed for greater freedom in Virginia and like others cited the Act of Toleration in his defense. Congregationalist minister Elisha Williams penned an eloquent and now much-studied work advocating liberty of conscience in the context of the revivals: *The Essential Rights and Liberties of Protestants* (1744). Williams drew from scripture, Locke's theory of natural rights, and the Toleration Act of 1689 to protest the Connecticut ban on itinerancy. However significant Williams' work appears in hindsight, however, it was not popular at the time.[103]

[102] Gooch's speech is included in John Burk, *The History of Virginia: From Its First Settlement to the Present Day* (Petersburg, VA: Dickson & Pescud, 1805), 3:119–121.

[103] Ellis Sandoz notes in his introduction to Williams's essay that Williams was criticized by Old and New Lights and lost reelection to the Supreme Court. English scholar John Dunn praised Williams's work as a "doctrine of startling originality." See Sandoz, ed., *Political*

Broadly speaking, the First Great Awakening advanced religious toleration and liberty in significant ways. Its emphasis on spiritual experience and conversion was egalitarian in nature and planted the roots of American evangelicalism by deemphasizing the denominational and doctrinal differences that had been essential for religious establishment and exclusion. The itinerant habits of many revivalists, some of whom preached in fields and didn't blush to attack local ministers as insufficiently pious or spiritual, suggested that the work of the Spirit could not be confined to pastor, building, parish, or locale – four other essential ingredients for religious establishment. Baptists, Methodists, and Presbyterians, denominations that would exploit the westward movement of colonists, were also more generally accepting of the egalitarian and pietistic elements of revivalism. All three denominations grew into the late eighteenth and early nineteenth centuries while Congregational and Episcopal (Anglican) churches, those churches enjoying establishment, would fall behind in growth.[104]

The Awakening also encouraged a nascent civil religion opposing divisive establishments. Aversion to division catalyzed by the Awakening prompted some to express, largely in magazines (a growing media format in America), that piety should be concerned more with civic norms and virtue as these were traits shared by all Christians.[105] The zealous energies of the revival, after religious enthusiasms had waned, were eventually channeled into the colonial wars of the period, especially the French and Indian War. In many political sermons preached during these wars, ministers unleashed rhetorical fire that summoned citizens to an existential defense of British Protestantism against bloodthirsty French and Spanish Catholic foes. These sermons subsumed denominational differences into

Sermons of the American Founding Era 1730–1805 (Indianapolis, IN: Liberty Fund, 1991), 52, 54.

104 Fine studies of the Great Awakening, including its sectarian character and its role in shaping American evangelicalism, include Thomas Kidd, *The Great Awakening: The Roots of Evangelical Christianity in Colonial America* (New Haven, CT: Yale University Press, 2009); Timothy Hall, *Contested Boundaries: Itineracy and the Reshaping of the Colonial American Religious World* (Durham, NC: Duke University Press, 1994), and John Howard Smith, *The First Great Awakening: Redefining Religion in British America 1725–1775*, (Madison, NJ: Fairleigh Dickinson University Press, 2015).

105 On the proliferation of a common-denomination Christianity beginning in the 1740s, see Keith Pacholl, "'Between God and Our Own Souls': The Discussion over Toleration in Eighteenth-Century America," in *The Lively Experiment*, ed. Beneke and Grenda, 117–132. On the proliferation of magazines in *advancing* revivalism see Frank Lambert, *Inventing the "Great Awakening"* (Princeton, NJ: Princeton University Press, 1999).

a common Protestant identity sanctifying civil rights and liberties against papist foes in France and Spain.[106] According to the implicit reasoning of these sermons, religious divisions could even be seen as unpatriotic.

The revivalist movement, a movement that continued into the Second Great Awakening, also privileged a spirit of religious liberty by joining the converting work of God to the individual heart of the believer. As Williams's *Essential Rights and Liberties of Protestants* implicitly demonstrates by its Lockean character, revivalism emphasized that individual Christian souls were directly accountable only to God for religious questions. They could not be bound to obey civil or ecclesiastical intermediaries who had partnered to create religious establishments. Williams took the Reformed idea of the magistrate as a "Nursing Father" and reformulated it in such a way as to make prior establishments a violation of the laws of God and man.

Conclusion: Free Exercise and Establishment

By modern standards, "free exercise" for many believers in colonial America was a thin gruel. All but four colonies (Pennsylvania, Delaware, New Jersey, and Rhode Island) had an established church that was either Anglican or Congregationalist – though some Anglican establishments were admittedly not that robust. Those not part of established churches came to enjoy only a negative liberty – a liberty to be left alone. Even in the wake of the 1689 Act of Toleration, that "toleration" still obliged ministers and congregants in many colonies to jump through one or another hoop to obtain this negative liberty: oaths of allegiance or supremacy, subscription to some variation of the Thirty-Nine Articles, registration of meeting houses, conducting services without privacy, or securing licenses or permits. Such was the lot of the nonconformist or dissenter under an established church.

[106] Glenn A. Moots, "Samuel Cooper's Old Sermons and New Enemies: Popery and Protestant Constitutionalism," *American Political Thought*, 5, no.3 (Summer 2016): 391–420; Nathan Hatch, *The Sacred Cause of Liberty: Republican Thought and the Millennium in Revolutionary New England* (New Haven, CT: Yale University Press, 1977).

Many were still thankful for this negative liberty, however. For example, when Charles II unilaterally granted toleration to Protestant nonconformists and Catholics on March 15, 1672, nonconformist Protestant leaders (including John Owen and Thomas Manton) met with the king to express their gratitude – despite the fact that tithes continued to be paid to the Church of England and nonconformists were disqualified from holding office.[107] Likewise, as restrictive as the Act of Toleration was, it was still celebrated for a long time by Congregationalists, Presbyterians, and Baptists on both sides of the Atlantic. Though dissenters failed to repeal the Test and Corporation Acts in the 1730s, they still enjoyed what the era defined as liberty of conscience: unimpeded public worship.[108] Such liberty in no way meant a "separation of church and state" suggested first by Williams, then Jefferson, then made a legal principle by Justice Black in *Everson* v. *Board of Education* (1947). No one at the time thought or spoke in such terms.[109] Even the various "walls" prescribed by Williams, Jefferson, and Black are not the same.

While it has been rightly said that Protestantism defined America, it can also be said that the experience of America defined its Protestants. Confessions and doctrinal statements of early Protestant Christendom did not shape America as much as America shaped them. The Thirty-Nine Articles adopted by the American Episcopal Church in 1801 rejected the Erastianism of its 1571 predecessor and proclaimed, "The Power of the Civil Magistrate extendeth to all men, as well Clergy as Laity, in all things *temporal*; but hath *no authority in things purely spiritual.*"[110] The aforementioned Chapter 23 of the Westminster Confession of 1646 was modified for American churches in 1788. The new version removed the confession's previous charge to the magistrate to suppress blasphemies, heresies, corruptions, or abuses, and the magistrate was instead to give no "preference to any denomination of Christians above the rest." Rather, "all ecclesiastical persons whatever shall enjoy the full, free, and unquestioned liberty of discharging, every part of their sacred functions, without violence or danger." Furthermore, "no law of any commonwealth, should

[107] Peter Toon, *God's Statesman: The Life and Work of John Owen, Pastor, Educator, Theologian* (Milton Keynes: Paternoster Press, 1971), 149.

[108] Hutson, *Church and State*, 51–53.

[109] Hutson makes this point, citing William McLouglin, Philip Hamburger, and R.E. Harkness in his defense, in *Church and State*, 92–93.

[110] Emphasis is mine.

interfere with, let, or hinder, the due exercise thereof." Confessional traditions were no longer compelling statements of truth; they became instead voluntary professions of one's own belief.

This principle of free exercise in confessional statements no doubt echoes to some degree the prohibition of legal establishment in the First Amendment. Such confessional and legal supports for free exercise were born of a dedicated legal and cultural struggle. This chapter demonstrates that the struggle was not a "national" struggle. Though changes in British law and religion changed the shape of toleration and liberty in the American colonies, the long-standing contest for toleration and liberty "on the ground" in North America was internecine, waged among various Christian communities, argued on grounds of conscience and expediency, and more or less local in origin. Congregations and individuals appealed for their rights, and those appeals had legal and social consequence for counties, provinces, colonies, and whole regions. Some conflicts arguably had an influence that reached *back* across the Atlantic.

Until the Revolution, there was no "nation" in which the right of free exercise could be protected. However, when the opportunity arose to create "a more perfect Union" promoting the general welfare and the blessings of liberty, how could the framers of that new union not recall the long struggle over true faith and practice, the human cost, and the damage to both civil peace and commercial progress?[111] A century and a half after its first settlements, Americans considered religious liberty a prudent and noble cause.

[111] Benjamin J. Kaplan argues that a similarly pragmatic and charitable motive, born particularly of the experiences of everyday people, spurred toleration in Europe in *Divided by Faith: Religious Conflict and the Practice of Toleration in Early Modern Europe* (Cambridge, MA: The Belknap Press of Harvard University Press, 2009).

5 The Historical Context of the Religion Clauses of the First Amendment

Chris Beneke

On New Year's Day, 1802, President Thomas Jefferson was presented with a half-ton block of cheese, an offering made by the Baptist farmers of Cheshire, Massachusetts. One of their ministers, John Leland, who happened to be an unstinting proponent of religious liberty and a stalwart Jefferson ally, had escorted this "Mammoth Cheese" all the way from that Berkshire valley town to the White House. A charmed President Jefferson thanked them for the labor invested in the unusual gift and echoed their praise for the federal Constitution's prohibition on religious tests and the amending process.

The cheese has been immortalized, but not Jefferson's remarks about it. Instead, we remember another reply that the President dispatched that same day to a group of Connecticut dissenters, the Danbury Baptist Association. Jefferson chose his words in that letter carefully, consulting advisors and meticulously revising the original composition. He knew that his response would shape perceptions of what the First Amendment meant and where the federal government stood on the matter of religious establishments and church–state interaction. Displaying his flair for bracing imagery, Jefferson posited that the amendment erected "a wall of separation between Church & State."[1]

One of the most important findings in church–state scholarship over the last three decades is that the First Amendment cannot be reduced to Jefferson's terse metaphor. The relationship between church and state, we have discovered, was neither entirely separate nor entirely straightforward.[2] The resulting confusion has opened the door for other

[1] Thomas Jefferson to the Danbury Baptist Association, January 1, 1802, *Founders Online*, National Archives, last modified June 13, 2018, http://founders.archives.gov/documents/Jefferson/01-36-02-0152-0006.

[2] Jefferson himself intimated that the "wall" might not be impermeable when he attended Rev. Leland's sermon in the House of Representatives two days later. On the significance of Jefferson's joining religious services in a government building, see James H. Hutson,

fictions: that the country was established on an exclusively Christian foundation or, at the opposite extreme, that the founders were devout secularists.[3] In the courts and among legal scholars, the center has held. Jurists and constitutional scholars now recognize that the founders were both (1) opposed to the federal government's promoting one particular faith at the expense of others and (2) dedicated to protecting religious worship and expression for a widening variety of groups.[4] Though unsatisfactory to partisans, this sums up the messy, historical reality.

When it came to the details, contemporaries were as divided as we are today. They disagreed about whether state governments should mandate public support for churches and ministers, and whether conscientious objectors should be exempted from military service. In Massachusetts, where the Congregational church establishment survived the Revolutionary era, citizens disagreed about whether unincorporated churches could collect tax

"Thomas Jefferson's Letter to the Danbury Baptists: A Controversy Rejoined," *William and Mary Quarterly* 3rd ser. 56, no. 4 (October 1999): 786–789.

[3] For a critique of the Christian founding myth, see Steven K. Green, *Inventing a Christian America: The Myth of the Religious Founding* (New York: Oxford University Press, 2017). For an example of a secular reading of the founders' approach to church–state matters, see Brooke Allen, *Moral Minority: Our Skeptical Founding Fathers* (Chicago: Ivan R. Dee, 2009).

[4] A few works reflecting this consensus view are Noah Feldman, *Divided by God: America's Church-State Problem and What We Should Do about It* (New York: Farrar, Straus and Giroux, 2005); Michael Meyerson, *Endowed by Our Creator: The Birth of Religious Freedom in America* (New Haven, CT: Yale University Press, 2012); Vincent Philip Muñoz, *God and the Founders: Madison, Washington, and Jefferson* (Cambridge, MA: Cambridge University Press, 2009); Stephen Waldman, *Founding Faith: Providence, Politics, and the Birth of Religious Freedom in America* (New York: Random House, 2008); and John Witte Jr. and Joel A. Nichols, *Religion and the American Constitutional Experiment*, 4th edition (New York: Oxford University Press, 2016). Other important recent works on late eighteenth-century American church–state history include Derek H. Davis, *Religion and the Continental Congress, 1774–1789: Contributions to Original Intent* (New York: Oxford University Press, 2000); Donald L. Drakeman, *Church, State, and Original Intent* (New York: Cambridge University Press, 2010); Daniel L. Dreisbach, *Thomas Jefferson and the Wall of Separation between Church and State* (New York: New York University Press, 2002); Daniel L. Dreisbach, Mark D. Hall, and Jeffry H. Morrison, eds., *The Founders on God and Government* (Lanham, MD: Rowman & Littlefield, 2004); Steven K. Green, *The Second Disestablishment: Church and State in Nineteenth-Century America* (New York: Oxford University Press, 2010); Philip Hamburger, *Separation of Church and State* (Cambridge, MA: Harvard University Press, 2002); James S. Kabala, *Church-State Relations in the Early American Republic, 1787–1846* (Brookfield, VT: Pickering and Chatto, 2013); and Isaac Kramnick and R. Laurence Moore, *The Godless Constitution: The Case against Religious Correctness* (New York: W. W. Norton, 1996). For a helpful account of the founders' religious beliefs, see David Holmes, *Faith of the Founders* (New York: Oxford University Press, 2006).

levies from their members.[5] In Pennsylvania, which never had an establishment, they disagreed about whether antireligious speech should be protected.[6]

No one was more cognizant of those disagreements, nor keener to reconcile them, than James Madison. If Jefferson gave us the most forthright – albeit misleading – recapitulation of what the First Amendment was intended to accomplish, his friend and political ally, Madison, probably had the most to do with the fact that it existed at all. Religious liberty had many champions in the new nation, but none as formidable or effective as this quiet, diminutive scion of a Virginia plantation family. Madison graduated from the College of New Jersey (now Princeton University) in 1771, after completing his coursework in a lightning-fast two years. The studious Madison returned to his Montpelier home without well-defined career ambitions. What he did possess was a marked disposition for politics. Madison soon joined the Revolutionary Committee on Safety and became a vigorous defender of the Baptist ministers who were being harassed by mobs and imprisoned by Anglican authorities.[7]

That early foray into religious advocacy proved a harbinger of what lay ahead for the precocious Madison. In the late spring of 1776, at the age of twenty-five, he put his first indelible stamp on American life. Serving as a representative at the Virginia constitutional convention in Richmond, Madison drafted a revision of George Mason's proposed language on religion. Most notable about his modifications was the substitution of a more encompassing and unqualified endorsement of religious liberty ("all men are equally entitled to the full and free exercise" of religion) for Mason's more restrained language ("that all Men shou'd enjoy the fullest Toleration in the Exercise of Religion, according to the Dictates of Conscience"). Madison's support for religious liberty over toleration may have had something to do with his reservations about conventional religion and his immersion in eighteenth-century Enlightenment thought at

[5] John D. Cushing, "Notes on Disestablishment in Massachusetts, 1780–1833," *William and Mary Quarterly* 3rd ser. 26, no. 2 (April 1969): 169–190.

[6] Eric Schlereth, "A Tale of Two Deists: John Fitch, Elihu Palmer, and the Boundary of Tolerable Religious Expression in Early National Philadelphia," *Pennsylvania Magazine of History and Biography* 132, no. 1 (2008): 5–31.

[7] James Madison to William Bradford, January 24, 1774, *Founders Online*, National Archives, last modified March 30, 2017, http://founders.archives.gov/documents/Madison/01-01-02-0029.

Princeton. It may have owed still more to his revulsion at the harsh treatment meted out to local dissenters. After the Revolutionary War, Madison enlisted the support of evangelical leaders to help pass Jefferson's Statute for Religious Freedom. That bill declared religious freedom to be an inalienable "natural right" and specified that governments could neither force a man to attend or support a church, nor could they impose civil penalties as a result of "religious opinions or belief."[8]

Given these commitments, it was not unreasonable to expect that Madison would support calls to introduce religious liberty protections at the federal level. But he did not – at least not at first. Madison's initial opposition to amendments disappointed his evangelical allies and has puzzled many students of the era since. While Madison would come to cherish the protections that these amendments established, at the time he was just not confident that an enumeration of rights would be the barrier to tyranny that its proponents supposed. The institutions of government, he believed, were not themselves the primary threat. Instead, as Madison put it in a letter to Jefferson, "the real power lies in the majority of the Community."[9]

Like the ratification process itself, Madison's progress toward support for amendments was slow and halting. He gradually found his way there during the winter and spring of 1789. The most straightforward of political calculations figured into his decision. Unless Madison supported an amendment protecting religious liberty, the evangelicals who represented a growing constituency, voted as a block and insisted on protections for rights of conscience would cast their ballots for his opponent. Even with such intense political pressure on him, he demurred until the very end.

Whatever reservations Madison had about revising the Constitution when the First Congress convened in May 1789, he set them aside and made the case for amendments. It began as an uphill battle. Members of the Federalist-dominated Congress, several of whom had sweated through the 1787 Philadelphia convention, were unenthusiastic about the prospect of revising a mechanism that had been so delicately fashioned. Through

[8] [Virginia] Act for Establishing Religious Freedom, October 31, 1785, *Founders Online*, National Archives, last modified June 13, 2018, http://founders.archives.gov/documents/Madison/01-08-02-0206.

[9] James Madison to Thomas Jefferson, October 17, 1788, *Founders Online*, National Archives, last modified June 13, 2018, http://founders.archives.gov/documents/Madison/01-11-02-0218.

compromise and careful deliberation, its framers had crafted a governing instrument that was meant to withstand the wages of time. They were not eager to see it mangled by a hundred hastily conceived alterations.

Madison's speech introducing amendments cast a wide net that included military exemptions for pacifist sects, restrictions on state interference with religious liberty, and a prohibition against a federal establishment. The various proposals wound their way through committee in July and early August, and then to the open floor of the House and Senate in August. Congress voted to do some, but not all, of the things Madison had initially proposed. The idea of protecting citizens from state infringements on rights of conscience was a bold proposition that probably never stood a chance of passage. Meanwhile, the clause exempting conscientious objectors from military service was unceremoniously dropped from the amendment protecting the right to bear arms.

No other part of Madison's proposal proved more controversial or subject to revision than the stipulation that no "national religion be established." In response to the concerns that state establishments might be curtailed and religion thereby neglected, he proposed the insertion of "national" before "religion."[10] Because "national" suggested a consolidation of power that few besides Alexander Hamilton desired, the House settled on language that forbade *Congress* from making a law "establishing religion, or to prevent the free exercise thereof, or to infringe the rights of conscience."[11] That mid-August pruning of the establishment clause brought it very close to the language ultimately ratified.

Immediately after the Senate took up the proposed amendments. And there, something unexpected occurred. A matter that appeared to be resolved in the House – the relationship between the federal government and religion – became a point of contention. It is not entirely clear what happened in the Senate, because only the language that came to a formal vote survives.[12] Like the fossilized impression of some ancient creature, we can discern its general shape, but nothing of its substance. The blood and sinews of the floor debate are lost to us. What we do know is that on

[10] Neil H. Cogan, ed., *The Complete Bill of Rights: The Drafts, Debates, Sources, & Origins* (New York: Oxford University Press, 1997), 60 [August 15, 1788].

[11] Ibid., 62 [August 20, 1789].

[12] For a concise analysis of the process, see Michael J. Malbin, *Religion and Politics: The Intentions of the Authors of the First Amendment* (Washington, DC: American Enterprise Institute, 1978), 12.

September 3, 1789, the Senate considered a few different iterations of the amendment. The first would have prohibited Congress from "establishing any religious sect or society." It was voted down. And so was the next, which would have prevented Congress from making laws "establishing any particular denomination of religion in preference to another." A similar proposal to forbid Congress from making laws "establishing one religious society in preference to others" failed as well. Four days later, the Senate approved the following: "Congress shall make no law establishing articles of faith or a mode of worship, or prohibiting the free exercise of religion." The language put up for a vote suggests that the senators were torn between a general prohibition on congressional legislation regarding religion and a more circumscribed ban on the establishment of a single church or creed. Whatever the case, when the amendments moved to conference committee, the language reverted to something similar to what the House had agreed to on August 20. It forbade Congress from making a "law respecting an establishment of religion, or prohibiting the free exercise thereof."

The final language of the religious clauses was beguilingly vague. Its sweep and imprecision imparted an enduring mystery to American constitutional life. What did "respecting" mean? Was Congress prohibited from funding religious organizations in a non-preferential way? Did the protection of free exercise also protect irreligious speech? There were no straightforward answers at the time. Nor have there been since.

Free Exercise

The framers had various ways of fashioning the language protecting religious liberty. Several alternatives were in use during this period, including "liberty of conscience," "religious liberty," the "divine right of private judgment," and "toleration." The meanings of these terms often overlapped, and the terms were often used interchangeably. None of them seems to have fully captured the shifting range of privileges that religious majorities and civil authorities were willing to grant – and religious minorities inclined to seek – during the 1770s and 1780s.

The alternative that almost made it into the Constitution was "rights of conscience" (or "equal rights of conscience"). The House of Representatives and Senate both considered this phrasing before turning to "free exercise." Rights of conscience embodied an ideal, Protestant and republican in connotation, with which contemporaries identified most readily. It may not, however, have been so easy to implement. "Rights of conscience" was prone to wide-ranging and potentially unwanted readings. On the one hand, it might be interpreted less strictly than its framers intended, opening the way for exemptions from military service and other civil obligations based on claims of conscience. On the other hand, it might be interpreted more strictly than intended. In some contexts, rights of conscience only entailed the right to judge religious claims in private. This meant the right to harbor nonconforming beliefs in one's mind, certainly no further than the confines of one's house or place of worship. At some point during their separate deliberations, it must have dawned on members of both congressional bodies that rights of conscience represented a worthy aspiration but a dubious legal principle.

The term eventually endorsed in both houses, "free exercise," was something of a dark horse at the outset. Madison did not propose to incorporate the phrase into the Constitution, and the House only took it up near the end of their amendment deliberations. The Senate then proceeded to drop the term, before readopting it. Lacking the ideological allure of rights of conscience, free exercise had some useful practical qualities, namely concreteness and specificity. Free exercise typically referred to either individual or (more often) group religious autonomy. As a constitutional principle, its meaning was more reliable, and less controversial, than rights of conscience. And yet free exercise was also noticeably broader than rights of conscience.

For much of the seventeenth and eighteenth centuries, free exercise was a circumscribed liberty that granted clergy and churches the right to conduct worship in specific locations. Such grants effectively exempted groups from measures such as Parliament's Conventicle Acts (1664, 1670), which forbade nonconformists from gathering in groups of more than five outside their homes. Free exercise was often offered as a concession to particular groups, and as a mechanism for achieving certain secular ends, such as attracting merchants, settlers, or mercenaries. And it usually carried the qualification that these same groups refrain from public proselytizing or disputation.[13]

[13] For an example of free exercise being used in this restrictive sense, see Charles Fenton James, *Documentary History of the Struggle for Religious Liberty in Virginia* (Lynchburg, VA: J.P. Bell, 1900), 22.

Occasionally, free exercise was employed to more expansive ends. A handful of early colonies offered free exercise privileges to all Christians. Maryland's 1649 Act Concerning Religion, for example, stipulated that Christians would not be "Molested" in the "free exercise" of their religion. Similarly, Rhode Island's 1663 charter pledged subjects the "free exercise" of their "Christian faith and worship of God." However, even these liberal grants were hemmed in by stringent behavioral constraints. Maryland's act specified that the punishment for blasphemy and other impolite forms of religious speech was death and property forfeiture. Rhode Island's subjects enjoyed religious liberty on the condition that they behave "peaceablie and quietlie" and refrain from disturbing others.[14]

A latitudinarian wave sweeping across eighteenth-century Protestant communities made restricted understandings of free exercise less tenable. Increasingly, religious and civil leaders emphasized that minor differences in doctrine would need to be accommodated and that individuals should be permitted to form their own judgments and attend worship services that suited them. An influx of European nonconformists, a series of cross-denominational evangelical revivals, and rapidly expanding networks of print and trade extinguished any remaining hopes for theological uniformity in the British American colonies.

These changes help explain why the term "free exercise" acquired a more universal valence by the Revolutionary era. Making the case for broader religious protections in Virginia, Patrick Henry noted as early as 1766 how the population of some northern colonies had been augmented because they granted the "free exercise of religion" to white inhabitants.[15] Why would a Protestant fleeing persecution in Europe sail for Virginia when its northern counterparts offered much more generous terms?

Colonial leaders were even beginning to consider Roman Catholics, a group long reviled by Protestants, as entitled to nondiscriminatory treatment. A decade after Henry's speech, and just two months before the Virginia Convention drafted its Bill of Rights, the Continental Congress commissioned a small delegation (which included Roman

[14] Maryland Toleration Act, September 21, 1649, *The Avalon Project*, Yale Law School, http://avalon.law.yale.edu/18th_century/maryland_toleration.asp; Charter of Rhode Island and Providence Plantations, July 15, 1663, *The Avalon Project*, Yale Law School, http://avalon.law.yale.edu/17th_century/ri04.asp. Spelling modernized.

[15] William Wirt Henry, ed., *Patrick Henry: Life, Correspondence and Speeches* (New York: Charles Scribner's Sons, 1891), 1:116.

Catholic statesman Charles Carroll and his second cousin, the Roman Catholic priest John Carroll) to deliver a conciliatory message to their Quebecois neighbors. They offered assurances that Congress would not interfere with "the free and undisturbed Exercise" of religion among the province's Catholics, as long as Protestants were accorded the same treatment.[16]

Two months after the Canadian delegation departed on their mission, Virginia's provincial assembly drafted a Declaration of Rights. That is when James Madison introduced his famous revision, substituting "all men are equally entitled to the full and free exercise of [religion]" for "the fullest Toleration in the Exercise of Religion." Three states would later propose Madison's exact language for inclusion in the 1787 Constitution. And six states, not including Virginia, incorporated "free exercise" into their own constitutions between 1776 and 1792.[17]

Despite its increasing popularity and expanding application, "free exercise" was absent from Madison's original proposal for amendments at the 1789 Congress. However, the House and Senate made their way back to the phrase intermittently as they drafted and redrafted the religious clauses. Their members tried other possibilities, such as "Congress shall not make any law, infringing the rights of conscience" and "nor shall the equal rights of conscience be infringed." In yet another iteration, the federal legislature was forbidden from passing laws to "prevent the free exercise [of religion], or to infringe the rights of conscience."[18] None seems to have been satisfactory.

In the end, Congress voted for "free exercise." If the term lacked the idealistic appeal of rights of conscience, it encompassed a contemporary constellation of intuitions and associations that both the House and Senate could endorse. "Free exercise" still possessed a concrete practical meaning – referring to the right to worship in one's own way – but had escaped the confines of its seventeenth-century application.

[16] Instructions and Commission from Congress to Franklin, Charles Carroll, and Samuel Chase for the Canadian Mission, March 20, 1776, *Founders Online*, National Archives, http://founders.archives.gov/documents/Franklin/01-22-02-0228.

[17] The six other states were Pennsylvania (1776); Georgia (1777); New York (1777); Vermont (1777); South Carolina (1790); Delaware (1792).

[18] For a concise and comprehensive list, see Witte and Nichols, eds., *Religion and the American Constitutional Experiment*, 296–297.

No Law Respecting an Establishment of Religion

The establishment clause is no less a mystery than its free exercise counterpart. Congress settled on wording that prohibited it from making a law "respecting an establishment of religion." Whatever they meant by that phrase, it represented an unmistakable break with the regimes that preceded it. For centuries, western European states had been legally entangled with churches. As Glenn A. Moots points out in Chapter 4 of this volume, early modern Europeans and American colonists generally presumed that the magistrate should be a "nursing father" to the church, and the churches a faithful aide to the magistrate. Much of New England (Massachusetts, Connecticut, and New Hampshire) maintained a Congregational establishment through the colonial period, while the southern states (Georgia, Maryland, Virginia, and both Carolinas) supported an Anglican establishment.

The diversity among these regimes, as well as the sizable cleavages between colonial church–state arrangements and those in Europe, left Congress without a single, common understanding of what constituted an "establishment." In Massachusetts, Connecticut, and New Hampshire, the churches received local tax support and the state treated Protestant dissenters, such as Baptists and Quakers, like second-class citizens. But their governments imposed no creeds and generally stayed out of church affairs. The southern colonies operated within the loose parameters of English church–state arrangements, which mandated the reading of the Book of Common Prayer, directed tax receipts to parish vestries, and permitted only Anglican clergymen to administer the sacraments of baptism and marriage.

Despite – or perhaps because of – such differences, leading founders agreed that the federal government had no business erecting a religious establishment. They were generally averse to prescribing forms of worship, investing churches and clergy with civil privileges, or giving the state a formal role in church affairs.[19] At the same time, they did not think

[19] "I know," the Reverend Samuel Cooper wrote, "there is a diversity of sentiment respecting the extent of civil power in religious matters." Samuel Cooper, "A Sermon on the Day of the Commencement of the Constitution (1780)," in *Intestine Enemies: Catholics in Protestant America, 1605–1791*, ed. Robert Emmett Curran (Washington, DC: Catholic University of America Press of America, 2017), 258. John Witte, Jr. and Joel A. Nichols point out that "most founders understood the establishment of religion to mean governmental actions to

that the federal government should restrict state establishments and expressed few reservations about state laws limiting Sabbath activity and prohibiting blasphemy.

By the time the First Congress met in 1789, anti-establishment sentiment had been mounting for decades. The imperial controversy with Great Britain over colonial taxes and trade regulations sparked an intensive reevaluation of the customs and institutions associated with monarchical rule, including the Anglican Church's cozy relationship with the English state. During the Revolutionary War, prevailing opinion shifted decisively in favor of voluntary religious arrangements.

The most adamant opponents of establishments were located on opposite ends of the Protestant theological spectrum, inclining toward either rational deism or pious evangelicalism. They found common ground on the odious effects of church–state union, particularly for churches.[20] Amid the postwar debate over a general religious assessment in Virginia, for example, James Madison tried to redirect his colleagues' attention from the civic value of religion to what he referred to in his notes as the "True question." Not, "Is religion necessary?" but "are religious establishments necessary for religion?"[21] To answer positively, he suggested on another occasion, was to betray a lack of confidence in Christianity's potency, to attribute its successes to the artificial props of state regulation and mandatory support.[22] Madison's argument was probably designed to sway moderate

'settle,' 'fix,' 'define,' 'ordain,' 'enact,' or 'set up' the religion of the community – whether its religious doctrines and liturgies, its religious texts and traditions, or its clergy and property." See Witte and Nichols, eds., *Religion and the American Constitutional Experiment*, 59.

[20] James Kabala notes that "while opponents of entanglement between government and religion did not often speak of desiring 'a separation of church and state,' they did speak fairly frequently of their fear of the opposite, a 'union of church and state.'" See Kabala, *Church-State Relations in the Early American Republic*, 6.

[21] The original language is as follows: "True Question – Is Rel: necesy.? are Religs. Estabts. necessy. for Religion? no." See Madison's Notes for Debates on the General Assessment Bill, [Outline B], [December 23–24, 1784], *Founders Online*, National Archives, last modified July 12, 2016, http://founders.archives.gov/documents/Madison/01-08-02-0104-0003.

[22] Christian history, Madison argued, "disavows a dependence on the powers of this world." James Madison, "Memorial and Remonstrance against Religious Assessments," June 20, 1785, in Philip B. Kurland and Ralph Lerner, eds., *The Founders' Constitution* (Chicago, IL: University of Chicago Press, 1987), Vol. 5, Amendment I (Religion), Doc. 43, http://press-pubs.uchicago.edu/founders/documents/amendI_religions43.html.

Anglicans, though it also anticipated the Baptist preacher John Leland's bolder assertion that "all state establishments of Christianity in the world, are ... ANTI-CHRISTOCRACIES."[23] Both rationalists like Madison and evangelicals like Leland regarded establishments as resource-devouring institutions that stifled inquiry and perverted religious faith.[24] And both insisted that free citizens should have the right to worship according to the dictates of conscience. (Few, besides Leland, ever gave much consideration to the religious plight of enslaved people.)

Delegates to Virginia's 1776 Convention fired the first live volley at religious establishments. They adopted a Declaration of Rights that guaranteed equal treatment under the law. Though the Church of England got a reprieve when Madison's proposal to uproot the establishment was defeated, its position remained precarious. Over the next few years, the state legislature voted to continue the Church's funding. However, efforts by partisans to permanently reinstate their privileged position failed. Passage of Jefferson's Statute for Religious Freedom in 1786 relegated the newly named Protestant Episcopal Church to the same civil status as other religious groups in Virginia.

The church–state revolution soon spread to other states. All of them adopted provisions protecting religious liberty, and those with church establishments trimmed them back. That did not mean that early Americans opposed all government aid to religion. From the mid-1770s through the late 1780s, several legislatures and constitutional conventions either adopted or seriously considered religious assessments supporting Christian (or just Protestant) worship and ministration. Historians call these *nonpreferential* establishments because they did not give formal preference to any one church. In practice, such measures usually benefitted some more than others, especially those with long-standing ties to the state.

Contemporaries delivered another blow against establishments by abolishing or curtailing religious tests for office. Prior to the American Revolution, European and colonial governments required that officeholders swear an oath

[23] John Leland, "The Government of Christ a Christocracy (1804)," in *Writings of Late John Leland, Including Some Events in His Life*, ed. L.F. Greene (New York: G.W. Wood, 1845), 281.

[24] Thomas S. Kidd lays out the major points of consensus in Kidd, *God of Liberty: A Religious History of the American Revolution* (New York: Basic Books, 2010), 6–8.

testifying to their conformity with the established faith. Rather than mandating adherence to a particular church, the earliest state constitutions permitted all Christians, or at least all Protestants, to serve. Virginia's 1786 Statute for Religious Freedom prohibited all religious tests for office. Article VI of the US Constitution forbade such strictures as well, and over the next decade several states moved in the same direction.[25]

Less conspicuous features of the church–state establishment eroded during the latter half of the eighteenth century. Colleges declared themselves open to all Protestants, while churches and synagogues of every stripe gained the right to incorporate. Prior to independence, nonconformist groups were barred from initiating lawsuits, or even the privilege of holding and transmitting property, which left their congregations vulnerable. The passage of nonexclusive incorporation laws leveled the playing field for them.[26]

Despite vociferous objections, a tax-supported system of religion survived in New England (Rhode Island excepted) into the first decades of the nineteenth century. And every state maintained the rudiments of what John Witte called the "moral establishment," that is, laws forbidding nonreligious activities on the Sabbath and outlawing blasphemous expression.[27] But the new nation had reached an inflection point when it came to relations between church and state. Though never fully separated, the connection between them had been severely, and irrevocably, frayed.

Religious Diversity

As uncontroversial as the establishment clause was, the ban on religious tests for federal office stuck in the craw of some orthodox Christians. They regarded it as an open invitation to heretics and infidels. Didn't republican governments require virtuous leaders at their head? And didn't republican citizens require the backbone of Christian rectitude?[28]

[25] Daniel L. Dreisbach, "The Constitution's Forgotten Religion Clause: Reflections on the Article VI Religious Test Ban," *Journal of Church and State* 38, no. 2 (Spring 1996): 272.

[26] Mark Douglas McGarvie, *One Nation Under Law: America's Early National Struggles to Separate Church and State* (DeKalb, IL: Northern Illinois University Press, 2004).

[27] John Witte, Jr., "'A Most Mild and Equitable Establishment of Religion': John Adams and the Massachusetts Experiment," *Journal of Church and State* 41, no. 2 (Spring 1999): 240.

[28] "There are," writes James H. Hutson, "a multitude of statements after 1776 about Christianity's ability to make Americans 'good citizens,' 'good members of society,' 'the

The problem for those who wanted to maintain some kind of confessional regime, as for proponents of religious establishment more generally, was the sheer diversity of religious groups that policymakers now encountered. By the end of the American Revolution, a dizzying array of Protestants who had once been deemed "dissenters" comprised a majority of the colonial religious population. Few leaders were eager to see a test imposed that might tilt the balance in favor of one denomination or the other.

It is worth emphasizing that the primary form of religious discordance confronting the founders existed between Christians, especially Protestant Christians. Warnings about Jews, Muslims, and atheists seizing control of office were probably a rhetorical canard, more effective as metaphor than as a genuine source of contemporary concerns. When the Constitution was framed, there were roughly 2,000 Jews in a US population of three and a half million. Islam was mostly confined to surreptitious meetings of enslaved people, and, with very few exceptions, atheists kept their unbelief to themselves.

To our modern eyes, eighteenth-century Protestant denominations appear to be no more than a hair's breadth apart. Yet those differences seemed of vital importance at time – dangerous if allowed to fester, and absolutely vital to transcend. Consider what happened at the second session of Continental Congress in September 1774. A proposal was made to open deliberations with prayer. Two delegates objected that the group was too "divided in religious Sentiments, some Episcopalians, some Quakers, some Anabaptists, some Presbyterians and some Congregationalists," to worship as a body.[29] The colonies' religious fractures seemed, at least for the moment, unbridgeable.

But a more conciliatory approach ultimately prevailed. After listening to the objections offered by his counterparts, Massachusetts' Samuel Adams "arose and said he was no Bigot, and could hear a Prayer from a Gentleman of Piety and Virtue, who was at the same Time a Friend to his Country." Adams, a Congregationalist, moved that a Philadelphia Episcopalian read prayers the next day.[30] Over the ensuing years, members of Congress made a point of patronizing various Philadelphia churches, even attending

most industrious and wise citizens.'" See Hutson, *Church and State in America: The First Two Centuries* (New York: Cambridge University Press, 2008), 113.

29 John Adams to Abigail Adams, September 16, 1774, *Adams Family Papers*, Massachusetts Historical Society, accessed online August 6, 2018, www.masshist.org/digitaladams/archive/doc?id=L17740916ja.

30 Ibid.

a Catholic Mass, a practice that would have made their Protestant ancestors blanch.

The commander-in-chief of the Continental Army and first President of the United States promoted these ecumenical sentiments. During his first term, George Washington responded sympathetically to a host of congregations and denominational leaders. None were more notable than the letters his office penned to Jewish and Catholic leaders. Washington told his Catholic correspondents that he expected their fellow Americans to bear in mind their patriotism during the war, as well as the support of Catholic France. He also shared his optimism that people everywhere, especially in the United States, were becoming more "liberal."[31]

Washington might have cited his own example. Twelve months after Samuel Adams made the case for interdenominational piety in Congress, Washington instructed the commander of an invasion force headed to Roman Catholic Canada to "protect and support the free Exercise of the Religion of the Country and the undisturbed Enjoyment of the rights of Conscience in religious Matters, with your utmost Influence and Authority."[32] He was even more magnanimous with his Jewish correspondents. Washington assured Rhode Island's Newport congregation that every US citizen enjoyed "liberty of conscience and immunities of citizenship," and that this new government would offer "bigotry no sanction" and "persecution no assistance."[33]

Given the revolutionary fervor against foreign and anti-republican influences and the civil instability that often triggers religious violence, the new nation could have been a dangerous place for Catholics, Jews, and other unpopular religious groups. Widespread support for free exercise made America safer for them. The fact that these groups accommodated themselves to both republicanism and disestablishment made it safer still.

For Catholics and Episcopalians, whose hierarchical ecclesiastical structures and allegiance to kings and popes might have constituted fatal

[31] George Washington to Roman Catholics in America, c. March 15, 1790, *Founders Online*, National Archives, last modified June 29, 2017, http://founders.archives.gov/documents/Washington/05-05-02-0193.

[32] Instructions to Colonel Benedict Arnold, September 14, 1775, *Founders Online*, National Archives, last modified June 29, 2017, http://founders.archives.gov/documents/Washington/03-01-02-0356.

[33] George Washington to the Hebrew Congregation in Newport, Rhode Island, August 18, 1790, *Founders Online*, National Archives, last modified June 29, 2017, http://founders.archives.gov/documents/Washington/05-06-02-0135.

liabilities in the new republic, putting some distance between their churches and the old regime was essential. William White, the nation's first Presiding Bishop of the Episcopal Church, emphasized that the church being raised from the remains of the old Anglican foundation would be faithful to the new nation and its republican principles. White attested to his coreligionists' patriotism and disavowed the principle of divine right, along with "any spiritual jurisdiction, connected with the temporal authority of a foreign state."[34]

Catholic leaders proved at least as keen to demonstrate their enthusiasm for the United States and its republican experiment. They had little choice. Catholicism represented Protestantism's chief ideological adversary for much of the early modern era, and early national Protestants inherited a deep-seated enmity toward the Pope and his Church's teachings. Anti-Catholicism was a mainstream tenet. Every fourth year, Harvard's distinguished Dudleian lecturer was obligated to use his allotted time "for the detecting, and convicting, and exposing the idolatry of the Romish church; their tyranny, usurpations, damnable heresies, fatal errors, abominable superstitions, and other crying wickednesses in their high places; and finally to prove that the church of Rome is that mystical Babylon, that man of sin, that apostate church, spoken of in the New-Testament."[35]

American Catholics' unstinting support for the United States, along with Catholic France's gift of munitions, naval support, and whole regiments of soldiers, reconfigured the geopolitical situation. The religious conflicts were harder to smooth over, though they too diminished in intensity. As the United States gained its formal independence, Michael Breidenbach notes, the Vatican took the unusual step of permitting American Catholics to elect their first bishop (John Carroll) rather than appointing him. They did so out of deference to American republicanism and because of Carroll's pleas to that effect.[36]

American Jews had no foreign ecclesiastical jurisdictions to disavow. Yet because there were so few of them, and because European Christians had

[34] William White, "The Case of the Episcopal Churches in the United States Considered (1782)," ed. Richard G. Salomon, *Historical Magazine of the Protestant Episcopal Church* 22, no. 4 (December 1953): 448.

[35] John Lathrop, *A Discourse on the Errors of Popery* (Boston, 1793), 5–6, https://catalog.princeton.edu/catalog/2662404.

[36] Michael D. Breidenbach, "Conciliarism and the American Founding," *William and Mary Quarterly*, 3rd ser., 73, no. 3 (July 2016): 487.

persecuted them with such unrelenting viciousness for centuries, they had reason to be concerned. Once again, republican commitment on the part of the religious minority and tolerance on the part of the majority combined to ensure that this religious minority could, in the words of George Washington to Newport's Hebrew congregation, flourish under their "own vine and fig tree."[37] Like Catholics, America's Jews had proved model citizens during the Revolutionary years. Three served as officers in the upper tier of the Continental Army (a privilege, Jonathan Sarna notes, denied to them in Great Britain).[38] Their financial support was also indispensable. The Jewish merchant Haym Salomon arranged for an essential flow of funds both to the fledgling government and to some of its leading framers.

Even though prohibitions on Jewish office holding remained in some state constitutions, the American Revolution inaugurated an unmistakable shift in Christian treatment of their Jewish neighbors. Early national Jews were welcomed into postwar parades and genuine respect was paid to their dietary restrictions. While anti-Semitic bigotry abided in the dark recesses of American culture, it was beginning to subside from public discourse and polite conversation.

Subsequent social and political developments bore out Washington's hopes. Catholic and Jewish migrants streamed into the country during the nineteenth century. And upstart Protestant groups – in particular the Methodists and Baptists – overspread the country, for the most part dwelling peaceably under their own vines and fig trees.

The Meaning of Religion

By forbidding Congress authority over religious institutions and practices, the Constitution secured a privileged status for religion that it has not since relinquished. That fact has been a perpetual source of judicial and philosophical concern.[39] Not least of the resulting conundrums is this: What counts as religion? Does it include only institutional religion? Might constitutional protections for religion be extended to irreligion?

[37] Washington to the Hebrew Congregation in Newport.

[38] Jonathan D. Sarna, *American Judaism: A History* (New Haven, CT: Yale University Press, 2004), 31–33.

[39] See the chapters in Part I of this volume.

During the latter decades of the eighteenth century, leading liberals stretched the definition of religion beyond orthodox Protestantism and guarded against small-minded efforts to confine it to a narrow set of beliefs and practices. Thomas Jefferson famously (to some, infamously) wrote that it did not matter whether his neighbor believed in twenty gods or one. All that mattered was his civil behavior.[40] Madison shared Jefferson's outlook, and applied it to more practical matters. In 1785, for example, Virginia assembly members voted that funds derived from a general assessment should be directed toward "Christian" ministers rather than "religious" teachers generally. Madison spent more than a year fighting the proposed measure. Though he suspected that the Christian qualification could be "easily eluded," Madison vented to Jefferson that it was "obnoxious on account of its dishonorable principle and dangerous tendency."[41]

Jefferson and Madison seemed to appreciate that even a flexible understanding of rights of conscience meant little for religious minorities unless the state operated with a definition of religion encompassing a wide range of beliefs and mode of worship. The differences between liberals and conservatives on religious liberty often had more to do with their understanding of what constituted "religion" as it did their understanding of what constituted "liberty." The late eighteenth-century revolution in religious liberty was thus as much an experiment in comparative theology as it was one in republican constitutionalism, expanding the meaning of what it meant to be Christian and religious.

The earliest state constitutions tended to embody a more restricted approach. Framers of the 1780 Massachusetts Constitution, for example, declared that no would be "hurt, molested, or restrained . . . for worshipping GOD in the manner and season most agreeable to the dictates of his own conscience."[42] Over the ensuing paragraphs, they authorized the legislature to mandate church support and attendance. Then, in the final paragraph devoted to religious rights, they made it clear that the "religion"

[40] Thomas Jefferson, *Notes on the State of Virginia*, ed. Frank Shuffelton (New York: Penguin Books, 1999), 196.

[41] James Madison to Thomas Jefferson, January 9, 1785, *Founders Online*, National Archives, last modified June 13, 2018, http://founders.archives.gov/documents/Jefferson/01-07-02-0433.

[42] Massachusetts Constitution of 1780, in Philip B. Kurland and Ralph Lerner, eds., *The Founders' Constitution* (Chicago, IL: University of Chicago Press, 1987), Vol. 5, Bill of Rights, Doc. 6, http://press-pubs.uchicago.edu/founders/documents/amendI_religions43.html.

protected by the Constitution belonged to Christians alone. (One wry commentator compared the Massachusetts constitution to a "cow that gives a full pail of milk and then kicks it over."[43])

Some were even stingier in their guarantees. South Carolina's 1778 constitution stipulated that "all persons and religious societies who acknowledge that there is one God, and a future state of rewards and punishments, and that God is publicly to be worshipped, shall be freely tolerated." They also established the "Christian Protestant religion," limited office-holding to Protestants, and spelled out in very specific terms what its framers considered a legitimate church. That required at least fifteen adult males, who either identified with a Protestant denomination or possessed some other legally recognized name.[44] The general assessment bill proposed in Virginia in 1779 gave a similarly concrete and constricted scope to the "Christian Religion." Under the provisions of that bill only Protestant churches would have received funding. Catholic churches would have been ineligible.

Despite these narrow constitutional renderings of both religion and Christianity, it was becoming possible for late eighteenth-century Americans to see religion as a broad spectrum of beliefs and practices. Conversely, it was becoming impossible for them to plausibly assert that religion was identical with Protestantism. There were few more vivid illustrations of this enlarged perspective than Hannah Adams' 1784 encyclopedia of religious groups, *An Alphabetical Compendium of the Various Sects.* This remarkable work accorded surprisingly respectful treatment to hundreds of faiths. Though grounded in a Protestant Christian perspective, it offered readers a panoramic view of religious life across time and space.[45]

Some state establishments of religion endured into the nineteenth century. Yet the constitutions adopted in the 1780s and 1790s were more generous, both in terms of the liberty they protected and the varieties of religion they acknowledged. By 1790, South Carolina guaranteed "free exercise and enjoyment of religious profession and worship, without discrimination or preference."[46] That was it. The state had excised the once

[43] Quoted in Hutson, *Church and State in America*, 127–128.

[44] Constitution of South Carolina, March 19, 1778, *The Avalon Project*, Yale Law School, http://avalon.law.yale.edu/18th_century/sc02.asp.

[45] Hannah Adams, *An Alphabetical Compendium of the Various Sects Which Have Appeared in the World from the Beginning of the Christian Era to the Present Day* (Boston, 1784).

[46] Edwin S. Gaustad, *Faith of the Founders: Religion and the New Nation* (San Francisco: Harper & Row, 1987), appendix B: 172.

elaborate conditions required for official support and recognition. When it came to religious liberty, the new constitutions signaled their respect for conscience through subtraction rather than addition, paring back religious tests and other distinctions between believers.

Less clear was the status of nonbelievers and outspoken skeptics. Religion's special protected status in the Constitution did not auger well for the irreligious, nor did the anti-blasphemy laws that remained in state legal codes into the twentieth century. Belief in a future state of rewards and punishments was regarded as essential to the republic's long-term viability. After all, what deterred an officeholder from lying if deception and malfeasance could go eternally unpunished?[47]

Still, there is reason to believe that the founders did not mean to deprive nonbelievers of the rights extended to believers. In the years after the Constitution was framed, atheists and Deists were generally left alone unless they criticized Christian orthodoxy in public. And even then they could call upon state and federal protections for speech and the press. Anti-blasphemy statutes lurked on the statute books as a potential weapon against unbelief, but were seldom enforced.

This, of course, leaves another question unanswered: whether the religious clauses were secular in effect, or by design.

Belief and Unbelief

In the months and years after the US Constitution was written, pious critics charged that the framers had made a grievous omission: They had left out God. The nation's newly ratified charter contained no mention of the Father, Son, or Holy Ghost. Asked about their absence, Alexander Hamilton is said to have cracked: "We forgot."[48] Whether Hamilton's remark was a statement of fact about the Constitution's framers or an irreverent commentary on the question, it represented both a departure from the reflexive piety of the past, and a potent source of anxiety in the present.

That unease was already evident during Congress's deliberations over the First Amendment. When the religion clauses came before

[47] See Hutson, *Church and State in America*, 110.

[48] Quoted in Ron Chernow, *Alexander Hamilton* (New York: Penguin Books, 2004), 235.

the House in mid-August 1788, New York's Peter Sylvester raised what now seems a curious point: the possibility that the proposed language "might be thought to have a tendency to abolish religion altogether." Sylvester's concern resurfaced sometime thereafter when Connecticut's Benjamin Huntington expressed the fear that such an imprecisely worded amendment might be misconstrued as a prohibition on religious support, subjecting state and local support to federal court action.[49] Like his New York colleague, Huntington wondered whether Madison's proposal would only serve "to patronize those who professed no religion at all."[50]

We might dismiss these sentiments as the fleeting concerns of a late summer day. But a week later, while making the case against military exemptions for conscientious objectors, Pennsylvania's Thomas Scott raised the matter again. If the reports of religion's "decline" were true, the government would need "to guard against those who are of no religion." Otherwise, "when the time comes that there is no religion," nonreligious grounds would be used to secure exemptions.[51]

No religion? That seems like a remote possibility in a country that had experienced intense religious revivals in the preceding decades and where clergymen were alternately blamed and commended for inciting the American Revolution. Nonetheless, during and after the American Revolution, theological currents shifted in a rationalist direction.[52] The Virginia Statute for Religious Freedom appeared to sail on those tides. While the long-winded preamble gestured toward orthodox Christian doctrines (referencing "Almighty God" and the "Holy Author of Our Religion"), it also advanced the secular proposition that "civil rights have no dependence on our religious opinions, any more than our opinions in physics or geometry."[53] Moreover, the statute banned religious tests for office, doing away with the conventional requirement that officeholders needed to be Protestant, or at least Christian.

[49] Cogan, ed., *The Complete Bill of Rights*, 60 [August 15, 1789]. [50] Ibid.

[51] *Annals of Congress* 1789, 1st Cong., 1st sess., 796 [August 20, 1789], Library of Congress, https://memory.loc.gov/ammem/amlaw/lwac.html.

[52] See Amanda Porterfield, *Conceived in Doubt: Religion and Politics in the New American Nation* (Chicago, IL: University of Chicago Press, 2012); Christopher Grasso, *Skepticism and American Faith: From the Revolution to the Civil War* (New York: Oxford University Press, 2018).

[53] [Virginia] Act for Establishing Religious Freedom.

To some worried contemporaries, the abolition of religious tests for office in Virginia (and then at the federal level) confirmed that the United States was on the road to irreligion. "[I]t begins to be a growing idea," one prominent New England minister had complained in 1783, "that it is mighty indifferent ... whether a man be of this or the other religious sect ... and that truly deists, and men of indifferentism to all religion are the most suitable persons for civil office."[54] Shortly after passage of the Virginia statute, a Philadelphia merchant warned that the statute's ban on religious tests had cleared the way for anti-Christian measures and legislators, including atheists, Muslims, or those "of any other creed, however unfriendly to liberty or the morals of a free country."[55]

As to the practical question of whether Americans were regularly attending church or not, and what they believed or doubted, the jury is still out. No Gallup or Pew Foundation polls were conducted during the colonial area. The best that some very good historians have been able to do is assemble anecdotal accounts of church attendance and pair these with scattered data about the number of pews available for sitting in the late eighteenth century.[56] In other words, we have a prodigious unknown built into our understanding of the period's religious life.

Perhaps more relevant to our understanding of the religious clauses are the particular convictions of those who framed them. Early national conventions and legislatures included a mixture of more-or-less conventional believers and moderate, skeptical deists. Everyone was deeply immersed in Bible language and tropes, though not everyone believed what they read there.[57]

[54] Ezra Stiles, *The United States Elevated to Glory and Honor* (New Haven, 1783), 70.

[55] John Swanwick, *Considerations on Act of the Legislature of Virginia* (Philadelphia, 1786), iii.

[56] For arguments against the presumption that late eighteenth-century America was light on religious attendance, see James H. Hutson, "The Christian Nation Question," in *Forgotten Features of the Founding: The Recovery of Religious Themes in the Early American Republic* ed. Hutson (Lanham, MD: Lexington Books, 2003); Patricia U. Bonomi and Peter R. Eisenstadt, "Church Adherence in the Eighteenth-Century British American Colonies," *William and Mary Quarterly*, 3rd ser., 39, no. 2 (April 1982): 245–286. Mark David Hall provides an update in "Vindiciae, Contra Tyrannos: The Influence of the Reformed Tradition in the American Founding," in *Faith and the Founders of the American Republic*, ed. Daniel L. Dreisbach and Mark David Hall (Oxford: Oxford University Press, 2014), 45–46.

[57] "[L]ate-eighteenth-century Americans remained biblically literate," writes Daniel L. Dreisbach, "and, contrary to the claims of modern scholarship, the Bible informed public culture. Biblical language pervaded the rhetoric of not only pious founders, such as Samuel Adams, Patrick Henry, John Jay, Roger Sherman, and John Witherspoon, but also those

Devout Christians, such as Henry Laurens, Elias Boudinot, John Jay, Roger Sherman, George Mason, and Patrick Henry, took leading roles in the creation and ratification of constitutions.[58] But so did rationalists such as George Washington, Thomas Jefferson, and James Madison, who conveyed doubts about revelation (Jefferson), avoided explicit references to God (Washington), or repeatedly challenged religious authority (Madison).

For decades, the rationalists have received much of the credit for the founders' achievements, which lent a secular tint to First Amendment interpretation. Why not, Mark David Hall asks, assign comparable importance to other states and other imperatives – as well as other individuals, such as Sherman, an orthodox Connecticut Protestant? After all, Sherman won most of the battles that he fought in the constitutional convention and played a key role in the First Congress, as well as church–state matters in his home state.[59]

Adopting more nuanced narratives does not, of course, mean that we have to abandon the well-documented conclusion that evangelical voters and rationalist-leaning statesmen played a critical role in reshaping church–state relations. But we also cannot presume that the cultural environment in which the religious clauses were forged was dominated by Deists, intent on separating church from state.

Conclusion: Interpretations and Aspirations

When it comes to our understanding of the past, the more we know, the more complicated things become. Rigorous historical study of the First Amendment's religious clauses began in the postwar era. Among the chief

figures most influenced by the Enlightenment, including Benjamin Franklin and Thomas Paine." See Dreisbach, "The Bible and the Political Culture of the American Founding," in *Faith and the Founders*, ed. Dreisbach and Hall, 145. See also Dreisbach, *Reading the Bible with the Founding Fathers* (New York: Oxford University Press, 2017).

58 On these men, see Hutson, *Church and State in America*, 95.

59 See Mark David Hall, "Madison's Memorial and Remonstrance, Jefferson's Statute for Religious Liberty, and the Creation of the First Amendment," *American Political Thought* 3, no. 1 (Spring 2014): 57–58. "If jurists and scholars are really interested in the 'generating history' of the Establishment Clause," Hall writes, "it is a mistake to assume that Jefferson's and Madison's approaches to these issues reflect the views of their peers" (p. 36). Donald L. Drakeman writes: "Whatever the Congress, the ratifiers, or the people thought the establishment clause meant, there is no evidence that any of those groups believed that it encompassed Madison's Memorial or Jefferson's Statute." See Drakeman, *Church, State, and Original Intent*, 259.

causes was judicial necessity. To sort out some difficult church–state questions, the Supreme Court began digging into the religious clauses' "generating history," as Justice Wiley Rutledge called it.[60] Unencumbered by the thousands of articles and books that have been published over the past half century, the postwar Court treated the purposes behind the religious clauses as relatively straightforward. Writing for the majority in the same 1947 case (*Everson* v. *Board of Education of the Township of Ewing*), Justice Hugo Black observed that the amendment's language was the "culmination" of a liberalizing process that first manifested itself in Virginia. Black attributed the First Amendment's protections to a recent intensification of the western world's long-standing tradition of religious persecution and conflict. The founders, he reasoned, designed a system to keep such horrors at bay. In what seemed like a counterintuitive ruling, Black and four other members of the Court approved a local school board's reimbursement transportation costs to the parents of students attending Catholic schools in the district.

The court's dissenters did not dispute the majority's historical observations so much as the conclusions drawn from them. Justice Rutledge contended that the First Amendment was designed "to create a complete and permanent separation of the spheres of religious activity and civil authority by comprehensively forbidding every form of public aid or support for religion."[61] Justice Robert Jackson agreed that the Constitution had raised a "wall of separation," an impassable barrier "between religion and almost every other subject matter of legislation."[62] Therefore, they concluded, the town should not reimburse costs that had some religious bearing. The specifics of the Court's decision in *Everson* had little impact on the shape of the controversies that followed. What stuck was the supposition that the founders had intended to prevent the mixing of these two categorically different pursuits. This, we have since learned, was a somewhat dubious conclusion.

Church–state jurisprudence and scholarship became more sophisticated, and more contentious, over the succeeding decades. Two insights inspired meaningful revisions in historical interpretation. The first should have seemed obvious all along: When the religious clauses were drafted, they only applied to the federal government. State establishments remained

[60] *Everson* v. *Board of Education*, 330 U.S. 1 at 33 (1947). [61] Ibid. at 31–32.
[62] Ibid. at 26.

legally insulated from their impact, and state authorities could still infringe on free exercise if their own constitutions permitted it. The second insight was subtler: Early national Americans were comfortable with the presence of religion in public life. They "accommodated" religion in a number of different ways, including government-funded missionary efforts, religious oaths, and congressional prayer (scholars and jurists who emphasize this position are known as "accommodationists"). Neither of these revelations threatens the well-supported conclusion that the Constitution's framers set the federal government on a largely secular foundation. They just make it difficult to maintain that the intent was to strip public institutions and public spaces (schools, prisons, courthouses, etc.) of their religious trappings.

Another provocative, albeit less common, view holds that the free exercise and establishment clauses were *only* exercises in federalism. That is, they allowed the framers to punt substantive religious liberty questions to the states. "[S]omething like the free exercise clause would have to be stated or implied," Steven D. Smith writes, "in order to effect an essentially federalist solution to the religious question."[63] While there may be some truth to that assertion, Smith's view discounts the deep, popular convictions and simmering anxieties that prompted Madison and the founders to consider an amendment protecting religious liberty, and ultimately motivated them to finish the job. Madison understood as well as anyone that federal power was severely circumscribed. That was one of the reasons he opposed amendments in the first place. Federal protections for religious liberty were inadequate in themselves. To actually shield believers from state impositions, he believed, required complementary action on the state level.

Inadequate, however, was not the same thing as irrelevant. Madison's May 1789 speech on behalf of amendments made that point. While "unimportant" in themselves, he conceded, the combination of these constitutional revisions with complementary state measures was likely to have a "salutary tendency."[64] Madison's visionary friend, Thomas Jefferson, floated the same idea a few weeks before when he noted that even if

[63] Steven D. Smith, *Foreordained Failure: The Quest for a Constitutional Principle of Religious Freedom* (New York: Oxford University Press, 1995), 43.

[64] James Madison, "Speech in Congress Proposing Constitutional Amendments," in *James Madison: Writings*, ed. Jack N. Rakove (New York: Library of America, 1999), 445.

a Bill of Rights failed to block all government infringements on liberty, "it is of great potency always, and rarely inefficacious."[65]

Whatever the intentions behind them, the First Amendment communicated an unambiguous signal that the new national government would be a partisan of religious liberty. Religious minorities showed their appreciation almost immediately. Members of Newport Rhode Island's Touro Synagogue wrote to George Washington in August 1790, lauding the new federal government, which gave "bigotry ... no sanction" and "persecution no assistance."[66] Roman Catholic leaders did the same, expressing their confidence that the new regime would protect religious liberties.[67] By the 1820s, the nation's first Catholic newspaper featured the religious clauses on its masthead.[68]

The First Amendment's winding route to legal relevance in the mid-twentieth century resembled the process by which they were originally framed, representing both an accommodation to the needs of vocal religious minorities and the reluctant codification of widely held principles. Jehovah's Witnesses forced the nation's hand in the 1930s and 1940s, much as Baptists had forced it during the republic's early years. In both instances, beleaguered religious groups capitalized on shared intuitions regarding the sanctity of conscience and the value of tolerance, giving them explicit and material form. If their petitions were not as pungent as a certain giant cheese shipped from Cheshire, Massachusetts to Washington, DC, in the waning days of 1801, they were nonetheless employed to great effect.

[65] Thomas Jefferson to James Madison, March 15, 1789, *Founders Online,* National Archives, last modified March 30, 2017, http://founders.archives.gov/documents/Jefferson/01-14-02-0410. On the "admonitory" character of the Bill of Rights, see Stephen L. Schechter and Richard B. Bernstein, "Editor's Introduction: Restoring the Contexts of the Bills of Rights," in *Contexts of the Bill of Rights*, ed. Schechter and Bernstein (Albany: New York State Commission on the Bicentennial of the United States, 1990), 9, 14.

[66] Washington to the Hebrew Congregation in Newport.

[67] See endnote to George Washington to Roman Catholics in America, c. March 15, 1790, *Founders Online,* National Archives, last modified November 26, 2017, http://founders.archives.gov/documents/Washington/05-05-02-0193.

[68] Peter Clarke and James Lowell Underwood, "Bishop John England and the Compatibility of the Catholic Church and American Democracy," in *The Dawn of Religious Freedom in South Carolina*, ed. James L. Underwood and W. Lewis Burke (Columbia: University of South Carolina Press, 2006), 188.

6 Religious Tests, Loyalty Oaths, and the Ecclesiastical Context of the First Amendment

Michael D. Breidenbach

On the morning of April 6, 1789, Daniel Carroll opened the front door of his apartment and stepped onto Maiden Lane in New York City.[1] A gentleman of considerable landholdings, he had recently traveled over 200 miles from Maryland to New York in order to join the other newly elected members of the first Federal Congress. Walking in the rain against a "violent Wind" that had greeted pedestrians that morning, he turned left onto Nassau Street, named after the royal dynasty that included King William III and a reminder of the anti-Catholic Revolution of 1688 that the Dutch monarch had helped to secure.[2] Yet four blocks later Daniel Carroll entered a new institution, the US House of Representatives, where he would challenge this anti-Catholic legacy. Within the history of Anglo-American politics, Daniel Carroll's presence in the newly remodeled Federal Hall for the first session of Congress was a quiet but momentous occasion. He was Catholic, yet he held a political office whose equivalent position in Britain had been denied to Catholics since the English Reformation. Carroll's presence in Congress signaled a remarkable double transformation: an American political culture more accessible to Catholics and a Catholic political theology now supportive of church–state separation and religious liberty.[3]

These two transformations had culminated in the no religious test clause in Article VI of the US Constitution, the first nonestablishment clause of the new Constitution. In Britain and the American colonies, the religious tests that had barred Catholics were the clearest manifestation of

The author would like to thank Mitchell Edward Oxford and Daniel Suhr for their helpful edits.

1 Samuel A. Otis to John Adams, April 21, 1789, in Charlene Bangs Bickford et al., eds., vol. 15: *Correspondence: First Session: March–May 1789*, in *Documentary History of the First Federal Congress of the United States of America, March 4, 1789–March 3, 1791*, 20 vols. (Baltimore, MD: The Johns Hopkins University Press, 1972–2012), 307–308.

2 Bickford et al., eds., vol. 15: *Correspondence: First Session: March–May 1789*, 206.

3 On early American Catholics' acceptance and promotion of church–state separation and religious liberty, see Michael D. Breidenbach, "Conciliarism and the American Founding," *William and Mary Quarterly*, 3rd ser., 73, no. 3 (July 2016): 467–500.

state sovereignty over religion and were often composed with the specific intent of making dissenters conform to the state religion or at least excluding them from positions of authority.[4] Yet Article VI stipulated that all federal and state legislative, executive, and juridical officers "shall be bound by Oath or Affirmation, to support this Constitution; but no religious Test shall ever be required as a Qualification to any Office or public Trust under the United States."[5] Therefore, when the Federal Congress passed its first act, it codified a simple oath for officeholders, one without any doctrinal demands, condemnations of papal power, or even a mention of God. While much of the contemporary discourse about church–state relations and religious liberty has been preoccupied with the First Amendment, that amendment was a later outcome of what had already been set down in Article VI.

When Congress codified religious liberty in the First Amendment, it was based on what the previous Congress had already stated in 1783: that powers in "purely spiritual" matters were "reserved to the several States, individually."[6] Congress had declared this principle in response to the Holy See's request for it to approve Daniel Carroll's brother, John, as a Catholic bishop in the United States. Congress's statement served as one of the few instances in which it made a policy decision concerning church–state relations. Privy to this correspondence between Congress and the Holy See, John Carroll later commented in 1786 that "the American Congress does not wish to treat of matters which concern one or another group of Christians, but to those who profess a certain creed it allows full liberty, without governmental interference, with respect to whatever pertains to its cult, discipline and internal organization, provided however that no harm ensues to the Republic."[7]

[4] See Oath of Supremacy, 1534, 26 Hen. VIII, c. 1; Oath of Allegiance, 1606, 3 Jac. 1, c. 4; Oath of Abhorrence, 1691, 3 W. & M., c. 2; and Oath of Abjuration, 1703, 2 Ann. c. 6. For religious tests before disestablishment among the colonies and the process of their disestablishment, see *Disestablishment and Religious Dissent: Church-State Relations in the New American States, 1776–1833*, ed. Carl H. Esbeck and Jonathan Den Hartog (Columbus: University of Missouri Press, 2019).

[5] U.S. Constitution, Article VI, Section 3.

[6] December 22, 1783, in Gaillard Hunt, ed., *Journals of the Continental Congress* (Washington, DC: Government Printing Office, 1922), 25: 825–826.

[7] John Carroll to [John Hock], [1786], in *The John Carroll Papers*, ed. Thomas O'Brien Hanley (South Bend, IN: University of Notre Dame Press, 1976), 1: 199 [hereafter, *JCP*].

Congress's statement to the Holy See and the issue of bishops generally serve as important contexts to the original meaning of the First Amendment. At the same time that Catholics were organizing the American Catholic Church in a way that accommodated the new Republic, the American founders were also framing the Constitution with the particular needs of churches in mind. In the autumn of 1789, when John Carroll was appointed the first Catholic bishop in the United States and Congress finalized the text of the First Amendment, both the Catholic Church and the American Republic had settled on an independent relationship to one another.

In doing so, the First Federal Congress, following its 1783 predecessor, renounced one of the key rights of patronage, or *ius patronatus*, that civil governments traditionally held over ecclesiastical affairs. As discussed in widely read texts in the American founding, *ius patronatus* included the right of the government to present and approve bishops in a country. Although "an establishment of religion" could mean many things – governmental command over doctrines, liturgy, and ministers; church attendance requirements or restrictions; financial support for the established church; the performance of "mixed" functions such as marriages and welfare programs; religious tests for public offices; and other restrictions on nonconformists – the one element of a church establishment that Congress had already explicitly and definitively denied was the right of a government to present or approve bishops.[8] The original meaning of the establishment clause, therefore, included at least this: Congress shall not present or approve the installation of a bishop.[9] The underlying principle of this policy was that "spiritual matters" were within the jurisdiction of states, not the federal government. The First Amendment, debated around the time that bishops were being installed in America, represented a fundamental change in church–state relations from Europe, where civil rulers routinely approved clerics for ecclesiastical offices. In this respect, the establishment clause sanctioned liberty of the church at the federal

[8] This list is an adaptation from Esbeck and Den Hartog, eds., *Disestablishment and Religious Dissent.*

[9] Chief Justice John Roberts recently pronounced that "the Religion Clauses ensured that the new Federal Government . . . would have no role in filling ecclesiastical offices." Roberts did not single out bishops, however. *Hosanna-Tabor Evangelical Lutheran Church and School* v. *Equal Employment Opportunity Commission*, 565 U.S. 171 (2012).

level: the freedom to determine its own internal affairs, including the selection of bishops.[10]

Religious Tests and Article VI of the US Constitution

Discussions over Article VI of the US Constitution expressed two contradictory fears. On the one hand, there was the fear of church–state unity – in the most extreme case, of popes becoming presidents. On the other hand, there was a fear of government without the leaven of a common religion. Article VI could not legally prevent the first fear and in some ways hastened the second. Oaths in general and religious tests in particular signaled a *lack* of trust between oath tenderer and taker and therefore attempted to quell fears from a breach of trust. Yet *removing* the religious test oaths did not necessarily indicate a *greater* trust in officeholders. Indeed, the disquiet over the possibility of "papists," "Jews," "Turks," and "Infidels" holding office demonstrated the profound distrust some Americans had of potential officeholders.[11]

The ban on religious tests for federal office had passed the Constitutional Convention of 1787 "by a great majority of the convention, and without much debate," yet opposition did appear in the state ratification debates, oftentimes with a decidedly anti-Catholic hue.[12] For instance, a Massachusetts representative worried that "a Papist or an infidel was as eligible as a Christian" to serve in the federal government.[13] Another representative "shuddered at the idea" that with the ratification of Article VI "Popery and the Inquisition may be established in America."[14] The first

[10] The scholarship on religious liberty has generally focused on individual religious liberty rather than on the liberty of the church. Honorable exceptions include Richard W. Garnett, "The Freedom of the Church," *Journal of Catholic Social Thought* 4, no. 1 (2007): 59–86, and the "Freedom of the Church in the Modern Era" symposium organized by Steven D. Smith in *Journal of Contemporary Legal Issues* 21 (2013).

[11] Gerard V. Bradley, "The No Religious Test Clause and the Constitution of Religious Liberty: A Machine that Has Gone of Itself," *Case Western Reserve Law Review* 37, no. 4 (1987): 691.

[12] Luther Martin, "Genuine Information," November 29, 1787, in *The Records of the Federal Convention of 1787* (New Haven, CT: Yale University Press, 1911), 3: 227.

[13] Quoted in John Gilmary Shea, *Life and Times of the Most Rev. John Carroll . . .* (New York: printed by author, 1888), 346–347.

[14] Speech by Reverend Thacher in *Debates and Proceedings in the Convention of the Commonwealth of Massachusetts, Held in the Year 1788*, ed. Bradford K. Pierce et al. (Boston, MA: William White, 1856), 251.

North Carolina convention, which refused to ratify the Constitution, witnessed one delegate claiming that under Article VI, the pope could become president of the United States.[15] Another representative, Baptist minister Henry Abbott, worried that if America signed a treaty with a Catholic country, it would result in the coerced conversion of America to Catholicism. Yet future Supreme Court Justice James Iredell disabused his fellow delegates of such a prospect by detailing the amusingly improbable path from priesthood to presidency: A native-born American would need to spend the first fourteen years of his life in the United States, study in Europe, become a priest, ascend the church's hierarchy eventually to be elected pope, and only then return to the United States to win the presidency.[16] Apparently no one demanded that James White, a Catholic educated at the Jesuit College of St. Omer, should step down from his position as a delegate to the North Carolinian ratifying convention, or stated that he had unworthily served as a member of the North Carolina General Assembly or a delegate to the Continental Congress.[17] Part of this anti-Catholic rhetoric was the reliable pabulum of Protestant prejudices. Yet these speeches, representative of a broader Protestant political culture, did express a particular concern about the direct political implications of Catholicism, such as papal inquisitions and claims to temporal power in other countries.

To assuage these anxieties and to support a ban on religious tests for public officeholders, John Carroll published a widely read letter in the New York *Gazette of the United States* in June 1789. A recent anonymous article in defense of religious tests served as Carroll's pretext to publish his reply in the most influential Federalist paper in the union right before North Carolina's second ratifying convention. He clearly intended to intervene in these ratification debates by persuading Federalists to support the religious test ban. Under the irenic pseudonym "Pacificus," Carroll argued that Catholics should not be excluded from public office, forfeit "the common rights of nature," or lose "the stipulated rights of the political society" "merely

[15] This observation seemed to be more appropriate for Article II, Section 1 of the Constitution, which prescribed an oath for the president.

[16] Speeches by Henry Abbott, William Lancaster, James Iredell, and Zachias Wilson in Jonathan Elliot, ed., *The Debates in the Several State Conventions on the Adoption of the Federal Constitution, as recommended by the General Convention at Philadelphia, in 1787*, 5 vols. (Washington, DC: printed by editor, 1836), 4: 192, 215, 196, 212.

[17] "White, James, (1749–1809)," *Biographical Directory of the United States Congress*, accessed June 25, 2018, http://bioguide.congress.gov/scripts/biodisplay.pl?index=W000377.

on account of their religious opinions." He did not respond directly to the claims about papal power – which he thought formed no part of the Catholic faith anyway – but instead leaned on the fact that Catholics had fought for an American government of "justice, peace, plenty, good order and civil and religious liberty."[18] Concerns about foreign or papalist Catholics were answered by appeals to the patriotism and loyalty of American Catholics.

In the end, the state ratification conventions passed the religious test ban at the federal level. But was this federal ban passed *despite* some states' own religious tests, or *because* of them? As a matter of principle or underlying political philosophy, it would seem contradictory for the same legislator – such as George Read of Delaware – to reject a religious test at the federal level but at the same time uphold one at the state level.[19] How then should we understand the situational irony of an elected Catholic representative such as Daniel Carroll seated in Federal Hall in New York City when, in the same state, Catholics were denied public office in the state assembly?

According to the federalist interpretation of Article VI, the federal religious test ban paradoxically *protected* state religious tests. Proponents of federalism maintained that if a government had any jurisdiction with respect to religion, then such power rested in the states, not the federal government. Therefore, a federal religious test would usurp state sovereignty.[20] (Of course, this interpretation slices both ways: A federal no religious test clause protected bans on religious tests in some states as much as it protected religious tests in others.) Another possible reason why the states ultimately ratified Article VI was that enough power would be distributed across the constitutional structure so no one religious group could impose their religion on others. This second federalist interpretation likewise promises to resolve the apparent contradiction between having state religious tests and banning federal religious tests.[21]

[18] Pacificus [John Carroll], [New York] *Gazette of the United States*, June 10, 1789, [1], in *JCP*, 1: 365–368 at 1: 366, 1: 365. John Carroll's letter was an immediate response to an anonymous article that implicitly argued for religious tests against non-Protestants. See E. C., "The Importance of the Protestant Religion politically considered," *Gazette of the United States*, May 9, 1789, [1].

[19] Bradley, "No Religious Test Clause," 689–690.

[20] Daniel L. Dreisbach, "The Constitution's Forgotten Religion Clause: Reflections on Article VI Religious Test Ban," *Journal of Church and State* 38, no. 2 (1996): 286–289.

[21] See speech by Edmund Randolph in *Debates in the Several State Conventions on the Adoption of the Federal Constitution*, 3: 204; Bradley, "No Religious Test Clause," 703, 706; and Dreisbach, "Constitution's Forgotten Religion Clause," 286.

But there is a complementary, yet simpler, explanation: Catholics Daniel Carroll and Thomas Fitzsimons of Pennsylvania were *already* in the Constitutional Convention. This state of affairs ensured that a sectarian test for federal office – any more than a belief in God that was already implied by swearing an oath – would contradict current practice if not standing principle. At the very least, such a test would have required the embarrassing recusal of two elected delegates. More importantly, it would have contradicted the will of the states that had elected these Catholics to be their delegates – and therefore would be a breach of federalism. If the people were sovereign, and legislators represented the people, then to exclude certain religious believers from public office implied that such religious believers were not part of that civil body. (This federalist principle was double-edged: Because Article I of the Constitution stipulated that US senators were chosen by state legislatures, states could levy a religious test on some federal officeholders anyway.[22])

Whatever the individual reasons of the framers and ratifiers, the religious test ban was passed despite everyone's acknowledgment that "papists," "Jews," "Turks," and "Infidels" could now hold federal office legally.[23] (Atheists were still considered barred from federal public office, since Article VI required an oath to support the Constitution, and, in the eighteenth century, to require an oath was a de facto acknowledgment of a Supreme Being.[24]) Since the paradigm case for religious tests were the British religious test oaths, which were explicitly intended to exclude Catholics from holding public office, one of the main consequences of Article VI was that Catholics in particular were now offered a freedom previously denied to them. Such legal and political possibilities indicate the vast extent to which the new American constitutional arrangement differed from the British penal laws and its established church.

[22] U.S. Constitution, Article I, Section 3. After the 1913 ratification of the Seventeenth Amendment, US senators were elected through the popular vote.

[23] Bradley, "No Religious Test Clause," 691.

[24] The only state ratifying convention to offer an amendment for Article VI was South Carolina, which proposed the addition of "other" to read "no *other* religious test" would be mandated. This implied that the oath was a religious test insofar as it required a belief in God. Donald L. Drakeman, "The Antifederalists and Religion," in *Faith and the Founders of the American Republic*, ed. Mark D. Hall and Daniel L. Dreisbach (New York: Oxford University Press, 2014), 127.

Loyalty Oaths: The First Act of Congress

The first bill that Congress considered concerned an oath for federal office. When the first Federal Congress passed the Oath Bill – HR-1, its first piece of legislation – it bore little resemblance to previous British and colonial oaths. The House committee had initially proposed the following text: "I, A B, a Representative of the United States in the Congress thereof, do solemnly swear (or affirm, as the case may be) in the presence of Almighty GOD, that I will support the Constitution of the United States. So help me God."[25] The Constitution had not required that God be featured in the oath text – indeed, besides the perfunctory dating "in the Year of our Lord," God did not enjoy a place in the Constitution itself – but the religious representatives who drafted it evidently believed a more explicit attestation to God was appropriate. Representative Lambert Cadwalader's own *imprimatur* – that the oath could be affirmed – was a subtle nod to his fellow Quakers' scruples against swearing oaths and a signal to other religious minorities of Congress's measured liberality. Yet no requirement from the English Oath of Allegiance to renounce the old "damnable doctrine" of papal deposition power remained; no acknowledgment of the head of state as also head of an established church was admitted; no stipulation that all citizens had to take the oath was imposed. Instead, the US oath required a *positive* affirmation, rather than a denial of doctrines or beliefs as required in the English Oath of Allegiance. And perhaps unique in the history of the West, the new US oath was impersonal: Officeholders did not propose to swear or affirm allegiance to the head of state, who had not even been sworn into office, but to uphold a mere seven articles of a written constitution.

After several more months of deliberations, Congress passed the final text: "I, A. B. do solemnly swear or affirm (as the case may be) that I will support the Constitution of the United States."[26] This first bill in the first Federal Congress was relatively uncontroversial – "Harmony has hitherto prevailed," wrote one senator – and passed with a yawn, starkly contrasting the controversy over British religious tests.[27] Even the removal of the

[25] *Annals of Congress*, 1st Cong., 1st sess., 101.

[26] "An Act to Regulate the Time and Manner of Administering Certain Oaths," *United States Statutes at Large*, vol. 1, 1st Cong., 1st sess., ch. 1, section 1, p. 23.

[27] Ralph Izard to Gabriel Manigault, June 9, 1789, in Bickford et al., eds., vol. 16: *Correspondence: First Session: June–August 1789*, 729. See also Abraham Baldwin to Governor Edward Telfair, June 17, 1789, in Bickford et al., eds., vol. 16: *Correspondence:*

word "God" from the House's first proposed formula apparently did not cause public ire. But perhaps what was most remarkable about the Oath Bill was that its scope was limited to officeholders as a pure pledge of civil allegiance. Unlike the English Oath of Allegiance, its reach did not extend to the whole citizenry, nor was it intended to reinforce or reject religious doctrines or propositions, nor could it exclude certain members from full citizenship or public office. The oath was so minimal that any religious believer – and even any quiet nonbeliever – could take it. When Catholics Daniel Carroll, Charles Carroll, and Thomas Fitzsimons took the new oath, it did not capture the attention of contemporary reporters.[28] The old fear of papists seemed to have quietly retreated at least in the halls of Congress.

Yet Congress's oath could have been much different, even within the parameters of Article VI. The Constitution did not ban *all* test oaths for public office, only religious tests. And because the English Oath of Allegiance had often been considered a political test, rather than a religious one, Congress arguably could have imposed similar clauses in their new oath. After all, King James I had argued that, despite its clauses against papal power, his Oath of Allegiance was a merely civil oath – a claim that Cecil Calvert, the founder of Maryland, himself had asserted.[29] Why, then, did the Oath Bill not require federal officeholders to renounce all other temporal allegiances, especially concerning the pope? Perhaps Congress believed that citizenship and adhering to the Constitution assumed a belief in the principles of the Declaration of Independence, which had prohibited other temporal loyalties. Or perhaps the other clause of Article VI – that "[t]his Constitution, and the Laws of the United States . . . shall be the supreme Law of the Land" – was understood as meaning that no other political power is supreme in the United States. Or perhaps most members of Congress simply trusted leading Catholics such as the Carrolls when they averred they did not have any temporal

First Session: June–August 1789, 795; Erkuries Beatty to Josiah Harmar, April 13, 1789, Bickford et al., eds., vol. 15: *Correspondence: First Session: March–May 1789*, 257–258.

28 April 8, 1789, *Annals of Congress*, 1st Cong., 1st sess., 106.

29 "Objections answered touching Mariland," 1633, Stonyhurst College MSS, Anglia A, iv. ff. 206–209, no. 108E, reprinted in Thomas Hughes, *History of the Society of Jesus in North America*, 4 vols. (New York: Longmans, Green, and Co., 1907–1917), vol. 1, part 1, pp. 12, 14–15.

allegiance with the pope. Either way, the final text of the Oath Bill was clear of all the clauses that had given British and American Catholics such trouble.

Beyond its significance for Catholics, Article VI and the Oath Bill represented a fundamental transformation in church–state relations. While other oaths had reinforced an established church, Article VI and the Oath Bill elided any notion of a "Church of the United States" – even before the First Amendment had confirmed its prohibition. The framers of the US Constitution deliberately rejected an important element of an established church: a religious test for public office. A religious test was not always coupled with tithe requirements, mandatory church attendance, state-funded ministers, or other elements of a church establishment. But while a church establishment might include many such elements, no such arrangement had previously *prohibited* a religious test for public office. The no religious test clause was the clearest prohibition of an established church, for even the later First Amendment did not explicitly proscribe laws that would prevent religious citizens from serving in public office.

Article VI and the Oath Bill – like the First Amendment later – were *juridical* determinations about ecclesiastical establishments, not necessarily philosophical or theological statements about whether a state should be "secular" or "religious" (even though the framers and ratifiers certainly had views on those questions). The prohibition of a religious test and the absence of the word "God" from the Constitution did not imply that the framers and ratifiers wanted federal officeholders to not believe in God, or that they were apathetic whether they did.[30] The final oath for federal officeholders, as all oaths were understood in the eighteenth century, still implied that the oath-taker believed in God.

Despite their seeming secularity, Article VI, the Oath Bill, and the First Amendment still allowed legislators much latitude in creating a moral establishment. Neither the religious test ban nor the later nonestablishment clause of the First Amendment could preclude the possibility of de facto church–state unity. To be sure, Article VI denied that officeholders needed to adhere to one religion in particular, and the First Amendment's

[30] Previous scholars have conducted a keyword search for "God" in the US Constitution and, after yielding zero results, have baptized it a "godless document." Isaac Kramnick and R. Laurence Moore, *The Godless Constitution: The Case Against Religious Correctness* (New York: W. W. Norton, 1996), 26–45 at 27.

nonestablishment clause denied federal legislation that would create a nationally established church.[31] But those injunctions could not preclude church–state unity, since a government could still consist of officeholders of the same religion through election. Moreover, Congress could infuse law with its members' religious-inspired principles, pay ministers for "civilizing" missions, elect and support congressional chaplains, erect religious iconography in federal buildings, and, of course, allow states to have established churches and religious tests. For much of American history, Protestantism was that moral establishment.[32] Of course, Catholics like Daniel Carroll could now legally enjoy these benefits as much as Protestants, thereby creating the possibility of political harmony among Christians without an established church. But while Article VI offered Catholics and other religious believers the freedom to work within that moral establishment, the debates over that article's ratification indicated that religious minorities would continue to face religious, political, and cultural, if not legal, resistance against their public service.

The history of religious tests in early America indicates that religious liberty was not one persistent note or a harmonious chordal progression but often discordant, modulated, and improvisational. Leading American Catholics, including the Carroll cousins who had helped to shepherd Article VI and the First Amendment, understood that loyalty remained a critical prerequisite to securing religious liberty. This was especially evident in a letter that they wrote to the recently elected president, George Washington, in the early spring of 1790.[33] The Catholics' letter to

[31] On religious tests and state authority over religion, see David E. Mass, "The Philosophical and Theological Roots of the Religious Clause in the Constitution," in *Liberty and Law: Reflections on the Constitution in American Life and Thought*, ed. Ronald A. Wells and Thomas A. Askew (Grand Rapids, MI: William B. Eerdmans, 1987), 6–7; John F. Wilson, "Religion, Government, and Power in the New American Nation," in *Religion and American Politics: From the Colonial Period to the 1980s*, ed. Mark A. Noll and Luke E. Harlow (New York: Oxford University Press, 1990), 88.

[32] Philip Hamburger, *Separation of Church and State* (Cambridge, MA: Harvard University Press, 2004); David Sehat, *The Myth of American Religious Freedom* (New York: Oxford University Press, 2011).

[33] The editors of both the John and Charles Carroll papers date the memorial to March 15, 1790, or, more vaguely, March 1790, but the signatories wrote it earlier that spring, since Washington *received* it on March 15. See *JCP*, 1: 409–11; *The Diaries of George Washington*, ed. Dorothy Twohig (Charlottesville, VA: University Press of Virginia, 1976–1979), 6: 46n; and *Writings of George Washington*, 12: 147–169; *Papers of George Washington*, 6: 284–286. Catholic historians have speculated, wishfully and wrongly, that the Catholic memorial was the basis for the First Amendment. See C. I. White, "Sketch of

Washington expressed their desire to receive the promise and protection of full religious liberty in both federal and state governments.[34] John Carroll included sections in the letter that argued for religious test bans in all states as well.[35] In support of their cause, they reminded Washington that Catholics had fought alongside Protestants under his command and therefore "shall have a well founded title to claim from her [the United States] justice equal rights of citizenship." While Catholics had fought against Protestants in European wars of religion, American Catholics joined their fellow Christians in an important test of loyalty: the willingness to fight and die for one's country. The Catholics' memorial was written before the states' ratification of the First Amendment and was more an expression of hope that they would actually be protected in their equal rights, rather than a statement that all Catholics were now protected.

In his reply, Washington thanked Catholics for their "patriotic part" in the American Revolution. Contrary to the hopeful tenor of the Catholics' letter, Washington assured that Catholics were already "realising, instead of anticipating, the benefits of the general government." He articulated his vision of America as a great example of a nation protecting all creeds under civil law, and he hoped that "the members of your Society in America, animated alone by the pure spirit of christianity, and still conducting themselves as the faithful subjects of our free government," will "enjoy every temporal and spiritual felicity."[36] On the one hand, Washington's letter was a ringing endorsement of civil and religious liberty for all – something that he articulated in his responses to other religious groups' congratulatory letters as well. According to Washington, the Catholic Church was neither established nor marginalized; instead, it was simply

the Origin and Progress of the Catholic Church in the United States of America," in *A General History of the Catholic Church: From the Commencement of the Christian Era until the Present Time*, ed. J. E. Darras (New York: P. O'Shea, 1865), 6: 610–611; "The Constitution of the United States and Religious Liberty," *American Catholic Historical Researches* 2, no. 4 (April 1886): 122–125; John Gilmary Shea, *History of the Catholic Church in the United States* (New York: printed by author, 1886), 1: 348.

34 Roman Catholic Committee to George Washington, [March?] 1790, George Washington Papers, Library of Congress, Washington, DC. I thank the editors of the Charles Carroll of Carrollton papers for this reference.

35 John Carroll to Charles Plowden, February 24, 1790, in *JCP*, 1: 432.

36 George Washington to the Roman Catholics in the United States of America, [March 15,] 1790, George Washington Papers, Library of Congress, Washington, DC, reprinted in Richard H. Clarke, "George Washington in his Relations with Catholics," *American Catholic Quarterly Review* 21, no. 83 (1896): 651–652.

another "Society in America" whose members should enjoy the same rights and privileges as members of any other association. On the other hand, Washington's reply made it clear that their enjoyment of civil and religious rights was contingent on their remaining "faithful subjects" of the United States – a term that evoked obedience to a king more than a republic of laws. Loyalty came before liberty.

Revisiting the Historical Record of the Establishment Clause

Because the US Constitution respected the sovereignty of states to decide matters of religious liberty, Catholic statesman Charles Carroll of Carrollton, like most Federalists, did not believe that further amendments to the Constitution were needed to secure civil and religious liberties.[37] As a principal drafter of the Maryland Declaration of Rights in 1776, Charles Carroll had already eliminated taxation for the support of the Church of England, which effectively disestablished the church – an act as yet without parallel in the other states.[38] James Madison, who also worked to disestablish the Church of England in his state, shared Carroll's belief that the Constitution did not require an amendment enumerating protections for religious liberty. But Madison also thought that certain amendments, including provisions for religious liberty and nonestablishment, would reconcile Anti-Federalists to the Constitution. Charles Carroll and his second cousin Daniel agreed. After Madison proposed his first draft of what would become the First Amendment, Daniel Carroll was the only Congressman to support the measure explicitly. In his speech in Congress on August 15, Daniel Carroll expressed a similar sense that the amendment merely articulated what was the general sentiment concerning the right to

[37] Charles Carroll wrote that the US Constitution of 1787, before any amendments, would allow "the miserable from every quarter" to enjoy "civil & religious liberty" and to "adore thy beneficent Providence in sincerity & truth." Charles Carroll of Carrollton, "Remarks on the Proposed Constitution," January 23, 1788, in Edward C. Papenfuse, "An Undelivered Defense of a Winning Cause: Charles Carroll of Carrollton's 'Remarks on the Proposed Federal Constitution,'" *Maryland Historical Magazine* 70, no. 2 (1976): 245.

[38] For more on disestablishment and religious liberty in Maryland, see Michael D. Breidenbach, "Church and State in Maryland: Religious Liberty, Religious Tests, and Church Disestablishment," in *Disestablishment and Religious Dissent*, ed. Esbeck and Den Hartog.

religious liberty. In the *Congressional Register*, journalist Thomas Lloyd reported Carroll as stating:

> As the rights of conscience are in their nature of peculiar delicacy, and will little bear the gentlest touch of the governmental hand; and as many sects have concurred in opinion that they are not well secured under the present constitution, he said he was much in favor of adopting the words; he thought it would tend more toward conciliating the minds of the people to the government than almost any other amendment he had heard proposed. He would not contend with gentlemen about the phraseology, his object was to secure the substance in such a manner as to satisfy the wishes of the honest part of the community.[39]

In Lloyd's hands, Carroll's remarks were elevated to oratory compared with the statements by other congressmen.[40] Whereas Lloyd introduced other comments with "Mr. Gerry said" or "Mr. Madison thought," Lloyd began Carroll's speech: "Mr. Carroll. As the rights of conscience . . . ."[41] In fact, Lloyd was the only reporter to record Carroll's comments at all. The *Gazette of the United States* noted that Carroll and other congressmen "made some observations" on the amendment; *The Daily Advertiser* did not mention him at all.[42]

Almost all of what we know about these congressional debates, including on the First Amendment, comes from a Catholic. The London-born Lloyd learned shorthand while studying at St. Omer, the same Jesuit College that Daniel Carroll, his brother John Carroll, and their cousin Charles Carroll had attended. John Carroll taught the young Lloyd there

[39] *The Congressional Register* ... 2nd Edition (New York: Hodge, Allen, and Campbell for T. Lloyd, 1790), 2: 195. See also *Debates in the House of Representatives, First Session: June-September 1789*, ed. Charlene Bangs Bickford, et al. (Baltimore, MD: The Johns Hopkins University Press), 11: 1261. The Gales and Seaton version excluded "the" in "of the governmental," and has slightly different punctuation and capitalization. Compare August 15, 1789, *The Debates and Proceedings in the Congress of the United States* ..., ed. Joseph Gales (Washington, DC: Gales and Seaton, 1834), 1: 757–758.

[40] I thank Don Drakeman for this point.

[41] *The Congressional Register* ..., 2: 194–197 at 195. Gales' and Seaton's version inserted a hyphen: "Mr. Carroll. – As the rights of conscience ..." Compare August 15, 1789, *Debates and Proceedings*, ed. Gales, 1: 757–758 at 757.

[42] *Gazette of the United States*, August 19, 1789, in *Debates in the House of Representatives, First Session: June-September 1789*, ed. Charlene Bangs Bickford, et al. (Baltimore, MD: The Johns Hopkins University Press), 11: 1257; *The Daily Advertiser*, August 17, 1789, in *Debates in the House of Representatives, First Session: June–September 1789*, ed. Charlene Bangs Bickford, et al. (Baltimore, MD: The Johns Hopkins University Press), 11: 1254.

just before the pupil immigrated to Maryland.[43] They all had attended St. Omer because religious liberty had been denied to them at home. Now in Congress, two St. Omer Catholics helped to pass the First Amendment while another wrote its first history. Lloyd gave Catholics a "literal advantage."[44]

Did Lloyd give his fellow college alumnus's speech pride of place in the *Congressional Register*? Like all English students at St. Omer, Lloyd had experienced religious persecution; he might have seen a Catholic with the ability to shape the First Amendment as momentous. Perhaps Carroll supplied Lloyd a written copy of his remarks to ensure a standout rendition of his speech. After all, James Madison later acknowledged that congressmen sometimes revised their speeches before they were printed.[45] Certainly, the Carrolls and Lloyd knew one another, and Daniel Carroll and Lloyd would have seen each other the day of Carroll's speech at St. Peter's Church in New York City for the feast day of the Assumption of the Blessed Virgin Mary, for which all Catholics were obligated to attend Mass.[46] And since it

[43] Lloyd volunteered in Maryland regiment during the Revolutionary War, oversaw the publication of the Continental Congress's *Journals*, served in the US Treasury, and recorded proceedings of the Pennsylvania House of Assembly and the Pennsylvania and Maryland ratifying conventions. Ibid., 521–524.

[44] Jill Lepore coined this term to describe the advantage given to those who printed their version of history. Jill Lepore, *The Name of War: King Philip's War and the Origins of American Identity* (New York: Vintage, 1998), 52.

[45] Marion Tinling, "Thomas Lloyd's Reports of the First Federal Congress," *William and Mary Quarterly*, 3rd ser., 18, no. 4 (October 1961): 527–530; James Madison to Edward Everett, January 7, 1832, in *Founders Online*, National Archives, last modified June 13, 2018, http://founders.archives.gov/documents/Madison/99-02-02-2503; James Madison to Gales and Seaton, August 5, 1833, Series 1, General Correspondence, 1723–1859, The James Madison Papers, Library of Congress, accessed online January 19, 2019, www.loc.gov/item/mjm021348/; James Madison to Isaac S. Lyon, September 20, 1834, Series: Series 1, General Correspondence, 1723–1859, The James Madison Papers, Library of Congress, accessed online January 19, 2019, www.loc.gov/item/mjm021498/. Madison also complained about Lloyd's inaccurate recording of many speeches that were not revised.

[46] Charles, Daniel, and John Carroll subscribed to Lloyd's publication of [Richard Challoner], *The Unerring Authority of the Catholic Church, in Matters of Faith* … (Philadelphia: T. Lloyd, 1789). For the list of subscribers, see Ibid., [209–212 at 209]. John Carroll helped Lloyd find subscribers in early 1789. John Carroll to Thomas Lloyd, January 12, 1789, in *JCP*, 1: 246–247. Charles Carroll remained his acquaintance decades later. See Thomas Lloyd, "Book of signatures and accounts," Lloyd Family, American Catholic Historical Society Historic Papers, Digital Library@Villanova University, accessed online, January 31, 2019, https://digital.library.villanova.edu/Item/vudl:253518, [6].

took Lloyd weeks to convert his shorthand into printed text, there would have been time for Carroll to review and amend Lloyd's record.

Or perhaps Lloyd himself embellished Carroll's speech.[47] After all, when Carroll apparently said that "[h]e would not contend with gentlemen about the phraseology, his object was to secure the substance," the same could be said about Lloyd's approach to his own work. From his skeletal stenography, Lloyd's account of the congressional debates was written with the license of Thucydides – memory, interpretation, interpolation.[48] Lloyd was not as concerned with the exact words of the speech but rather its essence, and the rhetorical flourishes in Carroll's remarks would not have been recorded exactly anyway. Lloyd had been accused previously of favoring his fellow Federalists in recording the Pennsylvania and Maryland ratifying conventions; perhaps his *Congressional Register* had favored his fellow Federalist Catholic as well.[49]

Either way, Daniel Carroll's unusually prominent and polished speech was a calculated response to Anti-Federalist demands that he and Madison had faced during the ratification debates. Carroll's mollifying words matched the ameliorative ends of the religion clauses, intended for "conciliating the minds of the people to the Government than almost any other amendment he had heard proposed."[50] From the beginning of the movement to revise the Articles of Confederation, he had sought to reconcile Anti-Federalists to the Constitution. He had informed Madison of popular sentiment regarding the proposed Constitution and strategized how best to achieve its passage.[51] After ratification, several Anti-Federalists still did not think that the Constitution sufficiently secured religious liberty and nonestablishment.[52] For instance, during

[47] Lloyd often "subjected" the speeches "to a good deal of embellishment." Tinling, "Thomas Lloyd's Reports," 531.

[48] Ibid., 538–539. [49] Ibid., 523–527. [50] *The Congressional Register* . . ., 2: 195.

[51] Daniel Carroll to James Madison, March 13, 1787, Series 1, General Correspondence, 1723–1859, The James Madison Papers, Library of Congress, accessed online, January 22, 2019, http://hdl.loc.gov/loc.mss/mjm.02_0619_0620; Daniel Carroll to James Madison, April 28, 1788, Series 1, General Correspondence, 1723–1859, The James Madison Papers, Library of Congress, accessed online, January 22, 2019, http://hdl.loc.gov/loc.mss/mjm.03_0386_0387; Daniel Carroll to James Madison, May 28, 1788, Series 1, General Correspondence, 1723–1859, The James Madison Papers, Library of Congress, accessed online, January 22, 2019, http://hdl.loc.gov/loc.mss/mjm.03_0448_0449. See also Mary Virginia Geiger, "Daniel Carroll: A Framer of the Constitution" (Ph.D. Dissertation, Catholic University of America, 1943), 141.

[52] Drakeman, "The Antifederalists and Religion."

the Maryland ratifying convention, William Paca led Anti-Federalists in drafting a list of constitutional amendments, including "[t]hat there be no National Religion established by Law; but that all Persons be equally entitled to Protection in their religious Liberty."[53] Daniel Carroll enclosed a copy of those amendments for Madison and wrote that although they "will be of little consequence" in Maryland – the Federalists had rejected them – they might "be of some [consequence] with you to hear both sides" as the Virginia ratifying convention met.[54] Lloyd's record of the House debates makes it clear that the introduction of the First Amendment was a coordinated effort between James Madison and Daniel Carroll – not the singular effort of Madison – to answer Anti-Federalist objections. If Madison was the "Father of the Constitution," Carroll was the First Amendment's godfather.

Daniel Carroll had spoken in favor of the amendment on Saturday, the first day of the debate in the House, and the discussion resumed on Monday. In refraining from meeting on Sunday, Congress implicitly recognized the Christian Sabbath even as they debated the establishment clause.[55] Several weeks passed before the House and the Senate agreed on the final text. The sparse record by Lloyd and others did not note Congress's reasons for adopting the final language of the religion clauses, or why other proposals – Congress shall make no law establishing "religious doctrine," "infring[ing] the rights of conscience," "establishing any particular denomination of religion in preference to another," and "establishing articles of faith or a mode of worship" – fell out of favor.[56] The conference committee formed to finalize the text included Senate members Charles Carroll, William Paterson of New Jersey, and Oliver Ellsworth of Connecticut, and House members James Madison, Roger Sherman of

[53] William Paca, "Amendments Proposed by William Paca in the Maryland Convention," April 29, in vol. 5, *Commentaries on the Constitution: Public and Private*, in vol. 17 of *The Documentary History of the Ratification of the Constitution*, ed. John P. Kaminski, et al. (Madison: State Historical Society of Wisconsin, 1995), 241; William Paca, et al., "Address of a Minority of the Maryland Ratifying Convention," May 1, 1788, Ibid., 245.

[54] Daniel Carroll to James Madison, May 28, 1788, Series 1, General Correspondence, 1723–1859, The James Madison Papers, Library of Congress, accessed online, January 22, 2019, http://hdl.loc.gov/loc.mss/mjm.03_0448_0449.

[55] The Constitution likewise implicitly acknowledged the Sunday Sabbath in its exemption of Sundays from the number of days that a president has to veto legislation. U.S. Constitution, Article 1, Section 7.

[56] For a survey of the debates and proceedings, see Chapter 5 of this volume.

Connecticut, and John Vining of Delaware.[57] Within a week that committee settled on the final language: "Congress shall make no law respecting an establishment of religion, or prohibiting the free exercise thereof."[58]

Ius Patronatus and the Ecclesiastical Context of the Establishment Clause

A breathtaking volume of scholarship has sought to explain what the constitutional framers and ratifiers meant by the religion clauses of the First Amendment. Interpreting the establishment clause has been particularly fraught. The most minimal reading of its original meaning, based on the available evidence of the framers' collective intention, is that Congress should not establish a "Church of the United States" akin to the Church of England.[59] Even if that reading is correct, however, the problem remains that there was disagreement about what was essential about the Church of England (and, *a fortiori*, a hypothetical "Church of the United States"). Anglicans, especially in the American colonies, disputed whether bishops were a necessary feature of the Church of England, and whether paying ministerial salaries, religious tests for public office, state ownership of church land, and so on were necessary for establishing the Church of England. If the nonestablishment clause meant no "Church of the United States," there was no unanimous agreement recorded on what *that* meant.

To understand what the establishment clause prohibited, we need to turn to Congress's actual policy decisions before the First Amendment was passed. The most significant choice that Congress made on matters of church establishment, one that indicated Congress's collective will on church–state matters, came in 1783. The Holy See had requested that Congress permit the establishment of a native Catholic vicar apostolic bishop in the United States.[60] In its reply, Congress laid down its first

[57] Donald L. Drakeman, *Church, State, and Original Intent* (New York: Cambridge University Press, 2010), 210.

[58] "The First Ten Amendments to the Constitution, or the Bill of Rights," 1789, in Bruce Frohnen, ed., *The American Republic: Primary Sources* (Indianapolis, IN: Liberty Fund, 2002), 349–450 at 349.

[59] See Drakeman, *Church, State, and Original Intent*, 260 and Chapter 13 of this volume.

[60] Benjamin Franklin had forwarded a translation of the papal nuncio's request to Congress. Daniel Carroll and Thomas Fitzsimons were members of the Princeton-based Congress at the time that Franklin forwarded the letter, but it arrived two months later when both of the

principle of church–state relations: that Congress had no jurisdiction, power, or authority in "purely spiritual" matters such as electing a Catholic ecclesiastical leader. The committee members responsible for the statement to the Holy See – Thomas Jefferson of Virginia, Elbridge Gerry of Massachusetts, and Hugh Williamson of North Carolina – held divergent religious commitments but could agree on the same distinction between temporal and "purely spiritual" matters that Anglo-American Catholics had offered.[61] Congress concluded that these powers in "purely spiritual" matters were, in a nod to the principle of federalism, "reserved to the several States, individually."[62]

At the same time that Catholic and Anglican bishops were renouncing power over political affairs, Congress was forswearing power over ecclesiastical affairs.[63] In so doing, Congress rejected what European governments had traditionally exercised: the rights of patronage over churches, or *ius patronatus*. Throughout the centuries in Christian Europe, *ius patronatus* constituted an established church. Since the Middle Ages, these patronage rights of the civil authority included *placet*, or veto power over ecclesiastical affairs within the civil ruler's territory; *exequatur*, or enforcement power over directives accepted by the local bishop; *ius praesentandi*, or nomination power of local ecclesiastics; and *ius exclusivae*, or the power to veto papal candidates in a conclave.[64] By the early modern period, *ius patronatus* was the paradigm for both Catholic and Protestant established churches. Popes granted monarchs power over ecclesiastical temporalities, first to Spain and Portugal with *Inter caetera* (1493) and later to Francis I of France with the Concordat of Bologna (1516). Protestant countries, including England, soon appropriated these rights for their own churches. The Peace of Augsburg's political settlement of *cuius regio, eius*

Catholic representatives had left Congress. Benjamin Franklin, "To the President of Congress," September 13, 1783, in *The Diplomatic Correspondence of the United States of America, from the Treaty of Peace to the Adoption of the Present Constitution* (Washington, DC: Blair & Rives, 1837), 4: 168–169. It often took two months before Congress acknowledged receipt of Franklin's letters.

61 See Breidenbach, "Conciliarism and the American Founding."

62 December 22, 1783, in Gaillard Hunt, ed., *Journals of the Continental Congress*, 25: 825–826.

63 Breidenbach, "Conciliarism and the American Founding," 496–499.

64 Russell Hittinger, "Introduction to Modern Catholicism," in *The Teachings of Modern Roman Catholicism: On Law, Politics, and Human Nature*, ed. John Witte Jr. and Frank S. Alexander (New York: Columbia University Press, 2007), 1–38, esp. 4–5.

religio solidified these established churches in the tradition of *ius patronatus*.

Congress's 1783 declaration was the first in British North America to reject a national government's right to nominate or approve a cleric for a bishopric. (The next country to do so was Belgium in 1831.[65]) Congress's refusal of *ius patronatus* was a knowing one. Governmental patronage of bishops was part of the legal lexicon of the American founders and was widely practiced in the Atlantic World. William Blackstone, to whom the American founders consistently turned for legal guidance, discussed the rights of patronage – or the rights of advowson, as it was called in the Church of England – as the proper prerogative of the civil government over ecclesiastical appointments.[66] A similar discussion appeared in the *Encyclopædia Britannica*, whose subscribers numbered George Washington, Charles Carroll of Carrollton, Thomas Jefferson, Aaron Burr, and Alexander Hamilton.[67]

While this reading of the establishment clause might seem too narrow, it in fact adds and provides greater specificity to its meaning. Prohibiting the establishment of a "Church of the United States" did not necessarily forbid Congress from nominating or accepting bishops in the United States. After all, government control over bishops could be found not only in establishments but also in nonestablishments. (The Chinese government today claims the power to appoint bishops, but is officially atheistic.) Governments with established churches even intervened in the affairs of bishops from other churches, as was the case with Britain claiming *ius patronatus* not only over the Church of England but also over the Catholic Church in some of their colonies. For instance, the British Governor of Minorca, Richard Kane, claimed the right of *placet* in order to expel two Catholic vicars general in that colony who were under the Spanish-controlled Bishop of Majorca. The governor also pressed for the patronage right of *exequatur*, so that all

[65] Belgium Constitution, 1831, art. 16 [now art. 21] Const. coord.

[66] William Blackstone, *Commentaries on the Laws of England*, 4th Edition (Dublin: John Exshaw, Boulter Grierson, Henry Saunders, Elizabeth Lynch, and James Williams, 1771), bk. 2, ch. 3, pp. 21–23. See also William Blackstone, *Commentaries on the Laws of England*, 4th Edition (Dublin: John Exshaw, Henry Saunders, Boulter Grierson, James Williams, and John Milliken, 1771), bk. 3, ch. 7, p. 91 and ch. 16, pp. 242–253.

[67] "Patronage," in *Encyclopædia Britannica* ..., 3rd Edition (Edinburgh: A. Bell and C. Macfraquhar, 1797), 14: 45–46. On the subscribers to the *Encyclopædia*, see James M. Wells, *The Circle of Knowledge: Encyclopedias Past and Present* (Chicago: Newberry Library, 1968).

ecclesiastical actions in Minorca and all papal bulls had to be approved by him.[68] When the Minorcan Catholics finally obtained their own bishop, Britain insisted that his diocese was under British authority and that he answer to the pope through a royal attaché even in spiritual matters. Britain's strategy in the Catholic-majority territory of Gibraltar was similar: to separate Catholics' existing ties to the Spanish Diocese of Cádiz and to insist that all ecclesiastical correspondence and power flow through the British governor.[69]

The United States charted a different path. From the very beginning, all the Anglican and Catholic bishops were consecrated and installed without any legal interference at the state or federal levels. The establishment clause of the First Amendment that Charles Carroll helped to finalize confirmed the policy that the Annapolis-based Congress had stated to the Holy See: The federal government does not have cognizance over any ecclesiastical affairs and thereby has no right to nominate or confirm a bishop, since authority in "purely spiritual" matters rested within the individual states. To be sure, there was no written discussion of bishops in the truncated record of the First Federal Congress's deliberations, and since the Congress in 1783 was under the older Articles of Confederation, not the US Constitution, one Congress's decisions did not necessarily bind another's. Yet insofar as the First Federal Congress never collectively defined what a "Church of the United States" might look like, we are left with constructing the constitutional text.[70] The most reasonable place to start is what the previous national legislative body had definitively denied: the power to appoint or approve bishops.

Church Establishments and Nonestablishments in the Early Republic

The federal government sustained this interpretation in the early national period. After the Louisiana Purchase in 1803, the federal government

[68] Desmond Gregory, *Minorca, the Illusory Prize: A History of the British Occupations of Minorca between 1708 and 1802* (Cranbury, NJ: Fairleigh Dickinson University Press, 1990), 112, 114–115, 128.

[69] Edward G. Archer, *Gibraltar, Identity and Empire* (Abingdon: Routledge, 2006), 94; Stephen Constantine, *Community and Identity: The Making of Modern Gibraltar Since 1704* (Manchester: Manchester University Press, 2009), 73–74.

[70] For the necessity of "constructing" a constitutional text, see Keith Whittington, *Constitutional Construction: Divided Powers and Constitutional Meaning* (Cambridge, MA: Harvard University Press, 2001).

confronted the question of whether it could exercise patronage rights over the approval of a Catholic bishop in New Orleans. In 1806, the St. Louis Cathedral in New Orleans, now in US territory, was rent apart over who would become bishop. The trustees of the cathedral wanted French Emperor Napoléon Bonaparte to exercise his claimed right of patronage to select Spanish Capuchin Antonio de Sedella. Pope Pius VII, embroiled in controversy with Napoléon, heard about the plan and directed John Carroll to administer the diocese instead. In an effort to install a permanent bishop in New Orleans, however, Carroll wrote to Secretary of State James Madison to ensure that his choice for bishop, a Frenchman "who has long resided amongst us, and is desirous of continuing under this government," could assume the role "without disapprobation" of President Thomas Jefferson.[71] Madison replied that "as the case is entirely ecclesiastical it is deemed most congenial with the scrupulous policy of the Constitution in guarding against a political interference with religious affairs, to decline the explanations which you have thought might enable you to accommodate the better, the execution of your trust, to the public advantage." Madison and Jefferson trusted that Carroll's "due attachment to the independence, the constitution and the prosperity of the United States" would ensure his selection of an excellent candidate for bishop.[72] Carroll most likely had anticipated Madison's answer but probably wanted to receive official assurance concerning a politically sensitive topic after the Louisiana Purchase. In a private letter to Carroll that same day, however, Madison wrote that he wished Carroll would become bishop of New Orleans and that the cathedral trustees' "foreign interposition" in soliciting Napoléon was "manifestly reprehensible."[73] Carroll continued to administer the diocese until 1812.

The federal government also rejected other forms of patronage, including the ownership of ecclesiastical property. Before the Louisiana Purchase was finalized, Thérèse de St. Xavier Farjon, mother superior of the Ursuline convent in New Orleans, worried whether ownership of her convent would be protected under US law and requested an act of Congress to ensure its incorporation. The convent had been under state control since its

[71] John Carroll to James Madison, November 17, 1806, in *JCP*, 1: 535–536.

[72] James Madison to John Carroll, November 20, 1806, in *Records of the American Catholic Historical Society of Philadelphia* 20 (1909): 63–64.

[73] Ibid., 64–65.

establishment. King Louis XV had authorized the founding of the convent in 1726, and the French colonial government had built it in 1734.[74] Since 1791, however, the French government shuttered most convents in France and assumed state ownership of those remaining under the Concordat of 1801.[75] The Ursulines' property in New Orleans had been spared. But would the nuns' property transfer from one government's ownership to another? A month before the official transfer from France to the United States was complete, Sister Farjon sent her concern to John Carroll (who forwarded her letter to Secretary of State James Madison) and later to President Thomas Jefferson.[76] Jefferson promised the nuns that the US government took no interest in owning their property. The US Constitution, he wrote, was "a sure guarantee" that their property "will be preserved to you sacred and inviolate, and that your institution will be permitted to govern itself according to its own voluntary rulers, without interference from civil authority." The social benefits of the "charitable objects" of their order, he concluded, "cannot fail to ensure it the patronage of the government it is under. Be assured that it will meet with all the protection which my office can give it."[77] With knowledge of the history of *ius patronatus*, Jefferson redefined what he called "patronage" in a church–state context.[78] The only

[74] Heloise H. Cruzat, "The Ursulines of Louisiana," *Louisiana Historical Quarterly* 2, no. 1 (1919): 8, 12.

[75] I thank Kate Marsden for our discussion of these points.

[76] Mary Teresa Farjon to John Carroll, November 1, 1803, Baltimore Cathedral Archives, Case 11-06, cited in Peter Guilday, *The Life and Times of John Carroll: Archbishop of Baltimore, 1735–1815* (New York: Encyclopedia Press, 1922), 482; John Carroll to Thomas Jefferson, December 14, 1803, not extant, in *JCP*, 2: 426; John Carroll to James Madison, January 14, 1804, in *JCP*, 2: 431; John Carroll to Mary Teresa Farjon, February 14, 1804, not found, cited in Guilday, *Life and Times of John Carroll*, 482; Thérèse de St. Xavier Farjon to Thomas Jefferson, June 13, 1804, Series 1: General Correspondence. 1651–1827, The Library of Congress, accessed online December 11, 2016, www.loc.gov/item/mtjbib013530/; William C. C. Claiborne to Thomas Jefferson, June 15, 1804, Series 1: General Correspondence. 1651–1827, Library of Congress, accessed online December 11, 2016, www.loc.gov/item/mtjbib013529/; and James Madison to John Carroll, July 20, 1804, in Archives of the Archdiocese of Baltimore and Associated Archives at St. Mary's Seminary & University, Baltimore, MD.

[77] Thomas Jefferson to Thérèse de St. Xavier Farjon, July 13, 1804, Series 1: General Correspondence, 1651–1827, The Library of Congress, accessed online, December 11, 2016, www.loc.gov/item/mtjbib013625/.

[78] Thomas Jefferson, 1762–1767, Legal Commonplace Book, Series 5: Commonplace Books, The Thomas Jefferson Papers, The Library of Congress, accessed online, January 18, 2019, www.loc.gov/item/mtjbib026466/. Jefferson copied this section in his commonplace book in Thomas Jefferson to Thomas Cooper, February 10, 1814, in *The Papers of Thomas*

"patronage" the US government granted religious organizations was the allowance for them to continue their religious mission uninhibited by civil interference or legal discrimination.

While the federal government abstained from intervening in ecclesial appointments or patronizing any one particular religious institution with government funds, it was willing to fund religious activities non-preferentially as long as such activities also expressed a secular purpose. Such was the policy of Congress when, after John Carroll's lobbying efforts, it authorized and appropriated the 1793 Civilization Fund to pay Christian missionaries to educate and evangelize Native Americans. A year before, Carroll had explained to President George Washington that when "Indian tribes received formerly some instruction in the principles and duties of Christianity … a strong attachment was formed in their minds towards the nation." Carroll therefore asked the president that he and Congress "make for a few years, a small allowance for the necessary subsistence of clergymen employed in disseminating the principles of Christianity amongst the natives of the Western Territory."[79] Washington told Carroll that he supported efforts to use "the mild principles of religion and philanthropy" to ensure "the permanent attachment of our savage neighbors."[80]

The Civilization Fund earmarked $20,000 per year (and $15,000 per year in 1796, 1799, and 1802) to fund presidentially appointed "temporary agents, to reside among the Indians, as he [the president] shall think proper."[81] These agents were often religious ministers, and John Carroll obtained some of this federal money for his missionary priests on the

Jefferson, Retirement Series, vol. 7, *28 November 1813 to 30 September 1814*, ed. J. Jefferson Looney (Princeton, NJ: Princeton University Press, 2010), 190–191.

79 John Carroll to George Washington, March 20, 1792, in *JCP*, 2: 24–25.

80 George Washington to John Carroll, April 10, 1792, in *The Writings of George Washington*, ed. Jared Sparks (Boston, MA: American Stationers, 1837), 10: 228–229.

81 An Act to Regulate Trade and Intercourse with the Indian Tribes, March 1, 1793, 2nd Cong., 2nd sess.; An Act to Regulate Trade and Intercourse with the Indian Tribes, and to Preserve Peace on the Frontiers, May 19, 1796, 4th Cong., 1st sess.; An Act to Regulate Trade and Intercourse with the Indian Tribes, and to Preserve Peace on the Frontiers, 1779, 5th Cong., sess. 3; An Act to Regulate Trade and Intercourse with the Indian Tribes, and to Preserve Peace on the Frontiers, 1802, 7th Cong., sess. 1, *1789–1875* and *1799–1813*, ed. Richard Peters, vols. 1 and 2 of *Statutes at Large* (Boston: Charles C. Little and James Brown, 1845), 1: 331, 472, 747, 2: 143. See Drakeman, *Church, State, and Original Intent*, 310–311; R. Pierce Beaver, *Church, State, and the American Indians* (St. Louis, MO: Concordia Publishing House, 1966), 85.

Western frontier. In 1800, he reported that at least two priests in the Native American territories received salaries from the US federal government to "tend to their [the Native Americans'] civilisation, and teach them the advantages of the Xtian [Christian] religion."[82]

Carroll continued to appeal for federal funds throughout the decade. In 1809, he recommended French-born Catholic priest Gabriel Richard to President-elect James Madison for obtaining federal funds "to unite with the duties of his religious ministry . . . the diffusion of useful knowledge" to not only Native Americans but also American settlers.[83] In addition to Carroll's letter to Madison, Richard petitioned Congress to support "the education & civilization of the Indians" in the Michigan territory.[84] Although little materialized from these efforts, Richard became a nonvoting US representative for the Michigan Territory from 1823 to 1825 – the first American Catholic priest to serve as a member of Congress. That any cleric would serve in public office was unusual: Many states prohibited ministers from holding a seat in their legislatures, and the Vatican also disapproved of clerics in civil roles.[85] Despite, or perhaps because of, this church–state cooperation, Richard later remarked to Alexis de Tocqueville that "[t]he greatest service one can do to religion is to separate it from temporal power."[86]

[82] John Carroll to [Samuel Dexter], September 15, 1800, in *JCP*, 2: 320–321.

[83] John Carroll to James Madison, January 6, 1809, James Madison Papers, 1723–1836, Library of Congress, accessed May 31, 2011, http://hdl.loc.gov/loc.mss/mjm.10_0914_0915. Originally from France, Richard immigrated to Baltimore in 1792 and was appointed pastor of St Anne's Church in Detroit from 1802 to 1832 by Carroll. See Stanley McCrory Pargellis, *Father Gabriel Richard* (Detroit, MI: Wayne University Press, 1950) and Michael Pasquier, *Fathers on the Frontier: French Missionaries and the Roman Catholic Priesthood in the United States, 1789–1870* (Oxford: Oxford University Press, 2009).

[84] Gabriel Richard to U.S. Congress, January 19, 1809, qtd. in Frank B. Woodford and Albert Hyma, *Gabriel Richard: Frontier Ambassador* (Detroit, MI: Wayne State University Press, 1958), 69.

[85] James Hennesey, *American Catholics: A History of the Roman Catholic Community in the United States* (New York: Oxford University Press, 1981), 30; Luca Codignola, "Roman Catholic Conservatism in a New North Atlantic World, 1760–1829," *William and Mary Quarterly*, 3rd ser., 64, no. 4 (2007): 742–743; and Edwin S. Gaustad, "Religious Tests, Constitutions, and 'Christian Nation,'" in *Religion in a Revolutionary Age*, eds. Ronald Hoffman and Peter J. Albert (Charlottesville, VA: United States Capitol Historical Society by the University Press of Virginia, 1994), 223.

[86] Quoted in Alexis de Tocqueville, *Journey to America*, ed. J. P. Mayer, trans. George Lawrence (New Haven, CT: Yale University Press, 1960), 135.

Yet George Washington, members of Congress, and Secretaries of War John Marshall and Samuel Dexter (who distributed the Civilization Fund monies) apparently did not consider funding clergy for their religious missions to Native Americans as constituting a federal establishment of religion. (Nor apparently did John Carroll see his activity in soliciting federal funds as breaching his "purely spiritual" role as bishop.) The federal funds were limited to religious missions to Native Americans and were intended to curry favor with them, not for the purposes of proselytization as such. In the eyes of the federal officials, religious education was simply a means to a secular end. The federal funding for religious missionary work was a "mixed case" that did not clearly establish a religion. Throughout the nineteenth century, the federal government continued to grant Catholics and Protestants federal funds and control of Native American territory for their evangelizing efforts, especially during the Grant administration in the 1860s and 1870s, even as Grant pushed the Blaine Amendment against Catholics.

Viewing the establishment clause in light of American Catholic history reveals several new insights into First Amendment jurisprudence. Although anti-Catholic movements in the nineteenth century interpreted Catholicism as hostile to the First Amendment, early American Catholics actually supported the juridical separation of church and state. Locating the First Amendment within the context of the United States' relationship with the Holy See indicates that the framers of the US Constitution denied Congress the rights of patronage that had traditionally defined an established church. In particular, the establishment clause, at the very least, prohibited Congress from nominating or accepting bishops in the United States. Traditional patronage rights had implied a certain cognizance or competency over religious affairs, which the federal government claimed it did not have. Instead, Congress's "patronage" took the form of protecting religious organizations in order for them to fulfill their religious missions and charitable functions, and funding activities with both religious and secular purposes. While the American founders insisted on bishops without temporal power and a national government without ecclesiastical power, no interpretation can accurately claim that the establishment clause amounted to a strict church–state separation.

What many Christians had maintained is the ideal, and what had been a precondition for trust and cohesion in British political governance – a common religion, often sanctioned by religious tests – was no longer a legal requirement under the US Constitution. Instead, appealing to the lowest common denominator – civil religion – attempted to fill the vacuum left by an established church. The promise of civil religion was that it would minimize religious conflict by offering a common set of beliefs, images, and traditions, while prohibiting religious coercion by civil authorities. But the allowance of increased religious propagation and evangelization also offered more chances for religious flashpoints. Moreover, Americans continued to vote for and against politicians precisely on the basis of their religion or lack of religion – a religious test of another sort. After disestablishment, much of American contemporary church–state and religious liberty controversies – whose rights, which dignity? – have been about attaining social and political harmony through means other than an established church, or measures just short of reestablishing one.

7 Church and State in the Nineteenth Century

Jonathan Den Hartog

In 1801, a group of Connecticut Baptists wrote to the newly elected President Thomas Jefferson, with the hope that he would affirm their religious liberty and oppose the Congregationalist church establishment in their state. These leaders of the Danbury Baptist Association asserted to Jefferson that "[o]ur Sentiments are uniformly on the side of Religious Liberty . . . That no man ought to suffer in Name, person or effects on account of his religious Opinions."[1] Jefferson saw in the letter an opportunity to make his opinions clear, "sowing useful truths & principles among the people."[2] Jefferson and various cabinet members carefully edited his reply. The result was his Letter to the Danbury Baptists, where Jefferson famously stated:

> Believing with you that religion is a matter which lies solely between Man & his God, that he owes account to none other for his faith or his worship, that the legitimate powers of government reach actions only, & not opinions, I contemplate with sovereign reverence that act of the whole American people which declared that *their* legislature should "make no law respecting an establishment of religion, or prohibiting the free exercise thereof," thus building a wall of separation between Church & State, adhering to this expression of the supreme will of the nation in behalf of the rights of conscience, I shall see with sincere satisfaction the progress of those sentiments which tends to restore to man all his natural rights, convinced he has no natural right in opposition to his social duties.[3]

More than just affirming existing conceptions of religious liberty, Jefferson staked out a definition of a "wall of separation" that was intended

[1] The Danbury Baptist Association to Thomas Jefferson, October 7, 1801, in *The Sacred Rights of Conscience: Selected Readings on Religious Liberty and Church-State Relations in the American Founding*, ed. Daniel L. Dreisbach and Mark David Hall (Indianapolis, IN: Liberty Fund, 2009), 526.

[2] Thomas Jefferson to Levi Lincoln, January 1, 1802, in *Sacred Rights of Conscience*, 527.

[3] Thomas Jefferson to Messrs. Nehemiah Dodge, Ephraim Robbins, and Stephen S. Nelson, January 1, 1802, in *Sacred Rights of Conscience*, 528.

to divide the operations of the church and the state much more fully than American society had previously accepted.[4]

For thinking about – and even adjudicating – the First Amendment, Jefferson's letter has assumed outsize importance. In the mid-twentieth century, Jefferson's phrase "wall of separation" became the dominant theory for understanding church–state issues. Jefferson's wall became the controlling metaphor in *Everson* v. *Board of Education* (1947). In discussing the "establishment of religion," the Court declared, "Neither a state nor the Federal Government ... can pass laws which aid one religion, aid all religions, or prefer one religion over another." After quoting Jefferson's words, Justice Hugo Black, writing for the majority, asserted, "That wall must be kept high and impregnable. We could not approve the slightest breach."[5] This approach was reiterated in subsequent Supreme Court cases, such as *McCollum* v. *Board of Education* (1948). It also impacted cases considering Sabbath observation in *McGowan* v. *Maryland* (1961) and *Braunfeld* v. *Brown* (1961).[6] This case law laid the groundwork for contemporary Supreme Court jurisprudence on matters of church and state.

Yet, should Jefferson's metaphor – one directed at a single religious organization, by someone not in the country during the debate over the First Amendment – carry such weight? A much more diverse set of interpretations of the First Amendment can be found in the history of the nineteenth century, as individuals considered the implications of both the establishment clause and the free exercise clause. At the same time, the nineteenth century also witnessed the First Amendment being deployed to sideline two unpopular religious minorities, Roman Catholics and Mormons. In these ways, the history of the nineteenth century suggests the need to appreciate a wider field for understanding the First Amendment than Jefferson's "wall" metaphor allows.[7]

[4] James H. Hutson, "Thomas Jefferson's Letter to the Danbury Baptists: A Controversy Rejoined," *William & Mary Quarterly*, 3rd ser., 56, no.4 (October 1999): 775–790; Daniel Dreisbach, *Thomas Jefferson and the Wall of Separation between Church and State* (New York: New York University Press, 2002).

[5] *Everson* v. *Board of Education*, 330 U.S. 15–18 (1947).

[6] *McCollum* v. *Board of Education*, 333 U.S. 203 (1948); *McGowan* v. *Maryland*, 366 U.S. 429–440 (1961); and *Braunfeld* v. *Brown*, 366 U.S. 602–604 (1961).

[7] For two treatments of the nineteenth century in tension with the argument presented in this article, see Steven K. Green, *The Second Disestablishment: Church and State in Nineteenth-Century America* (New York: Oxford University Press, 2010) and David Sehat, *The Myth of*

The outlooks of Americans across the political spectrum differed strikingly from Jefferson's proposed vision of a "wall of separation." In a telling way, the early Baptists who were Jefferson's political allies as Democratic-Republicans refused to endorse Jefferson's view. Although the Danbury Baptists received Jefferson's reply, they made no formal acknowledgment of it – a silence that suggests less than full agreement with Jefferson's claims. The general Baptist outlook was to advocate for religious liberty – meaning no state establishment – while still desiring a great deal of Christian influence in the government and Christian recognition by the government. South Carolina Baptists, for instance, asserted "that as nations are indebted to God for their security and prosperity that they ought to acknowledge him as nations." Quoting Proverbs 14:34 ("righteousness exalteth a nation but sin is the reproach of any people"), they also warned against neglecting gratitude and virtue being offered to God. Thus, the nation corporately had a responsibility before God, just as collective punishment would be earned for ignoring that duty.[8]

Other Democratic-Republicans concurred. Baptist preacher John Leland had worked with James Madison to secure religious disestablishment in Virginia, but he continued to press for public expressions of faith. Having returned to New England, he rallied the town of Cheshire, Massachusetts, to create a "Mammoth Cheese" in support of Jefferson and disestablishment. Having accompanied the cheese to Washington, DC, he preached a sermon connecting religion and politics in the largest meeting hall in the city – the Chamber of the House of Representatives. For Leland, even while supporting disestablishment, there was no division of religion and political concerns.[9] This approach was also evident among Methodists, such as the independent Methodist Lorenzo Dow. He supported Jefferson

American Religious Freedom (New York: Oxford University Press, 2011). Green supports a more Jeffersonian understanding of the debates over religious liberty, advocating for a more secular reading of American political institutions. By contrast, Sehat acknowledges religious involvement in legal and political affairs in the nineteenth century but decries them as coercive and exclusionary.

8 Circular Letter, in Minutes of the Savannah Baptist Association, Held at Black Swamp, in the State of South Carolina (Savannah, GA [?]: np, 1804), 5.

9 Daniel Dreisbach, "Thomas Jefferson, a Mammoth Cheese, and the 'Wall of Separation between Church and State,'" in *Religion and the New Republic: Faith in the Founding of America*, ed. James Hutson (Lanham, MD: Rowman & Littlefield, 2000), 65–114; Thomas Kidd, *God of Liberty: A Religious History of the American Revolution* (New York: Basic Books, 2010), 238–243.

politically and trumpeted a democratic faith in the common man, but he also believed that citizens should use that political liberty as a means of advancing the Gospel and shaping the political nation.[10] For these religious supporters of Jefferson, no wall existed in their minds.

If religious Democratic-Republicans refused to see an absolute division between religious beliefs and actions and the operation of the federal government, there was even less a sense of a divide among Jefferson's opponents, the Federalists. The Federalists had claimed their name in the struggle to ratify the Constitution, and in the disputes of the new nation, they were firm supporters of the federal government. They claimed leaders with sterling revolutionary credentials such as John Adams, John Jay, Charles Cotesworth Pinckney, and Gouverneur Morris, men who would have a justified sense of what the Constitution mandated or allowed. As an integral part of their political culture, the Federalists advanced a vision of public religiosity, whereby the federal government was not indifferent to religious claims but could actively encourage religious practice among the citizens, encouraging a generic Protestantism. In these endeavors, Federalists worked closely with ministers like Timothy Dwight of Connecticut, Jedidiah Morse of Massachusetts, and William Linn of New York – pastors who articulated the public good of religious expression. The Federalists and their allies believed that Christianity in particular helped to create the virtue needed for republican citizens, in addition to the spiritual benefits of religious practice. It thereby helped preserve the republic and served as a check to the violent revolution the Federalists watched transpiring in France.[11]

These Federalists saw the First Amendment as still legitimating nonsectarian religious activity by the federal government. Just as the Continental Congress and the Confederation Congress had issued official calls for Days of Thanksgiving and Days of Fasting and Prayer, so the First Congress considered whether to continue it. The Federalist Elias Boudinot stated he "could not think of letting the session pass over without offering an opportunity to all the citizens of the United States, of joining, with one voice, in returning to Almighty God their sincere thanks for the many

[10] Nathan Hatch, *The Democratization of American Christianity* (New Haven, CT: Yale University Press, 1989), 36–40, 184–189.

[11] For religion and the Federalists generally, see Jonathan Den Hartog, *Patriotism and Piety: Federalist Politics and Religious Struggle in the New American Nation* (Charlottesville, VA: University of Virginia Press, 2015), 1–20, 201–206.

blessings he had poured down upon them." In his resolution, he and the House of Representatives called upon President George Washington to declare "a day of public Thanksgiving and Prayer."[12] Although a few representatives resisted this measure, it passed handily, and Washington approved. The Federalists had thus begun an annual practice which John Adams would follow – and which Thomas Jefferson would be at pains to justify discontinuing. As president, Adams also issued national, religious statements (even though others wrote them). Still, Adams did not hesitate to declare, officially, that "[o]ur Constitution was made only for a moral and religious people. It is wholly inadequate to the government of any other."[13] Publicly religious statements and proclamations were acceptable, because they were nonsectarian under an acknowledged public Christianity: while endorsing Christianity's place in the republic, they refused to single out any particular denomination.

In the period after the War of 1812, some reformers pushed even further, as they saw no conflict between the First Amendment and their desires for an even more sacralized politics. In New York in 1827, for instance, the Presbyterian minister Ezra Stiles Ely called for "*a Christian Party in Politics*." He advocated for an electoral coalition of orthodox Christian denominations to elect Christian rulers to implement Christian policies. He insisted, "We are a Christian nation: we have a right to demand that all our rulers in their conduct shall conform to Christian morality."[14] A moral issue of the 1820s whose appeal reached beyond Ely's proposal was the delivery of mail on Sunday, regarded as the Sabbath by the vast majority of Christians. Christian reformers saw it as a federal intrusion upon the Day of Rest, given its tendency to disturb the peace, force labor on postal workers and postmasters, and contravene state and local Sunday-closing laws. They argued for a federal cessation of Sunday mail on religious grounds and mounted a concerted campaign from 1827 to 1831. Their efforts were

[12] Ibid., 99–100.

[13] John Adams, "To the Officers of the First Brigade of the Third Division of the Militia of Massachusetts" in *The Works of John Adams, Second President of the United States*, ed. Charles Francis Adams, 10 vols. (Boston: Little, Brown, 1850–1856), 9:228–229. See also Den Hartog, *Patriotism and Piety*, 127–129.

[14] Ezra Stiles Ely, *The Duty of Christian Freemen to Elect Christian Rulers: A Discourse Delivered on the Fourth of July, 1827, in the Seventh Presbyterian Church, in Philadelphia* (Philadelphia, PA: Wm F. Geddes 1828), 8, 14. See also Dreisbach, *Religion and Politics in the Early Republic*, 7–11; James Kabala, *Church-State Relations in the Early American Republic, 1787–1846* (New York: Routledge, 2015), 70–82.

unsuccessful, however, and the federal government continued to deliver the mail throughout the nineteenth century.[15]

A similar impulse of promoting greater recognition of Christianity in public life was on display in a widely debated sermon by Episcopal priest Jasper Adams. In 1833, Adams addressed the South Carolina Convention of the Protestant Episcopal Church on the topic *The Relation of Christianity to Civil Government in the United States*. Raised in New England and a graduate of the Federalist Andover Theological Seminary, Adams reflected continued belief in a privileged place for public Christianity. Part of his argument was practical. He asserted that the nation needed public Christianity. "No nation on earth," he asserted, "is more dependent than our own, for its welfare, on the preservation and general belief and influence of Christianity among us. . . . We must be a Christian nation, if we wish to continue a free nation."[16] The proper relations of government and citizenry required the virtue that only Christianity could inculcate. At the same time, Christianity stood as a barrier against the forces that would undermine the state. In this warning, he asked rhetorically, "Are we not convinced, that if our religion is once undermined, it will be succeeded by a decline of public and private morals?"[17] The nightmare vision in Adams' mind was revolutionary France, where loss of faith had preceded social disintegration. "Encouragement of the infidel [unbelieving] system among us, will dissolve all the moral ties which unite men in the bonds of society." Building off of Edmund Burke's *Reflections on the Revolution in France* and Timothy Dwight's warnings against "Infidelity," Adams desired a public Christianity as a public good.[18]

[15] Wayne Fuller, *Morality and the Mail in Nineteenth-Century America* (Urbana, IL: University of Illinois Press, 2003), 1–97; Daniel Walker Howe, *What Hath God Wrought: The Transformation of America, 1815–1848* (New York: Oxford University Press, 2007), 229–230.

[16] Jasper Adams, *The Relation of Christianity to Civil Government in the United States*, in Dreisbach, *Religion and Politics in the Early Republic: Jasper Adams and the Church-State Debate* (Lexington: University of Kentucky Press, 1996), 51–52.

[17] Ibid., 54.

[18] Ibid., 57. For Burke, see Edmund Burke, *Reflections on the Revolution in France* (Indianapolis, IN: Hackett Publishing, 1987 [1790]). Timothy Dwight preached much against infidelity, but Adams likely is referring to Dwight's *The Nature, and Danger, of Infidel Philosophy, Exhibited in Two Discourses, Addressed to the Candidates for the Baccalaureate, in Yale College, By the Rev. Timothy Dwight, D.D. President of Yale College; September 9th, 1797* (New Haven, CT: George Bunce, 1798). For Dwight and infidelity, see Den Hartog, *Patriotism and Piety*, 45–69.

In support of that goal, he considered the status of religion under the Constitution. He argued that the American religious settlement rejected preferential support for a single Christian denomination but did not eliminate an endorsement of Christianity. He stated this in a capital declaration: "THE PEOPLE OF THE UNITED STATES HAVE RETAINED THE CHRISTIAN RELIGION AS THE FOUNDATION OF THEIR CIVIL, LEGAL AND POLITICAL INSTITUTIONS; WHILE THEY HAVE REFUSED TO CONTINUE A LEGAL PREFERENCE TO ANY ONE OF ITS FORMS OVER THE OTHER."[19] Adams further asserted, "Thus, while all others enjoy full protection in the profession of their opinions and practice, Christianity is the established religion of the nation, its institutions and usages are sustained by legal sanctions, and many of them are incorporated with the fundamental law of the country."[20] Although Adams may have meant Christianity was the "settled" religion, rather than meaning it was "established" in the legal sense, still he was prioritizing Christianity for the public realm. In this, he insisted that the Constitution gave no right for Congress to interfere with Christianity. "They have no commission to destroy or injure the religion of the country."[21] The First Amendment did not grant power to Congress to innovate in religious matters, but to protect the liberty and prominence of religion, especially Christianity. To the argument that the Constitution was silent on his Christian claims, Adams asserted that it should be read in harmony with the public opinion at its ratification.[22]

Adams' claims sparked significant public debate. An unsigned essay in the *American Quarterly Review* took Adams to task for his privileging Christianity. This author declared himself "decidedly opposed to any connexion between church and state."[23] Similarly, when James Madison received a copy of the sermon, he insisted that the more separationist position he had staked out in his "Memorial and Remonstrance" in the 1780s was still the wisest course.[24] By contrast, two sitting Supreme Court Justices endorsed the sermon. John Marshall assented, "The American population is entirely Christian, & with us, Christianity & Religion are identified. It would be strange, indeed, if with such a people, our

[19] Adams in Dreisbach, *Religion and Politics*, 46. [20] Ibid., 49. [21] Ibid., 47.

[22] Ibid., 47 n21. [23] "Immunity of Religion" in Dreisbach, *Religion and Politics*, 128.

[24] James Madison to Jasper Adams, September 1833, in Dreisbach, *Religion and Politics*, 120–121. For the Memorial and Remonstrance, see Dreisbach and Hall, *Sacred Rights*, 309–313.

institutions did not presuppose Christianity, & did not often refer to it, & exhibit relations with it."[25] Marshall, although not an evangelical believer, still endorsed intersections of Christianity with law and politics. An even stronger reply came from the learned jurist Joseph Story, who confessed, "My own private judgement has long been, (& every day's experience more & more confirms me in it,) that government can not long exist without an alliance with religion *to some extent*; & that Christianity is indispensable to the true interests & solid foundations of all free governments."[26] Thus Story, who was famous for his *Commentaries* on the Constitution, endorsed a public, nonsectarian Christianity. These statements reveal that even Adams' bold claims received much public support.

Adams' claims also met challenges from several sides. Some Christians argued that the Constitution did not go far enough because of its lack of public endorsement of Christianity. On this side, a small Presbyterian sect, the Scots Covenanters, argued that the Constitution was flawed because it was not explicitly Christian. One voice supporting this complaint came from James R. Willson, who insisted that the Constitution had disregarded the claims of "Prince Messiah." He continued, "It is, indeed, astonishing, that in a Christian commonwealth, where the great majority of the citizens were attached to some Protestant church, a constitution of government could have been framed, with only two very remote and indirect allusions merely to the law and Bible of God." Given such scanty reference, Willson feared that the First Amendment would be read in opposition to Christian faith and expression.[27]

In a marked contrast to such approaches, however, freethinkers and skeptics protested that this public Christianity was oppressive to their justifiable disbelief. Although religious skeptics were few in number, they were insistent on removing public and official expressions of religion. They both doubted the truth of religious claims and questioned the public benefits of privileging Christianity while arguing for much greater neutrality in religious matters. They thus crafted an argument against a public

[25] John Marshall to John Adams, May 9, 1833 in Dreisbach, *Religion and Politics*, 113.

[26] Joseph Story to Jasper Adams, May 14, 1833 in Dreisbach, *Religion and Politics*, 115–118.

[27] James R. Willson, *Prince Messiah's Claims to Dominion over All Governments: and the Disregard of His Authority by the United States, in the Federal Constitution*, in Dreisbach and Hall, *Sacred Rights*, 360–363. For the Covenanters, see Joseph S. Moore, *Founding Sins: How a Group of Antislavery Radicals Fought to Put Christ into the Constitution* (New York: Oxford University Press, 2015).

endorsement of Christianity. Some of these freethinkers brought back arguments from Thomas Paine from previous decades, while others made their claims on the basis of reason alone. Many were influenced by skeptical currents in Europe, while others drew primarily on religious doubts found in domestic publications. This strain of argument culminated in "the Great Agnostic," Robert Ingersoll, who made articulate, public attacks on both religion and the legal structures of society that would support it. For these skeptics, a strong position of separation – an actual wall of separation – was the appropriate response.[28]

After the Civil War, Ingersoll joined with other individuals such as Francis Ellingwood Abbot in the National Liberal League to push for an even stronger standard of separation. Rooted in religious skepticism, the Liberal League argued for a full separation of church and state, and they sought to amend the First Amendment to create a clear definition of complete separation, at both the federal and state level. They warned about any entanglements of government with religious concerns. The League sought to apply this blanket approach of separation to all religious groups – Protestant and Roman Catholic. Significantly, the League adopted a new name in the 1880s, the American Secular Union. Although their ideas gained little traction in the nineteenth century, they would gain much more attention by the middle of the twentieth century.[29]

Simultaneously, some Democrats did begin to champion Jefferson's wall of separation, and they did so for two distinct reasons. First, they did so because the idea came from Jefferson, and the political culture of the party celebrated Jefferson's memory as a means of building identity and community. Second, and more significantly, some of these separationists began to invest in American politics – especially in Democratic politics – the significance of religious meaning. The New York Democrat William Leggett argued in 1836, "In framing our political institutions, the great

[28] Susan Jacoby, *Freethinkers: A History of American Secularism* (New York: Metropolitan Books, 2004); Susan Jacoby, *The Great Agnostic: Robert Ingersoll and American Freethought* (New Haven, CT: Yale University Press, 2013); Eric R. Schlereth, *An Age of Infidels: The Politics of Religious Controversy in the Early United States* (Philadelphia: University of Pennsylvania Press, 2013), 171–236; and Leigh Eric Schmidt, *Village Atheists: How America's Unbelievers Made Their Way in a Godly Nation* (Princeton, NJ: Princeton University Press, 2016).

[29] Philip Hamburger, *Separation of Church and State* (Cambridge, MA: Harvard University Press, 2002), 287–296, 302–321.

men to whom that important trust was confided, taught, by the example of other countries, the evils which result from mingling civil and ecclesiastical affairs, were particularly careful to keep them entirely distinct."[30] Separation would clear the way for American democracy to spread its own millennial benefits.[31]

Despite such objections, strong religious strains continued in both major political parties throughout the antebellum period. An important part of Whig political culture, carried over somewhat from the Federalists, was to shape both government and society according to Christian concerns. Moral reform would come about as Christian citizens used elements of government to shape all of society.[32] At the same time, many Democrats continued a moralistic, Christian vision for the laws of society, and this sense appealed to the populist ethos of ordinary believers in the party. Although the denominations that tended to support each party differed – Episcopalians, Presbyterians, and Congregationalists for the Whigs; Baptists and Methodists for the Democrats – their moral visions actually grew closer together.[33] This cooperation was enabled as the final state church establishments were removed – New Hampshire in 1817, Connecticut in 1818, and Massachusetts in 1833.[34] No longer divided over church establishments in the states, both sides demonstrated greater agreement on an informal Protestant establishment throughout the nation. This conception was even stronger in fringe movements, such as the Anti-Mason Party, which was explicitly Protestant.[35] Moreover, the critiques of the nation leveled by Protestant pastors in this period still assumed the

30 William Leggett, "Thanksgiving Day," December 3, 1836, in *A Collection of the Political Writings of William Leggett*, ed. Theodore Sedgwick, Jr. (New York: Taylor & Dodd, 1840), 2:113–114.

31 For a picture of this optimism, see John L. O'Sullivan, "The Great Nation of Futurity," *The United States Democratic Review* (November 6, 1839): 426–430. Philip Hamburger traced earlier roots of this optimism in *Separation of Church and State*, 133–143.

32 Daniel Walker Howe, *The Political Culture of the American Whigs* (Chicago, IL: University of Chicago Press, 1979), 150–180.

33 For an in-depth analysis of how religious belief suffused both parties and affected voting behavior, see Richard J. Carwardine, *Evangelicals and Politics in Antebellum America* (New Haven, CT: Yale University Press, 1993).

34 On the long-term process of disestablishment, see Carl H. Esbeck and Jonathan Den Hartog, eds., *Disestablishment and Religious Dissent: Church-State Relations in the New American States, 1776–1833* (Columbia, MO: University of Missouri Press, 2019).

35 Howe, *What Hath God Wrought*, 266–271. Paul Goodman, *Towards a Christian Republic: Antimasonry and the Great Transition in New England, 1826–1836* (New York: Oxford University Press, 1988).

right of the churches to direct national priorities.[36] Put together, they represented a sense of a Protestant establishment which channeled religious concerns into politics and which maintained the First Amendment, as long as no individual denomination received special privileges.

This push was also present in the political reform movements of the era. Although not all were explicitly Christian, they still borrowed from Christian principles for actions to be taken in the national realm. This impulse appeared in the grass-roots opposition to Andrew Jackson's Indian Removal policy, as women across the nation drew on their moral and religious status as women to condemn forced removal of the Cherokees from their homeland. This campaign had at least one prominent origin in the efforts of Catharine Beecher, daughter of Lyman Beecher, himself a reforming clergyman who viewed politics as responsible to Christian convictions. As an educator, Catharine felt a moral and Christian obligation to object to the theft of Cherokee lands, and she deployed communication networks to build support for their cause.[37] Lyman's daughter and Catharine's sister, Harriet Beecher Stowe, also became a proponent of abolition and did much to advance it with her novel *Uncle Tom's Cabin*.[38] In the antislavery cause, not all proponents were religious, but some abolitionists did reach that position through distinctly Christian principles. Charles Finney, Theodore Dwight Weld, William Jay, and Arthur and Lewis Tappan, although disagreeing on style and emphasis, still arrived at abolition through an analysis of Christian duties. By the 1840s, some abolitionists came to believe in the need for a dedicated political party to advance abolition – the Liberty Party.[39]

The Civil War touched off intense reflections on the nature of the Union and its relationship to Christianity. The debates from the first half of the nineteenth century were echoed in Confederate treatment of religious matters. In the Confederate Constitution, the two provisions about religion from the US Constitution – the First Amendment and the no religious test

[36] Mark Y. Hanley, *Beyond a Christian Commonwealth: The Protestant Quarrel with the American Republic, 1830–1860* (Chapel Hill, NC: University of North Carolina Press, 1993).

[37] Mary Hershberger, "Mobilizing Women, Anticipating Abolition: The Struggle against Indian Removal in the 1830s," *Journal of American History* 86 (June 1999): 15–40. For Lyman Beecher, see Howe, *Political Culture*, 150–180.

[38] Nancy Koester, *Harriet Beecher Stowe: A Spiritual Life* (Grand Rapids, MI: Eerdmans Publishing Company, 2014).

[39] Den Hartog, *Patriotism and Piety*, 190–200.

clause – were reproduced exactly.[40] However, the Confederate Constitution changed the Preamble significantly, as it placed the Confederate enterprise under "Almighty God," invoking His favor and guidance. Groups such as the Covenanters might have celebrated this religious development, even as they would have decried the explicitly pro-slavery aspects of the Confederate Constitution.[41]

Confidence in the institutionally Christian character of the Confederacy would also shape the development of its public culture.[42] President Jefferson Davis was much more willing than Abraham Lincoln to call for days of fasting and prayer or Thanksgiving. He proclaimed approximately nine such days over four years.[43] Southern ministers would use such days to shape public interpretation of events through their sermons. These ministers endorsed the goals of the Confederacy and the continuation of slavery but also preached jeremiads calling for further reform – often in the treatment of slaves.[44] Preaching by Christian chaplains encouraged the Confederate army's prosecution of the war and helped promote many Christian revivals in the ranks.[45] After their defeat in the war, this Christian language also nourished the "Lost Cause" mentality, along with the belief that had the Confederacy been more virtuous and Christian in practice, their efforts would have received divine favor and success.[46]

40 The First Amendment became embedded in the Confederate Constitution as Article I, Sec. 9, provision 12. Meanwhile, the prohibition of any religious test for office became Article VI, Sec. 4.

41 "Constitution of the Confederate States," March 11, 1861, *The Avalon Project: Documents in Law, History and Diplomacy*, accessed April 26, 2018, http://avalon.law.yale.edu/19th_century/csa_csa.asp.

42 For religion and Confederate Nationalism generally, see Drew Gilpin Faust, *The Creation of Confederate Nationalism: Ideology and Identity in the Civil War South* (Baton Rouge, LA: Louisiana State University Press, 1988, 1995), 24–34; John Fea, *Was America Founded as a Christian Nation? A Historical Introduction* (Louisville, KY: Westminster John Knox Press, 2011), 17–21; and George C. Rable, *God's Almost Chosen Peoples: A Religious History of the American Civil War* (Chapel Hill, NC: University of North Carolina Press, 2010), 59–64, 73–83.

43 Harry Stout, *Upon the Altar of the Nation: A Moral History of the Civil War* (New York: Viking, 2006), 35–52.

44 Mark Noll, *The Civil War as a Theological Crisis* (Chapel Hill, NC: University of North Carolina Press, 2006), 75–86.

45 For a hagiographic report of these revivals, see J. William Jones, *Christ in the Camp; or, Religion in Lee's Army* (Richmond, VA: B.F. Johnson, 1888).

46 Charles Reagan Wilson, *Baptized in Blood: The Religion of the Lost Cause, 1865–1920*, 2nd ed. (Athens: University of Georgia Press, 2009).

In the North, the Union was sacralized still further, as Christians rallied to defend it. The New York Baptist pastor John F. Bigelow called down "the curse . . . scathing with fires of Perdition, fall upon that man, or that class of men, whoever they may be, whether from the South or the North, from East or the West, who shall lift the hand for the overthrow, or the rupture of this *God founded* Republic."[47] Even as pastors and orators advanced a Christian vision of the Union, this thinking filtered down to ordinary Northerners. Not only did Union citizens and soldiers think of the Nation in Christian terms, they also thought about their fighting in Christian terms. Thus the standards of fighting the war energetically but with moral restraint emerged from a sense of Christian nationalism.[48] As the war dragged on and intensified, observers came to see it through the lens of forging a stronger Christian nation. The theologian Horace Bushnell, in particular, interpreted the war in terms of Romantic Nationalism in the European style – a nationalism whereby Christianity would be taken up as a natural part of the organic whole.[49] With the war's conclusion, Henry Ward Beecher (another child of Lyman Beecher) could declare, "Republican institutions have been vindicated in this experience as they never were before . . . God, I think, has said, by the voice of this event to all nations of the earth, 'Republican liberty, based upon true Christianity, is firm as the foundation of the globe.'"[50] With slavery ended and the Union restored, many in the North marched forward believing that Christianity was an integral part of both the American nation and its government.

All of this religious nationalism confronted challenges from religious minorities who did not match up to its Protestant expectations. One objection came from a small, radical group, the Mormons. Another came from the largest religious minority in the country, Roman

[47] Qtd. in John Fea, *Was America Founded as a Christian Nation?*, 17. For religion and the North, see Rable, *God's Almost Chosen Peoples*, 51–59, 65–68, 83–89.

[48] D. H. Dilbeck, *A More Civil War: How the Union Waged a Just War* (Chapel Hill, NC: University of North Carolina Press, 2016), 6–7, 78–80, 123–127.

[49] Robert Bruce Mullin, *The Puritan as Yankee: A Life of Horace Bushnell* (Grand Rapids, MI: Wm. B. Eerdmans Publishing Company, 2002), 208–233.

[50] Henry Ward Beecher, "Abraham Lincoln" in *Patriotic Addresses in America and England, 1850–1885, On Slavery, the Civil War, and the Development of Civil Liberty in the United States* (New York: Howard & Hulbert, 1888). For a contextualization of Beecher, see Mark Noll, *America's God: From Jonathan Edwards to Abraham Lincoln* (New York: Oxford University Press, 2002), 422–438.

Catholics. Although Catholics had been in America since colonial days, their numbers had remained small, and they had largely worked out an accommodation with American republican sensibilities.[51] That arrangement began to give way as the numbers of Catholics grew, with the upsurge of immigration in the 1830s and 1840s, when many German and Irish Catholics emigrated to the United States. Tensions again increased as Catholic immigration grew after the Civil War. In addition to seeming foreign, Catholic immigrants raised significant issues of church and state and whether Catholics could be responsible, independent republican citizens or whether the Catholic hierarchy of pope and bishops held such firm control over them that their voting habits would lead to Catholic control of the United States. The Vatican did not help American perceptions, either. During the middle of the nineteenth century, the Catholic hierarchy was particularly ultramontane and antiliberal as they protested against the modern world. The *Syllabus of Errors* by Pope Pius IX in 1864 condemned free speech, separation of church and state, free public schools, Bible societies, and Protestantism itself – opinions guaranteed to offend Americans.[52]

These tensions explain the very real violence encountered by Roman Catholics in nineteenth-century urban America. In 1834, in Charleston, Massachusetts, mobs burned a local convent, after scurrilous rumors had circulated about the women held there against their will. A decade later in July 1844, violence broke out in Philadelphia. Protestants set fire to Catholic churches and neighborhoods. When they attempted to destroy the St. Philip Neri Catholic Church, a pitched battle ensued, in which both sides even wielded small-bore cannons. Approximately twenty were killed in these Philadelphia riots. Then, in New York in 1861, a riot broke out on "Orange Day," celebrating the victory of Protestant King William of Orange over the Catholic James II. This time, over sixty Catholics died.[53] Less physically violent but still indicative of the cultural animosities was the

[51] Jay Dolan, *The American Catholic Experience: A History from Colonial Times to the Present* (Garden City, NY: Doubleday & Company, 1985), 101–126; Maura Jane Farrelly, *Papist Patriots: The Making of an American Catholic Identity* (New York: Oxford University Press, 2012); and Michael D. Breidenbach, "Conciliarism and the American Founding," *William & Mary Quarterly*, 3rd series, 73, no. 3 (July 2016): 467–500.

[52] John Corrigan and Lynn S. Neal, *Religious Intolerance in America: A Documentary History* (Chapel Hill, NC: University of North Carolina Press, 2010), 54–55.

[53] Ibid., 51, 63.

minister during the 1884 election campaign who proclaimed that citizens should vote against the Democratic Party, the party of "Rum, Romanism, and Rebellion."[54]

The distinctiveness of Catholics living in the republic was felt in two related battles: over Bibles and over schools. Public schools at the state and local level in the nineteenth century endorsed daily reading of the Bible by teachers, but at issue was the version to be read. The Protestant-dominated schools read from the King James Version and asserted that since it was accepted by all Protestant denominations, it could be read without problems. Such assumptions collided with the Roman Catholic preference for a different English Bible, the Douay-Rheims translation. This conflict led to public protests from Catholic students, most famously the Eliot School Rebellion in Boston in 1859, when Thomas Whall refused to recite the Protestant version of the Ten Commandments, leading to a mass walkout of Catholic students.[55] The issue of Scripture in the classroom pointed to the larger issue of schooling. Protestant advocates of the public school movement (inspired by figures such as Horace Mann) asserted a universal respect for religious expression, but they did so in ways that were indifferent or actively hostile to Roman Catholic identity. Such an approach prompted American Catholic bishops to lead the way in forming their own schools, connected closely to parishes, which came to be called a "parochial" school system. The literal "price" for fostering such schools intended to maintain a separate identity was the loss of any public support of them. States allowed the schools, but refused to pay for them – in a sharp contrast to many European countries where all religious schools equally received funding.[56]

Issues surrounding the place of Catholics within American political institutions and state funding grew after the Civil War. This popular concern about Catholics inspired James G. Blaine of Maine to try to score

[54] Mark Wahlgren Summers, *Rum, Romanism, and Rebellion: The Making of a President, 1884* (Chapel Hill, NC: University of North Carolina Press, 2000).

[55] John McGreevy, *Catholicism and American Freedom: A History* (New York: W.W. Norton, 2003), 7–15.

[56] Ibid., 19–42. Steven K. Green provides an extended presentation of educational debates, focusing especially on the period 1869–1876, in *The Bible, the School, and the Constitution: The Clash that Shaped Modern Church-State Doctrine* (New York: Oxford University Press, 2012). Green, echoing themes in *The Second Disestablishment*, argues approvingly of separating religious concerns from public education – a stance that would have been quite foreign to many in the nineteenth century.

more political points and position himself for a run to the presidency with anti-Catholic legislation. Representative Blaine in 1875 proposed a constitutional amendment that would have applied the First Amendment to the states. It was clearly intended to prohibit Catholic institutions from receiving public funds. Blaine's measure failed on a national level, but the idea was adopted by a number of states, leading to state "Blaine amendments."[57]

Constitutional disputes over Catholicism's standing led to several important court cases. In the years before the Civil War, the Catholic Church faced a case of free exercise that went to the Supreme Court. Bernard Permoli was a Catholic priest in New Orleans. Although New Orleans had passed a law prohibiting the public presentation of bodies for Catholic funeral services, Permoli nevertheless conducted a Catholic funeral service in the St. Augustine Church. When fined, he took the case first to the Louisiana state courts and then to the Supreme Court, in *Permoli* v. *Municipality No. 1 of City of New Orleans* (1845).[58] In defending against the ordinance, Permoli's attorney argued that the law singled out significant Catholic religious observation and so should be overturned on the basis of religious liberty. "[I]f there be aught essentially characteristic of religious liberty, it is the exemption of ecclesiastical discipline ... from secular control," he argued. Just as faith and doctrine were beyond the power of government, so church discipline, which flowed from doctrine, should be likewise protected. He concluded with the warning that "there never was an arbitrary change introduced by governments into the religious opinions of a community, which was not masked by a pretended reform of exterior observances."[59] In the end, the Court dismissed the case because it related to state considerations of religion. The Court claimed to have no jurisdiction, as the First Amendment applied only to the federal government, leaving religious matters to the states.[60] Before the use of the Fourteenth Amendment to incorporate First Amendment protections for

[57] Hamburger, *Separation of Church and State*, 296–302, 321–328. The recent Supreme Court case *Trinity Lutheran Church of Columbia, Inc.* v. *Comer*, 582 U.S. ___ (2017) revolved around a Missouri Blaine amendment.

[58] *Permoli* v. *Municipality No. 1 of City of New Orleans*, 44 U.S. 589 (1845). For background, see Michael W. McConnell, "Schism, Plague, and Late Rites in the French Quarter: The Strange Story Behind the Supreme Court's First Free Exercise Case," Stanford Public Law Working Paper No. 1675213, accessed April 26, 2018, http://dx.doi.org/10.2139/ssrn.1675213.

[59] *Permoli* v. *New Orleans*, 599.

[60] See the decision of Justice Catron, Ibid., 609.

the states, this ruling stood, thereby limiting the application of the First Amendment.

By contrast, the liberty of another Catholic priest, John Cummings of Missouri, was preserved. Following the Civil War, Missouri rewrote its constitution to require a test oath denouncing anyone who had previously supported the Confederacy or opposed the Union in word or deed. Those who would not take the oath were prohibited from practicing "as an attorney or counsellor at law; nor . . . as a bishop, priest, deacon, minister, elder, or other clergyman of any religious persuasion, sect, or denomination, to teach, or preach, or solemnize marriages, unless such person shall have first taken, subscribed, and filed said oath."[61] Cummings refused to take the oath and continued his work as a priest in Missouri until he was arrested and fined the exorbitant sum of $500. Cummings and his attorneys argued that the test oath was both an *ex post facto* law and served as a Bill of Attainder (a law directed at an individual or group to punish without a trial, prohibited by the Constitution). Justice Stephen J. Field argued, "Depriving Mr. Cummings of the right or privilege, whichever it may be called, of preaching and teaching as a Christian minister, which he had theretofore enjoyed, and of acting as a professor or teacher in a school or educational institution, was in effect a punishment."[62] The Supreme Court, divided 5–4, found in favor of Cummings and cited the *ex post facto* nature of the test oath. Cummings' character as a Catholic priest was not central, but the Court found the fact that Missouri was interfering with qualifications set by religious bodies to be problematic.

At the end of the century, the Catholic Church's public status via incorporation was challenged but protected in the case *Bradfield* v. *Roberts* (1899).[63] Providence Hospital in the District of Columbia had contracted with the District to build a new building, provide general hospital services, and receive District funds for caring for patients. Since this contract occurred in Washington, DC, these funds would be federal funds. A Washington, DC, resident, Joseph Bradfield, had objected to this contract because Providence Hospital was owned and operated by the Sisters of Charity, a Catholic religious order. Such payment looked to the complainant like an undue establishment of religion. The Court, in its 9–0 ruling, held that, by rules of incorporation, the hospital was not under the

[61] *Cummings* v. *Missouri*, 45 U.S. 281 (1866). [62] Ibid., 286.

[63] *Bradfield* v. *Roberts*, 175 U.S. 291 (1899).

direction of the Sisters or of the Catholic Church, but under its own Board of Directors. With these conditions, the Court asserted,

> Whether the individuals who compose the corporation under its charter happen to be all Roman Catholics, or all Methodists, or Presbyterians, or Unitarians, or members of any other religious organization, or of no organization at all, is of not the slightest consequence with reference to the laws of its incorporation, nor can the religious beliefs of the various incorporations be inquired into.[64]

Thus, the Catholic Church found its public charters protected and its ability to operate in the United States confirmed.

A second religious minority who found its religious rights limited was the Church of Jesus Christ of Latter-Day Saints, popularly known as the Mormons. In the 1820s in upstate New York, Joseph Smith claimed to have received a revelation by the angel Moroni. This angel directed him to find buried gold plates, which, when translated, told the story of religious happenings in pre-Columbian America, including the religion set up by Jesus Christ, when he visited the Americas after his resurrection. This translation became the *Book of Mormon*, and Smith began to gather a following. This growing group soon emigrated from New York to Kirtland, Ohio, where it built its first temple.[65]

After their time in Ohio, Mormons moved to frontier Missouri in 1837. Their rapidly growing numbers, however, sparked tension with other settlers. Missourians' fears were stoked still further in 1838 when Mormon leader Sidney Rigdon warned opponents that "a war of extermination" would follow any violence against the Mormons. Fighting actually broke out at Crooked Ridge, which led the governor of the state, Lilburn Boggs, to issue an executive order to the state militia that "[t]he Mormons must be treated as enemies, and must be exterminated or driven from the state if necessary for the public peace – their outrages are beyond all description."[66] The state of Missouri sanctioned violence against the Mormons by ordering militia and volunteer groups to attack the believers.

[64] *Bradfield* v. *Roberts*, 298.

[65] On Joseph Smith, see Richard Lyman Bushman, *Joseph Smith: Rough Stone Rolling* (New York: Knopf, 2005). One of the clearest introductions to Mormonism is Jan Ships, *Mormonism: The Story of a New Religious Tradition* (Urbana, IL: University of Illinois Press, 1985).

[66] Lilburn Boggs to Gen. John B. Clark, October 26, 1838, qtd. in Corrigan and Neal, *Religious Intolerance*, 82–83.

After another violent exchange at Haun's Mill, the Mormons fled east across the Mississippi River to their new settlement in Nauvoo, Illinois.

Mormonism continued to encounter resistance during its time in Illinois – although there the opposition was more private and social. For several years, Smith succeeded in building Nauvoo. The growing Mormon movement channeled its followers to Nauvoo, which was one of the largest cities in Illinois at the time. Smith's ambitions were larger: he even declared himself a candidate for the presidency in 1844. However, the control of Nauvoo by Mormon leadership became an issue. When a non-Mormon newspaper editor moved to Nauvoo and set up his press, he found that the cost of criticizing Smith was to have his press destroyed. Joseph and his brother Hyrum were arrested and held in the county courthouse. A lynch mob formed, and both men were killed.

After Smith's death, leadership fell to Brigham Young.[67] Young reorganized the Mormon community and led them overland to the shores of the Great Salt Lake to found the Mormon community of Deseret. The location had the benefit of being under very loose Mexican control. That would soon change, following the Mexican War, as the Treaty of Guadalupe Hidalgo ceded the territory of Utah to the United States. Although Young was named the first governor, his position – and Mormon dominance of the region – soon came under attack.

In these years, a developing distinction for the Mormon church was the practice of polygamy or "plural marriage." Polygamy would prove to be an affront to the mainstream American culture. It offended majority Christian beliefs, general Victorian morality, and the law of marriage. Joseph Smith introduced the concept of plural marriage as early as his time in Kirtland, Ohio. It became an open secret practiced more broadly among the leadership during their time in Missouri and Illinois. Brigham Young made it public knowledge and doctrine for the entire community during the trek westward. Thus, by the time the Mormons were settled in Utah, plural marriage had become publicly identified as a distinctive religious tenet of the movement.[68]

[67] For Young's life, the best study is John G. Turner, *Brigham Young: Pioneer Prophet* (Cambridge, MA: The Belknap Press of Harvard University Press, 2012).

[68] For women in early Mormonism, see Laurel Thatcher Ulrich, *A House Full of Females: Plural Marriage and Women's Rights in Early Mormonism, 1835–1870* (New York: Alfred A. Knopf, 2017).

By the 1850s, there had developed strong opposition in public opinion to Mormon polygamy. Republicans opposed Mormon polygamy from the beginning. Indeed, in their 1856 platform, they claimed "it is both the right and imperative duty of Congress to prohibit in the Territories those twin relics of barbarism – Polygamy and Slavery."[69] Similarly, the Roman Catholic writer Orestes Brownson wrote, "The Mormon reason and conscience are incompatible with the maintenance of the American state. Mormonism teaches that the dominion of the world belongs to the Saints, and that the Saints are the Mormons." Brownson went on to enumerate Mormon transgressions: their claims to exterminate their opponents, their desire to confiscate non-Mormon property, and their practice of polygamy. Put together, these reasons justified the suppression and non-toleration of Mormonism.[70]

With such growing opposition, President James Buchanan launched "the Mormon War" of 1857–1858 to reassert American control in Utah Territory. Domestically, anger rose further after the Mountain Meadows Massacre, in which Mormons and Native Americans killed unarmed members of a wagon train headed for California.[71] Buchanan dispatched American troops to Utah Territory with the aim of removing Brigham Young as governor of the territory. Buchanan justified sending troops to Utah as dealing with treason. He foreswore any religious interference. "Do not deceive yourselves," he addressed the Mormons, "that this is a crusade against your religion. The Constitution and laws of this country can take no notice of your creed, whether it be true or false. This is a question between your God and yourselves, in which I disclaim all right to interfere."[72] In the end, the military force was sufficient, and for a time federal control was restored. The government was prohibited from exerting further force, however, by the Civil War.

After the Civil War and Reconstruction, with one of the "twin relics of barbarism" – slavery – dealt with, American reformers turned their

[69] Quoted in Evan C. Rothera, "The Tenacious 'Twin Relic': Republicans, Polygamy, and *The Late Corporation of the Church of Jesus Christ of Latter-Day Saints v. United States*," *Journal of Supreme Court History* 41 (March 2016): 23.

[70] Orestes Brownson, "Christianity and the Church Identical," *Brownson's Quarterly Review*, July 1857, qtd. in Corrigan and Neal, *Religious Intolerance*, 87.

[71] Ronald W. Walker, Richard E. Turley, and Glen M. Leonard, *Massacre at Mountain Meadows* (New York: Oxford University Press, 2008).

[72] James Buchanan, "Proclamation on the Rebellion in Utah," qtd. in Corrigan and Neal, *Religious Intolerance*, 91.

attention back to Mormonism, and public opposition grew in intensity. For example, in 1877 *Scribner's Monthly* decried Mormonism as "an essentially foreign theocracy." The spiritual rule of Mormon civil life led to an inherent conflict with American rule of law. The editorial continued, "[S]omething peculiar to Mormonism takes it out of the sphere of religion and necessarily brings it into conflict with a republican people and their institutions." If this was the case, the temporal power needed, by law and force if necessary, to strip the civil power from Mormon leadership. The aim should thus be to "reduce the institution from a government to a church, and establish a republic in Utah . . ."[73] During the Gilded Age, then, American attention shifted to Mormonism and to issues of religious free exercise.

These issues would also play out in the courts' efforts to adjudicate constitutional standing.[74] Since Utah was still a territory, federal law and federal courts decided all matters. The central test came from George Reynolds, the secretary to Brigham Young. Reynolds had been convicted of knowingly undertaking a second marriage. Reynolds had appealed as part of his free exercise rights. So, the court had to weigh whether polygamy, understood as religious practice, could be legal. In *Reynolds* v. *United States* (1879), the court found 9–0 against Reynolds.[75] It then had to reason through why the Courts could penalize a clear tenet of belief. The court made clear that "[r]eligious freedom is guaranteed everywhere throughout the United States," but then had to reason how that would function.[76] The court made an attempt to use a basic originalist interpretation to understand how "religious freedom" was understood in the Founding Era. It turned to Madison's "Memorial and Remonstrance" and to Jefferson's Virginia Bill for Establishing Religious Freedom and then applied that concept through the First Amendment. The Court even quoted Jefferson's Letter to the Danbury Baptists.[77]

Looking at the law of marriage, the court declared, "Polygamy has always been odious among the northern and western nations of Europe," and "at common law [polygamy was] an offence against society."[78] The

[73] "The Mormon Theocracy," *Scribner's Monthly*, July 1877, qtd. in Corrigan and Neal, *Religious Intolerance*, 92–93.

[74] For the fullest consideration of the constitutional questions involved, see Sarah Barringer Gordon, *The Mormon Question: Polygamy and Constitutional Conflict in Nineteenth-Century America* (Chapel Hill, NC: University of North Carolina Press, 2002).

[75] *Reynolds* v. *United States*, 98 U.S. 145 (1879). [76] Ibid., 162. [77] Ibid., 164. [78] Ibid.

regulation of marriage was appropriate for the state. "Marriage, while from its very nature a sacred obligation is nevertheless . . . a civil contract, and usually regulated by law." Marriage structured social relations and obligations, which brought it into the legal and political realm.[79] With a view to evaluating marriage law, the court considered whether such regulation was a violation of freedom. It concluded, "Laws are made for the government of actions, and while they cannot interfere with mere religious belief and opinions, they may with practices."[80] In the face of religious claims, the court found that general law could trump the religious claim to polygamy. In defense of a common good, the court made a ruling that dramatically adversely impacted what Mormons considered their religious free exercise.

Following the Court's ruling in *Reynolds*, Congress responded with even stronger legislation, including the Edmunds Act of 1882, which made polygamy a felony on the federal level. For both Utah and Idaho territory, Congress also required voters to swear an oath that they were not polygamists. Such a requirement was upheld for Utah in *Murphy* v. *Ramsey* (1885).[81] Meanwhile, in Idaho, Samuel Davis, a Mormon polygamist, falsely swore the oath. When charged, he appealed again on religious free exercise grounds. In *Davis* v. *Beason* (1890), the court was swift, finding unanimously against Davis and largely reiterating the *Reynolds* decision.[82] It addressed the guarantees of the First Amendment with a reiteration that it enabled all "to entertain such notions respecting his relation to his Maker and the duties they impose as may be approved by his judgment and conscience, and to exhibit his sentiments in such form of worship as he may think proper, not injurious to the equal rights of others. . . ."[83] While such belief was always to be protected, the court held that such claims could not be unlimited. The court reasoned, "It was never intended or supposed that the amendment could be invoked as a protection against legislation for the punishment of acts inimical to the peace, good

[79] Ibid., 165. [80] Ibid., 166.

[81] *Murphy* v. *Ramsey*, 114 U.S. 15 (1885). Interestingly, in *Murphy* the court wrote, "For certainly no legislation can be supposed more wholesome and necessary in the founding of a free, self-governing commonwealth, fit to take rank as one of the coordinate states of the Union, than that which seeks to establish it on the basis of the idea of the family, as consisting in and springing from the union for life of one man and one woman in the holy estate of matrimony; the sure foundation of all that is stable and noble in our civilization; the best guarantee of that reverent morality which is the source of all beneficent progress in social and political improvement." Ibid., 45.

[82] *Davis* v. *Beason*, 133 U.S. 333 (1890). [83] Ibid., 342.

order, and morals of society."[84] Because the Court judged polygamy outside the bounds morally, it imposed a limiting factor on religious free exercise. It was a moral consensus in the United States that provided guidelines for what was acceptable.

The final official blow to Mormon polygamy came almost simultaneously with *Davis* v. *Beason* in the case *The Late Corporation of the Church of Jesus Christ of Latter-Day Saints* v. *United States* (1890).[85] In its legal fights with the Mormon church over polygamy (pursuant to another federal law, the Edmunds-Tucker Act of 1887), the US government had begun to seize the assets and property of the Mormon church. The church appealed this ruling, but the court held, 6–3, that this was a legitimate action.[86] With this ruling, the Saints leadership began to see the inevitable results of persisting in polygamy. Later that year, the president of the church issued a new revelation officially ending the practice of plural marriage. That decision preserved the church and opened the way for it to become a more "normal" participant in American religious life in the twentieth century.

Even so, as Utah attained statehood in 1896, Mormons faced one additional challenge: non-Mormon acceptance of their new legislators they were sending to Washington, DC. This issue only took two years, when B.H. Roberts, who continued to practice polygamy, was elected to the House of Representatives in 1898. His standing became a test case of whether the United States would tolerate both the practice and the religion it represented. Roberts was a warning, according to a critic, of how Mormons "have turned from American liberty and American morality and have taken the initial step towards the establishment of a hierarchy, foreign to our institutions and our social laws, in the midst of our republic . . ."[87] With the protests, Roberts was not seated in the House. Just four years later, the issue was raised again with the election to the US Senate of Reed Smoot. Smoot was not just a Mormon, but a Mormon Apostle, one of the Quorum of the Twelve who advised Mormon President Lorenzo Snow. After several

[84] Ibid.

[85] *The Late Corporation of the Church of Jesus Christ of Latter-Day Saints* v. *United States*, 136 U.S. 1 (1890).

[86] Rothera, "Tenacious 'Twin Relic,'" 28–36.

[87] Eugene Young, "Address to the Women's Board of Home Missions of the Presbyterian Church," *New York Evangelist*, December 22, 1898, qtd. in Corrigan and Neal, *Religious Intolerance*, 94–95.

years of hearings and trials, the Senate did seat Smoot, marking at the beginning of the twentieth century an armistice between Mormonism and American religious concerns.[88]

In the last decade of the nineteenth century, yet one more case involving the First Amendment came before the Supreme Court. The Church of the Holy Trinity, an Episcopal church in New York, sought to hire as their rector an Anglican priest and British national. The church was fined for violating a recently-passed law, the 1885 Alien Contract Labor Act, which prohibited American corporations from contracting with foreign nationals to come to the United States to perform "labor or service of any kind." Did the statute apply to the church, seeking to bring in a new pastor?[89] The court admitted that the language of the statute would seem to limit even the importation of Episcopal priests, but it then examined the legislative history to conclude, "It was never suggested that we had in this country a surplus of brain toilers, and least of all, that the market for the services of Christian ministers, was depressed by foreign competition." The Court therefore discounted the letter of the law in an attempt to apply the spirit of the law, and the Court concurred 9–0 in this decision, *Church of the Holy Trinity v United States* (1892).[90]

Even more interesting than the issues surrounding immigration and employment was the commentary that the united court gave, articulated by Justice Josiah Brewer, about the place of religion in the United States. Regarding the 1885 statute under dispute, Brewer asserted, "no purpose of action against religion can be imputed to any legislation, state or national, because this is a religious people. This is historically true."[91] The court then launched into its own historical survey, paying attention to the many state constitutions as well as the culture of America to assert the universal endorsement of religious affirmation. "Even the Constitution of the United States," through the First Amendment, the court asserted, was to be read as validating and protecting religious liberty.[92] These surveys culminated in two significant claims. First, the court concluded, "There is

[88] Kathleen Flake, *The Politics of American Religious Identity: The Seating of Senator Reed Smoot, Mormon Apostle* (Chapel Hill: University of North Carolina Press, 2004).

[89] For this background, see Vincent Phillip Muñoz, *Religious Liberty and the American Supreme Court: The Essential Cases and Documents* (Lanham, MD: Rowman & Littlefield, 2013), 18.

[90] *Church of the Holy Trinity* v. *United States*, 147 U.S. 457 (1892) at 464. [91] Ibid., 465.

[92] Ibid., 470.

no dissonance in these declarations. There is a universal language pervading them all, having one meaning; they affirm and reaffirm that this is a religious nation. These are not individual sayings, declarations of private persons: they are organic utterances; they speak the voice of the entire people."[93] Calling such declarations organic is significant, not only in the late nineteenth century when biological language was common, but because of the way the court viewed the endorsement of religion as rooted in the basic nature of the Constitution. Even more stunning was the final specificity the court leant to this religiosity, when Brewer declared, "These, and many other matters which might be noticed, add a volume of unofficial declarations to the mass of organic utterances that this is a Christian nation."[94] Brewer's statement thus endorsed, at the end of the century, reading Christianity as integral to the nation.

With Justice Brewer, the United States had come a long way from Jefferson's proposal for a "wall of separation" at the beginning of the century. What this survey of the nineteenth century suggests is that Jefferson's metaphor was known and discussed but not endorsed broadly or practiced as Jefferson intended. At most, Americans desired a one-way wall that protected religious bodies from governmental interference but allowed much religious influence for shaping policy and politics. This attitude explains why there were relatively few First Amendment cases in the nineteenth century, and why religious issues that did come up tended to touch on other issues, such as contracts or incorporation. Thus the general practice in the nineteenth century was to read the First Amendment primarily through the free exercise clause, with much less concern about establishments, as long as the federal government stayed away from creating a national church.

At the same time, the First Amendment and the place of religion in government and society were debated and contested. In the process, future issues were raised, though not resolved. The most significant challenges came from minority religious groups who found themselves in uncomfortable positions in a public culture dominated by Protestants. Roman Catholics observed that public policies that claimed to be nonsectarian Christian still implied a Protestant character – realities revealed in debates over schooling and which version of the Bible should be read in public schools. Mormons also objected that their free exercise should include

[93] Ibid. [94] Ibid., 471.

plural marriage. These objections were overlooked due to the dominant Protestant character of the public culture, but largely the responses failed to wrestle with religious pluralism. What would happen if a Protestant consensus broke down? Indeed, what would happen if a pro-religious consensus broke down? These questions would arise with increasing urgency in the twentieth century.[95]

Still, the nineteenth century suggests that a Jeffersonian "wall of separation" is not sufficient either to describe the First Amendment in the century after its drafting or as an interpreting metaphor for ongoing jurisprudence. Instead, the experiences of the century offer alternative possibilities for understanding ways that free exercise can be protected that would not constitute an establishment. It also suggests that the government need not be neutral on the question of the public value of religion or the recognition of the religious motivations of its citizens.

[95] Tisa Wenger, in *Religious History: The Contested History of an American Ideal* (Chapel Hill, NC: University of North Carolina Press, 2017), argues that a new era of religious liberty debates began with the Spanish-American War in 1898.

8 The First Amendment Religion Clauses in the United States Supreme Court

Zoë Robinson

Introduction

The First Amendment religion clauses provide that "Congress shall make no law respecting an establishment of religion, or prohibiting the free exercise thereof."[1] For most Americans, the two clauses – referred to independently as the establishment clause and the free exercise clause – exemplify the concept of individual rights and the capacity of individuals to restrain government overreach in matters of personal choice. The terms of the religion clauses are viewed as capturing the liberal ideal of religious freedom, and act to enshrine the perception of the United States as a bastion of religious tolerance, where persons can seek refuge in the face of persecution elsewhere.[2] This idealized narrative of the Constitution's religion clauses as a bulwark of religious liberty against religious majoritarianism, which has persisted since the colonization of the United States, permeates the narrative of the development of America as a nation.[3] And it is against this backdrop that the Constitution's religion clause jurisprudence, and the picture of the Supreme Court as a bulwark of religious liberty for all religious Americans, has developed. Yet, this picture is at best incomplete.

This chapter examines the Supreme Court's landmark First Amendment religious liberty cases to show how the judiciary has come to terms with the disputes that arise over religious liberty. The chapter takes the view that in examining key constitutional religious liberty cases emanating from the Court, it is impossible to separate the cases from the trajectory of the Court's broader constitutional rights jurisprudence and the wider political

Thanks to Cameron Custard for outstanding research assistance and Dr. M. J. Fox for her excellent editing.

[1] US Constitution Amendment I.

[2] Arlin M. Adams and Charles J. Emmerich, *A Nation Dedicated to Religious Liberty: The Constitutional Heritage of the Religion Clauses* (Philadelphia: University of Pennsylvania Press, 1990), 32.

[3] Ibid., 3–31.

landscape, both as it relates to judicial politics as well as contemporary social discourse. To that end, in its discussion on these core religious liberty cases, this chapter endeavors to situate the Court's jurisprudential developments in the religious liberty space in their appropriate context. Indeed, constitutional doctrine is, in many ways, the exemplification of the Court's political engagement – and religious liberty cases are no exception to this. Ultimately, once we examine the Court's constitutional religious liberty jurisprudence in context, it becomes apparent that, except for a short period between 1960 and 1979, the scope of religious liberty epitomizes constitutional majoritarianism. That is, First Amendment religious liberty jurisprudence "roughly mirrors contemporary public opinion, the views of the political branches, and the positions held by powerful social institutions (e.g. corporations)."[4]

In justifying this claim, the chapter traces the development of constitutional religious liberty from the Court's first religion clause decision to the time of writing this chapter in 2018. To do so, it will highlight select cases that best represent the overall arc of the Court's approach to constitutional religious liberty in any given period. The chapter proceeds in five sections. The first section begins with the Court's inaugural religion clause decision in *Reynolds* v. *United States*, which sets the foundation for the Court's approach to constitutional religious liberty going forward.[5] The second section examines the Court's dramatic expansion of religious liberty, largely prompted by the tenure of Chief Justice Earl Warren in the context of his expansion of individual rights more generally. This section outlines those cases that represent the apex of both the establishment clause and the free exercise clause, in terms of protection from and for religion. The third section discusses the gradual restriction of individual religious liberty under the Constitution under the Warren Court, which reflected the rise of social and political conservatism in the United States beginning in the 1970s. The fourth section outlines the culmination of the Court's doctrinal rollback and the

[4] Zoë Robinson, "Constitutional Personhood," *George Washington Law Review* 84, no. 3 (June 2016): 646. On the concept of constitutional majoritarianism, see, for example, Darren L. Hutchinson, "The Majoritarian Difficulty: Affirmative Action, Sodomy, and Supreme Court Politics," *Law & Inequality* 23, no. 1 (2005): 2 (claiming that the Supreme Court is a majoritarian, rather than a countermajoritarian, institution) and Thomas R. Marshall, *Public Opinion and the Supreme Court* (London: Unwin Hyman, 1989), 192 ("Overall, the evidence suggests that the modern Court has been an essentially majoritarian institution").

[5] *Reynolds* v. *United States*, 98 US 145 (1878).

reestablishment of religious majoritarianism. This period outlines those decisions that reflect the current state of religious liberty for individuals under the Constitution. The final section discusses the Court's contemporary religious liberty jurisprudence and highlights the rise of religious institutionalism and the predominance of religious protectionism under the Constitution.

Religious Liberty's Majoritarianism

Along with the remainder of the Bill of Rights provisions, the First Amendment religion clauses were drafted by the First Congress in 1791.[6] The early amendment of the new Constitution to include a Bill of Rights was in fulfillment of the Federalist's promise during the Constitution ratification debate.[7] Contrary to contemporary popular understanding of the religion clauses specifically, and the Bill of Rights more generally, the inclusion of constitutional rights was not to endow individuals with rights but rather to protect the states' capacity to organize its citizenry in the manner of its choosing.[8] Prior to the Civil War and the passage of the Reconstruction Amendments, the Bill of Rights very clearly applied to restrict federal government action.[9] That is, it did not restrict state conduct and no person could raise a First Amendment claim that a state violated the religion clauses.[10] In the context of the religion clauses, this meant, for example, that a state could continue its established religion, without fear of federal interference.[11] This initial purpose

[6] US Constitution Amendment I; Library of Congress, *Religion & the Founding of the American Republic*, www.loc.gov/exhibits/religion/rel06.html (last visited September 20, 2017).

[7] See Kent Greenawalt, *Religion and the Constitution: Free Exercise and Fairness* (Princeton, NJ: Princeton University Press, 2006), 22n43 and accompanying text; Michael McConnell, "The Origins and Historical Understanding of Free Exercise of Religion," *Harvard Law Review* 103, no. 7 (May 1990): 1481.

[8] See Arthur Wilmarth, "The Original Purpose of the Bill of Rights: James Madison & the Founders' Search for a Workable Balance between Federal & State Power," *American Criminal Law Review* 26, no. 4 (Spring 1989), 1261–1294.

[9] William Brennan, "State Constitutions & the Protection of Individual Rights," *Harvard Law Review* 90, no. 3 (January 1977): 493.

[10] *Barron* v. *Mayor of Baltimore*, 32 US 243, 249–250 (1833) (confirmed in context of RC in *Permoli* v. *Mun. No. 1 of City of New Orleans*, 44 US 589, 609 (1845)).

[11] Charles Warren, "The New 'Liberty' under the Fourteenth Amendment," *Harvard Law Review* 39, no. 4 (February1926): 431–436.

and understanding of the religion clauses goes a long way toward explaining the dormancy of the clauses in litigation. In fact, it was not until 1878 that the Supreme Court handed down its first substantive religion clause decision, in *Reynolds* v. *United States*, where the Court interpreted the free exercise clause for the first time since the ratification of the Bill of Rights in 1791.[12]

Yet, while the interpretation of the free exercise clause in *Reynolds* is relegated to a historic footnote, the case remains important as an exemplification of the limit of the Court's interpretive methodology when faced with religion clause challenges. *Reynolds* demonstrates that the core driver in the Court's interpretation of the religion clauses was, and remains, political, religious, and social majoritarianism. *Reynolds* involved a challenge to Section 5352 of the Revised Statutes of the Territory of Utah, which criminalized bigamy and stipulated a punishment of a $500 fine and five years in prison.[13] George Reynolds, a member of the Church of Latter Day Saints (LDS), had two wives in accordance with then LDS doctrine and was charged under the statute. In his defense, Reynolds argued that his practice of polygamy was protected by the First Amendment's free exercise clause.[14] Reynolds' constitutional challenge was part of a broader battle over the practice of polygamy in the United States. In the period between 1852 (when Brigham Young proclaimed that Mormons both believed in and practiced polygamy) and 1890 (when the church, cowed by the power of the majoritarianism emanating from all government institutions, renounced polygamy), the American public and its institutions waged a war against the LDS and polygamy.[15]

In a decision that highlights the Court's majoritarianism and, relatedly, institutional limits, the Supreme Court denied that the prohibition of bigamy violated Reynolds' religious liberty.[16] The Court stated that the issue was "whether religious belief can be accepted as a justification of an overt act made criminal by the law of the land."[17] In answering its own question, the Court stated that while Congress is "deprived of all legislative power over mere opinion," it retains power over "actions which were in

[12] *Reynolds* v. *U.S.*, 98 US 145 (1878). [13] Ibid. at 146.

[14] Ibid. at 161. On the history of Mormonism, and the relationship between politics and Mormonism, see Sarah Barringer Gordon, *The Mormon Question: Polygamy and Constitutional Conflict in Nineteenth Century America* (Chapel Hill, NC: University of North Carolina Press, 2002).

[15] Gordon, *Mormon Question*, 1. [16] *Reynolds*, 98 US at 166–167. [17] Ibid. at 162.

violation of social duties" or were "subversive of good order."[18] That is, the Court held that when it comes to judging the legality of religious action, political majoritarianism is determinative as to the scope of religious liberty. Moreover, in establishing majoritarianism as the touchstone for religious liberty determinations, the Court undercut any power of the religion clauses to protect minority religious belief. For the *Reynolds* Court, religious liberty is protected *by* those generally applicable laws enacted by the political branches. That is, the law itself reflects the boundary of religious tolerance and religious liberty, and the idea that the Constitution would require the law to accommodate minority religious practices was incomprehensible. As a matter of constitutional doctrine, then, the Court's decision rendered the free exercise clause a blunt and binary instrument, where the coverage of the right extends only to belief, which is absolutely protected.[19] Conversely, in practice, religious action falls outside the coverage of the clause entirely; that is, burdens on religious conduct are not protected by the free exercise clause.[20] In the case of *Reynolds*, then, the Court deferred to the judgment of the political branches of government and affirmed the prohibition against bigamy on the grounds that polygamy was subversive of good order due to its "odious" nature and entrenchment of patriarchal principles.[21]

[18] Ibid. at 164.

[19] On the concept of "coverage" and "protection" in rights discourse generally, see Frederick Schauer, "The Boundaries of the First Amendment: A Preliminary Exploration of Constitutional Salience," *Harvard Law Review* 117, no. 6 (April 2004) (discussing the determinants of the boundaries of constitutional categories); Frederick Schauer, "Categories and the First Amendment: A Play in Three Acts," *Vanderbilt Law Review* 34 (1981) (discussing the importance of categorization in the context of the First Amendment). On the coverage and protection of the First Amendment religion clauses specifically, see Zoë Robinson, "Hosanna-Tabor after Hobby Lobby," in *The Rise of Corporate Religious Liberty: Hobby Lobby and the New Law of Religion in America*, ed. Zoë Robinson, Micah Schwartzman, and Chad Flanders (Oxford: Oxford University Press, 2016), 173–191.

[20] On the Court's early interpretation of the religion clauses, see, for example, Douglas Kmiec, "The Original Understanding of the Free Exercise Clause & Religious Diversity," *University of Missouri-Kansas City Law Review* 59 (1990–1991); Carl H. Esbeck, "Dissent and Disestablishment: The Church-State Settlement in the Early American Republic," *Brigham Young University Law Review* 2004, no. 4 (2004).

[21] *Reynolds* was followed by the 1890 decision of *Davis* v. *Beason*, 133 US 333, which reinforced the *Reynolds'* Court action-belief dichotomy, holding that held that while the free exercise clause is intended to allow all people "to entertain such notions respecting his religious relations to his Maker," "the duties they impose as may be approved by his judgment and conscience," and "to exhibit his sentiments in such form of worship as he may think proper," the free exercise clause cannot be invoked as a protection against

Combined with the limited applicability of the religion clauses to restrict federal action only, the Court's majoritarian interpretive approach virtually ensured the dormancy of the religion clauses for decades. That changed with the advent of the "incorporation" of the religion clauses, where the Court determined that the Fourteenth Amendment Due Process Clause "incorporated" both the free exercise clause and the establishment clause such that the provisions applied with equal force to restrict state conduct, as well as federal conduct.[22] Incorporation opened up new possibilities for the scope of the religion clauses. In addition, World War II, and the moral irony of fighting for racial and religious freedom abroad while sustaining discriminatory majoritarianism at home, raised expectations of a broader interpretation of the religion clauses that would step beyond the majoritarianism of *Reynolds* and potentially protect minority religious practices.[23] These hopes and expectations proved accurate. Following the incorporation of the free exercise clause in the 1940 decision of *Cantwell* v. *Connecticut*, and the establishment clause in the 1947 decision of *Everson* v. *Board of Education*, a steady flow of religion clause cases came before the Supreme Court.[24] The Court responded with an expanding interpretation that, at least briefly, signaled the possibility of robust constitutional protections for religious minorities in America.

The Expansion of Religious Liberty

The Supreme Court's expansion of religious liberty maps onto the Court's general expansive interpretation of constitutional rights following World War II. Under the leadership of Chief Justice Earl Warren, both the free exercise clause and the establishment clause developed such that religious minorities could expect to be free from the constraints of religious

legislation for punishment of acts inimical to peace, order, and good governance and/or societal morals. Ibid. at 342.

22 While the narrow concept of liberty of conscience and worship was incorporated in 1923 in *Myer* v. *Nebraska* (referenced by Brennan in *Sch. Dist. of Abington Tp., Pa.* v. *Schempp*, 374 US 203, 250 (1963)), the free exercise clause was formally incorporated in 1940 in *Cantwell* v. *Connecticut*, 310 US 296, 303–304 (1940), and the establishment clause in 1947, in *Everson* v. *Bd. of Educ.*, 330 US 1, 15–16 (1947).

23 Mary Ann Glendon, "Law, Communities, & the Religious Freedom Language of the Constitution," *George Washington Law Review* 60 (1991–1992).

24 *Cantwell*, 310 US at 303–304; *Everson*, 330 US at 15–16.

majoritarianism. However, while Warren was appointed to lead the Court in 1953, it was not until 1962, with the retirements of Justices Whittaker and Frankfurter, that Warren gained the liberal majority necessary to usher in dramatic interpretive changes in the religion clauses.[25]

Yet, even before the 1962 watershed shift in judicial personnel, the Court began to expand the scope of the religion clauses.[26] In 1961, the Court decided a case concerning the free exercise clause that would set the scene for the Warren Court's expansive interpretation over the subsequent decade. In *Braunfeld* v. *Brown*, an Orthodox Jew challenged a Pennsylvania criminal statute proscribing Sunday retail trading as violating his free exercise of religion.[27] Braunfeld argued that his faith required the closing of his business from nightfall Friday until nightfall Saturday, and that the Sunday closing law prevented him from recouping the Saturday trading losses.[28] In a 6–3 decision, the Court dismissed Braunfeld's challenge. Even in doing so, however, the Court quietly expanded the coverage of the free exercise clause beyond the narrow *Reynolds'* holding that religious action did not fall within the protective auspices of the right. Instead, the plurality opinion in *Braunfeld* stated that while religious action "is not totally free from legislative restriction," a "law is constitutionally invalid" if its "purpose or effect ... is to impede the observance of one or all religions." If a generally applicable law forces an individual to abandon her religious principles under threat of prosecution, the free exercise clause provides coverage, and the Constitution requires the state to enact an exemption for the claimant where "the State may accomplish its purpose by means which do not impose such a burden."[29]

In 1963, the Court expanded the *Braunfeld* holding in the seminal case of *Sherbert* v. *Verner*, with a dramatic expansion of the scope of both the coverage of the free exercise clause and the level of protection applied to alleged violations of the provision.[30] *Sherbert* arose out of South Carolina's

[25] Lawrence Baum, "Membership Change and Collective Voting Change in the United States Supreme Court," *The Journal of Politics* 54, no. 1 (February 1992): 10.

[26] *Braunfeld* v. *Brown*, 366 US 599 (1961); *McGowan* v. *Maryland*, 366 US 420 (1961).

[27] *Braunfeld*, 366 US at 600–602. [28] Ibid. at 601–602.

[29] Ibid. at 603, 607. Notably, the Court's holding was more limited than the quote indicates. The majority suggested that the Constitution only requires a legislative exemption from a generally applicable law burdening religion when the burden is direct (e.g., a criminal penalty). The majority stated that where the burden is indirect, the Constitution does not mandate an exemption. Ibid. at 603.

[30] *Sherbert* v. *Verner*, 374 U.S. 398 (1963). For an in-depth discussion of the case, see Greenawalt, *Religion and the Constitution*, 410n7.

denial of unemployment benefits to Adele Sherbert, a Seventh-day Adventist who by virtue of her religious faith could not work on Saturdays. The state held that Sherbert had failed "without good cause" to accept work offered to her, rendering her ineligible for unemployment benefits.[31] In his majority opinion, Justice William Brennan held that where a generally applicable law has the effect of violating a person's religious liberty by, in this case, denying her a state benefit because of her religious tenet, the free exercise clause compels the state to enact an exemption from that law unless the state meets a strict scrutiny standard – that is, unless the state can show a compelling interest for burdening religious liberty.[32] The Court thereby made two significant doctrinal moves. First, it expanded the coverage of the free exercise clause beyond burdens on religious liberty that force a person to choose between their religion and formal sanctions (so-called direct burdens). The Court's holding additionally held that the free exercise clause extends to cover so-called indirect burdens, when a generally applicable law burdens a person's religion by making the practice of that religion more difficult.[33] Second, the Court moved beyond the general standard of review applied to statutes – that the law lacks a "rational basis" – which is extremely easy for the government to satisfy.[34] Instead, the Court held that the appropriate standard of review is strict scrutiny, a standard that had proved extremely difficult for the government to meet in the context of other rights.[35] In *Sherbert*, South Carolina could not meet this standard and the Court held that its failure to enact a religious exemption was unconstitutional.[36]

As many scholars have noted, the adoption of a strict scrutiny standard of review in the context of the free exercise clause appeared to herald an era of robust judicial protections for religious minorities.[37] This sense of robust judicial protection of religious liberty pursuant to the free exercise clause was amplified by the Court's 1972 decision in *Wisconsin* v. *Yoder*,

[31] Ibid., 400. [32] Ibid., 403–404. [33] Ibid. [34] Ibid., 406–407. [35] Ibid.

[36] Ibid., 405–406. Notably, the majority opinion in *Sherbert* picked up on Justice Brennan's dissenting opinion in *Braunfeld* v. *Braun*, where he had stated that the critical question was the *effect* of the law. Ibid., 612–614. Brennan specified that where the effect of the law is that a person's religious free exercise is burdened by generally applicable law, that burden is sufficiently substantive that the Constitution requires an exemption from the law unless there is a compelling government interest for its imposition. Ibid.

[37] Jesse Choper, "The Rise & Decline of the Constitutional Protection of Religious Liberty," *Nebraska Law Review* 70 (1991); Milner Ball, "Judicial Protection of Powerless Minorities," *Iowa Law Review* 59 (1974).

a case that served to illustrate the Court's application of strict scrutiny in the free exercise clause context.[38] *Wisconsin* v. *Yoder* involved a challenge by Amish parents to a Wisconsin law requiring attendance at school until the age of sixteen. The Amish claimed that the law burdened their religion because the Amish believe that schooling beyond eighth grade exposes their children to worldly influences that are contrary to the Amish faith and would undermine the insularity of the Amish community that is integral to their beliefs.[39] While accepting that the compulsory school attendance law did burden the Amish religion, Wisconsin argued that it had a compelling interest in the law.

In rejecting Wisconsin's claim of a compelling interest in compulsory school attendance, the Court clarified the nature of the inquiry. Wisconsin initially argued that, as a general matter, compulsory school attendance is critical.[40] The Court rejected this justification and held that in the context of the free exercise clause the state's claim of compelling interest cannot be general, but instead it must be articulated at the claimant level.[41] In other words, while the government may be able to justify the need for the law generally, the question is whether it can justify the need for the law *as applied* to the claimant. That is, the state has to provide a justification (a compelling interest) for not enacting an exemption and instead imposing the challenged burden on the claimant. In *Wisconsin* v. *Yoder*, then, an interest in compulsory education was insufficient; instead, the compelling interest in this as-applied standard required Wisconsin to justify its interest was in forcing the Amish to go to school beyond eighth grade. In its attempt to meet this as-applied standard, Wisconsin claimed that requiring Amish children to attend school until the age of sixteen was necessary to prepare teenagers to prepare them to be "self-reliant and self-sufficient participants in society."[42] The Court rejected this justification, stating that the Amish are a "highly successful social unit" that produces productive and law-abiding members of society who reject welfare of any kind.[43] The Court stated that even if the Amish leave the faith, they would find work using their vocational skills. Having failed to demonstrate a compelling interest for burdening the Amish, the Court held that the free exercise clause compelled Wisconsin to enact an exemption from the compulsory school attendance laws. Together, *Sherbert* v. *Verner* and *Wisconsin*

[38] *Wisconsin* v. *Yoder*, 406 US 205 (1972). [39] Ibid. at 207. [40] Ibid. at 221.
[41] Ibid. at 220–221. [42] Ibid. at 221. [43] Ibid. at 222.

v. *Yoder* represent an expansive interpretation of the free exercise clause in this period. Ultimately, the Court's approach to the free exercise clause in this period enshrines a principle of protection of religious minorities from majoritarian burdens imposed by the political branches and an institutional vision that included a robust role for the judiciary in protection of individual rights.

Alongside the Court's dramatic expansion of the scope of the free exercise clause, the Court's establishment clause doctrine also quickly developed into a robust prohibition on the state benefiting religion, either intangibly (e.g., religious symbolism, religious teaching), or tangibly (e.g., financial aid). The first major establishment clause battleground occurred in the context of religion in public schools, specifically prayer in schools and curriculum with religious content. The Court's first decision in this area was in the 1962 case of *Engel* v. *Vitale*, where the Board of Education of the Union Free School District in New York directed the school principal to have a school prayer said every day in the presence of a teacher.[44] Holding the government-sponsored prayer was a violation of the establishment clause, the Court stated that an official government prayer raised a significant constitutional concern about the fusion of church and state, namely that powerful groups would control the views ultimately put forward by the government and that less powerful groups would be ostracized.[45] For the Court what was critical was the government's *participation* in the undisputed religious activity.

Only a year later in *Abington School District* v. *Schempp*, the Court extended this holding to Bible reading in public schools.[46] Pennsylvania law required at least ten verses from the Holy Bible to be read without comment at the opening of every public school every day.[47] The Court held that because the Bible reading occurred on state property, during school hours, under the supervision of state employees (i.e., teachers), and in a place where children are required to be by law, the state acted to benefit a specific religious denomination.[48] The state, the Court opined, must be neutral among religions.[49] Responding to Justice Potter Stewart's dissenting opinion that children could be excused from the reading and therefore

[44] *Engel* v. *Vitale*, 370 US 421 (1962). The prayer was: "Almighty God, we acknowledge our dependence upon Thee, and we beg Thy blessings upon us, our parents, our teachers, and our Country." Ibid. at 422.

[45] Ibid. at 431–436. [46] *Sch. Dist. of Abington Tp., Pa.* v. *Schempp*, 374 US 203 (1963).

[47] Ibid. at 205. [48] Ibid. at 223. [49] Ibid. at 226.

were not coerced to participate, the Court held that the psychic coercion faced by children to engage in the prayers was sufficient.[50] That is, the capacity to "opt-out" of the religious activity is insufficient to save the provision from constitutional infirmary because of the indirect pressure on children to participate. The Court specified that any law that has as its purpose or effect the advancement or inhibition of any religion violates the establishment clause.[51] The Court affirmed this doctrinal approach of examining both the purpose and the effect of a law in the 1968 decision of *Epperson* v. *Arkansas*, where the Court held that the purpose of an Arkansas law forbidding the teaching of evolution or the adoption of a textbook that teaches evolution was clearly to advance religion.[52] The Court stated that the law was driven by "fundamentalist sectarian conviction was and is the law's reason for existence."[53]

While the doctrinal standard for establishment clause challenges in the public school prayer and curriculum cases was now relatively settled, the Court had dealt with establishment clause challenges in other areas, including tangible aid to public schools, in a more ad hoc manner. The 1971 case *Lemon* v. *Kurtzman*, however, represents the Court's attempts to establish a robust, comprehensive standard (or test) for determining the validity of laws pursuant to the establishment clause, regardless of the nature of whether the aid to religion was intangible or tangible in nature.[54] Pursuant to the *Lemon* test, for a law to be valid it must (1) evidence a secular purpose, (2) have no religious effect, and (3) not foster excessive entanglement of the state with religion.[55] Applying this standard in *Lemon*, the Court invalidated a Rhode Island statute authorizing a direct payment supplementing the salary of teachers of secular subjects in nonpublic schools, including parochial schools.[56] The Court held that while the law

[50] Ibid. at 224–225. [51] Ibid. at 222. [52] *Epperson* v. *Arkansas*, 393 US 97 (1968).

[53] Ibid. at 108.

[54] *Lemon* v. *Kurtzman*, 403 US 602 (1971). On the "Lemon test," see Herbert Kritzer, "Jurisprudential Regimes & Supreme Court Decision-making: The Lemon Regime & Establishment Clause Cases," *Law and Society Review* 37 (2003); John Valauri, "The Concept of Neutrality in Establishment Clause Doctrine," *University of Pittsburgh Law Review* 48 (1987).

[55] *Lemon*, 403 US at 612–613.

[56] Ibid. at 602. The eligibility was: (1) Teacher must teach in school where average per-pupil expenditure on secular education is less than public school; (2) eligible schools have to submit financial data and, if the per-pupil limit is exceeded, then records must be examined for the percentage spent on secular/sacred subjects; and (3) teachers must teach secular subjects only and use secular teaching materials and not teach religion while receiving the supplement.

clearly had the secular purpose of enhancing the quality of education in all Rhode Island schools, the effect of the law was to advance religion and to entangle religion and the state.[57] The Court stated that the nature of the aid – a salary subsidy to teachers employed at religious schools – had the effect of fostering religion by essentially giving funding to the religious school itself.[58] In addition, the Court considered a variety of factors that indicated an effect of advancing religion and entangling the state and religious institutions, including the locality of the schools vis-à-vis the church, the religious symbolism in the schools, and the general religiosity of the schools.[59] The Court concluded that all of these characteristics made the schools a "powerful vehicle for transmitting [religion] to the next generation."[60] Finally, the Court noted that the statute required continuous monitoring of the religious schools by the state to ensure that the funding is not going directly to religious purposes. This, the Court noted, created an entanglement between the institutions of church and state and risked political divisiveness.[61]

Together, the Court's free exercise clause and establishment clause jurisprudence in this period is representative of the dominance of ideological liberalism on the part of a majority of the justices.[62] The ideological perspective of a majority of justices who served on the Court in this period directed a doctrinal position that would ensure that the power of the majority would not be readily used against powerless minorities in the United States. Relatedly, the Court's religion clause jurisprudence also reflected some level of protectionism of the countermajoritarian role that the justices had begun to carve out for the Court in terms of rights protections. For the Court, the prior decades of rights jurisprudence represented a significant co-opting of judicial power and the consolidation of the institutional role of the Supreme Court in American government. This is not a claim that the Supreme Court was engaged in a nefarious power grab. Rather, the argument is that, reflecting on twenty-five or so years of rights jurisprudence, the Court saw its role as a bulwark against majoritarianism as a critical one in the scheme of American government. The Court's

[57] Ibid. at 615–620. [58] Ibid. at 619–620. [59] Ibid. at 615–616. [60] Ibid. at 616.

[61] Ibid. at 619–620.

[62] See, for example, Herbert Kritzer, "Jurisprudential Regimes & Supreme Court Decision-making: The Lemon Regine & Establishment Clause Cases," *Law and Society Review* 37 (2003); Joseph Ignagni, "Explaining & Predicting Supreme Court Decision Making: The Burger Court's Establishment Clause Decisions," *Journal of Church and State* 36 (1994).

religion clause jurisprudence in this period fits neatly into this narrative and, considered in this broader jurisprudential context, it is easier to understand the Court's doctrinal moves.

Bounce Back: The Gradual Constriction of Individual Constitutional Religious Liberty

The Court's gradual roll back of both the broad protectionist scope of the religion clauses and the Court's involvement in protection of religious liberty came on the back of the rise of social conservatism in the United States. From around 1980, the new conservative appointments on the Supreme Court began to quietly and strategically limit the scope of the previously established religion clause jurisprudence.[63]

In the context of the free exercise clause, three major objections were raised about the constitutional exemption model that the Court adopted in *Sherbert* v. *Verner*. First, commentators complained that constitutionally mandated exemptions necessarily favor religion over nonreligion and persons with secular justifications were unfairly burdened by the requirement of religious exemptions. Second, robust scholarship began to emerge arguing that the original understanding of the free exercise clause did not support the idea of constitutionally mandated exemptions, and thus the Court's *Sherbert* approach was inconsistent with the framer's vision for religious liberty. Third was the claim that the exemptions doctrine was exclusionary.[64] This was possibly the most persuasive argument against the constitutional exemption model and the implementation of strict scrutiny in free exercise clause cases. Specifically, the concern was that the combination of the constitutional exemption model and the strict scrutiny standard of review resulted in a judicially mandated space for a limited group of persons where the law would not apply. This was quite different than the result of an application of strict scrutiny review in other judicial rights (e.g., speech or equal protection) where the result of a successful application of strict scrutiny was the voiding of the law, not the

[63] See, for example, Frederick Mark Gedlicks, "The Improbability of Religion Clause Theory," *Seton Hall Law Review* 27 (1997); Choper, "The Rise and Decline."

[64] See, generally, William P. Marshall, "In Defense of Smith and Free Exercise Revisionism," *University of Chicago Law Review* 58, no.1 (1991).

inapplicability of the law to a narrow subset of the political community. Animated by these concerns, although facially applying the *Sherbert* standard, the Supreme Court began to limit the scope of the test in order to avoid granting religious exemptions.

The Court's 1982 decision of *United States* v. *Lee* demonstrates one way the Court subtly limited the scope of strict scrutiny in the context of the free exercise clause.[65] *Lee* involved a challenge by an Amish employer who argued that Social Security tax law requiring him to pay into a fund for his Amish employees violated the Amish faith.[66] While the Court accepted that the law violated the Amish faith, it held that the government had a compelling interest in a generally applicable social security system for a host of reasons, including "assuring mandatory and continuous participation in and contribution to the social security system," the fact that a voluntary system would be unworkable, and the difficulty of administering the wide range of exemptions that might be claimed.[67] Yet, when examining the government's claimed compelling interest, the Court only assessed that interest at the general level; that is, the Court did not examine the compelling interest as applied to the claimant, as it stipulated was necessary in *Yoder.*[68]

The Court's 1986 decision in *Goldman* v. *Weinberger* demonstrates another technique the Court adopted to avoid applying the *Sherbert* test on its own terms.[69] In *Goldman*, the Court denied an Orthodox Jewish Air Force psychologist's claim that the ban on wearing head gear indoors violated the free exercise clause.[70] The Court held that, in the context of free exercise clause challenges to military decisions, strict scrutiny is not the appropriate standard of review due to the need for judicial deference to military regulations.[71] The Court held that in the military context there is a strong need for obedience, unity, and commitment, and dress codes are particularly important because it encourages subordination of personal preferences in favor of the group.[72] Deferring to the military, then, the Court upheld the regulation as constitutional, despite the clear impact on religion.[73]

Finally, in *Lyng* v. *Northwest Indian Cemetery Protective Association*, the Court avoided *Sherbert's* strong standard by denying that there was

[65] *United States* v. *Lee*, 455 US 252 (1982). [66] Ibid. at 254–255. [67] Ibid. at 257–259.
[68] Ibid. at 259–261. [69] *Goldman* v. *Weinberger*, 475 US 503 (1986).
[70] Ibid. at 504–505. [71] Ibid. at 507. [72] Ibid. at 508. [73] Ibid. at 509–510.

a burden on the claimant's religion.[74] *Lyng* involved a challenge to a proposed road through a Native American spiritual site, which the claimants alleged burdened their religion.[75] Rejecting the challenge, the Court suggested that, similar to *Braunfeld*, the claimants in *Lyng* were not being coerced by the government to violate their religious beliefs, for only their spiritual actions would be interfered with.[76] This, the Court held, meant that there was no constitutional burden on the claimant's freedom of religion.[77] Instead, the Court held that the burden in *Lyng* represented only "incidental effects" of government programs that only make it more difficult to practice religion.[78]

Similar incremental doctrinal narrowing can be seen in the context of the establishment clause, with the Court quietly limiting the scope of one or more of the prongs of the *Lemon* test. In the 1983 decision of *Mueller* v. *Allen*, for example, the Court was faced with a challenge to the constitutionality of a Minnesota tax deduction, which permitted taxpayers to deduct tuition, textbook, and transportation expenses from their state income tax payment.[79] The deduction was not limited to public school expenses, and a group of taxpayers alleged that the deduction "violated the Establishment Clause by providing financial assistance to sectarian institutions."[80] Writing for the majority, Justice William Rehnquist significantly restricted the scope of the first two prongs of the *Lemon* standard: evidence of a secular purpose and no religious effect. In *Allen*, the Court stated that the government needed only to show a *plausible* secular motive on the face of the statute to satisfy the secular purpose inquiry.[81] This contrasted earlier cases in which the Court had examined the challenged statutory provision in its context when ascertaining whether an impermissible purpose existed. The *Allen* inquiry, then, was significantly more limited than a standard that enables the Court to look beyond the text of the statute and, in essence, renders the inquiry into a secular purpose a nullity.

In addition, Rehnquist's opinion sharply limited the effects inquiry. Whereas prior to *Allen* the Court engaged in a robust analysis of the actual effect of the law (i.e., the as-applied or substantive effect of the law), *Allen* limited the effects inquiry to the face of the law.[82] That is, the Court held

[74] *Lyng* v. *Northwest Indian Cemetery Protective Ass'n*, 485 US 439 (1988).
[75] Ibid. at 441–443. [76] Ibid. at 449. [77] Ibid. at 447–448. [78] Ibid. at 450.
[79] *Mueller* v. *Allen*, 463 US 388 (1983). [80] Ibid. at 392. [81] Ibid. at 394.
[82] Ibid. at 401.

that when examining the effect of the law, it would only look to whether the law on its face has the effect of advancing religion. Where the law is neutral on its face, as in the *Allen* decision itself, the law will survive constitutional challenge under the establishment clause.[83] Looking at the challenged law in *Allen*, the Court held that the Minnesota legislature grants the aid equally to all parents, not to a religious institution or only to religious parents. While the aid might indirectly advance religion, the establishment clause cannot limit the impact of the private choice of citizens.[84]

The Court solidified this narrower version of the *Lemon* standard the following year in *Lynch* v. *Donnelly*, a case involving a challenge to a government Christmas display that included a crèche depicting the birth of Jesus.[85] Referring to the role of religious traditionalism in American culture with approval, Chief Justice Warren Burger's majority opinion proceeded to apply the *Lemon* standard with the caveat that the Court is "unwilling to be confined to any single test or criterion in this sensitive area."[86] The majority's application of the *Lemon* test proved to be a signal of the Court's unwillingness to deploy the standard in its most robust form.[87] As in *Mueller* v. *Allen*, the majority specified that the *Lemon* test's criterion of a secular purpose was limited to examining the purpose *on the face of the law*.[88] Similarly, applying the effects prong of the *Lemon* test, the majority stipulated that the question was whether the effect of advancement of religion was merely "indirect, remote, and incidental," and, if so, then no constitutional violation exists.[89] Finally, on the entanglement prong, the majority opinion held that the question of entanglement is limited to an inquiry as to whether the law creates political friction.[90] Applying this narrow standard, the Court concluded that the crèche was a passive symbol that engenders friendly community spirit, and not a violation of the establishment clause.[91] Of some importance is the concurring opinion of Justice Sandra Day O'Connor, who stated that she wrote separately to "clarify" the *Lemon* test but in fact adopted an entirely new standard for measuring alleged establishment clause violations.[92] For O'Connor, the question is whether the law has the purpose or effect of conveying a message that the government endorses religion, as judged by

[83] Ibid. [84] Ibid. at 401–402. [85] *Lynch* v. *Donnelly*, 465 US 668 (1984).
[86] Ibid. at 679. [87] Ibid. at 678–685. [88] Ibid. at 679–681. [89] Ibid. at 683.
[90] Ibid. at 684–685. [91] Ibid. at 685–686. [92] Ibid. at 686–694.

an objective observer.[93] In *Lynch*, she held that there was no evidence of an intent to endorse religion, only evidence that the government wanted to celebrate the holiday.[94]

In the same year, the Court decided *Marsh* v. *Chambers*, which involved an establishment clause challenge to the Nebraska legislature's practice of opening each session with a prayer by a chaplain, paid by the state.[95] The Court declined to apply the *Lemon* test and stipulated that the practice of legislative prayer was so steeped in history and tradition in the United States that the establishment clause was inapplicable.[96] In other words, a "traditional" practice, regardless of its religiosity, was "carved out" of the applicable coverage of the establishment clause.[97] The Court justified this holding on the basis that the practice of legislative prayer coexisted with disestablishment and religious freedom, that courts open with a "God save this Court" announcement, that the First Federal Congress adopted a policy of opening with a prayer by a chaplain and enacted a statute providing for payment of chaplains in 1789, and that this practice had continued with an unbroken history of more than 200 years.[98] For the Court, legislative prayer is representative of a tradition that is merely a "tolerable acknowledgement" of "widely held" American beliefs.[99]

It was somewhat surprising, then, that in the 1987 decision of *Edwards* v. *Aguillard*, the Court struck down a Louisiana statute for violating the establishment clause.[100] *Edwards* involved a statute that required the "balanced treatment" of evolution and creationism in schools and stipulated that evolution could not be taught unless it was accompanied by teaching of creation science.[101] Writing for the Court, Justice Brennan stated that the standard governing the Court's assessment of constitutionality under the establishment clause was the *Lemon* test.[102] Justice Brennan also noted the "special context" of establishment clause violations in public elementary and secondary schools.[103] As would become clear a number of years later, the locus of public schools was particularly impactful for Justice John Paul Stevens, who joined the majority opinion, despite signing on with his more conservative brethren in the earlier cases narrowing the scope of the *Lemon* inquiry. And despite the Court's

[93] Ibid. at 690. [94] Ibid. at 691. [95] *Marsh* v. *Chambers*, 463 US 783 (1983) at 784–785.
[96] Ibid. at 785–795. [97] Ibid. at 786–792. [98] Ibid. at 786. [99] Ibid. at 792.
[100] *Edwards* v. *Aguillard*, 482 US 578 (1987). [101] Ibid. at 580–581.
[102] Ibid. at 582–583. [103] Ibid. at 583.

decisions in *Allen* and *Lynch*, the Court engaged in a robust analysis of the purpose of the statute, examining the legislative history of the law, before concluding that despite Louisiana's claim that the purpose of the law was to promote academic freedom, the purpose of the law clearly was to reform the science curriculum in order that it conform with a specific religious perspective.[104] Justice Antonin Scalia's dissent (which Justice Rehnquist joined) aggressively disputed the majority's use of the purpose test in this way.[105] For Justice Scalia, any examination of purpose that goes beyond the face of the law involves judicial subjectivity as to legislator motives.[106] Besides, Justice Scalia argued, academic freedom is a secular purpose on the face of the law, and even if there is a religious purpose, the law is saved from constitutional infirmary by the presence of a single secular purpose.[107] For Justice Scalia, the context of public schools is inconsequential to determine the applicable standard to adjudicate alleged establishment clause violations.[108]

Justice Scalia and the other conservative justices swiftly moved from dissent to majority in the Court's decision in *Bowen* v. *Kendrick*, a 1998 case involving the funding of religious organizations pursuant to the Adolescent Family Life Act (AFLA).[109] Under AFLA, the government provided grants to organizations for research as well as provision of services concerning premarital sex and pregnancy.[110] Notably, the statute excluded abortion counseling, services, or referrals, as well as family planning from the scope of its funding grants.[111] The statute was challenged as a violation of the establishment clause as it enabled religious organizations to receive government funds.[112] As in *Lynch* v. *Donnelly*, the Court applied the *Lemon* test in a significantly narrowed form.[113] Justice Rehnquist's majority opinion reiterated the *Lynch* interpretation of the purpose prong that limited the inquiry to the purpose on the face of the law and, in addition, explicitly picked up on Justice Scalia's *Aguillard* dissent on the purpose prong and held that a single secular purpose on the face of the law is sufficient to meet the standard.[114] More subtly, the Court limited the purpose inquiry further by articulating the question as to whether there is a purpose of endorsing religion.[115] Prior to *Bowen*, the standard had been

[104] Ibid. at 585–596. [105] Ibid. at 610–611. [106] Ibid. at 635–639.
[107] Ibid. at 627–631. [108] Ibid. [109] *Bowen* v. *Kendrick*, 487 US 589 (1988).
[110] Ibid. at 593–594. [111] Ibid. at 597–598. [112] Ibid. at 598. [113] Ibid. at 602.
[114] Ibid. at 602–607. [115] Ibid. at 604.

more broadly stated as endorsing *or advancing.* Given that "advancing" captures more government conduct than a sole endorsement standard, this narrowing was significant. On the facts of *Bowen*, the Court held that on its face AFLA evidenced a clear secular purpose.[116]

The Court similarly narrowed the scope of the effects inquiry, stating that the inquiry was whether the Act, *on its face*, had the effect of *endorsing* religion.[117] Again, the Court answered in the negative, holding that on its face the Act had no requirement that grantees be affiliated with religious denomination, that the services provided were not religious in character, and that there was no suggestion that religious organizations were uniquely qualified to carry out the service.[118] Finally, the Court limited the application of the entanglement prong of the *Lemon* standard, holding that the political divisiveness that is the hallmark of entanglement is limited to the context of primary and secondary schools.[119] As in *Lynch*, the four dissenting justices, Justices Harry Blackmun, Brennan, Thurgood Marshall, and Stevens, looked beyond the form of the statute and focused on the actual effect, applying the *Lemon* standard in its pure form, and ultimately holding that the risk of religious use of government funds is significantly higher in *Bowen* than in other financial aid contexts that the Court had faced.[120]

The Court began to abandon the pretense of adhering to the *Lemon* standard in the 1989 decision of *County of Alleghney* v. *ACLU.*[121] The case involved a challenge by the American Civil Liberties Union (ACLU) to two religious displays: a nativity scene erected on the main stairway of the Allegheny County Courthouse in Pittsburgh, and an eighteen-foot Hanukkah menorah, installed outside the city council building.[122] Four justices – Justice Rehnquist, Byron White, Scalia, and Anthony Kennedy – held that both displays were constitutional. These justices held that in order for there to be an establishment clause violation the state must coerce citizens to participate in religion.[123] Notably, the nature of the coercion the

[116] Ibid. at 617. [117] Ibid. at 604–606. [118] Ibid. at 606–615. [119] Ibid. at 615–617.

[120] Ibid. at 625–652. [121] *County of Allegheny* v. *ACLU*, 492 US 573 (1989).

[122] Ibid. at 578. The first was a nativity scene erected on the main stairway of the Allegheny County Courthouse in Pittsburgh, which was donated by the Holy Name Society, a Catholic group. Over the manger there was a banner, and over the angel "glory to god." The second was an eighteen-foot Hanukkah menorah owned by a Jewish group that was installed outside the city council building next to the Christmas tree with a message, "Salute to liberty."

[123] Ibid. at 593–594.

justices considered necessary to meet this new standard was not the "psychic" coercion standard set down by the Court in its earlier establishment clause cases involving religion in schools.[124] Instead, the nature of the coercion required under the standard articulated in *County of Alleghney* was formal coercion, which would not be violated by the government merely passively acknowledging religion in the form of religious symbolism, as in *County of Alleghney.*[125] Justice O'Connor, who held the menorah display constitutional and the crèche display unconstitutional, applied her new symbolic endorsement approach to establishment clause violations, which she continued to pose as an exemplification of the effects prong of the *Lemon* standard.[126] O'Connor stated that the relevant question for the Court was whether an objective observer, "acquainted with the Free Exercise Clause and the values it promotes and with the text, legislative history, and implementation of the statute, would perceive the law as a state endorsement" of religion.[127] Representative of a more neutral approach to establishment clause violations than the formal coercion standard applied by the conservative wing of the Court, O'Connor's endorsement standard was also applied by Justices Blackmun and Stevens. Ironically, while all three justices held the crèche unconstitutional, Justices Blackmun and O'Connor held the menorah constitutional, while Justice Stevens held it unconstitutional, demonstrating the entrenched subjectivity of the standard.[128] Only two justices, Justices Brennan and Marshall, continued to apply the *Lemon* standard and held both displays unconstitutional.[129]

This period, then, is ultimately marked by doctrinal "breadcrumbs" that would enable the Court to undertake a wholesale revision of both religion clause doctrine and the nature of constitutional religious liberty in America.

Consolidation: (Re)Enshrining Religious Majoritarianism

The year 1990 was a watershed year for religious liberty in the United States. Empowered and emboldened by a decade of incremental limiting of the constitutional exemption model established in *Sherbert* v. *Verner*, the

[124] Ibid. [125] Ibid. at 627–629. [126] Ibid. at 631–637.
[127] *Wallace* v. *Jaffree*, 472 US 38, 83 (O'Connor, J., concurring) (1985).
[128] County of Allegheny, 492 US at 632–633, 637–638. [129] Ibid. at 637–655.

Court outright rejected the general applicability of *Sherbert* in the seminal case of *Employment Division* v. *Smith.*[130] *Smith* arose out of Oregon's refusal to pay unemployment benefits to two members of the Native American Church who were fired from their jobs because they had ingested peyote at a worship ceremony of the church.[131] The state maintained that they were fired for misconduct and, as such, were ineligible for unemployment benefits.[132]

In his opinion for the Court, Justice Scalia held that while laws directly regulating religion (i.e., laws that ban acts that are only engaged in for religious reasons or because of the religious beliefs that they display) fall within the coverage of the free exercise clause, generally applicable laws that have a deleterious effect on religion do not fall within the protective auspices of the First Amendment.[133] Citing the Court's foundational case of *Reynolds* v. *Davis,* Justice Scalia stated that the Court has consistently held that to permit a person to be excused from compliance with the law would be to permit religion to trump the law.[134] Justice Scalia declared that the free exercise clause does not permit an individual to be exempted from the application of generally applicable laws because of their religious belief.[135] Scalia rationalized the Court's contradictory holdings in both *Sherbert* and *Wisconsin* v. *Yoder* by holding that these cases represent exceptions to the general rule stated in *Reynolds* and affirmed in *Smith.*[136] *Sherbert* v. *Verner,* Scalia argued, epitomized an exception that holds when the government makes an individualized determination about an individual's entitlement to government benefits such as unemployment compensation, the free exercise clause extends to cover those exercises of government power, and strict scrutiny review will apply.[137] *Yoder,* Justice Scalia stated, involved a "hybrid right," in which the free exercise claim was coupled with the parents' right to direct their child's education.[138] As commentators have noted, Justice Scalia did not elaborate on what is required to bring a hybrid claim, and it is difficult to understand the "exception" as anything other than a post hoc rationalization of an opinion that stood in the way of the Court's preferred approach to free exercise clause claims.

The Court's decision in *Smith* sharply limits the reach of the free exercise clause and squarely places the responsibility of protection of religious

[130] *Employment Div. Dept. of Human Resources of Oregon* v. *Smith*, 494 US 872 (1990).
[131] Ibid. at 874. [132] Ibid. [133] Ibid. at 877–878. [134] Ibid. at 879. [135] Ibid. at 882.
[136] Ibid. at 881–885. [137] Ibid. at 883. [138] Ibid. at 881–882.

minorities in the hands of the legislature. Congress immediately responded to *Smith* by passing the Religious Freedom Restoration Act (RFRA) in order to "restore the compelling interest test ... guarantee its application in all cases where free exercise of religion is substantially burdened; and to provide a claim or defense to persons whose religious exercise is substantially burdened by government."[139] In a potential show of pique, the Court struck down RFRA as applied to the states on the basis that Congress lacked legislative power to pass the law.[140] However, RFRA remains valid as applied to federal law, and a significant number of states have passed either constitutional amendments to enshrine the *Sherbert* standard or state-level RFRAs designed to do the same.[141]

While in many ways *Smith* and RFRA mark the end of the Court's free exercise clause journey, at least as it relates to individual religious liberty, the Court continued to struggle over the scope and limits of the establishment clause. Over a nearly two-decade period, the conservative members of the Court continued to pare back the broad scope of the establishment clause doctrine and successfully limited the applicability of the establishment clause. One exception to this was in the area of prayer in public schools. In 1992, the Court decided the case of *Lee* v. *Weisman*, where a middle school student objected to the school's practice of a standing prayer at graduation, attendance at which was voluntary.[142] In a 5–4 decision, the Court held that the graduation prayer violated the establishment clause.[143] For the majority, whose opinion was authored by Justice Kennedy and joined by Justices Blackmun, Stevens, O'Connor, and David Souter, the presence of "psychic coercion" to participate in the prayer was the touchstone of unconstitutionality.[144] The majority held that in the context of public schools, the pressure to attend and stand during invocation and benediction at such a significant life event as graduation rendered the psychic coercion as real as any formal coercion.[145] Justice Scalia's dissenting opinion rejected the concept of psychic coercion as "precious"

[139] Religious Freedom Restoration Act of 1993 (RFRA), 42 USC § 2000bb(b) (2000).

[140] *City of Boerne* v. *Flores*, 521 US 507 (1997).

[141] Christopher C. Lund, "Religious Liberty after Gonzales: A Look at State RFRAs," *South Dakota Law Review* 55 (2010).

[142] *Lee* v. *Weisman*, 505 US 577, 581–582 (1992).

[143] Ibid. at 599.

[144] Ibid. at 593–594.

[145] Ibid. In their concurring opinion, Justices Blackmun and Souter held that coercion was not necessary, but sufficient. Ibid. at 619–622.

and "incoherent," ultimately overextending the reach of the establishment clause.[146] For the dissenters, it is permissible to require respect for the beliefs of others by standing silently to mark an important occasion with prayer. Justice Scalia stated that the establishment clause would only be violated in this context if formal coercion was present; that is, if the students would face punishment if they did not attend and participate in the prayer.[147]

Contrary to the public school prayer cases, establishment clause doctrine in the context of tangible aid continued the Court's earlier trajectory of narrowing the scope of government conduct that would give rise to a constitutional concern. For example, in the 1997 case of *Agostini* v. *Felton*, the Court lifted an injunction on public school employees teaching remedial classes to children in inner-city sectarian schools.[148] The employees had been barred because, as the Court had reasoned in the 1985 case of *Aguilar* v. *Felton*, the monitoring required to ensure that religion was not taught would create an entanglement of religion and the state.[149] In overturning the *Aguilar* decision, the Court relied on its jurisprudence holding that formal neutrality was the standard against which a law would be assessed.[150] That is, if the law itself is neutral on its face and identifies secular criteria that neither favors nor disfavors religion, then the aid does not violate the establishment clause.[151]

This formal neutrality standard also directed the outcome in the 2000 case of *Mitchell* v. *Helms*, where the Court held that loans of instructional materials to students, such as computer software, could be made to religious schools under the Education Consolidation and Improvement Act of 1981, so long as the aid was granted to all individuals equally, and not statutorily directed to religious schools.[152] The determinative concurring opinion of Justice O'Connor, joined by Justice Stephen Breyer, reinforced that this kind of indirect aid, where the private choice of individuals determines the ultimate use of the funding, was constitutionally permissible.[153] However, Justice O'Connor reiterated that the legislative

[146] Ibid. at 636–646. [147] Ibid. at 643. [148] *Agostini* v. *Felton*, 521 US 203 (1997).

[149] Ibid. at 232–235. [150] Ibid. at 230–232.

[151] The Court does suggest some possible qualifiers, implying that the aid must be supplemental and cannot be too substantial and that money cannot be paid directly to religious schools ("no [government] funds ever reached the coffers of religious schools.") Ibid. at 228.

[152] *Mitchell* v. *Helms*, 530 US 793, 801 (2000). [153] Ibid. at 883–844.

diversion of tangible aid for religious use would continue to present an establishment clause problem because the aid would advance a religious mission.[154] For Justice O'Connor, the substance of the aid must be secular to avoid diversion to a religious use. For example, the funded school computers could not be used for religious purposes, and the government had the burden of establishing adequate safeguards against this possibility.[155] The plurality opinion of Justice Clarence Thomas, joined by Chief Justice Rehnquist and Justices Scalia and Kennedy, disagreed with Justice O'Connor on this point, and would have held that any religious use of aid was inconsequential to the constitutional validity of the aid.[156] For the plurality, so long as tangible aid is formally neutral and generally available based on secular criteria articulated in the statute, it would survive an establishment clause challenge.[157] The plurality's jurisprudential vision represents, according to Kent Greenawalt, a "sweeping reconceptualization that would open the door to virtually all aid."[158]

The formal neutrality approach of the plurality was doctrinally entrenched in the 2002 case of *Zelman* v. *Simmons-Harris*, in which an Ohio program provided tuition aid for children in elementary or middle school to attend a public or private school of their choosing.[159] The program specified that a family could choose to send their child to any private school, religious or not, so long as the school agreed not to discriminate or foster hatred.[160] In the 1999–2000 school year, fifty-six private schools participated, 82 percent of which were religiously affiliated.[161] In upholding the aid, Chief Justice Rehnquist's opinion for the Court held that the program did not have the effect of advancing religion because the aid was not only generally available based on neutral criteria, but it was indirect and the individual recipients made a private choice as to how to direct the funds; any advancement of religion is, then, not attributable to the government.[162] For the Court, the government permitting funds to be directed to religious use via an individual intermediary presents no constitutional problem. It remains to be seen whether the Court's reasoning will be applied in any future direct aid cases, as many justices would have held in *Mitchell* v. *Helms*.

[154] Ibid. [155] Ibid. at 857–864. [156] Ibid. at 821–825. [157] Ibid. at 809–814.
[158] Greenawalt, *Religion and the Constitution*, 410n7.
[159] *Zelman* v. *Simmons-Harris*, 536 US 639, 643–644 (2002). [160] Ibid. at 645.
[161] Ibid. at 647. [162] Ibid. at 653–655.

The conservative plurality continued to press for a more permissible establishment clause standard in the public symbols cases. In 2005, the Court handed down two cases involving public displays, *McCreary County*, which involved two counties in Kentucky displaying the King James Version of the Ten Commandments on their courthouse walls, and *Van Orden* v. *Perry*, where Texas displayed a six-foot-high monument on the grounds of the Texas State Capitol.[163] In each case, a coalition of Chief Justice Rehnquist and Justices Scalia, Thomas, and Kennedy stated that the establishment clause is not implicated when the government acknowledges "the Creator"; instead, the display is representative of a passive, historic recognition of America's heritage.[164] Yet, this approach was contradicted by the majority opinion in *McCreary County*, in which Justices Souter, Stevens, O'Connor, Ruth Bader Ginsberg, and Breyer held that in light of both its sectarian content and historical context the display conveyed a message of government endorsement of religion in violation of the establishment clause.[165] Further, while the conservative coalition was in the majority in *Van Orden* v. *Perry*, upholding the Texas Ten Commandments display as constitutionally permissible, their jurisprudential approach commanded only a plurality of the Court.[166] Instead, the governing opinion was that of Justice Breyer, who held that while the display had a religious message, the context of the display – including the long historical presence in the Capitol grounds and the physical setting of the display surrounded by other historic monuments – rendered it constitutionally permissible.[167] Justice Scalia's dissent in *Van Orden* exemplifies the approach of the conservative wing of the Court. Justice Scalia emphasized that where the government simply acknowledges "the creator," (e.g., by displaying religious symbols or messages) there is no establishment of religion. Of course, the problem with this approach to the establishment clause is that it enshrines religious majoritarianism and implicitly drives a wedge in the community between (majority) believers and nonbelievers.

[163] *McCreary County* v. *ACLU*, 545 US 844 (2005); *Van Orden* v. *Perry*, 545 US 677 (2005).

[164] *Van Orden*, 545 US at 686–692.

[165] *McCreary*, 545 US at 871–881.

[166] Ibid. Notably, in separate concurrences, Justice Scalia emphasized that passive governmental acknowledgment of God would always be constitutionally permissible, and Justice Thomas claimed that not only would passive acknowledgment of religion always be constitutionally permissible, but only formal coercion into religion would present an establishment clause issue.

[167] Ibid.

Contemporary Religious Liberty and the Rise of Religious Institutionalism

The combination of a static ideological coalition and the relatively settled nature of both the free exercise clause and establishment clause doctrine resulted in very few individual religious liberty cases after 2005, and those few cases that did arise did not result in either sharp doctrinal shifts or indications of incremental moves away from the relatively settled status quo. Yet, while cases involving *individual* religious liberty were rare, contemporary constitutional religious liberty is marked by the rise of religious institutionalism and the amplification of religion clause protections for religious institutions. While the Court's jurisprudence reflects a decline in the capacity of individuals to call on the religion clauses to protect their religious freedom, the Court has proved remarkably receptive to comparable claims of religious institutions. A trio of cases decided in 2012, 2014, and 2017 evidences the fundamental shift in the Court's religion clause jurisprudence.

The rise of religious institutionalism is marked by the Court's 2012 watershed decision in *Hosanna-Tabor Evangelical Lutheran Church & School* v. *EEOC*.[168] Hosanna-Tabor was a Lutheran Church and school operating in Michigan, and offered a "Christ centered education" from Kindergarten to Grade 8.[169] Teachers at the school were designated as either "lay" teachers or "called" teachers, where called teachers were considered to be called to the vocation by God and received the endorsement of their Synod district and were "called" (voted on) by their congregation.[170] Upon receiving an affirmative vote of the congregation, the called teachers received the title "Minister of Religion: Commissioned."[171] Cheryl Perich was a called teacher at Hosanna-Tabor before becoming ill and taking disability leave.[172] When her doctor cleared her as fit for work, the school resisted her return, and Perich threated to sue for discrimination on the basis of her disability.[173] Hosanna-Tabor consequently terminated Perich and the congregation rescinded her call for "insubordination," "disruptive behavior," and the damage she had done to her working relationship with the school by threatening to sue the school.[174] When Perich filed a complaint under the Americans with Disabilities Act with the EEOC, Hosanna-Tabor

[168] *Hosanna-Tabor Evangelical Lutheran Church & School* v. *EEOC*, 565 US 171 (2012).
[169] Ibid. at 177. [170] Ibid. [171] Ibid. [172] Ibid. at 178. [173] Ibid. at 179. [174] Ibid.

defended the complaint on the basis that the First Amendment religion clauses barred the suit.[175] Specifically, Hosanna-Tabor claimed that the religion clauses enshrine a "ministerial exception," pursuant to which a religious institution has the right to make decisions about ministerial employment without the involvement of the state.[176]

In an 8–1 decision, the Court in *Hosanna-Tabor* held that the First Amendment religion clauses grant "special solicitude" to religious institutions, part of which ensures that religious institutions can fire ministers without regard for generally applicable employment laws.[177] Notably, at least in the context of employment discrimination, the Court was clear to state that a "minister" is not limited to the head of a religious congregation, nor is the exemption limited to those persons who perform exclusively religious functions.[178] Rejecting the obvious analogy to the *Smith* decision, the Court claimed that there is a constitutional difference between an institutional claimant claiming an exemption to ensure protection for its internal church decisions, and an individual claimant looking for an exemption to do a physical act contrary to general law.[179] With this decision, the Supreme Court enshrined an exclusive, and potentially potent, constitutional right for religious institutions, which has the potential to change the landscape of constitutional rights in the United States.[180] What the Court's decision in *Hosanna-Tabor* left open, however, were critical definitional questions with potentially significant implications for constitutional religious liberty, namely who or what is a religious institution entitled to claim status as an institutional rights-holder, as well as the scope of the right, specifically whether it extends beyond employment discrimination.[181]

The Court faced some of these complicated issues in *Burwell* v. *Hobby Lobby Stores*.[182] *Hobby Lobby* involved the claim of Hobby Lobby Stores that the Affordable Care Act's so-called "Contraception Mandate," mandating that all health insurance plans include coverage for contraception and

[175] Ibid. at 179–180. [176] Ibid. at 180. [177] Ibid. at 189–191. [178] Ibid. at 193.

[179] Ibid. at 189–99.

[180] See Zoë Robinson, "What Is a 'Religious Institution'?," *Boston College Law Review* 55, no. 1 (2014), 182; Zoë Robinson, "The Contraception Mandate and the Forgotten Constitutional Question," *Wisconsin Law Review* 2014 (2014); Richard Schragger and Micah Schwartzman, "Against Religious Institutionalism," *Virginia Law Review* 99, no. 5 (September 2013): 919–921.

[181] See Robinson, "Hosanna-Tabor."

[182] *Burwell* v. *Hobby Lobby Stores*, 134 S. Ct. 2751 (2014).

abortifacients, violated their religious liberty.[183] While the Court's ultimate decision in Hobby Lobby was not based on First Amendment grounds – instead resolving the litigation under the Religious Freedom Restoration Act (RFRA) – the broader Hobby Lobby litigation efforts illustrate the direction in which many proponents of broad constitutional rights for religious institutions are attempting to expand those protections. Many challengers to the "contraception mandate" have argued that they should be exempt from the mandate because it interfered with the institution's right to make decisions about its internal affairs, a right the claimants argue was established in *Hosanna-Tabor*. While the Court's decision did nothing to resolve the complicated doctrinal questions, the potential of *Hosanna-Tabor* is evidenced in the broader *Hobby Lobby* litigation. For example, among the groups claiming that they were entitled to "special solicitude" under the First Amendment were hospitals, schools, charities, various not-for-profit groups, and religious lobby groups.[184] Further, these various groups who claimed to be rights-holders of the exclusive right for religious institutions claimed that the scope of First Amendment religious institutionalism extends beyond the facts of *Hosanna-Tabor* – that is, beyond the context of employment discrimination – to any decisions made by religious institutions relating to the internal functioning of the institution.[185]

The contemporary rise of religious institutionalism has been buttressed by the Court's most recent religion clauses decision in *Trinity Lutheran* v. *Comer*.[186] There, Trinity Lutheran School was denied a Missouri Department of Public Resources grant to subsidize the cost of playground resurfacing from scrap rubber tires.[187] The state had a policy of excluding Church applications based on the Missouri State Constitution's prohibition on public funding of churches and other houses of worship.[188] The Church claimed that the categorical exclusion of churches violated the free exercise clause.[189] The Court agreed, holding that "the exclusion of Trinity Lutheran from a public benefit for which it is otherwise qualified, solely because it is a church, is odious to our Constitution all the same, and cannot stand."[190] For the Court, "denying a generally available benefit solely on account of religious identity imposes a penalty on the free exercise of religion that can be justified only by a state interest 'of the highest

[183] Ibid. at 2759. [184] Robinson, "Hosanna-Tabor." [185] Ibid.
[186] *Trinity Lutheran* v. *Comer*, 137 S. Ct. 2012 (2017). [187] Ibid. at 2016.
[188] Ibid. at 2018. [189] Ibid. [190] Ibid. at 2025.

order'."[191] Missouri's justifications for denying the Church the grant failed the Court's application of strict scrutiny, and the denial of the grant was held a violation of the free exercise clause.[192] The import of this decision is potentially far-reaching. As one commentator has noted, the decision implies that "any denial of aid to religious schools is unconstitutional when assistance is provided to public schools. Or for that matter, it would make it unconstitutional to deny religious institutions any aid that is provided to secular institutions."[193]

Taking *Hosanna-Tabor*, *Hobby Lobby*, and *Trinity Lutheran* together implies the constitutional predominance of religious institutions; not only do religious institutions now have exclusive rights not available to individuals under the religion clauses, but *Trinity Lutheran* appears to constitutionalize a right to benefits for religious institutions, which had previously been recognized as a violation of the establishment clause. Buttressing this trio of free exercise clause cases and the inherent religious protectionism within is the establishment clause decision in *Town of Greece* v. *Galloway*.[194] There, the Court held that a town's practice of opening its board meetings with a prayer delivered by a member of the clergy did not violate the establishment clause if the practice is consistent with tradition, does not discriminate against minority faiths when deciding who can offer a prayer, and does not coerce nonadherent participation.[195] Writing for the plurality, Justice Kennedy stated that "[a]bsent a pattern of prayers that over time denigrate, proselytize, or betray an impermissible government purpose, a challenge based solely on the content of a particular prayer will not likely establish a constitutional violation."[196] Taken together, the contemporary establishment clause and free exercise clause cases indicate a model of religious liberty that reflects an asymmetrical form of unitary separationism, whereby religious institutions can avail themselves of the Constitution's protections in order to ensure that general law imposes no burdens, yet provides equal benefits.

[191] Ibid. at 2019. [192] Ibid. at 2024.

[193] Erwin Chemerinsky, "Symposium: The Crumbling Wall Separating Church & State," SCOTUSblog, June 27, 2017, www.scotusblog.com/2017/06/symposium-crumbling-wall-separating-church-state/.

[194] *Town of Greece* v. *Galloway*, 134 S. Ct. 1811 (2014). On the decision generally, see Lisa Shaw Roy, "The Unexplored Implications of *Town of Greece v. Galloway*," *Albany Law Review* 80, no.2 (2016).

[195] *Town of Greece* 134 S. Ct. at 1824. [196] Ibid.

Conclusion

This chapter has identified the Supreme Court's fundamental decisions as to the function and scope of the First Amendment religion clauses. More specifically, the chapter has highlighted the complex relationship between the Court's interpretation of those clauses and the broader social and political mores. Tracing the Court's jurisprudence from its inaugural religion clause case through to its most modern decisions, it is possible to see that the Court's interpretation of both the free exercise clause and establishment clause is representative of constitutional majoritarianism – reflective of contemporary public opinion on questions of religious liberty. Viewed this way, it is possible to see that rather than functioning as a protective device for countermajoritarian interests, by and large the Court's interpretation of the religion clauses means that the core protection for religious liberty in the United States ultimately privileges the majority.

Part III

Law, Politics, and Economics

9 Religious and Secular Presuppositions in First Amendment Interpretations

Paul E. Kerry

The sixteen words on religion in the First Amendment – "Congress shall make no law respecting an establishment of religion, or prohibiting the free exercise thereof" – have generated voluminous, and vociferous, scholarly interpretations, particularly in the twentieth century. These disagreements strike at the heart of the role of religion in American public life. How are we to decide which interpretation of the First Amendment is correct? Answers to this question have been laden with presuppositions, or tacit assumptions – for example, a postulate or premise – made before the start of an argument. Presuppositions are not always a part of the propositional content of an argument, but they do set the direction of the argument. This chapter is an interdisciplinary analysis of recent historical, political, legal, and philosophical writing on the First Amendment to illustrate how key presuppositions inform the approach to scholarly arguments about the meaning, scope, and intent of the First Amendment. The chapter will first outline the contextual and philosophical problems of interpreting the First Amendment. It will then evaluate several providentialist, secular (including pragmatic) presuppositions that have guided scholarly interpretations. Ultimately, the chapter will argue that there has not been a single understanding of the relationship between church and state in America, but that investigating these presuppositions can help us better appreciate the dynamic nature of religion, politics, and jurisprudence in America.

It is important to note at the outset that this is not an examination of a "hidden Constitution" but an interdisciplinary and selective analysis of largely contemporary historical and philosophical writing on the First Amendment to illustrate how presuppositions inform the approach in arguments about the meaning, scope, and intent of the First Amendment.[1] What emerges can be roughly placed into two competing

[1] Laurence Tribe, *The Invisible Constitution (Inalienable Rights)* (New York: Oxford University Press, 2008). Tribe investigates what is invisible within the Constitution (10) in

understandings of religious freedom. Steven Smith called these secularist and providentialist understandings, the former shaped largely by Enlightenment ideals of progress and rationalism toward a state free from any particular religious influence, and the latter shaped by a belief that religion constitutes a foundational public good and deserves protection.[2] Previous scholarship has acknowledged some interpenetration of these ideas during the American revolutionary period, but recent scholarship has emphasized that religion was and remains a dynamic force that provides essential resources for contributing to the continuing vitality of the republic, and hence the urgent need for religious freedom.[3]

The Problems of Finding the Meaning of the First Amendment

Scholars routinely turn to historical evidence to answer the question of the meaning of the First Amendment. Sometimes this relies on a minute reconstruction of the 1787 Constitutional Convention in Philadelphia. Some take a broader view and begin to catalogue the lifelong statements of various founders and constitutional framers of the new American republic. And others turn for further insight to the political, jurisprudential, and theological thought produced in British and European history. There is also the problem of changing rhetoric in early America and how to evaluate the influence of particular ideas. And finally there can be a tendency in studies of American history, when interpreted from an exceptionalist standpoint, to read the development of the American Constitution teleologically.

Opinions on the meaning of the First Amendment run a spectrum. Michael McConnell held that the free exercise clause of the First Amendment is the "most philosophically interesting and distinctive feature of the American Constitution ... because it represents a new and

connection to the fundamental traditions and beliefs that undergird it, whereas I am interested in the presuppositions of scholarly arguments.

2 Steven D. Smith, *The Rise and Decline of American Religious Freedom* (Cambridge, MA: Harvard University Press, 2014), 8–10.

3 Ruth H. Bloch, "Religion and Ideological Change in the American Revolution," in *Religion and American Politics: From the Colonial Period to the Present*, ed. Mark A. Noll and Luke E. Harlow (New York: Oxford University Press, 2007), 48.

unprecedented conception of government and its relation to claims of higher truth and authority."[4] These higher claims about government were based in the sovereignty of the people and the "laws of nature" as found in the Declaration of Independence, which could be construed, as David Novak proposed, as the "true preamble to the Constitution."[5]

Other scholars reserve judgment about its meaning, philosophical and otherwise, since the historical record is so sparse and opaque. Michael Meyerson called the language of the First Amendment "ill defined" and rejected using the drafting history as effective "because we do not know why the proposals were rejected."[6] James Hutson held that there is little in the historical record of the congressional debate on the First Amendment, perhaps owing to the silence of congressmen "who did not think amendments necessary in the first place." He also blamed the "incompetent" shorthand reporters in the record.[7] David Sehat called the wording of the First Amendment "garbled at best and meaningless at worst."[8] Martha Nussbaum conceded a middle ground: "It seems clear . . . that the text the framers chose does make religion (whatever that includes) special for the purposes of the Free Exercise Clause, fair or unfair."[9]

Donald Drakeman acknowledged the paltry congressional record and concluded that, given the evidence, the First Amendment "was specifically designed to protect the established churches in states from federal interference." Although broad ideals are sought for in the language of the First Amendment, including freedom of conscience and equality of religious denominations, the language of the First Amendment prohibits only "a federal ecclesiastical enterprise" and one cannot derive from that language

[4] As quoted in Ellis Sandoz, "Religious Liberty and Religion in the American Founding Revisited," in *Religious Liberty in Western Thought*, ed. Noel B. Reynolds and W. Cole Durham, Jr. (Atlanta, GA: Scholars Press for Emory University, 1996), 275.

[5] David Novak, *In Defense of Religious Liberty* (Wilmington, DE: ISI Books, 2009), 41. For an incisive reading of the Declaration of Independence as "a creed in American thought and history," see Owen Anderson, *The Declaration of Independence and God: Self-Evident Truths in American Law* (New York: Cambridge University Press, 2015), 1.

[6] Michael I. Meyerson, *Endowed by Our Creator: The Birth of Religious Freedom in America* (New Haven, CT: Yale University Press, 2012), 240, 172.

[7] James H. Hutson, *Church and State in America: The First Two Centuries* (New York: Cambridge University Press, 2008), 160.

[8] David Sehat, *The Myth of American Religious Freedom* (New York: Oxford University Press, 2011), 49.

[9] Martha C. Nussbaum, *Liberty of Conscience: In Defense of America's Tradition of Religious Equality* (New York: Basic Books, 2008), 102.

"any broad-based set of American principles that were shared by the founding generation" and, further, that "it is difficult to find any originalist support for the enhanced or 'turbocharged' federalism argument. It may be an attractive approach to a 'plain meaning' interpretation, but, in the end, the contemporary documentary record argues strongly against the enhanced federalism interpretation as the original meaning of the establishment clause."[10] Hutson's assessment is somewhat similar: "All indications are that in debating the religion clause of what became the First Amendment, Congress only considered the issue of federalism as it related to the propriety of religious taxes levied by New England state governments."[11]

Perhaps no other metaphor for the meaning of the First Amendment has proved as powerful as Thomas Jefferson's "wall of separation between Church & State." In his letter to the Danbury Baptists, he wrote:

> Believing with you that religion is a matter which lies solely between Man & his God, that he owes account to none other for his faith or his worship, that the legitimate powers of government reach actions only, & not opinions, I contemplate with sovereign reverence that act of the whole American people which declared that their legislature should "make no law respecting an establishment of religion, or prohibiting the free exercise thereof," thus building a wall of separation between Church & State.[12]

Philip Hamburger argued that this phrase presents such a clear image that, ripped from its context, and deployed increasingly in the nineteenth century, culminating in its 1947 use by the US Supreme Court, has displaced its historical meaning or philosophical nuance.[13] He made the case that this has become, in fact, the dominant presupposition in understanding the meaning of the Constitution's religion clause.[14] As Daniel

[10] Donald Drakeman, *Church, State, and Original Intent* (New York: Cambridge University Press, 2010), 232; 261–262; 246. See also Chapter 11 of this volume. This is underscored by Michael Klarman's argument that Madison, in initially opposing the Bill of Rights, was concerned that it might actually circumscribe "the rights of religious consciences." Michael J. Klarman, *The Framers' Coup: The Making of the United States Constitution* (New York: Oxford University Press, 2016), 561.

[11] Hutson, *Church and State in America*, 160.

[12] Library of Congress, Jefferson's Letter to the Danbury Baptists, 1802, accessed online, www.loc.gov/loc/lcib/9806/danpre.html.

[13] Philip Hamburger, *Separation of Church and State* (Cambridge, MA: Harvard University Press, 2002), 488.

[14] This Tribe would call a part of the invisible Constitution.

Dreisbach likewise observed, "separation of church and state" and "wall of separation" have overshadowed the amendment's more expansive wording of "free exercise."[15] John Wilson concluded that the "separationist paradigm" comes into play only in the mid-twentieth century "through the application of the due process clause of the Fourteenth Amendment."[16] This gave rise to at least two ways of understanding religious liberty: the separationist understanding, which held a negative view of liberty that favored the "absence of government constraint upon individuals in matters of religion," and the accommodationist view of freedom for religion, the understanding of religious liberty as a positive right and that preferential treatment by the federal government was all that needed to be avoided.[17] As Christopher Eisgruber and Lawrence Sager put forward, the "distinction between removing a burden and conferring a benefit is vanishingly thin," and it is in this interstitial space that the debate on the First Amendment's religion clauses has been hottest most recently.[18]

Steven Smith proposed yet another reason for the religion clauses, that "[t]he central purpose of the clauses was to simply reaffirm the jurisdictional status quo." The religion "clauses did not reflect the acceptance by Americans of any commitment to religious equality, secular government, or governmental neutrality in matters of religion." There would be no national church because it would be outside the jurisdiction of the national government: "Over time ... this jurisdictional purpose came to be largely forgotten, leaving the nation with what seemed to be more substantive constitutional commitments."[19] Thus, Smith concluded that these broader commitments have been read back into the First Amendment.

Smith characterized the "American settlement" as the "separation of *church from state* ... not *religion from government*." He furthermore saw that "entrenched in the nation's ... constitutive practices and self-understandings, was one not of secularism or neutrality but rather of open contestation."[20] This open contestation is underscored by Teresa

[15] Daniel L. Dreisbach, *Thomas Jefferson and the Wall of Separation between Church and State* (New York: New York University Press, 2002), 5, 22–23.

[16] John F. Wilson, "Religion, Government, and Power in the New American Nation," in *Religion and American Politics: From the Colonial Period to the Present*, ed. Mark A. Noll and Luke E. Harlow (New York: Oxford University Press, 2007), 80.

[17] Ibid., 80–82.

[18] Christopher L. Eisgruber and Lawrence G. Sager, *Religious Freedom and the Constitution* (Cambridge, MA: Harvard University Press, 2007), 25.

[19] Smith, *The Rise and Decline of American Religious Freedom*, 8. [20] Ibid., 9.

Bejan's account of how evangelical free speech maps onto the idea of free exercise. She provocatively asserted that there is perhaps more a legacy of Roger Williams and his commitment to robust evangelical free speech in the "free exercise" and "free speech" clauses of the First Amendment than John Locke's liberalism and polite discourse. Indeed, Bejan propounded that although Locke has been casually understood in the US context as supporting a modern view of pluralism and diversity for its own sake, he was in fact coming from an establishment position – that is, with the view that religious enthusiasts and dissenters could potentially become supporters of the state.[21] Normally, it is the religious in a polity who are seen to proselytize, but here her thought seems to suggest that the state may have an interest in seeking converts to liberalism and secularism.

Alexandra Walsham concluded that the older chronological political and intellectual history approach to toleration, in contrast to recent studies, is inevitably teleological.[22] Newer studies tend to focus on local communities and to throw into relief the social interactions of different religious groups.[23] Joachim Whaley's work is exemplary in this regard.[24] Examining local communities and their practical interactions disrupts the narrative of an unstoppable "rise of toleration." Although these scholarly debates are not irrelevant when examining the American context, the First Amendment is already set in a political and philosophical context by its status in the US Constitution and its continuing jurisprudential use.

[21] Teresa M. Bejan, *Mere Civility: Disagreement and the Limits of Toleration* (Cambridge, MA: Harvard University Press, 2017), 122–123.

[22] Ursula Henriques, *Religious Toleration in England, 1787–1833* (London: Routledge and Kegan Paul, 1961) would fit this category on Walsham's view, although she makes allowances for Kamen's standard account as well as for Coffey's more recent efforts. Henry Kamen, *The Rise of Toleration* (London: Weidenfeld and Nicolson, 1967) and John Coffey, *Persecution and Toleration in Protestant England, 1558–1689* (Harlow: Pearson, 2000). Peter Zagorin would fit into the crosshairs of Walsham's critique: *How the Idea of Religious Toleration Came to the West* (Princeton, NJ: Princeton University Press, 2003).

[23] Alexandra Walsham, *Charitable Hatred: Tolerance and Intolerance in England, 1500–1700* (Manchester: Manchester University Press, 2006). See also Benjamin J. Kaplan, *Divided by Faith: Religious Conflict and the Practice of Toleration in Early Modern Europe* (Cambridge, MA: Belknap Press, 2007).

[24] Joachim Whaley, *Religious Toleration and Social Change in Hamburg 1529–1819* (Cambridge: Cambridge University Press, 1985). Christopher Dawson reminds us that it was the transregional practice of philosophers and scientists that helped to overcome religious and national differences. *Progress and Religion: An Historical Enquiry* (London: Sheed and Ward, 1929).

One must be on guard, however, not to press the First Amendment into other teleological narratives. Carl Nederman contended that it is an ideology of political liberalism to connect toleration exclusively to itself – a move that ignores older, medieval arguments on toleration that are routinely discarded as illiberal.[25] Moreover, Alan Levine reasoned that liberal attempts to ground toleration are problematic, whether on prudential, metaphysical, or political grounds.[26] William Cavanaugh observed that a myth of religious violence (including the notion that religions and religious people have a propensity to be violent) has been constructed to justify political liberalism and create a militant religious Other. More relevant here is that this myth is used to assert flatly a simplistic thesis that "the transfer of power from the church to the state was the solution to the wars of the sixteenth and seventeenth centuries."[27]

Religious, Secular, and Pragmatic Interpretations

Despite the historiographical, rhetorical, and philosophical challenges, scholars have attempted to make sense of the First Amendment and its context. Smith's hermeneutic is helpful: we can divide the scholarship into religious (or providentialist) understandings and secularist understandings. Providentialist understandings cast America as a covenantal nation with a typology set in biblical metaphors and language and where early Christian influences could be given expression.[28] The role of religion and Judeo-Christian virtues in civil society is important to this reading of the context of the First Amendment. On the secularist understanding, there is

[25] Cary J. Nederman, *Worlds of Difference: European Discourses of Toleration c. 1100–c. 1550* (University Park, PA: The Pennsylvania State University Press, 2000), 117. See also *Beyond the Persecuting Society: Religious Toleration before the Enlightenment*, ed. John Christian Laursen and Cary J. Nederman (Philadelphia: University of Pennsylvania Press, 1998).

[26] Alan Levine, "Introduction: The Prehistory of Toleration and Varieties of Skepticism," in *Early Modern Skepticism and the Origins of Toleration*, ed. Alan Levin (Lanham, MD: Lexington Books, 1999), 1–20.

[27] William T. Cavanaugh, *The Myth of Religious Violence: Secular Ideology and the Roots of Modern Conflict* (Oxford: Oxford University Press, 2009), 11.

[28] Although scholarship has read different American colonists, particularly in New England, as seeing themselves as being a part of the New Jerusalem, not all did, including Cotton Mather. Jan Stievermann, *Prophecy, Piety, and the Problem of Historicity: Interpreting the Hebrew Scriptures in Cotton Mather's* Biblia Americana (Tübingen: Mohr Siebeck, 2016), 102, 158, 214–215.

the context of radical Freethinkers who detached religion from politics, culminating in Jefferson's linguistic achievement of the "wall of separation" between church and state. This view turns toward the Classics to understand the role of virtue in civil society and extends the Enlightenment aspiration and articulation of religious freedom to protect religious minorities and sees religious liberty ultimately as a principle of equality. Yet, there are other interpretations as well that might fall under the umbrella of "pragmatic." This view in some ways revisits the concept of religious toleration and its modern extension, tolerance. The First Amendment is understood as a pragmatic statement of governance and at most maintaining a juridical status quo vis-à-vis federalism. This perspective considers First Amendment religious freedom a political expedient, given the religious pluralism of the population of the young republic.[29] The multiplicity of religions and values made "free exercise" a practical, if not a principled, necessity.

Smith presented two narratives that have come to dominate the backstory to the First Amendment. The first is the "standard story" with a liberal progressive view that Enlightenment thinking transformed or moved on from religious toleration to religious freedom and from thence to equality and fairness. This view held that government was neutral with respect to religious and nonreligious viewpoints and that religion should be separated from government. The second narrative is what he called the "revised story" that posits two distinct authorities, sacred and secular, as well as the realm of conscience. Under this arrangement, there has been a persistent contestation among these authorities up to the present day. To recapitulate Smith's argument, the First Amendment originally meant that there was no need to adopt any principles of religious freedom on the national level because governmental jurisdiction did not extend to religion. In essence, the First Amendment on Smith's understanding aimed at no establishment of religion nationally; nevertheless, the amendment came to be freighted through accidental and indirect changes with imported meanings such as "church-state separation and religious freedom" that have now become the basis of constitutional jurisprudence concerning the religion clauses.[30] Particularly

[29] A new book elucidates the economic incentives that helped to create the conditions for religious liberty. See Noel D. Johnson and Mark Koyama, *Persecution and Toleration: The Long Road to Religious Freedom* (Cambridge: Cambridge University Press, 2019).

[30] Smith, *Rise and Decline of American Religious Freedom*, 49–52.

intriguing is Smith's deeper argument that the "American settlement operated to ensure that both the providentialist and secularist interpretations would have a continuing place at the constitutional table."[31] What is innovative here is that rather than argue, as most accounts do, that the presuppositions are either religious or secular, Smith posits that by design the presuppositions are meant to incorporate both.

Smith's argument dovetails with Akhil Amar's reconstruction thesis: "Originally centered on protecting a majority of the people from a possibly unrepresentative government, the Bill has been pressed into the service of protecting vulnerable minorities from dominant social majorities."[32] This undergirds the claim that the original purpose was to ensure the rights of the majority against a minority in control. James Madison, however, was fearful of a popular majority and sought to include protections of the rights of minority groups. Madison's vision came to fruition in the Fourteenth Amendment.

Yet, such appeals to the framers of the US Constitution, typical in scholarly discussions of religious liberty, elide many important definitions. What constitutes that group known as "the framers"? Would it be only the signers of the US Constitution? There were seventy appointed individuals to the Constitutional Convention. Rhode Island famously did not appoint any delegates. Of the fifty-five delegates who did attend, only thirty-nine signed the Constitution. What of those on state legislatures, many of whom were Antifederalists? What of ministers of religion whose opinions held great sway with the public? These are contested, polemical issues. Some of the delegates appeared to have said little, while others who did not attend – for example, Thomas Jefferson, who was in Paris as the successor to Benjamin Franklin as trade minister – are nearly always cited as an authoritative source.

According to the secularist narrative, these American founders framed a liberal democracy that allowed for religious freedom. This liberal religious environment was shaped by Enlightenment ideas.[33] In particular, the

[31] Ibid., 9.

[32] Akhil Reed Amar, "The Creation and Reconstruction of the First Amendment," in *Religious Liberty: Essays on First Amendment Law*, ed. Daniel N. Robinson and Richard N. Williams (New York: Cambridge University Press, 2016), 39.

[33] Robert Faulkner, "Faiths of Our Modern Fathers: Bacon's Progressive Hope and Locke's Liberal Christianity," in *Resistance to Tyrants, Obedience to God: Reason, Religion, and*

Enlightenment view of human nature was one in which, as Michael Novak stated, "our ability to choose gives us the power either to make ourselves into the highest developed creatures our consciousness longs for us to become, or, to turn aside in a stunted, self-destructive direction. We direct our own future, for good or evil."[34]

Inherent in this argument is that the establishment of religious freedom is a significant move from religious toleration as practiced in early modern and Enlightenment Europe, where tolerance was a privilege of the sovereign.[35] Bejan called attention to the fact that in the early modern period of the European Reformation "no one considered toleration to be an adequate solution to the problem of coexistence."[36] Hans Erich Bödeker noted that notions of tolerance and sufferance were bound up with prioritizing difference related to the central question of what it means to be human. Religion as such was only one category; other discourses, such as anthropology, created other criteria for judgment.[37] Thus, although tolerance became an ethical category for many Enlightenment thinkers, toleration was unable to resolve issues of, for example, race (interactions between Europeans and other cultures) and gender (male and female equality). Presuppositions of religious freedom as a "first freedom" are nested on the secular view in new claims of equality that could allow people not only of different faiths but also of different cultures and sexes to have an ideological currency for their claims of equality.[38]

Religious freedom is said to shift the philosophical basis of equality by no longer prioritizing difference (racial, social, gender), as toleration would, but by showing the way to equal respect before the law. Nussbaum mooted that the idea of equality was associated with religious liberty in virtually all of the colonies.[39] Ellis Sandoz called this the

Republicanism at the American Founding, ed. Dustin Gish and Daniel Klinghard (Lanham, MD: Lexington Books, 2013), 19–41.

[34] Michael Novak, "The First of All Freedoms is Liberty of Conscience," in *Religious Liberty: Essays on First Amendment Law*, ed. Daniel N. Robinson and Richard N. Williams (New York: Cambridge University Press, 2016), 176.

[35] Hans Erich Bödeker, "Prologue: Towards a Reconstruction of Discourse on Tolerance and Intolerance in the Age of Enlightenment," in *Discourses of Tolerance and Intolerance in the European Enlightenment*, ed. Hans Erich Bödeker, Clorinda Donato, and Peter Hanns Reill (Toronto: University of Toronto Press, 2009), 19.

[36] Bejan, *Mere Civility*, 33. [37] Bödeker, "Prologue," 22.

[38] See Tisa Wenger, *Religious Freedom: The Contested History of an American Ideal* (Chapel Hill, NC: University of North Carolina Press, 2017).

[39] Nussbaum, *Liberty of Conscience*, 84.

progressive idea of evolving religious liberty, the move from toleration to liberty of conscience to the perfect freedom of belief and practice.[40] The resulting claim in the liberal narrative is that religious freedom is but a stepping-stone on the way to the full freedom of conscience against all forms of discrimination.

The religious narrative is not altogether different; rather, it views freedom of conscience as the "first freedom" and the basis for all human rights and therefore the foundation of equality before the law.[41] Hertzke asserted that "Philosophically … religious liberty is the 'first freedom' because it embodies a person's highest, especially transcendent, obligations – especially sacred duties – which flow from an authority higher than the state." He quoted Madison's 1785 "Memorial and Remonstrance against Religious Assessments": "Before any man can be considered a member of civil society, he must be considered as a subject of the Governor of the Universe." Consequently, according to Madison, "Religion, or the duty which we owe to our Creator … is precedent, both in order of time and in degree of obligation, to the claims of civil society. … In matters of religion," therefore, "no man's right is abridged by the institution of Civil Society."[42] Thus, the presupposition of the transcendent nature of religious freedom and the liberty of conscience is crucial to understanding the relevance of the First Amendment today. On the secularist account, it is a necessary but insufficient link to greater forms of freedom that supersede the merely religious. As we have seen, on the providentialist account it is the wellspring from which all other freedoms flow.[43] And "flow," which

40 Ellis Sandoz, "Religious Liberty and Religion in the American Founding Revisited," in *Religious Liberty in Western Thought*, ed. Noel B. Reynolds and W. Cole Durham, Jr. (Atlanta, GA: Scholars Press for Emory University, 1996), 267.

41 Paul Tiedemann, *Religionsfreiheit – Menschenrecht oder Toleranzgebot? Was Religion ist und warum sie rechtlichen Schutz verdient* (Heidelberg: Springer, 2012), 55.

42 Allen D. Hertzke, "Introduction: A Madisonian Framework for Applying Constitutional Principles on Religion," in *Religious Freedom in America: Constitutional Roots and Contemporary Challenges*, ed. Allen D. Hertzke (Norman, OK: Oklahoma, 2015), 9.

43 Novak, "The First of All Freedoms is Liberty of Conscience," *passim.* See also Christian Walter, "Die Religionsfreiheit als individuelles Menschenrecht und als Grundpfeiler demokratischer Verfassungsordnungen," in *Glauben in Bedrängnis. Religionsfreiheit als Menschenrecht*, ed. Volker Kauder and Hans-Gert Pöttering (Freiburg: Herder, 2017), 23–35. Religion is individual, communal, and corporate (24–25), but one challenge is that the state plays a significant role in recognizing what constitutes a religious community (26–27).

conjures images of a stream, is an apt metaphor as these two accounts draw on Enlightenment and Christian streams of thought.[44]

Under one providentialist account, Harry Stout identified a covenantal framework that informed the revolutionary Americans, that of a "sacred pretense of a covenanted people." This covenant, a promise between God and his people, was simple and compelling: "If Americans were to inherit the millennial promise, they must keep the covenant." Thus, the creation of the Constitution and the Bill of Rights did not change the course of this vector of American identity; rather, "[a]longside the celebration of religious liberty, separation of church and state, and the privatization of religious conscience lay a competing rhetorical world."[45] This competing rhetorical world is found, for example, in the biblical language of the English Puritan attorney and first governor of the Massachusetts Bay Colony, John Winthrop's well-known "city upon a hill" metaphor. He explicitly envisioned the colony as entering into a covenant: "Thus stands the cause between God and us. We are entered into covenant with him for this work."[46]

Some examinations of the First Amendment contextualize its genesis in the religious freedom discourse over millennia and trace its origins to ancient Christian influence. "It was Christian thinkers," wrote Robert Wilken, "who first set forth notions of freedom of religion in the ancient world and defended the dignity of the human person; it was Christian philosophers and theologians who developed an understanding of liberty of conscience; and it was the dualism of political and spiritual authority within the Christian tradition that provided a foundation for the idea that civil government and religious beliefs must be kept separate."[47] Sandoz wrote that the "key problem underlying the matter of religious liberty is the theoretical question of the right relationship between the temporal and spiritual realms of reality."[48] The relationship between church and state is

[44] *The Separation of Church and State: Writings on a Fundamental Freedom by America's Founders*, ed. Forrest Church (Boston: Beacon Press, 2004), x.

[45] Harry S. Stout, "Rhetoric and Reality in the Early Republic," in *Religion and American Politics. From the Colonial Period to the Present*, ed. Mark A. Noll and Luke E. Harlow (New York: Oxford University Press, 2007), 73–76.

[46] *Reading the American Past: Volume I: To 1877: Selected Historical Documents*, ed. Michael P. Johnson (Boston: Bedford/St. Martin's, 2012), 59.

[47] See Robert Louis Wilken, "The Christian Roots of Religious Freedom," in *Christianity and Freedom: Historical Perspectives*, vol. 1, ed. Timothy Samuel Shah and Allen D. Hertzke (New York: Cambridge University Press, 2016), 82–83.

[48] Sandoz, "Religious Liberty and Religion in the American Founding Revisited," 275.

seen to have its origins in the New Testament teachings of Jesus Christ and, later, St. Paul.[49] Revolutionary American Christian understandings of the Hebrew Bible are said to underlie the thinking of the constitutional framers.[50] The particular contribution of dissenting Protestants is highlighted, namely, "the right of private judgment in matters of biblical interpretation – a corollary of the Protestant doctrine of the priesthood of believers – led to a respect for individual conscience that propelled the idea of religious liberty and disestablishment in the early modern West."[51] According to Martin Fitzpatrick, some of the "central ideas relating to conscience," including the "need to give ease to tender consciences, to allow conscience to operate free of the interference of the state, and the suggestion that conscience could not be forced, could all be found in the early Christian church."[52]

John Coffey opined that although accounts of toleration in the West tend to rely on political or philosophical language, it is really biblical language that drenched the discourse, even though modern scholars have often turned a blind eye toward those parts of the key writings of John Milton, Thomas Hobbes, or John Locke, for example.[53] Biblical religious thought on this account influenced the development of American culture during the colonial era. It was a frequent source of inspiration referenced by many authors of the period, and biblical phrases and stories were a part of the warp and weft of the founding-era discourse. Dustin Gish and Daniel Klinghard averred, "[T]here is a uniquely American perspective and political thought that emerges" from the generative friction between religion and reason. This "creative tension" between secularity and providentialism

[49] Daniel N. Robinson, "Introduction," in *Religious Liberty: Essays on First Amendment Law*, ed. Daniel N. Robinson and Richard N. Williams (New York: Cambridge University Press, 2016), 2.

[50] Eran Shalev, "Evil Counselors, Corrupt Traitors, and Bad Kings: The Hebrew Bible and Political Critique in Revolutionary American and Beyond," in *Resistance to Tyrants, Obedience to God: Reason, Religion, and Republicanism at the American Founding*, ed. Dustin Gish and Daniel Klinghard (Lanham, MD: Lexington Books, 2013), 105–114.

[51] Nicholas P. Miller, *The Religious Roots of the First Amendment. Dissenting Protestants and the Separation of Church and State.* (New York: Oxford University Press, 2012), 1.

[52] Martin Fitzpatrick, "Toleration in the Enlightenment Movement," in *Toleration in Enlightenment Europe*, ed. Ole Peter Grell and Roy Porter (Cambridge: Cambridge University Press, 2000), 26.

[53] John Coffey, "Scripture and Toleration between Reformation and Enlightenment," in *Religious Tolerance in the Atlantic World. Early Modern and Contemporary Perspectives*, ed. Eliane Glaser (Houndsmill: Palgrave Macmillan, 2014), 16–18.

pervaded political thought and action of the period. It was in this environment and with these cultural, literary, philosophical, and religious influences that the framers of the Constitution developed their views and doctrines regarding the relationship between civil society and religious institutions and the roles each had to play.[54] Jefferson, to give one example, as Timothy Shah has shown, connected his ideas on the natural right of religious liberty to his reading of Tertullian.[55]

The liberal progressive reading, in contrast, is that religious liberty was not initially a true liberty, but rather there existed "a mutually accepting plurality within an overwhelmingly Protestant consensus." Early court cases still relied on biblical teachings and laws that would only allow tolerance of Christian beliefs. This led the more radical thinkers to push America to "detach morality from theology." While they recognized the role of religion in encouraging moral behavior, they saw a need for a more complete religious liberty. Jefferson was among these so-called radical thinkers and held that freedom from religion was as important as the freedom of religion. The framework for this American radicalism was stimulated by Unitarian ideas and European radical thought and on differing interpretations of the meaning of the American Revolution.[56]

These two strands of interpretation, the religious and the secular, can be detected microcosmically through examining how scholars have understood ideas of intolerance and coercion in religious matters as they relate to Samuel von Pufendorf and John Locke.[57] John Dunn maintained that the need for tolerance developed as the question arose regarding the extent to

[54] Dustin Gish and Daniel Klinghard, "The Mutual Influence of Biblical Religion and Enlightenment Reason at the American Founding," in *Resistance to Tyrants, Obedience to God: Reason, Religion, and Republicanism at the American Founding*, ed. Dustin Gish and Daniel Klinghard (Lanham, MD: Lexington Books, 2013), 12.

[55] Timothy Shah, "The Roots of Religious Freedom in Early Christian Thought," in *Christianity and Freedom: Historical Perspectives*, ed. Timothy Samuel Shah and Allen D. Hertzke (New York: Cambridge University Press, 2016), 1:57.

[56] Jonathan Israel, "The Radical Enlightenment's Critique of the American Revolution," in *Resistance to Tyrants, Obedience to God: Reason, Religion, and Republicanism at the American Founding*, ed. Dustin Gish and Daniel Klinghard (Plymouth, UK: Lexington Books, 2013), 53–54.

[57] Locke has been compared to other contemporaries, of course, and productively with William Penn and Roger Williams – all three published key treatises and had varying degrees of input into actually existing North American colonies. See Andrew R. Murphy, *Liberty, Conscience, and Toleration. The Political Thought of William Penn* (New York: Oxford University Press, 2016), chap. 8.

which Christian rulers had to enforce Christian beliefs and practice through coercion (defined narrowly as forced conversions). Religious tolerance became a political principle to block the "hallowed Augustinian judgement that forceful assertion of Christian truth towards the obtuse or recalcitrant was a clear religious duty."[58] This crisis in authority led to the possibility of heterogeneity with tolerance as the regulating principle. In America, a broader form of coercion, not necessarily restricted to forced conversions, remained a central concern of some founders, as Jefferson's "Bill for Establishing Religious Freedom" in 1779 illustrates:

> Well aware that the opinions and belief of men depend not on their own will, but follow involuntarily the evidence proposed to their minds; that Almighty God hath created the mind free, and manifested his supreme will that free it shall remain by making it altogether insusceptible of restraint; that all attempts to influence it by temporal punishments, or burthens, or by civil incapacitations, tend only to beget habits of hypocrisy and meanness, and are a departure from the plan of the holy author of our religion, who being lord both of body and mind, yet chose not to propagate it by coercions on either, as was in his Almighty power to do, but to extend it by its influence on reason alone.[59]

Pufendorf and Locke both justified intolerant "coercions," but not forced conversions, in religious matters, but from different perspectives, broadly speaking from a religious and liberal one, respectively. Coercion is neglected in the American story because many miss, as Michael McConnell asserted, that "religious coercion" is "the fundamental evil against which the [establishment] clause is directed."[60] Indeed, one element of the argument of those who supported Amendment VIII of the US Constitution, which explicitly forbade the federal government from inflicting "cruel and unusual punishments," was the fear that "Congress might repeat the abuses of 'that diabolical institution, the Inquisition.'"[61]

58 John Dunn, "The Grounds for Toleration and the Capacity to Tolerate," in *Natural Law and Toleration in the Early Enlightenment*, ed. Jon Parkin and Timothy Stanton, for The British Academy (New York: Oxford University Press, 2013), 202.

59 National Archives, Founders Online, 82. A Bill for Establishing Religious Freedom, accessed online, https://founders.archives.gov/documents/Jefferson/01-02-02-0132-0004-0082.

60 Michael McConnell, "Coercion: The Lost Element of Establishment," *William and Mary Law Review* 27 (1986): 933.

61 National Constitution Center, Amendment VIII, accessed online, https://constitutioncenter.org/interactive-constitution/amendments/amendment-viii.

Thomas Ahnert analyzed Pufendorf's views in this regard as intolerant since Pufendorf justified that princes might, for example, expel religious dissidents or refuse to grant residence to religious refugees who might have been persecuted and driven from another kingdom. Pufendorf was against forced conversions, but only because it would produce "hypocrites and secret heretics." It is, of course, coercive to force a person to leave family, friends, home, livelihood, and civic identity through expulsion, but Ahnert's fine point was that it is not quite compelling a conversion (although he conceded that it "may seem rather unconvincing and, indeed, hypocritical" to view these as distinct, but it was "not unusual in Pufendorf's own time").[62] Pufendorf preferred orthodox Christianity as the core element of a virtuous, confessional state and saw toleration as an artificial circumstance: "Toleration . . . is of the Nature of a Truce in War, which suspends the Effects of it, and the actual Hostilities, while the State and the Cause of the War do remain."[63] Ahnert can be seen to be warning against reading modern liberalism back into Pufendorf by misunderstanding his reasons for toleration and his seemingly contradictory justification of intolerance and coercive measures.

Pufendorf viewed a polity of traditional Christian homogeneity as the ideal state. He held Christianity's aims to be in harmony with the aims of a civil society and necessary for the maintenance of morality. Thus, Pufendorf did not seek to deconfessionalize society but rather to maintain the superior position of Christianity and to deploy toleration where circumstances required it. This position helps to shed light on the American Antifederalists who sought to maintain the privileges of certain Christian denominations in individual states. Andrew Murphy pointed out that this view does not support a liberal political narrative, for early modern toleration "was not a state based upon broad notions of social egalitarianism or equal respect, but a *modus vivendi* system that protected rights of Dissenting congregations to gather and worship."[64]

[62] Thomas Ahnert, "Samuel Pufendorf and Religious Intolerance in the Early Enlightenment," in *Natural Law and Toleration in the Early Enlightenment*, ed. Jon Parkin and Timothy Stanton, for The British Academy (New York: Oxford University Press, 2013), 22–24.

[63] As quoted in Ahnert, "Samuel Pufendorf and Religious Intolerance in the Early Enlightenment," 32–33.

[64] Andrew R. Murphy, *Conscience and Community: Revisiting Toleration and Religious Dissent in Early Modern England and America* (University Park, PA: The Pennsylvania State University Press, 2001), 210.

Locke on coercion is particularly intriguing as scholars have challenged the view that from his thought on toleration a straightforward genealogy can be traced to modern liberalism. Locke rebooted the toleration discussion with a new epistemology – that humans were a *tabula rasa* at birth – and with the notion that force was wrong and useless in the case of dissenters.[65] Yet, as Ian Harris pointed out, in an effort to rescue Locke from Millian, Straussian, and Rawlsian interpretations, for Locke there were cases in which intolerant coercive measures were necessary, especially as these concerned the protection of the commonwealth: "Locke infprotection end of government its duty to coerce belief and behaviour that either threatened people's lives and related concerns, or compromised its own continuance."[66] Locke considered religious toleration as appropriate only in those circumstances where belief and practice were consonant in support of the *respublica*. Harris submitted that for Locke coercion is "not about the irrationality of coercing religious tenets as such." Nevertheless, "[s]ome religious positions *were* proper objects of coercion … because they contradicted the ends which the commonwealth existed to serve."[67] Locke excluded Catholics and atheists from toleration.[68] Yet, as Mark Goldie explained, this was not about belief as such for "[a]lthough Catholics held absurd beliefs [on Locke's view], such as transubstantiation, the absurdity of another's belief is not, in itself, a ground for coercion. What rendered Catholics unable to be tolerated was that they held political and moral positions that fundamentally threatened civil society."[69] Coercion could be justified on grounds that Catholics, for example, were held to be loyal to a foreign sovereign, the Pope.[70]

The foregoing touches on how philosophical presuppositions drawn from a liberal or religious perspective are complicated to prove when it comes to the contested idea of influence. And why does this matter to discussions on the First Amendment? David Sehat captured a key aspect of

65 Martin Fitzpatrick, "Toleration in the Enlightenment Movement," 40.

66 Ian Harris, "John Locke and Natural Law: Free Worship and Toleration," in *Natural Law and Toleration in the Early Enlightenment*, ed. Jon Parkin and Timothy Stanton, for The British Academy (New York: Oxford University Press, 2013), 92–93.

67 Ibid., 94. For a comprehensive view on Locke and toleration, see John Marshall, *John Locke, Toleration and Early Enlightenment Culture: Religious Intolerance and Arguments for Religious Toleration in Early Modern and "Early Enlightenment" Europe* (New York: Cambridge University Press, 2009).

68 Mark Goldie, "Locke on Toleration," Online Library of Liberty, accessed online, https://oll.libertyfund.org/pages/locke-on-religious-toleration-by-mark-goldie.

69 Ibid. 70 Harris, "John Locke and Natural Law: Free Worship and Toleration," 94–95.

the paradoxical difference between the religious and secular worldviews succinctly and how they are *not* answered directly in the First Amendment: "What was the point of protecting religious liberty, however understood? Was it that it formed an individual and essential right . . . Or was it that such protection was a means of encouraging religious expression to shore up social morality and thereby strengthen the state?"[71] All of this stands apart from the historical-critical standards that must apply when one evaluates concepts of toleration, religious freedom, and liberty of conscience. Certainly, as Bejan reminded, these are not synonyms and not to be solely linked to disestablishment.[72] One might ask if Locke, Pufendorf, and the parade of early modern political thinkers who are called on for philosophical support of one or the other reading of the First Amendment can be genuinely helpful at all.

There seem to be practical understandings of the First Amendment that escape the need of finding deeply principled reasons for the religion clauses. John Murrin asserted that there was a "mosaic of competing denominations" in the British North American colonies and that this diversity caused a necessary toleration.[73] Certainly, the religious diversity of the thirteen states required an experiential vision to maintain some kind of unity. This was a lesson already learned in Europe, which forced the hand of even those who wished to maintain the superiority of a dominant faith in a state. So, for example, even after the Revocation of the Edict of Nantes (1685) it proved exceedingly difficult and counterproductive to enforce the explicitly anti-Protestant laws in Paris where Protestants were integrated in different layers of society. Paris was home to the embassies of other states with Protestant ambassadors and the Catholic population of Paris itself could not understand "why respected men and women, law-abiding neighbours, should be punished for their religious beliefs, however misguided these might be. Local and workplace loyalties, the interests of the community, often outweighed confessional differences and official hostility."[74] Willem Frijhoff held this to be "the ecumenicity of

[71] Sehat, *Myth of American Religious Freedom*, 49. [72] Bejan, *Mere Civility*, 169.

[73] John M. Murrin, "Religion and Politics in America from the First Settlements to the Civil War," in *Religion and American Politics. From the Colonial Period to the Present*, ed. Mark A. Noll and Luke E. Harlow (New York: Oxford University Press, 2007), 29.

[74] David Garrioch, *The Huguenots of Paris and the Coming of Religious Freedom, 1685–1789* (New York: Cambridge University Press, 2014), 263–264. Yet, Grell and Porter noted that mere diversity did not always "unequivocally clinch the case for toleration" and toleration

everyday life."[75] Goethe called this *Zusammenleben*, community life or the acceptance that comes when persons regularly interact and dwell together in civil society.[76]

Although most New England Puritans came, according to Murrin, "not to establish religious liberty, but to practice their own form of orthodoxy," New England Puritanism was offset by Chesapeake Catholicism and other religions in the Middle Atlantic colonies. Eventually, churches came to be seen as voluntary societies that did not admit of governmental coercion.[77] Sally Schwartz pointed out that the thirteen new states, in particular Pennsylvania, were a "mixed multitude" of religions and cultures, making it difficult for the imposition of any one denomination to be established.[78] This harmonized well with the remedy to factions proposed in *The Federalist*, particularly 51, as Matthew Franck judged: "The solution is to turn the country's religious diversity to account as a contributor to peace and justice among the sects, rather than a cause of conflict and injustice."[79]

Franck's view is related to the question of the role of virtue in a republic that had been posed by Montesquieu and others. The

was nowhere in the eighteenth century "unequivocally and comprehensively embraced in either theory or practice." Ole Peter Grell and Roy Porter, "Toleration in Enlightenment Europe," in *Toleration in Enlightenment Europe*, ed. Ole Peter Grell and Roy Porter (Cambridge: Cambridge University Press, 2000), 1, 4.

75 As quoted in Garrioch, *The Hugeunots of Paris and the Coming of Religious Freedom*, 264.

76 Paul E. Kerry, "*Zusammenleben:* Goethe's Ideas on Community Building: Transforming Religious Festivals in the Wake of the Napoleonic Wars," *Global Intellectual History*, 2019, accessed online, https://doi.org/10.1080/23801883.2019.1586775. For Goethe's essays on "Zusammenleben" see Paul E. Kerry, "Religion and the Late German Enlightenment: Four New Translations of Schiller and Goethe," in *New Approaches to Religion and the Enlightenment*, ed. Brett C. McInelly and Paul E. Kerry (Vancouver: Fairleigh Dickinson University Press, 2018), 336–341.

77 Ibid., 24–26. See also David Little, "Constitutional Protection of the Freedom of Conscience in Colonial America: The Rhode Island and Pennsylvania Experiments," in *Christianity and Freedom: Historical Perspectives*, vol. 1, ed. Timothy Samuel Shah and Allen D. Hertzke (New York: Cambridge University Press, 2016), 235–263.

78 Sally Schwartz, *"A Mixed Multitude:" The Struggle for Toleration in Colonial Pennsylvania* (New York: New York University Press, 1987). See also Jan Stievermann, "Defining the Limits of American Liberty: Pennsylvania's German Peace Churches during the Revolution," in *A Peculiar Mixture: German-Language Cultures and Identities in Eighteenth-Century North America*, ed. Jan Stievermann and Oliver Scheiding (University Park, PA: The Pennsylvania State University Press, 2013), 207–245.

79 Matthew J. Franck, "Christianity and Freedom in the American Founding," in *Christianity and Freedom. Historical Perspectives*, ed. Timothy Samuel Shah and Allen D. Hertzke (New York: Cambridge University Press, 2016), 1:276.

Constitution was framed with the intent to foster republican liberty, that is, to preserve the common good of people.[80] American constitutional framers learned from European experience and avoided creating a "confessional public sphere,"[81] and this had a salubrious side effect of fostering a "legitimization of diversity."[82] This diversity need not lead to disharmony if, as Nederman pointed out, the major presupposition of religious freedom is that "truth (including religious truth) cannot be grasped without respect for differing opinion and rites."[83] In addition to this enlightened reasoning, the actual pressures of a religiously diverse population were real. The well-known English Toleration Act of 1689, similar to the First Amendment, was not an intellectual tolerance, but a utilitarian one, necessitated by England's geopolitical situation.[84]

Thus, the diverse and growing population in the newly united colonies was an impetus to the religion clauses. At their inception, the Spartan language of the First Amendment was construed not as abstract principles but rather as statements of governance. At heart, Roger Scruton submitted, there was a heuristic purpose to the Establishment Clause given the varieties of Christianity and different forms of worship in the states: "To attempt to impose a single established church on all the states would have led to the breakdown of the Union."[85] John Wilson reached the same conclusion, but with a slightly different nuance: "The founding fathers' overriding concern was to neutralize religion as a factor that might jeopardize the achievement of a federal government."[86] The First Amendment's Establishment Clause rendered state coercion much less a threat. The multiplicity of religions and values made "free exercise" a practical necessity.

80 M. N. S. Sellars, *The Sacred Fire of Liberty: Republicanism, Liberalism and the Law* (New York: New York University Press, 1998), 100.

81 Joris van Eijnatten, *Liberty and Concord in the United Provinces: Religious Toleration and the Public in the Eighteenth-Century Netherlands* (Leiden: Brill, 2003), 9.

82 Willem Frijhoff, "Religious Toleration in the United Provinces: from 'Case' to 'Model,'" in *Calvinism and Religious Toleration in the Dutch Golden Age*, ed. R. Po-Chia Hsia and Henk van Nierop (New York: Cambridge University Press, 2002), 45.

83 Nederman, *Worlds of Difference*, 118.

84 Scott Sowerby, *Making Toleration: The Repealers and the Glorious Revolution* (Cambridge, MA: Harvard University Press, 2013), 251.

85 Roger Scruton, "Religious Freedom in the World Today," in *Religious Liberty: Essays in First Amendment Law*, ed. Daniel N. Robinson and Richard N. Williams (New York: Cambridge University Press, 2016), 165.

86 Wilson, "Religion, Government, and Power," 86.

Conclusion

As one can see from the foregoing, there are several philosophical presuppositions that guide arguments on religious liberty and on the First Amendment. John Murrin claimed that the "revolutionary generation never shared a single set of fundamental values." Rather, as Murrin has detailed, "[a]t least six discernible value systems competed for the allegiance of Americans: Calvinist orthodoxy, moralism, civic humanism, classical liberalism, Tom Paine radicalism, and Scottish moral sense and commonsense philosophy." In addition, there were others present in the polity, including Roman Catholics and Jews.[87] As in many accounts of the American founding, Catholics are often positioned as being merely present, a static religious Other. Yet, as Michael Breidenbach has shown, American Catholics drew fruitfully on their own tradition of conciliarism, which dovetailed with republican thought along with a distinctive nonhierarchical understanding of church and state.[88] Catholicism contained its own dynamic and fecund intellectual resources that enabled it to contribute to the early American polity – an important reminder and illustration that religion can be a creative and constructive force. Thus, there were competing value systems and not one dominant narrative in early America.

Stout called this a period of "competing" rhetoric,[89] Enlightenment and religious, which accords with notions of overlapping symbols and vocabulary of religion and politics during the 1770s. On top of this, Ruth Bloch noted that a "new dimension of American public life, neither church nor state, characterized by voluntary moral and social activism" was coming into being.[90] This more robust civic sphere meant that neither the state nor church could take up all of the social space. New meanings could imbue familiar words. Some of the framers could operate in this space and deploy language that different constituencies would understand in different ways and construct meanings that supported their views. Chris Beneke argued, for example, that the use of the word "religion," the word used in the First Amendment, had many resonances, and it was the broadest category that

87 Murrin, "Religion and Politics in America from the First Settlements to the Civil War," 30.

88 Michael Breidenbach, "Conciliarism and the American Founding," *William and Mary Quarterly* 73, no. 3 (2016): 467–500. See also Chapter 6 of this volume.

89 Stout, *Rhetoric and Reality in the Early Republic*, 76.

90 Bloch, "Religion and Ideological Change in the American Revolution," 52–53, 60.

could be found, one that was not denominational, yet also not strictly speaking Christian. Thus, many in the new republic could see themselves in the word, even if they had some fears that it might include non-Trinitarian Christians or Jews.[91] Washington's "Farewell Address" exemplifies this turn toward the inclusive vocabulary of religion:

> Of all the dispositions and habits which lead to political prosperity, religion and morality are indispensable supports. In vain would that man claim the tribute of patriotism, who should labor to subvert these great pillars of human happiness, these firmest props of the duties of men and citizens. The mere politician, equally with the pious man, ought to respect and to cherish them. A volume could not trace all their connections with private and public felicity. Let it simply be asked: Where is the security for property, for reputation, for life, if the sense of religious obligation desert the oaths which are the instruments of investigation in courts of justice? And let us with caution indulge the supposition that morality can be maintained without religion. Whatever may be conceded to the influence of refined education on minds of peculiar structure, reason and experience both forbid us to expect that national morality can prevail in exclusion of religious principle.[92]

What is perhaps most important to recognize is that there was no single understanding among the framers of the Constitution about the relationship of church and state. Their views on religious liberty were influenced by the legal, historical, political, and theological writings of the period. It is in the analysis of their differences that we begin to see where religious and secular presuppositions in scholarship derive. Vincent Phillip Muñoz maintained that in considering the differing philosophical thoughts of the founding generation we are better able to understand how constitutional principles relate to modern society.[93] They held no unified position on the relationship of the religious and the secular realms of authority: "Whatever the merits of history-based jurisprudence, the Founders' disagreement means that there is no single church–state position that can claim exclusive authority of America's founding history and that no one Founder's position can be

91 Chris Beneke, *Beyond Toleration: The Religious Origins of American Pluralism* (New York: Oxford University Press, 2006), 162–165. See also Chapter 5 of this volume.

92 Washington's Farewell Address, 1796, The Avalon Project, Yale Law School, http://avalon.law.yale.edu/18th_century/washing.asp.

93 Vincent Phillip Muñoz, "The Founding Founders' Disagreements about Church and State," in *Resistance to Tyrants, Obedience to God: Reason, Religion, and Republicanism at the American Founding*, ed. Dustin Gish and Daniel Klinghard (Plymouth, UK: Lexington Books, 2013), 180. See also Chapter 10 of this volume.

assumed to reflect the original meanings of the religion clauses."[94] Thus, according to Muñoz, a Madisonian approach would "prevent the State from engaging religion directly," a Washingtonian approach would "favour religion the most," and a Jeffersonian view would favor religion the least.[95]

The meaning of the First Amendment's religion clauses continues to be interpreted differently over time because, as Jon Meacham professed, the Constitution is a part of the political process, both as its guide and as its product. It does not in itself distinguish and interpret, but we, the people, must.[96] Marc DeGirolami also warned against an overreliance on monistic and reductive theories, of falling prey to the academic temptation of trying to fit full-bodied lived reality, with its "untidy welter of values that are encompassed in the social and legal practice of religious liberty," into flattened theory. Instead, he proposed a "gradualist and incremental" approach, "a particular cast of mind or disposition – a quality more than a theory" that eschews both "hard skepticism" and a "reliance on reductive and systematic justifications."[97] Hutson observed a similar untidiness in the immediate aftermath of accepting the Bill of Rights when the president of Congress, Elias Boudinot, recommended a day of public prayer and thanksgiving just one day after the House adopted the amendments to the Constitution. His recommendation passed overwhelmingly in both chambers of Congress. Huston saw in this not only the acceptance of religious language, but read into it Boudinot's attempt "that under the Constitution … the national government could assume, without objection, that it possessed undelegated, inherent powers to conduct religious activities, which trumped the principle of federalism as well as the language of the just minted Third Amendment, prohibiting an establishment of religion."[98]

Meyerson expressed it plainly: "Neither the Constitution nor the First Amendment created the American understanding of freedom of religion."[99] He proposed that the "framers expected that the real

94 Vincent Phillip Muñoz, *God and the Founders: Madison, Washington, and Jefferson* (New York: Cambridge University Press, 2009), 206–207.

95 Ibid., 160–163.

96 Jon Meacham, *American Gospel: God, the Founding Fathers, and the Making of a Nation* (New York: Random House, 2006), 228. Klarman emphasized the lived realty and political aspects of this process throughout his account of *The Framers' Coup*.

97 Marc O. DeGirolami, *The Tragedy of Religious Freedom* (Cambridge, MA: Harvard University Press, 2013), 2–3. See also Chapter 14 of this volume.

98 Hutson, *Church and State in America: The First Two Centuries*, 160–161.

99 Meyerson, *Endowed by our Creator,* 180.

meaning ... would be derived from the practices of those charged with fulfilling its promise."[100] What "creates" the understanding of the First Amendment's religion clauses are to some degree the presuppositions – including historical, philosophical, linguistic, and religious – we bring to the Amendment, its text, logic, structure, and plain history. All understanding is relative to presuppositions, so the more closely examined and interrogated these are in connection to professed arguments, the more clearly we will be able to understand disagreements, particularly in contested, charged, and untidy, even messy, areas of the polity such as those concerning the religion clauses of the First Amendment.

It is crucial to remember that religion has been and remains a dynamic and constructive force in the lives of citizens since the founding era. As Robert George wrote, religion is "an intrinsic and constitutive aspect of our integral flourishing as human persons, *and also* a good that plays a shaping and integrating role with respect to all other intrinsic and constitutive aspects of human well-being and fulfillment."[101] To return to DeGirolami, he would have all who walk the path of seeking to understand or adjudicate the "frequently conflicting goods of religious liberty" to be prepared to embrace "contingency and conditionality" and "proceed with caution on the delicate terrain." In a subtle turn of phrase he asked readers to bear in mind the "context independence" of "the multitude of values of religious liberty."[102] Perhaps this framing comes close to what Brad Gregory reminded readers of in *Salvation at Stake*, namely that religious faith is not merely epiphenomenal, but is about actual lived belief and transcendental obligations and duties.[103]

This may be on some views "messy," and the allure to construct artificial static boundaries in the polity and impose "clean" monolithic metaphors

100 Ibid., 240.

101 Robert P. George, "Two Concepts of Liberty ... and Conscience," in *Religious Liberty: Essays in First Amendment Law*, ed. Daniel N. Robinson and Richard N. Williams (New York: Cambridge University Press, 2016), 18.

102 DeGirolami, *The Tragedy of Religious Freedom*, 3.

103 Brad S. Gregory, *Salvation at Stake: Christian Martyrdom in Early Modern Europe* (Cambridge, MA: Harvard University Press, 2001). Thomas Carlyle explained the meaning of lived religious belief in this way, that "it is believed, that it is practically acted upon from day to day & from hour to hour; taken as a very fact, the neglect or contradiction of which will vitiate and ruin all other facts of the day and of the hour." Yale University Library Beinecke Rare Book and Manuscript Library, *Past and Present*: autograph manuscript, GEN MSS 677.

such as a "wall of separation" can be great. Nevertheless, building such walls may not only harm the individuals and communities that the First Amendment protects, but also sterilize the creative and imaginative élan that religion provides to sustain a vibrant republic and foster human flourishing.[104]

[104] "The unopposable freedom to imagine – and to believe in the prospects made evident by the imagination – would seem to be the first freedom rendering liberty itself intelligible." Daniel N. Robinson, "Religious Liberty: the First Freedom?" in *Religious Liberty: Essays in First Amendment Law*, ed. Daniel N. Robinson and Richard N. Williams (New York: Cambridge University Press, 2016), 35.

10 Two Concepts of Religious Liberty

The Natural Rights and Moral Autonomy Approaches to the Free Exercise of Religion

Vincent Phillip Muñoz

Despite the consternation over the Supreme Court's recent *Burwell* v. *Hobby Lobby Stores* ruling, the right to religious liberty is generally understood in contemporary American political and legal thought to mean that individuals and institutions deserve exemptions (or, at least, strong consideration for exemptions) from generally applicable laws that burden sincerely held religious beliefs and exercises.[1] Take the dispute surrounding the Affordable Care Act's "contraception mandate." Hobby Lobby advocates contend that the Obama administration advanced a "crabbed view" of religious freedom because it failed to extend exemptions to all those who sought them.[2] They did not claim that the administration rejected religious exemptions altogether, because Obamacare's HHS preventive care regulations did include some exemptions for some religious groups; critics simply wanted more, which they eventually received under the Trump administration.[3] The disagreement, in other words, was over how extensively exemptions should be granted, not whether religious liberty requires them.

This broad consensus reflects the last fifty years of judicial and scholarly thought about religious free exercise. While the exemption approach has not always been embraced by the Supreme Court,[4] since *Sherbert* v. *Verner*

Vincent Phillip Muñoz, "Two Concepts of Religious Liberty: The Natural Rights and Moral Autonomy Approaches to the Free Exercise of Religion," *American Political Science Review* 110, no. 2 (May 2016): 369–381, reproduced with permission.

1 *Burwell* v. *Hobby Lobby Stores*, 573 U.S. ___ (2014).

2 Mark Rienzi, "Religious Liberty 9, President Obama 0," *National Catholic Register*, January 12, 2012, www.ncregister.com/daily-news/religious-liberty-9-president-obama-0/.

3 Religious Exemptions and Accommodations for Coverage of Certain Preventive Services under the Affordable Care Act, 83 Fed. Reg. 57,536, 57,536 (November 15, 2018) ("Final Religious Exemption"); Moral Exemptions and Accommodations for Coverage of Certain Preventive Services under the Affordable Care Act, 83 Fed. Reg. 57,592 (November 15, 2018) ("Final Moral Exemption").

4 See, notably, *Employment Division* v. *Smith*, 494 U.S. 872 (1990).

in 1963 it reflects the dominant understanding of how religious free exercise is protected.[5] Moreover, it is commonly thought that exemptionism, as I shall call it, is supported both by the American founders' philosophy of religious freedom and by modern interpretations of freedom of conscience. That view, I shall argue, is partially mistaken.

The first section of this chapter recounts the founders' understanding of the inalienable natural right to religious liberty and their attendant social contract constitutionalism. The second describes modern free exercise exemptionism, first as it developed in constitutional practice and then its scholarly defenses that appeal to notions of autonomy. The third compares the founders' natural rights free exercise constitutionalism with modern autonomy exemptionism. I reject Michael McConnell's influential interpretation that the founders' political philosophy counsels constitutional exemptionism and, instead, argue that the opposite is true: The founders' jurisdictional understanding of religious liberty denies the idea of a constitutional right to religious exemptions. Constitutional exemptionism, I conclude, is more properly understood and defended by appeals to secular notions of autonomy.

America's constitutional tradition offers two distinct conceptions of religious liberty: the founders' inalienable natural right of free exercise and modern moral autonomy exemptionism. The approaches are grounded upon divergent philosophical understandings of human freedom and competing notions about freedom's place in the moral order of the universe. They present different views of what religious liberty is, how it is threatened, and, accordingly, how it is best protected. This chapter does not advocate natural rights free exercise or moral autonomy exemptionism. Rather, it aims, first, to identify and distinguish the two leading accounts of and approaches to religious free exercise in our constitutional tradition; second, to challenge the widely accepted conclusion that the founders' political philosophy espouses constitutional exemptionism; and, third, to clarify how our modern approach expands the protection of religious liberty in some ways but limits it in others.

[5] *Sherbert* v. *Verner*, 374 U.S. 398 (1963). Andrew Koppelman notes that "hardly anyone doubts" it is appropriate for some branch of government to possess authority to extend religious exemptions. The arguments, he continues, "are about who ought to draw those lines." *Defending Religious Neutrality* (Cambridge, MA: Harvard University Press, 2013), 11.

The Founders' Natural Rights Constitutionalism of Religious Liberty

The American Founders' Philosophy of an Inalienable Natural Right to Religious Liberty

The American founders generally held that religious free exercise is a natural right that belongs to all individuals. Article II of Delaware's 1776 Declaration of Rights, for example, states "that all men have a natural and unalienable right to worship Almighty God according to the dictates of their own consciences and understandings."[6] The same or similar natural rights language can be found in several of the early state constitutions – including Pennsylvania (1776), North Carolina (1776), and New Hampshire (1784) – and other significant founding-era documents.[7] George Washington's 1790 letter to the Hebrew Congregation at Newport, Rhode Island, captures the founders' common understanding. "All possess alike liberty of conscience and immunities of citizenship," Washington writes. He then continues:

> It is now no more that toleration is spoken of as if it were the indulgence of one class of people that another enjoyed the exercise of their inherent natural rights, for, happily, the Government of the United States, which gives to bigotry no sanction, to persecution no assistance, requires only that they who live under its protection should demean themselves as good citizens in giving it on all occasions their effectual support.[8]

By "inherent," Washington means that the right of religious liberty inheres in the individual absent of, and prior to, any state recognition or state action. As a natural right, religious liberty is not understood to be created by the state or by the mutual consent of citizens. Rather, the founders locate religious liberty in man's created nature and his pre-political obligations to his creator.

[6] Philip B. Kurland and Ralph Lerner, eds., *The Founders' Constitution* (Indianapolis, IN: Liberty Fund, 2001 [1987]), 5:70.

[7] Benjamin Perley Poore, ed., *The Federal and State Constitutions, Colonial Charters, and Other Organic Laws of the United States* (Washington, DC: Government Printing Office, 1878), 1541, 1410, and 1281.

[8] *George Washington: A Collection*, ed. William B. Allen (Indianapolis, IN: Liberty Fund, 1988), 548.

Many founding-era documents acknowledge this understanding (without further explanation), as is the case in Washington's letter. Some set forth religious liberty in terms of individual rights, such as the aforementioned Delaware declaration; others include a statement of man's duties to the divine. Article XVI of Virginia's 1776 Declaration of Rights, for example, declares

> [t]hat religion, or the duty which we owe to our Creator, and the manner of discharging it, can be directed only by reason and conviction, not by force of violence; and therefore all men are equally entitled to the free exercise of religion, according to the dictates of conscience.[9]

Maryland's 1776 Declaration of Rights also derives religious freedom from the "duty of every man to worship God in such manner as he thinks most acceptable to him."[10] For the founders, the natural right to religious liberty and the duty to worship God are different sides of the same coin. Because an individual has a duty to worship God with conviction, he has a right among men to do so according to conscience.

This reciprocal relationship between duties to the creator and the moral norms arising from the created order of nature on the one hand and rights on the other can be seen in the most philosophical of the founding-era documents. In his Virginia Statute for Religious Freedom, Thomas Jefferson starts with the observation that "Almighty God hath created the mind free."[11] He then proceeds, following Locke, to derive religious freedom from the nature of the mind's operations, operations that reflect God's "supreme will" and "Almighty power."[12] James Madison adopts that argument and adds another. In his Memorial and Remonstrance against Religious Assessments, he presents two reasons why men have an "unalienable" right to exercise religion according to conviction and conscience. First, following Jefferson, "the opinions of men, depending only on the evidence contemplated by their own minds, cannot follow the dictates of other men," and second, "it is the duty of every man to render to the Creator such homage and only such as he believes to be acceptable to him."[13]

[9] Kurland and Lerner, eds., *Founders' Constitution,* 5:3. [10] Ibid., 5:70.

[11] *Thomas Jefferson: Writings*, ed. Merrill D. Peterson (New York: The Library of America, 1984), 346.

[12] Sanford Kessler, "Locke's Influence on Jefferson's 'Bill for Establishing Religious Freedom,'" *Journal of Church and State* 25, no. 2 (1983): 231–252.

[13] James Madison, *The Mind of the Founder: Sources of the Political Thought of James Madison*, ed. Marvin Meyers (Hanover, NH, and London, UK: Brandeis University Press, 1981), 7.

Because we have a divinely imposed duty to worship God according to conviction and conscience, Madison concludes, we have an inalienable right among our fellow men to do so.

According to the Memorial, religious exercise can be directed only by "reason and conviction," a presumption also shared by Jefferson's Statute. Madison does not attempt to demonstrate the truth of this understanding of religion, which has led some commentators to conclude he offers a distinctly Protestant account.[14] This may be true, and Madison may have thought it sufficient to rely on the religious beliefs of his immediate audience, but without too much trouble, we can reconstruct the philosophical steps that also might have led him to his understanding of religion.

Both Jefferson's and Madison's arguments recognize the freedom of the human mind, by which they mean our capacities of reason and free will. Men's capacities for reason and freedom allow us to be self-directed moral agents, not simply unreflective slaves of our instincts or passions. As Jefferson says in his Virginia Statute, even God, "lord both of body and mind," chose not to coerce man but rather to teach him by and through reason.[15] Our ability to apprehend moral principles (including those that are divinely revealed) and our freedom to choose to follow them makes possible a distinctly human manner of worship. Man can worship God freely, according to his conviction and conscience. This capacity to worship freely – which, of course, includes the capacity to choose not to worship – suggests that if men do have the duty to worship God, that duty can only be discharged through worship animated by conscientious conviction. Worship short of this, whether coerced or somehow otherwise prompted, would fail to reflect the full capacities of man's created nature. It therefore would not be fitting homage to a god that created mankind with freedom and reason. A god that creates a man capable of the exercise of freedom governed by reason would seem to settle for nothing less than freely given worship that reflects conscientious convictions. As Madison declares in one of his official presidential proclamations calling for a day of "public humiliation and prayer":

[14] Lance Banning, *The Sacred Fire of Liberty: James Madison and the Founding of the Federal Republic* (Ithaca, NY: Cornell University Press, 1995), 436 n. 68; Gary Rosen, *American Compact: James Madison and the Problem of Founding* (Lawrence, KS: University Press of Kansas, 1999), 23. Cf. Vincent Phillip Muñoz, *God and the Founders: Madison, Washington, and Jefferson* (New York: Cambridge University Press, 2009), 29–32.

[15] *Jefferson,* ed. Peterson, 346.

If the public homage of a people can ever be worthy [of] the favorable regard of the Holy and Omniscient Being to whom it is addressed, it must be that, in which those who join in it are guided only by their free choice, by the impulse of their hearts and the dictates of their consciences.

Only religion "freed from all coercive edicts" and "free-will offerings of humble supplication, thanksgiving and praise," Madison continues, "can be acceptable to Him whom no hypocrisy can deceive, and no forced sacrifices propitiate."[16]

Jefferson's and Madison's argument for religious freedom assumes a creator God and the normative status of nature.[17] Given these assumptions – that God created nature (including human nature) and that this created nature establishes moral guidelines for human behavior – they philosophically deduce that religious duties can only be fulfilled according to conviction and conscience. And from that conclusion, they reason that all men have a natural right to religious freedom.

The Founders' Social Compact Constitutionalism: Limited State Jurisdiction with Discretionary Exemptions

Whether or not all the framers self-consciously adopted the natural theology just set forth, their natural rights philosophy clearly structured their constitutional design. The framers held that individuals do not alienate their natural right to religious liberty when they join the social compact and, therefore, the natural right to religious liberty is not part of the state's jurisdiction.

The clearest expression of the framers' social compact political philosophy can be seen in founding-era state declarations of rights. After recognizing "[t]hat all men have a natural and unalienable right to worship Almighty God according to the dictates of their own consciences and understandings," the declarations of rights of Delaware (1776), Pennsylvania (1776), and Vermont (1777) immediately announce that "no authority can or ought to be vested in, or assumed by any power

[16] *The Papers of James Madison: Presidential Series*, ed. J. C. A. Stagg, et al. (Charlottesville, VA: University of Virginia Press, 1984), 6:458–459.

[17] For a parallel account of the role of divine creation in Locke's thought, see Adam Seagrave, *The Foundations of Natural Morality: On the Compatibility of Natural Rights and the Natural Law* (Chicago, IL: University of Chicago Press, 2014), 24–55.

whatever, that shall in any case interfere with, or in any manner control the right of conscience in the free exercise of religious worship."[18] Religious free exercise possesses a particular status in the framers' social compact constitutionalism. Although individuals themselves are parties to and members of the social contract, their religious exercises as such are not.

The framers approached religious liberty in terms of sovereignty and jurisdiction. Since individuals retain exclusive sovereignty over that which belongs to the natural right of religious liberty, the state lacks jurisdiction over such matters. Leaving aside for now the difficult question of what exactly is covered within the inalienable natural right to religious free exercise, the framers held that whatever belongs exclusively to that right remains beyond the government's direct prohibition and regulation.

Understanding the framers' social compact theory reveals a crucial mistake made by Professor Michael McConnell, the former Tenth Circuit Court of Appeals judge who is widely regarded as one of the nation's leading church–state scholars. McConnell has argued that constitutional exemptionism follows from the founders' natural rights philosophy of religious liberty. His account has been extraordinarily influential, in no small part because of its scholarly prominence (lengthy articles in the *Harvard Law Review* and *University of Chicago Law Review*[19]), its timing (surrounding the Supreme Court's controversial free exercise clause decision in *Employment Division* v. *Smith* (1990)), and its impact (forming the basis of Justice Sandra Day O'Connor's dissenting opinion in *City of Boerne* v. *Flores* (1997), which sought to reverse *Smith*).

McConnell offers a wide range of historical evidence to support his exemptionist account of the free exercise clause, but, for our purposes, his interpretation of the founders' natural rights philosophy is most relevant. McConnell begins by linking the idea of the natural right of religious freedom to the original meaning of the free exercise clause. "[T]here is reason to believe that this inalienable right understanding [of the founders]," he writes, "is the genuine theory of the Religion Clauses of the First Amendment." He then summarizes that teaching as follows:

[18] Kurland and Lerner, eds., *Founders' Constitution,* 5:70, 5:71, and 5:75.

[19] Michael McConnell, "The Origins and Historical Understanding of Free Exercise of Religion," *Harvard Law Review* 103, no. 7 (1990): 1409–1517; Michael McConnell, "Free Exercise Revisionism and the *Smith* Decision," *University of Chicago Law Review* 57, no. 4 (1990): 1109–1153.

> The reason the rights of conscience were deemed inalienable is that they represented *duties to God* as opposed to *privileges of the individual.* Thus the Free Exercise Clause is not an expression of the will of the sovereign but a declaration that the right to practice religion is jurisdictionally beyond the scope of civil authority. This, then, *is* an anarchic idea: that duties to God, perceived in the conscience of the individual, are superior to the law of the land.[20]

It is "anarchic," McConnell says, because the inalienable natural right of religious liberty means the civil law is subordinate to the perceived religious obligations of the individual rights-bearer. To fulfill his duties to God, the individual has a right not to obey civil laws he conscientiously believes to be incompatible with his religious precepts.

McConnell more fully explicates his "anarchic" interpretation of the inalienable right of religious liberty through an analysis of Madison's Memorial and Remonstrance. Quoting the Memorial, McConnell writes,

> Madison claimed that this duty to the Creator is "precedent both in order of time and degree of obligation to the claims of Civil Society," and "therefore that in matters of Religion, no man's right is abridged by the institution of Civil Society." This striking passage illuminates the radical foundations of Madison's writings on religious liberty. While it does not prove that Madison supported free exercise exemptions, it suggests an approach toward religious liberty consonant with them. If the scope of religious liberty is defined by religious duty (man must render to God "such homage . . . as he believes to be acceptable to him"), and if the claims of civil society are subordinate to the claims of religious freedom, it would seem to follow that the dictates of religious faith must take precedence over the laws of the state, even if they are secular and generally applicable.[21]

McConnell constitutionalizes (and thereby tames) the founders' "anarchic" understanding by transforming Madison's natural right to disregard laws that impede a believer's perceived religious obligations into a constitutional right to a presumed exemption along the lines of the Supreme Court's Sherbert test.

If correct, McConnell's interpretation of Madison would offer a powerful natural rights and originalist argument for constitutional exemptionism. But McConnell, I believe, misinterprets the founders' understanding of the natural right to religious liberty – a misreading that, in turn, leads him to

[20] McConnell, "Free Exercise Revisionism and the *Smith* Decision," 1151 (emphasis in the original).

[21] McConnell, "Origins and Historical Understanding," 1453.

misinterpret the founders' social compact teaching regarding religious free exercise.

To see McConnell's mistake, it will be helpful to review the two analytically distinct stages of the framers' social compact political philosophy. Madison set forth a clear statement on the subject in his letter to N. P. Trist:

> Although the old idea of a compact between the Government and the people be justly exploded, the idea of a compact among those who are parties to a Government is a fundamental principle of free Government.
>
> The original compact is the one implied or presumed, but nowhere reduced to writing, by which a people agree to form one society. The next is a compact, here [in the United States] for the first time reduced to writing, by which the people in their social state agree to a Government over them.[22]

At stage one, individuals initially agree to leave the state of nature and to form a political society. Madison, following Locke, calls this the "original compact."[23] The original compact is among all the individuals who are members to it, not between the government and the people. At stage two, in Madison's words, "the people in their social state agree to a Government over them." The second stage of social compact theory involves the adoption of a form of government and constitutional rules. A political society specifies how the power of the community will be arranged, divided, exercised, etc. According to Locke and Madison, unanimity establishes (and then simple majority rule governs) the initial political society; constitutions, however, can legitimately empower one person, a few, many, or some combination thereof.[24]

With these two stages in mind – we can call them the "original compact" and the "constitutional compact" – let us return to Madison's Memorial and Remonstrance. The first article pertains to the formation of the "original compact." Madison holds that men have a natural right to religious free exercise, a right that follows from the nature of their religious obligations to the Creator. Those duties, he says, are "precedent . . . in order of time . . . to the claims of Civil Society" because they exist in the state of nature, i.e.,

22 *Letters and Other Writings of James Madison* (Philadelphia, PA: J. B. Lippincott & Co, 1865), 63.

23 Rosen, *American Compact,* 3, 6, 10, 88.

24 James Madison, *The Writings of James Madison*, ed. Gaillard Hunt (New York, NY: G.P. Putnam's Sons, 1900), 9:570–571. See also John Locke, *Two Treatises on Government*, ed. Peter Laslett (Cambridge, MA: Cambridge University Press, 2010), 331–332, 354.

before the "original compact" is formed. Madison also says these religious duties are "precedent ... in degree of obligation, to the claims of Civil Society." The importance of this becomes apparent in his subsequent reasoning. When men enter into civil society and form the "original compact," Madison says, they "reserve their allegiance to the Universal Sovereign." Here Madison qualifies the initial political society's jurisdiction, clarifying that, when individuals leave the state of nature, they do not include within the "original compact" their natural right pertaining to the discharge of religious duties.[25] This is why Madison emphasizes that the right of religious exercise is an "unalienable" natural right. Authority over religious exercises is not conferred to civil society and, therefore, Madison concludes, "[r]eligion is wholly exempt from its cognizance."[26]

If authority over religious free exercise is not part of the original compact, it cannot be within the authority of any subsequent government that the political society forms at the second stage of the social compact, what we have labeled the "constitutional compact." Madison begins Article 2 of the Memorial and Remonstrance accordingly:

> Because if Religion be exempt from the authority of the Society at large, still less can it be subject to that of the Legislative Body. The latter are but the creatures and viceregents of the former.[27]

Since the jurisdiction of the constitutional compact (including any governing bodies created by it) is derived from the original compact, what the latter lacks, the former cannot acquire.

Let us now return to McConnell's "anarchic" reading of the Memorial. McConnell interprets Madison's assertion that religious obligations are "precedent ... in degree of obligation to the Claims of Civil Society" to mean that citizens have a right not to obey civil laws they conscientiously believe to be incompatible with their religious duties. Such a position supports constitutional exemptionism, McConnell says, because "if the claims of civil society are subordinate to the claims of religious freedom,

[25] Elisha Williams, the influential mid-eighteenth-century preacher, made the exact same point using similar language in his 1744 essay, "A Seasonable Plea for the Liberty of Conscience and the Right of Private Judgment in Matters of Religion," in *Political Sermons of the American Founding Era, 1730–1805*, ed. Ellis Sandoz (Indianapolis, IN: Liberty Fund, 1990), 61. See also the religious liberty articles Isaac Backus proposed in 1779 for the Massachusetts state declaration of rights, in Edwin S. Gaustad, *A Documentary History of Religion in America to the Civil War*, 2nd Edition (Grand Rapids, MI: Eerdmans, 1993), 268.

[26] Madison, in Meyers, *Mind of the Founder*, 7. [27] Ibid.

it would seem to follow that the dictates of religious faith must take precedence over the laws of the state, even if they are secular and generally applicable."[28]

McConnell mistakenly conflates Madison's jurisdictional limitations on the original compact with legal rules for the constitutional compact. When Madison says that members of civil society must reserve their "allegiance to the Universal Sovereign," he does not suggest, as McConnell contends, that citizens should receive exemptions from civil laws. Rather, Madison means that authority over religious exercise as such does not become part of the original compact. Religious obligations remain outside the social compact and, therefore, beyond the jurisdiction of any constitutional authority created to govern it. McConnell's failure to distinguish the two stages of social compact theory leads him to assume that Madison is discussing stage-two constitutional rules about the operations of government power, when Madison is actually demarcating stage-one jurisdictional authority. The Memorial does not teach that individuals have a right to exemptions from burdensome civil laws; rather, it concludes that civil authorities lack sovereignty over the natural right of religious free exercise.

This lack of sovereignty means that legislators lack authority to prohibit that which belongs to the natural right of religious liberty. It also means that judges – who, too, are agents of the state – lack authority to balance elements of the natural right to religious liberty against other state interests. The act of balancing itself assumes jurisdiction: The "balancer" places the competing free exercise right and state interests on a scale. Even if the scale is tilted toward religious freedom (as McConnell would have it), the act of weighing assumes an authority that the founders deny. In this context, Madison's use of the word "cognizance" is telling. A state that must remain non-cognizant of the natural right of religious liberty cannot make it the subject of legislative or judicial balancing. As we shall discuss momentarily, this does not mean that all laws that incidentally burden religious interests are unconstitutional but, rather, that the state may never legitimately exercise direct sovereignty over elements of the natural right to religious liberty.

This jurisdictional approach corresponds to the language of the First Amendment's free exercise clause. The text imposes an absolute ban on Congress; it can "make *no law . . . prohibiting* the free exercise" of religion.

[28] McConnell, "Origins and Historical Understanding," 1453.

Unlike the Fourth Amendment's protection against "unreasonable searches and seizures," or the Fifth Amendment's protections against deprivations of life, liberty, and property "without due process of law," the First Amendment affords no constitutional space for "reasonable" prohibitions of religious free exercise if "due process" is afforded or, to use modern terminology, "compelling state interests" are pursued. The categorical character of the free exercise clause comports with the idea that the state lacks jurisdiction over the non-alienated right to religious liberty and, therefore, that the state can never directly prohibit any element of it.

In this sense, the framers understood and protected the natural right of religious liberty differently from most other natural rights. Take property, for example. The framers held that it is reasonable for individuals to exchange their natural right to property for a civil right to property, even with the knowledge that the state may tax and even take their property under some circumstances. As Article III of the 1784 New Hampshire Declaration of Rights states:

> III. When men enter into a state of society, they surrender up some of their natural rights to that society, in order to insure the protection of others; and, without such an equivalent, the surrender is void.[29]

Individuals alienate their natural right to property in order to better secure their rights, including property rights, because without government most rights remain insecure. But the framers held that individuals make no such exchange regarding their natural right to religious liberty. Article IV of the 1784 New Hampshire Declaration of Rights continues:

> IV. Among the natural rights, some are in their very nature unalienable, because no equivalent can be given or received for them. Of this kind are the RIGHTS OF CONSCIENCE.[30]

The framers held that it would never be reasonable for an individual to alienate sovereignty over his or her religious practices because the nature of religious worship itself, unlike the use of property, requires the

[29] Poore, ed., *Federal and State Constitutions*, 1280.

[30] Ibid., 1280–1281. Such reasoning was not limited to arguments articulated at the state level. See, for example, the Anti-Federalist Brutus, [pseud.]: "But it is not necessary . . . that individuals should relinquish all their natural rights. Some are such a nature that they cannot be surrendered. Of this kind are the rights of conscience, the right of enjoying and defending life, etc." Quoted in Kurland and Lerner, eds., *Founders' Constitution*, 451.

individual to act according to conscience and conviction. "But our rulers can have authority over such natural rights only as we have submitted to them," Jefferson writes. "The rights of conscience we never submitted, we could not submit. We are answerable for them to our God."[31]

The framers' jurisdictional approach to religious free exercise also includes a second distinction McConnell fails to make. While the framers held that all elements of the natural right to religious liberty remain beyond the jurisdiction of the state, they did not hold that all matters pertaining to religion are part of the natural right to religious liberty. The framers distinguished aspects of the natural rights of religious liberty from what we might call religious "interests."

Clear evidence of this distinction can be seen in the drafting of what became the Second Amendment. During the constitutional ratification debates, three states (VA, NC, RI) proposed an amendment that would protect religious objectors from military service. This led Congressman Madison to propose the following:

> The right of the people to keep and bear arms shall not be infringed; a well armed and well regulated militia being the best security of a free country: but no person religiously scrupulous of bearing arms shall be compelled to render military service in person.[32]

On August 17, 1789, the House considered an amended version of Madison's initial proposal. Egbert Benson from New York moved to have the "religiously scrupulous" exemption removed because,

> No man can claim this indulgence of right. It may be a religious persuasion, but it is no natural right, and therefore ought to be left to the discretion of the Government.[33]

Three days later, the House resumed consideration of the exemption provision. Thomas Scott from Pennsylvania repeated Benson's point, contending that the matter was "a legislative right altogether."[34] The congressional record is not sufficiently detailed to confirm whether Benson's and Scott's specific concern led to the ultimate defeat of the militia conscientious exemption proposal, but it does reveal that the drafters of the Bill of

[31] *Jefferson*, ed. Peterson, 285.

[32] *Annals of the Congress of the United States, 1789–1834* (Washington, DC: Gales and Seaton, 1834–1856), 1:451.

[33] Ibid., 1:780. [34] Ibid., 1:796.

Rights were cognizant of – and that some sought to craft amendments in light of – the distinction between the natural right of religious liberty and matters of "religious persuasion."

The distinction between the natural right of religious liberty on the one hand and religious interests subject to state jurisdiction on the other also explains the seemingly curious fact that the First Congress considered a religious exemption in the context of drafting the Second Amendment, not the First. At no time did the advocates for the militia exemption contend that it was a part of (or required by) the text protecting religious free exercise. Moreover, the case for adding the conscientious objector exemption was pressed *after* the House had already adopted text that would become the First Amendment. Immediately prior to the August 20 debate on the militia exemption for the religiously scrupulous, the House had approved text protecting "free exercise" and the "rights of conscience."[35] If "free exercise" was understood to include religious exemptions, the subsequent debate would have been superfluous; a constitutional right for religious exemption already would have been secured.[36] The debate continued because the drafters of the Bill of Rights understood exemptions and matters of religious free exercise to be analytically distinct legal subjects.

The distinction between free exercise and exemptions evinced in the First Congress's drafting record reflects the framers' two-track constitutional design to protect religious freedom. Boundaries on governmental sovereignty, demarcated by provisions in state declarations of rights and the federal First Amendment, were written to protect the inalienable natural right of religious freedom. This aspect of religious freedom remained, as it were, beyond the Constitution and thus out of reach of governmental power. Other facets of religious freedom, including conscientious exemptions from military service, were to be protected through the democratic political institutions established under the Constitution.[37] Representation,

[35] Ibid.

[36] Vincent Phillip Muñoz, "The Original Meaning of the Free Exercise Clause: The Evidence from the First Congress," *Harvard Journal of Law and Public Policy* 31, no. 3 (2008): 1117–1118; Ellis West, "The Right to Religion-Based Exemptions in Early America: The Case of Conscientious Objectors to Conscription," *Journal of Law and Religion* 10, no. 2 (1993–1994): 397. Cf. McConnell, "Origins and Historical Understanding," 1501.

[37] For a history of legislative and judicial actions taken (and not taken) to protect religious interests before, during, and immediately after the founding era, see McConnell, "Origins and Historical Understanding" 1503–1511; West, "Right to Religious Exemptions"; and

checks and balances, the separation of powers, federalism, an independent judiciary, and all the other features of the American constitutional system – including, of course, the multiplicity of interests and sects encouraged by the sheer size and entrepreneurial character of the American nation – would help to protect religious interests and, perhaps, afford religious individuals exemptions from burdensome laws. This two-track constitutional framework was designed, first and foremost, to recognize and protect the underlying non-alienated natural right to religious freedom, a right the founders held to limit the state's sovereignty and jurisdiction.

Before proceeding to a discussion of modern autonomy exemptionism, three further observations about the founders' constitutionalism of religious liberty are warranted. I have tried to sketch the framers' broadly shared understanding; the further one digs for details, the more one finds disagreement. To take the most prominent example, I have left aside the question of what exactly belongs to the natural right to religious free exercise. I have done so, in part, because I am aware of no place where the founders defined with precision the exact contours of the right. My analysis of the founding-era state constitutions points to a general consensus that acts of worship as such made up the core of the non-alienated natural right to religious liberty, but whether the state could legitimately impose religious taxes (and thereby extend its jurisdiction over the funding of religion) or use religious affiliation to limit political rights (such as office holding) appears to have remained a matter of dispute.[38]

Second and relatedly, given its "non-balanceable" character, the scope of the natural right of religious exercise can be expected to be deep but not necessarily wide. Several of the founding-era state constitutions indicate this textually. Article II of the 1780 Massachusetts Declaration of Rights, for example, states:

> No subject shall be hurt, molested, or restrained, in his person, liberty, or estate, for worshipping God in the manner and season most agreeable to the dictates of his own conscience, or for his religious profession or sentiments, provided he doth not disturb the public peace or obstruct others in their religious worship.[39]

Gerard V. Bradley, "Beguiled: Free Exercise Exemptionism and the Siren Song of Liberalism," *Hofstra Law Review* 20 (1991): 272–306.

[38] Vincent Phillip Muñoz, "Church and State in the Founding-Era States," *American Political Thought* 4 (2015): 1–38.

[39] Poore, ed., *Federal and State Constitutions,* 957.

The founders understood the natural right of religious liberty to have natural limits – namely, at the points where legitimate state jurisdiction begins, i.e., protecting public peace and the rights of others.[40]

Third, given its grounding in the nature of man, the framers did not expect the natural right to religious liberty to evolve, grow, or change over time. The framers had a relatively fixed conception of human nature and, along with it, a stable notion of the rights that belonged to it.[41]

Modern Moral Autonomy Exemptionism

To understand the founders, we began with their idea of the natural right of religious freedom and proceeded to the constitutional practice that followed. The modern approach is easier to understand in reverse: A new jurisprudence of religious liberty emerged in the middle of the twentieth century, which was then defended by theoretical justifications. To be sure, the new jurisprudence reflected earlier philosophical criticism of natural rights and social compact theory; but modern religious freedom, much like the philosophy that animates it, can be understood as an evolving process of practical adaptation to meet changing social conditions.

The Judicial Establishment of Moral Autonomy Exemptionism

The Supreme Court first adopted exemptionism in *Sherbert* v. *Verner* (1963).[42] The case involved a provision of the South Carolina Unemployment Compensation Act that denied benefits to claimants who failed, without good cause, to accept available employment. The state's unemployment commission found that Adell Sherbert had refused available work and, accordingly, rejected her application for benefits. Sherbert

[40] Philip Hamburger, "A Constitutional Right of Religious Exemptions: An Historical Perspective," *George Washington Law Review* 60 (1992): 918–921; Philip Hamburger, "Natural Rights, Natural Law, and American Constitutions," *Yale Law Journal* 102 (1993): 922–930; Philip Hamburger, "More is Less," *Virginia Law Review* 90 (2004): 835–892. Cf. McConnell, "Origins and Historical Understanding," 1461–1466.

[41] Harvey Mansfield, Jr., "Responsibility versus Self-Expression," in *Old Rights and New*, ed. Robert A. Licht (Washington, DC: The AEI Press, 1993), 97.

[42] Earlier calls for "accommodation" under the free exercise clause can be found in the joint dissenting opinion of Justices Black, Douglas, and Murphy in *Jones* v. *Opelika*, 316 U.S. 584 (1942), and Justice Brennan's opinion in *Braunfeld* v. *Brown*, 366 U.S. 599 (1961).

contended that the state's denial of benefits violated her rights of religious freedom. Every job available to her required Saturday hours; as a Seventh-Day Adventist, she testified, accepting any of them would have required her to violate the Sabbath. The South Carolina Supreme Court was unsympathetic, upholding the denial of benefits while finding that the challenged statute "places no restriction upon the appellant's freedom of religion nor does it in any way prevent her in the exercise of her right and freedom to observe her religious beliefs in accordance with the dictates of her conscience."[43]

The Supreme Court disagreed. In an opinion by Justice William Brennan, the Court declared that South Carolina's ruling

> forces her [Sherbert] to choose between following the precepts of her religion and forfeiting benefits, on the one hand, and abandoning one of the precepts of her religion in order to accept work, on the other hand. Government imposition of such a choice puts the same kind of burden upon the free exercise of religion as would a fine imposed against appellant for her Saturday worship.[44]

The decisive facts driving Justice Brennan's opinion were, first, that Sherbert was engaged with a state-sponsored program and, second, she was left worse off than she otherwise would have been on account of her religious practice. The Court adopted the doctrine – now known as the Sherbert test – that, absent a properly pursued compelling state interest, the free exercise clause prohibits the state from infringing individuals' religious exercises, even indirectly.

By focusing on the effects of a law as experienced by the particular religious individual, Justice Brennan and the Court implicitly rejected the framers' natural rights jurisdictional framework. That approach focuses on the law itself (not its effects) and asks whether the state has improperly exercised jurisdiction over the natural right of religious liberty. The absence of legal cognizance of religion, presumably, would have been prima facie evidence that the state had not entered the religious space jurisdictionally denied to it. Justice Potter Stewart noted that the South Carolina statute had not targeted religion and that South Carolina's stated reasons for denying Sherbert benefits did not include a religious rationale. "We do not have before us," he wrote in his opinion,

[43] *Sherbert* v. *Verner*, 374 U.S. at 401. [44] Ibid. at 404.

> a situation where a State provides unemployment compensation generally, and singles out for disqualification only those persons who are unavailable for work on religious grounds. This is not, in short, a scheme which operates so as to discriminate against religion as such.[45]

Nonetheless, Stewart concurred with the Court that acts of omission could be as constitutionally sinful as those of commission.

Sherbert's focus on how state action actually affects religious individuals expanded the range of behaviors protected by the free exercise clause. Not just elements of the natural right of religious liberty but any religious activity that a sincere religious individual perceives to have been burdened became eligible for constitutional protection. Even if, as discussed in the first section, the framers left unclear the precise boundaries of the natural right of religious free exercise, those lines were marked by reference to the state's legitimate jurisdiction; legislation that was unquestionably within the state's jurisdiction presumptively did not violate the natural right to religious liberty. In *Sherbert*, the Court severed the connection between free exercise and fixed jurisdictional boundaries.

A second expansion soon followed. To extend exemptions to religious individuals, the Court first has to identify those individuals as "religious." Ms. Sherbert's religious status was not at issue in her case, but the issue of who, exactly, counts as "religious" would quickly reach the Supreme Court.

That dispute arose under *United States* v. *Seeger* (1965), a case involving conscientious objector status from military service. After World War II, federal law exempted from combat service individuals whose conscientious opposition to war was based on "religious training and belief," a phrase that Congress defined as "an individual's belief in a relation to a Supreme Being involving duties superior to those arising from any human relation, but does not include essentially political, sociological, or philosophical views or a merely personal moral code."[46] Under that definition, Daniel Seeger's claim for conscientious objector status was denied, because he had been unwilling to confirm that his beliefs were grounded in belief in a "Supreme Being."

The Court resolved the issue by creatively crafting the following "Supreme Being test":

> The test of belief "in a relation to a Supreme Being" is whether a given belief that is sincere and meaningful occupies a place in the life of its possessor parallel to

[45] Ibid. at 416. [46] Universal Military Training and Service Act, 50a U.S.C. §§ 451–473.

> that filled by the orthodox belief in God of one who clearly qualifies for the exemption. Where such beliefs have parallel positions in the lives of their respective holders we cannot say that one is "in a relation to a Supreme Being" and the other is not.[47]

What was important, according to the Court, was whether Seeger's beliefs were sincerely held and, "*in his own scheme of things*, religious."[48]

Seeger was litigated primarily under a federal statute and not on First Amendment grounds, but the underlying extension of who is eligible for religious liberty protection would become, as we shall discuss below, a central feature of the philosophy of modern autonomy exemptionism. In awarding Seeger conscientious objector status, the Court severed any necessary connection between "religion" and the divine. Those who believed in God were still identified as "religious," but so, too, were those who, in their "own scheme of things," possessed deep, life-shaping convictions not attached to the divine. Under *Seeger*, the authority animating legal respect for conscientious convictions was no longer a transcendent deity but, rather, the individual himself and his or her ability to generate sincere and authentic meaning.

If any questions remained about whether religious liberty protections required belief in a transcendent god, the Court put them to rest five years later. In *Welsh* v. *United States* (1970), the Court awarded conscientious objector status (which, according to statute, was still based on "religious training and belief") to an individual who could not affirm belief in God and denied that his opposition to war was based on religious training. Young men, the Court said, might not be "fully aware of the broad scope of the word 'religious'" as set forth by the Court. "A registrant's statement that his beliefs are nonreligious," the Court explained, "is a highly unreliable guide for those charged with administering the exemption."[49]

The expansion of what practices could be protected, along with the extension of who was eligible for protection, led the Court to devise a framework to limit the availability of "religious" exemptions. The most important constraint was set forth in *Sherbert* when Justice Brennan noted that the imposition of an indirect burden on religious exercise "may be

[47] *United States* v. *Seeger*, 380 U.S. 163, 165–166 (1965).
[48] Ibid. at 185 (emphasis in the original).
[49] *Welsh* v. *United States*, 398 U.S. 333, 314 (1970).

justified by a 'compelling state interest in the regulation of a subject within the State's constitutional power to regulate.'"[50] Chief Justice Burger, in his subsequent implementation of the approach, used the image of balancing. Governmental interests, he said, would "overbalance" religious liberty when the state adopted "the least restrictive means of achieving some compelling state interest."[51]

The balancing approach to free exercise rights was concomitant with the Court's move to expand religious liberty protections. After *Sherbert*, activities within the state's traditional jurisdiction were eligible for free exercise clause protections. To prevent exemptions from lifting all legal limits on religious individuals, a mechanism to impose state authority was required. In a sense, the modern Supreme Court did no more than develop legal language to adjudicate the same matter the founders addressed when considering Second Amendment exemptions for conscientious objectors. The founders recognized that, for what we deemed "religious interests" in the first section, "discretion" was needed to allow some state authority to extend some exemptions to some religious believers from some legitimate laws. "Compelling state interest" analysis (sometimes accompanied with a "least restrictive means" requirement)[52] formalized that discretionary process, allowing courts to affirm the state's legitimate jurisdiction and "compelling" interests while, at the same time, affording religious individuals consideration for protection from some burdensome laws.

The Supreme Court was not exactly following the founders, however. Most obviously, the framers explicitly had left discretionary authority over matters of "religious persuasion" in the hands of the legislature. *Sherbert* and the cases that followed transferred that authority to the judiciary: What is religion, who is "religious," and what constitutes an overriding "compelling state interest," ultimately, would be decided by courts. Exemptionism, moreover, rejected the framers' two-track constitutional design by shifting nearly all religious liberty claims into a single balancing

[50] *Sherbert* v. *Verner*, 374 U.S. at 403, quoting *NAACP* v. *Button*, 371 U.S. 415, 448 (1963).

[51] *Wisconsin* v. *Yoder*, 406 U.S. 205, 215 (1971); *Thomas* v. *Review Board of the Indiana Employment Security Division*, 450 U.S. 707, 718 (1981).

[52] For a discussion of the role of the "least restrictive means" prong in the Court's free exercise clause jurisprudence, see Jillian T. Weiss, "The First Amendment Right to Free Exercise of Religion, Nondiscrimination Statutes Based on Sexual Orientation and Gender Identity, and the Free Exercise Claims of Non-Church-Related Employees," *Florida Coastal Law Review* 12 (2010): 15–46.

framework. This move quietly eviscerated the framers' categorical, jurisdictional protection for the nonbelief elements of the natural right of religious liberty.

The case most clearly marking this shift, *Church of Lukumi Babalu Aye* v. *City of Hialeah* (1993), involved a Florida city's attempt to outlaw the religious practice of animal sacrifice by members of the Santeria religion. The Supreme Court found that the City of Hialeah had drafted ordinances that "by their own terms target . . . religious exercises" and "had as their object the suppression of religion."[53] A unanimous Court, accordingly, struck down the ordinances. It did so, however, only after conducting "compelling state interest" and "narrowly tailored" means analysis. As stated by the Court:

> If the object of a law is to infringe upon or restrict practices because of their religious motivation, the law is not neutral; and it is invalid unless it is justified by a compelling interest and is narrowly tailored to advance that interest.[54]

Under this doctrinal standard, a law that prohibits religious exercises as such could be constitutional if it was designed to narrowly pursue a compelling state interest. Justice Anthony Kennedy, the author of the Court's opinion in *Lukumi Babalu Aye*, implicitly acknowledged this when he recognized that only "a law targeting religious *beliefs* as such is never permissible."[55]

The distinction between beliefs and actions in the Court's religious liberty jurisprudence goes back to at least *Reynolds* v. *United States* (1879),[56] but it is not one easily supported by the First Amendment's text, which protects religious "exercises" from prohibition, or the founding-era state constitutions, which uniformly use the language of "worship," not "beliefs." Even if the framers did not mark with precision all that belongs to the natural right of religious liberty, religious worship as such seems to have been part of it and, therefore, remains outside of the state's jurisdiction (along with religious beliefs). *Lukumi Babalu Aye* confirmed that, under the exemptionist balancing approach, the state can directly prohibit specific forms of worship, or the worship of specific religious sects, if it has a compelling reason to do so.

[53] *Church of the Lukumi Babalu Aye* v. *City of Hialeah*, 508 U.S. 520, 542 (1993).
[54] Ibid. at 533. [55] Ibid. at 533 (emphasis added).
[56] *Reynolds* v. *United States*, 98 U.S. 145 (1879).

The Philosophy of Free Exercise Exemptionism

As noted earlier, the practice of exemptionism came before its philosophical defense and explication. Justice Brennan's opinion proceeded as if it were self-evident and uncontroversial that denying Adell Sherbert unemployment benefits was the same as fining her for keeping the Sabbath. His *Sherbert* opinion does not attempt to justify exemptionism philosophically, nor does it attempt to explain its consistency with (or even opposition to) the founders' natural rights constitutionalism. Extended legal and philosophical defenses, however, would soon follow.

With the prominent exception of Michael McConnell, most contemporary philosophical defenses of exemptionism center their arguments on a modern notion of human autonomy.[57] Jocelyn Maclure and Charles Taylor offer a particularly cogent example of the approach in their recent book *Secularism and Freedom of Conscience*.[58] Maclure and Taylor propose "freedom of conscience" and "equality of respect" as the two principal ends of a well-functioning liberal democracy. By "freedom of conscience," they mean an individual should be allowed "to choose and realize his or her own conception of what a successful life is."[59] Martha Nussbaum, to take another leading defender of autonomy free exercise, reaches a similar conclusion by grounding the special status of what she calls "liberty of conscience" in "the faculty with which each person searches for the ultimate meaning of life." This faculty itself, she says, "is of intrinsic worth and

[57] This is not to say that every defense of exemptionism is philosophical or that all philosophical defenses focus on autonomy. For examples of the latter, see John H. Garvey, "An Anti-Liberal Argument for Religious Freedom," *Journal of Contemporary Legal Issues*, 7 (1996): 275–291; Christopher Wolfe, "Free Exercise, Religious Conscience, and the Common Good," in *Challenges to Religious Liberty in the Twenty-First Century*, ed. Gerard V. Bradley (New York: Cambridge University Press, 2012) 93–110; and Christopher Tollefsen, "Conscience, Religion, and the State," in *Challenges to Religious Liberty in the Twenty-First Century*, ed. Gerard V. Bradley (New York: Cambridge University Press, 2012), 111–135. Nonphilosophical defenses of exemptionism tend to appeal to history. For example, see Justice O'Connor's dissenting opinion in *City of Boerne* (1997); Douglas Laycock "Formal, Substantive, and Disaggregated Neutrality Toward Religion," *DePaul Law Review* 39 (1990): 993–1022; Douglas Laycock, "Continuity and Change in the Threat of Religious Liberty: The Reformation Era and the Late Twentieth Century," *Minnesota Law Review* 80 (1996): 1047–1102; and Michael McConnell, "Accommodation of Religion: An Update and a Response to the Critics," *George Washington Law Review* 60 (1992): 685–742.

[58] Jocelyn Maclure and Charles Taylor, *Secularism and Freedom of Conscience* (Cambridge, MA: Harvard University Press, 2011).

[59] Ibid., 71.

value, and is worthy of respect whether the person is using it well or badly."[60] While not all scholars adopt Nussbaum's particular emphasis on human cognition,[61] her focus on the individual's personal quest to identify and assert meaning is typical. William Galston nicely captures the essence of autonomy free exercise in his notion of "expressive liberty": the freedom for individuals to live their lives in ways that express their deepest beliefs about what gives meaning or value to life.[62] All these accounts have an underlying normative conception of human liberty that revolves around the individual developing his or her own deep, meaning-giving convictions.

To allow the individual to live according to those convictions, all these scholars contend that exemptions are needed.[63] Maclure and Taylor emphasize that formal equality before the law offers insufficient protection in practice, because norms and laws of general applicability inevitably impose unfair burdens on some individuals' conscientiously held beliefs.[64] Nussbaum emphasizes the plight of numerical minorities. In a democratic polity, "differential favorable treatment" is required to ensure substantive equality among all individuals deserving "equal respect."[65] For autonomy to be realized in practice, individuals need sufficient space to follow their self-constructed moral identities. Exemptions with due limits are the

[60] Martha Nussbaum, *Liberty of Conscience: In Defense of America's Tradition of Religious Equality* (New York: Basic Books, 2008), 168–169.

[61] Cf. Maclure and Taylor, *Secularism,* 96.

[62] William Galston, *Liberal Pluralism: The Implications of Value Pluralism for Political Theory and Practice* (New York: Cambridge University Press, 2002), 28.

[63] Not all scholars concerned with liberty of conscience, of course, champion exemptions. Brian Leiter, for example, agrees with the proposition that nonreligious claims of conscience ought to be treated equally to religious claims but denies that most claims of conscience ought to receive exemptions from generally applicable laws, in *Why Tolerate Religion?* (Princeton, NJ: Princeton University Press, 2013). John Locke, of course, also opposed exemptions in *A Letter Concerning Toleration,* ed. James H. Tully, (Indianapolis, IN: Hackett, 1983), 48–49.

[64] Maclure and Taylor, *Secularism,* 66. This point and the one that follows are made by nearly every defender of exemptionism. For a particularly cogent example, see Michael McConnell, "Free Exercise Revisionism and the *Smith* Decision," *University of Chicago Law Review* 57, no. 4 (1990): 1133–1136. For a systematic analysis of formal neutrality and its perceived shortcomings, see Douglas Laycock, "Formal, Substantive, and Disaggregated Neutrality," 993–1022 and Douglas Laycock, ""Substantive Neutrality Revisited," *West Virginia Law Review* 110 (2007): 51–88. Micah Schwartzman helpfully points out that appeals to equality alone are not sufficient to require exemptions, in "What If Religion Is Not Special?", *University of Chicago Law Review* 79 (2012): 1401.

[65] Nussbaum, *Liberty of Conscience,* 21–25.

constitutional means prescribed to maximize autonomous freedom in a diverse and pluralistic political community.

The autonomous notion of human freedom is joined by what Nussbaum and Maclure and Taylor label "equality of respect."[66] All individuals, Maclure and Taylor state, possess equal moral value and dignity. Their notion of freedom of conscience, accordingly, extends to all individuals, who, they say, should have equal opportunity to choose and realize their deep convictions about the meaning of life.[67] Nussbaum advances the same idea through what she labels "the equality principle." When added to the autonomous notion of conscience, "equality of respect" and "the equality principle" require that the privileges of conscience be extended beyond religiously informed consciences alone.[68] "Within the context of contemporary societies marked by moral and religious diversity," Maclure and Taylor write, "it is not religious convictions in themselves that must enjoy a special status but, rather, all core beliefs that allow individuals to structure their moral identity."[69] They emphasize that, to the extent that religious convictions receive special protections, it is because of "the role they play in people's moral lives rather than from an assessment of their intrinsic validity."[70] Nussbaum's account sharpens the focus of this expansive notion of conscience by calling for accommodations for all convictions surrounding "what one might call ultimate questions, questions of life and death, the meaning of life, life's ethical foundations, and so forth."[71] Under both accounts, religious individuals can receive protections from burdensome laws, but those protections are not limited to religious individuals alone. The autonomous conscience is protected, not religion as such.

The priority of the individual's conscience apart from any necessary religious conviction is reinforced by another foundational commitment of the autonomy school: the idea that the state should be neutral regarding competing conceptions of the good. Maclure and Taylor make the point repeatedly on the first pages of chapter 1 of their volume.[72] "In a society that is both egalitarian and diverse," they write, "the state must be separate from the churches, and political power must be neutral toward religions."

[66] Ibid., 19; Maclure and Taylor, *Secularism*, 20. [67] Maclure and Taylor, *Secularism*, 71.
[68] Nussbaum, *Liberty of Conscience*, 22. [69] Maclure and Taylor, *Secularism*, 89.
[70] Ibid., 81. [71] Nussbaum, *Liberty of Conscience*, 68.
[72] Maclure and Taylor, *Secularism*, 10–11.

The state must also "treat equally citizens who act on religious beliefs and those who do not; it must, in other words, be neutral in relation to the different worldviews and conceptions of the good – secular, spiritual, and religious – with which citizens identify." As Micah Schwartzman bluntly concludes, treating atheists or agnostics differently than religious citizens "has absurd consequences" insofar as these secular doctrines "cannot be distinguished on normative, epistemic, or psychological grounds from their religious counterparts."[73] For autonomy scholars, state neutrality accommodates the reality that moral and religious diversity cannot be overcome, what John Rawls calls "the fact of reasonable pluralism."[74] The limits of human rationality and its inability to decisively adjudicate competing conceptions of the good make state neutrality a necessary requirement of any well-functioning modern liberal state. State neutrality fosters the commitment to individual autonomy, which, when coupled with the practice of exemptions for all core beliefs, complements and reinforces the norm of neutrality.

Natural Rights Free Exercise and Moral Autonomy Free Exercise Compared

Due to the influence of Michael McConnell, exemptionism is generally thought to be compatible with, if not dictated by, the church–state philosophy of the founding. But if, as I have argued, McConnell misreads the founders, at least two competing accounts of religious free exercise exist within the American constitutional tradition. This section attempts to further clarify those traditions by explaining the philosophical and practical differences between the framers' inalienable natural rights approach and modern autonomy exemptionism.

Different Understandings of the Nature of Freedom and the Meaning of Religious Liberty

The most significant philosophical difference between the two lies in their conceptions of human freedom and the place of that freedom in the moral

[73] Schwartzman, "What If Religion Is Not Special?", 1416–1421.

[74] John Rawls, *Political Liberalism* (New York: Columbia University Press, 1993).

order of the universe. The framers derive the idea of a natural right to religious liberty from duties to God and the moral fabric of human nature, which itself is understood to be created by God. Their conception of religious freedom is oriented toward the divine; individuals require freedom so they can worship according to conscience. This does not imply that the founders thought political authorities could legitimately suppress religious freedom if individuals blasphemed or committed idolatry – they understood this freedom itself to be a gift from God and an inalienable right. But it does suggest that, though establishing religious liberty is a great political accomplishment, it is not the final end or even an end in and of itself. The *telos* of the founders' understanding of religious freedom is the proper worship of God according to conviction and conscience. The right of religious liberty establishes the political means to facilitate that end.

The autonomy defense of exemptionism brings the *telos* of religious freedom down to man. The individual's autonomy becomes an end in itself. The free human being is the individual who finds his own meaning and then lives accordingly. Being sincere and authentic to oneself and one's own "core" principles is the foundation and overarching purpose of liberty of conscience. The Supreme Court articulated this conception of freedom with brilliant clarity in *Planned Parenthood* v. *Casey*:

> At the heart of liberty is the right to define one's own concept of existence, of meaning, of the universe, and of the mystery of human life.[75]

Casey, of course, adjudicated a different legal matter, but the Court's plurality reached its decision by employing the same understanding of freedom as embraced by autonomy exemptionism.

The autonomy notion of freedom also expands the meaning of religious liberty. While both approaches embrace the dignity of the individual, the founders' account of religious freedom is tethered to the worship of God. The natural right to religious freedom, as discussed, pertains to matters concerned exclusively with the divine. The concept of autonomy encompasses traditional notions of religion but is not limited to them. Nussbaum and Maclure and Taylor all draw our attention to this by including the word *conscience* in the titles of their books. The focus on *conscience* (as opposed to *religion*) conveys the idea that the object of protection is the individual's

[75] *Planned Parenthood* v. *Casey*. 505 U.S. 833, 851 (1992).

ability to search for ultimate meaning, a quest that may or may not involve worship, religion, or a sense of the divine. Liberty of conscience includes, in Maclure and Taylor's words, "different philosophical conceptions that stand as the secular equivalents of religions."[76]

Different Understandings of How Religious Freedom Is Threatened and, Therefore, Protected

These different conceptions of freedom lead to different conceptions of how religious liberty is best protected. In the framers' social contract constitutionalism, the state is viewed primarily as a potential threat to religious freedom. In particular, regarding the elements of the natural right of religious free exercise, the state is generally thought to be incapable of enabling or increasing freedom. To protect liberty, then, requires strict limitations.

It lies beyond the scope of this chapter to specify all the elements of the natural right of religious freedom in the framers' understanding; but, in general, it would seem that the regulation of religious exercise as such would remain beyond the state's competence. Perhaps an obvious violation would be the enforced prescription or prohibition of religious practice as such: say, a law that explicitly prohibited or required a particular religious observance on a day of the week that was legally specified as the Sabbath. If South Carolina had imposed a fine on Adell Sherbert specifically for attending religious services on Saturday, for example, it would seem to have violated her natural right of religious liberty. Another violation might have occurred if the state had specified the articles of faith necessary for Sherbert's church to be legally incorporated or if it required her pastor to obtain a state-issued preaching license.

In the framers' natural rights understanding, that which lies beyond the jurisdiction of the state also cannot legitimately be balanced against competing state interests, even if they are compelling and properly pursued. Regarding *Lukumi Babalu Aye*, once it was determined that the city had attempted to prohibit Santeria religious exercises as such, the ordinances in question would have been struck down. No compelling state interest or narrowly tailored means analysis would have been required. To further the preaching license example: say South Carolina had experienced

[76] Maclure and Taylor, *Secularism*, 13.

an epidemic of scam artists masquerading as prophets. At the same time, the state found itself in the midst of a dramatic influx of out-of-state, religiously intolerant sects advocating hatred toward any number of minority groups. Because of earlier efforts to increase respect for diversity, those new religious groups were deemed to be the only anti-diversity groups operating in the state. In the interests of preventing fraud and safeguarding cultural diversity, South Carolina establishes a licensing requirement for any minister who preaches in a house of worship (defined according to IRS tax exemption regulations). Those interests might very well be compelling, and, given the circumstances, the licensing requirement might even be the least restrictive means to prevent "religious" fraud and to safeguard the diverse populations targeted by "hate preaching." Under the jurisdictional approach to religious liberty, however, it would seem that such considerations would not and could not factor into judicial decision-making. Natural rights constitutionalism would ask only if the state exercised jurisdiction over elements of the natural right to religious liberty. If it had – and, presumably, requiring preclearance from the state to preach in a house of worship would be an example of an impermissible exercise – the statute would be struck down, regardless of any extenuating compelling state interests.

Modern exemptionism does not deny that state action can threaten religious freedom, but it recognizes that affirmative state action can help secure it and that rights of autonomy must be balanced against other competing rights and interests. Autonomous free exercise imposes limits on some (primarily legislative and executive) exercises of state power by empowering other (primarily judicial) state officials to neutralize and offset burdensome state actions. Instead of strict enforcement of the state's jurisdictional limits, exemptionism calls for superintendence of the exercise of all state power. Freedom is achieved not simply through the absence of state power but by a judicious and dynamic oversight of state action with regard to its impact on conscience. This more expansive role is called for because, it is held, laws and regulations that do not target religion as such can still deny liberty of conscience in practice.

Exemptionism, for perhaps obvious reasons, goes hand in hand with the modern administrative state. In the name of protecting individuals in advanced, culturally diverse, free-market economies, the modern state regulates much of what, at one time, was considered private. The more areas of life the state regulates, the more it will affect religious individuals and institutions. Take, for example, the regulation of employment. State licensing requirements imposed on pharmacists may require activities that some professionals find conscientiously objectionable. Employment nondiscrimination laws may intrude on the autonomy of churches and their ability to define their internal governing structures. In the view of autonomy free exercise, this expansion of what has become public and subject to state regulation necessitates a concomitant expansion of protections for matters of conscience.

Expanding the rights of conscience to include protection from the actual impact of law on religious belief necessitates a balancing approach to that right. Furthermore, as the notion of "religious" belief is expanded to include all beliefs involving "the ultimate meaning of life," potential conflicts between generally applicable laws and individuals' consciences rapidly multiply. Almost any law or regulation can impose burdens on the "core" beliefs of some individual, which means that every law can potentially be subject to liberty-of-conscience litigation. As a practical matter, some form of rights-balancing is necessary, given the complexities and demands of modern political life. Since not every burden on conscience can be relieved, the balancing approach allows exemptionism to maximize the liberty of conscience while recognizing the necessities of the modern state.

Conclusion: Trading the Depth of Natural Rights for the Breadth of Modern Autonomy

When the Supreme Court introduced the modern era of exemptionism, it offered no defense for its break with the founders' natural rights constitutionalism, probably because it was concerned neither with the founders nor the idea of natural rights. While *Sherbert*'s precedential value has been curtailed by *Employment Division* v. *Smith* (1990),[77] the exemptionist approach it adopted still governs some Free Exercise case law, including the issues litigated in *Lukumi Babalu Aye* (1993)[78] and *Hosanna-Tabor* (2012),[79] and it guides a fair amount of federal and state legislation. Among scholars, moreover, exemptionism remains the dominant

[77] *Employment Division, Department of Human Resources of Oregon* v. *Smith*, 494 U.S. 872 (1990).

[78] *Church of the Lukumi Babalu Aye* v. *City of Hialeah*, 508 U.S. 520 (1993).

[79] *Hosanna-Tabor Evangelical Lutheran Church and School* v. *Equal Employment Opportunity Commission*, 565 U.S. 171 (2012).

understanding of what religious free exercise demands in a pluralistic liberal democracy.

At least prior to the Supreme Court's *Hobby Lobby Stores* (2014) ruling, exemptions for conscience remained one of the few bipartisan issues across politics, law, and academic scholarship. An astonishing coalition was formed to pass the exemptionist Religious Freedom Restoration Act (1993), with support ranging from the American Civil Liberties Union to the Traditional Values Coalition. What was done politically has been reinforced intellectually by an equally diverse range of scholars, from philosophical champions of liberal autonomy to the nation's leading conservative originalist church–state scholar. The modern coalition in favor of exemptionism would seem to be a model of Rawlsian overlapping consensus.

Exemptionism can be said to facilitate social harmony in other ways, as well. Much modern civil rights legislation probably would not have been possible (or, at least, would have been much more difficult to pass) without religious exemptions. Title VII of the 1964 Civil Rights Act, for example, exempts religious employers from the statute's prohibition against workplace discrimination on account of religion. Without the religious exemption, the provision certainly would have faced opposition from religious institutions focused on protecting their religious character and mission. The same is probably true of contemporary legislation to protect homosexual rights. Though same-sex marriage remains divisive, one can imagine the social rancor that would ensue if traditionally oriented churches were forced to ordain homosexual unions. Religious exemptions from conducting homosexual marriages in houses of worship no doubt lessen at least some opposition to the extension of marriage equality. The expansion of the rights of conscience to include the "core beliefs" concerning questions of "ultimate meaning," moreover, furthers the notion of state neutrality between religion and nonreligion and, in the lexicon of its proponents, "equal respect" for all citizens.

The corollary of "equal respect" is the absence and abandonment of the idea of special protection for religion more narrowly or traditionally designated. The argument for natural rights free exercise is founded on, and limited to, the individual's duties to God. It extends only to those beliefs and actions that flow from those duties, not a more generalized notion of "ultimate meaning." In the natural rights tradition, religion is different because the character of authentic human worship itself makes it impossible and irrational for individuals to cede authority over their natural right of religious liberty: Forced worship is not worship at all. That right, as discussed, is narrow; it excludes from state jurisdiction only elements of the natural right of religious liberty. It does not offer constitutional protection from incidental burdens on religious practice but, rather, subjects what we have called religious "interests" to the democratic political process. Autonomy free exercise offers far more constitutional breadth, protecting against direct and indirect burdens on religious exercise, as well as covering conscientious actors in addition to traditional religious believers. This breadth is exchanged for depth, as a properly pursued compelling interest justifies state burdens on religion, whether direct or indirect.

In exchanging breadth for depth, modern free exercise exemptionism transforms the idea of limited government. Natural rights free exercise maintains that there are some interests the state can never pursue, no matter how "compelling." It holds that the individual retains a realm of unbreachable religious liberty that the state may never trespass. Modern exemptionism erases this categorical understanding of limits. The state is not limited in its reach, only in how it proceeds.

Whether this constitutes a worthy trade lies beyond the scope of this chapter. That question cannot be addressed, however, without clarity about the different approaches to free exercise within America's constitutional tradition. This chapter has attempted to shed light on those differences and thereby facilitate further reflection and choice about the most prudent and most proper way to protect our "first freedom."

11 The Economic Origins of Religious Liberty

Anthony Gill

Introduction

Looking across the vast expanse of human history, true religious liberty has been a rare occurrence. Historically, most societies maintained regimes that heavily favored a single religious confession (e.g., pre-1900 Latin America), allowed for some pluralism among a narrowly defined denominational range (e.g., the Roman Empire), or tried to stamp out religion entirely (e.g., the Soviet Union). Today, in the early twenty-first century, the picture looks much better. Various empirical studies have shown movement toward greater freedom of conscience around the world, especially compared to a century or more in the past.[1] Problems still remain, and backtracking has occurred, but the religious rights of majorities and minorities have moved in positive conjunction with the expansion of other political and economic freedoms across nations.

The general progress toward greater religious freedom offers up a social science mystery: Why would any political authority grant greater religious freedoms to their citizens when the typical state of the world has been to have a tightly controlled religious landscape? This question tracks well with the broader study of political liberalization over the past two centuries, which is not surprising given that basic civil liberties surrounding rights of conscience are hallmarks, if not cornerstones, of democracy. Using insights from the general study of political economy, this chapter will present a case that the origins of religious liberty in the modern world originate in the incentives of political actors facing a changing economic environment. Rulers who wish to retain power, increase tax revenue, and promote economic growth in countries or regions with increasing religious pluralism will warm to the idea of deregulating the spiritual marketplace

[1] Jonathan Fox, *A World Survey of Religion and the State* (Cambridge, MA: Cambridge University Press, 2008).

or, in more common parlance, increase the rights to believe and worship as one chooses.

Religious Liberty Understood from an Economic Perspective

If religious beliefs and institutions are powerful motivators of human action, why would rulers ever willingly yield control over the religious landscape? This is the essential question surrounding the origins of religious freedom. If ruling a nation is essentially about exercising political authority over constituents, allowing individuals to have greater autonomy in their personal and collective (congregational) lives represents a diminution of power, something mainstream political economists see as inimical to the interests of government officials. Indeed, relinquishing any sort of power to citizens tends to be unusual in human history and the key puzzle to be explained.[2]

Several scholars have argued that religious liberty is an inherently good thing[3] and that if enough world leaders came to that realization – by direct diplomacy,[4] the diffusion of ideas across borders,[5] or observing the success of other nations[6] – religious freedom would expand globally. Ideas do matter, as many scholars have argued. The rise of religious freedom in the United States, the place where it was first *constitutionally* codified,[7] has

[2] Cf. Douglass C. North, John Joseph Wallis, and Barry R. Weingast, *Violence and Social Orders: A Conceptual Framework for Interpreting Recorded Human History* (Cambridge, MA: Cambridge University Press, 2009).

[3] Timothy S. Shah, *Religious Freedom: Why Now? Defending an Embattled Human Right* (Princeton, NJ: Witherspoon Institute, 2012).

[4] Thomas F. Farr, *World of Faith and Freedom: Why International Religious Liberty Is Vital to American National Security* (Oxford: Oxford University Press, 2008).

[5] Daniel Philpott, *Revolutions in Sovereignty: How Ideas Shaped Modern International Relations* (Princeton, NJ: Princeton University Press, 2001).

[6] John M. Owen, *The Clash of Ideas in World Politics: Transnational Networks, States, and Regime Change 1510–2010* (Princeton, NJ: Princeton University Press, 2010).

[7] Technically speaking, religious liberty, or at least toleration, was codified into law in Europe prior to the ratification of the US Constitution. The prime examples are the Edict of Nantes (1598), giving French Protestants some guarantees of safety in limited geographical areas, and the Act of Toleration (1688), providing limited freedom of worship to non-Anglican Protestants. Both of these documents were rather limited in scope and were not part of official constitutions, which neither country had at the time. Moreover, while the Act of Toleration eventually expanded to promote greater liberties for religious minorities in Britain, the Edict of Nantes lasted only until 1685, when it was revoked and initiated

been viewed within the intellectual lineage of the Protestant Reformation and Enlightenment, with John Locke taking center stage in influence over James Madison. As Cole Durham argues, the diffusion of ideas was the primary motivating factor for the rise of religious freedom in America:

> Locke revolutionized politics by suggesting how religious (and by extension, political) freedom could sow political order from religious seeds that had always been assumed to be the ultimate source of anarchy. *The Lockean insight thus opened up the possibility of seeing the political cosmos from a new perspective.* By placing respect for freedom at the center of the constellation of values, and by recognizing that respect for freedom and dignity of individuals is itself a moral end religious truth of the highest order, this revolution transformed the grounds for legitimizing and stabilizing political communities . . . This idea was initially theoretical, but it became a central aspect of the "lively experiment" with religious freedom in the United States.[8]

Legal scholars Arlin Adams and Charles Emmerich saw this ideational influence much more broadly, dating back to the early Reformation thinkers and Catholics.

> The American Founders were influenced greatly by theologians and philosophers who reflected on the religious conflicts that occurred in the wake of the Reformation. From Martin Luther and John Calvin they inherited the view that God had instituted "two kingdoms" – a heavenly one where the church exercised spiritual authority and an earthly one where the civil magistrates exercised temporal authority. A liberal Roman Catholic tradition represented by Erasmus and Thomas More also exerted influence in the colonies, inspiring the Lords Baltimore and the Carrolls of Maryland to rethink the proper relationship between church and state.[9]

Similar arguments that emphasized the causal role of ideas have been common in the literature on the origins of religious liberty given that

a new wave of persecution against French Protestants. As such, the First Amendment of the US Constitution represents the first broad-based declaration of religious freedom in modern times.

[8] W. Cole Durham Jr., "Perspectives on Religious Liberty: A Comparative Framework," in *Religious Human Rights in Global Perspective: Legal Perspectives*, ed. Johan D. van der Vyver and John Witte Jr. (The Hague: Martinus Nijhoff Publishers, 1997), 8–9 (emphasis added).

[9] Arlin M. Adams and Charles J. Emmerich, *A Nation Dedicated to Religious Liberty: The Constitutional Heritage of the Religion Clauses* (Philadelphia: University of Pennsylvania Press, 1990), 3.

religion is viewed almost primarily from an ideational and behavioral standpoint in the social sciences.[10]

But ideas don't exist in a vacuum, and history is replete with "good ideas" that never are codified into law. Moreover, ideas are often contested and the ones that become actual policy do not necessarily win because their partisans scored more points in forensic debates. To wit, none other than Patrick Henry, the stalwart patriot of political liberty in the eighteenth century and a super rhetorician, faced off against James Madison in debating religious freedom clauses in the Virginia constitution. The key issue was whether or not to disestablish the Anglican Church, to which Henry objected and Madison favored. Madison was not known for his public speaking skills, and the forces for and against religious liberty appeared evenly divided across the colony, yet it was Madison's side that eventually prevailed.[11] With a population split evenly on an issue, there is no guarantee that the "best idea" will win. This prompts the social scientist to look for additional causes that might give rise to why one side prevailed.

Enter political economy, a science that emphasizes the role of interest-based incentives. For the political economist, human decisions and actions are more often attributed to the shifting costs and benefits than to changes in one's preferences or intellectual perspective. This does not mean that tastes and viewpoints are immutable; an inventory of our own lives over time would easily convince us otherwise. We do change our minds, though perhaps not as much as we may think. Political economists, as a matter of methodological choice, assume a stability of preferences over a narrowly defined period of time (usually the period of decision-making) and then search for changes in relative prices that would incentivize individuals to choose differently. Changes in relative prices could come from alterations

[10] Cf. J. Christopher Soper, Kevin R. den Dulk, and Stephen V. Monsma, *The Challenge of Pluralism: Church and State in Six Democracies* (Lanham, MD: Rowman and Littlefield, 2017); Ahmet T. Kuru, *Secularism and State Policies toward Religion: The United States, France, and Turkey* (Cambridge, MA: Cambridge University Press, 2009); Marc M. Arkin, "The Intractable Principle: David Hume, James Madison, Religion and the Tenth Federalist," *The American Journal of Legal History* 39, no. 2 (1995): 148–176; Owen Chadwick, *The Secularization of the European Mind in the 19th Century* (Cambridge, MA: Cambridge University Press, 1975); and S. Gerald Sandler, "Lockean Ideas in Thomas Jefferson's Bill for Establishing Religious Freedom," *Journal of the History of Ideas* 21, no. 1 (1960): 110–116.

[11] Thomas E. Buckley, *Church and State in Revolutionary Virginia, 1776–1878* (Charlottesville, VA: University Press of Virginia, 1977), 38–99.

in environmental constraints (e.g., a budgetary windfall or debt) or from the strategic actions of other individuals who are also goal-oriented and competing for a similar set of resources or lobbying for changes in the rules of the game. These other individuals may be newcomers to a situation and upset the equilibrium that previous occupants had enjoyed over time, forcing the latter to make different choices to preserve the things they valued.

When discussing religious liberty, political economists view that concept as a set of laws, regulations, or general rules that define what religious individuals can or cannot do. Such a definition goes beyond simply declaring it as a "right of conscience" or "right of exercise," though these notions do help to point us in the right direction. In an earlier work, I framed the concept of religious freedom in terms of governmental regulatory policy with respect to any law that raised the cost of believing or practicing one's faith privately or in a public setting.[12] A cost imposed on an individual from a government making it more difficult to worship as one pleases would represent a diminution of religious freedom, whereas any law (or removal of a law) that makes it easier to worship indicates greater religious freedom. This definition places the notion of religious liberty on a continuum (as compared to a simple dichotomy) that allows social scientists to craft rough measures of this admittedly amorphous concept.[13] It also allows us to understand fluctuations in religious liberty over time. Ratifying the Bill of Rights did not automatically guarantee that the United States was now religiously free. We know from history that even with the First Amendment in place, various levels of government (local, state, and federal) have imposed restrictions on different religious groups that made it difficult for them to exercise their full freedom. From Blaine

[12] Anthony Gill, *The Political Origins of Religious Liberty* (Cambridge, MA: Cambridge University Press, 2008), 9–21. Note that this definition does not include extra-legal or societal-based religious persecution. Citizens acting on their own, without government support or against existing law, can burn churches and harass or physically assault members of different denominations. Such persecution is often episodic and difficult to detect. This is a serious problem, but one that is not taken up directly in this study. Brian Grim and Roger Finke take up the issue of persecution in their well-documented book. For present purposes of this chapter, my focus is on official government policy on religious freedom such as is stated in the US Constitution's First Amendment and subsequent Congressional actions. Brian J. Grim and Roger Finke, *The Price of Freedom Denied: Religious Persecution and Conflict in the Twenty-First Century* (Cambridge, MA: Cambridge University Press, 2010).

[13] Cf. Fox, *World Survey*.

Amendments enacted by different states in the nineteenth century that restricted access to educational funding for Catholics, to efforts to chase Mormons across the continent, to limits on speech from the pulpit via 501 (c)3 regulations, the United States has moved back and forth with respect to how free religious individuals and groups actually are.[14]

The additional benefit of conceptualizing religious liberty within a cost-benefit regulatory framework is that it points us in the direction of where to look for clues when explaining its emergence (or recession). And the possibilities are endless. Not only will governments create laws that outright ban certain denominations, but politicians will also enact more subtle laws that impose differential costs on denominations, making regular religious activity more difficult. For instance, zoning regulations are used frequently to prevent a congregation from building a worship center.[15] If a congregation cannot build a sanctuary close to where their parishioners live, the chances for that organization flourishing diminish substantially.[16] The mere governmental definition of what constitutes a "religious organization" also has an impact on religious freedom as it can determine an entity's tax status, ability to purchase real estate, or to merely exist. A rather blatant example of this occurred in the Czech Republic in 2003 when their parliament passed legislation that defined a legal church to be one that had at least 0.1 percent of the population in membership and has existed for ten years.[17] While a seemingly low threshold, the previous size to obtain legal status was 300 parishioners; the 0.1 percent marker raised that bar to roughly 10,000 members. This law dramatically favored the historically existing Catholic Church, which aggregated its membership across hundreds of parishes, and made it difficult for smaller, independent

[14] Cf. Mark David Hall, "Jeffersonian Walls and Madisonian Lines: The Supreme Court's Use of History in Religious Clause Cases," *High Court Quarterly Review* 5 (2009): 109–153.

[15] Anthony Gill, "The Political Economy of Religious Property Rights," *Forum for Social Economics* (April 2016), accessed online, www.tandfonline.com/doi/full/10.1080/07360932.2015.1128347.

[16] I often like to point out how precipitously church attendance will drop after a Saturday evening snowfall. People are reacting to changes in their expected costs (e.g., getting in an accident on a slippery road). Moving a church a few miles away can have a dramatic impact on attendance as well. Ibid. As any good commercial realtor knows, the keys to business success are location, location, location.

[17] Petr Pajas, "The Impact of the New Czech Laws on Churches," *The International Journal of Not-for-Profit Law* 6, no. 1 (2003), accessed online, www.icnl.org/research/journal/vol6iss1/special_6.htm.

congregations to get building permits and tax-exempt status on equipment purchases.[18]

There is no end to the creativity in which governments can restrict religious freedom. The most blatant forms of such violations come in the form of outright prohibitions on all religious expression to explicit favoritism and endorsement of one confession (e.g., an established state church) over all others. Violations may also be subtler, from zoning "inconveniences" regulating the location, size, and use of houses of worship to lighting, noise, and parking ordinances that make gathering together difficult.[19] Visa restrictions on missionaries, import bans on spiritual items, and speech codes in public spaces are also common. Less obvious forms of religious favoritism and discrimination include the mandatory collection of tithes (via religious taxes) that are directed to one specific denomination. Any new upstart sect seeking to break into the spiritual marketplace will be facing a population that is already paying once for religious services; convincing potential congregants to "give again" voluntarily presents an uphill battle. The latter tactic was used by the Congregationalists in colonial British America as a means not only of funding their own churches but to make it harder for groups like the Quakers, Methodists, and Baptists to gain a foothold in New England.[20] It was the issue of mandatory religious taxation directed toward Congregationalists that motivated a group of Baptists in Danbury, Connecticut, to petition Thomas Jefferson for help, resulting in the president's famous *Letter to the Danbury Baptists*.[21] All of these examples represent imposed costs upon an individual or group's ability to worship as they choose.

Finally, it is important to note that most imposed costs on free exercise are generally directed toward collective worship, limiting the ability of individuals to gather together in communal prayer. It is significantly more difficult to regulate individual conscience, but considering that an individual's faith is often reinforced by ritualized and regular participation in a group, limiting the rights of groups has the effect of reducing (but not

[18] Within the political economy literature, this is referred to as "rent seeking," a process wherein a private entity (e.g., the Catholic Church) lobbies the government to enact laws or provide subsidies that give them an advantage over their competition. To prove how incentives work, a number of independent Protestant congregations began to combine themselves under broad umbrella organizations to meet the 0.1 percent threshold. See Pajas, "Impact."

[19] See Gill, "Political Economy." [20] Gill, *Political Origins*, 105–108.

[21] Hall, "Jeffersonian Walls," 109–153.

altogether eliminating) religious faith among individuals. And to be realistic, some regulatory limitations on religious free exercise will always exist merely because the actions of some groups may impose significant costs upon others, what political economists call "negative externalities."[22] Murderous cults practicing human sacrifice are generally not permitted in societies as murder, quite obviously, imposed costs upon others.[23] All societies, via their governing regimes, will have to decide how to regulate religion, and the extent to which they all do varies across time and space.

The Economic Logic of Church–State Relations and Religious Liberty

If we conceptualize religious liberty as a regulatory issue, the next step is to ask the question of why a government would regulate or deregulate the religious economy (i.e., the marketplace where potential denominations compete for members and resources). Increased regulations placed upon religious activity imply a decrease in religious liberty for some, if not all, religious actors and institutions. Decreased regulations signify the opposite – i.e., an increase in religious freedom. To explain why governments would increase or decrease regulations over religious groups and individuals, we begin by making some general assumptions about the motivations regarding the three primary actors in this regulatory game – political rulers, religious leaders, and the general population.[24] A presentation of these assumptions reveals a certain political logic wherein secular leaders have an incentive to favor one particular religious faith over others, and why the leaders of that particular denomination will want to have the religious economy tightly regulated in their

[22] Cf. Ronald H. Coase, "The Problem of Social Cost," *Journal of Law and Economics* 3, no. 1 (1960): 1–44.

[23] I include this seemingly silly observation because I was sometimes confronted by a colleague who argued that religious liberty is a legal fiction and no society could ever have such freedom. For this colleague, a nation was not religiously free if the government restricted cannibalistic vampire cults from freely exercising their beliefs. That was *literally* the example given to challenge arguments about whether a country truly had religious freedom or not. Such an assertion relies upon a dichotomous notion of religious freedom: You either have it or not. A concept based upon a scaled continuum seems to make more common sense.

[24] For a more extensive and nuanced version of this argument, see Gill, *Political Origins*.

favor. Close church–state relations favoring a single established denomination tend to be the historical equilibrium.[25] Outlining how this equilibrium is upset and moves toward greater religious liberty for (nearly) all spiritual groups will be the more difficult explanatory task, but it will be seen how the same assumptions used to explain the lack of religious liberty can illuminate the right conditions under which greater freedom emerges.

The Motivations of Politicians, Pastors, and the Pious Public

Political economy generally begins with the assumption that politicians – be they dictators or democrats – are rational, self-interested individuals who are goal-oriented.[26] There is little room for the altruistic and disinterested philosopher kings found in Plato's *Republic*. While politicians may vary somewhat in their character traits with respect to "greediness" or "altruism," reflective of the population as a whole,[27] there is one primary goal that motivates them beyond all else: the acquisition and maintenance of power.[28] While rulers may have a broad policy platform on which they seek to implement, they cannot implement that agenda unless they are in power. Political survival comes first and foremost. Second to this goal is the need to collect tax revenue as

[25] I use the term "church" in church–state relations for rhetorical simplicity. This argument could be applied to other forms of religious institutions that do not use the term "church" to designate their congregations. Cf. Ani Sarkissian, *The Varieties of Religious Repression: Why Governments Restrict Religion* (Oxford: Oxford University Press, 2015) and Kuru, *Secularism and State Policies.*

[26] James M. Buchanan, "Politics without Romance: A Ketch of Positive Public Choice Theory and Its Normative Implications," in *The Collected Words of James Buchanan, Vol. 1* (Indianapolis, IN: Liberty Fund, 1999).

[27] Having studied public choice theory, I may be willing to accept an assumption that those entering the political arena are actually less altruistic than the general population, on average. The allure of power is seductive.

[28] Cf. David Mayhew, *Congress: The Electoral Connection* (New Haven, CT: Yale University Press, 1974). Mayhew's seminal work argued that US Congressional representatives are motivated by their desire to be reelected to office. This assumption can easily be translated to parliamentarians, presidents, and even military dictators who need not face pressure at the electoral booth, but who still need to stave off palace coups and revolutions. Cf. Barbara Geddes, *Politician's Dilemma: Building State Capacity in Latin America* (Berkeley, CA: University of California Press, 1994).

fulfilling one's agenda, and staying in power will depend upon financing government agencies that provide basic public goods, including national defense and an internal justice system. Leaders who cannot fund an army to fend off invaders are usually conquered, and countries without a system of policing internal chaos are quick to fall into revolution. The third, and final goal for our purposes, is economic growth. An economy that is growing generally promotes a content population (that will keep the current leaders in power) and increases the tax base from which government officials can draw revenue.

Religious leaders (broadly defined as those in charge of resources under control of religious institutions) also desire to retain their positions of authority. To accomplish this, they need to ensure a stable, if not growing, number of adherents who give purpose to the organization and provide economic resources for the institution's survival. To state this simply, religious leaders are "parishioner maximizers." This is true whether one considers the clergy to be theologically motivated, wherein they want to proselytize "The Word" to as many people as possible, or self-interested, meaning they are out to protect the institution that guarantees them a professional living. Pastors, rabbis, and imams do have to eat, after all, and dismissing the material motives of the priestly class would be shortsighted on the part of the social scientist. Theological and career motivations are not antithetical to one another, however; clergy can be motivated by both objectives, much the way politicians with idealistic agendas still must think about remaining in office. And like politicians, religious leaders also are interested in increasing funding for their institution via tithing or other means. (A stable or expanding membership base affects the ability to collect funds, ceteris paribus.) A well-funded church can better serve congregants, grow or maintain the organization, and help forward the professional goals of the clergy, ceteris paribus.[29]

Considering the relatively low costs of starting a religion, churches that are hegemonic within a population will prefer restrictions on upstart sects, much the way older businesses will seek regulations that make entry into

[29] Of course, the world is not ceteris paribus, and a well-funded clergy could veer away from its theological roots and alienate its parishioner base. Many of the well-endowed mainline Protestant churches in the United States and Europe are seeing increasing gulfs between their leadership and members, resulting in significant rifts.

their sector more difficult.[30] On the contrary, new religious groups trying to gain a foothold in that market will prefer such restrictions be liberalized to their competitive advantage.[31] Leaders of upstart sects, missionary groups, and other religious minorities are typically those who favor religious freedom. If spiritual entrepreneurs believe they can meet the needs of the religious population better than the hegemonic confession, they will want to lower every possible barrier and reduce all unnecessary costs standing in their way. This isn't a matter of theological conviction, but one of self-interest (based upon the desire to proselytize). The Catholic Church has been a vigorous proponent of religious freedom in places such as Africa, China, and Russia where they are expanding their missionary reach, but have been quick to lobby for restrictions on Protestants in Latin America, where the Vatican's forces are on the defensive and losing ground to evangelicals.[32] This is true even after the publication of *Dignitatis Humanae* at the end of Vatican II (1965), a document intended to make church policy consistent with respect to religious freedom and pluralism. Actual application of that policy depended heavily on whether Catholics were in the majority or minority.

Last, but not least, are the members of the general population. Economists of religion typically assume that consumers of religious goods and services (e.g., sermons, counseling, fellowship) will want a high-quality product at a reasonable price,[33] as is true with consumer purchases in other arenas. It is further assumed that there is a variety of religious tastes among the population. Some people prefer "fire and brimstone" faith, whereas others enjoy a comforting "pajama and bunny slippers" theology. Religious tastes may also include stylistic factors such as the type of music, architecture of buildings, and personality of the clergy. And some individuals may even prefer "no religion" as their spiritual preference. In short, the religious

[30] See Anne O. Krueger, "The Political Economy of the Rent-Seeking Society," *American Economic Review* 64, no. 3 (1974): 291–303.

[31] Gill, *Political Origins*, 44–46.

[32] Ibid. and Anthony Gill, *Rendering unto Caesar: The Catholic Church and the State in Latin America* (Chicago, IL: University of Chicago Press, 1998).

[33] "Price" may seem an odd term here as churches typically rely upon voluntary donations. Those donations, though, represent a price that is determined by the consumer and not set by the producer (although some congregations do set minimal contribution limits for full membership). Another aspect of "price" is the time that a religious consumer devotes to attending services, participating in small groups, or volunteering labor.

marketplace – like any consumer marketplace – is pluralistic and often changing, making it difficult for a single institutional entity to satisfy every demand.[34] This means that in a spiritually free market – i.e., one with high levels of religious liberty – religious institutions and their leaders will face competition for parishioners and provide attentive service to their needs. Adam Smith, the grandfather of modern economics, even made this observation in his monumental tome *The Wealth of Nations*.[35] Religious liberty also supports the needs and wants of atheists and agnostics amid a religious population in that such freedom encompasses the free exercise of faith, which includes choosing not to exercise a faith. The bottom line is that religious freedom is beneficial to the population writ large.[36]

Now that we have the major actors and their presumed preferences laid out, we can build a logic regarding the historical nature of church–state relations and hypothesize about how such arrangements may change with an eye toward increasing liberalization. This, in turn, will be followed by a discussion of how this theory helps explain the gradual evolution of religious freedom in the United States.

[34] Rodney Stark, *For the Glory of God: How Monotheism Led to Reformations, Science, Witch-Hunts, and the End of Slavery* (Princeton, NJ: Princeton University Press, 2003), 17–20. While it may seem easy to refute this pluralism claim by pointing to the hegemonic culture of Catholicism or Islam within some countries, it should be noted that both of those faith traditions are not monolithic in their "flavors." Islam is a highly fissiparous confession that includes a wide variety of theological interpretations with individual imams competing with one another. Catholicism, while uniting a billion adherents under the ostensible authority of the Vatican, is also quite diverse with groups from the orthodox Opus Dei to progressive Sojourners, and a smattering of Catholic Charismatics here and there, representing different Catholic tastes. For more on religious pluralism, see Anthony Gill, "Lost in the Supermarket: Comments on Beaman, Religious Pluralism and What It Means to Be Free," *Journal for the Scientific Study of Religion* 42, no. 3 (2003): 327–332.

[35] Adam Smith, *An Inquiry into the Nature and Causes of the Wealth of Nations* (Indianapolis, IN: Liberty Fund, 1976 [1776]), 788–808. See also Laurence R. Iannaccone, "The Consequences of Religious Market Structure: Adam Smith and the Economics of Religion," *Rationality and Society* 3, no. 2 (1991): 156–177.

[36] One of the more common arguments against religious freedom is that a certain nation is historically rooted to X denomination and allowing freedom for new sects to proselytize would undermine the society's culture. But this is somewhat absurd on its face considering that if the ancient faith was deeply historically rooted in the soul of the country, any attempts to proselytize by upstart groups would fail. After all, if the historical confession was serving the needs of the population, one would not have to keep competitors out by coercion; they would fail on their own merits.

The Logic of Religious Establishment and Limited Spiritual Freedom

Secular rulers want to stay in power. Religious institutions and clergy can assist in that goal by promulgating moral codes regarding proper human behavior that have a beneficial effect on social stability. Adam Smith noted, "the clergy ... could easily keep the peace without the support or assistance either of the king or of any other person; and neither the king nor any other person could keep the peace [in Europe] without the support and assistance of the clergy."[37] A society that is peaceful is less costly and more secure for a secular ruler's tenure than one in open chaos. Furthermore, clergy have the ability to endorse politicians and confer an increased degree of legitimacy on rulers by proclaiming them morally just and worthy of obedience. This includes priests encouraging people to be good citizens and pay their taxes or comply with military conscription, advice that helps to lower the government's enforcement costs and minimizes tax evasion.[38] Given that citizens often have little knowledge about the quality of a leader and will seek information from trusted sources, the clergy can exercise influence over elections or quell passive or active (rebellious) resistance to autocratic regimes. On the flipside, critical words from clergy can threaten to unseat secular rulers, as was evident during the Iranian Revolution of 1979.

Ideological legitimacy is not the only thing clergy can offer secular leaders. Religious institutions excel in organizing collective action; their "business model" essentially revolves around enticing people to attend worship services voluntarily and to pay for the maintenance of the institution. This collective action power has been harnessed for a wide array of social movements throughout history, including the Mexican War of Independence and the Taiping Rebellion in China. In the United States, churches often served as focal points for rallying militia and motivating rebellion during the American War of Independence.[39] And religious mobilization of all stripes played a role in the abolition of slavery, women's

[37] Smith, *Wealth of Nations*, 801.

[38] Cf. Margaret Levi, *Consent, Dissent, and Patriotism* (Cambridge, MA: Cambridge University Press, 1997). Military conscription is a form of taxation wherein the tax comes in the direct provision of labor dedicated to a certain cause (i.e., military service).

[39] Thomas Kidd, *God of Liberty: A Religious History of the American Revolution* (New York: Basic Books, 2012).

suffrage, the prohibition of alcohol, civil rights for racial minorities, and support for Republican electoral victories. If a ruler fully understands the power of religious collective action, and its ability to provide legitimacy to a regime, it is not surprising that secular leaders would want to be on good terms with the dominant religious players in society, if not wield significant regulatory control over those institutions.[40]

Religious leaders, for their part, are interested in receiving support from the state. There are fairly low barriers of entry into a religious market. Simply consider the proliferation of storefront churches and street preachers where there are few legal restrictions to creating a church. During the First Great Awakening in the United States, Methodist and Baptist preachers only needed some horses, a wagon or two, and a few tents to travel from town to town and plant churches. If a single, hegemonic church proves institutionally incapable of meeting all the latent spiritual preferences of a population, the only way it can maintain membership in the face of new spiritual movements would be to coercively restrict their entry into the market. As Adam Smith observed how the Church of England responded to an onslaught of dissenting sects in the seventeenth century, the Anglican clergy's "first demand was generally, that [the king or local magistrate] should silence and subdue all their adversaries," a tendency that he saw elsewhere in history as well.[41] But Smith also observed that smiting one's enemies physically was not nearly enough. A church that could gain a competitive advantage over others was one that was financed via coercive taxation by the state; thus, the clergy also demanded that the magistrate "should bestow an independent provision on themselves"[42] and shelter them financially from the lost tithing that would be skimmed off by upstart sects. State-enforced religious taxation helps preserve the dominant religious confession. Government officials can block new spiritual

[40] One other option is to destroy the religious institutions entirely. This was tried in the Soviet Union and succeeded to a large, although not entirely successful, extent. Paul Froese, *The Plot to Kill God: Findings from the Soviet Experiment in Secularization* (Berkeley, CA: University of California Press, 2008). The Russian Bolsheviks could not "make nice" with the Russian Orthodox Church because of their atheist ideology and because the Orthodox clergy was firmly on the tsarist and, later, White Russian side of the battle over Russia. Gill, *Political Origins*, 180–182. A similar tension has played out in China and Russia, with the regimes in both countries sponsoring "official" Christian faiths while tamping down all other faiths. Karrie J. Koesel, *Religion and Authoritarianism: Cooperation, Conflict, and the Consequences* (Cambridge, MA: Cambridge University Press, 2014).

[41] Smith, *Wealth of Nations*, 792. [42] Ibid., 801.

entrants by banning missionaries, denying building permits to minority religious groups, or physically repressing religious dissenters. History is replete with such examples of this, from the French and English monarchies persecuting confessional minorities in the seventeenth century to attempts to limit Protestant evangelization in Latin America in the nineteenth and early twentieth centuries.[43] Such repression exists throughout our contemporary world, and the oppression is often politically strategic to bolster both an existing regime and its favored faith.[44]

Beyond offering the hegemonic religion protection from religious competitors, the state may also offer the clergy positive support for their institution by financing it directly from government coffers, making laws enforcing tithing, or granting them privileged access to various institutions (e.g., schools, the military) that other denominations are denied. Official endorsement (or establishment) of a specific faith also helps a particular confession secure its position in the religious marketplace relative to other groups. It is difficult for religious minorities to compete with a church that citizens already pay for via mandatory taxation. Even in contemporary and seemingly secular Europe, historic churches still receive significant government endorsement and financial benefits that give them a competitive advantage over religious minorities, although some nations do offer support for the nondominant faith.[45] While secular governments could offer similar financial support to all religious institutions, such a system could become rather costly over time, which is why there are usually a variety of regulatory requirements determining what groups constitute legitimate religions.[46]

When examining the various benefits that religious leaders can offer secular rulers and vice versa, it is not difficult to understand the strong affinity for church–state cooperation throughout history. An understandable bargain suggests itself. Churches provide legitimacy for a regime and agree to keep the citizens peaceful and supportive of the government in

[43] Gill, *Political Origins*; Gill, *Rendering unto Caesar.*

[44] See Sarkissian, *Varieties of Religious Repression* and Grim and Finke, *Price of Freedom.*

[45] Soper, den Dulk, and Monsma, *Challenge of Pluralism.*

[46] One of the major problems facing Europe is how to bring Islam into their corporatist religious structure. While historical Protestant or Catholic churches are often supported (and made placid) with government funds, this is difficult with Islam, which is highly decentralized and doesn't have a "pope" to speak for all adherents. Steven Pfaff and Anthony Gill, "Will a Million Muslims March? Muslim Interest Organization and Political Integration in Europe," *Comparative Political Studies* 39, no. 7 (2006): 803–828.

exchange for protection from spiritual competitors and for financial assistance to maintain their institution (including paying the salaries of clergy).[47] If a paucity of religious freedom is typical of world history, and if there is such a symbiotic relationship between church and state, why would religious freedom ever emerge? The answer revolves around the shifting environment affecting the political calculus of secular rulers and the reluctant acceptance of a clergy facing an increasingly pluralistic environment.

The Economic Origins of Religious Liberty

If religious establishment and restrictions on the rights of religious minorities are a political calculus based upon the desire of a politician to retain power and enhance tax revenue, then those same factors should also play a role in incentivizing a ruler to promote greater liberalization. The question is under what conditions the incentives (or cost-benefit calculations) of a politician shift toward granting more religious freedoms. The first essential ingredient to the recipe is an increasingly pluralistic spiritual landscape. If there was only one religious institution and all citizens were wedded happily to this confession, there would be little need for any laws regulating religious minorities since they would not exist. As noted above, though, the underlying structure of the religious marketplace is assuredly diverse. Entrepreneurs who tap this diversity by offering different products catered to the needs of different niches will likely find success in challenging the reach of the dominant faith.[48] Within a country only being served

[47] While institutionally logical for clergy to seek support of the government in exchange for legitimacy, this arrangement can often chisel away at the proselytizing effectiveness of the clergy. Smith understood this well when he said that priests were likely to be found "reposing on their benefices" and being "indolent" in several pages of passages that rank among the best rhetoric of the Scottish Enlightenment. Smith, *Wealth of Nations*, 788–793. Worse yet for the institution, hitching one's wagon to an unpopular secular regime that serves its citizenry poorly often leaves the religious population disillusioned with their spiritual leadership and the faith itself. Gill, *Rendering unto Caesar.*

[48] One need only consider the explosion of religious pluralism in Africa over the past half century, or the myriad "flavors" of house churches in China (against the risk of persecution), to understand the natural diversity of religious tastes. Philip Jenkins, *The Next Christendom: The Coming of Global Christianity* (Oxford: Oxford University Press, 2011) and Rodney Stark and Xiuhua Wang, *A Star in the East: The Rise of Christianity in China* (West Conshohocken, PA: Templeton Press, 2015). Even what appears to be religiously

by a single religious institution that cannot cater to every spiritual preference, there are potential gains to be made by adventurous entrepreneurs willing to risk proselyting to underserved populations. Religious freedom is most necessary in a pluralistic environment, be it actual or latent.

But how does religious pluralism manifest itself in the first place, especially if the market is heavily restricted to favor one confession? One possibility is that there are not restrictions on religious practice, one confession is serving the population, and then suddenly, by surprise, new religious entrepreneurs appear. This may happen by an internal schism arising from the extant institution,[49] by entirely new theological ideas put forth by domestic religious entrepreneurs,[50] or by foreign missionaries. In such instances, leaders of the dominant church will scramble to create barriers to these groups expanding by appealing to the government for assistance. Political leaders then must decide whether or not they should yield to these demands. The bigger mystery, though, is how religious minorities gain a foothold in a spiritual marketplace that already has significant barriers of entry in place. In such a situation, the dominant church has probably worked hand in hand with secular rulers to trade off a monopolistic religious position for granting legitimacy to the government. Breaking into the new market would seem a difficult, if not impossible, task, *unless* government leaders were not willing to fully enforce the restrictions on religious minorities. With lax enforcement, spiritual entrepreneurs can "sneak into" the market. Again, the onus now lies with the state as to whether secular officials will enforce these rules or allow for greater liberalization within the spiritual marketplace.

monolithic Islamic countries have an amazing diversity in schools of thought and emphases of worship as the decentralized nature of that faith allows for independent mosques to compete with one another. Many Islamic nations provide adequate amounts of freedom for these autonomous mosques to flourish, though there are heavy restrictions on other faith traditions. Rodney Stark, *Why God?: Explaining Religious Phenomenon* (West Conshohocken, PA: Templeton Press, 2017), 145.

49 For an extensive discussion of this in medieval European Christianity, see Stark, *For the Glory of God*. Far from being a monolithic faith, the Church faced a continual onslaught of theological innovations ("proto-reformations," if you will). The Vatican proved remarkably good at either stomping these movements out (e.g., Jan Jus) or incorporating them into the broader umbrella of Catholicism (e.g., Franciscan monks).

50 Consider the Church of Jesus Christ of Latter Day Saints. While they could possibly be seen as a schismatic movement within Christianity, the extensive theological development in the Book of Mormon seems to categorize it as a relatively unique faith.

The decision to restrict religious liberties at a time of growing pluralism will depend on how much the new minorities are a threat to the power of the rulers, how much the restriction on religious freedom would damage economic growth and tax collection. Creating, monitoring, and enforcing restrictions on the rights of minorities come at a cost to any regime and must be balanced against the benefits they receive from religious pluralism and the legitimacy they gain from the dominant church. Banning religious missionaries who come for the sole (or "soul") purpose of making converts and nothing else is the least costly scenario for secular leaders. If those missionaries come with valuable resources to the population such as schools, infrastructure improvement projects (e.g., irrigation wells), disaster relief, or medical clinics, the decision is a bit more difficult because all of those services provided by missionaries help to improve the overall economy. By providing these types of public goods, the government saves its financial resources for other tasks and the citizenry will be better off and less rebellious, ceteris paribus. Moreover, if those missionaries also come along with merchants who connect the country to valuable trade networks, the government might be willing to relax any restrictions on religious minorities (or not impose them in the first place). Any increase in economic activity – production or trade – will enhance the government's tax revenue. A country dependent upon import and export tariffs will be more tolerant of merchants who come to the country with alternative religions. I demonstrated that this was the case in Latin America during the late nineteenth and early twentieth centuries; the countries that were most trade dependent – namely Argentina, Brazil, Chile, and Uruguay – were the first to introduce greater religious freedoms for Protestants from the United States and Europe based upon concerns over trade.[51] Finally, since people are an economic resource and countries sometimes encourage immigration to build a workforce when labor shortages exist, restrictions on religious minorities are likely to be overlooked if the few sources of labor are from lands with people of different faiths. Following World War II, Europe faced a significant shortage of male labor and opened the doors to Muslim immigration from North Africa and Turkey.[52]

[51] Gill, *Political Origins*, 135–146.

[52] Joel S. Fetzer and J. Christopher Soper, *Muslims and the State in Britain, France, and Germany* (Cambridge, MA: Cambridge University Press, 2005).

The rise of *domestic* religious pluralism is a bit trickier for political leaders as it is difficult to prohibit physical entry of new proselytizers who are already citizens. (There is no foreign place to send them back to!) The option for government officials then is to persecute them via physical attacks or imprisonment, or restrict their basic worship activities by denying building permits or other public amenities. Leaders who are insecure in their tenure and needing the support of the nation's dominant religious leaders may find such policies worthwhile, and various minority groups have been used as scapegoats throughout history to bolster the majority standing of a regime, particularly if minorities are seen as potential pockets of political resistance.[53] Much like foreign missionaries, though, if these domestic upstart sects do not threaten the political survival of rulers and provide tangible benefits to the population that would otherwise have to come from government coffers, there is little incentive to restrict their behavior. Protestant missionaries from the United States and Europe were quick to indigenize the leadership of their denominations in Latin America in the mid-twentieth century, and these missionaries often provided important services such as schooling to poor neighborhoods.[54] As such, several governments were reluctant to persecute them, particularly those in the more stable states (at the time) of Brazil, Chile, El Salvador, Nicaragua, and Uruguay.[55]

[53] Ani Sarkissian, "Religious Regulation and the Muslim Democracy Gap," *Politics and Religion* 5, no. 3 (2012): 501–527, and Ani Sarkissian, "Religious Reestablishment in Post-Communist Polities," *Journal of Church and State* 51, no. 3 (2009): 472–501. Religious minorities may be financially valuable to secular rulers as well. Both Mark Koyama and Colleen Haight have amazingly insightful analyses of why Jewish minorities were considered economically valuable citizens in medieval England and the nineteenth-century United States, respectively. Koyama provides an additional analysis of how financial innovations made Jews less valuable over time, which led to their persecution and exile. Mark Koyama, "The Political Economy of Expulsion: The Regulation of Jewish Moneylending in Medieval England," *Constitutional Political Economy* 32, no. 4 (2010): 374–406 and Colleen Haight, "Hostile Territory: High Tension Religion and the Peddler," *American Journal of Economics and Sociology* 66, no. 5 (2007): 1005–1027. Timur Kuran and Jared Rubin also explore the economic value of Christian and Jewish minorities in his work in Islamic financial systems. Timur Kuran and Jared Rubin, "The Financial Power of the Powerless: Socio-Economic Status and Interest Rates under Partial Rule of Law," *Economic Journal* 128, no. 609 (2018): 758–796.

[54] Gill, *Rendering unto Caesar*, 85–91.

[55] All of these nations have turbulent histories beginning in the 1960s, but the Protestant advances typically came before then. And "stable" does not necessarily mean "democratic."

Once religious pluralism begins to take root, and advances to a point where any persecution might incite civil conflict, government leaders who value their security will be more likely to expand religious liberties to expanding religious minorities. Lessons learned from civil conflict that involve a religious dimension often prompt governments to pursue a path of religious toleration, gradually leading to expanded freedoms. This was the case following the religious wars in France that led to the Edict of Nantes (1598) and, eventually, the Act of Toleration (1689) following the English Civil War (1642–1651) and the uncertainty surrounding the religious motivations of the Restoration monarchs. Of course, increasing religious pluralism does not always lead to peace, particularly if religious minorities remain geographically or demographically separated or if there is political gain to be made from discriminating against a certain group.[56] The most fertile ground for the emergence of religious liberty tends to be an environment where there are several religious factions that carefully balance one another out, with none holding a majoritarian sway over the population. In many respects, this is the religious equivalent of factions checking each other, discussed by James Madison in *Federalist* 10. All of this should be taken in a probabilistic light with an eye toward understanding the costs and benefits of political actors, religious leaders, and the citizenry. What the economic perspective provides is a framework for looking at historical evidence and evaluating a plausible explanation of the rise (or fall) of religious freedom. We now turn to an analytic narrative of the emergence of religious freedom in the British American colonies and its eventual codification in the US Constitution's First Amendment (and subsequent state constitutions).

The Economic Foundations of American Religious Freedom

The history of religious freedom in the United States usually begins with reference to the Pilgrims escaping persecution in England, traveling to the Netherlands, and eventually planting the symbolic flag of liberty on Plymouth Rock. Such a precedent eventually leads to the ratification of the US Constitution and its all-important First Amendment. While the first

[56] Steven Wilkinson, *Votes and Violence: Electoral Competition and Ethnic Riots in India* (Cambridge, MA: Cambridge University Press, 2006).

constitutional declaration of religious liberty in modern history owes a great deal to courageous individuals advocating for this essential freedom, the process was not automatic and the United States experienced setbacks in the rights of conscience and worship during the colonial era.[57] The Puritans (or Congregationalists as they became known) who followed on the heels of the Mayflower in the early- to mid-seventeenth century were quick to set up their own religious establishment, much like the Church of England back in the homeland, and passed laws making it difficult to deviate from their newly defined orthodoxy. Anglicans did likewise in the Southern colonies. How the Founders eventually came to agree on the priority of religious freedom at the national level, with individual states following suit over time, was a story of increasing religious pluralism, the need for immigration, the importance of commerce and tax revenue, and the security of a nation struggling for independence.

The economic story of America's religious freedom actually begins in Europe, most notably with the Protestant Reformation that manifested a latent religious diversity that was brewing on the continent at the time. The Reformation raised religious conflict to new levels of warfare until the Peace of Westphalia (1648) brought a calm and allowed kingdoms to declare their own religious sovereignty.[58] France itself realized this prior to Westphalia and through the Edict of Nantes (1598) declared a "tolerant truce" between Catholics and Protestants (the Huguenots). Such a peace was necessary to eliminate the devastation the Wars of Religion wrought upon the region's economy. Despite peace across Europe, some nations still experienced conflict brought upon by growing religious diversity, most notably England in the decades leading up to its Civil War (1642–1651). Some dissenters in England (derisively called the Puritans) fled persecution at the hands of the Church of England in the early seventeenth century and made their way to the Netherlands, where the first major connection between economic growth and religious toleration took root.

[57] Setbacks for religious liberty did not end with the ratification of the US Constitution. As noted above, religious freedom should be viewed as a continuously dynamic continuum. Over the past two and a half centuries, the United States experienced several periods where Catholics, Mormons, Jehovah's Witnesses, Jews, and Muslims faced restrictions on their activity. Such restrictions can still be felt today across a wide swathe of all religious groups. Gill, "Political Economy."

[58] Philpott, *Revolutions in Sovereignty*.

The Netherlands were not lands of great natural resources that many rulers valued as the source of great riches. However, the Dutch realized that they could improve their wealth by excelling in the art of commerce, becoming a crossroads for merchant traffic.[59] The wealth of commerce attracted an amalgamation of ethnically and religiously diverse individuals, and the Low Countries became a mix of Calvinists, Lutherans, Catholics, and Jews. Attracting such merchants meant that the Dutch had to tolerate religious differences lest individuals with different skills and wares avoided the nation. Merchants who are continually arrested for merely practicing their brand of worship generally don't want to engage in "tradesies" with those persecuting them. As one scholar has noted, "Tolerance was after all conducive to the trade interests of the [Dutch] merchant elite that ruled the cities and eventually the state itself."[60] And such a welcoming environment also encouraged those who were being persecuted abroad, including the English Pilgrims and French Huguenots,[61] to establish businesses in the Netherlands. It was generally the wealthiest and most entrepreneurial individuals who ended up moving to Amsterdam and Leiden, adding to the bustling Dutch economy.[62] Religious toleration, largely an informal norm rather than a formal policy at the time, encouraged commerce and immigration, which in turn paid handsome dividends for the Dutch and became a lesson learned in the American colonies.[63]

While the Pilgrims found a safe haven from British persecution, a looming war potentially involving the Netherlands against Spain prompted another move, and one that proved important for the development of religious pluralism and freedom in the United States. In the first several decades of the seventeenth century, King James I was feeling the pressure of religious

[59] Angus Maddison, *The World Economy: A Millennial Perspective* (Paris: OECD Development Centre Studies, 2001), 77–80.

[60] Joke Spaans, "Religious Policies in the Seventeenth-Century Dutch Republic," in *Calvinism and Religious Toleration in the Dutch Golden Age*, ed. R. P. Hsia and H. F. K. van Nierop (New York: Cambridge University Press, 2002), 78.

[61] Despite the Edict of Nantes, French Protestants faced ongoing harassment and pressure from Catholic figures such as Cardinals Richelieu and Mazarin, who both held important posts in the French monarchy. In 1685, the Edict of Nantes was revoked sending a large number of Huguenot into exile with the Netherlands benefitting the most, but with some also seeking asylum in the increasingly free British American colonies.

[62] Anthony Gill and John M. Owen IV, "Religious Liberty and Economic Prosperity: Four Lessons from the Past," *Cato Journal* 37, no. 1 (2017): 115–134.

[63] Evan Haefeli, *New Netherland and the Dutch Origins of American Religious History* (Philadelphia: University of Pennsylvania Press, 2012).

conflict abroad (Thirty Years' War) and at home with an increasing number of "dissenting sects" challenging the authority of England, not to mention having to juggle relations between Catholics in Ireland, Presbyterians in Scotland, and the Church of England. Thanks to the Age of Exploration and a desire to grab colonial territory, a solution for diffusing tensions prevented itself to the king: Send the Dissenters to America! This policy solved two problems at once. First, it created a foothold in America against potential encroachment from Spain and France. Second, it helped to remove potential vocal opponents to himself and the Church of England, and thus bolstered his chances at political survival.[64] Recruiting individuals to start anew in an uncharted wilderness is never an easy task, so having a group of religious "nonconformists" populate the territory was a blessing, and the Puritans were happy to oblige this policy. James' successor, Charles I, followed suit by allowing Catholics to establish their own outpost in Maryland. While "Maryland was established first and foremost as a commercial enterprise, with profit, not religion, the primary impulse," the settlers of the colony realized that as religious minorities they would have to promote toleration of other denominations if only to preserve relations with the neighboring Anglicans in Virginia.[65] The Dutch settlement of New Amsterdam explicitly promoted a policy of religious toleration to encourage immigrants, as the directors of the West India Company advised Governor Peter Stuyvesant: "[A]lthough we heartily desire that these [Quakers] and other sectarians remained away from [New Amsterdam] ... we doubt very much, whether we can proceed against them rigorously without diminishing the population and stopping immigration, which must be favored at so tender stage of the country's existence."[66] If you want to let people into your country, don't chase them away with religious intolerance.

[64] Political survival was rather tenuous at this time and several attempts to dethrone James I, or cause turmoil, were in the air, including the famous "Gunpowder Plot" of Guy Fawkes (an ironically popular character among anarchists nowadays).

[65] Jay P. Dolan, *The American Catholic Experience: A History from Colonial Times to the Present* (Notre Dame, IN: University of Notre Dame Press, 1992), 72, 76. In one of the great ironies of religious freedom in the colonial United States, Maryland's policy of religious toleration allowed Protestants to settle the territory and eventually they became numerous enough to take over the governance of the colony and place restrictions on Catholic worship by the early 1700s. Thomas J. Curry, *The First Freedoms: Church and State in American to the Passage of the First Amendment* (Oxford: Oxford University Press, 1986), 51.

[66] Quoted in George L. Smith, *Religion and Trade in New Netherland: Dutch Origins and American Development* (Ithaca, NY: Cornell University Press, 1973), 230.

The result of an immigration policy that encouraged dissenters to leave was that it laid the groundwork for religious diversity across the (eventual) thirteen colonies, an essential ingredient for religious freedom. Although each particular confession had their stronghold (e.g., Congregationalists in New England, Anglicans in Virginia, Quakers in Pennsylvania), by the eve of the American War of Independence, no single denomination held a majority position among the population. This diversity fostered the ability of new sects (e.g., Methodists, Baptists) to spring up "between the cracks" of colonial religious establishments and proselytize. The Great Awakening was as much of a function of incipient religious toleration as it was a furtherance to greater religious liberty, which begat a greater need for toleration.[67] A "balance of power" among minority religions guaranteed that no single establishment could have been approved of in the new country, and thus at the federal level the result was the nonestablishment clause of the First Amendment.

Immigration was not the only economic motivation behind the promotion of religious tolerance and (eventually) freedom. Like the Netherlands, colonists quickly realized that in a sparsely populated land, any and all commercial contact with outsiders is valuable, irrespective of religious affiliation. Early attempts to imprison Quakers almost led to a trade war between Connecticut and Rhode Island that was forestalled by allowing Quakers to continue commercial trade if they did not preach.[68] While a limitation on the rights of proselytization, this was certainly preferred to imprisoning, exiling, or executing Quakers. William Penn picked up on the importance of linking economic trade to religious freedom when he petitioned King Charles II to have all colonists practice a Christian toleration toward one another. "Consider Peace, Plenty, and Safety, the three great Inducements to any Country to Honour the Prince . . . as well as the best Allurements to Foreigners to trade with it . . . are utterly lost by such Partialities [religious establishments and restrictions on minorities] . . . Plenty will be hereby exchanged for Poverty, by the Destruction of many thousand Families within this Realm, who are greatly instrumental for the carryon on of the most substantial Commers therein."[69] Penn went further

[67] Gill, *Political Origins*, 74. [68] Curry, *First Freedoms*, 22–23.

[69] William Penn, *The Political Writings of William Penn* (Indianapolis, IN: Liberty Fund, 2002), 58.

to link explicitly the flourishing of trade with greater tax revenue for the crown.[70] Samuel Davies, an itinerant preacher during the Great Awakening in the mid-eighteenth century, argued for expanded religious liberties and exemptions from mandatory tithing by making an explicit appeal to the British Board of Trade, noting that "a free Exercise of Religion is so valuable a branch of true liberty, and so essential to the enriching and improving of a Trading Nation, it should ever be held sacred in His Majesty's Colonies."[71] The Congregationalists of New England implicitly understood this connection between religious freedom and the enriching benefits of trade given that Boston, the colony's thriving port city, was exempted from mandatory tithing laws as early as the 1650s,[72] something that famed Baptist preacher Isaac Backus pointed out a century later: "[T]he multitude of people in Boston, have been left entirely free, these eighty-five years, to choose what worship they would attend upon, and not to be compelled to pay a farthing to support any that they did not chuse [*sic*]: And there were proofs [*sic*] enough to show, that this liberty has greatly contributed to the welfare and not the injury of the town."[73] And none other than America's first political economist Tench Coxe (writing shortly after the ratification of the US Constitution) observed, "In those states [allowing expanded religious freedoms] . . . agriculture, commerce, manufactures, the fisheries, and navigation, afford comfortable sustenance and ample rewards of profit to the industrious and well disposed, amidst the blessings of civil and religious liberty."[74] Religious freedom is simply good for a growing economy, which in turn allows the civil magistrate to collect greater tax revenues, ceteris paribus.[75] All of this helps to strengthen popular support for the leaders as well.

[70] For extended quotations on trade and religious freedom from Penn, see Gill, *Political Origins*, 98–100.

[71] Quoted in Rhys Isaac, "Religion and Authority: Problems of the Anglican Establishment in Virginia in the Era of the Great Awakening and the Parsons' Cause," *The William and Mary Quarterly* 30, no. 1 (1973): 27.

[72] William G. McLoughlin, *New England Dissent 1630–1833: The Baptists and the Separate of Church and State* (Cambridge, MA: Harvard University Press, 1971), 118.

[73] Isaac Backus, *Government and Liberty Described and Ecclesiastical Tyranny Exposed* (Boston: Powars and Wills, 1778), 11.

[74] Tench Coxe, *A View of the United States of America, in a Series of Papers* (Philadelphia: William Hall and Wrigley and Berriman, 1794), 74.

[75] For a more extensive discussion of the connection between religious liberty and economic growth that extends to other parts of the globe and historical eras, see Gill, *Political Origins.*

It should be noted that the economic causes that gave rise to denominational pluralism and (eventually) liberty in the United States were primarily focused on Protestant Christianity. While the first few decades of the Maryland colony provided some breathing space for Catholics, the Protestant majority of the nation did not smile kindly on those who were considered "papists." The philosophical grounding for such freedom certainly had its limits. But the need to gain the support of France during the War of Independence dictated that discriminatory policies toward Catholics be rolled back.[76] Hanson's book is entitled *Necessary Virtue: The Pragmatic Origins of Religious Liberty in New England*, which underscores the notion that while ideas do have a force in history, it is often economic and political incentives – for gaining wealth or winning wars – that push many ideas that would otherwise go ignored at the forefront.

Eventually, and slowly, pockets of resistance to expanded religious freedoms broke down. While the Congregationalists played a "defensive" game over time by way of imprisonment, fines, or religious taxes against the Quakers, Methodists, Baptists and other dissenters, the growing religious diversity of American society brought home the realization that restrictions on one group could be easily brought to bear on others, including one's own particular faith. A balance of power ensued over time among Protestants, leading to an agreement codified in the First Amendment that no one (or plurality) of religions should be established over any other. Some state constitutions continued to support official establishments into the early nineteenth century, but those too quickly fell as the reality of religious diversity and the economic benefits of such pluralism became apparent. Alas, this realization of freedom's benefit was not to be practiced uniformly, and Catholics, Mormons, Jehovah's Witnesses, and others faced societal hostility and legislative burdens throughout the 1800s and into the next century.[77] Religious liberty exists on a continuum, and the United States continually witnesses progress and regress, but the understanding of the manifest benefits of spiritual freedom to all realms of society has preserved a benchmark for which to always strive.

[76] Charles P. Hanson, *Necessary Virtue: The Pragmatic Origins of Religious Liberty in New England* (Charlottesville, VA: University of Virginia Press, 1998).

[77] David Smith, *Religious Persecution and Political Order in the United States* (Cambridge, MA: Cambridge University Press, 2015).

Conclusion

The drive for greater religious liberty is an admirable goal. Efforts to promote religious freedom, though, often are pursued from the "top-down," either through legislative mandates or foreign diplomacy at the highest level. While such efforts may assist in getting religious freedoms codified on paper, the actual enforcement of those laws and the day-to-day practice of toleration on the ground may not result unless the involved parties in the equation have the proper incentives to follow those dictates. There are plenty of counter-incentives pushing against the broadening of individual and group freedoms. Dominant churches or those losing members to upstart sects will try to make it more difficult for minority groups to worship as they choose. Politicians in an insecure tenure and beholden to the legitimation of the hegemonic confession may often oblige those demands by suppressing the new faiths. It is only when these actors fully understand that it is in their own political and economic interests to mutually agree to open societies that true freedom will take root, not only on the religious landscape, but across the broad plain of political and economic society as well. Such a lesson is important to the extent that scholars and activists desire to extend the rights of religious expression to our own societies or other nations. An appeal to our "better angels" is a good method of convincing people about the glory of our natural rights, but an appeal to our "better angels" combined with a reminder of how freedom can serve our material interests will be the manner in which liberty is fully embraced.

12 Corporate Religious Liberty and the Culture Wars

Steven D. Smith

Supreme Court decisions that appear friendly to the idea of corporate religious liberty have lately generated controversy and consternation. Two decisions in particular have provoked criticism. In *Burwell* v. *Hobby Lobby*, the Court ruled that statutory rights afforded by the Religious Freedom Restoration Act (RFRA) could extend to a business corporation.[1] And in *Hosanna-Tabor Evangelical Lutheran Church and School* v. *Equal Employment Opportunity Commission*, the Court held that the so-called ministerial exception grounded in the First Amendment's religion clauses insulated a church-associated school against federal legislation regulating employment.[2] The decisions have been denounced by progressive critics – and dissenting justices – as a novel and dangerous jurisprudential development.[3]

I will argue in this chapter that these criticisms are mostly misconceived – and also misleading with respect to the deeper complaints and agendas that are being advanced. Corporate religious freedom is not a novel or radical development; what is new, rather, is an increasingly intense opposition to religious freedom itself, or at least to any special legal accommodation of religious commitments.[4] Indeed, upon close examination, familiar complaints

I thank Barb Fick for helpful and challenging comments on an earlier draft, and John Mysliwiec for citation assistance.

[1] *Burwell* v. *Hobby Lobby*, 573 U.S., 134 S. Ct. 2751 (2014).

[2] *Hosanna-Tabor Evangelical Lutheran Church and School* v. *Equal Employment Opportunity Commission*, 565 U.S. 161 (2012).

[3] Justice Ginsburg denounced the *Hobby Lobby* decision as "of startling breadth," "extraordinary," and "radical," and she predicted that the decision would cause "havoc." 134 S. Ct. at 2787 (Ginsburg, J., dissenting). See also Elizabeth Sepper, "Contraception and the Birth of Corporate Conscience," *J. Gender, Social Policy and the Law* 22 (2014): 303, 304 (describing development as "dangerous"). For a collection of views, see *The Rise of Corporate Religious Liberty*, ed. Micah Schwartzman et al. (New York: Oxford University Press, 2016). Although the essays reflect diverse perspectives (including my own), the majority of the contributions are critical or skeptical of the ostensible "Rise."

[4] Douglas Laycock observes that "[f]or the first time in nearly 300 years, important forces in American society are questioning the free exercise of religion *in principle* – suggesting that

about *Hobby Lobby* and *Hosanna-Tabor* do not for the most part turn on anything peculiar to the corporate form. They are better understood as manifestations of an emerging, deep-seated opposition to the traditional American commitment to religious freedom as a distinctive legal right. And this opposition is itself part of a broader effort decisively to repudiate the vestiges of an older religious or biblical conception of American community, as described in Robert Bellah's influential scholarship on American "civil religion,"[5] in favor of a different conception that might be described as "secular" or "progressive."[6]

We should note at the outset that the term "corporate religious liberty" conflates two questions that need to be distinguished, if only so that they may be reconnected later at a deeper level. One question asks whether corporations, and in particular business corporations, enjoy a right to religious freedom. (Or at least that is a familiar way of formulating the question, although I will suggest that this formulation is obfuscating and mildly tendentious.) A different question asks whether there are institutions describable as "churches" (or even as "the church," in the singular[7]) that, whether or not formally incorporated, are deserving of deference from the law and the government.

While both *Hobby Lobby* and *Hosanna-Tabor* offered affirmative answers to each question, they are nevertheless independent questions: someone might well answer the first question "no" and the second "yes" (as several justices did), or vice versa, without committing logical or practical inconsistencies. And yet the questions are not unrelated. Each question is a manifestation of a fundamental conflict about the nature of American community.

In this chapter, I will begin with the question addressed in *Hobby Lobby* – the question of religious freedom rights for business corporations. I will suggest that the Supreme Court's conclusion – that under proper circumstances a business corporation can assert a right of religious freedom – was,

free exercise of religion may be a bad idea, or at least, a right to be minimized." Douglas Laycock, "Sex, Atheism, and the Free Exercise of Religion," *Detroit-Mercy Law Review* 88 (2011): 407.

5 See, for example, Robert N. Bellah, *The Broken Covenant: American Civil Religion in Time of Trial*, 2nd Edition (Chicago, IL: University of Chicago Press, 1975).

6 See Steven D. Smith, *Pagans and Christians in the City* (Grand Rapids, MI: Wm. B. Eerdmans, 2018).

7 On this usage, see Steven D. Smith, *The Rise and Decline of American Religious Freedom* (Cambridge, MA: Harvard University Press, 2014), 163–166.

far from being "radical" (as Justice Ruth Bader Ginsburg and others suggested), thoroughly conventional and commonsensical. Strident criticisms of the decision reflect the fact that the question of corporate religious freedom was intertwined in public perceptions and advocates' rhetoric with other fraught issues, including contraception, sexual morality, gender equality, and religious freedom as a general proposition.

This chapter will then consider the second question, which was at the center of the decision in *Hosanna-Tabor*, and which implicates perennial issues associated with the ancient idea of "freedom of the church." In the course of the examination, we will see how the debate over this second question, like the controversy over the first question, is a manifestation of fundamental disagreements about the nature of American community.

The Religious Rights of Corporations

Hobby Lobby involved the application of a federal statute, the RFRA, which declares that "[g]overnment shall not substantially burden a person's exercise of religion even if the burden results from a rule of general applicability." RFRA provides that a "person" so burdened is entitled to be accommodated by being excused from compliance with the burdensome rule, unless the government demonstrates a compelling interest in compliance that cannot be achieved in some less restrictive way.[8]

When enacted in 1993, RFRA was understood to be reinstating (hence the "Restoration"), as a statutory matter, a right that had long been recognized in constitutional free exercise doctrine until the Supreme Court disavowed it in *Employment Division* v. *Smith* (the "peyote case").[9] *Smith*'s cutback in protection for religious freedom, clumsily and (as some perceived the matter) disingenuously rationalized in Justice Antonin Scalia's majority opinion, had been widely condemned by liberals and conservatives alike.[10] Hence, the statute restoring the accommodation requirement had been adopted with virtual unanimity in Congress and with the support of a spectrum of diverse groups, from the American Civil Liberties Union (ACLU) to the National Council of Churches. In signing

[8] 42 U.S. C. sec. 2000bb-1 (2006) *et seq.* [9] 494 U.S. 872 (1990).

[10] See, for example, Michael W. McConnell, "Free Exercise Revisionism and the *Smith* Decision," *University of Chicago Law Review* 57 (1990): 1109.

the statute, President Bill Clinton delivered an eloquent address praising religious freedom as "perhaps the most precious of all American liberties" and urging Americans to "fight to the death to preserve the right of every American to practice whatever convictions he or she has."[11]

Although the Supreme Court later ruled that Congress lacked power to impose the statute on states,[12] RFRA has been applied in numerous cases involving federal laws – usually with little fanfare or public controversy. For example, in *Gonzalez* v. *O Centro Espírita Beneficente União do Vegetal*, the Supreme Court ruled that RFRA mandated an exemption for a Brazil-based religious group that used a tea containing a hallucinogenic substance (hoasca) that was on the government's list of forbidden substances. *O Centro Espírita* was a unanimous decision that elicited little or no criticism.[13]

Hobby Lobby and a spate of similar cases provoked greater dissension, by contrast, for two principal reasons. First, the religious objectors were resisting application of a federal regulation – the so-called contraception mandate requiring employers (subject to a variety of qualifications) to include contraception in their insurance plans – that was viewed by many as vital to the achievement of gender equality in the workplace. Second, the religious objectors were not mere individuals, or even churches or primarily religious associations (like the group in *O Centro Espírita*), but rather business corporations.

Hobby Lobby itself, for example, is a national chain of craft supply stores with the central purpose, presumably, of making a profit for its owners.[14] But Hobby Lobby is owned and managed by members of a family – David and Barbara Green and their three children – who have made it clear in corporate documents and policies that the business is to be operated in accordance with Christian principles. One of those principles, the Greens believe, is respect for the Sabbath day. At a loss of millions of dollars, therefore, Hobby Lobby stores do not open on Sundays. Another principle is opposition to abortion. Although willing to provide insurance coverage

[11] William J. Clinton, Remarks on Signing the Religious Freedom Restoration Act of 1993, November 16, 1993, accessed online, www.presidency.ucsb.edu/ws/?pid=46124.

[12] *City of Boerne* v. *Flores*, 521 U.S. 507 (1997).

[13] *Gonzalez* v. *O Centro Espírita Beneficente União do Vegetal*, 546 U.S. 418 (2006).

[14] The facts recited here are taken from the *Hobby Lobby* majority opinion. See *Burwell* v. *Hobby Lobby Stores*, 573 U.S.__, 134 S. Ct. 2751 (2014).

for a variety of contraceptives, therefore, the Greens object to subsidizing particular contraceptives that they regard as abortifacients.

The Supreme Court ruled that Hobby Lobby and similar businesses could claim the protection of RFRA. From this conclusion it does not automatically follow that such businesses should be granted exemptions: They still need to prove that a law imposes a "substantial burden" on the exercise of a sincere religious commitment, and even then the government can prevail by demonstrating a "compelling interest" that cannot be achieved in a less burdensome way. Under a similar standard, religious objectors in the pre-peyote case era had rarely succeeded in winning exemptions. In *Hobby Lobby*, however, a 5–4 majority ruled that the contraception mandate did impose a substantial burden on the business's religious commitments and that even if the government's interest was deemed compelling, that interest could be achieved in a less burdensome way – namely, through the same procedure that the government was already using for "non-profit" religious corporations.[15] Hobby Lobby was accordingly excused from complying with the mandate.

While this result provoked indignation in some quarters, I will suggest that, viewed as an exercise in statutory interpretation and application, the Court's ruling was blandly sensible. Insofar as critics have expressed outrage at the idea of giving religious freedom rights to a business corporation, those criticisms are unpersuasive and probably misleading. They are better understood as manifestations of other emerging and powerful concerns to which the matter of "corporate" status is largely peripheral.

Corporations and Rights

Corporations are typically viewed as artificial creations of positive law,[16] and they are routinely regarded as possessing "rights" of various kinds. In American constitutional law, this approach is sometimes traced back to Chief Justice John Marshall's seminal ruling, in the *Dartmouth College* case, which accepted a corporation's right to invoke the constitutional

[15] *Hobby Lobby*, 134 S. Ct. at 2782.

[16] In fact, scholars and jurists have proposed a variety of different conceptions of the nature of a corporation, ranging from the "real entity" theory to the view that a corporation should be viewed simply as a nexus of contracts. For discussion, see Ronald J. Colombo, "Rights and Responsibilities of the American Business Corporation," in *Business and Human Rights*, ed. Manoj Kumar Sinha (Thousand Oaks, CA: Sage Publications, 2012).

prohibition on the impairment of contracts.[17] Often the attribution of rights to corporations seems wholly unproblematic. For example, hardly anyone doubts that corporations properly enjoy the rights to own property, to enter contracts, or to sue and be sued. But sometimes the ascription of a right can provoke opposition. Thus, the Supreme Court's ruling in *Citizens United* v. *Federal Election Commission* that corporations enjoy a right of free speech has been much criticized.[18] (Although hardly anyone questions that corporations should enjoy free speech rights in other contexts, such as in defamation suits. The Court's ruling in *New York Times Company* v. *Sullivan* – notice the "Company" – is in that respect hardly controversial.[19])

Attempting to portray *Hobby Lobby* as a novel extension, critics argued that the Supreme Court's First Amendment jurisprudence had not previously ruled that corporations enjoy rights to religious freedom.[20] But neither had the Court ever indicated otherwise: Some religious freedom cases had involved corporate claimants, and the Court had never suggested that religious freedom rights were thereby forfeited.[21] On the contrary, that possibility hardly seems to have occurred to the justices, or to others. Should it have? Suppose, say, that Jacob is the owner and sole proprietor of a business to which religious freedom protections might sometimes be relevant – a business that engages in the slaughter of animals for kosher foods, perhaps.[22] And suppose that for practical reasons, Jacob decides to incorporate his business. Should this utterly routine decision regarding the form of the business, available as a matter of right to any citizen willing to fill out the proper papers and pay the registration fee, cause Jacob to forfeit his or his business's constitutional protections?

Hobby Lobby itself turned not on the Constitution but rather on the interpretation of a federal statute – RFRA – which gave more explicit guidance than the free exercise clause does. More specifically, as noted, in enacting RFRA Congress extended statutory religious freedom rights to

[17] *Trustees of Dartmouth College* v. *Woodward*, 17 U.S. 518 (1817).
[18] *Citizens United* v. *Federal Election Commission*, 558 U.S. 310 (2010).
[19] *New York Times Company* v. *Sullivan*, 376 U.S. 254 (1964).
[20] *Hobby Lobby*, 134 S. Ct. at 2794 (Ginsburg, J., dissenting).
[21] See, for example, *Corporation of the Presiding Bishop* v. *Amos*, 483 U.S. 327 (1987) and *NLRB* v. *Catholic Bishop of Chicago*, 440 U.S. 490 (1978).
[22] Congress has granted limited exemptions from laws regulating the treatment of animals for kosher slaughter. For a critical discussion, see Melissa Lewis, "The Regulation of Kosher Slaughter in the United States," *Lewis & Clark Law Review* 16 (2010): 259.

"persons" – a term that to a lay observer might mean flesh-and-blood human beings. When used in positive law, however, the term "persons" commonly, though not always, includes both "natural" persons and "artificial" or juristic persons, including corporations.[23] Thus, almost a century and a half ago, the Supreme Court indicated that the term "persons" as used in the Fourteenth Amendment's conferral of rights normally includes corporations.[24] And in the so-called Dictionary Act, Congress expressly instructed that when used in federal statutes, the term "persons" includes "corporations, companies, associations, firms, partnerships, societies, and joint stock companies, as well as individuals," unless the context indicates otherwise.[25]

Nothing in the legislative history of RFRA reveals any congressional intention to use the term "persons" in other than its usual statutory sense. Nor had the question come to the forefront in earlier cases. Was the religious group that sued under RFRA leading to the Court's unanimous decision in *O Centro Espírita* incorporated? Did anyone care? Should anything have turned on the question? Understandably, therefore, the *Hobby Lobby* majority considered itself bound to follow the Dictionary Act's instruction. Far from radical, the Court's ruling was yawningly unadventurous.

Perhaps that was the problem: Perhaps the justices should not have treated the case as a mundane exercise in statutory interpretation, but should instead have been more ambitious or searching in their inquiry?[26] In any case, critics now exerted themselves to articulate reasons why, in the face of congressional instruction and of standard legal usage, a corporation should nonetheless not be deemed a legal "person" in this context. We must consider the principal reasons that have been proposed.

(Corporate) Form and Legal Substance

Critics have argued that there is something about the corporate form that makes it inherently incapable of supporting a right to religious freedom.

23 See Colombo, "Rights and Responsibilities," 75–76 (describing "the law's practice of treating the corporation as a *persona ficta* – an artificial fictitious person, but a person nonetheless when it comes to the assessment of legal status, rights, and obligations").

24 *Santa Clara Co.* v. *Southern Pac. Railroad*, 118 U.S. 394 (1886).

25 1 U.S.C. sec. 1.

26 See Kent Greenawalt, "*Hobby Lobby*: Its Flawed Interpretive Techniques and Standard of Application," in *The Rise of Corporate Religious Liberty*, 146 (arguing that RFRA is "more complex" than most statutes, and criticizing the Court for not adopting a "more comprehensive and context-oriented analysis" taking account of "multiple factors").

One version of this objection focuses on the *legal* features of corporate status. Another more common and substantial version emphasizes what we might call the *ontological* nature of the corporation, arguing that a corporation simply does not have the capacity to exercise religion.

In the *Hobby Lobby* case itself, an amicus brief signed by forty or so law professors pressed the first objection, arguing that corporate status is inherently incompatible with a right to religious freedom.[27] But the brief consisted largely of a platoon of truisms escorting a *non sequitur*. Thus, the academic amici emphasized that a corporation is a legal entity that is independent of its owners, that a corporation's liabilities do not normally carry over to the owners or shareholders personally (so that incorporation affords shareholders the advantage of limited liability), and that unlike the mortal human beings who create, own, and manage it, a corporation can enjoy perpetual existence. These are all familiar propositions of corporate law, but none of them entails that a corporation cannot possess rights of various kinds, including a right of religious freedom. No one says to the owners and editors of the *New York Times*: "As long as you publish as individuals, you enjoy the free speech protections of the First Amendment (in defamation lawsuits, for example), but if you choose to incorporate, thereby gaining the benefits of limited liability and so forth, you forfeit those rights." Why should religious freedom rights be any different? Critics typically concede that *some* corporations can claim rights to religious freedom – churches, for example, or even religious nonprofit corporations. Yet that concession effectively vitiates the claim that there is something about the legal status of being a corporation that precludes a right to religious freedom.

The more common and substantial argument is more ontological in character: The claim is that a corporation is not the kind of entity that can do the sorts of things that "religion" involves – believing, praying, worshipping. Elizabeth Sepper's argument is typical:

> How can a business have beliefs, religious or otherwise? What does it mean for a business to hold a faith? How can a corporation exercise religion? How does it show sincerity? Can a single-minded obligation to maximize profits meld with religious devotion?[28]

[27] Amicus Curiae Brief of Corporate and Criminal Law Professors in Support of Petitioners, accessed online, www.americanbar.org/content/dam/aba/publications/supreme_court_preview/briefs-v3/13-354-13-356_amcu_cclp.authcheckdam.pdf.

[28] Sepper, "Contraception," 315–316.

As an analogy, one might cogently argue that a corporation is incapable of enjoying a right to abortion – not because corporations cannot possess legal rights, but because having an abortion is the kind of thing that only a "natural person" or human being can do. The same, critics say, is true for religion, and hence for religious freedom – or so say the critics.

This objection might have force against the ambitious claim that a *corporation in and of itself* can exercise religion, and thus can claim a right to religious freedom. Indeed, a few theorists do offer versions of this ambitious claim by drawing on sophisticated philosophical theories of group agency or intentionality.[29] But we need not pursue that interesting philosophical question here, because the *Hobby Lobby* Court explicitly disclaimed any such position. On the contrary, the Court adopted the more commonsensical position that although a corporation is an artificial entity that does not *in itself* worship or exercise faith, endowing the corporation with a right to religious freedom is a way of respecting the interests of the human beings who create and own the corporation – the organizers and shareholders.[30]

This conclusion seems utterly unremarkable. The law routinely endows the artificial entities called "corporations" with rights to own property (which enjoy the support of constitutional protections), to sue and be sued (subject to constitutional due process constraints and protections), and to enter into contracts (subject to constitutional protections against unlawful impairment, as Chief Justice Marshall emphasized in the *Dartmouth College* case). The law does this not because corporations are in some mystical sense soulful or mindful entities possessed of intrinsic dignity and deserving of respect and protection, but rather, and more mundanely, because corporate status is a legal construction that promotes the interests of the human beings who create and use such corporations. Rights are legally attributed to *the corporation*, but the purpose of the attribution is to serve the interests of *human beings*. The same is true with respect to religious freedom.[31]

29 See, for example, John Iuliano, "Do Corporations Have Religious Beliefs?," *Indiana Law Journal* 90 (2015): 47.

30 *Hobby Lobby*, 134 S. Ct. at 2678 ("A corporation is simply a form of organization used by human beings to achieve desired ends . . . When rights, whether constitutional or statutory, are extended to corporations, the purpose is to protect the rights of these people.").

31 For elaboration of the point, see Amy J. Sepinwall, "Corporate Piety and Impropriety: Hobby Lobby's Extension of RFRA to the For-Profit Corporation," *Harvard Business Law Review* 5 (2015): 173, 177, 202.

Or at least it *might be* true. Nothing in the fact of corporate status counts against the conclusion. Critics can of course coherently oppose corporate religious freedom as a *normative* matter, arguing that the law *should not* ascribe rights of religious freedom to business corporations. But there is no *ontological* obstacle – nothing in the corporate form – that counts against the possibility of such an ascription. And so the familiar, earnest refrain that "a corporation does not *believe*, does not *pray*, does not *worship*" turns out to be quite possibly true – and also wholly beside the point. Such protestations are little more than, as Amy Sepinwall remarks, a "red herring."[32]

The question, in short, is not whether a business corporation *can* be endowed with a right to religious freedom – the answer to that question is emphatically "yes" – but whether it *should* be. Critics address that latter question as well, obviously. But the standard formulation of the question – something like "Do business corporations have a right to religious freedom?" – obscures the normative question and trades illicitly on the rhetorically beguiling but analytically misconceived ontological objection. We would do well, therefore, to avoid that confusion by posing the question in a more explicitly normative form: *Should people who own and operate a business be required to forfeit whatever religious freedom protections they and their business would otherwise enjoy if they choose to operate the business in corporate form?* Perhaps they should. Many advocates today appear to think so. But why?

Religion and the Pursuit of Profits

Probably the most common complaint objects to giving religious freedom rights not to *corporations*, exactly, but rather to *business* (or "for-profit") corporations. A corporation's profit-making aspirations are said to negate any claims to religious freedom it otherwise might have. But why should that be so? Although the reasoning is often less than clear, sometimes the critics seem to be making a point about *religion*; at other times they seem to be making a point about *corporations*. In either version, however, the point does not stand up to scrutiny.

In one version, the objection suggests that the pursuit of profit is somehow foreign to or incompatible with "religion." But there is nothing in the notion or the practice of "religion" that requires any such conclusion. In

[32] Ibid., 184.

perhaps the most familiar and frequently recited of all religious prayers, believers address the deity and implore that "Thy will be done," and then they request divine assistance in obtaining their "daily bread" and in steering clear of "temptation."[33] Mundane and utilitarian purposes are thoroughly intermixed with more spiritual or "religious" ones. Is there anything suspicious, or even surprising, about this intermixing? Indeed, for believers who live in the world, is it even imaginable that the situation could be otherwise? The notion that religious believers should or could segregate their religious commitments from the pursuits of mundane matters – the earning of "daily bread" (or of "profits" with which to buy that bread) – seems a crude distortion of the religious vocation. And in fact the major Western religions of Judaism, Christianity, and Islam all impose religious obligations on the conduct of business.[34] Moreover, even if the posited cleavage between living one's religion and making a profit were plausible, the objection would have nothing to do with questions of corporate form. It would apply equally to the lone business person pursuing a profit-making trade in his or her personal capacity.

But the objection can be reinterpreted as making a point about the nature of corporations. Thus, one might argue that although a *human being* can attempt simultaneously to earn a living (or "make a profit") and to honor religious obligations, a *corporation* cannot do this. Once a corporation chooses to pursue profits, profit-making must thereafter become its sole purpose, to the exclusion of other (or at least religious?) considerations.

Hobby Lobby's critics sometimes seem to take this position. We have already noted Elizabeth Sepper's rhetorical question: "How can a single-minded obligation to maximize profits meld with religious devotion?"[35] And yet the position is starkly inconsistent both with current law and with contemporary thinking about the purpose and obligations of business corporations. As the *Hobby Lobby* opinion noted, current law does not require that business corporations be solely devoted to profit-making to the exclusion of other concerns and aspirations.[36] And the school of thought often described as "Corporate Social Responsibility" insists that corporations not only may but *should* be guided by ethical considerations that go beyond "the bottom line."[37]

33 Matt. 6:9–13 (King James Version).

34 See Mark L. Rienzi, "God and the Profits: Is There Religious Liberty for Moneymakers?," *George Mason Law Review* 21 (2013): 66–73.

35 Sepper, "Contraception," 315–316.

36 *Hobby Lobby*, 134 S.Ct. at 2770–2771.

37 See Colombo, "Rights and Responsibilities," 70–75.

Hence, corporations today often adopt ethical purposes and constraints in their charters or policies and forego potentially profitable opportunities in order to honor these ethical commitments.[38] They refrain from activities that would pollute the environment, for example, or that would exploit vulnerable populations.[39] There is no reason at all why such purposes and constraints could not reflect religious commitments. This is not just a possibility: as in the old joke about baptism by immersion, we've seen it done – often.[40] Thus, a corporation like Hobby Lobby manifestly does have such commitments.

Such behavior is usually applauded, not condemned. Thus, the same progressive critics who assail Hobby Lobby for tempering its quest for profits with religious commitments would likely berate the company for pursuing profits at the expense of damaging the Amazon rain forest or exploiting underpaid workers in developing countries. In short, the claim that a for-profit corporation is obligated to engage in the single-minded, Scroogish pursuit of money is simply untenable. Even business corporations *may* – and, most critics would say, *should* – take other ethical constraints into consideration. And there is no reason why such constraints cannot be grounded in religion.

Or is there?

Corporate Governance and Religious Difference

Critics sometimes suggest that religious commitments are distinctively problematic in corporations, for two related but independent reasons. First, owners of a corporation – shareholders, basically – might disagree about religion.[41] Some shareholders, like the Greens, might oppose abortion; others might not. So, then, how would such disagreements be resolved? Whose religion would prevail?

38 See Sepinwall, "Corporate Piety," 182 (noting that "owners otherwise committed to maximizing profits might object to profits earned through child labor, or the sale of arms to genocidal rebels, or the exploitation of poor and vulnerable populations").

39 See Rienzi, "God and the Profits," 81–84.

40 Alan Meese and Nathan Oman point out that corporations often adopt shareholders' religious values and precepts. For example, corporations sometimes close on Sundays, or before sundown on Fridays, in honor of the Sabbath; they decline to sell alcohol or comply with kosher requirements; or they play Christian music in their stores. Alan J. Meese and Nathan B. Oman, "Hobby Lobby, Corporate Law, and the Theory of the Firm: Why For-Profit Corporations Are RFRA Persons," *Harvard Law Review* 127 (2014): 273, 278–282.

41 See, for example, Sepper, "Contraception," 319.

There is an obvious and straightforward answer to such questions. Shareholders of a corporation might indeed disagree in matters of religion – just as they might disagree about all manner of other ethical and economic matters that potentially affect the corporation. Such disagreements are utterly routine, and they are hardly debilitating: They are resolved in the manner that state law and corporate articles and by-laws prescribe.[42] So, yes, shareholders might diverge regarding the permissibility of subsidizing particular contraceptives that are deemed abortifacients; they might also clash over whether it is unethical to invest in South African diamond mines or to produce a profitable product that might cause adverse climate change. And they resolve such disagreements by voting, in the prescribed fashion. In this respect, there is nothing distinctive about potential religious disagreements.[43]

As a practical matter, to be sure, the possibility of religious differences among shareholders or others who manage and control a corporation makes it unlikely that many business corporations – especially large public corporations – will actually embrace a religious self-understanding that would potentially give rise to religious freedom claims. Such claims are most likely to come from family owned or closely held corporations like Hobby Lobby, as the Supreme Court observed.[44] There is nothing in principle that would categorically confine religious freedom in this way. Giving free rein to our imaginations, we can perhaps conceive of, say, a large publicly held pharmaceutical corporation in which a majority of the shareholders happen to be "pro-life" Catholics who object to producing abortion-inducing drugs. If we are realistic, though, we will not hold our breath waiting for this to happen. IBM and AT&T will not likely invoke RFRA anytime soon.[45]

A second, though related, objection asserts that a corporation like Hobby Lobby that asserts a religious constraint thereby imposes burdens on third parties who may not share the owners' religious commitments. This concern is hardly distinctive to religious constraints: The corporation that foregoes profitable opportunities because of scruples about despoiling

42 Hobby Lobby, 134 S.Ct. at 2775. See also Sepinwall, "Corporate Piety," 200.

43 See Meese and Oman, "Hobby Lobby," 291–292 (arguing that actual experience provides little support for progressive fear that religion will be disruptive or corporate enterprise or governance).

44 *Hobby Lobby*, 134 S.Ct. at 2774.

45 For further discussion, see Meese and Oman, "Hobby Lobby," 288.

the rain forest or exploiting workers in developing countries may suffer reduced earnings, leading to reduced dividends for shareholders who do not embrace these ethical commitments (and who might likely include unknowing and economically straitened retirees whose retirement accounts are handled through mutual funds). Still, the effects on third parties are easy to visualize in a case like *Hobby Lobby*, because it is easy to understand that the company's Christian commitments could mean (at least unless and until the government provides an alternative means of coverage) that employees might be deprived of contraception coverage as part of their employee insurance plans, even if they do not personally have any moral or religious objection to contraception or abortion.

Virtually everyone concedes that under RFRA, this sort of impact on third parties is central among the factors that a court should consider in deciding whether the government has a "compelling interest" in requiring compliance even by religious objectors.[46] How that balance is to be resolved will surely vary with the facts of different cases. For now, two general observations are pertinent.

First, once again, the concern about third-party effects is not intrinsically related to the question of corporate form.[47] If Christian entrepreneurs like the Greens chose not to incorporate but rather to operate through, say, a business partnership, exactly the same issue about third-party effects would be presented.

Second, from the nation's inception, commitments to religious freedom have always implicated concerns about effects on third parties. For every Quaker who has been excused from serving in the military because of his religious scruples, some other person will presumably have been called upon to serve (and perhaps die). Nor is the concern in any way limited to *religious* accommodation: Governments attempt to accommodate all sorts of people for all sorts of reasons – medical conditions, physical or psychological disabilities, family emergencies, economic hardship, the birth of children – and such accommodations virtually always have effects on third parties. The school district that is legally required to allocate substantial resources to accommodate particular students with learning disabilities has fewer resources to devote to other students, or to pay teachers and staff, or to support the school's athletic teams. The business that spends large amounts of money to accommodate employees with physical disabilities

[46] See Sepinwall, "Corporate Piety," 201–202. [47] See Ibid., 202.

has less money to pay to its owners, other employees, and shareholders. In this respect, there is nothing distinctive about accommodations based on commitments to religious freedom.

Or is there? Could it be that although governments act permissibly and even nobly when they accommodate all sorts of special needs and concerns, even though such accommodation imposes costs on third parties, religion is somehow different in this respect? Should third-party harms preclude *religious* accommodation, even though they do not preclude other kinds of accommodation?

Although weakly grounded in tradition and case law,[48] just this argument has gained momentum in recent years.[49] The argument seems to have been inspired by, and arisen during, the controversy over the contraception mandate. Once again, though, there is nothing in the argument that intrinsically turns on the corporate status of a religious objector. Third-party effects can follow from accommodating individuals just as surely as from accommodating corporations: think again of the exemptions from military service for religious pacifists. And, again, the same issue would arise if the Greens operated their business through a partnership instead of a corporation. And yet it seems that a case like *Hobby Lobby* has provided a convenient and favorable context for the promotion of this third-party harm argument. That fact is instructive in understanding the underlying cultural significance of the debates provoked by the case.

Corporate Religious Freedom amid the Culture Wars

We noted earlier in this section how RFRA enjoyed nearly unanimous support when it was enacted, and how it was effusively praised by President Clinton. By the time of *Hobby Lobby*, however, the cultural climate had changed, drastically. This change was vividly manifest in the virulent reaction in 2015 to the enactment in Indiana of a statute virtually identical in its substance to RFRA. A commitment to religious freedom that nearly all Americans and politicians had enthusiastically supported in 1993 now triggered passionate opposition from politicians, pundits,

[48] See Marc O. DeGirolami, "Free Exercise by Moonlight," *San Diego Law Review* 53 (2016): 105, 131–144.

[49] See, for example, Frederick M. Gedicks and Rebecca Van Tassell, "RFRA Exemptions from the Contraception Mandate: An Unconstitutional Accommodation of Religion," *Harvard Civil Rights-Civil Liberties Law Review* 49 (2014): 343.

CEOs, late-night entertainers, athletic associations, and of course academics.[50]

Exactly what produced this change is no doubt a complex question, not to be satisfactorily answered in a short chapter like this one. But a few tentative observations seem necessary. Douglas Laycock, who has been not only a leading scholar but also a litigator and lobbyist in the area since the 1980s, attributes the reversal to two main causes. One is demographic – namely, the increase in nonbelievers as a proportion of the population. When nearly everyone was a religious believer of one kind or another, Laycock observes, religious freedom was viewed as "a sort of mutual non-aggression pact" that was beneficial to all. Today, by contrast, "[m]uch of the nonbelieving minority sees religious liberty as a protection only for believers. On that view, a universal natural right morphs into a special interest demand."[51] The other main cause, Laycock thinks, has been the gay rights movement and, more generally, the campaign to embody the results of the Sexual Revolution in law. "[G]roups committed to sexual liberty naturally view traditional religion as their principal enemy," he contends. "If traditional religion is the enemy, then it might follow that religious liberty is a bad thing, because it empowers that enemy."[52]

Both of these developments are associated with the broader conflict often described as the "culture wars."[53] The term was given contemporary prominence by a book of that title by the sociologist James Davison Hunter, whose diagnosis seems if anything more cogent today than when the book was published in 1991.[54] Hunter found that across a variety of issues ranging from education to family to media to law and politics, Americans were coalescing into two contending camps, which he labeled "orthodox" and "progressive."[55] This conflict, Hunter suggested, was not confined to merely private disagreements; it was a struggle, as his subtitle put it, to "define America."

[50] For a brief recounting, see Patrick J. Deneen, "The Power Elite," *First Things*, June 2015, accessed online, www.firstthings.com/article/2015/06/the-power-elite.

[51] Laycock, "Sex, Atheism," 422. [52] Ibid., 415.

[53] The following argument is developed at much greater length in Steven D. Smith, *Pagans and Christians in the City* (Grand Rapids, MI: William B. Eerdmans 2018), chap. 11.

[54] James Davison Hunter, *Culture Wars: The Struggle to Define America* (New York: Basic Books, 1991).

[55] Ibid., 43–44.

The orthodox party, Hunter explained, is committed to the view that "moral and spiritual truths have a supernatural origin beyond ... human experience."[56] In accordance with this view, the party's conception of American community hearkens back to the national self-understanding captured in Will Herberg's classic *Protestant-Catholic-Jew*,[57] and it resonates with the "civil religion" that had been described in the 1960s and 1970s in Robert Bellah's influential writings. Until relatively recently, Bellah explained, "[Americans] saw themselves as being a 'people' in the classical and biblical sense of the word."[58] Citing the appeals to deity in the Declaration of Independence, Bellah argued:

> It is significant that the reference to a suprapolitical sovereignty, to a God who stands above the nation and whose ends are standards by which to judge the nation and indeed only in terms of which the nation's existence is justified, becomes a permanent feature of American political life ever after.[59]

A succinct abbreviation for this understanding might be the phrase used in the Gettysburg Address and later added to the Pledge of Allegiance, taken at face value and in its traditional sense: We are "this nation [or, in the Pledge, one nation], under God."

By contrast, the "progressive" party is distinguished, Hunter argued, by its rejection of transcendent moral authority in favor of more secular and "innerworldly sources of moral authority."[60] Progressives accordingly resist the "civil religion" conception of American community and reject or attempt to deflate (as Justice Sandra Day O'Connor did in the Pledge of Allegiance case[61]) the idea of "one nation, under God," sometimes even attempting surreptitiously to excise the phrase from Abraham Lincoln's revered address.[62]

Hunter observed that in struggling to maintain their respective conceptions of American community, both the orthodox and progressive parties appreciate the crucial importance of public symbols.[63] As Benedict

[56] Ibid., 120.

[57] Will Herberg, *Protestant-Catholic-Jew* (Chicago, IL: Chicago University Press, 1983 [1955]), 87. Herberg studied and described "the conception of the three 'communions' – Protestantism, Catholicism, Judaism – as three diverse, but equally legitimate, equally American, expressions of an over-all American religion." Ibid., 87.

[58] Bellah, *Broken Covenant*, 2. [59] Ibid., 174. [60] Hunter, *Culture Wars*, 124.

[61] *Elk Grove School Dist.* v. *Newdow*, 542 U.S. 1, 35 (2004) (O'Connor, J., concurring).

[62] See Robert P. George, *Conscience and Its Enemies: Confronting the Dogmas of Liberal Secularism* (Wilmington, DE: ISI Books, 2013), 147–152.

[63] Hunter, *Culture Wars*, 58.

Anderson explains, communities are not physical facts, but rather are constructed, or "imagined" entities,[64] and the imaginings that construct a community arise around public symbols. Symbols, in other words, do not merely *express* a community; they help to *constitute* it.[65] Consequently, each side in the culture wars "struggles to *monopolize the symbols of legitimacy.*"[66]

These observations help to illuminate the debates – both their shape and their intensity – in a case like *Hobby Lobby*. After all, two especially powerful symbolic embodiments of the older, biblical conception of the American community were its official legal norms of sexuality and its traditional commitment to religious freedom. So it is hardly surprising that these would be central targets of progressive efforts to recast the conception of American community. As late as the 1950s or even later, American law reflected a traditionally biblical view of sexual morality. Fornication was still a criminal offense in all but ten states, adultery in all but five, sodomy in all fifty states. Seduction was both a tort and a crime. The distribution of contraceptives was forbidden in most places.[67] The fact that these laws were retained even though they were routinely disregarded and almost never enforced underscored their primarily symbolic function, consistent with the biblically oriented conception of community discerned by Bellah. To the progressive faction, conversely, that conception is alienating and offensive. Over the past half-century, accordingly, all of the traditional legal norms have been subjected to sustained challenge, as constitutional and statutory law has aggressively replaced them with the progressive norms of the so-called Sexual Revolution.[68]

Perhaps more than anything else, legal and readily available contraception has been the central symbol of liberation from older, biblical norms of sexuality.[69] So even though earlier prohibitions on contraception were for the most part purely symbolic, and even though contraceptives are today readily available and affordable in comparison to other less symbolically fraught necessities that government typically does *not* supply or

[64] Benedict Anderson, *Imagined Communities* (New York: Verso, 1991).

[65] The point is elaborated at much greater length in Smith, *Pagans and Christians*.

[66] Hunter, "Culture Wars,"147 (emphasis in original).

[67] Robert E. Rodes, *Law and Chastity* (Durham, NC: Carolina Academic Press, 2006), 9–22.

[68] Geoffrey R. Stone, *Sex and the Constitution* (New York: Liveright, 2017).

[69] John D'Emilio and Estelle B. Freedman, *Intimate Matters: A History of Sexuality in America*, 3rd Edition (Chicago, IL: University of Chicago Press, 2012), 242–255, 338.

subsidize (cell phones, laptops), it is not surprising that contraception has been at the center of progressive legal efforts "to monopolize the symbols of legitimacy."[70] Nor is it surprising that challenges to this newer pro-contraception regime, like Hobby Lobby's, evoke especially intense opposition.

But more generally, the traditional American commitment to religious freedom, or to special protection for, or accommodation of, religion,[71] has been more than just a policy for dealing with religious diversity; it has been a central constitutive symbol of the commitment to "one nation, under God." James Madison's celebrated justification for religious freedom emphasized that our duties to "our Creator" are prior in time and importance to any duties we may assume to civil society and government.[72] Thomas Jefferson justified his seminal Virginia Statute for Religious Freedom by declaring that "Almighty God hath created the mind free" and that coercing people in matters of religion was "contrary to the plan of the holy Author of our religion."[73] Consistent with Bellah's later description, both men conceived of the nation (including in its public policies) as subject to a transcendent authority – the "Creator" or "Almighty God." Moreover, these theistic rationales were offered as justifications for freedom of religion.

But as the traditional and "orthodox" conception of "one nation, under God" has come to be rejected in favor of a more secular and "progressive" understanding, it was likely inevitable that the commitment to religious freedom would be challenged as well. Although relatively recent, that challenge is by now far advanced in the academy and in the culture generally. The reaction to the Indiana laws and to similar measures in

[70] Hunter, *Culture Wars*, 147.

[71] Paul Horwitz observes that "[a]ccommodation of religion is an aboriginal feature of American public law. From the earliest days of the Republic, exemptions from legally imposed burdens on religious belief and practice 'were seen as a natural and legitimate response to the tension between law and religious conviction.'" Paul Horwitz, "Comment: The *Hobby Lobby* Moment," *Harvard Law Review* 128 (2014): 154, 167, partially quoting Michael W. McConnell, "The Origins and Historical Understanding of Free Exercise of Religion," *Harvard Law Review* 103 (1990): 1409, 1466.

[72] James Madison, "Memorial and Remonstrance against Religious Assessments," in *The Sacred Rights of Conscience* ed. Daniel L. Dreisbach and Mark David Hall (Indianapolis, IN: Liberty Fund, 2009), 309.

[73] Virginia Act for Religious Freedom, reprinted in *Church and State in the Modern Age: A Documentary History*, ed. J. F. MacClear (New York: Oxford University Press, 1995), 63, 64.

Arizona, Georgia, and elsewhere attest to this fact. So does the intense criticism of the *Hobby Lobby* decision.

In *Hobby Lobby*, the specific issue of corporate religious freedom was caught up in a more general struggle over religious freedom itself, which is itself merely one theater in a broader cultural and political war to "define America," as Hunter put it. In such fundamental struggles, combatants (on both sides) will instinctively resort to any political, legal, or rhetorical resources that may serve their purposes. They may engage in pervasive mendacity.[74] They will invent new arguments, such as the third-party harm argument. Even though religious accommodation has always involved effects on third parties, and even though all kinds of accommodation – of physical disabilities, for example, or childbirth – impose costs on third parties, it will suddenly come to seem intolerable that *religious* burdens should be accommodated at the expense of third parties.

I do not mean to suggest that the advocates in these conflicts are being merely opportunistic or cynical. They are often true believers. Convinced of the rightness of their conception of the American community (which may be so deeply and instinctively held that they may scarcely be conscious of it), they will naturally regard claims and arguments that resonate with and support that conception as correct. More than correct, actually – righteous, and just.

Passionate but dubious arguments over "corporate religious liberty" become understandable when viewed in this context. In a cultural climate in which a commitment to religious freedom enjoyed general and robust support, it would seem profoundly counterintuitive to say that business people should forfeit religious freedom protections if they choose to incorporate. Why would we want to exact such a perverse price for the exercise of a privilege – incorporation – that is routinely available to anyone for just about any licit purpose? Conversely, if religious freedom comes to be viewed as an anachronistic and discriminatory special privilege inherited from the past, then such a forfeiture may come to seem entirely sensible. Why *not* make people pay for the benefits of incorporation by giving up a special privilege that in principle they probably should not have anyway?

[74] Douglas Laycock, "The Campaign against Religious Liberty," in *The Rise of Corporate Religious Liberty*, 231, 248 ("The public debate over the Indiana RFRA presented mostly falsehood from both sides").

What drives the argument, in sum, is not actually any cogent concern about the corporate form per se, but rather a deeper opposition to religious freedom as a special and symbolically constitutive constitutional commitment. The issue of corporate rights merely provides a convenient context for that deeper opposition to assert itself.

From Corporations to Churches

The *Hosanna-Tabor* case was like *Hobby Lobby* in one central respect: The entity invoking religious freedom was not a solitary individual but rather a collective entity. But the religious claimant in *Hosanna-Tabor* was not a business corporation but rather a *church*. More precisely, it was a school so intimately associated with a Lutheran congregation in Redford, Michigan, that it was treated as part of the church (including in the case caption). So the question as posed was not whether a *corporation* can claim a statutory right to religious freedom but whether a *church* (which might or might not be incorporated as a technical matter) enjoys some kind of special constitutional protection.

The question emerged from a dispute between the Hosanna-Tabor school and a fourth-grade teacher, Cheryl Perich.[75] Teachers at the school were divided into "called" teachers and "lay teachers." "Called" teachers were required to complete a course of theological training and to be "called" by the congregation; once called, they were given the title of "Minister of Religion, Commissioned." Perich had begun at the school as a lay teacher and had later advanced to the status of "called" teacher. But the congregation revoked this designation and the school terminated her contract after she insisted on returning from a disability leave mid-semester and earlier than expected, and then in open confrontation refused to accept the school's judgment that she was not ready to return to work.

The Equal Employment Opportunity Commission sued the school on Perich's behalf, contending that her termination violated the Americans with Disabilities Act. Considering Perich's position to be ministerial in character, the school defended by invoking a legal doctrine known as the

[75] These facts are taken from the Court's majority opinion. *Hosanna-Tabor Evangelical Lutheran Church & School* v. *Equal Employment Opportunity Commission*, 565 U.S. 171 (2012).

"ministerial exception." Under this doctrine, which had been accepted by numerous lower federal courts[76] but had not previously been addressed by the Supreme Court, employment decisions with respect to ministerial employees are treated as insulated against federal legislation regulating employment (including prohibitions on employment discrimination). Where the exception applies, the usual inquiries – whether a religious employer's stated reasons for an adverse employment decision are pretextual, for instance – are preempted. Under the doctrine, decisions to appoint or discharge ministers are, basically, the church's business, not the government's.

Ruling that the ministerial exception applied to Perich's case, the district court granted summary judgment in favor of the school.[77] The Sixth Circuit reversed, concluding that, notwithstanding her title, Perich's duties were mostly nonreligious in character and that the ministerial exception therefore did not apply.[78] On appeal to the Supreme Court, however, the Commission backed away from this argument on which it had prevailed in the Sixth Circuit. Instead, the Commission primarily urged the Court to reject the ministerial exception altogether and to treat religious employers in such cases just like other nonreligious employers.[79]

This seemed an audacious strategy, as the Court's stern rejection of the Commission's position would eventually confirm.[80] Without something like the ministerial exception, after all, it would seem that an entity such as the Roman Catholic Church that maintains a male-only priesthood might be subject to a barrage of lawsuits for sex discrimination. The Commission tried to fend off this implication by suggesting that such a church would be protected not by religious freedom but rather by the implied right of freedom of association. But that right has done little to shield other associations that have tried to maintain male-only policies,

[76] See, for example, *Combs* v. *Central Texas Conference*, 173 F.3d 343 (5th Cir. 1999); *Natal* v. *Christian and Missionary Alliance*, 878 F.2d 1575 (1st Cir. 1989).

[77] *Equal Employment Opportunity Commission* v. *Hosanna-Tabor Evangelical Lutheran School*, 582 F.Supp.2d 881 (E.D. Mich. 2008).

[78] *Equal Employment Opportunity Commission* v. *Hosanna-Tabor Evangelical Lutheran School*, 597 F.3d 769 (6th Cir. 2010).

[79] Hobby Lobby, 132 S. Ct. at 706.

[80] Ibid. The Court described the Commission's position as "untenable" and "remarkable" – words which in the understated vocabulary of Supreme Court opinions typically mean something like "absurd" or "preposterous."

including the Rotary Club and the Jaycees.[81] Unless a church receives some special protection *qua* church, why would it not suffer the same fate?[82]

In another sense, though, the Commission's decision to oppose the ministerial exception was understandable. After all, even supporters of the exception had acknowledged that the doctrine's constitutional grounding was uncertain and that its compatibility with more general free exercise doctrine was debatable.[83] The case thus touched on elusive and far-reaching constitutional questions.

Authorities Modern and Ancient

Unlike the right claimed in *Hobby Lobby*, the ministerial exception did not derive from any statute, and, as noted, its constitutional grounding was uncertain. But the most plausible candidate for a supporting legal text, it seemed, was the free exercise clause of the First Amendment, under which Congress (and, by later extension, government generally) is forbidden to "prohibit the free exercise [of religion]." Before 1990, lower courts had comfortably invoked this provision as a basis for forbidding governmental interference in a church's decisions about the ministers who would constitute, govern, and instruct the church.[84] Then, in *Employment Division* v. *Smith*, the aforementioned peyote case, the Supreme Court had ruled that as long as a law is "religiously neutral" and "generally applicable," constitutional free exercise requirements are thereby satisfied. Federal antidiscrimination and disabilities laws regulating employment would seem to meet these conditions: Such laws do not target or single out religious employers.[85] Consequently, post-*Smith* courts and commentators, while continuing to invoke and apply the ministerial exception, had

[81] See, for example, *Board of Directors of Rotary International* v. *Rotary Club*, 481 U.S. 537 (1987); *Roberts* v. *United States Jaycees*, 468 U.S. 609 (1984).

[82] For a determined effort to answer these questions, and indeed to interpret *Hosanna-Tabor* itself as accepting the position that the Court appears to have explicitly rejected – namely, that a church cannot be protected by any special right of *religious* freedom but only by a more general freedom of (intimate) association – see Larry Sager, "Why Churches (and, Possibly, the Tarpon Bay Women's Blue Water Fishing Club) Can Discriminate," in *The Rise of Corporate Religious Liberty*, 77.

[83] For a masterful review of the debate, see Christopher C. Lund, "In Defense of the Ministerial Exception," *North Carolina Law Review* 90 (2011): 1, 4 n.6.

[84] See, for example, *McClure* v. *Salvation Army*, 460 F.2d 553 (5th Cir. 1972).

[85] *Employment Division* v. *Smith*, 494 U.S. 872 (1990).

found themselves embarrassed in attempting to articulate a solid constitutional basis for that doctrine.[86]

Partly for this reason, perhaps, the Supreme Court in *Hosanna-Tabor* was not content to begin its analysis with the free exercise clause, or even with the Constitution. Instead, the Court looked farther back – much farther back – to the Magna Carta. The very first clause in that venerable document, the Court noted, had provided that "the English church shall be free, and shall have its rights undiminished and its liberties unimpaired."[87] The Court then traced this idea of freedom of the church to early America before connecting it with *both* the Establishment and free exercise clauses of the First Amendment.[88]

Although it may seem unusual for the Supreme Court to trace a constitutional commitment back to 1215, the Court's narration in fact had started in the middle of the full story of church–state relations. A more complete version[89] would need to begin with the biblical account in which Jesus, in response to a question about the permissibility of paying taxes, declared that there are *two* authorities that we are obligated to respect: the temporal authority, but also the spiritual authority. "Render unto Caesar the things that are Caesar's," Jesus enjoined, "and unto God the things that are God's."[90] The political dualism inherent in this view was elaborated by later Christian thinkers, including Augustine with his doctrine of the "two cities," Pope Gelasius with his declaration that there are two authorities,[91] and, much later, by Martin Luther and John Calvin with their doctrine of the "two kingdoms."[92] The idea of *libertas ecclesiae* or "freedom of the church," reflected in the Magna Carta and other precedents recited by the Court in *Hosanna-Tabor*, was the product of the creative tension between the spiritual and temporal jurisdictions in the West. And the medieval commitment to *libertas ecclesiae* led in discernible if circuitous fashion to

86 Richard Garnett observed that the doctrine had "something of an imprecise emanations-and-penumbras air about it." Richard W. Garnett, "Religion and Group Rights: Are Churches (Just) Like the Boy Scouts?," *St. John's Journal of Legal Commentary* 22 (2007): 515, 526.

87 *Hosanna-Tabor,* 565 U.S. at 182.

88 Ibid., 182–185.

89 For a somewhat more detailed rendering, see Smith, *Rise and Decline*, 14–47.

90 Matt. 22:20–21 (King James Version).

91 See Hugo Rahner, *Church and State in Early Christianity* (San Francisco, CA: Ignatius Press, 1992 [1961]), 174.

92 See John Witte, Jr., *Law and Protestantism: The Legal Teachings of the Lutheran Reformation* (New York: Cambridge University Press, 2002), 87–117.

the American system of "separation of church and state" and religious freedom.

A shamelessly abbreviated synopsis might go like this: The medieval struggle over *libertas ecclesiae* produced its legendary battles – the confrontation in the empire between Henry IV and Pope Gregory VII, the clash between Henry II of England and Archbishop Thomas Beckett, the conflict between Henry VIII and the deeply devout former Lord Chancellor Thomas More. Then, following the effective takeover of national churches by monarchs in England and elsewhere in the sixteenth century, and now more under the direction of Protestant Christians, the "freedom of the church" modulated into the "freedom of conscience" – conscience becoming a sort of "internal church" as the new locus of God's essential interaction with humans.[93]

Deference previously given to the *church* as an independent jurisdiction was now extended to the individual *conscience*. Indeed, early proponents of the freedom of conscience sometimes defended the commitment in explicitly jurisdictional terms. The government, they argued, had *no jurisdiction* over the conscience, which was Christ's kingdom.[94] This commitment to conscience was energetically expounded by seventeenth-century figures such as Roger Williams, William Penn, and John Locke.[95]

Later, in the eighteenth century, American founders such as James Madison and Thomas Jefferson took up the idea. We have already noticed how Madison's and Jefferson's seminal statements on religious freedom reflected that dualistic and explicitly theistic conception. The First Amendment's establishment and free exercise clauses, respectively denying governmental jurisdiction over institutional religion (or establishments of religion) and over the "exercise [of religion]," reflected both the older commitment to institutional separation and the more modern commitment to freedom of conscience, the internal church. In this way, the Christian

93 See Smith, *Rise and Decline*, 36–38.

94 See, for example, Elisha Williams, *The Essential Rights and Liberties of Protestants: A Seasonable Plea for the Liberty of Conscience, and the Right of Private Judgment, In Matters of Religion, Without any Controul from Human Authority* (Boston: S. Kneeland and T. Green, 1744), 12 (arguing that "[i]f CHRIST be the Lord of Conscience, the sole King in his own Kingdom; then it will follow, that all such as in any Manner or Degree assume the Power of directing and governing the Consciences of Men, are justly chargeable with invading his rightful Dominion; He alone having the Right they claim").

95 See Smith, *Rise and Decline*, 36–38.

commitment to dual jurisdictions – Caesar and God – wound its meandering way into the American political order.

But most of this history is obviously very old: pre-Constitution. Should these old or even ancient commitments – to freedom of the church, to freedom of conscience – carry over into contemporary constitutional law?

American Constitutional Law and the Freedom of the Church

One can argue, quite plausibly, that they should – and also that they shouldn't. More specifically, modern constitutional doctrine is fashioned from various sources.[96] One important source is the constitutional text, understood at least in part in terms of its original meaning or understanding. Another source is judicial precedent. Still another source is current and long-standing American political practice and sensibilities. And these conventional legal authorities provide the rhetorical material to affirm the idea of "freedom of the church." Or to reject it.

I have argued elsewhere that the original meaning and purpose of the First Amendment religion clauses was simply to deny Congress any power ("Congress shall make no law . . . ") over central aspects of religion that fall within the scope of the "establishment" and the "exercise" of "religion."[97] The former phrase in particular is plausibly understood as referring to institutional religion – a religious "establishment" (much like a "business establishment") designating religion in an institutionalized form (or, in short, a church).[98] The clause might be read to say, in essence, that "Congress [and, by later interpretation, government generally] shall make no law respecting a church." The religion clauses – the establishment clause in particular, and reenforced by the free exercise clause – can plausibly be read as ratifying the ancient idea of "freedom of the church" from governmental control. And if one wanted a succinct slogan for this idea, one could hardly do better than to embrace the classic Jeffersonian

[96] For one oft-cited study of the diverse sources and modes of constitutional interpretation, see Phillip Bobbitt, *Constitutional Fate* (New York: Oxford University Press, 1984).

[97] See, for example, Steven D. Smith, "The Jurisdictional Establishment Clause: A Reappraisal," *Notre Dame Law Review* 81 (2006): 1843.

[98] For further development, see Steven D. Smith, "The Establishment Clause and the 'Problem of the Church,'" in *Challenges to Religious Liberty in the Twenty-First Century*, ed. Gerard V. Bradley (New York: Cambridge University Press, 2012), 3.

formulation: The religion clauses raised a "wall of separation between church and state."[99]

But then, as we also know, modern advocates who are fond of Jefferson's phrase typically do not read it to mean what it actually says, or to effect a separation of *church* and *state*. Instead, they read the phrase to mandate something like a separation of government from "religion," which in turn may be taken to mean primarily that government must not advance or promote "religion."[100] It might follow from this interpretation that government *can* interfere in churches so long as "religion" is not thereby advanced and, extending the logic, that government cannot *refrain* from interference in churches if such detachment would mean that government was thereby "advancing religion."[101] Perversely, perhaps, the "wall of separation between church and state," which on its face would seem calculated to keep government *out* of churches, might thus come to mean that, at least in situations in which other comparable institutions are regulated, government not only may but *must* intervene equally in the affairs of churches. A similar conclusion might be reached on the common premise that the Constitution means government must be strictly "neutral" toward religion.[102] If government regulates other institutions, how can it refrain from regulating religious institutions?

Such readings (or misreadings) are evident, if ambiguously so, in modern judicial interpretations of the establishment clause. Modern doctrine (the so-called *Lemon* test[103]) primarily forbids government to act for religious purposes or in ways that will unduly advance religion. To be sure, the doctrine also forbids excessive "entanglement" between government and religion – a prohibition that might well provide grounding for a modern

[99] For a helpful discussion of the context and meaning of the metaphor, see Daniel L. Dreisbach, *Thomas Jefferson and the Wall of Separation between Church and State* (New York: New York University Press, 2002), 66.

[100] See, for example, Jean L. Cohen, "Rethinking Political Secularism and the American Model of Constitutional Dualism," in *Religion, Secularism & Constitutional Democracy*, ed. Jean L. Cohen and Cecile LaBorde (New York: Columbia University Press, 2016), 113, 124.

[101] See Ibid., 142–144.

[102] See, for example, *Epperson* v. *Arkansas*, 393 U.S. 97, 103, 106 (1968).

[103] So named after *Lemon* v. *Kurtzman*, 403 U.S. 602, 612–613 (1971). Under the test, a challenged law must (1) have a secular purpose, (2) have a principal or primary effect that neither advances nor inhibits religion, and (3) avoid excessive entanglement between government and religion.

"freedom of the church"[104] – but both courts and commentators have often been at a loss to figure out what this last provision entails.[105] And courts and commentators often insist that government must be "neutral" in matters of religion.[106]

If we look instead to precedent and practice, we again receive mixed signals. Establishment clause precedents have attempted to elaborate and apply the various "prongs" of the *Lemon* test, including the prong forbidding government to advance religion but also the prong forbidding excessive entanglement of religion. In at least one case before *Hosanna-Tabor*, the Supreme Court somewhat ambivalently construed the latter precept to protect a church institution from governmental regulation.[107] Conversely, in a lengthy and intricately reasoned decision, a lower federal court invoked the prohibition on "advancing" religion to invalidate a provision in which Congress had exempted religious institutions from some federal employment discrimination requirements.[108] Although this ruling was ultimately reversed,[109] the Supreme Court's pronouncements in this and other cases exude uncertainty about just how the "no advancement" and "no excessive entanglement" precepts mesh with each other and with the free exercise doctrine.

There is also a venerable line of cases dealing with internal church disputes, often over property, that provides quite emphatic support, both in its results and in its rhetoric, for the idea that government ought not to intervene in the internal affairs of churches.[110] But this line of cases has

[104] I have argued for this proposition at length in Steven D. Smith, "Separation and the 'Secular': Reconstructing the Disestablishment Decision," *Texas Law Review* 67 (1989): 955.

[105] See, for example, David E. Steinberg, "Alternatives to Entanglement," *Kentucky Law Review* 80 (1991/1992): 691, 699 (asserting that "[i]f the Court's opinions on administrative entanglement are inconsistent, its political divisiveness decisions are virtually incomprehensible").

[106] See Andrew Koppelman, *Defending American Religious Neutrality* (Cambridge, MA: Harvard University Press, 2013), 1. For criticism of the neutrality theme, see Smith, *Rise and Decline*, 128–138.

[107] *NLRB* v. *Catholic Bishop of Chicago*, 440 U.S. 490 (1978). The Court reasoned that possible conflict with the establishment clause provided a reason to construe the relevant statute not to confer jurisdiction over Catholic schools on the NLRB.

[108] *Amos* v. *Presiding Bishop*, 594 F. Supp. 791 (D. Utah 1984).

[109] *Corporation of the Presiding Bishop* v. *Amos*, 483 U.S. 327 (1987).

[110] For discussion of these cases, see Richard W. Garnett, "'Things That Are Not Caesar's': The Story of Kedroff v. St. Nicholas Cathedral," in *First Amendment Stories*, ed. Richard Garnett and Andrew Koppelman (New York: Foundation Press, 2012), 171.

never been well integrated into more general establishment clause doctrine or jurisprudence.

Meanwhile, on the state level, Sarah Barringer Gordon has shown that throughout the nineteenth century, states often regulated churches – in their internal organization, for example, or in their rights to hold property – in ways that seem incongruent with any genuine commitment to freedom of the church.[111] These practices mostly occurred before the First Amendment religion clauses had been treated as incorporated against the states. One might argue, therefore, that they have little or no significance as a basis for construing those clauses. Such practices are nonetheless suggestive insofar as "tradition" or "practice" is accepted as a legitimate source for constitutional interpretation.

In sum, on the basis of conventional legal materials and reasoning, one can make a perfectly respectable argument that the Constitution supports a commitment to "freedom of the church." Or that it doesn't. In *Hosanna-Tabor*, the Court essentially drew the first conclusion, upholding the ministerial exception and grounding it in both religion clauses. The Court's critics draw the second conclusion. Both sides can offer reasoned arguments for their conclusions. So then how should this impasse be resolved? Confronted with competing arguments that are respectable but less than compelling, how do courts or citizens choose sides?

Freedom of the Church and American Community

I have already suggested that underlying the uncompelling and sometimes quite feeble arguments in the contemporary debates lie competing conceptions of what the American community is or should be. There is nothing novel in this situation (even if the contours of the current controversy over national identity *are* a relatively new development). We have already seen how both Madison and Jefferson appealed to theistic premises in their seminal justifications of religious freedom. In doing so, they necessarily relied on a conception of the political community as a "nation under God" (to borrow Lincoln's later formulation).

Madison understood as well that this conception was relevant not only to the particular question of religious freedom but also, more broadly, to

[111] Sarah Barringer Gordon, "Religious Corporations and Disestablishment, 1780–1840," in *The Rise of Corporate Religious Freedom*, 63.

our general understanding of the relation between government and the individual, and hence to the question of rights generally. He accordingly argued that if religious freedom is not respected as sacrosanct, all other rights will be placed in jeopardy as well. The right to religious freedom, Madison argued,

> is held by the same tenure with all our other rights . . . Either, then, we must say that the will of the Legislature is the only measure of their authority, and that in the plenitude of this authority, they may sweep away all our fundamental rights; or, that they are bound to leave this particular right untouched and sacred.[112]

This conception of the nation as subject to a higher, divine authority has guided the nation through much of its history.[113] The Supreme Court gave a classic expression to this view in 1952, declaring, "We are a religious people whose institutions presuppose a Supreme Being."[114] But this conception of political community is fiercely contested today. It is that contest – between "orthodox" and "progressive" factions – that underlies and energizes the current "culture wars" struggle to "define America," as James Davison Hunter explained.[115] So, then, can we say that Americans who accept the orthodox "one nation under God" conception will automatically and necessarily embrace the outcome in *Hosanna-Tabor* and more generally the idea of "freedom of the church"? And that Americans who reject the orthodox understanding in favor of a more secular or progressive conception of community will automatically and necessarily reject *Hosanna-Tabor*?

Not quite. As usual, the issues are more complicated. The premise of "one nation under God" does not lead inexorably to freedom of the church. Probably other supplemental premises are necessary – for example, the idea that government has no business deciding which among the competing churches is the best or true one. Conversely, an agnostic *could* favor a policy of strict governmental noninterference with churches on prudential grounds, libertarian principles, originalism, or by taking Jefferson's "wall of separation" metaphor seriously and at face value. Though much criticized, *Hosanna-Tabor* was, after all, a unanimous decision.

[112] Madison, *Memorial and Remonstrance*, 313.

[113] Bellah, *Broken Covenant*, 12 ("Biblical imagery provided the basic framework for imaginative thought in America up until quite recent times and unconsciously, its control is still formidable.").

[114] *Zorach* v. *Clauson*, 343 U.S. 306 (1952).

[115] Hunter, *Culture Wars*, 43–44.

But we can say this much with moderate confidence. As an intellectual matter, a firm commitment to freedom of the church seems most defensible on the foundation of a providential conception of community. Moreover, as a historical matter, that commitment symbolically expresses the providential conception as it developed in the pluralistic context of American democracy. Conversely, on purely secular assumptions, a special commitment to freedom of the church becomes not indefensible but at least much more tenuous. When the issue arises in the context of our current culture wars, therefore, it is predictable which party will most often favor which conclusion. And arguments made by the contending parties that may seem frail when examined just on their merits become more understandable if appreciated in our context of cultural struggle.

Conclusion

Recent Supreme Court decisions favoring the idea of corporate or collective religious freedom, though portrayed by critics as a novel development, are in fact more accurately understood as a reaffirmation of traditional and even ancient understandings traceable to the nation's Christian heritage and to the conception of American political community as "one nation, under God." Current debates have intensified not because there is anything radical about the idea that corporations might enjoy a right to religious freedom, or that churches deserve deference in their internal affairs, but rather because the conception of the political community that inspires these ideas is currently embattled.

13 Which Original Meaning of the Establishment Clause Is the Right One?

Donald L. Drakeman

"No provision of the Constitution is more closely tied to . . . its generating history than the religion clause," proclaimed Justice Wiley Rutledge in the 1947 *Everson* v. *Board of Education* case.[1] The justice's ode to church–state originalism was not necessarily true when he sat down to write his dissenting opinion, but it soon became a self-fulfilling prophecy. His extensively footnoted draft opinion propelled Justice Hugo Black to rewrite the majority opinion so that it would also examine the "background and environment of the period in which the constitutional language was fashioned and adopted."[2] The two opinions divided on the constitutionality of busing children to religious schools, but they were united in the belief that James Madison and Thomas Jefferson held the key to the meaning of the establishment clause. With all nine justices signing on to one or the other of these history-laden opinions, the jurisprudential stage was set for dozens of subsequent cases to mine the eighteenth-century records for clues about the first clause of the First Amendment: "Congress shall make no law respecting an establishment of religion."

Justices, lawyers, historians, political scientists, and numerous others over the past seventy years have written about the origins of the establishment clause. Most have confidently pointed to the obvious original meaning. A fair summary of this extensive literature leads to several contradictory conclusions about the clause's meaning: that it built an impermeable wall between church and state ("strict separationism"); that it allowed evenhanded government support of religion ("nonpreferentialism"); that it was essentially a pro-establishment clause designed to protect tax-supported churches in the states from the risk of federal interference

[1] *Everson* v. *Board of Education*, 330 US 1 (1947) at 33. [2] Ibid. at 8.

("federalism"); or that it merely confirmed that there would be no formal Church of the United States.[3]

In these lively and contentious debates, there have been serious scholarly disputes over the meaning of at least seven of the ten words in the clause, including "an."[4] When we look to the documentary record for ways to resolve these interpretive disagreements, it turns out to be surprisingly sparse. As Leonard Levy has observed, "At the very least, one would expect frequent expressions of fear and concern on the subject [of an establishment of religion]. Yet the startling fact is that it was rarely mentioned at all and then only briefly."[5] Historical battles over church and state have thus been fought primarily over which elements of a very limited pool of evidence provide what Hugo Black called the "background and environment" of the clause, and which are irrelevant or extraneous.[6] Exploring the establishment clause can thus provide an opportunity not only to consider what its original meaning was, but also to see how competing interpretive methodologies can generate different outcomes from the same evidence. As a result, often obscure theoretical battles between old and new originalists, for example, come to life through the Court's nearly four-score years of struggling with the establishment clause.

The purpose of this chapter is to examine how these methodological issues have helped to drive conflicting conclusions, even while the participants in these debates rarely acknowledge that they are actually arguing about competing theories of interpretation. Instead, these scholars typically exchange epithets and allegations of various forms of historical malpractice, from the relatively mild accusation of "law office history" to sharper claims that someone's argument is "false," in "error," "flawed," or, in one case, "historical fiction masquerading as scholarship."[7] Yet the charges of

[3] For a summary of these debates, see Donald L. Drakeman, *Church, State, and Original Intent* (New York: Cambridge University Press, 2010), 1–20. Some of the themes of this chapter appear at much greater length in this book.

[4] Compare Michael J. Malbin, *Religion and Politics: The Intentions of the Authors of the First Amendment* (Washington, DC: American Enterprise Institute for Public Policy Research, 1978) and Douglas Laycock, "The Origins of the Religion Clauses of the Constitution: 'Nonpreferential' Aid to Religion: A False Claim about Original Intent," *William and Mary Law Review* 27 (1986): 875–923.

[5] Leonard Levy, *The Establishment Clause: Religion and the First Amendment* (New York: Macmillan, 1986), 67.

[6] *Everson*, 330 US at 8.

[7] For examples of these criticisms, see Drakeman, *Church, State, and Original Intent*, 15.

falsehood and fiction do not cite evidence that has been made up or forged; instead, they are assertions that the scholar-in-error has emphasized the wrong evidence and, therefore, has come to the wrong conclusion.

Figuring out which evidence is relevant to the question of original constitutional meaning is the key to resolving these disputes. My goal is to set aside the invective in favor of exploring the competing arguments to determine their assumptions, usually unstated, about the proper approach to constitutional interpretation, and how those assumptions relate to the text and its historical context. Such an analysis raises interesting issues not only for the meaning of the establishment clause but also for the leading candidates for methodological dominance, especially since interpretive theory and historical facts do not, in this case, mesh as well in practice as they do in the abstract. Ultimately, my aim is to consider whether there are good reasons to favor any particular approach to interpreting the establishment clause besides the most obvious one, which is to pick the outcome that we like the best.

Church and State in the States before the Constitution

As Hugo Black has suggested, we need to understand the environment that gave rise to the establishment clause to understand the clause itself. That environment was shaped by the need for new state charters following the American Revolutionary War. This process led to a number of public debates over church–state issues. These disputes were perhaps most sharply contested in Virginia and Massachusetts. These two influential states represented over a quarter of the US population, and they were home to the country's first six presidents.[8] They also provide abundant evidence that the nation was sharply, even bitterly, divided on church–state issues. To identify the original meaning of the establishment clause, we need to figure out how it could have emerged in the midst of such fundamental disagreements about the proper relationship between religion and government.

[8] For the 1790 census, see *Return of the Whole Number of Persons within the Several Districts of the United States* ... (Philadelphia: J. Phillips, 1793). For the number of presidents, see "The Presidents," The White House, accessed November 4, 2017, www.whitehouse.gov /1600/Presidents.

The debates in these two commonwealths involved essentially the same issue in both states: whether to levy taxes to support whatever Christian churches were designated by the various towns (Massachusetts) or by the taxpayers themselves (Virginia). These were especially controversial political questions, and prominent statesmen may be found on both sides. Opponents of the Virginia taxes included James Madison and Thomas Jefferson, both of whom have featured prominently in the Supreme Court's church–state opinions, but the justices have often overlooked the fact that Patrick Henry and future Chief Justice John Marshall took the other side.[9] Meanwhile, Massachusetts debated a constitution drafted by John and Samuel Adams that included taxes in support of religion that were opposed by many Baptists, including the well-known spokesman for religious liberty, Isaac Backus.[10]

Virginia

Revolutionary fervor threatened to weaken Virginia's tax-funded Anglican establishment, especially since many of the clergy remained loyal to the crown. Other wartime factors also contributed to the political environment for Virginia's discussion of church–state issues. The rapidly growing population of Baptists, Presbyterians, and other dissenters had often felt oppressed by both church and state. They complained not only of explicit legal prejudice, such as the fact that their ministers were not allowed to perform marriages, but also of the improper use of what now are often called "generally applicable laws," such as when government officials interfered with the dissenters' religious practices by imprisoning evangelists for sedition, public nuisance, or disturbing the peace.[11] The dissenters regularly

[9] Thomas J. Buckley, *Church and State in Revolutionary Virginia, 1776–1787* (Charlottesville, VA: University Press of Virginia, 1997), 192–200.

[10] Samuel Eliot Morison, "The Struggle over the Adoption of the Constitution of Massachusetts, 1780," *Proceedings of the Massachusetts Historical Society* 50 (1917): 353–411, esp. 356. See also Jacob C. Meyer, *Church and State in Massachusetts from 1740–1833* (Cleveland, OH: Western Reserve University Press, 1930).

[11] Monica Najar, "Sectarians and Strategies of Dissent in Colonia Virginia," in *From Jamestown to Jefferson: The Evolution of Religious Freedom in Virginia*, ed. Paul Rasor and Richard E. Bond (Charlottesville, VA: University of Virginia Press, 2011), 108–137. For contemporary jurisprudence on "generally applicable laws" and church–state issues, see *Employment Division, Department of Human Resources of Oregon* v. *Smith*, 494 US 872 (1990).

sought greater legal protection for their religious rights, and they did not miss the opportunity to push for more religious freedom in return for their support of the war effort when partisans of independence sought to recruit more troops for General George Washington's army.[12]

The Commonwealth of Virginia was among the first of the states to consider adopting a new constitution. Within weeks of Virginia's motion in the Continental Congress on May 15, 1776, in favor of American independence, the commonwealth began to create a new constitution, including a Declaration of Rights.[13] George Mason's original draft promised the "fullest toleration" of religion, which James Madison had amended so that it would instead grant "all men . . . the free exercise of religion." Madison was not, however, able to muster sufficient support to add language that would ban any "privileges" on "account of religion."[14] The unresolved issue of religious privileges would be a persistent one, especially since the ecclesiastical tax in support of the Anglican Church often exceeded the amount of a citizen's regular county taxes.[15] According to one historian, Baptists, Presbyterians, Quakers, and other dissenters could have "their own ministers and meeting houses but were not exempted from [taxes for the Anglican Church] or the requirement that they seek out the Anglican parson when they desired to be married."[16] During the next legislative session, in the fall of 1776, a series of petitions demanded the end of Anglican privileges, commencing a lively and extensive press war.[17] Another historian has estimated that "over 10 percent of the adult white male population" signed the "10,000 name" petition from "the Dissenters from the Ecclesiastic establishment."[18] Petitions from both sides poured into the Virginia legislature, and they were accompanied by a lively debate in Virginia's newspapers and in the legislature.[19] Thomas Jefferson later called these debates

[12] See, in particular, John A. Ragosta, *Wellspring of Liberty: How Virginia's Religious Dissenters Helped Win the American Revolution and Secured Religious Liberty* (New York: Oxford University Press, 2010).

[13] Buckley, *Church and State*, 17. [14] Ibid., 19.

[15] John K. Nelson, *A Blessed Company: Parishes, Parsons, and Parishioners in Anglican Virginia, 1690–1776* (Chapel Hill, NC: University of North Carolina Press, 2001), 4. Nelson notes that the tax in support of the Anglican Church was "on average . . . two-and-one-half times greater annually than the county levy." Ibid. What had been the Church of England during the colonial era would become the Episcopal Church of America following the American Revolution. Herein, it will sometimes be referred to as the "Anglican Church."

[16] Ibid., 6. [17] Ibid., 22. [18] Ragosta, *Wellspring*, 56.

[19] For a summary of the arguments and a sample of the rhetoric, see Buckley, *Church and State*, 23–27.

over what would happen with Virginia's tax-funded church "the severest contests in which I have ever been engaged."[20] Because of the extent of the disagreements, only a temporary compromise emerged. Dissenters would be exempted from the ecclesiastical taxes that supported the Anglican Church. The taxes themselves were suspended temporarily but not repealed, and the legislature explicitly reserved judgment as to whether there would be a general assessment (essentially a replacement tax) for the benefit of a wider range of Christian churches.[21]

After only a brief respite, the petition war continued, as neither side was content with the compromise. The Anglican Church wanted its prior position restored, and many proponents of establishment petitioned in 1779 for a "general assessment for the support of Religious Worship."[22] Meanwhile, the dissenters urged the passage of Jefferson's bill for establishing religious freedom, which would formally end privileges for any church.[23] Although the dissenters made steady political progress over time, it was not until 1780 – several years after the Declaration of Rights had proclaimed religious freedom – that the ministers of dissenting churches obtained the right to perform marriages, and, even then, only a limited number could do so in any one county.[24] The issue of religious taxes remained unresolved.

As the Anglican Church was faced with the difficulty of determining how to pay their previously tax-supported clergy, many of its supporters focused on a general assessment tax that would support all Christian ministers.[25] The rationale for such an assessment was not simply to find a way to pay Anglican priests, however. In Virginia and elsewhere, many people believed that religion was necessary to provide a moral foundation for society, as stated in Virginia's 1784 general assessment bill: "Christian knowledge hath a natural tendency to correct the morals of

[20] Thomas Jefferson, *The Autobiography of Thomas Jefferson, 1743–1790*, ed. Paul Leicester Ford (Philadelphia: University of Pennsylvania Press, 2005), 62.

[21] Ragosta, *Wellspring*, 60. [22] Quoted in Ragosta, *Wellspring*, 66.

[23] Jefferson's bill was "part of a general revision of the laws ordered by the legislature in 1776." Buckley, *Church and State*, 46. See also Daniel L. Dreisbach, "A New Perspective on Jefferson's Views on Church-State Relations: The Virginia Statute for Establishing Religious Freedom in its Legislative Context," *American Journal of Legal History* 35, no. 2 (1991): 172–204.

[24] Ragosta, *Wellspring*, 69, 109.

[25] Supporters of the Anglican Church also sought the right to incorporate so as to be able to own property in corporate form, including their churches. Ibid., 116.

men, restrain their vices, and preserve the peace of society; which cannot be effected without a competent provision for learned teachers."[26] With the arrival of numerous pro-tax petitions, momentum for an assessment began to build. The Virginia House, sitting as a Committee of the Whole, "voted forty-seven to thirty-two that there should be a moderate tax or contribution annually for the support of the Christian religion, or of some Christian church, denomination, or communion of Christians, or of some form of Christian worship," and the committee referred the matter to a committee chaired by Patrick Henry to draft the necessary language.[27]

The opposition soon mobilized its forces, and James Madison and others in the House worked to delay the bill. These efforts led to what John Ragosta has called "massive petitioning of the General Assembly," including what would become one of the most famous petitions in American history, Madison's "Memorial and Remonstrance Against Religious Assessments." This now-iconic document hardly deserves the credit that it has often been given for being the pivotal argument that carried the day. Numerous Baptist and Presbyterian petitions, bearing many more signatures, overshadowed Madison's anonymous petition.[28] An active public debate again ensued, and the assessment bill dominated the legislative campaign of 1785. In the end, the results were very close, with "the proposal to bring the assessment forward for a third reading [in the legislature] defeated by only three votes."[29] Instead, the House adopted Jefferson's Bill for Establishing Religious Freedom, and even that famous document generated what Madison called "warm opposition."[30] The most notable observation from this lengthy battle to eliminate church taxes is how sharply Virginians at the time were divided over these church–state questions, with the legislature split almost exactly equally on the issue.[31]

[26] "A Bill Establishing a Provision for Teachers of the Christian Religion," 1784, quoted in Buckley, *Church and State*, 188–189.

[27] Buckley, *Church and State*, 119.

[28] See John T. Noonan, Jr., *The Lustre of Our Country: The American Experience of Religious Freedom* (Berkeley, CA: University of California Press, 1981), 74.

[29] Ragosta, *Wellspring*, 125–131.

[30] James Madison to James Monroe, December 17, 1985, quoted in Ragosta, *Wellspring*, 133.

[31] Buckley, *Church and State*, 192–200. Buckley divides the 1784–1785 House of Delegates based on those favoring or opposing "Church–State Relationships."

Massachusetts

The story in Massachusetts was quite similar, except that the results came out the other way, and its general assessment tax endured into the 1830s. The first attempt to create a Massachusetts constitution came in 1777, when the General Court prepared a proposed constitution. It granted the "free exercise and enjoyment of religious profession and worship" to Protestants only but was silent on religious taxes, which meant that the long history of providing such financial support for Congregationalist churches in Massachusetts was bound to continue.[32] By this time, the Baptists were already sufficiently disappointed by how the state had been dealing with church–state matters that they had formed an official "Grievance Committee." They launched a petition drive to add a provision to the Constitution specifying "that religious ministers shall be supported only by Christ's authority, and not at all by assessment and secular force."[33] The proposed 1777 constitution failed to be ratified for a variety of reasons, ranging from issues of representation to those of religion.[34] The disputes over religious taxes would continue to be battled in the courts and the legislature, as well as in sermons, letters, and pamphlets, and it would reappear in earnest in the debates over the next draft of a Massachusetts constitution.[35]

When the General Assembly called a constitutional convention in 1779, the most controversial provision was Article III, which would essentially require towns to have religious taxes to support "public Protestant teachers of piety, religion, and morality" so as to promote "the good order and preservation of civil government."[36] As in the case of the proposed Virginia

[32] William G. McLoughlin, *New England Dissent, 1630–1833: The Baptists and the Separation of Church and State* (Cambridge, MA: Harvard University Press, 1971), 1:594–595. See also Samuel Eliot Morison, *History of the Constitution of Massachusetts* (Boston: Wright & Potter, 1917).

[33] Meyer, *Church and State*, 100–101. See also McLoughlin, *New England Dissent*, 1:595–596.

[34] Meyer, *Church and State*, 103.

[35] See, for example, John D. Cushing, "Notes on Disestablishment in Massachusetts, 1780–1833," *William and Mary Quarterly*, 3rd series, 26, no. 2 (1969): 169–190; McLoughlin, *New England Dissent*, 1:596–599.

[36] "Massachusetts Constitution," 1780, in *The Sacred Rights of Conscience: Selected Readings on Religious Liberty and Church-State Relations in the American Founding*, ed. Daniel L. Dreisbach and Mark David Hall (Indianapolis, IN: Liberty Fund, 2009), 246. See also Theophilus Parsons, Jr., *Memoir of Theophilus Parsons, Chief Justice of the Supreme*

assessment, the language emphasized the importance of religion's role in promoting the moral foundation of society. The proposed constitution was sent to the towns for ratification, where virtually all of the published commentary related to issues of religion and, in particular, to the debate over religious taxes.[37] As in Virginia, petitions were circulated, pamphlets were written, and letter writers battled in the newspapers.[38]

Ultimately, Article III did not command the necessary two-thirds majority but, according to Samuel Eliot Morison, "the Convention deliberately juggled the returns in order to make it appear that there was" and declared that it had passed anyway.[39] Once again, as in Virginia, there were vigorous debates in a variety of public forums, and the final vote was split nearly in half.

The Remaining States

The results in the other states divided along geographical lines.[40] New England, New Hampshire, Vermont, and Connecticut continued to have religious taxation, and these taxes engendered less controversy than occurred in Massachusetts.[41] In the South, South Carolina eliminated religious taxes but enacted a constitutional provision that "established Protestantism," although the Palmetto State framers failed to define the term, and there were no provisions for religious taxes. North Carolina and Georgia both eliminated taxes for the Anglican Church, although Georgia's constitution expressly permitted people to be taxed to support their own churches. Maryland "devised the least clear system," in Thomas Curry's words, but provided for the possibility of religious taxation, which was never implemented.[42] "Delaware, New Jersey, and Pennsylvania . . . maintained few official connections between religion and government," as was

Judicial Court of Massachusetts (Boston: Ticknor and Fields, 1859), 201–203. Parsons was a member of the Article III committee. Morison, "Struggle," 360–369.

37 Morison, "Struggle," 368. 38 Ibid., 375–381.

39 Ibid., 400–401. Article III received 8,885 of the 16,235 votes. Ibid., 411.

40 For a state-by-state comparison, see Vincent Phillip Muñoz, "Church and State in the Founding-Era State Constitutions," *American Political Thought* 4, no. 1 (2015), 1–38.

41 Thomas J. Curry, *The First Freedoms: Church and State in America to the Passage of the First Amendment* (New York: Oxford University Press, 1986), 105–177.

42 Ibid., 148–158. For the significant role of Roman Catholicism in Maryland's approach to church and state, see Michael D. Breidenbach, "Conciliarism and the American Founding," *William and Mary Quarterly*, 3rd series, 73, no. 3 (2016): 467–500.

also the case in Rhode Island, and therefore according to Curry the "Revolution precipitated no movements . . . calling for an extensive rearrangement of Church-State relations."[43] Meanwhile, New York's prior church–state arrangements had differed from county to county, and its 1777 constitution eliminated any religious taxes.[44]

The Federal Constitution

The religious taxes debates that roiled Virginia and Massachusetts make it clear that church–state issues remained highly controversial leading up to the federal constitutional convention just a few years later. Since these issues had stimulated unusually heated debates in the legislatures and in the press, modern historians have been surprised that establishment issues were completely ignored at the federal Constitutional Convention, and, even when the establishment clause was included in the Bill of Rights, it generated no controversy, no petitions, and impressively little in the way of either support or opposition.[45]

At the Constitutional Convention, no one proposed that there should be a "Church of the United States," or a tax in favor of any or all religions, nor did the Convention consider forbidding any such things. The only substantive discussion relating to religion was whether there would be a religious test for public office.[46] As a result, the Constitution, as sent out for ratification by the states, made no reference to establishments of religion. Since the establishment clause later became a part of the First Amendment – and has often been hailed, misleadingly, as one of America's "first freedoms" – we might expect that when the Antifederalists battled for amendments, church–state issues would be prominent.[47] But that was not the case, either. The leading Antifederalist publications typically ignored the issue altogether. Among the most widely circulated writings by

[43] Curry, *First Freedoms*, 159, 162. [44] Ibid., 161. [45] Levy, *Establishment Clause*, 67.

[46] Gerard V. Bradley, "The No Religious Test Clause and the Constitution of Religious Liberty: A Machine that Has Gone of Itself," *Case Western Reserve Law Review* 37, no. 4 (1987): 674–747.

[47] See, for example, Curry, *First Freedoms*, and *First Freedoms: A Documentary History of the First Amendment Rights in America*, ed. Charles C. Haynes, Sam Chaltain, and Susan M. Glisson (New York: Oxford University Press, 2006).

Antifederalists, over three-quarters failed to raise *any* issues of religion, and not one of them mentioned religious establishments.[48]

There were very few comments on the subject of religious establishments during the ratification debates, and the same basic themes appeared in various states where they did occur. Someone would express a concern that there could, in the future, be a national establishment of one church to the detriment of the others. In response, defenders of the Constitution pointed out that Congress has no power over religion, and that America's religious diversity would prevent the establishment of a national religion. The ratifying conventions in three states – Virginia, North Carolina, and New York – eventually proposed amendments in almost identical language: "no particular religious sect or society ought to be favored or established by law in preference to others," largely because Virginia's proposed amendment was adopted nearly verbatim by the other two. New Hampshire proposed, "Congress shall make no laws touching religion."[49] In all of these cases, the nonestablishment amendment was part of a long list of proposed amendments, many of which involved issues that had been far more prominent in the ratification debates.[50]

In running for Congress, James Madison had promised his Baptist constituents that he would address their concerns about church–state issues.[51] Therefore, when he assembled a Bill of Rights for consideration by the Congress, he included both a clause recognizing the rights of conscience and a nonestablishment clause: "nor shall any national religion be established." In introducing the first version of the establishment clause to the First Federal Congress, he was reported as saying, "Whether the words are

[48] Donald L. Drakeman, "The Antifederalists and Religion," in *Faith and the Founders of the American Republic*, ed. Mark David Hall and Daniel L. Dreisbach (New York: Oxford University Press, 2014), 124. It is important to note, however, that religious freedom concerns were raised, even where there was no discussion of establishment-related concerns.

[49] Neil H. Cogan, *The Complete Bill of Rights: The Drafts, Debates, Sources, and Origins* (New York: Oxford University Press, 1997), ch. 1.

[50] "Of the 210 separate amendments recommended either officially or unofficially by the states, covering almost one hundred substantive items, only six of the states had dealt with the subject of religion; four of these included non-establishment clauses, and one state, Maryland, specifically rejected such a provision." Bernard Schwartz, *The Bill of Rights: A Documentary History* (New York: Chelsea House, 1971), 2:983, cited in Drakeman, *Church, State, and Original Intent*, 197.

[51] Richard Labunski, *James Madison and the Struggle for a Bill of Rights* (New York: Oxford University Press, 2006), ch. 7.

necessary or not, he did not mean to say, but they had been required by some of the State Conventions, who seemed to [think that Congress might have the power] to establish [a religion]."[52] An Antifederalist did not like the use of the word "national," which was then removed, and the proposal was slightly revised to read, "No religion shall be established by law."[53]

The House discussions were very brief, especially compared to the petition-filled controversies in Virginia and Massachusetts. Daniel Carroll from Maryland, one of two Roman Catholics in the House, made the only supportive comment. He said, "[M]any sects have concurred ... that they are not well secured under the present constitution." He would not "comment ... about phraseology" since he just wanted to satisfy the community's wishes. No one else in the legislature spoke in favor of the clause. Roger Sherman said it was unnecessary because "Congress had no authority ... to make religious establishments." Elbridge Gerry wanted to revise it to say, "no religious doctrine shall be established by law," but Madison emphasized that the amendment meant "that congress should not establish a religion, and enforce the legal observation of it by law." Connecticut's Samuel Huntington agreed with Madison's meaning but worried that the federal courts might read it in a way that would prevent them from enforcing financial pledges for the support of local churches. In response, Madison offered to reinsert "national" to clarify that only a "national religion" was being discussed. New Hampshire's Samuel Livermore offered his state's "no touching" provision, saying that "the sense of both provisions was the same," but he, too, was concerned that Madison's language could be subject to "misconstruction." Livermore's language passed thirty-one to twenty votes. A few days later, however, it was replaced by language from Fisher Ames of Massachusetts, which became the House's final version. It read, "Congress shall make no law establishing religion."[54]

The Senate, for which we do not have a record of the debates, responded with: "Congress shall make no law establishing articles of faith or a mode of worship."[55] The Conference Committee came up with the final version, "Congress shall make no law respecting an establishment of religion," which more closely resembled the House's version ("no law establishing

[52] *Annals of Congress: The Debates and Proceedings in the Congress of the United States*, ed. Joseph Gales (Washington, DC: Gales & Seaton, 1834), 1:758.

[53] Ibid., 1:757. [54] All quotations are in Cogan, *Complete Bill of Rights*, ch. 1.

[55] Curry, *First Freedoms*, 116.

religion") than the Senate's. Where the "respecting an" language came from, and what it was intended to mean, is a mystery that will be discussed further below.[56]

Beyond the accounts of the congressional debates over the establishment clause that appeared in newspapers and the Congressional Record, we have virtually no contemporaneous commentary.[57] There were no petitions, speeches, or letters to the newspapers. The few private letters from members of Congress and other influential Federalists described the proposed Bill of Rights in phrases like a "tub to the whale" and "frothy and full of wind" – noncontroversial language that could be used to address the Antifederalists' demand for amendments.[58] In interpreting the clause, it is, therefore, important to consider that the new nation agreed effortlessly and quietly on the establishment clause even when church–state issues had so recently created such bitter political battles in the states. Moreover, the final language of the clause was able to satisfy not only Roger Sherman and Oliver Ellsworth, staunch supporters of Connecticut's religious taxes, but also James Madison, the leader of the anti-assessment forces in Virginia.[59] There can be no question that these men – and the states they represented – disagreed sharply on the general principle of whether governments should foster religion, yet they could agree on the establishment clause.

[56] As discussed below, some scholars have focused on "respecting" to argue in favor of a "jurisdictional" or federalism approach to interpreting the establishment clause. See, for example, Steven D. Smith, "The Jurisdictional Establishment Clause: A Reappraisal," *Notre Dame Law Review* 91 (2006): 1843–1894; Smith, *Foreordained Failure: The Quest for a Constitutional Principle of Religious Freedom* (New York: Oxford University Press, 1999); Vincent Phillip Muñoz, "The Original Meaning of the Establishment Clause and the Impossibility of its Incorporation," *University of Pennsylvania Journal of Constitutional Law* 8, no. 4 (2006): 585–639; and Akhil Reed Amar, *The Bill of Rights: Creation and Reconstruction* (New Haven, CT: Yale University Press, 1998), 33–42.

[57] The Congressional Record was not an official federal publication. The note-taker present at the debates published the materials in the Record, which was fairly widely available by subscription. Marion Tinling, "Thomas Lloyd's Reports of the First Federal Congress," *William and Mary Quarterly*, 3rd series, 18, no. 4 (1961): 519–545. See also James H. Hutson, "The Creation of the Constitution: The Integrity of the Documentary Record," *Texas Law Review* 65 (1986): 1.

[58] Kenneth R. Bowling, "'A Tub to the Whale': The Founding Fathers and Adoption of the Federal Bill of Rights," *Journal of the Early Republic* 8, no. 3 (1988): 244, 250.

[59] See, for example, William Casto, "Oliver Ellsworth's Calvinism: A Biographical Essay on Religion and Political Psychology in the Early Republic," *Journal of Church and State* 36, no. 3 (1994): 507–525; Mark David Hall, *Roger Sherman and the Creation of the American Republic* (New York: Oxford University Press, 2012).

Originalism

Originalism Old and New

Over the last few decades, commentators have typically linked all forms of originalism with politically conservative views, whereas progressives are expected to favor an evolutionary "living Constitution."[60] But perhaps the most remarkable aspect of the Supreme Court's church–state jurisprudence is that justices generally considered very liberal (e.g., Black, Rutledge, Brennan, and Sotomayor) as well as those categorized as quite conservative (e.g., Rehnquist, Scalia, and Thomas) have all embraced a historical approach to the establishment clause.[61] Church–state constitutional battles seem almost invariably to be about the founding era. Since everyone is examining the same historical record but reaching inconsistent and even contradictory conclusions, the establishment clause offers an unusually good opportunity to consider which potential evidence of original meaning is (or should be) constitutionally authoritative. In short, which original meaning is the right one?

There are various schools of thought within the field of originalism, but it is probably reasonable to say that originalists unite at least around the concept that the meaning of the text of the Constitution was fixed when it became the supreme law of the land in the eighteenth century.[62] Two primary methodological approaches fall under the broad umbrella of originalism. One is often called "Old Originalism," and it derives originalism's fixed meaning from a search for the intentions of the constitutional

[60] See Aaron Blake, "Neil Gorsuch, Antonin Scalia and Originalism, Explained," *Washington Post*, February 1, 2017, www.washingtonpost.com/news/the-fix/wp/2017/02/01/neil-gorsuch-antonin-scalia-and-originalism-explained/.

[61] For Justices Black and Rutledge, see the opinions in the *Everson* case discussed above; for Justice William Brennan, see his concurring opinion in *Abington School District* v. *Schempp*, 374 US 203 (1963); and for Justice Sotomayor, see her dissenting opinion in *Trinity Lutheran Church of Columbia, Inc.* v. *Comer*, 582 US ___ (2017), in which she wrote, "This Court has consistently looked to history for guidance when applying the … Religion Clauses." For Justice Rehnquist, see the majority opinion in *Marsh* v. *Chambers*, 463 US 783 (1983); for Justice Thomas, see his concurring opinion in *Town of Greece* v. *Galloway*, 572 US ___ (2014); and for Justice Scalia, see his dissenting opinion in *McCreary County* v. *American Civil Liberties Union of Kentucky*, 545 US 844 (2005).

[62] Lawrence Solum calls this the "fixation thesis": "The linguistic meaning … was fixed at the time each provision was framed and ratified." Lawrence B. Solum and Robert W. Bennett, *Constitutional Originalism: A Debate* (Ithaca, NY: Cornell University Press, 2011), 3.

framers. The other, dubbed "New Originalism," does not focus on what the framers intended; instead, it holds that the original meaning is based on the "meaning that the words and phrases had (or would have had) to ordinary members of the public."[63] Whereas Old Originalism searches for the subjective intentions of the framers in the legislative history, and sometimes in various framers' writings outside the constitutional context, New Originalism seeks the objective public meaning of the language itself by looking at dictionaries and commentaries from the founding era and, increasingly, at pamphlets, tracts, and other eighteenth-century texts. Elements of both of these major schools of originalist thought have appeared in Supreme Court opinions, often without the justices acknowledging the sometimes-heated methodological debates among originalist scholars.

Separationism and Nonpreferentialism

Establishment clause opinions favoring a strict separation of church and state have generally followed the *Everson* lead of looking specifically at the writings of two individuals: Thomas Jefferson and James Madison, especially Jefferson's "Virginia Statute for Religious Liberty" and Madison's "Memorial and Remonstrance." For the justices in *Everson*, the fundamental principle expressed in the establishment clause can be found by combining the provisions prohibiting religious privileges in Jefferson's "Statute" and Madison's "Memorial," which condemn the idea of governments forcing citizens to make contributions of even "three pence" to a religious establishment.[64] The shorthand version of these principles is often found in Jefferson's 1802 letter to a group of Connecticut Baptists saying that the First Amendment had built "a wall of separation between Church & State."[65]

Invoking the views of Madison, Jefferson, and other individuals to define constitutional provisions represents a classic example of Old Originalism. Such a method is subject to the potent criticism of all intent-based interpretations: How do we know that the views of any one or two

[63] Ibid., 2–3. [64] *Everson*, 330 US at 40.

[65] Thomas Jefferson to Messrs. Nehemiah Dodge, Ephraim Robbins, and Stephen S. Nelson, January 1, 1802, in *Sacred Rights of Conscience*, ed. Dreisbach and Hall, 528. See Daniel L. Dreisbach, *Thomas Jefferson and the Wall of Separation between Church and State* (New York: New York University Press, 2002).

individuals fairly represent the intentions of the First Federal Congress, which framed the language, let alone the many more involved in the ratification process? Madison was only one of dozens of members of the House of Representatives, and Jefferson, who was serving as minister to France, was not even in the country when the First Amendment was adopted.

Hugo Black and Wiley Rutledge proposed different rationales for invoking these particular founders and their church–state writings. Their arguments bear detailed consideration not only because of their influence on *Everson*'s legacy of strict separationist opinions, but also because even many opponents of separationism have agreed that the views of Madison and Jefferson are authoritative. Despite this enthusiasm on various sides of the debate for resolving church–state constitutional questions by looking at these two Virginians, it is difficult, in light of the historical evidence, to conclude that their church–state views represent either the understandings of the framers as a whole or the public meaning of the language.

Black arrived at the works of Madison and Jefferson because of what he saw as Virginia's central and "catalytic" role in American disestablishmentarianism, which is ultimately expressed in the First Amendment. He began by noting that many immigrants came to America "to escape the bondage of laws which compelled them to support government favored churches." Nevertheless, religious dissenters in America also often had to pay religious taxes, which "became so commonplace as to shock the freedom loving colonials into a feeling of abhorrence," and those "feelings ... found expression" in the First Amendment. Although Black conceded that "[n]o one locality ... can rightly be given entire credit," Virginia nevertheless "provided a great stimulus and able leadership for the movement," and, as a result, "the controversy upon this general subject ... culminate[d]" in Virginia's battle over the proposed general assessment. He then quoted Jefferson's "Statute" at length, since "the First Amendment, ... the drafting and adoption of which Madison and Jefferson played such leading roles, had the same objective ... as the Virginia statute."[66] Then, citing also Jefferson's "wall of separation" letter, Black concluded that the establishment clause "means at least this: Neither a state nor the Federal Government ... can pass laws which aid one religion, aid all religions, or prefer one religion over another."[67]

[66] *Everson*, 330 US at 13. [67] Ibid., 16–17.

Whereas Black began with early colonial history and traced American church–state thinking forward to the First Amendment, Rutledge argued first that Madison was the author of the religion clauses, and then he worked back to the Virginia documents. For Rutledge, "[a]ll the great instruments of the Virginia struggle for religious liberty ... became the warp and woof of our constitutional tradition ... by the common unifying force of Madison's life, thought and sponsorship," which was "the compact and exact summation of its author's views formed during his long struggle for religious freedom." Rutledge then interpreted the establishment clause as if it had essentially codified the "Memorial and Remonstrance," since "the matter had become so well understood as to have been taken for granted [by the First Congress] in all but formal phrasing."[68]

The first major historical counterattack against the *Everson* arguments did not challenge the fundamental premise that the church–state views of Madison and Jefferson should define the meaning of the establishment clause, but instead argued that the justices had misinterpreted these two founders. J.M. O'Neill's approach (echoed later by Robert Cord and others) was an extended historical argument for nonpreferentialism – the idea, which had been explicitly rejected by Hugo Black, that the Constitution allows the government to provide aid evenhandedly to all religions.[69] O'Neill's book featured prominently in the oral arguments in *McCollum* v. *Board of Education* (1948), the Court's next major church–state case.[70] O'Neill acknowledged that Jefferson played such a critical role in "the movement against the establishment of any religion ... that a careful discussion ... cannot omit ... Jefferson's actions and statements," and that Madison was "the one man who had most to do with the phraseology of the First Amendment."[71] O'Neill then tried to show that neither founder opposed nonpreferential aid to religion, as can be seen in a number of their actions, including Madison's role in appointing congressional chaplains, and both Madison's and Jefferson's willingness to appropriate federal

[68] Ibid., 42.

[69] Robert L. Cord, *Separation of Church and State: Historical Fact and Current Fiction* (New York: Lambeth Press, 1982).

[70] J. M. O'Neill, *Religion and Education Under the Constitution* (New York: Harper & Bros., 1949), as described in Robert F. Drinan, *Religion, the Courts and Public Policy* (Westport, CT: Greenwood Press, 1963), 76–77.

[71] O'Neill, *Religion and Education*, 247, 253.

funds for religious activities for Native Americans.[72] While the justices in *McCollum* rejected this nonpreferentialist argument, Chief Justice William Rehnquist embraced it decades later in a dissenting opinion in which he called the wall of separation "a metaphor based on bad history." Yet, even as Rehnquist rejected the metaphor, his argument revolved around what he believed was a better understanding of the views of Madison and Jefferson.[73] In fact, as recently as 2005, both the majority and dissenting opinions in a case involving the display of the Ten Commandments on public property fought primarily over how to interpret Madison and Jefferson.[74]

Despite the centrality of Madison and Jefferson to church–state jurisprudence, an originalist analysis could have come to a very different conclusion. An equally good argument could be made that American church–state thinking was better represented by the debates over the Massachusetts constitution. The battles over religious taxes were at least as lively as they were in Virginia, where the general assessment tax merely died in committee. Meanwhile, constitutionally required tax-supported churches endured in Massachusetts for nearly half a century after the federal Bill of Rights was adopted. If Hugo Black's goal was to identify a common American attitude about church–state interactions at the time of the Constitution, there is no particular reason to choose the Virginia approach over the one in Massachusetts. In fact, distinguished nineteenth-century commentators can be found on both sides. On the one hand, law professor and Supreme Court Justice Joseph Story said that, at the time of the First Amendment, any "attempt to level all religions, and to make it state policy to hold all in utter indifference, would have created universal disapprobation."[75] On the other hand, prominent historian George

[72] For an opposing argument calling the "O'Neill thesis . . . the official position of the Catholic Church" and a "cavalier construction of the Constitution," see Leo Pfeiffer, "Church and State: Something Less Than Separation," *University of Chicago Law Review* 19 (1951): 3–7. Since *Everson*, many books have refought these battles. For a summary, see Drakeman, *Church, State, and Original Intent*, ch. 4.

[73] *Wallace* v. *Jaffice*, 472 U.S. 38 (1985).

[74] *McCreary County*, 545 U.S. For an in-depth analysis of Madison and Jefferson, see Vincent Phillip Muñoz, *God and the Founders: Madison, Washington, and Jefferson* (New York: Cambridge University Press, 2009).

[75] Joseph Story, *Commentaries on the Constitution of the United States . . .* (Boston: Little, Brown, and Company, 1833), 3:78. Story went even further to say that "the general, if not universal, sentiment . . . was, that Christianity ought to receive encouragement from the state." Ibid.

Bancroft wrote that Jefferson's "Virginia Statute on Religious Freedom" "shows the opinion of the leading American Statesmen in 1785."[76]

Since the outcomes in Virginia and Massachusetts were both slim and hotly debated, it may be most accurate to say that founding-era Americans were divided almost equally between two competing principles. One held, with Madison, that "employ[ing] Religion as an engine of Civil policy is . . . an unhallowed perversion of the means of salvation."[77] The other, as Massachusetts Chief Justice Theophilus Parsons said in extolling his commonwealth's approach, is that "[c]ivil government . . . availing itself only of its own powers, is extremely defective," and, therefore, "the people . . . adopted and patronized a religion, which . . . might cooperate with human institutions, to promote and secure the happiness of the citizens."[78] The importance of religion to the state, argued Parsons, is that it "tend[s] . . . to make every man . . . a better . . . neighbor, citizen, and magistrate."[79]

Today's battle between strict separationists and nonpreferentialists is often a modern reflection of these opposing views of how religion and government should relate to each other. It is, therefore, very tempting to favor those framers' views that match our own, and then search for an argument for why our preferred framers spoke for all the rest, much as Wiley Rutledge admitted to doing in *Everson*. In a strongly worded memorandum to the other justices, Rutledge wrote, "We all know . . . that this is really a fight by the Catholic schools to secure this money from the public . . . . It is aggressive and on a wide scale."[80] In later explaining his historically focused dissenting opinion, he wrote to a friend, "I felt pretty strongly about the Everson case but tried to keep the tone . . . moderate and also to avoid pointing . . . in the direction of any specific sect. The Virginia history was admirable for the latter purpose."[81]

[76] Quoted in C. Peter Magrath, "Chief Justice Waite and the Twin Relic: Reynolds v. United States," *Vanderbilt Law Review* 18, no. 2 (1965): 526, 567. For a discussion of how this letter profoundly influenced church–state jurisprudence, see Drakeman, *Church, State, and Original Intent*, ch. 2.

[77] [James Madison], "A Memorial and Remonstrance Against Religious Assessments," 1785, in *Sacred Rights of Conscience*, ed. Dreisbach and Hall, 311.

[78] *Barnes* v. *Falmouth*, 6 Mass. 401 (1810) at 405–406. [79] Ibid., 46.

[80] Wiley Rutledge, Memo after Conference, Wiley Rutledge Papers, Box 143, p. 5, quoted in Drakeman, *Church, State, and Original Intent*, 130.

[81] Wiley Rutledge to Ernest Kirschten, February 20, 1947, Wiley Rutledge Papers, Box 143, quoted in Drakeman, *Church, State, and Original Intent*, 131.

Not everyone is as quick to confess to doing "law office history" as Rutledge was, but our continued national division over church–state issues can make it easy to fall prey to Judge Leventhal's memorable description of the judicial use of legislative history: It is like "looking over a crowd and picking out your friends."[82] Yet, if we set the search for friends aside, it is hard to reach any conclusion other than the fact that Americans at the time of the Constitution did not share one view of the proper relationship of church and state. Instead, there was very considerable support for two opposing views, which divided the citizens of the various states as well as their representatives in the House and Senate.

Black's culmination-in-Virginia argument failed to account for the views that prevailed in New England and that had even attracted the votes of nearly half of the Virginia legislature.[83] Meanwhile, Rutledge offered a different, but equally unpersuasive, reason for coalescing all relevant church–state constitutional thinking into the themes of the "Memorial and Remonstrance": his assertion that Madison was the author of the establishment clause. If authorship is meaningful, perhaps we should look instead to Fisher Ames of Massachusetts, since the House rejected Madison's proposal, and ultimately adopted Ames' proposal instead. The Ames version – "Congress shall make no law establishing religion" – formed the textual foundation for the final version rather than Madison's "nor shall any national religion be established."[84] If authorship is central to a proper originalist interpretation, then the church–state views of Ames, and his fellow Massachusetts supporters of that state's ecclesiastical "standing order," may resonate better than Madison's "Memorial" as the "warp and woof" of the First Amendment. From a purely methodological point of view, however, it is hard to see why the opinions of one person, even if he is the provision's author, should constitute strong evidence of the original meaning of the First Amendment, especially where those opinions were expressed several years before in an entirely different context involving a different level of government and were dramatically different than the beliefs of many others in Congress.

[82] Quoted in Patricia M. Wald, "Some Observations on the Use of Legislative History in the 1981 Supreme Court Term," *Iowa Law Review* 68, no. 2 (1983): 214.

[83] Ragosta, *Wellspring*, 125–131.

[84] Madison biographer Irving Brant suggests that Madison wrote the Ames version and had it proposed by Ames. There is no evidence to support that speculation, and is very unlikely to be the case. See Drakeman, *Church, State, and Original Intent*, 143–144.

Concerns about whether it makes sense to attribute the personal opinions of one or two individuals to an act of either the Congress or the ratifiers is often called the "summing problem," and it is one of the issues that has driven New Originalists away from Old Originalism and the Framers.[85] Yet, if the arguments for separationism and nonpreferentialism focus too much attention on Madison and Jefferson, where should we look for the original meaning instead?

The Original Public Meaning

Many contemporary originalists question whether seeking the framers' understandings is useful at all. The First Amendment did not become law until it was ratified, so they argue that the framers' specific understandings are largely irrelevant.[86] New Originalists seek the objective meaning of the words rather than the intentions of the framers, an approach that is based on the assumption that there is a single, identifiable original semantic meaning. In this case, however, there are at least two equally good candidates for such a meaning. One approach is based on the concept of federalism. As Phillip Muñoz has written, "The key to unlocking the meaning of the Establishment Clause lies in understanding the words 'respecting an'."[87] Since "respecting" means "regarding; having regard to; relating to," according to Noah Webster's 1828 American dictionary, a federal law banning state establishments would be unconstitutional because it would be a law relating to "an establishment of religion."[88] The point of the clause is thus to allocate jurisdiction over church–state issues to the state governments.

[85] On the "summing problem," see, for example, Paul Brest, "The Misconceived Quest for the Original Understanding," *Boston University Law Review* 60 (1980): 214. On skepticism of Old Originalism, see, for example, Antonin Scalia, *A Matter of Interpretation: Federal Courts and the Law*, ed. Amy Gutmann (Princeton, NJ: Princeton University Press, 1998).

[86] See, for example, Vasan Kesavan and Michael Stokes Paulsen, "The Interpretive Force of the Constitution's Secret Drafting History," *Georgetown Law Journal* 91 (2003): 1113–1214.

[87] Muñoz, "Original Meaning," 630.

[88] "Respecting," in Noah Webster, *An American Dictionary of the English Language ...* (New York: S. Converse, 1828). The *Oxford English Dictionary* (OED) defines "respecting" as "with reference or regard to," citing, among others, Thomas Paine's letter to the Abbé Raynal. *Oxford English Dictionary,* s.v. "Respecting," accessed November 6, 2017, www.oed.com/view/Entry/275608?rskey=KRDUuP&result=3. See Steven D. Smith, *The Rise and Decline of American Religious Freedom* (Cambridge, MA: Harvard University Press), 59–60.

Justice Clarence Thomas has been the most prominent advocate of the federalism interpretation. In his concurring opinion in *Town of Greece* v. *Galloway* (2014), he interpreted the establishment clause as meaning that "Congress could not interfere with state establishments, notwithstanding any argument that could be made ... under the Necessary and Proper Clause."[89] Noting the differing approaches to religion and government in the various states in the founding era, he concluded, "[T]he relationship between church and state in the fledgling republic was far from settled at the time of ratification."[90] This "lack of consensus ... suggests that the First Amendment was simply agnostic on the subject of state establishments." As a result, the question of whether "to establish or disestablish religion was reserved to the States," and the clause only "*probably* prohibits Congress from establishing a national religion."[91] That is, Thomas is so certain that federalism animates the establishment clause that he is unsure whether it puts any limits on the ability of the federal government to create an established church.

Because Thomas believes that the clause was meant to allow the states to make church–state decisions free of federal interference, the "federalist logic ... poses a special barrier to its mechanical incorporation against the States through the Fourteenth Amendment."[92] According to Thomas, the Supreme Court's decisions to apply the provisions of the Bill of Rights to the states via the Fourteenth Amendment would, in the case of the establishment clause, reverse its original mandate that church–state decision-making would be reserved to the states. Although the First Amendment protections of the free exercise of religion, free speech, and so on can be seen to benefit individuals, Thomas argued, the states, rather than individuals, are the "particular beneficiaries of the [establishment] clause," and incorporation would thus "give rise to a paradoxical result": a clause meant to give the states freedom of choice in church–state matters would end up limiting (or eliminating) that choice.[93]

The second candidate for New Originalism's objective meaning is that the clause was meant simply to prohibit the formation of a national church by forbidding laws on the subject of a national establishment. On this reading, "respecting" still means "relating to," and "an establishment of religion" refers to a national church along the lines of the Church of

[89] *Town of Greece*, 572 US at 2. [90] Ibid., 3, citing Muñoz, "Original Meaning," 605.
[91] *Town of Greece*, 572 US at 1, 2 (emphasis added). [92] Ibid., 3. [93] Ibid., 4.

England. Proponents of the federalism interpretation counter that the no-national-church reading fails to account adequately for the inclusion of "respecting." Why, asks Steven Smith, reject the House's "no law establishing religion," and adopt "this more convoluted wording?"[94] A potential answer is that one or more members of the Conference Committee who added the "respecting" language was worried that prohibiting Congress from making laws "establishing religion" could cause confusion.

The phrase "establishing religion" was not as common as "an establishment of religion" in the founding era. A search of the 200,000 volumes in the Eighteenth-Century Online Collections database shows that "establishing religion" appears fewer than thirty times, and it carried various meanings based on the context. They include some clear references to a legally established national church, as in Francis Plowden's *Jura Anglorum*, where he discussed "the laws establishing religion" that created "established religions" in England and Scotland, and in Thomas Lyttelton's 1774 letter on the Quebec Act published in New York, which mentioned "the moment Parliament had established the Protestant religion."[95] But there are also descriptions of "the great aim of God in establishing religion," and, in a 1793 letter from Benjamin Carpenter, there is a reference to "the principle of establishing religion in general, without any exclusive establishment, on which the Americans have acted."[96]

Meanwhile, "establishment of religion" was a more common phrase that appears over ten times more frequently than "establishing religion" in the same eighteenth-century collection. The phrase "establishment of religion" is often used in connection with institutional relationships between church and state, as when Theophilus Philadelphus, in his *Sequel to Common Sense*, argued that a true religious revival is impossible where there is a "political establishment of religion" because "in all national establishments the showy appearance of duty, pompous rites and ceremonies, take off from . . . men's reverence for . . . reality."[97] Similarly, in 1763, Reverend

[94] Smith, *Rise and Decline*, 59.

[95] Francis Plowden, *Jura Anglorum: The Rights of Englishmen* (London: E. and R. Brooke, 1792), 84, 94; William Meredith, *A Letter from Thomas Lord Lyttelton, to William Pitt, Earl of Chatham, on the Quebec Bill* (Boston: M[il]ls and Hicks for Cox and Berry, 1774), 13.

[96] Richard Lucas, *An Enquiry after Happiness* . . . 6th Edition (London: R. Gosling, W. Innys, R. Manby, and T. Longman, 1734), 1:188; Benjamin Carpenter, *A Letter to the Rev. R. Foley, M.A. Rector of Oldswinford: In Answer to the Charges Brought Against the Dissenters in Stourbridge* . . . (Stourbridge: R. Baldwin and T. Pearson, [1793?]), 24.

[97] Theophilus Philadelphus, *A Sequel to Common Sense* . . . (Dublin: Alex Stuart, 1777), 67.

Henry Caner concluded that the Massachusetts Bay Colony did not have a "civil establishment of religion" because there were no "express words" in the charter granting "a power ... of instituting an ecclesiastical establishment."[98]

In light of these varying usages, it is not surprising that congressmen Huntington and Livermore, both of whom represented states with close ties between church and state, had worried that the "No religion shall be established" proposal could be misconstrued and not be interpreted to achieve the goal Madison had specified, which was to prohibit the formation of a national church. Although "establishing religion" was used synonymously with "an establishment of religion" by Plowden and Lyttelton, the former phase could also be interpreted more broadly – as possibly prohibiting laws that promote or support religion but fall short of a formal legal establishment, as the Carpenter letter suggested. Perhaps the framers replaced the phrase no law "establishing religion" with no law "respecting" (on the subject of) "an establishment of religion" in order to emphasize that the clause would only relate to laws involving formal, institutional links along the lines of a national church, as in the common description of the Church of England as "the church established by law."[99]

Some scholars have offered a third potential reading of the clause. "Respecting," they argue, expands the reach of the clause. As John Witte has observed, the "respecting an establishment" language could arguably be read as forbidding "laws that would 'point toward,' 'anticipate,' or 'reflect' ... an establishment."[100] This approach means that the clause's prohibition of governmental action is, according to Leo Pfeffer, "almost unlimited in scope."[101] Such an interpretation is considerably less likely than the others based on eighteenth-century English usage. Because "respecting," as used at that time, simply pointed to the subject matter of the clause, it is hard to see how the addition of that word would perform

[98] Henry Caner, *A Candid Examination of Dr. Mayhew's Observations* ... (Boston: Thomas and John Fleet, Green & Russell, and Edes & Gill, 1763), 32.

[99] This interpretation would help to answer Steven Smith's question about why the framers used the more ambiguous word "respecting" in the establishment clause. See Smith, *Rise and Decline*, 59.

[100] John Witte, Jr., *God's Joust, God's Justice: Law and Religion in the Western Tradition* (Grand Rapids, MI: Wm. B. Eerdmans, 2006), 198.

[101] See, for example, Leo Pfeiffer, "No Law Respecting an Establishment of Religion," *Buffalo Law Review* 2 (1952–1953): 237.

any sort of expanding or amplifying function.[102] Moreover, changing "establishing religion" to "respecting an establishment of religion" more likely narrows, rather than broadens, the range of applications because "an establishment of religion" typically had an institutionally related meaning. There were disagreements over whether particular laws, such as the provisions for New England religious taxes, constituted "establishments." Additionally, in some regions, but not others, legally incorporating religious institutions was seen as the creation of churches "established by law," an interpretation Madison followed in a presidential veto message.[103] But those official legislative links with formal ecclesiastical institutions are a far cry from the wide range of religious activities that have been the subject of the Supreme Court church–state opinions over the past seventy-five years.

Although the expansive, "almost unlimited" interpretation of the "respecting an establishment" language is considerably less plausible than the others, there are still at least two reasonable interpretations for a New Originalist focused on dictionaries and word usage, and it is hard to find a compelling reason to choose one over the other based simply on the meaning of the words.[104] Yet, these two contenders for the objective original meaning could lead in different directions in light of the incorporation doctrine. The no-national-church reading could potentially be incorporated to mean no-state-churches. Thomas' federalism version, however, would prevent the incorporation of the establishment clause and would allow states to make their own church–state choices. It might even allow Congress to create a national church if federalism is the only purpose of the clause.

One of the difficulties with the New Originalism methodology is that it does not include a method for deciding which of the two equally plausible semantic readings of a constitutional text is the correct one. This problem surfaced in the Supreme Court's first case of judicial review in 1796, and continues today.[105] In that case, *Hylton* v. *U.S.*, Justice William Paterson

[102] As I have previously written, in "twenty uses of the word 'respecting' in works published in America between 1750 and 1770 and available in the Sabin Americana collection, I was unable to identify any use of the word other than as a synonym for 'regarding' or 'on the subject of.'" Drakeman, *Church, State, and Original Intent*, 245, n. 153.

[103] Ibid., 274. [104] Pfeiffer, "No Law," 237.

[105] Joel Alicea and Donald L. Drakeman, "The Limits of New Originalism," *University of Pennsylvania Journal of Constitutional Law* 15, no. 4 (2013): 1161–1219.

resolved such a dilemma relating to the tax clauses by referring to the compromise made at the Constitutional Convention (where he was a delegate) that had led to the clause in question.[106] That is, he focused on the policy choice made by the framers as essentially the tie-breaker for competing semantic meanings. Following this (really quite) Old Originalism method of looking at what the framers decided when they agreed upon the establishment clause leads to the public meaning that best matches the framers' understandings, which is that they were preventing Congress from setting up a national church. Moreover, because the framers' debates about the Bill of Rights were publicly available at the time of ratification, their understanding of what the establishment clause was meant to accomplish also provides strong evidence of what the ratifiers and the public thought it meant.

The record is quite clear. Madison actually said what he thought his proposal meant, and it had nothing to do with the principled analysis of church–state issues contained in his "Memorial and Remonstrance." Congress, he said, "should not establish a religion, and enforce the legal observation of it by law." He had introduced the provision because some "people feared one sect might attain a pre-eminence, or two combine together, and establish a [national] religion to which they would compel others to conform."[107] Madison's description of the provision's purpose and meaning is consistent with both the ultimate House version ("Congress shall make no law establishing religion"), the Senate version ("no law establishing articles of faith or a mode of worship"), and the final ratified version ("no law respecting an establishment of religion"). Two of the six members of Congress who spoke about the establishment clause, Livermore of New Hampshire and Huntington of Connecticut, both said that they thought the proposed amendment meant what Madison said it did, i.e., no national religion.

Adopting language that was understood as a ban on a national church would not have required either the framers or the ratifiers to resolve their long-standing and deeply held disagreements over the proper relationship of religion and government. Moreover, because Madison repeatedly said that the goal of the establishment clause was just to prohibit the formation of a national religion and "enforce the legal observation of it by law," the First Federal Congress, which was heavily distracted by the task of setting

[106] *Hylton* v. *United States*, 3 US 171 (1796). [107] Cogan, *Complete Bill of Rights*, 60.

up an entire government, had neither the time nor the inclination to contemplate what exactly had been excluded. To be sure, a tax-funded Church of the United States, with federal employees acting as the clergy and laws specifying rites and doctrines, would not be constitutional. This is the classic definition of a religious establishment. A formal religious establishment required institutional links between church and state that were so substantial that the New Hampshire and Connecticut courts held that their own states, which had religious taxes similar to those in Massachusetts, did not actually have religious establishments.[108] They based these decisions on the grounds that, according to the Granite State's Chief Justice Jeremiah Smith, a "religious establishment is where the State prescribes a formulary of faith and worship for the rule and government of all the subjects."[109] If we ask what question the members of the First Federal Congress believed they were addressing, the answer was no-national-church, i.e., that Congress would not have the power to create a Church of the United States, unlike the British Parliament which had passed laws to establish the Church of England.

As a result, although the federalism approach is a reasonable candidate for being *an* objective meaning of the text, it is unlikely to be *the* objective *public* meaning. That is, people at the time may not have understood that Congress had adopted the establishment clause with the specific goal of allocating church–state decision-making power to the states. Beyond the public availability of the debates, which point to the no-national-church interpretation, the two state court decisions described above suggest that federalism was not understood to be the key to the establishment clause. As noted above, two of the three New England states that maintained ecclesiastical taxes, Connecticut and New Hampshire, declared that they did not have religious establishments. It would have been in their interest to admit to having a church establishment if the establishment clause was publically understood to protect such establishments. Disavowing an establishment,

[108] McLoughlin, *New England Dissent*, 1:863–870, 991. At about the same time, Massachusetts Justice Theophilus Parsons called his state's ecclesiastical tax an "establishment," which is what Madison's "Memorial and Remonstrance" called the proposed Virginia general assessment, even if Parsons and Madison held opposite opinions of whether establishments were a good thing.

[109] *Muzzy* v. *Wilkins*, 1 Smith's (1803), citing several scholarly sources. See also McLoughlin, *New England Dissent*, 1:864. Judge Zephaniah Swift similarly said that Connecticut's prior establishment had ended when, in 1784, the state eliminated support of specific churches and "civil endorsement to the Savoy Confession of Faith." Ibid., 1:923–924.

as New Hampshire and Connecticut did, would be the equivalent of refusing whatever protection a federalism-inspired clause was offering against federal legislative interference. Rather than explicitly turning down this constitutional protection, however, the New Hampshire and Connecticut courts probably did not read the establishment clause as having anything to do with church–state activities in the states.

The no-national-church interpretation is also the most consistent with the context in which the clause arose. There was no evidence of widespread public concern that Congress would try to interfere with state religious establishments, and the final House and the Senate versions of the establishment clause that appeared in the newspapers did not contain the word "respecting" or any other federalism-related language.[110] It is unlikely that the ratifiers or the public would have expected the conference committee to shift the meaning from one designated to eliminate the possibility of a national church to one that specifically sought to protect state establishments. Such an approach would require the conference committee to have a considerable amount of discretion to change a constitutional amendment, something one scholar has called "wildly implausible" in light of well-known eighteenth-century parliamentary procedures.[111]

The historical evidence indicates that the clause was understood by those who framed and ratified it, as well as by the public, as relating to the prohibition of a national church. It would not have encompassed any broad church–state principle of strict separationism or nonpreferentialism, and it was not directed toward insulating state establishments from congressional interference. As Connecticut congressman Timothy Pitkin, a lawyer and historian who wrote a two-volume *Political and Civil History of the United States*, said about the establishment clause on the floor of Congress in 1811, it was "intend[ed] to prevent the establishment of a National Church, such as the Church of England – a refusal to subscribe to the tenets of which was to exclude a citizen from office, etc."[112]

[110] For a discussion of the lack of many historical materials showing concern for specific protections for the state religious establishments, see Drakeman, "Antifederalists."

[111] William R. Casto, "Oliver Ellsworth's Calvinist Vision of Church and State in the Early Republic," in *The Forgotten Founders on Church and State*, ed. Mark David Hall, Daniel L. Dreisbach, and Jeffry Morrison (South Bend, IN: University of Notre Dame Press, 2009).

[112] *Annals*, 22:995–999. See Timothy Pitkin, *A Political and Civil History of the United States of America . . .*, 2 vols. (New Haven, CT: Hezekiah Howe and Durrie & Peck, 1828).

Conclusion: The Contemporary Importance of the Federalism Interpretation

To interpret the establishment clause solely in light of the most likely candidate for original meaning – the prohibition of a national church – may, unfortunately, be contrary to the policy outcome the framers and ratifiers believed would result from its adoption. Even though the framers and the public may not have seen the states as the explicit beneficiaries of the clause, the federalism interpretation is almost certainly the modern approach that most closely tracks the constitutional outcome anticipated by the framers and understood by the public. American religious pluralism was well known in the founding era, and it was manifested in the diverse array of church–state arrangements in the states. States were the locus of church–state interactions, and even the citizens of the New England states that had ecclesiastical taxes expected that even more localized governments – individual cities and towns – would allocate those taxes based on the communities' desires. Freeing those community-based decisions from the complications and competition that would result from a national church was one of the underlying premises of the establishment clause. The clause was designed to ensure that a national church would not be superimposed on whatever other church–state choices might be made by states, cities, and towns.

The reason that congressmen with impressively diverse church–state views could agree on the clause is that its anti-establishment reach would extend only as far as the national government. It was not a statement in favor of a general policy of nonestablishment. It thus differed from the remainder of the First Amendment, which was a series of statements in favor of the general principles of free exercise of religion, freedom of speech, freedom of the press, and so on. There was no equivalent nonestablishment value underlying the establishment clause. That is, whereas the Congress demonstrated a belief in free speech rights and the rights of conscience in general – and, in fact, the House voted to prohibit the states from infringing them[113] – there was no indication that the Congress sought to adopt a broad anti-establishment principle. Rather, the establishment clause was a decision that there would not be an

[113] *Annals*, 1:783–784.

establishment of a national church.[114] To extend the reach of the establishment clause via the incorporation doctrine to prohibit actions by state governments is to read into the clause a principle of nonestablishment that was neither the framers' original understanding nor the original public meaning.

Accordingly, although the federalism interpretation may not reflect how members of the First Congress and the public explicitly understood the goal of the clause, in today's environment, it nevertheless best captures the policy choices implicit in its prohibition of a national church. As the draft version of Jefferson's Second Inaugural Address, penned by Madison, said, "[R]eligious exercises, could … be neither controlled or prescribed by us. They have … been left as the Constitution found them, under the direction and discipline acknowledged within the several states."[115] These sentiments echo Madison's recorded statements during the Virginia debates over ratifying the Constitution, where he said, "There is not a shadow of right in the general government to intermeddle with religion," an observation he made in recognition of the fact that a "particular state might concur in one religious project."[116]

Because of the widespread view that the national government could not "intermeddle" with "religious project[s]" in the states, the federalism interpretation did not appear until over a century later, when scholars responded to the Supreme Court's announcement of the incorporation doctrine.[117] In a post-incorporation constitutional environment, which has enabled the Supreme Court to intermeddle in church–state policies in the states on a regular basis, a federalism approach that continues to prohibit a national church, but which also leaves the states free to address their own church–state issues, most closely tracks both the explicit understandings and the implicit assumptions contained in the establishment clause. In *Everson* and the cases following it, the Supreme Court has essentially rewritten the establishment clause twice: once through the

[114] In Jack Balkin's terminology, it was a rule, not a principle or a standard. Jack Balkin, *Living Originalism* (Cambridge, MA: Harvard University Press, 2014), 6, 14.

[115] James Morton Smith, ed., *The Republic of Letters: The Correspondence Between Thomas Jefferson and James Madison 1776–1826* (New York: W. W. Norton, 1995), 3:1364.

[116] Cogan, *Complete Bill of Rights*, 71.

[117] The oldest scholarly source cited by both Phillip Muñoz and Steven Smith is a 1954 article (i.e., post-*Everson*): Joseph M. Snee, "Religious Disestablishment and the Fourteenth Amendment," *Washington University Law Quarterly* 1954, no. 4 (1954): 371–407.

incorporation doctrine, which has revised "Congress shall make no law" to include any actions of any state or local governmental authority, and again by reading "respecting an establishment of religion" as if it said "anything where government is involved with religious beliefs, practices or institutions." The federalism/no-national-church interpretation is, in this evolutionary environment, the approach most likely to restore the establishment clause's original meaning and effect.

Whether originalism is the best way to interpret the Constitution is a complex jurisprudential issue well beyond the scope of this chapter. Even for those who take the original meaning seriously – which includes an increasing number of scholars as well as the vast majority of the American public – it is essential to focus on which historical evidence is the most relevant to determining a constitutional meaning.[118] In the case of the establishment clause, different methodological choices about what constitutes the most relevant evidence can lead to different outcomes. But the best understanding of the original meaning comes from examining the text in light of the specific policy choices made by the framers and understood by the public, which, in this case, is the no-national-church interpretation. Because of the effects on constitutional interpretation resulting from the Supreme Court's incorporation doctrine and its expansive reading of "establishment," however, the no-national-church interpretation *plus* the federalism interpretation may, in our current post-incorporation, constitutional environment, come closest to matching the policy outcomes for which the clause was designed.

[118] For the popular consensus for originalism, see Donald L. Drakeman, "What's the Point of Originalism?" *Harvard Journal of Law and Public Policy* 37 (2014): 1124–1150.

14 The Two Separations

Marc O. DeGirolami

Introduction

The advantage of "separation" as an ideal of church–state relations is that its view of the right relationship between church and state is plain. Combination, congruence, and harmony must be avoided. Distance, division, and even discord must be fostered. The separationist desires the disintegration of religion and civil government in the etymologically correct sense – by splitting apart one from the other. Integration is the chief danger and segregation the chief objective.

As a model for individual or collective life, separation is not innately attractive. Separation is perhaps most often used in ordinary conversation to describe the breakdown of a marriage before the formality and finality of divorce – not a self-evidently desirable state of affairs. Pursuing separation is not like pursuing knowledge or friendship, whose ends are intrinsically good. Separation must be justified by some contingent reason. Indeed, though the US Constitution speaks of the free exercise and nonestablishment of "religion," much of the confusion about separation as an American civic ideal results from a failure to focus on the specifically historical and contingent justifications for it. These justifications for separation concern not "religion" in general or in the abstract but Christianity specifically – Christianity being, as a historical and cultural matter, the central religious tradition in the United States.

These historical justifications have taken two cardinal forms. The first concerns the politico-theological benefits that are believed to devolve onto Christian churches, or onto Christian believers, from a division from the state, and the general social and political advantages derived therefrom. The second involves the secular benefits to the liberal democratic state of unbreachable barriers against the civic and cultural influence of Christianity. The first justification is more ancient, but the second is more powerful today. The

Thanks to Samuel Bray, Michael D. Breidenbach, Nathan Chapman, Richard Garnett, Mark Movsesian, Jeffrey Pojanowski, Steven Smith, and Kevin Walsh for comments.

first is oriented positively and the second negatively, toward the cultural and political value of Christianity in the United States. The first sees Christianity as socially and politically valuable – even precious. The second sees it as irrelevant or even obnoxious.

But separation is generally thought to be waning. It is supposed by many scholars of law and religion that the direction of American church–state constitutional law in the last generation has been away from separation and toward other aspirations – especially equality and nondiscrimination. Many scholars claim that approaches of equality or nondiscrimination are in tension, if not in outright conflict, with separation. Of late, the Supreme Court seems to have made its choice decisively in favor of norms of equality and nondiscrimination and against separation.

This chapter takes a different position. Equality and nondiscrimination are fundamentally variations on the second type of separation – the view that Christianity is at best irrelevant and at worst obnoxious to the secular liberal state. Though there has been a real doctrinal shift, that change has masked an underlying unity of justification, application, and often outcome in approaches of separation and equality. Talk of equality and nondiscrimination has served to continue to push the law from the first type of separation to the second.

This chapter distinguishes and explores the two separations – separation as a specifically Christian piece of political theology, in large part for the benefit of a Christian civil society, and separation as a specifically secular position for the benefit of a liberal society that wishes to divest from and repudiate Christianity. This chapter then describes the allure of equality and nondiscrimination as church–state ideals, their ascendancy in late twentieth-century constitutional law, and the sense in which they are believed to have supplanted the first version of separation.

But neither equality nor nondiscrimination delivers what it promises: a valueless perspective on the social and political worth of Christianity. In fact, their perspective is decidedly negative. To see how, it is helpful to compare the use of these principles in other areas of constitutional law. Equality and nondiscrimination are constitutional touchstones in the contexts of race and sex discrimination, where the overriding assumption is that race and sex are fundamentally irrelevant considerations, and obnoxious and illegitimate bases on which to make laws and to order society. Transposed to the context of religion – and, as this chapter argues, the transposition in reality concerns Christianity specifically – a similar assumption holds: that Christianity is fundamentally an irrelevant, or even an obnoxious, and illegitimate, influence in the making of laws or the structuring of the cultural and political realms. Indeed, in a society in which Christianity has had such overwhelming predominance, insisting on equality is tantamount to squelching Christianity. This view is not neutral as to the value of Christianity in contemporary American politics and society. It is nothing less than an expression of the second separation.

The First Separation: Christianity as Precious

Separation of church and state is neither universal nor inevitable. Many civilizations have enjoyed relatively stable arrangements in which religion and civil government have been united in various ways and degrees. For example, civil and religious offices have been held together, states have established official religions, and civil authorities have made religious appointments. Some governments continue to use such arrangements. True, most of the liberal democratic nations of Western Europe as well as the United States today espouse some type of separation, even if the forms of separation among these countries differ significantly. But in each of these nations, it is the Christian tradition (not abstracted "religion") that occupies the central historical position from which these societies desired separation, and it is likewise the Christian tradition (not abstracted "religion") that itself provided the earliest justifications for separation.

Indeed, as a legal matter, "religion" by itself has been credibly criticized as a useless category for understanding the sources and justifications of American separation. It is true that the Constitution proscribes laws "respecting an establishment of religion" and enjoins Congress not to prohibit the "free exercise" of religion. But the meager evidence concerning the original meaning of the establishment clause (the clause that is generally used today to police church–state matters) discloses little about either the word "religion" or the sense in which it (whatever it is) must be "separated" from civil government.[1] The meaning of religion within the

1 See, for example, Donald L. Drakeman, *Church, State, and Original Intent* (New York: Cambridge University Press, 2009), 196–216 ("There were no eloquent speeches extolling the virtues of the strict separation of church and state or the importance of religion to the federal government.").

First Amendment was not debated by the constitutional drafters; it seemingly was widely assumed to include "a plurality of Protestant Christian faiths," but one will search in vain for a definition of religion, either in the constitutional text or in its history.[2] As Leonard Levy has said, "The debate [in Congress concerning the religion clauses] was sometimes irrelevant, usually apathetic, and unclear. Ambiguity, brevity, and imprecision in thought and expression characterize the comments of the few members who spoke."[3] To the extent that framers including James Madison spoke of "religion," they generally tended to assume, discuss, and react against distinctively Christian expressions of it.[4] As for the meaning of the *separation* of religion from civil government, that, too, is difficult to pin down, since, as Philip Hamburger has put it, "the constitutional authority for separation is without historical foundation."[5]

This murky state of affairs has not been clarified in the least by the Supreme Court, which has steadfastly, even willfully, refused to offer any constitutional criteria at all for identifying what counts as religion.[6] To the contrary, it has insisted throughout the twentieth century that religion is a legal category with no fixed criteria and that sincere expressions of religion must be taken without inquiry and on judicial faith as authentic examples of it.[7] The academy has done little better: sociologists of religion continue to do battle over the

[2] John Witte, Jr., *God's Joust, God's Justice: Law and Religion in the Western Tradition* (Grand Rapids, MI: Wm. B. Eerdmans Publishing, 2006), 205 ("[P]recisely what constituted religion and nonreligion, and where the line was to be drawn between them, the congressional record simply does not say.").

[3] Leonard W. Levy, *The Establishment Clause: Religion and the First Amendment* (Chapel Hill, NC: University of North Carolina Press, 1986), 79.

[4] See, for example, James Madison, "Memorial and Remonstrance Against Religious Assessments" (1785), in which Madison deploys distinctively Christian phrases like "duty we owe to our Creator" and engages in a theological apology for a certain understanding of "the Christian religion itself, for every page of it disavows a dependence on the powers of this world."

[5] Philip Hamburger, *Separation of Church and State* (Cambridge, MA: Harvard University Press, 2002), 481.

[6] The closest the Court has come to a definition did not concern the constitutional text at all, but a congressional selective service statute in which the Court drew from the Protestant theologian Paul Tillich's functionalist account of religion to hold that in using the term "religious training or belief," Congress aimed to exempt those with any "belief that is sincere and meaningful [and that] occupied a place in the life of its possessor parallel to that filled by the orthodox belief in God." *United States* v. *Seeger*, 380 US 163, 166 (1965).

[7] See, for example, *Thomas* v. *Review Board of the Indiana Employment Security Division*, 450 US 707 (1981).

cogency of religion as a category,[8] and legal scholars debate its validity and its claims to "special" or distinctive constitutional protection as well.[9] A conceptual category with no legal definition and no generally accepted criteria – indeed, whose very existence continues to be disputed among scholars across disciplines and which may well have been invented for scholarly purposes – can do very little explanatory work, let alone justify a particular church–state ideal like separation.[10]

To understand separation, Christianity, not religion, must be the focus. That is because, unlike the history of "religion," Christian history contains a rich deposit of politico-theological explanations for separation. Some historical accounts of religious freedom in America treat separationism as beginning with Thomas Jefferson's Letter to the Danbury Baptists or perhaps extend slightly further back to Roger Williams, but separation has a much longer and richer lineage.[11] Indeed, separation is fundamentally a distinctive piece of political theology dating from the origins of Christianity, an account of the relationship between divine and civil authority.[12] As John Witte observes, "Separation of Church and State was … an ancient Western principle of religious liberty, rooted in the Bible and subject to all manner of complex theological and political interpretations in the two millennia before the First Amendment was forged."[13]

The nature of the Christian political theology supporting separation is complicated and variegated, however. Witte has individuated no less than five conceptions of separation that eventually influenced American

[8] For classic skeptical sociological treatments, see Jonathan Z. Smith, *Imagining Religion: From Babylon to Jonestown* (Chicago, IL: University of Chicago Press, 1982) and Talal Asad, *Genealogies of Religion: Discipline and Reasons of Power in Christianity and Islam* (Baltimore, MD: Johns Hopkins University Press, 1993). For recent efforts to give substance to the category, at law and otherwise, see Christian Smith, *Religion: What It Is, How It Works, and Why It Matters* (Princeton, NJ: Princeton University Press, 2017) and Kathleen A. Brady, *The Distinctiveness of Religion in American Law: Rethinking Religion Clause Jurisprudence* (New York: Cambridge University Press, 2015).

[9] Compare Micah Schwartzman, "What if Religion is Not Special," *University of Chicago Law Review* 79 (2012): 1351 with Christopher C. Lund, "Religion is Special Enough," *Virginia Law Review* 103 (2017): 481.

[10] Smith, *Imagining Religion.*

[11] See, for example, John Fea, *Was America Founded as a Christian Nation? A Historical Introduction* (Louisville, KY: Westminster John Knox Press, 2011), 163.

[12] See Nicholas Wolterstorff, *The Mighty and the Almighty: An Essay in Political Theology* (Cambridge: Cambridge University Press, 2012), 2 ("[A]t the core of traditional political theology was the question of how God's authority is related to the authority of the state.").

[13] Witte, *God's Joust*, 209.

understandings: separation to protect the church from the state; the state from the church; the individual conscience from church or state; the ecclesiastical jurisdictions of the several states of the union from the federal government; and society from untoward religious influence.[14] Certainly "separation" is an umbrella term; underneath it one will find nuances and historical distinctions of many kinds, and it is well beyond the ken of this chapter even to survey, let alone to identify, each of these varieties.

Yet, what unites the first four out of Witte's five conceptions of separation, and, indeed, what represents an overriding justification for separation for most of its history is a view about the relationship between Christianity and the civil authority:

- Christianity is precious for the cultural and political community in which it is situated.
- Christianity demands a special place of independent authority in relation to the state – perhaps above the state, but at least distinct and, to some extent, insulated from it.
- The specifics of the relationship between Christianity and the state – the quality of the "special place" of authority – may vary over time, but the sense that Christianity is precious does not.

It should be emphasized that this distillation makes no claims about whether a country and a people are essentially Christian, or whether a nation was "founded" as Christian or is fundamentally identified with Christianity. Indeed, it is capacious enough to describe periods during which Christianity was more or less aligned with the dominant state power and those in which Christianity was at odds with it. Again, it is well beyond the scope of this chapter to offer a complete treatment of Christian sources discussing separation over the centuries. Its more modest aim in this part is to show that this first sense of separation is a common theme that recurs (though with distinctive emphases) at different moments over the history of Christianity.

Consider only a very few examples of the early Christian period before, and just after, the Edict of Milan and the conversion of the Emperor Constantine to Christianity. This period was marked by conflict between a nascent Christianity and a decadent Roman Empire. Perhaps the best-

[14] Ibid., 224–237.

known and most-quoted separationist Biblical injunction is Christ's statement in the Gospels of Matthew, Mark, and Luke to "[r]ender therefore unto Caesar the things that are Caesar's, and unto God the things that are God's."[15] The imagery is one of dual and distinctive authority: God's things, to be rendered to God during life in this world, must be disambiguated and set apart from the things not appertaining to God but instead to the political authority. Christ is moved to draw this distinction in answering the questions of the scribes and Pharisees as to the source of Christ's authority: "By what authority doest thou these things, or who is he that gave thee this authority?"[16] His response is a statement of political theology: the separation of authority into two types.

Several scholars have noted similar dualistic affirmations of Christian and political authority by subsequent apostolic and patristic writers of this period.[17] The work of Tertullian, a second-century Christian convert and apologist in the Roman Empire, is rarely highlighted but particularly illuminating for its modern resonances. Tertullian's *Apologeticum* is directed at local Roman governors and protests the persecution of Christians.[18] Most of the tract is a mix of philosophy and polemic designed to obtain privileges for Christians that other religious sects enjoyed in the Empire. But in Chapter XXIV, Tertullian argues for Christian toleration – and, in fact, for what he calls "libertatem religionis," or freedom of religion[19] – on two bases: first, the pragmatic ground that "no being, not even a man, will desire to be worshipped by an unwilling person"; and second, that by singling out Christianity for especially bad treatment, the Romans are essentially depriving themselves of the true faith, of communion with the Christian God.[20] This is an argument for religious liberty that connects separation and tolerance. It concerns the limits of Roman political

[15] Matthew 22:21; Mark 12:17; and Luke 20:25 (King James Version).

[16] Luke 20:2 (King James Version).

[17] Witte, *God's Joust*; Oliver O'Donovan, *The Desire of the Nations: Rediscovering the Roots of Political Theology* (Cambridge: Cambridge University Press, 1996); Lester L. Field, Jr., *Liberty, Dominion, and the Two Swords: On the Origins of Western Political Theology* (Notre Dame, IN: University of Notre Dame Press, 1998).

[18] Tertullian, *Apologeticum*, trans. Alexander Souter (Cambridge: Cambridge University Press, 1917).

[19] The eminent church historian Robert Wilken writes that Tertullian's may be the earliest use of "religious liberty" by any writer. Robert Louis Wilken, *Liberty in the Things of God: The Christian Origins of Religious Freedom* (New Haven, CT: Yale University Press, 2019).

[20] Tertullian, *Apologeticum*, Chapter XXIV ("We offend the Romans and are not considered Romans because we do not worship the god of the Romans. It is well that there is a God of

authority and the reservation of space within the Empire for Christian belief, not only for the practical reason that the state cannot effectively coerce worship (this is a theme that will recur in much later arguments), but also, and more centrally, for the specifically theological reason that the Christian religion is the true one and that it would greatly benefit the Romans to reject their own false divinities and accept the true God.

But perhaps the best-known expositor of separation in the early Christian period is Augustine, whose metaphor of the two cities – the earthly and the heavenly – has come to represent one of the archetypal Christian ideas of separation: "Two cities have been formed by two loves: the earthly by the love of self, even to the contempt of God; the heavenly by the love of God, even to the contempt of self."[21] As Miles Hollingworth writes in his study of Augustine, "From its inception, Christianity had always had to negotiate the ancient expectation that religion and politics should form a single piece."[22] A Christian citizen was untrustworthy, from the Roman perspective, and therefore dangerous. The post-lapsarian condition of Christians prevented them from treasuring earthly things as ultimate ends, whereas the Romans idealized this world, precisely because they had no other world to praise.[23] As Peter Brown has noted, "Committed to the fragile world they had created, [non-Christian Romans] were forced to idealize it[.]"[24]

Augustine, who wrote *City of God* after the conversion of Constantine, distinguished the two realms of authority and explained that Christians had an important role to play in the earthly city. Christians were not to withdraw from that city, "for the earthly city, which shall not be everlasting . . . has its good in this world, and rejoices in it with such joy as things can afford."[25] Rather, in perpetually longing for something beyond the earthly city, and in "establish[ing] their identity by refusing to be engulfed in the unthinking habits of their fellows," Christians could

all, to whom willy nilly we all belong. But among you it is lawful to worship anything except the true God, as if He to whom we all belong were not rather the God of all.").

21 Augustine of Hippo, *The City of God*, trans. Marcus Dods (New York: Penguin Random House, 2013), XIV, 24.

22 Miles Hollingworth, *Saint Augustine of Hippo: An Intellectual Biography* (New York: Oxford University Press, 2013), 12.

23 Augustine of Hippo, *The City of God*, III.

24 Peter Brown, *Augustine of Hippo: A Biography* (Berkeley, CA: University of California Press, 1967), 307.

25 Augustine of Hippo, *The City of God*, XV, 4.

contribute to the earthly city's improvement – to its progress – while never losing sight that the earthly city was never completely perfectible and that it could never become the heavenly city.[26] Separation, for Augustine, followed from the Christian's primary allegiance to and full-fledged citizenship in the heavenly city. Augustine's commitment to the earthly city and to improving its goods was derivative of this primary loyalty.[27] His argument for separation depends upon the value of Christianity and its important role in the earthly realm.

The early Christian period witnessed the first separation of Christianity from the civil power. This separation occurred even as Christianity changed, by degrees, from the religion of an oppressed minority to the religion of the prevailing political power. The first separation likewise modulated from a "separation of survival" to a "separation of preemption."[28] Yet in both cases, the dynamics of separation were similar: Christianity was precious and, as a result, demanded a distinct sphere of authority that could not be colonized by the political power. Many scholars have noted Pope Gelasius's rebuke in 494 of the theological pretensions of Anastasius, the Eastern Roman Emperor, during the eastern-western Acacian schism as an emblematic moment, in which the pope not only distinguished the "two powers" of Christian and civil authority, but also ranked the "priestly power" as superior.[29] Here, the separation of Christianity implied an authority over and above the civil power, even if not a union with it.[30]

26 Brown, *Augustine of Hippo*, 322.

27 Augustine of Hippo, *The City of God*, XIX, 17: "The earthly city, which does not live by faith, and the end it proposes, in the well-ordered concord of civic obedience and rule, is the combination of men's wills to attain the things which are helpful to this life. The heavenly city, or rather the part of it which sojourns on earth and lives by faith, makes use of this piece only because it must, until this mortal condition which necessitates it shall pass away."

28 Witte, *God's Joust*, 216.

29 Michael W. McConnell, "Non-State Governance," *Utah Law Review* 2010 (2010): 7, 8. Witte, *God's Joust*, 214; Harold J. Berman, *Law and Revolution: The Formation of the Western Legal Tradition* (Cambridge, MA: Harvard University Press, 1983), 92; Brian Tierney, "Religious Rights: A Historical Perspective," in *Religious Liberty in Western Thought*, ed. Noel B. Reynolds and W. Cole Durham (Grand Rapids, MI: Wm. B. Eerdmans Publishing, 1996), 34–36.

30 There is scholarly debate about whether Gelasius intended to subordinate civil authority to the pope. Compare Walter Ullmann, *A Short History of the Papacy in the Middle Ages* (New York: Routledge, 2003), 35 with Brian Tierney, *The Crisis of Church and State 1050–1300* (Toronto: University of Toronto Press, 1964), 14–15.

Likewise, Harold Berman's masterpiece, *Law and Revolution*, makes the "Papal Revolution" of the eleventh to the thirteenth century the centerpiece of his history of Western legal thought.[31] While "the church in the year 1000 . . . was conceived as the Christian people . . . which was governed by both secular and priestly rulers," a succession of popes including Leo IX, Nicholas II, Alexander II (whose election was conducted for the first time without the assent of the Holy Roman Emperor), and (most importantly) Gregory VII "proclaimed the legal supremacy of the pope over all Christians and the legal supremacy of the clergy, under the pope, over all secular authorities."[32] This *libertas ecclesiae*, several law and religion scholars have recently suggested, undergirds many present-day doctrines of constitutional law, very much including the separation of powers as well as contemporary notions of "church autonomy."[33]

To be sure, the controversy over "investiture" – over the power of high ecclesiastical appointments – was both theological and political. Yet to label the series of confrontations between popes and emperors in this period as "political" *instead* of "theological" – "theology as power play," in Paul Horwitz's phrase – itself reflects a particular and highly contestable political theology that understands Christianity as ideally cut off politics.[34] This "political" view adopts Christian political powerlessness as a baseline. But the Christian historical experience has rarely reflected that sort of political theology, even if theology and politics are sometimes imagined today as hermetically sealed off from one another. Indeed, the first separation instantiates a specific type of Christian political theology – a view of Christianity as precious, and a perspective on the proper allocation of authority between civil and Christian powers. It is no criticism to call variations of that view political, and it misses the point to deprecate those that reflect comparatively greater power on the part of Christian clerics as "a bid for dominance, not separation."[35] All political theologies work against the backdrop of existing political arrangements of power,

[31] Berman, *Law and Revolution*. [32] Ibid., 91, 94.

[33] See, for example, Richard W. Garnett, "'The Freedom of the Church': (Towards) an Exposition, Translation, and Defense," *Journal of Contemporary Legal Issues* 21 (2013): 33 and Steven D. Smith, *The Rise and Decline of American Religious Freedom* (Cambridge, MA: Harvard University Press, 2014), 31–36.

[34] Paul Horwitz, "Freedom of the Church Without Romance," *Journal of Contemporary Legal Issues* 21 (2013): 59, 74.

[35] Ibid.

which, at the time of Gregory VII, were decidedly with the civil authority, and all prescribe reallocations of it.

At any rate, if the Christian medieval period reflected a "separation of preemption" that sits at the heart of the first separation, early Protestant Reformation perspectives offer an equally vital separation of cooperation.[36] Our next stop – one that regrettably necessitates leapfrogging the centuries of the late medieval period[37] – is the sixteenth century and John Calvin's *Institutes of the Christian Religion*, a colossally influential source for the religious views of many early Americans, particularly for Baptists and in the New England colonies and states through the mid-nineteenth century.[38] What is striking about the structure of the *Institutes* is that while the overwhelming majority of the work is devoted to theological profundities concerning the knowledge of God and of humanity, the study of Scripture, Augustinian-inflected reflections on original sin and predestination, the nature of Christian faith, and so on, the final chapter of Book IV deals explicitly with church–state relations and separation.

Calvin's understanding of separation is distinctive, but is also a distinctive variety of the first separation. Throughout the *Institutes*, he intersperses observations that "in man government is twofold: the one spiritual, by which the conscience is trained to piety and divine worship; the other civil, by which the individual is instructed in those duties which, as men and citizens, we are bold to perform," that "these two are always to be viewed apart from one another," that there is "a great difference between the ecclesiastical and the civil power," and that "neither does the Church

[36] Witte, *God's Joust*.

[37] For discussion of "conciliarism" as important in the tradition of Christian church–state separation and as influential on the American founding generation, see Michael D. Breidenbach, "Conciliarism and the American Founding," *The William and Mary Quarterly* 73 (2016). For the Christian history of separation during the period omitted by this chapter, see Oliver O'Donovan and Joan Lockwood O'Donovan, eds., *From Irenaeus to Grotius: A Sourcebook in Christian Political Thought, 100–1625* (Grand Rapids, MI: Wm. B. Eerdmans Publishers, 1999). On the importance of Martin Luther for separation, see Brad S. Gregory, *Rebel in the Ranks: Martin Luther, the Reformation, and the Conflicts that Continue to Shape Our World* (San Francisco, CA: HarperCollins Press, 2017).

[38] Roger Finke and Rodney Stark, *The Churching of America, 1776–2005: Winners and Losers in Our Religious Economy* (New Brunswick, NJ: Rutgers University Press, 2005); Mark A. Noll, *America's God: From Jonathan Edwards to Abraham Lincoln* (New York: Oxford University Press, 2002), 293–329; and Witte, *God's Joust*, 219.

assume anything to herself which is proper to the magistrate, nor is the magistrate competent to what is done by the church."[39]

Yet, while these are certainly arguments against unification of the civil and ecclesiastical realms, Calvin also is clear that there must be cooperation – particularly by the civil authority on behalf of the church. "[T]hey ought," he wrote, "to combine their efforts."[40] This separation of cooperation is explicit in the last chapter of Book IV, "Of Civil Government." Here, Calvin wrote that while civil and ecclesiastical authority "are distinct from one another . . . they are not adverse to each other," for:

> The former [civil law] . . . begins the heavenly kingdom in us, even now upon earth, and in this mortal and evanescent life commences immortal and incorruptible blessedness, while to the latter [civil courts] it is assigned . . . to foster and maintain the external worship of God, to defend sound doctrine and the condition of the Church, to adapt our conduct to human society, to form our manners to civil justice, to conciliate us to each other, to cherish common peace and tranquility.[41]

Indeed, Calvin goes further: the principal function of civil government is to arrange matters so as to ensure "that a public form of religion may exist among Christians, and humanity among men" in order to prevent "the true religion, which is contained in the law of God, from being violated."[42] No polity, he continues, "can be successfully established unless piety be its first care, and . . . those laws are absurd which disregard the rights of God, and consult only for men . . . Christian princes and magistrates may be ashamed if they make it not their care."[43] It is "folly" for civil authorities "to neglect the care of divine things, and devote themselves merely to the administration of justice among men."[44]

Calvin says in the same breath that while "the spiritual kingdom of Christ and the civil government are . . . very widely separated," they must act in mutual concert and reinforcement "within a unitary local Christian commonwealth."[45] This is a distinctive and highly influential (at least for the early American republic) variation on the first separation, one that, as

39 John Calvin, *Institutes of the Christian Religion*, trans. Henry Beveridge (Edinburgh: Calvin Translation Society, 1846), Book III, chapter 19.15; Book IV, chapter 11.3.

40 Ibid., Book IV, chapter 11.3.

41 Ibid., Book IV, chapter 20.2.

42 Ibid., Book IV, chapter 20.3.

43 Ibid., Book IV, chapter 20.9.

44 Ibid.

45 Ibid., Book IV, Chapter 20.1; Witte, *God's Joust*, 219. See also John Calvin, *Thought on Economic and Social Issues and the Relationship of Church and State*, ed. Richard C. Gamble (New York: Garland Publishing, 1992).

with all of the other examples of the first separation, depends on the cultural and political preciousness of Christianity.

Separation in Enlightenment sources somewhat destabilized the central position of Christianity. The key proponents of separation during this period were no longer theologians and churchmen but political men and thinkers. And yet Christianity remained an object of their reflections concerning separation, and Christianity was still very much presupposed to be the basic religious framework structuring civil society. Separation for John Locke, George Washington, James Madison, and Thomas Jefferson – distinct from one another as they are – can be understood as variants of the first separation. In fact, in some cases they echo earlier views.[46]

For example, Locke's *Letter Concerning Toleration* specifically addressed "the mutual toleration of [C]hristians in their different professions of religion."[47] Locke wrote that "toleration is the chief characteristical mark of the true church" and that expressions of Christian faith that do not arise from conscientious conviction, "far from being any furtherance, are indeed great obstacles to our salvation ... add[ing] unto the number of our sins those also of hypocrisy ... and contempt of his Divine Majesty."[48] In a distinctive echo of Tertullian, who had argued more than a millennium earlier that compelled belief was worthless to the worshipped being (whether divine or human), Locke continued in a pragmatic vein: "True and saving religion consists in the inward persuasion of the mind, without which nothing can be acceptable to God."[49] Yet just as in Tertullian, the pragmatic argument for separation, which need not be intelligible only to Christians, is immediately conjoined in Locke with the distinctively Christian claim that even if the force of law could change a person's mind, "yet [it] would not ... help at all to the salvation of their souls. For, there being but one truth" – the Christian truth – there is only "one way to heaven," which can only be reached by obedience to the dictates of "conscience."[50] As in Tertullian's *Apologeticum*, Locke united Christian soteriology with pragmatic considerations to complete his argument for separation.[51] John Witte has rightly

[46] And they are distinct, notwithstanding the modern tendency to bunch them all together. See Vincent Phillip Muñoz, *God and the Founders: Madison, Washington, and Jefferson* (New York: Cambridge University Press, 2009), 2–7.

[47] John Locke, *John Locke: A Letter Concerning Toleration and Other Writings*, ed. Mark Goldie (Indianapolis, IN: Liberty Fund, 2010).

[48] Ibid., 5. [49] Ibid., 11. [50] Ibid., 12.

[51] For further discussion, see Wilken, *Liberty in the Things of God*, chapter 9.

noted that Locke's arguments "presupposed a magistracy and community committed to a common Christianity."[52] Even more than this, however, Locke's arguments for separation depend upon Christian theological claims about the salvation of souls.

Once one turns to the American understanding of separation as filtered through some of its most renowned leaders, the quality of the first separation takes on a distinctively civic cast, and the functions of separation take a more republican direction.[53] George Washington's views in some ways are the mirror image of Calvin's, inasmuch as Washington envisioned a separation of cooperation but (unlike Calvin) one principally for the benefit of the republican polity. According to Muñoz, Washington "thought that the state could and should nurture citizens' religious beliefs and encourage religious practices."[54] Washington wrote in his Farewell Address, "Of all the dispositions and habits which lead to political prosperity, religion and morality are indispensable supports."[55] Daniel Dreisbach remarks that this particular view of the relationship of Christian morality and civil government "was a virtually unchallenged assumption of the age."[56] This Christian republicanism, Mark Noll has written, "held that religion could and should contribute to the morality that was necessary for the virtuous citizens, without which such a republic could not survive."[57] Washington effected his own separation by diluting the Christianity that, he believed, was so necessary for civic health, by using "nonsectarian" but nevertheless distinctively Christian language in his public pronouncements.[58] Nevertheless, the "non-preferentialist" support

[52] Ibid., 11. For arguments that Locke's arguments for equality likewise presuppose Christian theological understandings, see Jeremy Waldron, *God, Locke, and Equality: Christian Foundations in Locke's Political Thought* (Cambridge: Cambridge University Press, 2002).

[53] I am cognizant that I have sampled only Virginians in what follows, omitting the church state views of northerners in the early republic. Part of the reason is that one is apt to find less support for separation among northern statesmen such as John Adams. John Witte Jr., "A Most Mild and Equitable Establishment: John Adams and the Massachusetts Experiment," *Journal of Church and State* 41 (1999): 213.

[54] Muñoz, *God and the Founders*, 50.

[55] George Washington, "Farewell Address," 1796, in *Writings of George Washington*, ed. Worthington Chauncey Ford (New York: G.P. Putnam's Sons, 1889), 13:307.

[56] Daniel L. Dreisbach, "Defining and Testing the Prohibition on Religious Establishments in the Early Republic," in *No Establishment of Religion: America's Original Contribution to Religious Liberty*, ed. T. Jeremy Gunn and John Witte Jr. (New York: Oxford University Press, 2012), 258.

[57] Noll, *America's God*, 203. [58] Muñoz, *God and the Founders*, 57.

for religion advocated by most of the founding generation did not entail support for any conceivable religion, Biblical or otherwise. It meant support for Christianity – whether of a distinctively Protestant denomination or of an indistinct, general variety.[59]

James Madison's separation was quite different. What has been described as Madison's principle of religious "noncognizance" need not appertain to Christianity specifically, and Madison's was certainly a rigorous and severe separation.[60] Still, though Madison speaks of a generic "duty we owe to our Creator," his arguments in favor of separation in the *Memorial and Remonstrance* are directed explicitly to Christianity and depend upon the views Madison ascribes to a Christian God. To violate the freedom of religion protected by the Virginia Constitution by moving in the direction of establishment was not only to offend the state but also, and more vitally, to offend God Himself. "If this freedom be abused," Madison wrote, "it is an offence against God, not against man," and it was therefore to God, and not to man, that violators of this natural right would have to render accounts.[61] Whether Madison's theology in the *Memorial and Remonstrance* incorporates and assumes "a Christian point of view,"[62] or, instead, merely "adopts a theology compatible with many forms of Christianity,"[63] Madison aspired to ground separation in a theological view, the centerpiece of which was Christianity as he understood it – a Christianity that served the American republic best by its privatization.

Even Thomas Jefferson, "hardly an orthodox Christian," spoke in the register of Christianity – though, to be sure, "a benign and freedom-favoring interpretation" of Christianity – when advocating for a separation that was no longer one of cooperation (as in Calvin and Washington) but of an impregnable "wall" of division.[64] As Thomas Buckley writes in his history of Virginia's Statute for Establishing

[59] Thomas G. West, *The Political Theory of the American Founding: Natural Rights, Public Policy, and the Moral Conditions of Freedom* (Cambridge: Cambridge University Press, 2017), 212.

[60] Ibid., 121. [61] Madison, "Memorial and Remonstrance."

[62] Lance Banning, *The Sacred Fire of Liberty: James Madison and the Founding of the Federal Republic* (Ithaca, NY: Cornell University Press, 1995), 436. See also Gary Rosen, *American Compact: James Madison and the Problem of Founding* (Lawrence: University of Kansas Press, 1999), 23 (noting the "obvious Protestant subtext" of the Memorial and Remonstrance).

[63] Muñoz, *God and the Founders*, 31. [64] Smith, *Rise and Decline*, 40.

Religious Freedom, the separation between church and state envisioned by Jefferson was complete, in large part because "Jefferson regarded the church as an institution of little value, nor did he see the clergy as fulfilling a significant role in society."[65] Yet his understanding of separation was nevertheless propelled by a particular and positive view of Christianity's role in the social sphere. It is difficult to read the phrase, "Almighty God hath created the mind free," in the preface to the Virginia statute without supposing that Jefferson had Christianity in mind, albeit a Christianity whose authority rested on individual reason and conscience alone.[66] Elsewhere, Jefferson would wonder whether "the liberties of a nation be thought secure when we have removed their only firm basis, a conviction in the minds of the people that these liberties are of the gift of God."[67]

Jefferson was, in Edwin Gaustad's assessment, "the most self-consciously theological of all America's presidents,"[68] and his theological aspirations were nothing short of separating "the gold from the dross" in the reformation of Christianity.[69] His was a fervently anticlerical Christianity in which separation was necessary so that the clergy might be "stripped of political power and influence"[70] and so that, in time, "truth will prevail over fanaticism, and the genuine doctrines of Jesus, so long perverted by his pseudo-priests, will again be restored to their original purity."[71] As Phillip Muñoz observes, however, Jefferson did not believe in Christ's divinity but in a "demystified Christianity," distilled and perfected in his "Jefferson Bible" (a heavily and eccentrically edited version of the original) containing "Jesus's pure and simple doctrines . . . supported by reason."[72]

Part of the enigma of Jefferson is that his theories so often deviated from his practice. As a public man, he was not averse to invoking a generic civil

[65] Thomas E. Buckley, *Establishing Religious Freedom: Jefferson's Statute in Virginia* (Charlottesville, VA: University of Virginia Press, 2013), 60.

[66] Ibid., 58. [67] Thomas Jefferson, *Notes on the State of Virginia*, 1787, Query 18.

[68] Edwin S. Gaustad, *Sworn on the Altar of God: A Religious Biography of Thomas Jefferson* (Grand Rapids, MI: Wm. B. Eerdmans Publishing, 1996), xiii.

[69] Thomas Jefferson to William Short, April 13, 1820, in *Memoir, Correspondence, and Miscellanies, from the Papers of Thomas Jefferson*, ed. Thomas Jefferson Randolph (Charlottesville, VA: F. Carr, 1829), 4:321.

[70] Muñoz, *God and the Founders*, 102.

[71] Thomas Jefferson to Jared Sparks, November 4, 1820, in *Jefferson's Extracts from the Gospels: The Papers of Thomas Jefferson*, ed. Dickinson W. Adams (Princeton, NJ: Princeton University Press, 1983), 401–402.

[72] Muñoz, *God and the Founders*, 103–104.

Christian-inflected Deism in his first presidential address to calm the political upheaval following the election of 1800: "And may that Infinite Power which rules the destinies of the universe, lead our counsels to what is best, and give them a favorable issue for your peace and prosperity."[73] Moreover, Jefferson's invocation of civil Christianity was not merely symbolic, as his use of federal funds to support the "civilizing" work of Christian missionaries in Indian territories shows.[74]

Nevertheless, other Virginians of the period, such as Patrick Henry, took the more traditional Washingtonian view that "the Christian religion provided an essential support for republican government" and were therefore inclined toward a less absolute separation.[75] However Jefferson's famous "wall of separation" phrase in the Letter to the Danbury Baptists was intended, it was not received enthusiastically in Connecticut.[76] As Philip Hamburger has noted, "[S]eparation was not what the Baptists wanted. Indeed, it was incompatible with their understanding of the pervasive value of Christianity."[77] Even in Virginia, Jeffersonian separation was quickly thought undesirable by Evangelical Christian ministers whose revivalist spirit would fuel the Second Great Awakening.[78] A few years before his death, Jefferson wrote with great certitude that "there is not a young man now living in the United States who will not die a Unitarian."[79] It seems he was quite wrong about that.

Jefferson stretches the first separation to its absolute limits, since his view of Christianity as socially and civicly precious was highly qualified, absolutely anticlerical, idiosyncratic, and perhaps just as much generically deistic as Christian. It is therefore certainly plausible to contend that he is in reality a second-separation figure. But it is possible to include him

[73] Quoted in Gaustad, *Sworn on the Altar of God*, 97.

[74] Ibid., 100–104; see also Nathan S. Chapman, "Money for Missionaries: Rethinking Establishment Clause History," University of Georgia School of Law Legal Studies Research Paper (2019): 32–36, at https://papers.ssrn.com/sol3/papers.cfm?abstract_id=3334148.

[75] Buckley, *Establishing Religious Freedom*, 61.

[76] Here, too, there are many interpretive difficulties, including whether the metaphor was originally intended substantively or jurisdictionally. Daniel Dreisbach, for example, has suggested that Jefferson meant the phrase to indicate the jurisdictional limits of national authority to interfere with state establishments. Daniel L. Dreisbach, *Thomas Jefferson and the Wall of Separation between Church and State* (New York: New York University Press, 2003), 4.

[77] Hamburger, *Separation of Church and State*, 163.

[78] Buckley, *Establishing Religious Freedom*, 165. [79] Quoted in Ibid., 166.

within the first separation and to identify the positions of Jefferson and Henry as internecine differences within the first separation. Still, Jefferson (and perhaps also Madison) may well represent a kind of bridge between the first and second separations. Indeed, the nineteenth-century religious controversies concerning the Bible and the education of American children are perhaps a clearer variant of the first separation than are Jefferson's own views. These battles over the proper variety and place of Christianity in the arena of education, though they certainly evinced hostility to what were at that time particular Christian minority groups (principally Catholics), presuppose the preciousness and worth of Christianity for the perpetuation of the American social and political commonwealth. They were in large part the work of partisans of "an aggressively Protestant 'Americanism.'"[80] This "theologically liberal" and anti-ecclesiastical Protestantism reflects one of the final clear expressions of the first separation.

The Second Separation: Christianity as Irrelevant or Obnoxious

The movement between the two separations did not happen instantly. In fact, it is still ongoing. In the United States, it began in earnest in the late nineteenth century and gathered speed and force in the second half of the twentieth. If the distinguishing mark of the first separation, in its vast historical complexity, is Christianity's preciousness, the second separation's much briefer history is distinguished by its hostility to Christianity as a cultural and political phenomenon in the United States, and reflects the following principles:[81]

- Christianity is an irrelevant or even an obnoxious influence on the American cultural and political community.
- Christianity's irrelevance or obnoxiousness demands laws that divest from and repudiate any cultural or political connections between Christianity and the United States.

[80] Hamburger, *Separation of Church and State*, 191.

[81] The claims about Christianity in this chapter focus on it as an American historical, cultural, and political artifact. Certainly, some of those who espouse second separationism may regard themselves as Christians, and they may believe that their views are consonant with Christianity. This chapter expresses no position on those matters.

- The specifics of the divestiture and repudiation of Christianity may vary over time, but the sense that Christianity is irrelevant or obnoxious as an influence on the American cultural and political community does not.

An important moment of transition in the United States[82] from the first to the second separation occurred when anti-Christian liberals modified and expanded arguments that had formerly been pressed by theologically liberal Protestants, who had espoused separation in the mid-nineteenth century in large part to oppose what they regarded as the dangerous political theology of Catholicism. In this period, as Philip Hamburger observes, "theologically liberal, anti-Christian secularists . . . prominently advocated separation . . .. The Liberals resented all clerical hierarchies, all churches, and even all religions, especially Christianity."[83] Indeed, just at about the moment when the anti-Catholic federal Blaine Amendment failed, organizations such as the so-called Liberal League recognized, and capitalized on, the thirst for a new separation, united by growing "fears and resentments of the influence of Christianity upon government."[84] This was to be a distinctively anti-Christian separation: "In contrast to earlier nativists and other Protestants, who adopted separation in opposition to Catholics, Liberals ecumenically applied it to all Christians."[85]

This new second separation, as initially envisaged by the Liberal League and its sympathizers, would keep all of government apart from Christianity, divest from it entirely, eliminate all exemptions from general laws for Christian believers, and even prohibit laws that imposed obligations coinciding with Christianity.[86] The League aspired to purify politics and civil society from Christian influence.[87] But once it became apparent that theological liberals – who would begin to call themselves "secular" during this period – could not muster sufficient political energy to change the Constitution or to enact their views into law, a new strategy emerged. They formed the second separation as an act of constitutional interpretation, at a time when both American religious pluralism and American sentiment were more favorably inclined toward the anti-Christian themes of the second separation.[88]

[82] Second separationism has a rather different, and older, genealogy in France, for example, as well as in most European countries, in which later Enlightenment influences were more powerful.

[83] Hamburger, *Separation of Church and State*, 287. [84] Ibid., 290. [85] Ibid., 302.

[86] Ibid., 305. [87] Ibid., 360. [88] Ibid., 294.

The history of the second separation resumed in earnest in 1947, the year commonly regarded as a watershed in the Supreme Court's jurisprudence when the Court began to strike down federal and state policies and laws as violations of the establishment clause. The impact of the famous *Everson* case, which concerned the constitutionality of using state tax dollars to reimburse parents whose children rode the bus to Catholic parochial schools, had little to do with its unobjectionable holding but instead with the separationist rhetoric in Justice Hugo Black's opinion for the Court. After identifying several practices that would violate the clause, Black invoked the famous Jeffersonian mural metaphor: "In the words of Jefferson, the clause against establishment of religion by law was intended to erect 'a wall of separation between church and State.'"[89]

In the years and decades that followed, the Court's primary establishment clause project was to discern the nature of the constitutional interest in separation. As is always the case, the Court both led and followed general cultural trends. *McCollum* v. *Board of Education*[90] – involving a program of "released-time" for religious instruction in public schools for parents of consenting students – followed on the heels of *Everson* and "made clear that the justices would go far beyond the Protestant separation of church and state"[91] and effectuate a specifically Christianity-focused expansion of it. Soon thereafter, separation was combined with a requirement that laws be "secular." Thus, the test devised in another funding case, *Lemon* v. *Kurtzman*, demanded that all government laws evince two indicia of secularism and one of church–state separation – a secular purpose, a primary secular effect of neither advancing nor inhibiting religion, and an absence of excessive government entanglement with religion.[92]

But as in the first separation, "religion" as such is of very limited value either in understanding the meaning of its putative opposite, "secularism," or in mapping the Court's second separationist trajectory. Religion's constitutional meaning, as we have seen, is utterly opaque, even intentionally so.[93] Steven Smith has remarked that "secular" has come in the Court's

89 *Everson* v. *Board of Education*, 330 US 1, 16 (1947).

90 *McCollum* v. *Board of Education*, 333 US 203 (1948).

91 Hamburger, *Separation of Church and State*, 476.

92 *Lemon* v. *Kurtzman*, 403 US 602, 612–613 (1971).

93 For discussion and criticism, see Marc O. DeGirolami, "Religious Accommodation, Religious Tradition, and Political Polarization," *Lewis & Clark Law Review* 20 (2017): 1127.

jurisprudence to mean "not religious," but since religion is itself a turbid category, it may be more accurate to say that "secular," as the term has come to be used in the case law, connotes something more like "not Christian."[94] The milder form of second separationism sees Christianity as irrelevant, while the stricter expression of it sees Christianity as obnoxious to American civic and cultural health.

Perhaps the key to understanding the second separation in constitutional interpretation is that since 1947 the laws and policies struck down by the Supreme Court on establishment clause grounds overwhelmingly have been explicit or implicit cultural or political supports for traditional forms of Christianity. Of the twenty-eight laws and policies struck down by the Court on establishment clause grounds since 1947, only three did not directly concern civic support (whether overt or implicit) for Christianity or otherwise reflect Christian influences on American politics and culture.[95]

To be sure, the Court has not framed its decisions striking down these policies and laws as overtly hostile to Christianity, as that would violate what it has said is protected by the free exercise clause, and at least some of these establishment clause cases were not exclusively about Christianity. Furthermore, often the type of Christianity supported by these laws and policies was diffuse or at least not theologically pristine: it reflected very much the same sort of generic or nondenominational Christianity invoked by George Washington, John Adams, Patrick Henry, and so many other early Americans as a necessary pillar of republican virtue and citizenship. This is especially the case in the Court's later decisions, after state and local governments had responded to the Court's initial separationist sallies by attempting to dilute their policies and laws of what they had been informed by the Court was an unconstitutionally concentrated Christian savor.

[94] Smith, *Rise and Decline*, 93.

[95] The exceptions are *NLRB* v. *Catholic Bishop of Chicago*, 440 US 490 (1979) (holding that the National Labor Relations Board did not have authority to compel schools operated by Catholic institutions to bargain with labor unions); *Board of Kiryas Joel* v. *Grumet*, 512 US 687 (striking down a New York statute creating school district for religious "enclave" of Satmar Hasidim); and *Hosanna-Tabor Evangelical Lutheran Church and School* v. *EEOC*, 565 US 2012 (holding that the ministerial exception to federal antidiscrimination laws prohibited the government from interfering in hiring and firing decisions of employees holding ministerial roles).

And yet in case after case, in the areas of state financial support of parochial schools;[96] state-sponsored religious displays;[97] the requirements for public office;[98] regulatory exemptions and licensing;[99] Bible-reading, prayer, and even moments of silence in public schools and school events;[100] public school curricular decisions;[101] and state accommodations of Sabbath observance,[102] the Court has intervened regularly to enforce a systematic political and cultural divestment from Christianity. It has spoken of "secularism" and "religion" without bothering to define these categories – indeed, while insisting that the category of religion has no criteria. Perhaps, as in the case of obscenity, the Court simply knows "religion" when it sees it, but it should come as no surprise that what it largely knows, and what it largely polices, is Christianity and Christian influence.[103] The Court, wielding the establishment clause, has become a kind of censor ensuring that policies and laws adopted across the country are not perceived to provide civic support for or approval of Christianity.[104] In some ways the overwhelming predominance of Christianity is not surprising in these cases, given Christianity's own historical predominance in American culture. Yet a comparison of free

[96] See, for example, *McCollum* v. *Board of Education*, 333 US 203 (1948); *Flast* v. *Cohen*, 392 US 83 (1968); *Board of Education* v. *Allen*, 392 US 236 (1968); *Lemon* v. *Kurtzman*, 403 US 602 (1971); *Committee for Public Education* v. *Nyquist*, 413 US 756 (1973); *Meek* v. *Pittenger*, 421 US 349 (1975); *Wolman* v. *Walter*, 433 US 229 (1977); *Aguilar* v. *Felton*, 473 US 402 (1985); and *City of Grand Rapids* v. *Ball*, 473 US 373 (1985). Some of these decisions were subsequently overruled in *Agostini* v. *Felton*, 521 US 203 (1987) and *Mitchell* v. *Helms*, 530 US 793 (2000).

[97] See, for example, *Stone* v. *Graham*, 449 US 39 (1980); *County of Allegheny* v. *ACLU*, 492 US 593 (1989) (striking down the display of a crèche, but not that of a menorah next to a Christmas tree); and *McCreary County* v. *ACLU*, 545 US 844 (2005).

[98] See, for example, *Torcaso* v. *Watkins*, 367 US 488 (1967).

[99] *Larkin* v. *Grendel's Den*, 495 US 116 (1982); *Texas Monthly* v. *Bullock*, 489 US 1 (1989) (striking down a Texas statute that exempted religious periodicals from sales tax).

[100] *Engel* v. *Vitale*, 370 US 421 (1962); *Abington* v. *Schempp*, 374 US 203 (1963); *Wallace* v. *Jaffree*, 472 US 38 (1985); *Lee* v. *Weisman*, 505 US 577 (1992); and *Santa Fe Indep. School Dist.* v. *Doe*, 530 US 290 (2000).

[101] *Epperson* v. *Arkansas*, 393 US 97 (1968); *Edwards* v. *Aguillard*, 482 US 578 (1987).

[102] *Estate of Thornton* v *Caldor*, 472 US 703 (1985).

[103] *Jacobellis* v. *Ohio*, 378 US 184 (1964).

[104] Even the establishment clause cases that the Court has agreed to hear, but in which it has ultimately found no constitutional violation, are overwhelmingly challenges to some state or local policy perceived to favor Christianity. See, e.g., *Town of Greece* v. *Galloway*, 572 U.S. 565 (2014); *The American Legion* v. *American Humanist Association*, 139 S. Ct. 2067 (2019).

exercise clause cases and cases brought before the Court under the Religious Freedom Restoration Act reveals a much greater variety of religious diversity in the Court's jurisprudence.[105]

The Court has not yet gone quite as far as the Liberal League might have liked. It has not invalidated laws which happen to coincide with Christian morality, though it has said that Christianity is an unconstitutional, "non-secular" influence on lawmaking – that lawmaking must remain "wholly apart" from Christian influence.[106] Legal scholars and advocacy groups have taken up these themes in arguing for more stringent versions of second separationism. They claim, for example, that the Constitution is "Godless"[107] – precisely in the sense that it abjures any Christian influence – or that those who continue to underscore the cultural and historical connections of Christianity and the United States are blinded by "Christian privilege"[108] or are "religionists"[109] (though the proper term of derogation should be "Christianists"). As Caroline Corbin has put it, "Their Sabbath defines the workweek, their sacred days define state and national holidays, their morality defines the family and determines when life begins, belief in their God characterizes patriotism, and invocation of their God solemnizes, dignifies, and authenticates."[110] The "Christian Right" has likewise become a favorite target of second separationists, though whether their odium is primarily directed at its politics or its Christianity is uncertain.[111] Similarly, powerful advocacy groups including "Americans United for Separation of

105 These cases have been brought by Native American, Jewish, Muslim, Santerian, Asatru, Wiccan, and Christian Spiritist religious individuals and groups, among others, as well as more traditional Christian groups.

106 See, for example, *Harris* v. *McRae*, 448 US 297, 319 (1980) ("That the Judaeo-Christian religions oppose stealing does not mean that a state or the Federal Government may not, consistent with the Establishment Clause, enact laws prohibiting larceny."); *McGowan* v. *Maryland*, 366 U.S. 420, 442 (1961).

107 Isaac Kramnick and R. Lawrence Moore, *The Godless Constitution: The Case Against Religious Correctness* (New York: W.W. Norton & Co., 1996).

108 See, for example, Caroline Mala Corbin, "Justice Scalia, the Establishment Clause, and Christian Privilege," *First Amendment Law Review* 15 (2017): 185.

109 See, for example, Steven K. Green, "Understanding the 'Christian Nation' Myth," *Cardozo Law Review De Novo* (2010): 245.

110 Caroline Mala Corbin, "Ceremonial Deism and the Reasonable Religious Outsider," *UCLA Law Review* 57 (2010): 1545, 1578–1579.

111 See, for example, Katherine Stewart, *The Good News Club: The Christian Right's Stealth Assault on America's Children* (New York: Hachette Book Group, 2012); Martha C. Nussbaum, *Liberty of Conscience: In Praise of America's Tradition of Religious Equality* (New York: Basic Books, 2008).

Church and State" – known at its founding in 1947 as "Protestants and Other Americans United for Separation of Church and State"[112] during separationism's late anti-Catholic phase – work tirelessly to erase any political or cultural symbolic recognition of Christianity.[113]

The law's object, on this account, is to sever these connections and to adopt non-or perhaps even anti-Christian alternatives – to create not so much a wall as a yawning and ever-broadening escarpment between Christianity and American civil society. This is the strongest form of separation in the second sense – separation as rejection or repudiation of Christianity as obnoxious to American civic health. It sees Christianity not merely as irrelevant but as positively harmful.

Variations of Second Separation: The Rise of Equality and Nondiscrimination

Since roughly the 1980s, however, the second separation that characterized the Court's establishment clause doctrine since the late 1940s has seemingly fallen into disfavor. Though *Lemon* has not been overruled, the Supreme Court has applied the *Lemon* test in fewer cases. Instead, it has elevated equality as the definitive value of the establishment clause in two principal ways: first, in the principle of religious nonendorsement; and second, in the principle of religious nondiscrimination. Nonendorsement is the approach used for issues concerning religion in the public square, such as state-sponsored religious displays and religious language and imagery, while nondiscrimination is preferred for matters concerning equal access and the distribution of public funds or resources.

The nonendorsement test was first articulated in a concurrence by Justice Sandra Day O'Connor in a case involving the display of "a Santa Clause house, reindeer pulling Santa's sleigh, candy-striped poles, a Christmas tree,

[112] The reliance of groups like Americans United on Jefferson's "wall" metaphor is some indirect evidence that Jefferson is an important bridge figure between the two separations.

[113] Americans United for the Separation of Church and State, accessed online December 26, 2017, www.au.org/. The "Our Issues" tab includes "Marriage and Reproductive Rights," "Religion in Public Schools," "Government Subsidies of Religion," "Official Prayer, Government Displays, and Ceremonial Religion," and "Fighting the Religious Right." On the history of Americans United, see John T. McGreevy, *Catholicism and American Freedom* (New York: W.W. Norton & Co., 2003), 213.

carolers, cut-out figures representing such figures as a clown, an elephant, a teddy-bear, hundreds of colored lights, a large banner reading 'SEASONS GREETINGS,' and a crèche" in the local shopping district of a Rhode Island municipality.[114] The endorsement test probes whether a "reasonable observer" of these kinds of pastiches would perceive that the state was thereby endorsing or disparaging religion in such a way as to convey a message of unequal membership or unequal status in the political community. It has been used in subsequent cases to hold that displays of a crèche and the Ten Commandments inside courthouses and public schools violate the establishment clause.[115] Though several members of the Court have recently voiced some skepticism about non-endorsement, it continues to influence the Court's approach to these issues.[116]

Nondiscrimination, or "neutrality," by contrast, is the test by which the Court generally evaluates questions of equal access and state funding of religion: a commitment to equality of treatment or neutrality among religions and between religion and nonreligion. As Kent Greenawalt has observed, the "dominant" understanding of neutrality requires that a law "not distinguish between religious individuals or groups and nonreligious ones,"[117] which is tantamount to a norm of nondiscrimination. Thus, for example, the Supreme Court has held that a municipality's school voucher program, in which participants could spend government funds to send their children to parochial schools as well as public schools, reflected a neutral fiscal allocation – one that treated religion and nonreligion equally.[118] Similarly, it has struck down policies that exclude religion from otherwise publicly available programs and grants, holding that an interest in appearing not to violate the establishment clause was insufficient in these contexts to justify the state's discriminatory treatment of religion.[119] These egalitarian commitments have hardened in the years following equality's

[114] *Lynch* v. *Donnelly*, 465 US 668 (1984).

[115] *County of Allegheny* v. *ACLU*, 492 US 593 (1989); *McCreary County* v. *ACLU*, 545 US 844 (2005).

[116] See *The American Legion* v. *American Humanist Association*, 139 S. Ct. 2067 (2019).

[117] Kent Greenawalt, *Religion and the Constitution: Free Exercise and Fairness* (Princeton: Princeton University Press, 2006), vol. 1.

[118] *Zelman* v. *Simmons-Harris*, 536 US 639 (2002).

[119] See, for example, *Good News Club* v. *Milford Central School*, 533 US 98 (2001); *Widmar* v. *Vincent*, 454 US 263 (1981); and *Trinity Lutheran Church of Columbia, Inc.* v. *Comer*, 137 S. Ct. 2012 (2017).

ascendancy. Notwithstanding the preponderance of establishment clause interpretive approaches, and with only a few exceptions (such as for the practice of legislative prayer or for very old religious monuments), courts today regularly find that the establishment clause requires adherence to ever more unyielding interpretations of nonendorsement and nondiscrimination. As Justice Elena Kagan put it in a dissenting opinion, at the heart of the establishment clause is a "breathtakingly generous" "norm of religious equality" that "does not translate[] ... into a bright separationist line."[120]

Many scholars believe that, as a result of these doctrinal changes, separation is waning as a church–state ideal.[121] Michael McConnell has written approvingly of this development: "[T]he old paradigm of 'strict separation' under the Establishment Clause has had to give way to ideas such as 'equal access,' 'neutral funding,' and 'accommodation.' If it had not, the expansion of government power, combined with the old insistence on 'strict separation,' would have been a relentless engine of secularization."[122] Other scholars bemoan it.[123] Running alongside this shift in the doctrine, influential accounts of equality as the foundational value of the religion clauses have emerged, which largely sideline or even reject separation.[124] Some claim that equality and separation are fundamentally incompatible,[125] while others, including Douglas Laycock, argue

120 *Town of Greece* v. *Galloway*, 134 S. Ct. 1811, 1841 (2014) (Kagan, J., dissenting).

121 One of the earliest pieces taking this view is Ira C. Lupu, "The Lingering Death of Separationism," *George Washington Law Review* 62 (1993): 230 ("Many of the cultural and political conditions that sustained the concept of separationism have eroded considerably in the past twenty years ..."). See also Frederick Mark Gedicks, "A Two-Track Theory of the Establishment Clause," *Boston College Law Review* 43 (2002): 1071, 1072–1073.

122 Michael W. McConnell, "Why Is Religious Liberty the 'First Freedom?'" *Cardozo Law Review* 21 (2000): 1243, 1261–1262.

123 See, for example, Alan Brownstein, "Protecting Religious Liberty: The False Messiahs of Free Speech Doctrine and Formal Neutrality," *Journal of Law & Politics* 18 (2002): 119, 120, 186.

124 See Christopher Eisgruber and Lawrence Sager, *Religious Freedom and the Constitution* (Cambridge, MA: Harvard University Press, 2010); Nussbaum, *Liberty of Conscience*; Nelson Tebbe, *Religious Freedom in an Egalitarian Age* (Cambridge, MA: Harvard University Press, 2017). For some discussion of this literature, see Marc O. DeGirolami, *The Tragedy of Religious Freedom* (Cambridge, MA: Harvard University Press, 2013), chap. 1.

125 See, for example, Noah Feldman, "From Liberty to Equality: The Transformation of the Establishment Clause," *California Law Review* 90 (2002): 673.

that there is an "underlying unity" of separation and its competitors, but only if separation is entirely reconceived as a principle of religious voluntarism.[126]

There is, in fact, an underlying unity of separation and equality. Equality and nondiscrimination are variations of the second separation. Though scholars including Michael McConnell are correct that there has been a shift in the Supreme Court's doctrinal approach (particularly in areas respecting government financial aid), that shift masks deeper and more fundamental similarities of justification and application in egalitarian and second-separationist approaches.

The ostensible appeal of equality as a church–state ideal is that it regards all religions and nonreligion as of identical value or nonvalue. Religion and nonreligion are exactly alike from the state's perspective: the state must offer no view as to the social or political worth of the religious or nonreligious phenomena under its superintendence. The state's perspective is value-less, or neutral.

Stated in these terms, however, equality is a hopelessly unpersuasive description of the relationship between Christianity and American government. The two separations that represent the long inheritance of the American church–state experience differ in their perspectives on Christian civic and cultural influence, but they align in adopting a definite perspective – positive or negative – on the cultural and political value of Christianity. Equality, by contrast, purports to be perspective-less: Christianity is said to be neither precious nor obnoxious as an influence on American culture and government.

But these claims are not sustainable. To see why, it is helpful to compare other constitutional contexts in which norms of equality and nondiscrimination are the analytical touchstones – in particular, the areas of race and sex discrimination. Long before equality and nondiscrimination gained traction in the religion clause context, the Supreme Court prohibited race discrimination on the basis of the Thirteenth and Fourteenth Amendments to the Constitution. As early as 1880, the Court held that "all persons, whether colored or white, shall stand equal before the laws of the States, and . . . that

[126] The most comprehensive of these accounts is in Douglas Laycock, "The Underlying Unity of Separation and Neutrality," *Emory Law Journal* 46 (1997): 43. See also Douglas Laycock, "Formal, Substantive, and Disaggregated Neutrality toward Religion," *DePaul Law Review* 39 (1990): 993.

no discrimination shall be made against them by law because of their color."[127] Beginning again in the twentieth century, the Court's Equal Protection Clause jurisprudence has mandated the equality of the races: it has prohibited segregation in schooling,[128] anti-miscegenation laws,[129] anti-cohabitation laws,[130] race-based redistricting,[131] and many other racially discriminatory laws and policies.[132] Laws that discriminate on the basis of race receive the Court's most exacting scrutiny and are almost always invalidated.

There are many justifications for the Court's approach to race-based discrimination – too many to explore here. But one nearly universal underlying assumption in the Court's jurisprudence is that the use of race in the making of laws and the ordering of society is fundamentally illegitimate, and that laws and policies that discriminate on racial bases are obnoxious to the American polity. In the words of Justice O'Connor, the object of the law in this area is to "eliminate[e] entirely from governmental decisionmaking such irrelevant factors as a human being's race."[133] But race is more than merely irrelevant: to consider it is to be swayed by an "invidious" influence on social and political life – iniquitous and grossly unjust.[134] Those that rely on race to make law or structure policy act on the basis of irrational "animus" – blind and unreasoned hatred. The "duty to confront racial animus" and root it out is one of the chief functions of both Congress and the courts.[135] Equality and nondiscrimination, the lodestars of the Court's equal protection jurisprudence, are therefore not neutral at all as to the use of race. Courts that are guided by equality and nondiscrimination norms are and must be clear that race is an altogether improper influence on law and American society.[136]

[127] *Strauder* v. *West Virginia*, 100 US 303 (1880).
[128] *Brown* v. *Board of Education*, 374 US 483 (1954).
[129] *Loving* v. *Virginia*, 388 US 1 (1967). [130] *McLaughlin* v. *Florida*, 379 US 174 (1964).
[131] *Gomillion* v. *Lightfoot*, 364 US 339 (1960).
[132] See, for example, *Palmore* v. *Sidoti*, 466 US 429 (1984); *Village of Arlington Heights* v. *Metropolitan Housing Development Corporation*, 429 US 252 (1979).
[133] See *City of Richmond* v. *J.A. Croson*, 488 U.S. 469, 495 (1989) (plurality opinion). See also *Hirabayashi* v. *United States*, 320 US 81, 100 (1943) (racial classifications are "in most circumstances irrelevant and therefore prohibited").
[134] Loving, 388 US at 9. [135] *Pena-Rodriguez* v. *Colorado*, 137 S. Ct. 855 (2017).
[136] There are complications, to be sure, in the area of affirmative action. There is long-standing disagreement about whether the use of race for emancipatory purposes in education (for example) is also illegitimate and obnoxious. But those need not detain us here, as they are narrow exceptions to the general rule.

The Court's doctrine regarding discrimination on the basis of sex proceeds on similar assumptions. Many political and cultural distinctions on the basis of sex, the Court has said, simply "perpetuate the legal, social, and economic inferiority of women."[137] While such distinctions do not receive quite the level of scrutiny reserved for race-based discrimination, the state must nevertheless offer "an exceedingly persuasive justification" in order for discrimination on the basis of sex to survive.[138] As Justice Ruth Bader Ginsburg has put it, the Court's task in this area is to eradicate and reverse outdated and "overbroad generalizations about the way men and women are."[139] The imperative of equality spurs the Court to ever more expansive applications of it, "for in interpreting the [e]qual [p]rotection [guarantee], [we have] recognized that new insights and societal understandings can reveal unjustified inequality ... that once passed unnoticed and unchallenged."[140] The Court has been at times less absolute about the cogency of sex-based differences than those based on race.[141] But in the main, just as in the race context, its object has been to dissolve these differences as irrelevant, passé, and obnoxious influences on law and American social structure. The egalitarian perspective on sexual distinctiveness as an influence on law and policy is therefore not neutral, but decidedly negative.

Transposed to the context of religion – and, as has been argued, the transposition in reality concerns not the black-box category of religion, but Christianity – the logic of equality and nondiscrimination holds constant. As in the cases of race and sex, Christianity, too, is at least an irrelevant influence on American law, politics, and society. Stated more strongly, although Christianity may once have been thought by some to be a positive influence, these are now outmoded notions, and the Court's responsibility today is to continue the work of civic divestment from Christian influence. Even more strongly: equality requires the flattening of any distinctions, the disowning of the past, and the forging of a future that continues the process of movement away from the first separation – in which Christianity was deemed socially and politically precious – toward

[137] *United States* v. *Virginia*, 518 US 515 (1996). [138] Ibid.

[139] *Sessions* v. *Morales-Santana* (2017).

[140] Ibid. (quoting *Obergefell* v. *Hodges*, 135 S. Ct. 2584 (2015)).

[141] See, for example, *United States* v. *Virginia*, 518 US at 533 ("Inherent differences between men and women, we have come to appreciate, remain cause for celebration.").

the second – in which it is deemed worthless and harmful to American culture and politics.[142]

Consider two contemporary examples that illustrate the effects of the egalitarian approach in the areas of "equal access" and religious exemptions. In both, courts and others have interpreted the overarching egalitarian mandate to reflect a variation, whether stronger or weaker, of the second separation.

With respect to "equal access," relying on the Supreme Court's nonendorsement test, one court has held that a state's interest in avoiding even the perception of violating the establishment clause justified its exclusion of a Christian group that desired after-hours access to public school classrooms, on the same terms as other groups, in order to engage in Christian worship.[143] Equality was what the Christian group desired, but "a constitutional interest in equality," the court ruled, justified the group's unequal treatment in order to avoid even the perception of favoritism that might, or might not, violate the establishment clause – a favoritism about which "reasonable observers" are likely to be especially sensitive in the case of Christianity because of its historical and cultural associations with the United States. From the equality of access, one moves seamlessly to hostility to Christianity.[144]

Not all cases involving similar issues take this stricter second separationist position. In one of its most recent religion clause rulings, the Supreme Court struck down Missouri's exclusion of a school operated by a Christian church from a program for playground resurfacing. The Court held that the state had engaged in "unequal treatment" in discriminating against "religious status."[145] True, the church won the case, but its victory depended on the fact that Christian belief and exercise was completely irrelevant to its claim: the church was not seeking funding "for a religious endeavor," but for an unequivocally secular one.[146] Had it instead pitched

[142] Steven D. Smith, "Justice Douglas, Justice O'Connor, and George Orwell: Does the Constitution Compel Us to Disown Our Past?," accessed online December 26, 2017, https://papers.ssrn.com/sol3/papers.cfm?abstract_id=728663.

[143] *Bronx Household of Faith* v. *Board of Education of City of New York*, 750 F.3d 184 (2d Cir. 2014). For Supreme Court authority on the issue of "interests in equality" and the establishment clause, see *Locke* v. *Davey*, 540 US 712 (2004).

[144] For further discussion, see Marc O. DeGirolami, "The Bloating of the Constitution: Equality and the U.S. Establishment Clause," in *The Social Equality of Religion or Belief*, ed. Alan Carling (London: Palgrave Macmillan, 2016).

[145] *Trinity Lutheran Church* v. *Comer*, 137 S. Ct. 2012 (2017).

[146] Ibid. at nn.3–4.

its claim in terms of Christian practice or belief, it would likely have lost, because the Court had previously held that a government exclusion of particular Christian exercises on the basis of egalitarian "establishment interests" was unproblematic.[147] This is the softer variant of second separation: an equality that ratifies Christianity's irrelevance to American law and policy.

On the issue of religious exemptions, in several recent high-profile cases involving the conflict between new egalitarian sexual norms and Christian morality, the permissive accommodation of religion has been criticized as an unlawful, and possibly unconstitutional, imposition on the interests of third parties. Exemptions from generally applicable laws have long been tolerated as essentially innocuous – a gesture of noblesse oblige toward exotic and politically powerless religious individuals or entities.[148]

But that is no longer the case, precisely because Christian sexual norms are now running headlong into ever-burgeoning legal mandates of sundry varieties of sexual equality.[149] It was just at the moment when conservative Christians began to invoke religious exemptions from these laws that they began to arouse public and academic controversy.[150] It is telling, for example, that in criticizing exemptions for Christian believers who object to contemporary sexual norms, Martin Castro, then chair of the United States Commission on Civil Rights, wrote that "[t]he government of the United States is not, in any sense, founded on the Christian religion."[151] Exempting Christians from laws that require them to participate in practices to which they object is, on this view, a type of religious establishment and an attempt to "deny others equality."[152] True equality requires choking these views off by not exempting from legal compliance the Christians who hold them. Rather, the government should compel them to obey.

147 See *Locke* v. *Davey*.

148 Marc O. DeGirolami, "Free Exercise by Moonlight," *San Diego Law Review* 53 (2016): 105.

149 See, for example, the many appellate courts that had ruled against for-profits and nonprofits in the contraceptive mandate litigation. See also the litigation that preceded and is now following *Masterpiece Cakeshop, Ltd.* v. *Colorado Civil Rights Commission*, 138 S. Ct. 1719 (2018); *Elane Photography, LLC* v. *Willock*, 309 P.3d 53 (2013).

150 Maimon Schwarzschild, "Do Religious Exemptions Save?," *San Diego Law Review* 53 (2016): 185.

151 "Peaceful Coexistence: Reconciling Nondiscrimination Principles with Civil Liberties" (statement of Martin Castro), accessed online December 26, 2017, www.usccr.gov/pubs/Peaceful-Coexistence-09-07-16.PDF. The line is quoted from Article XI of the Treaty of Tripoli of 1796.

152 Ibid.

Sometimes, Christian claimants have been successful in seeking religious exemptions from these laws. More often, however, they have not been, and if they continue to lose these cases, it will have as much to do with the ratification and extension of the egalitarian premises of the emerging new sexual norms as with the entrenchment and reaffirmation of a harsher form of second separation.

Conclusion

Separation of church and state is not a self-evident good. It is not an intrinsically valuable political ideal, and it does not depend upon anything in religion's essential nature – a nature that is to this day opaque and violently contested by courts and scholars alike. *Quid obscurum, quid divinum* can neither explain nor justify separation.

Rather, to understand the American inheritance of religious liberty is to trace the political and cultural history of America's relationship to Christianity in the two separations. Separation is, first, an idea appertaining to Christian political theology – a view about Christianity's political and cultural preciousness and the consequent necessity for divisions of authority in this world. And it is, second, a response by the secular liberal state to the political and cultural associations between itself and Christianity – a concerted effort to divest from and repudiate a Christian influence that is deemed either irrelevant or obnoxious to its own cultural and civic well-being. More recent ideals of equality and nondiscrimination in religion clause jurisprudence and elsewhere have not supplanted separation, but are themselves later-stage expressions and developments of the second separation. To insist on equality, in a society that has been permeated and structured by Christianity, is to suppress it.

15 The Challenge Ahead
Reconnecting Religion, Reason, and Truth

Gerard V. Bradley

Sometime in the last few years, for the first time in American history it became respectable to publicly oppose religious liberty and its overarching value in our political order. It is a remarkable, and portentous, turn. Religious liberty has been an axiom of our political culture. Americans have long regarded religious liberty not only as the "First Freedom" of our Constitution, but also as architectonic, somehow the linchpin or final guarantor of other civil liberties. They have cherished it because their religious convictions and their resolve to live by them have been the most important things in their lives. Religious liberty was their polity's promise of repose. It was also a promise that they could be *both* conscientious Americans *and* good Christians, or Jews, or adherents of some other worldview.

The concrete benefits of this defining commitment to religious liberty have thus been political and cultural, as well as more strictly spiritual and personal. One of many benefits includes churches' huge public works projects in the fields of education, healthcare, and charity. These mainstays of civil society have been a bulwark against overreaching government. They have also been a pathway to participation in civic life for many believers who might otherwise have hovered near sectarianism.

Americans have often opposed *particular* claims of religious liberty – by Latter-Day Saints concerning polygamy, for instance, or by Catholics who challenged Protestant observances in public school rooms, or by those conscientiously opposed to one or another of America's wars. No doubt, too, there have been some religious-liberty skeptics along the way. In past debates about the precise scope of religious liberty, though, no one publicly questioned the great value of religious liberty itself.

What's happening now is different. Opposition then was to a particular religious group's specific activity (e.g., Mormons' plural marriages). Today, the opposition is against a broader front of issues concerning religion, while respect for religious liberty as such is in decline. The brunt of this opposition is not, moreover, being borne now by isolated religious minorities. Christians who adhere to what was until recently America's common morality are the most conspicuous targets.

The most obvious cause of this remarkable change in Americans' understanding of their political culture is today's intense concern for "sexual minorities." Recently emboldened opponents say that "religious liberty" (often placed within gratuitous scare quotes) is just a "license to discriminate" against homosexuals and lesbians who want to marry. The next most obvious cause is the Obama Administration's strikingly unsympathetic concern for religious liberty. In 2012, the federal government maintained that a church had *no* religious liberty to hire and fire its own ministers. It argued in *Hosanna-Tabor* v. *EEOC* that churches had just the same rights of free speech and association that a social club or a labor union has – and there was an end to it.[1]

The Trump Administration is certainly friendlier to religious liberty than was Obama's. It surely matters who fills the next vacancy (and the one after that) on the Supreme Court. But focusing on the to-and-fro of constitutional litigation and judicial appointments impairs one's view of the deep and pervasive forces in both culture and law that have long been eroding religious liberty. These forces erupted in the crucible of argument about same-sex "marriage." They have been emboldened, not satiated, by *Obergefell* v. *Hodges.*[2]

Today's open opposition to religious liberty is actually the front of a broad movement of thought and action. The Obama Administration's stance in *Hosanna-Tabor* articulated a burgeoning opinion among academics, judges, and popular writers that religion should have no "special" – that is, particularly favorable – constitutional or legal status. This is the view that churches should be treated like other ideological associations, and that religious liberty for individuals is a lesser aspect of an encompassing liberty of individual self-definition within the private sphere of

[1] *EEOC* v. *Hosanna-Tabor*, 565 U.S. 171 (2012). The United States' position was so startling that the Court refuted it by observing that there happens to be a free exercise clause. The Court said that the government's position is "hard to square with the text of the First Amendment. ... We cannot accept the remarkable view that the Religion Clauses have nothing to say about a religious organization's freedom to select its own ministers." Ibid. at 189.

[2] *Obergefell* v. *Hodges*, 576 US ___ (2015).

social life. This ominous complex of views is now a structural feature of our social world.

The view of this new social world is that we live in a secularized public realm where religion is relegated to the *private* sphere of church, family, and individual psyche and that religion consists – *if* it consists of anything real – of ineffable spiritual experiences that (to paraphrase the Supreme Court's line of thought since World War II) may seem vital to some.[3] But to others, religious doctrines, creeds, and sacred texts are more or less arbitrary ways of talking about what is not real. The presupposition is that religion is and ought to be treated as an aspect of individual subjectivity – just one source among many of personal identity. The Supreme Court began to install this presupposition in our fundamental law more than seventy years ago.[4] If this complex of views is sound, then religious liberty is being treated – and valued and adjudicated – today pretty much as it ought to be. And *will* be, unless this whole structure of thought is uprooted.

It is true that religions *include* subjective experiences, as well as stories and prescriptions that are historical and contingent and, in that way, arbitrary. But religions are much more than this. They are more or less reasonable accounts of reality in all of its breadth, including its furthest reaches, visible and invisible. The indispensable criterion of a religion's value is whether it is *true*. The central value of religious liberty is the protection it offers to those who seek the truth about the cosmos and who resolve to live their lives in accord with what they believe to be the truth about all that there is. Sever it from this search, guided by reason, and religious liberty will wither and eventually disappear.

Tactical victories for religious liberty may be won by skillful argument that takes for granted, and exploits, the fact that religions include subjective experiences. Rhetoric based upon the tangible benefits of religious liberty for those who patronize soup kitchens and hospitals can be effective, too. Decline might be slowed, and the total disappearance of religious liberty could possibly be postponed for a considerable time. But nothing short of radical shifts in foundations can achieve strategic benefits, and preserve religious liberty for the long run.

[3] See the third section of this chapter.

[4] *West Virginia State Board of Education* v. *Barnette*, 319 US 624 (1943).

Friends of religious liberty must yank its subject, religion, out of the nest of subjectivity and irrationality to which it has been consigned.[5] They must reconnect religion and truth. Not with "truth," as if religious convictions might have a noncognitive validity or are simply revisable human articulations of seemingly compelling personal experiences. Religions rather should be judged by the metrics we predicate of other worldviews. The reconnection must be achieved by and through reason.

As a cultural undertaking, that reconnection is daunting and likely to take a long time. The more manageable agenda described in this chapter is to sketch out legal, mostly constitutional, strategies that would stanch the bleeding of religious liberty caused by severing the connection between religion and truth. That manageable project has two main components. One is to reestablish religion as a distinct public good, and not just as one of many privatized forms of personal satisfaction. The second is to reestablish religion as a distinct and, in important ways, more compelling private good, one that public authority could justifiably favor and encourage over lesser aspects of personal identity. The effort will pay dividends immediately. Because law so powerfully shapes our culture, pursuing this legal agenda will significantly contribute to the larger cultural reclamation.

We shall consider in the first section of this chapter the most distant precondition of the present crisis, the moment during Reconstruction when *atheism* emerged into public respectability. Relying extensively here upon the observations of a leading historian of "unbelief," we shall briefly explore how reputable atheism, even when very few people actually denied God's existence, transformed the entire culture.[6] This historical episode is instructive; we still live in its shadows. It is also a cautionary tale, for the transformative effects of respectable atheism owed principally, not to enemies of religion, but to its friends' half-witting but well-intentioned efforts to negotiate and adapt to unbelief. The second section then excavates the more proximate, *superstructural* condition of today's crisis of religious liberty: the Supreme Court's establishment of *secularism* in

[5] The present parlous state of religious freedom could not have come to pass in a country (ours) so largely populated by adherents to a religion that has always prized conspicuous public witness and discipleship, without considerable acquiescence – and some misguided help – from believers.

[6] James Turner, *Without God, Without Creed: The Origins of Unbelief in America* (Baltimore, MD: Johns Hopkins University Press, 1985).

a series of decisions from 1943 to 1948. The Court's handiwork included the wholesale privatization of religion. Section 3 takes up the key *infra-structural* element of the Court's new construct: the reduction of religion in law to the subrational and emotional levels of individual "experience." Section 4 brings the current crisis into sharper focus by examining a few snapshots of religious liberty today. The conclusion considers elements of a radical legal strategy to reclaim, and to preserve, religious liberty by reconnecting religion to truth via reason.

Atheism and Its Copernican Consequences

After the Civil War, Union veteran Robert Ingersoll came out of the theological closet. He began touring the lecture circuit, billing himself as "Colonel Ingersoll, the Atheist." Before then, "virtually everyone within the orbit of European culture [including America] agreed that a superhuman power was somehow responsible for the universe and that this fact determined the purpose of life."[7] Although that assertion by James Turner, in his meticulous chronicle of the rise of American unbelief, lacks a certain theological precision, he nonetheless comes close enough to the mark to guide us through Ingersoll's flouting of the sacred canopy that enveloped his society.[8]

This unanimity of belief had supplied a norm for the political culture, even if widespread natural religion does not entail a unity of mind of specific religious doctrines or a rule of public discourse and deliberation. With Ingersoll and other nonbelievers, however, our "web of shared assumptions" was battered, though not shattered. This respectable godlessness, despite its relatively few adherents, transformed a whole culture. The "option of godlessness," Turner noted, "dis-integrated our common intellectual life, both in formal disciplines like philosophy, science, and literature and in those informal habits of mind by which we, as a culture, experience and order our world."[9] "Belief became then for the first time, and remains still, *subcultural*," Turner wrote. Although "most Americans

[7] Ibid., xiv–xv.

[8] "Superhuman" would be better rendered as "transcendent," and "determined the purpose of life" would be more carefully expressed as "determined the ultimate source of meaning and value for humankind."

[9] Ibid., 263–264.

believe in God ... belief no longer functions as a unifying and defining element of that entire culture; it no longer provides a common heritage that underlies our diverse world views. Writing more than thirty years ago, Turner concluded that "our culture ... *now* lacks a center."[10]

When Turner began to chart the origins and causes of unbelief, he came across a "surprising picture," "a photographic negative" of what he expected to discover. He concluded that unbelief was *not* something that happened to religion. On the contrary, "religion caused unbelief." The respectability of unbelief unwittingly emerged as religious believers attempted "to adapt their religious beliefs to socioeconomic changes, to new moral challenges, to novel problems of knowledge, to the tightening standards of science ... If anyone is to be arraigned for deicide, it is not Charles Darwin but his adversary Bishop Samuel Wilberforce, not the godless Robert Ingersoll but the godly Beecher family."[11] Turner concluded that the various compromises and negotiations by *believers* "to deal with modernity by embracing it – to defuse modern threats to the traditional bases of belief by bringing God into line with modernity" – hastened and solidified the cultural effects of unbelief.[12]

Secularism and the Privatization of Religion

It is a curious (if not ironic) fact of our constitutional history that the plaintiffs for whom the Supreme Court began secularizing our public square were not atheists. They were not even secularists: that is, people who might believe in God but who lived practically as if there were none.[13] They were two Jehovah's Witnesses whose father had instructed them not to salute the flag, as they were required to do at their public grade school. They all regarded the flag as a "graven image." They could show no more personal fealty to it than they could show to any other aspect of human government. They believed that God's sovereignty over the universe was undivided and exclusive. Human government was therefore akin to

[10] Ibid., 263. [11] Ibid., xiii. [12] Ibid.

[13] One character in Georges Bernanos' *The Diary of a Country Priest* observes that "faith is not a thing one 'loses,' we merely cease to shape our lives by it." George Bernanos, *The Diary of a Country Priest* (Cambridge, MA: Da Capo Press, 2002).

blasphemy. These Witnesses were nearly theonomists; temporal affairs were to be governed directly by God's rules.

The Barnettes' refusal matured into the "second flag-salute case," decided by the Supreme Court in 1943.[14] In *Minersville School District* v. *Gobitis* three years earlier, the high court had sustained municipal authority to compel flag salutes. (This case also involved children who were Jehovah's Witnesses.)[15] In the course of reversing itself, the Court launched its project to secularize America's understanding of its Constitution, of its government, and of the permissible bases for lawmaking in our polity.

The epochal declaration in *Barnette* was this: "If there is any fixed star in our constitutional constellation, it is that no official, high or petty, can prescribe what shall be orthodox in politics, nationalism, religion or other matters of opinion."[16] *Barnette* cited *no* case – and no authority of any kind – to support this breathtaking claim. Harvard philosopher Michael Sandel proclaimed that *Barnette* marked the arrival of the "procedural republic."[17]

How was *Barnette* so transformative? After all, is it not self-evident that "officials" should not "prescribe" an "orthodoxy"? Yes, if the prescription is limited to what are truly matters of (mere) opinion and if it means that children cannot be expelled from school for declining to affirm publicly what they honestly do not believe. But the *Barnette* Court had much more in mind than that. The justices were laying down the blueprint of what was regularly called in those times "our democratic way of life."

The lineaments of the new constitution included the Court's assertion (plainly implicit in the "no-orthodoxy" passage) *that* "politics, nationalism, [and] religion" *are* matters of "opinion." These subject matters could no longer include propositions that, from the perspective of law and its makers, were simply true (or false). These assertions further entailed that any unity of "opinion" on such matters would be a consensus or a "prescri[ption]" – in either case, an "orthodoxy," a matter not of truth but of convention or stipulation. It is perhaps

[14] Barnette, 319 US 624 (1943).

[15] *Minersville School District* v. *Gobitis*, 310 US 586 (1940).

[16] Barnette, 319 US at 642.

[17] Michael J. Sandel, *Democracy's Discontent: America in Search of a Public Philosophy* (Cambridge, MA: The Belknap Press of Harvard University Press, 1996), 54.

most telling to note what the Court did *not* include among the now starkly relativized subjects: science and law.

There would be some risk of overinterpreting *Barnette* thus far were it not so clear that, read as a whole and in the context of plentiful additional signals about the Court's new constitutional vision, it meant to refound America's understanding of its constitution. For one thing, with computer-assisted research into Supreme Court opinions since the founding, one can see at a glance that in the early- to mid-1940s, the Court reimagined our form of government, its bases in truth and opinion, and its relationship to religion. Before 1943, there were very few uses of terms such as "orthodox," "dogma," "secularism," "irreligion," "no religion," "atheism," "inculcate," and "indoctrinate" – and, in some instances, none at all. "Atheist," for example, appears for the first time in the *McCollum* case in 1948 (and scores of times since).[18] The word "orthodoxy" appears for the first time in a Supreme Court opinion in 1943: *Barnette*.

Gobitis marked the debut of "indoctrinate" (or "indoctrination"), a word that became synonymous in constitutional law with the concept of teaching or transmitting religion. This particular verbal innovation substituted for alternatives like religious "instruction" or "education." It conveyed the Court's conviction that anyone who comes to embrace putative religious truths does so by dint of authority or manipulation, which in either event bypasses the initiate's freedom of thought and critical reason.[19]

The new democratic epistemology was on full display just two years after *Barnette*. In *Thomas* v. *Collins*, Justice Robert Jackson wrote (in his concurrence) that it "cannot be the duty, because it is not the right, of the state to protect the public against false doctrine."[20] "Doctrine" was not limited to theological speculation. In Jackson's usage, it referred to *all* manner of normative discourse – to free speech, free press, and freedom of religion. In these matters, Jackson warned, "every person must be his own watchman for truth." He treated *Barnette* as if it had erected a wall of separation between public authority and truth:

[18] *McCollum* v. *Board of Education*, 333 US 215, 234 (1948).

[19] Here as elsewhere from the 1940s through the 1970s, whenever the Court opined about church–state matters, the justices' fear of Catholic political power and cultural influence was never far from their thoughts. And Catholicism was their prototype of authoritarian religion which subsisted on fear and "indoctrination."

[20] *Thomas* v. *Collins*, 323 US 516 (1945).

> The very purpose of the First Amendment is to foreclose public authority from assuming a guardianship of the public mind through regulating the press, speech, and religion . . . [T]he forefathers did not trust any government to separate the true from the false for us.[21]

The whole *Thomas* court agreed that the theretofore discrete First Amendment freedoms now ran together in a unified theory of individual freedom and government relativism:

> It was not by accident or coincidence that the rights to freedom in speech and press were coupled in a single guaranty with the rights of the people peaceably to assemble and to petition for redress of grievances. All these, though not identical, are inseparable. . . .
>
> This conjunction of liberties is not peculiar to religious activity and institutions alone. The First Amendment gives freedom of mind the same security as freedom of conscience. Great secular causes, with small ones, are guarded. The grievances for redress of which the right of petition was insured, and, with it, the right of assembly, are not solely religious or political ones. And the rights of free speech and a free press are not confined to any field of human interest.[22]

If *Barnette* was the architect's vision of religion in our democracy, and *Collins* the blueprint, then *Everson* v. *Board of Education*, decided in 1947, was the master builder.[23] *Everson* was the Court's first confrontation ever with the establishment clause. We now live according to its mandate. *Everson* saddled every unit of public authority in the land, from the US Congress down to the Ewing Township Board of Education in New Jersey, with precisely the same constraints upon government's relationship with religion. In more specifically legal terms, the Court in *Everson* "incorporated" the establishment clause. The climactic passage in *Everson* pronounced:

> The "establishment of religion" clause of the First Amendment means at least this: neither a state nor the Federal Government can set up a church. Neither can pass laws which aid one religion, aid all religions, or prefer one religion over another. . . . No tax in any amount, large or small, can be levied to support any religious activities or institutions, whatever they may be called, or whatever form they may adopt to teach or practice religion. In the words of Jefferson, the clause against establishment of religion by law was intended to erect "a wall of separation between church and State."[24]

[21] Ibid. at 545. [22] Ibid. at 530–531. [23] *Everson* v. *Board of Education*, 330 US 1 (1947).
[24] Ibid. at 15–16.

Here the Court decreed that government had no authority to promote and encourage religion, even where it would do so without any favoritism to a particular religion. By stipulating that governments in America remain neutral between religion and what the Court over the years called "irreligion" or "non-religion," the justices effectively decreed a secular public sphere. The corollary of that *ukase* was the *privatization* of religion.

The most immediate casualty of this novel secularism, which the Court installed as the new foundation of religious liberty, was the old foundation. The American roots (at least) of religious liberty as a natural and civil right were *religious*. They were canonically articulated by James Madison, our fourth president and a moving force behind the enactment of our Bill of Rights, in his *Memorial and Remonstrance*, written in 1786 during the course of the Virginian debate over state support of religion teachers.[25] Madison's ode to religious freedom listed, as the first of fifteen grounds for opposing support, that "religion or the duty which we owe to our Creator and the Manner of discharging it, can be directed only by reason and conviction, not by force or violence."[26] This Madison affirmed, not as a hypothesis or as the lesson of experience or as the special deliverance of the distinctively political reflection or reason, but as *true*.

The founders understood that religious liberty was basically a matter of discerning the truth about God, adhering to it once discerned, and then doing one's duty as prescribed by God. This nest of convictions presupposed that religion is the kind of thing that can be either true or false, and in fact most founders maintained that one religion, Christianity, *was* true. The founders further held that religion was an important element of the political common good. The Supreme Court in 1963 – albeit, by then, possessed of a decidedly different worldview – accurately observed that the founders "believed devoutly that there was a God and that the unalienable rights of Men were rooted in Him." Religious liberty was the central "unalienable right."[27]

Squarely in the cross-hairs of the Court's new constitution of the 1940s was American political leadership's practice of affirming truths about divine matters, truths that were available to reason unaided by revelation or authoritative religious texts. When public authorities declared that there

[25] Even the Supreme Court has treated Madison's *Memorial* as the *Magna Carta* of religious liberty in America, mining it often (though always selectively and through secularized eyes) and even reprinting it in full as an appendix to its *Everson* opinion.

[26] James Madison, *Amendment to the Declaration of Rights* (May 29–June 12, 1776).

[27] *Abington School District* v. *Schempp*, 374 US 203, 213 (1963).

is a God (as in the National Motto or the Pledge of Allegiance), lawmakers did not abandon what would be called today "secular" purposes for lawmaking, either. "Secular" is a term deployed much later in our constitutional tradition; in this connection, "secular" made its debut in the 1940s. The founders did not use the word when they talked about religion and the polity, or even when they spoke (rarely, in fact) about the separation of church and state. For them, government care for the commonweal included care for religion. Religion was sublime. But it was nonetheless part of the temporal common good.

Where government promoted natural theology, it did not affirm any sects' distinctive message or practices. For what distinguished the various sects, one from the others, were matters added onto natural truths, such as the denominations' finer points of doctrine, modes of worship, and manner of church governance. On *these* matters the First Amendment stipulated the state to be agnostic. Public authority nonetheless contributed to the sects' *plausibility*, and to the *reasonableness* of their appeal. Where government affirmed that God providentially guided human affairs, one could further reasonably affirm that prayer and worship in community were fitting human responses to this Almighty God. Some further divine communication – revelation – could also reasonably be expected. The state's affirmation of natural theology, in other words, provided a *reasonable* prologue, or ramp, to the churches and their distinctive beliefs. Affirmations of the truths of natural religion signaled unmistakably that there is a Creator God who remains involved in human affairs, with whom it behooves humans to seek some sort of harmony.

Barnette and *Everson* unfortunately did not traffic in this differentiation between, on the one hand, reasoned affirmation of certain truths about God – natural religion or theology – and revealed religion. These cases did not recognize the distinction between religion and *sect* (or denomination). In fact they obliterated it. This effacement is most unfortunate, because without it the whole founding-era church–state settlement is unintelligible, as is the vast bulk of American constitutional and political thought up into the twentieth century.

In the year after *Everson,* Justice Felix Frankfurter buried this crucial distinction. The Court has never disinterred it.[28] After a brief recital of

[28] One indication of how deeply buried is this effacement is the innocence of the Court's greatest originalist, a man who was throughout his career also one of its greatest protectors

historical data in *McCollum* v. *Board of Education*, Frankfurter concluded "that long before the Fourteenth Amendment subjected the states to new limitations, the prohibition of furtherance by the state of *religious* instruction became the guiding principle, in law and feeling, of the American people." The Fourteenth Amendment in this regard "merely reflected," Frankfurter said, "a principle dominant in American life."[29]

There was no such "principle" operative at the founding. Or in 1868. Frankfurter's fatal misstep was his equation of non*sectarian* with non*religious*. But his nineteenth-century witnesses meant what they said: a separation of *sect* from education. "Sect" was used mainly with respect to Christianity and referred to what distinguished the various Christian bodies from each other, namely creeds, doctrines, worship, organization of church government, and internal rules of church discipline and communal life. In Frankfurter's historical fiction, Horace Mann's mid-nineteenth-century fight to bar "sectarian" teachings from common schools is consequently an exhortation to separate *religion* from education. A speech by President Ulysses S. Grant, as well as the Blaine Amendment, both seeking to end public funding of "sectarian schools," demonstrated to Frankfurter that by 1875 "the separation ... of the state from the teaching of *religion*, was firmly established in the consciousness of the nation."[30] But educational reformer Horace Mann firmly and always believed in "an education which instructed all children in the fundamental ethical norms which were the basis of all religions."[31] In fact, in the words of one historian of

of religious liberty. In his largely sound dissent from the Court's invalidation of a county's display of the Ten Commandments in *ACLU* v. *McCreary County*, Justice Scalia wrote: "If religion in the public forum had to be entirely nondenominational, there could be no religion in the public forum at all. One cannot say the word 'God,' or 'the Almighty,' one cannot offer public supplication or thanksgiving, without contradicting the beliefs of some people that there are many gods, or that God or the gods pay no attention to human affairs ... Historical practices ... demonstrate that there is a distance between the acknowledgment of a single Creator and the establishment of a religion." *ACLU* v. *McCreary County*, 545 US at 893 (Scalia, J., dissenting). Scalia is quite right that "historical practices" belie establishment clause objections to public declarations in favor of a Creator God. But the reason has nothing to do with "contradicting" some extant belief (or not). America's practices also do not support his view that "denominational" religion is publicly admissible because there is no other kind.

[29] *McCollum* v. *Board of Education*, 333 US at 215 (emphasis added).

[30] Ibid. at 217 (emphasis added).

[31] Vincent Lannie, *Public Money and Parochial Schools: Bishop Hughes, Governor Seward and the New York School Controversy* (South Bend, IN: University of Notre Dame Press, 1968), 80.

American schooling, "no great educational leader before the Civil War . . . would tolerate non-Christian beliefs in the school." This explanation of anti-sectarianism is evident in the language of the Blaine Amendment, which itself provided for Bible reading in the schools.[32]

Despite the consequences of the *Everson* decision, it is perhaps a tender mercy that its privatization of religion was limited to government action. After all, the First Amendment (even after it was "incorporated" in *Everson* and thus applied to the states as well as to the national government) only constrained what public authority could do or not do. But the aspects of our common life which the Constitution puts in government hands do not exhaust the whole common good of political society. Much of our common life is beyond the just care of government, and where that is so, care of common life devolves upon the institutions of civil society and, finally, the people. Unfortunately, the Supreme Court's "privatization" campaign pushed religion *entirely* outside the political common good.

To explain this transformation, it is necessary to return to the founders' astute vision of religion as both private and profoundly public. The founders asked the following question explicitly, and often, and with worry: Is there sufficient virtue among men for self-government? As Madison asked in *Federalist* 55, are "nothing less than the chains of despotism" required to "restrain [men] from destroying and devouring one another?" Madison's reply gave expression to the axiom that animated the whole founding generation: "[R]epublican government presupposes the existence of virtuous qualities" in citizens "in a higher degree than any other form" of government.[33] But how would these more "esteemed" qualities be cultivated in the citizenry, especially in a Protestant political community whose members maintained a healthy belief in original sin? This is what I call the *missing* Federalist Paper, one that would describe how a limited government in a free society could, somehow, rely upon virtues that it was largely powerless to produce.

[32] For a fuller account of the Blaine Amendment and Frankfurter's ham-handling of it, see Gerard V. Bradley, "The Blaine Amendment of 1876: Harbinger of Secularism?" *Engage* 8 (2007): 138.

[33] James Madison, *Federalist*, No. 55, in *The Federalist Papers* (1788). Madison famously wrote elsewhere in *Federalist*: "If men were angels, no government would be necessary. If angels were to govern men, neither external nor internal controls on government would be necessary. In framing a government which is to be administered by men over men, the great difficulty lies in this: you must first enable the government to control the governed."

The answer lay with the nongovernmental institutions of civil society, especially religion. The founders firmly believed that religion was part of the citizenry's republican equipment. Religion had to be free because that was the truth about religion. Religion had to be free, too, because the alternatives were politically oppressive. But religion had to be palpably present, taken very seriously, and had to be the sort that could bind men and women to the conscientious performance of their civic duties. Religion was a bulwark of the republic.

Among the testimonies to religion's inestimable public value was Washington's statement in his Farewell Address: "Of all the dispositions and habits which lead to political prosperity, Religion and Morality are indispensable supports."[34] He continued, "And let us with caution indulge the supposition, that morality can be maintained without Religion. Whatever may be conceded of the influence of refined education on minds of peculiar structure; reason and experience both forbid us to expect that national morality can prevail in exclusion of religious principle."[35] John Adams thought that "religion and virtue" were the foundations not only of republicanism, "but of social felicity under all governments and in all the combinations of human society."[36] Thomas Jefferson feared for a future America shorn of Christian morality. He said in 1781 that American liberty depended on a popular perception that it was the gift of God and thought it politically beneficial if Americans privately decided that there was "only one God, and he all perfect" and that there was a future state of rewards and punishments.[37]

The Court's second wave of privatization replaced the founders' vision with a secular version. I said earlier that *Barnette*'s kerygma was based on no authority whatsoever. But, if it was not based on authority, where did the radical new vision come from? Frankfurter said at the justices' *Everson* conference that the Court's "new trend" of decisions had already "shifted [its] latest views about our democracy."[38] What did he have in mind?

[34] George Washington, *Washington's Farewell Address to the People of the United States* (1813).

[35] Ibid.

[36] John Adams to Benjamin Rush, August 28, 1811, in *Founders Online,* accessed online, https://founders.archives.gov/documents/Adams/99-02-02-5678.

[37] Thomas Jefferson to Dr. Benjamin Waterhouse, June 26, 1822, in *American History: From Revolution to Reconstruction,* www.let.rug.nl/usa/presidents/thomas-jefferson/letters-of-thomas-jefferson/jefl268.php.

[38] Donald L. Drakeman, "*Everson v. Board of Education* and the Quest for the Historical Establishment Clause," *The American Journal of Legal History* 49, no. 2 (April 2007): 133.

The intellectual shift indicated by Frankfurter had its origins partly in violent global conflict. The world war then raging against fascism, and authoritarianism more generally, called forth among Americans a profound recommitment to their free institutions. That is what the "Greatest Generation" fought for. But they fought not only, or even primarily, for a set of political practices – elections, bicameralism, City Hall. They fought for "democracy," which the Court fashioned into a political *culture* with deep roots in character, belief, and psyche. It was a "way of life." "Democracy" indicated a significant modification of inherited political form, which had long been described as "our republican form of government." "Way of life" indicated that, for the first time in Supreme Court annals, the form of government called for – or even included – a corresponding culture. It was to be democracy all the way down, to where one could speak of a "democratic" (often, opposed to an "authoritarian") *personality.*[39]

But democratic theory was then indeterminate. One view of it held that democracy depended upon a citizenry possessed of moral truth. The other saw moral truth as a phantom, a superstition that, when possessed of citizens' minds, led straight to authoritarianism if not to outright fascism. These latter visionaries favored a pragmatic philosophical spirit, relativism in morals and a free market in ideas. And they won – in the Court, if not in public sentiment.[40]

Michael Sandel argued that *Barnette* was foundational because it affirmed the priority of fair procedures over substantive ends, a priority rooted in the

[39] The oral argument in *McCollum* is available in Gerard V. Bradley, "The Prodigal Argument," *Engage* 5 (2004). During it, on December 8, 1947, just ten months after the shocking *Everson* declaration against any and all government help to religion, even if the help was nondiscriminatory and noncoercive, Frankfurter made this point to John Franklin, representing (simply put here) the pro-religious liberty school board: "I put my question again: we have a school system of the United States on the one hand, and the relation it has to the democratic way of life. *On the other hand we have the religious beliefs of our people.* The question is whether any kind of scheme which introduced religious teaching into the public school system is the kind of thing we should in our democratic institutions." (Emphasis added.)

[40] See generally Paul Gottfried, *After Liberalism: Mass Democracy in the Managerial State* (Princeton, NJ: Princeton University Press, 1999). The Court's church–state decisions are mired in concerns about religion in our democracy. The justices most keenly worried that a politically and culturally assertive Catholic Church, authoritarian in its ecclesiology and long suspected of being despotic in its political thought, would be the undoing of "our democracy." See John McGreevy, *Catholicism and American Freedom* (New York: W.W. Norton, 2003), 166–188.

fact of disagreement about religious and moral ends among citizens. That is true enough. But Yves Simon more astutely diagnosed the political vision that animated, if only intuitively, the *Barnette* Court. This "liberalism" was an ideological construct that was coming to the fore in some Western societies. By its lights, the mind is vouchsafed no freedom from the requirements of "logical and experimental truth" and so none in regard to science (the synthesis of logic and experience). "As regards the so-called transcendental sphere . . . the individual should be granted an unlimited freedom of assertion and denial." Simon asserted that these "liberties cannot be safeguarded unless society adopts an attitude of complete indifference toward transcendental objects, and professes some kind of agnosticism."[41]

It was as if the atheist Robert Ingersoll had become the avatar of the Court's constitutional philosophy: "Experience, observation, and reason provide the only basis of knowledge," Ingersoll maintained. "I care nothing about the 'future' world."[42] Chief among the justices' innovations was their conviction that religion was all about inward experiences. William James was the justices' new tutor on matters religious. And he – they – left no doubt then that religion, like the "missing federalist," was history.

Democratic Religious "Experience": The Subjective Turn

In the mid-twentieth century, the Ballard family was convicted for using US mail to defraud. They had started the "I Am" religious movement and collected large sums of money from supporters who credited their claims to be divine messengers capable of miraculous healings. This claim was embedded in a larger story involving reincarnation, earthly appearances by Jesus, and even the return of George Washington. The legal issue was whether (as the indictment alleged) the Ballards "well knew" that their representations to donors were false. The First Amendment overlay was this: Assuming (as did both the government's and the Ballards' attorneys) that the truth or falsity of the Ballards' asserted *beliefs* was not to be considered, how should the jurors be instructed to gauge whether the

[41] Yves Simon, "Beyond the Crisis of Liberalism," in *Essays in Thomism* ed. Robert E. Brennan (New York: Sheed and Ward, 1942).

[42] Quoted in Turner, *Without God, Without Creed*, 195. Turner added, "knowledge aimed at precision; God was undefinable. Knowledge looked for what was tangible or observable; God was impalpable and invisible."

Ballards were frauds? More exactly: Could (should?) the jurors bring into their deliberations their convictions, based upon common sense and experience, that the *contents* of the Ballards' beliefs were indeed false? Or, to use the Court's own characterization of "I Am": Should the fact that the Ballards' contentions were "incredible, if not preposterous," count as some evidence that they could not have sincerely believed them?[43]

The *Ballard* Court split five-to-four on that question. The justices were *not* divided, though, about the metaphysics of religious beliefs. Writing for the majority, Justice William Douglas expressed two common themes: Men "may not be put to the proof of their religious doctrines or beliefs. Religious experiences which are as real as life to some may be incomprehensible to others."[44] Each of these assertions is close enough to being true to count as sound, *if* one takes the first to be a legal precept and not a general norm of discourse, and the second to be a matter of fact about certain incommunicable subjective states and *not* an exhaustive account of the contents of religion. But the Court stated them without qualification and connected the two thoughts by a silent, yet profound, *because*.

Justice Jackson expressed the common view most cogently in his brief dissent.[45] He dissented because he could "not see how we can separate an issue as to what is believed from considerations as to what is believable." He added: "The most convincing proof that one believes his statements is to show that they have been true in his experience."[46] Then Jackson turned to a conception of religion that, as if miraculously, was tailor-made for the Court's new "democracy":

[43] *United States* v. *Ballard*, 322 US 78, 87 (1944). [44] Ibid. at 86.

[45] Justices Roberts and Frankfurter joined Chief Justice Stone's dissent. Their key point was that the "state of one's mind is a fact as capable of fraudulent misrepresentation as is one's physical condition or the state of his bodily health." *United States* v. *Ballard*, 322 US at 90. Their metaphysics of religion was nonetheless fully in line with that of their brethren: "I cannot say that freedom of thought and worship includes freedom to procure money by making knowingly false statements about one's religious *experiences*"; the government alleged "conspiracy ... by false statements of their religious *experiences*"; "whether the alleged religious *experiences* had in fact occurred"; whether the "religious *experiences* alleged did or did not in fact occur"; "the question whether the religious *experiences* in fact occurred." *United States* v. *Ballard*, 322 US at 89–90. (All emphases added.)

[46] *United States* v. *Ballard*, 322 US at 92. ("Likewise, that one knowingly falsified is best proved by showing that what he said happened never did happen. How can the government prove these persons knew something to be false which it cannot prove to be false? If we try religious sincerity severed from religious verity, we isolate the dispute from the very considerations which, in common experience, provide its most reliable answer." Ibid.)

> [A]ny inquiry into intellectual honesty in religion raises profound psychological problems. William James, who wrote on these matters as a scientist, reminds us that it is not theology and ceremonies which keep religion going. Its vitality is in the religious experiences of many people. If you ask what these experiences are, they are conversations with the unseen, voices and visions, responses to prayer, changes of heart, deliverances from fear, inflowings of help, assurances of support, whenever certain persons set their own internal attitude in certain appropriate ways ... Such experiences, like some tones and colors, have existence for one, but none at all for another. They cannot be verified to the minds of those whose field of consciousness does not include religious insight. When one comes to trial which turns on any aspect of religious belief or representation, unbelievers among his judges are likely not to understand, and are almost certain not to believe him. ... All schools of religious thought make enormous assumptions, generally on the basis of revelations authenticated by some sign or miracle. The appeal in such matters is to a very different plane of credibility than is invoked by representations of secular fact in commerce. Some who profess belief in the Bible read literally what others read as allegory or metaphor, as they read Aesop's fables. Religious symbolism is even used by some with the same mental reservations one has in teaching of Santa Claus or Uncle Sam or Easter bunnies or dispassionate judges. It is hard in matters so mystical to say how literally one is bound to believe the doctrine he teaches, and even more difficult to say how far it is reliance upon a teacher's literal belief which induces followers to give him money.[47]

After *Ballard* it surely seemed that, in contemplation of law, the only things *real* about "religion" were ineffable subjective "experiences." This "religion" did not need to be privatized by rule; it was intrinsically as private as anything could be. The religions' putative larger "truths" (doctrines, worldviews, creedal assertions, scriptural witnesses) were, in truth, verbalizations of just so many subjective states. These expressions could aspire to no more than the truth of poetry. They might enjoy some protection as "opinions" in the (private) marketplace of ideas. But they could scarcely claim any more validity, value, or importance than that.[48]

[47] *United States* v. *Ballard*, 322 US at 93–94. The two footnotes omitted are both to works of William James. James famously defined "religion" in his seminal *Varieties of Religious Experience* (at page 36) as "the feelings, acts, and experiences of individual men in their solitude, so far as they apprehend themselves to stand in relation to whatever they consider the divine." William James, *Varieties of Religious Experience* (New York: Modern Library, 1999 [1901]), 36.

[48] The *Ballard* Justices were not pioneers of religious subjectivism. Audible expressions of it in America go back at least to the revivals of the early nineteenth century. Emerson (among others) welcomed the prospect of a religion freed from institutions and human forms, religion – and thus religionists – free to be fully spiritual: "What a fertility of projects for

Ballard meant that the law would treat religious claims about God, the universe, and human existence as opaque reports of someone's self-understanding. The Court made this clearer in its 1965 decision in *United States* v. *Seeger*.[49] The case was about "conscientious objection" to the draft in the early stages of the Vietnam War. Three men were denied exemptions by their draft boards, whose decisions were upheld by the federal trial courts. The objectors' claims foundered upon the governing statutory language, which required an objection based not on "essentially political, sociological, or philosophical views or a merely personal moral code" but on the basis of "religious training and belief." That term was defined as "an individual's belief in a relation to a Supreme Being involving duties superior to those arising from any merely human relation."

the salvation of the world!" *Selected Writings of Ralph Waldo Emerson* (New York: Modern Library, 1998), 402. Turner explains, "Religion had already become for Charles Eliot Norton by 1867 'the most private and personal part of the life of every man.' The idea that believing in God is a matter of individual choice would have sent Norton's Puritan forbears, even his Unitarian father, spinning in their graves. Yet, ever since Norton's generation, upbringing and experience have led some people to choose belief, others unbelief. The numbers inclining each way matter far less, from the historian's point of view, than the fact that the decision is open." Turner, Turner, *Without God, Without Creed*, 263. Jaroslav Pelikan begins his specific discussion of "The Theology of the Heart" in his magisterial history of Christian doctrine with a recitation of Kant's eighteenth-century confession (in his 1788 *Critique of Pure Reason)* of "awe" at two things: "the starry heavens above me and the moral law within me." Jaroslav Pelikan, *The Christian Tradition: A History of the Development of Doctrine*, vol. 5, *Christian Doctrine and Modern Culture (since 1700)* (Chicago, IL: University of Chicago Press, 1989), 118. To many believers thereafter, it seemed (to Pelikan) that God was closing one door to faith and opening another: God "permitted the external evidence of Christianity to be more or less clogged and encumbered" so that men might "look into themselves also and attend to the light shining in their hearts". Ibid., 118. Indeed, "Miracle, mystery, and authority, whose validity as objective realities seemed to have reached a dead end, took on new life when they became, instead, ways of speaking about the subjective validity of inward experience." Ibid., 119. Friedrich Schleiermacher gave what has often since been called this "liberal" Protestantism its most thematic and compelling expression. Liberal Christianity is *not* a reduction of Christian belief to what Pelikan aptly describes as "solipsistic self-fulfillment." But it is close enough to make that possibility not only become intelligible, but perilously real. The *Ballard* Court pioneered the entry of this "liberalism" into constitutional law. The cultural critic Philip Rieff wrote in 2005, "I think that the orthodox are in the miserable position of being orthodox for therapeutic reasons." Richard Neuhaus commented: "People who try to practice orthodox Christianity and Judaism today," according to Rieff, "inevitably remain trapped in the vocabulary of therapy and self-fulfillment." See Neuhaus' "Philip Rieff Has Died at Age 83," *First Things*, July 10, 2006, accessed online, www.firstthings.com/web-exclusives/2006/07/rjn-philip-rieff-has-die.

[49] *United States* v. *Seeger*, 380 US.

Except for the substitution of the term "Supreme Being" for "God," this was the traditional expression of the grounds for draft exemption, most lucidly given by Chief Justice Charles Hughes, albeit in dissent, in another such case, *United States* v. *Macintosh.*[50]

The objectors denied, with varying degrees of explicitness, that they believed in a Supreme Being at all. Daniel Seeger was "skeptical" about the existence of God; Arno Jakobson affirmed a "Supreme Reality" of sorts, but one that even a casual observer could see was scarcely distinguishable from a personal philosophy. Asked to define "religion" Jakobson replied: "The sum and essence of one's basic attitude to the fundamental problems of human existence." Defendant Forest Peter "hedged" (the Court's word) on the question of a Supreme Being. For him, "religion" was "the supreme expression of human nature; it is man thinking his highest, feeling his deepest, and living his best."[51]

The *Seeger* Court found that all three objectors were "religious" enough to qualify for exemption from the draft. The Court "believe[d] that its construction embraces the ever-broadening understanding of the modern religious community" of what "religion" was. Eight justices adopted this "modern" belief; *Ballard* author William Douglas embraced an even more *avant garde* understanding of religion. The Court sharply contrasted the old view (as the Court phrased it) of a "God up there." The opinion repeated the relativizing assertion from *Ballard*: "Religious experiences which are as real as life to some may be incomprehensible to others." Then the Justices opined that, save for the very few atheists in the universe, "everybody believes in some kind of God."[52] *Seeger* therefore redefined religion to include a "belief" or a "faith" that occupies in the life of the individual a place parallel to that of God in the lives of the more traditionally religious.[53] In *Seeger*,

[50] *United States* v. *Macintosh*, 283 US 605, 633–634 (1931) ("The essence of religion is belief in a relation to God involving duties superior to those arising from any human relation".).

[51] *United States* v. *Seeger*, 380 US at 169. [52] Ibid. at 182.

[53] Historian Jon Butler wrote that "Tillich's conviction [was] that religion was, at its essence, a philosophical and theological 'ground of being' whose redefined spiritual centeredness could successfully confront modern totalitarianism, religious bigotry, and racism even as it transcended the creedal orthodoxy and denominational distinctiveness that" traditionally was the hall mark of religion. Jon Butler, "Jack-in-the-Box Faith: The Religion Problem in Modern American History," *The Journal of American History* 90, no. 4 (2004): 1370.

the Court also introduced Paul Tillich's existentialist theology to a probably unaccustomed audience.[54]

Congress had modified the World War I–era draft exemption, so as to no longer make membership in a traditional "peace" church (such as the Mennonites or Quakers) a condition for conscientious objection, a change which the *Seeger* Court did not hesitate to follow and which it extended across the board to free-exercise claimants in the 1989 *Frazee* case.[55] It is worth special mention, too, that the *Seeger* Court referred to beliefs, not to belief systems, organized communities of believers, or to a personal relationship of any sort with the divine, however broadly understood. In 1981, the Court established that "religious belief need not be acceptable, logical, consistent, or comprehensible to others in order to merit First Amendment protection."[56]

[54] The inherited metaphysics of religion is evident in the following from *Seeger:*

> Few would quarrel, we think, with the proposition that in no field of human endeavor has the tool of language proved so inadequate in the communication of ideas as it has in dealing with the fundamental questions of man's predicament in life, in death, or in final judgment and retribution. This fact makes the task of discerning the intent of Congress in using the phrase "Supreme Being" a complex one. Nor is it made the easier by the richness and variety of spiritual life in our country. Over 250 sects inhabit our land. Some believe in a purely personal God, some in a supernatural deity; others think of religion as a way of life envisioning, as its ultimate goal, the day when all men can live together in perfect understanding and peace. There are those who think of God as the depth of our being; others, such as the Buddhists, strive for a state of lasting rest through self-denial and inner purification; in Hindu philosophy, the Supreme Being is the transcendental reality which is truth, knowledge and bliss. *United States* v. *Seeger*, 380 US at 174–175.

Justice Goldberg gave an odd testimony to this development at the justices' *Seeger* conference. "The only difference between Seeger and Buddhism is that Seeger isn't a Buddhist," Goldberg observed. Ibid. at 436.

[55] See *Frazee* v. *Illinois*, 489 US 829 (1989). "Frazee asserted that he was a Christian, but did not claim to be a member of a particular Christian sect. It is also true that there are assorted Christian denominations that do not profess to be compelled by their religion to refuse Sunday work, but this does not diminish Frazee's protection flowing from the Free Exercise Clause. . . . Undoubtedly, membership in an organized religious denomination, especially one with a specific tenet forbidding members to work on Sunday, would simplify the problem of identifying sincerely held religious beliefs, but we reject the notion that to claim the protection of the Free Exercise Clause, one must be responding to the commands of a particular religious organization. Here, Frazee's refusal was based on a sincerely held religious belief. Under our cases, he was entitled to invoke First Amendment protection." Ibid. at 834.

[56] *Thomas* v. *Review Board*, 450 US 707 (1981). Yale theologian George Lindbeck observed that the "privatism and subjectivism that accompanies the neglect of communal doctrines leads to weakening of social groups (*Gemeinschaften)* that are the chief bulwarks against chaos and against totalitarian efforts to master chaos." George A. Lindbeck, *The Nature of*

The *Ballard* and *Seeger* Courts made it clear the law would treat religions' claims about God, the universe, and human existence as opaque reports of someone's self-understanding. The Court made this unmistakably clear in 1992. The crowning moment of this convergence occurred in *Planned Parenthood* v. *Casey*, the 1992 Supreme Court decision that affirmed *Roe* v. *Wade*. "Religion" in constitutional law became each one's basic narrative arc, no matter what it is.[57] As this "religion" lost any essential transcendent referent and bent toward the temporal world, a host of other (nonreligious, by any recognizable measure) life options ascended the stairway to heaven. The Court in *Casey* tied together several lines of cases having to do with legal treatment of marriage, family, and sexual morality. Why, the Court asked, did the law "afford protection to personal decisions relating to marriage, procreation, contraception [and] family relationships?" The Court answered that these choices are "central to personal dignity and autonomy." It concluded, "*At the heart of liberty is the right to define one's own concept of existence, of meaning, of the universe, and of the mystery of human life.*"[58] Religion was thus subsumed within an encompassing project of individual self-definition, which was all soon assimilated into the "conscience" or "dignity" or "identity" of the acting person. The metric of value here is neither moral truth nor one's obligations to a greater-than-human source of meaning and value. It is instead authenticity – one's subjective sense of one's own deepest, and thus "true," self.

Doctrine: Religion and Theology in a Postliberal Age (Louisville, KY: Westminster John Knox Press, 1984), 77–78.

[57] *Seeger* foreshadowed, if it did not ordain, this rendezvous: "[P]utting aside dogmas with their particular conceptions of deity, freedom of conscience itself implies respect for an *innate conviction of paramount duty*. The battle for religious liberty has been fought and won with respect to religious beliefs and practices, which are not in conflict with good order, upon the very ground of the supremacy of conscience within its proper field." *United States* v. *Seeger*, 380 US at 176 (emphasis added).

[58] *Planned Parenthood* v. *Casey*, 505 US 833, 851 (1992) (emphasis added). James Turner anticipated this denouement, and recognized its roots conceptually in atheism: "For those who have accepted personally the agnostic option, the disappearance of God has meant still more. If divine purpose does not inhere in the cosmos, then human beings must define the meaning of their own brief lives amid a pointless vastness. Hence arises the distinctively modern angst." Turner, *Without God, Without Creed*, 264.

In most academic legal commentary, in much law, and to a significant extent in the minds of many ordinary people, religious acts have the same dignity and value as do other acts by which persons express and actualize their deepest selves, desires, or self-defining thoughts and emotions. The supreme and perhaps only universal value here is authenticity and, thus, "identity." As John Finnis aptly writes, religion's "status and immunities are as instances . . . of the only really basic human good, the only intrinsically worthwhile end at stake, setting for oneself one's stance in the world."[59] Religious liberty in the new dispensation, therefore, is really one subdivision, or set of exercises, of the One Great Liberty, which was given authoritative expression more than a quarter-century ago. Religious liberty is not thus so much redefined, as that it disappears into the maws of this colossus. The so-called Mystery Passage in *Casey* has consumed not only religion, but also sexual morality,[60] marriage,[61] and, arguably, the whole constitutional basis for morals laws.[62]

Scenes from the Crisis

The "Mystery Passage" concluded with this assertion: "Beliefs about these matters could not constitute the attributes of personhood were they formed under the compulsion of the state."[63] Of course, our status as *persons* does not depend upon any liberty offered or withheld by public authority. And it is not easy to visualize how "beliefs" could be formed under state "compulsion." But this second thought indicates that, although all sources of individual personal "identity" stand on equal footing by dint of someone's "authentic" appropriation of it, the

59 John Finnis, "Religion and State", in Religion and Public Reasons, vol. 5, *Collected Essays of John Finnis* (Oxford: Oxford University Press, 2011), 86.

60 The effect of *Lawrence* v. *Texas* is to assimilate sexual misconduct, at least insofar as it may be regulated by criminal law, to ambient norms of justice: consenting adults may do what they wish in private, and there is nothing distinctively *sexual* about legal regulation of intimate relationships.

61 *Obergefell* v. *Hodges*, 576 US, slip opinion at 13–15.

62 Justice Scalia wrote in his *Lawrence* dissent that the Court's Mystery-Passage-based invalidation of Texas' sodomy laws doomed state laws against "fornication, bigamy, adultery, adult incest, bestiality, and obscenity."

63 *Planned Parenthood* v. *Casey*, 505 US at 851.

"Mystery Passage" project correlates with a governmental duty of non-interference. It does not apparently imply or entail any duties upon other people. It seems to be a demand to leave people alone to work out their worldview. Call it "Identity Politics 1.0."

The Court's same-sex "marriage" decision revealed a very different correlative. *Obergefell* v. *Hodges,* decided in 2015, brought to the fore what we might call "Identity Politics 2.0." The radical autonomy championed in *Casey* could not have produced that holding by itself; the Court in *Lawrence* v. *Texas,* in an opinion authored by Justice Anthony Kennedy, said as much when it declared that it was *not* requiring any "formal recognition" of homosexual relationships.[64] But the *Obergefell* Court coupled the "Mystery Passage" with heaping portions of social and legal duties to "affirm" and to "recognize" these same relationships for the sake of "affirming" the choices of the two parties to them. By 2015, "recognition" was part of what it meant to have the "liberty" of self-definition. As the Court wrote, "Laws excluding same-sex couples from the marriage right impose stigma and injury of the kind prohibited by our basic charter," the Constitution.[65]

It also appears now that the state has some derivative duty to protect the "autonomous" choosing person from moral criticism by others. After noting in *Obergefell* that many oppose same-sex "marriage" based upon "decent and honorable religious or philosophical premises," the Court warned that, whatever rights such persons might have – in Justice Samuel Alito's tart reply to this part of the Court's opinion, to "whisper their thoughts in the recesses of their homes" – should those "decent" views become "enacted law and public policy," then the state will have put its own "imprimatur" "on an exclusion that soon demeans and stigmatizes."[66] Justice Alito put it this way: Should "decent" folks "repeat those views in public, they will risk being labeled as bigots and treated as such by governments, employers, and schools."[67]

This "Identity Politics 2.0" shapes the current crisis of religious liberty. Here is a snapshot from it. In *Elane Photography* v. *Willock*, the New Mexico Supreme Court ruled in favor of a lesbian couple who asserted that, under the state law outlawing discrimination on grounds of sexual orientation in all "public accommodations," a wedding photographer was bound to shoot

[64] *Lawrence* v. *Texas*, 539 US 558, 567 (2003).

[65] *Obergefell* v. *Hodges*, 576 US, slip opinion at 17–18. [66] Ibid. at 19. [67] Ibid., 7.

video at their "commitment ceremony."[68] Concurring in that result, Justice Richard Bosson recognized that the photographers – the Huguenins – acted out of a sincere Christian belief that the ceremony celebrated an immoral sexual relationship and that memorializing it in pictures made them complicit in the immorality. Justice Bosson wrote, tellingly, that the Huguenins are "free to think, to say, to believe, as they wish; they may pray to the God of their choice and follow these commandments in *their personal lives*." In the world of "the marketplace, of commerce, of public accommodation," however, they must "compromise." They "must channel their conduct, not their beliefs, so as to leave space for other Americans who believe something different." They must adhere to the "glue which holds us together as a nation, the tolerance that lubricates the varied moving parts of us as a people." This is "the price of citizenship." It looks then like the anthem of the new social arrangements might be: "carnival in private; conformity in public."[69]

The asymmetry of Christian moral life multiplies the effects of this predicament. Christians who adhere to the New Testament are not to judge that doing just one or two abortions, or performing even one same-sex wedding, is morally acceptable so long as doing so is needed to keep them in medical school, or in business, or simply to avoid a public penalty of some sort. Christians know that Saint Paul taught that no one may do evil so that good may come of it.[70] They also know that the entire tradition of martyrdom that

[68] *Elane Photography* v. *Willock*, 309 P. 3d, 53 (NM 2013), *cert denied,_US _(2014).*

[69] In his 2010 Christmas greeting to the Roman Curia, Pope Benedict XVI noted that in modern thinking, "the word 'conscience' signifies that for moral and religious questions, it is the subjective dimension, the individual, that constitutes the final authority for decision." In the modern world, however, it is "divided into the realms of the objective and the subjective." Religion and morals, the pope continued, "lie within the subjective realm. Here, it is said, there are in the final analysis no objective criteria. The ultimate instance that can decide here is therefore the subject alone," guided by and indeed governed by his "intuitions and experiences," and not, one might emphasize, objective *indicia* of truth. This division of the social world was adopted in most stark terms by an English law lord (named Law) who gave thematic expression to this development in a recent case; he denied relief to a Christian relationship counselor who could not endorse the same-sex acts of his potential clients. Her refusal was a prima facie case of sexual orientation discrimination. She sought an exception rooted in ambient legal norms of religious liberty. Lord Law declared that any exemption on religious grounds would be "unprincipled." He reasoned that it would "give effect to the force of subjective opinion" (read: religion) and thus could not "advance the general good on objective grounds." Benedict XVI, "Address of His Holiness Benedict XVI on the Occasion of Christmas Greetings to the Roman Curia," December 20, 2010, accessed online, http://w2.vatican.va/content/benedict-xvi/en/speeches/2010/december/documents/hf_ben-xvi_spe_20101220_curia-auguri.html.

[70] See Romans 3:8.

began with Jesus makes no sense unless there are certain acts (such as those proscribed in the Decalogue) which are never to be done, come what may. Christian moral life is like a sailing ship; even a tiny bit less than intact portends disaster. The Titanic missed all the icebergs but one. Thus, indifference to the conscience claims of Christians leads, not to wholesome or even grudging compromise, but rather to the forced eviction of so many dedicated professionals and workers from sundry walks of life.

For Christians, and for many other believers as well as some nonbelievers, moral life can be scuttled by a head-on collision with just *one* legally required, morally obnoxious duty – whether to certify a candidate to be euthanized, to pay for one abortion, to return one guilty verdict in a death penalty case, to dispense one prescription of "ella," or to help celebrate and thus morally ratify one same-sex wedding, or to knowingly promote even one unmarried couple's sexual intercourse by giving them a bed or a condom or a how-to-do-it talk. So too on the grander scale: several Catholic agencies have decided to close rather than place a child for adoption by a same-sex couple. More institutional martyrs are sure to follow.[71]

Conclusion

Almost all Americans had agreed during and since the American founding that religion was a singular public good and that it provided irreplaceable common benefits. Many Americans still think so. Our constitutional law has for two generations or more charted a very different course for our country. Popular convictions about religion, reason, morality, and the common good are not nearly what they once were. But they have not decomposed so far that it is too late to muster them as assets in the struggle to preserve religious liberty. It would seem, however, that time is not on the side of religious freedom.

[71] A new concept has been minted to give expression and ballast to the results in these and other cases like them, of contest between persons seeking to exercise the *same* great liberty of self-definition, namely, "dignitary harm." See, for example, Douglas Nejaime and Reva B. Segal, "Conscience Wars: Complicity-Based Conscience Claims in Religion and Politics," *Yale Law Journal* 124 (2015): 2516–2591 and Douglas Laycock, "Religious Liberty for Politically Active Minority Groups: A Response to NeJaime and Siegel," *Yale Law Journal* 125 (2016), accessed online, www.yalelawjournal.org/forum/religious-liberty-for-politically-active-minority-groups.

Someone might object that nothing short of a radical strategy could possibly preserve religious liberty. Many friends of religious liberty reasonably stress the wisdom, if not the necessity, of working *within* the parameters of thought and argument on offer. They seek, for example, not a breakout of religion into the public realm but, instead, fairer treatment of religion as a source of private edification. They regularly adopt, and seek to co-opt, the categories of thought given to them. Many of these friends are litigators and political strategists with professional obligations to seek success on a one-off basis, either for a particular client or in order to win the next vote. Tactical victory is certainly preferable to tactical defeat, but tactics are suited to small-unit engagements. The argument of this chapter is that fighting it out along a line drawn in our constitutional law nearly four-score years ago can do no more than slow down the pace of defeat. Religious liberty is caught in a great cultural shift. Nothing less than radical strategic action has any chance of preserving religious liberty beyond the foreseeable future.

Happily, there are several opportunities at hand. Establishment clause doctrine is a rotten door waiting to be kicked in. The core of it is the secularism entailed by the Court's notional "neutrality" between "religion" and some vague antithesis of it. This pseudo-neutrality is impossible to square with the free exercise clause, which the Court has noted many times over the years, unfortunately without making the doctrinal adjustments implied.[72] That religion must constitutionally be treated just as "non-religion" is treated is a proposition refuted by the text of the First Amendment itself. It is time to revisit with renewed determination the Court's privatization of religion.

Recognition of religion as an important and unique common good vitiates the Court's main establishment clause test for breaches of neutrality between religion and "non-religion," namely the "no-endorsement" test. First expressly articulated by Justice Sandra Day O'Connor in *Lynch* v. *Donnelly* (1984),[73] the most recent statement of its basic appeal is Justice

[72] *Hosanna-Tabor* is one example. See text accompanying note 2. See also *Cutter* v. *Wilkinson*, 544 US 709 (2005).

[73] *Lynch* v. *Donnelly*, 465 US 668, 688 (1984) (O'Connor, concurring) ("The second and more direct [establishment clause] infringement is government endorsement or disapproval of religion. Endorsement sends a message to nonadherents that they are outsiders, not full members of the political community, and an accompanying message to adherents that they are insiders, favored members of the political community. Disapproval sends the opposite message.")

Elena Kagan's, in the 2014 legislative prayer case: The First Amendment "promise[s] that every citizen, irrespective of her religion, owns an equal share in her government."[74] This broad claim has many possible meanings, many of them sound. But the precise meaning upon which its cogency in church–state cases depends is not sound; at least, its appeal depends entirely upon supposing that religion is a "private" satisfaction for some people. For so long as coercion is not at issue (and it is *not* an element of "no-endorsement" analysis), then the presence of public religion is no more productive of "inequality" than is the presence of public education, public health, industrial public works, military defense, or even government itself. Some conscientious people object to these manifestations of what the common good requires, and they may fairly be exempted from some of its requirements. But these objectors – whether Amish or Christian Scientists or Jehovah's Witnesses or Christian pacifists – do not possess a veto power over the political community's promotion of the common goods for the benefit of all. None of these objectors could summon a "no-endorsement" test to judicially invalidate, for example, Medicare and Medicaid (even if it might be fair to relieve some of personal participation in them). So too with those who complain about public religion, because religion too is part of the political common good.

Reestablishing religion as a distinct public good would secure a major premise of the second great strategic challenge, which is to distinguish religion from other pursuits and then to cement the case for its "special" compelling quality. Arguments about free exercise doctrine are secondary to, and perhaps not even entirely derivative of, this key point. For if religion is treated as distinct and compelling, the doctrine will follow. If, on the other hand, religion continues to fester within encompassing self-invention projects, no change in doctrine will itself catapult it to "special," or compelling, status.

There is a third strategic opportunity, or rather an imperative. The founders stipulated a sort of mental discipline for lawmakers. Lawmakers were obliged by the First Amendment to refrain from making the truth or falsity of theological propositions a basis for legislation. This could be difficult for members of the founding generation; by and large they held that such matters *were* propositions. The First Amendment meant that the

[74] *Town of Greece* v. *Galloway*, 572 US __ (2014) (Kagan, dissenting, joined by Breyer, Sotomayor, Ginsburg).

truth (or falsity) of such matters had to be put aside in civil affairs. The validity of these propositions was beyond the competences of public authority. The great challenge was to sustain and promote religious liberty within this framework, namely making religion-centric norms absolute ("Congress shall make no law ... ") and stipulating that officials are incompetent to judge religious claims, *all the while holding that not only was religion the sort of thing that is either true or false, but that America was in some crucial way founded upon the one religion which was true.*[75]

But whereas the founders saw *sectarian* distinctions as intelligible differences that one could and should judge to be true or false, the modern view has the virtue of making them utterly subjective. It is easy to supply a foundation for religious liberty in indifferentism and subjectivism. The problem is that, once founded on those bases, one soon discovers that it is not religious liberty at all that is propped up. The challenge of founding religious liberty upon truth is that no one – not a litigator, professor, judge, legislator, opinion writer, administrative official, or anyone else – should assert *anything* that implies or entails that the religions are all equally true (or false); or that none is true; or that they are all matters of individual experience; or that no one can be morally certain what is true about God and his will for us; and so on.

The project to restore reason to religion and to reconnect it to truth is surely daunting, and success is far from guaranteed. There will be some successes along the way. At the very least, the effort will do well what it always does in our society, which is to *teach* the truth about religion and truth. The strongest argument for joining this strategic effort is that there really is no alternative. Staying on the present path would be to just keep on sleepwalking along a death march.

[75] It is therefore only a rough approximation of the meaning of the establishment clause to say that it mandates "equality" among the various religions. The truths of natural religion cut across the religious landscape without concern for equality of any groupings. The "equality" of the various sects is not in any event like a dumb arithmetical function. It is rather the effect of the stipulated government incompetence with regard to matters such as doctrine, discipline, worship, and governance. Any sound approach to constitutional doctrine and its application must also be influenced to *some* extent by the fact that Americans have been, and are, predominantly a Christian people. Finally, to the extent that the "missing federalist" can be revived, an additional potential inequality is introduced: by now, many religions do not teach that there is an objective morality, or that there is any future state of rewards or punishments – or both. And *both* were and probably are ingredients of any religion which might serve as a bulwark of the free society.

Index

For EU product safety concerns, contact us at Calle de José Abascal, 56–1°,
28003 Madrid, Spain or eugpsr@cambridge.org.

www.ingramcontent.com/pod-product-compliance
Lightning Source LLC
LaVergne TN
LVHW052020200926
848481LV00005B/1535